INTRODUCTION TO
Management
FIFTH EDITION

WARREN **R**. **P**LUNKETT

Wright College

RAYMOND **F**. **A**TTNER

Brookhaven College

WADSWORTH PUBLISHING COMPANY ■ BELMONT, CALIFORNIA ■ A DIVISION OF WADSWORTH, INC.

To my sister, Ann Sheldon, and her son Tim
W.R.P.

To my wife, Deborah — my joy, my support, my partner
R.F.A

Publisher: Larry Alexander

Assistant Editor: Karen Mandel

Print Buyer: Barbara Britton

Designer/Art Director: Gary Palmatier

Copy Editors: Toni Murray, Elizabeth von Radics

Photo Researcher: Laurel Anderson, Photosynthesis

Technical Illustrator: Ideas to Images

Cover Illustrator: Boris Lyubner

Permissions Editor: Jeanne Bosschart

Compositor: Ideas to Images

Printer: Arcata Graphics / Hawkins County

International Thomson Publishing

The trademark ITP is used under license.

3 2280 00640 7324

Printed in the United States of America

1 2 3 4 5 6 7 8 9 10 — 98 96 95 94

Library of Congress Cataloging-in-Publication Data

Plunkett, W. Richard (Warren Richard)
    Introduction to management / Warren R. Plunkett, Raymond F.
  Attner. — 5th ed.
        p.   cm.
    Includes bibliographical references and index.
    ISBN 0-534-93321-1 (alk. paper)
    1. Management.   I. Attner, Raymond F.   II. Title.
HD31.P55   1994
658.4 — dc20   93-22708
                                                  CIP

Brief Contents

Detailed Contents

Part II: Planning and Decision Making 93

4 Organizational Planning 94

Part III: Organizing

Part V: Controlling

499

Part VI: Special Concerns   641

Preface

This fifth edition includes dramatic changes from previous editions. It is a more comprehensive survey of the principles and practices of management as they are currently being applied, in the United States and around the world. The number of chapters has been increased from seventeen to twenty-two in order to incorporate the most recent innovations and research on corporate culture, managers' environments, total quality management and productivity, operations management, managing teams, management information systems, and strategic planning and management.

With the help of reviewers, the authors have made every effort to keep this text objective, timely, and interesting to both the student and the instructor. Along with the shift to full color, all case problems, examples, and features portray actual companies and managers in action. Successes as well as failures are included to lend perspective and aid in understanding.

To the Student

Chapter Structure

This text is designed to introduce you to the terminology, theories, and principles at the core of business management. The book is broken into six comprehensive parts, comprising a variety of examples, applications, exercises, and devices. Each chapter begins with an outline showing the primary and secondary headings and contains the following components:

- A list of specific Learning Objectives—concepts to be mastered through the chapter content

- A list of Essential Terms defined within the chapter, at the end of each chapter, and in the glossary at the back of the book

- A Management in Action feature that highlights an actual manager's or company's experiences as they relate to the content of each chapter

- Exhibits designed to illustrate and summarize essential concepts

- An Issues and Ethics sidebar reporting on ethical issues currently facing organizations and their managers

- Photographs chosen to enrich the chapter content

- A Global Applications feature that demonstrates how the chapter content are applied in international businesses

- A Focus on Quality sidebar explaining how different people and enterprises are applying the concepts of total quality management

- A list of Future Trends at the end of each chapter that highlights predictions for expected evolutions over the next few years

- A Chapter Summary listing the chapter's key concepts

- Skill-Building exercises to help you apply one or more of the chapter's key concepts

- Review Questions designed to assist your mastery of the chapter's learning objectives

- Recommended Reading chosen to help you explore the chapter content in more depth and detail

- References detailing the sources of the chapter's research

- A Glossary of Terms containing the definitions of the essential terms introduced and defined in the chapter

- A Case Problem summarizing an actual manager's or company's problems as they relate to the chapter content

Throughout your study of this text, try to relate what you read and discuss to your own experiences. You have already been practicing—and perhaps violating—many of the principles of management. What you are about to learn is an extension and refinement of what you already know—a blending of it with the experiences of others.

Although you will be reading each chapter as a separate area of study, try to relate it to what you have experienced and read previously. By linking the content of each chapter to that which has preceded it, you will begin to appreciate that management is a tapestry with many threads that run parallel to and across one another. For example, planning relates to all the management functions; it is part of every management activity in much the same way that communicating is. Periodically step back from your study to see the "big picture" of which each chapter is but a part.

Upon completion of this text and course, you will have developed your own philosophy of management and be armed with the essentials necessary for improving your career. You will become a better manager of your own concerns as well as the work of others.

Organization of the Content

Part I: Management Concepts This section provides a basic overview; it examines the evolution of management thought and the various environments that affect the practice of management.

Chapter 1 explores what management is, why it is necessary, the kinds of managers found in organizations, management functions, management roles, and management skills.

Chapter 2 takes the student on a journey through the past, examining the evolution of management theory from the classical schools through today's contingency school. It assesses the worth and contributions made by each and explains the links among them.

Chapter 3 lists and defines the internal and external environments that affect and challenge the practice of management. Business as an open system and the demands of stakeholders are the major focuses.

Part II: Planning and Decision Making   The importance of the first function of management—planning—is examined from several perspectives in Chapters 4 and 5: organizational, contingency, strategic, and operational. The relationship of planning to all other management functions, and ways to make it more effective, are covered. The art of decision making is the focus of Chapter 6.

Chapter 4 explains the importance of planning, the framework for plans, types and uses of plans, and the planning process.

Chapter 5 explores the nature of strategic planning, elements of planning strategies, levels of strategic planning, and the strategic-planning process.

Chapter 6 guides the student through the steps for rational decisions, decision-making climates, quantitative methods, and the various influences on the manager's problem-solving efforts.

Part III: Organizing   Organizing is examined as a process along with why different organizations adopt different approaches to structuring their operations. Both the formal and informal organization are included in the discussions. Organizing principles are demonstrated with examples.

Chapter 7 looks at the formal organization, the organizing process, its key principles and concepts, and the informal organization.

Chapter 8 covers organizational design, the range of organizational-design outcomes, contingency factors affecting organizational design, and the structures in common use.

Chapter 9 features organizational culture and handling change. The manifestations of cultures and subcultures, creation of cultures, nature of change, managing and implementing change, and the concepts connected with organizational development are covered comprehensively.

Part IV: Staffing and Leading   This section develops the concepts of staffing, communication, motivation, leadership, team management, and conflict. Essential legal concepts are included along with the principles and practices that affect each.

Chapter 10 surveys staffing from human resource planning to employee separations. Social and cultural influences are addressed along with such activities as job analysis, job evaluation, training and development, and the practice of staffing in a union environment.

Chapter 11 focuses on communication—organizational and interpersonal. The communication process and barriers to it are demonstrated along with how managers can improve their communication efforts.

Chapter 12 explores motivation and the applications of the most relevant theories. Special concern is given to how managers can use their insights and principles to get the most from themselves, their subordinates, and team members.

Chapter 13 looks at leadership. Its importance and associations with power and authority are detailed. The roles leaders must play with their followers are reviewed along with the theories that govern the practice of leadership and the styles that leaders may adopt.

Chapter 14 examines team management and conflict. The nature and types of teams, philosophical approaches to team management, and how to establish team-based organizations are included. Conflict is defined, and the causes and methods for coping with it are discussed.

Part V: Controlling This comprehensive section contains four chapters, each of which examines and applies different aspects of the principles and theories of control.

Chapter 15 focuses on the nature of control, the control process, types of controls, and characteristics of effective controls. Special attention is given to the art of making controls effective.

Chapter 16 is an in-depth look at four kinds of controls: financial, budgetary, marketing, and human resource. Financial-statement analysis is followed by budget-development processes and types of budgets. Next, various marketing controls are scrutinized, followed by popular human resource controls.

Chapter 17 focuses on total quality management and productivity issues. Key contributors to TQM are chronicled, methods for implementing TQM detailed, and the link between quality and productivity explained. Factors that affect productivity are examined along with how to manage to increase it.

Chapter 18 looks at operations management—its nature, its link to planning, processes, and facilities, and how to manage operations. How to control operations for both quality and productivity is included.

Part VI: Special Concerns This section explores information management systems, international management, succeeding in one's career, and management ethics and social responsibility. Although all chapters include regular features on ethics and international applications, these important subjects merit further exploration.

Chapter 19 focuses on information flow and how it can be managed in organizations. Management information systems and their computerized applications are discussed in detail.

Chapter 20 explores the recent trends affecting businesses in global markets, the dependence of American businesses on foreign suppliers and customers, and the nature of multinational corporations. Each function of management is discussed as it applies to an international operation and environment.

Chapter 21 is concerned with career management. Stages in career development and steps in career planning are analyzed. These analyses are followed by several strategies managers can take to advance their career.

Chapter 22 examines ethical issues and the need to be proactive when managing for social responsibility. After defining both concepts, the chapter explores ethical tests, approaches to social responsibility, and the links between them and applicable legal requirements. The issues of responsibilities to stakeholders and of government regulation of business activities are dealt with as well.

Acknowledgments

We would like to thank the following reviewers who were helpful in preparing the previous editions of this text: A. M. Agnello (Solano Community College), Anthony J. Alesi (Passaic County Community College), Douglas Anderson (Ashland College), Gary Bacon (North Lake College), Sr. Marian Batho (Aquinas Junior College), Rex L. Bishop (Charles County Community College), Donna Bleck (Middlesex Community College), Gus Blomquist (Del Mar College), John Bohan (Clackamas Community College), Arnold J. Bornfield (Worcester State University), Bruce E. Bugbee (Glendale Community College), John Carmichael (Union County College), Charles Chanter (Grand Rapids Junior College), Linda M. Duckworth (Northeast Mississippi Community College), Jim Garaventa (Chemeketa Community College), William H. Graham, Jr. (Catawba Valley Community College), David A. Gray (University of Texas, Arlington), Theodore L. Hansen, Jr. (Salem State College), Dave Harris (Mission College). S. Miller Harrison (Durham Technical Community College), Ken Howey (Trident Technical College), Don Hucker (Cypress College), Samir T. Ishak (Grand Valley State University), W. J. Jacobs (Lake City Community College), Judith E. Kizzie (Clinton Community College), Gus L. Kotoulas (Morton College), Arthur La Capria, Jr. (El Paso Community College), Norbert Lindskog (Washington College), John E. McCarty (New Mexico Junior College), Vladimir G. Marinich (Howard Community College), Leonard Martyns (Chaffey College), Jim Lee Morgan (West Los Angeles College), Joyce P. Moseley (Trident Technical College), George Otto (Truman College), Quenton Pulliam (Nashville State Technical Institute), Carol Rowey (Community College of Rhode Island), Seiji Sugawara (Mendocino College), Ralph Todd (American River College), W. Emory Trainham (Ashland College), Sumner M. White (Massachusetts Bay Community College), Bob Willis (Rogers State College), Doug Ashby (Lewis and Clark Community College), Tom Birkenhead (Lane Community College), Rex L. Bishop (Charles County Community College), Felipe H. Chia (Harrisburg Area Community College), Edward Giermak (College of DuPage), Dennis Hansen (Des Moines Area Community College), Clay Lifto (Kirkwood Community College), Sylvia Ong (Scottsdale Community College), Dennis D. Pappas (Columbus State Community College), and Patricia Mink Rath (The International Academy of Merchandising and Design Ltd.—Chicago Campus).

We extend heartfelt thanks to the following reviewers who have been so helpful in preparing this fifth edition: Allen Bluedorn (University of Missouri, Columbia), C. Richard Paulson (Mankato State University), David W. Murphy (Madisonville Community College), Edwin A. Giermak (College of DuPage), Tom Shaughnessy (Illinois Central College), Bill Tinder (Greenville Tech), Ravi Sarathy (Northeastern University), Joseph C. Santora (Essex County College), Kehinde A. Adesina (Contra Costa College), Paul Hegele (Elgin Community College), Duane C. Brickner (South Mountain Community College), George Labovitz, Scott King (Sinclaire Community College), Helen A. Corley (Oxnard College), James B. Thomas (Pennsylvania State University), Martin S. St. John (Westmoreland County Community College), and Anthony B. Foster (Cloud County Community College).

With thanks,
Warren Plunkett
Ray Attner

A Strategic Guide

to the Fifth Edition of Plunkett & Attner's
Introduction to Management

Good planning and organization: These two elements are equally essential to successfully operating a business and writing a textbook—and using one! This six-page guide introduces you to the features in the text that are designed to help you master the management concepts fundamental to success in today's business environment.

Essential Terms are your introduction to the vocabulary of management. They are listed at the beginning of each chapter, then defined in context, as well as at the end of the chapter, and in a master glossary at the back of the book.

Management in Action cases highlight relevant experiences of actual companies and managers. This example, for instance, offers practical, real-world application of strategic planning for future growth.

E S S E N T I A L   T E R M S

budget	management by objectives	operational plan	rule
contingency planning	(MBO)	plan	single-use plan
forecasting	mission statement	planning	standing plan
linear programming	objective	policy	strategic objective
	operational objective	procedure	strategic plan
		program	tactical objective
			tactical plan

M A N A G E M E N T   I N   A C T I O N
McDonald's Plan for Global Dominance

f **CEO** Michael R. Quinlan's plans are successful, the golden arches and Ronald McDonald will be familiar in every country in the world. Quinlan expresses his ambition this way: "I don't know what we will be serving in the year 2000, but we'll be serving more of it than anyone else." His goal is simple and direct: "I want it all. That's all. I want it all."

To realize such an ambition—or even come close—you need a plan, which McDonald's has. Faced with the prospect of limited domestic growth, the world's largest food-service company is training its sights and energies on foreign markets. Today, McDonald's has more than 12,500 restaurants operating in 61 countries. But in preparation for expansion into new territories, it has established 7,000 trademarks in 130 additional nations.

The potential is enormous. Consider this: In the United States there is one McDonald's for every 29,000 Americans; in

Australia, Canada, England, France, Germany, and Japan—referred to by McDonald's as the Big Six countries—there is one set of golden arches for every 134,000 people. In Taiwan, 425,000 people must share a restaurant; in Brazil, the figure is two million. Not only are the potential numbers significant, but the profits abroad are growing nearly three times faster than at home.

McDonald's management plans to open 400 to 500 restaurants a year outside the United States throughout the decade. The company intends to build 1,000 restaurants in Europe in the next five years and add 70 per year for the next 10 years in Japan. Major investments will be made in Mexico, with the YASNY (You Ain't Seen Nothing Yet) development company.

If Michael Quinlan has his way and the plan is successful, perhaps we have not seen anything yet. For starters, Quinlan can add to his 20% share of an estimated $6-billion

Planning for future growth, McDonald's hopes that one day the golden arches will span the globe.

Words and Graphics Working Together

Thumb through the book and look at the colorful **charts**, **diagrams**, and **photographs** that appear on almost every page. Of course, these graphic elements make the book attractive and inviting, but they do more. The words and illustrations throughout are designed to reinforce each other; by organizing material and depicting it graphically, the text's concepts and theories become easy to understand, retain, and apply.

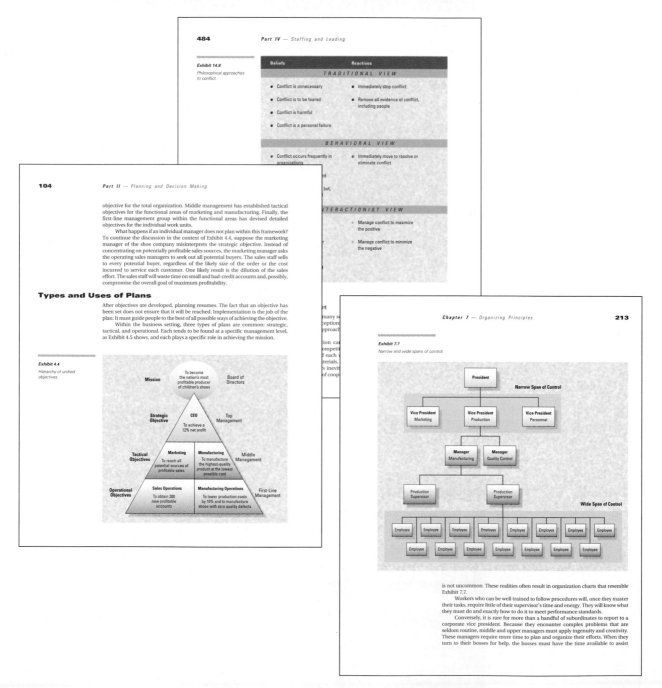

484   *Part IV — Staffing and Leading*

Exhibit 14.8
Philosophical approaches to conflict.

Beliefs	Reactions
TRADITIONAL VIEW	
• Conflict is unnecessary	• Immediately stop conflict
• Conflict is to be feared	• Remove all evidence of conflict, including people
• Conflict is harmful	
• Conflict is a personal failure	
BEHAVIORAL VIEW	
• Conflict occurs frequently in organizations	• Immediately move to resolve or eliminate conflict
INTERACTIONIST VIEW	
	• Manage conflict to maximize the positive
	• Manage conflict to minimize the negative

104   *Part II — Planning and Decision Making*

objective for the total organization. Middle management has established tactical objectives for the functional areas of marketing and manufacturing. Finally, the first-line management group within the functional areas has devised detailed objectives for the individual work units.

What happens if an individual manager does not plan within this framework? To continue the discussion in the context of Exhibit 4.4, suppose the marketing manager of the shoe company misinterprets the strategic objective. Instead of concentrating on potentially profitable sales sources, the marketing manager asks the operating sales managers to seek out all potential buyers. The sales staff sells to every potential buyer, regardless of the likely size of the order or the cost incurred to service each customer. One likely result is the dilution of the sales effort. The sales staff will waste time on small and bad-credit accounts and, possibly, compromise the overall goal of maximum profitability.

Types and Uses of Plans

After objectives are developed, planning resumes. The fact that an objective has been set does not ensure that it will be reached. Implementation is the job of the plan: It must guide people to the best of all possible ways of achieving the objective.

Within the business setting, three types of plans are common: strategic, tactical, and operational. Each tends to be found at a specific management level, as Exhibit 4.5 shows, and each plays a specific role in achieving the mission.

Exhibit 4.4
Hierarchy of unified objectives.

Mission — To become the nation's most profitable producer of children's shoes — **Board of Directors**

Strategic Objective — CEO — To achieve a 12% net profit — **Top Management**

Tactical Objectives — Marketing: To reach all potential sources of profitable sales — Manufacturing: To manufacture the highest-quality product at the lowest possible cost — **Middle Management**

Operational Objectives — Sales Operations: To obtain 200 new profitable accounts — Manufacturing Operations: To lower production costs by 10% and to manufacture shoes with zero quality defects — **First-Line Management**

Chapter 7 — Organizing Principles   **213**

Exhibit 7.7
Narrow and wide spans of control.

President

Narrow Span of Control

Vice President — Marketing
Vice President — Production
Vice President — Personnel

Manager — Manufacturing
Manager — Quality Control

Production Supervisor
Production Supervisor

Wide Span of Control

Employee × 8
Employee × 7

is not uncommon. These realities often result in organization charts that resemble Exhibit 7.7.

Workers who can be well trained to follow procedures will, once they master their tasks, require little of their supervisor's time and energy. They will know what they must do and exactly how to do it to meet performance standards.

Conversely, it is rare for more than a handful of subordinates to report to a corporate vice president. Because they encounter complex problems that are seldom routine, middle and upper managers must apply ingenuity and creativity. These managers require more time to plan and organize their efforts. When they turn to their bosses for help, the bosses must have the time available to assist

Fundamental Topics for Managers of the '90s

Two primary concerns of today are **total quality management** and adapting to a **global business environment**. You will discover the importance of these topics to every aspect of management as real-life examples in every chapter reveal how successful organizations and their managers are responding to these new challenges. All of these current and informative sidebars are unique to this edition (in fact, 95 percent of all the material is new).

Chapter 14 — Team Management and Conflict　　　**471**

F O C U S　　O N　　Q U A L I T Y
Quality Teams Reform the Workplace

Ann Combs's co-workers used to hate to come to work in the morning. "There was no morale, absolutely none," says the Navy travel manager. Vernedia Arlington, an X-ray worker at Sentara Norfolk General Hospital in Virginia, felt the same way. She was about to quit, burned out after 15 years

important, the team members convinced management to listen to them and act on their suggestions.

Each team made stunning improvements in the workplace, rejuvenated morale, slashed bureaucracy, and eliminated waste.

...son Federal Express team revamped a ...cess and saved the overnight-delivery ...early $1 million in 18 months. Prior to ...innovative problem solving, up to ...ages a month were missing flights.

...eam at U.S. Steel slashed shipments ...teel by 78% and prevented U.S. auto ...m dumping the plant as a supplier.

...Hospital, the doctors were waiting ...to get an X-ray image. When the ...m finished its analysis, the turnaround ...0 minutes.

...e of hourly employees at L S Electro ...literally run their company. They ...on the responsibility for planning, ...and quality assurance. The com- ...ductivity increased 20%, and quality ...programs saved the company ...one year.

...t the Naval Aviation Depot Operations ...amlined purchasing and maintenance ...aving the Navy $2 million a year. ▲

...ams," *USA Today,* April 10, 1992, pp. 1D–2D.

338　　*Part IV — Staffing and Leading*

G L O B A L　　A P P L I C A T I O N S
Staffing the Japanese Way

Staffing practices of American and Japanese companies differ in important ways. Each is a product of its country's culture; the shrinking business world, however, means that each must learn the strengths of the other. Here are some of the major distinctions of the Japanese way:

- Large Japanese companies competing in international markets offer lifetime employment to their employees. Once a person joins the company, its managers will do whatever is necessary to keep that person usefully employed.

- The Japanese prefer to train employees to do a variety of tasks. Job descriptions, where they exist, are usually broad and do not list specific duties. They focus instead on skills. People are expected to do what they know how to do when and where it is necessary.

- Before taking action, Japanese managers seek consensus—unanimous agreement by a group on what needs to be done and how to proceed. Even at the lowest level of a company, teams of workers conduct business in the same way.

- Japan lacks meaningful antidiscrimination laws; non-Japanese people as well as women are openly discriminated against. In foreign opera- tions, however, Japanese companies must abide by the host country's laws.

- In Japan, recruiting for entry-level management jobs takes place at schools and universities.

From then on, management jobs are usually filled from within. Japanese employers promote by tapping the pool of employees who intend to spend their careers with just one employer.

- Japanese companies tend to use the techniques of the assessment center to screen applicants. They rely heavily on in-depth interviews as well as hands-on exercises to determine applicants' attitudes, commitment, and talents.

- Job rotation as a means for training and development is more common in Japan than in the United States. Japanese employees move through jobs in one area and also cross functional lines. Japanese managers tend to stay in a job for a longer period of time than the typical American manager does.

- In Japan, employee appraisals are part of the mentoring process. Those who conduct the evaluations try hard not to embarrass an em- ployee. Japanese appraisals tend to be less formal than American appraisals.

- Salaries and promotions for Japanese employees are typically linked to seniority and experience. Wages and salaries are usually lower than they are in the United States.

- Forced retirements are still common in Japanese companies. They usually occur before an employee is over 60 years old. ▲

...rk team. Work-team members assume ...s and complementing each other. The ...exas Instruments, a Malcolm Baldrige ...teams in operation. Under the team ...ssemblies, and all members learn the

---

According to Ira Kay, a management consultant with the Hay Group (*Business Week,* January 27, 1992):

> [American CEOs of companies with revenues between $500 million and $800 million] enjoy pay levels that are 13.6 times those of entry-level professionals. For Italy, Germany, Britain, and Japan, such multiples are comparable, ranging from 12.1 to 13.1.

In recent years, however, discussion of "excessive" executive compensation has appeared in popular periodicals and the business press.

More New Coverage

Managers of the '90s must be able to identify ethical problems and adapt corporate policy accordingly. **Issues and Ethics** features not only discuss many moral dilemmas that face managers today, but also challenge you to resolve the conflicts that arise when profitability or expediency collide with ethics.

Each chapter includes an actual **Case Problem**, directly related to the chapter content. Some are success stories; others (like the one shown here) present unresolved problems. All of these case studies, however, allow you to apply what you have learned. There are no right or wrong answers— just workable solutions, based on the underlying principles of informed management decisions.

---

370   *Part IV — Staffing and Leading*

I S S U E S   A N D   E T H I C S
Do We Need to Leash Electronic Watchdogs?

n today's electronic environment, people often socialize by using the company's e-mail. Gossip, recipes, social invitations, and rumors all appear in electronic mailboxes. Employers have ways of accessing private e-mail once it is in the computer system. Some employees have been fired on the basis of information that was contained in their electronic mailboxes.

By looking at the contents of e-mail, for example, employers have discovered that employees were communicating confidential information to unauthorized persons or using company time to run a personal business.

Since 1986 a federal law has restricted third-person access to e-mail messages, but the law does not deal directly with an employer's right to scan the contents of e-mail.

For many years, employers have used electronic monitoring to keep track of how employees are using their computers. Many employees are evaluated, in part, on the findings of systems that keep track of computer keystrokes, number of orders processed, and the amount of time employees are actively using their computers. The issue with electronic eavesdropping and monitoring is one of privacy.

What do you think about an employer using a computer system to monitor your performance? Should supervisors be allowed to read the personal messages sent between employees at work? Do you see broader social or ethical conflicts in this issue? ▲

---

people to
much. The
providing
keeping co
that when
should ob

Change
When a ne
methods,
to cope wi
Group in
to people.
team play

Rank or
the higher
others. Ra
willing to
imagine t
listening t
In *R*
Wang Lab
an unwill

Chapter 7 — Organizing Principles   **231**

C A S E   P R O B L E M
Crises at GM

he future of General Motors is in the hands of President John Jack Smith—and he has his work cut out for him. The company continues to flounder. It lags behind its major competitors in almost every measure of efficiency. By some key standards—how many worker hours it takes to assemble a car, for example—GM is 40% less productive than Ford. In 1991 GM lost, on average, $1,500 on every one of the more than 3.5 million cars and trucks it made in North America. It ended 1991 with about 35% of the U.S. market; the company had sold fewer than 13 million new cars and light trucks that year. In comparison, in 1979 GM had commanded 46% of the market.

Salvaging GM, in the opinion of both insiders and outside observers, will require a radical restructuring. The company has a long tradition of being highly centralized and insulated from the rest of the industry. The current structure still reflects a time when the company had abundant time to work on any problem.

The organizational problems that Smith faces include:

- The existence of separate marketing operations for each of its six car divisions—Chevrolet, Pontiac, Oldsmobile, Buick, Cadillac, and Saturn.

- The fact that GM, unlike any other auto company in the world, has a chief of design and a head of research who do not report to the auto-making side of the business. Instead, both report to the head of R&D, who in turn reports to another executive—a top-level manager who runs the aerospace divisions. This arrangement penalizes GM in two ways. Because designers do not work closely with vehicle engineers, development is long and costly. Second, scientists do not work with the engineers, so GM is slow to apply new technologies—even when GM developed them.

- A past history of poor managerial performance without accountability. Fewer than 100 salaried workers out of well over 100,000 were dismissed annually for poor performance between 1977 and 1983.

- A nonfunctioning decision-making structure. Middle managers—sometimes referred to as the "frozen middle"—have often been unable or unwilling to make decisions.

Q U E S T I O N S

1. For each of the four situations noted, what organizational concepts apply? Explain.

2. As an advisor to President John Jack Smith, how would you resolve each situation?

For more about the crises at GM, see Alex Taylor, "Can GM Remodel," *Fortune*, January 13, 1992, pp. 26–29, 32–34.

Setting Goals and Reviewing Progress

A strategy for study appears at the beginning of each chapter. By keeping these **Learning Objectives** in mind while reading the text and relating them to the concepts discussed, you will gain full understanding of the principles of successful management.

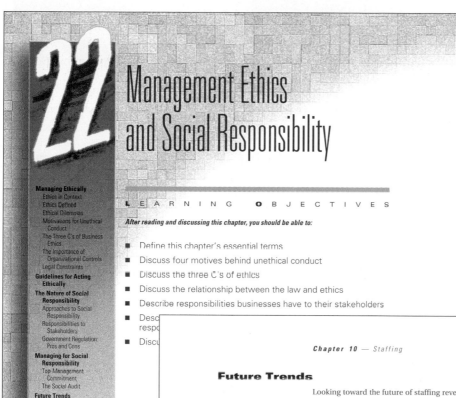

22 Management Ethics and Social Responsibility

Managing Ethically
Ethics in Context
Ethics Defined
Ethical Dilemmas
Motivations for Unethical Conduct
The Three C's of Business Ethics
The Importance of Organizational Controls
Legal Constraints

Guidelines for Acting Ethically

The Nature of Social Responsibility
Approaches to Social Responsibility
Responsibilities to Stakeholders
Government Regulation: Pros and Cons

Managing for Social Responsibility
Top Management Commitment
The Social Audit

Future Trends

L E A R N I N G   O B J E C T I V E S

After reading and discussing this chapter, you should be able to:

■ Define this chapter's essential terms

■ Discuss four motives behind unethical conduct

■ Discuss the three C's of ethics

■ Discuss the relationship between the law and ethics

■ Describe responsibilities businesses have to their stakeholders

■ Desc... respo...

■ Discu...

Effective management techniques are never static, so each chapter concludes with an overview of **Future Trends**. Based on emerging concerns, this survey provides insight into the environment that you, as a manager of tomorrow, will face.

The **Chapter Summary** is designed to check your grasp of the chapter's learning objectives as well as your ability to apply them effectively.

Future Trends

Looking toward the future of staffing reveals four areas that are likely to become increasingly more important:

● Top managers' compensation. A number of recent articles on this subject indicate that American executives' pay and benefits are out of line when compared with compensation systems around the world. The IRS and Congress are currently considering ways to cap executives' pay.

● Privacy issues. Concerns over privacy will grow in significance and begin to cost employers additional time and money. Tests for honesty, AIDS, drug use, and genetic predispositions to disease are just four of the hot topics that relate to privacy.

● Work force diversity. The growing numbers of Asian-, Hispanic-, and African-Americans bring special strengths and needs to the workplace. Forecasts show that businesses will become increasingly dependent on these protected groups. Programs in the workplace that respond to cultural diversity are in growing demand.

● Meeting employees' needs. Employers will be under greater pressure to modify tasks and work procedures to accommodate employees. Managers and organizations will have to become more flexible.

C H A P T E R   S U M M A R Y

■ People are an organization's most important asset. Staffing is the process of attracting, developing, rewarding, and retaining competent people.

■ Staffing is part of every manager's job. It requires expertise and a knowledge of applicable law. Managers must provide equal opportunity in all employment decisions, especially with respect to protected groups.

■ Many companies must make their human resource decisions in the context of agreements made with labor organizations and through collective bargaining.

■ Human resource planning begins with a job analysis. Performing a job analysis involves creating descriptions of all jobs in an area

P·A·R·T

Management Concepts

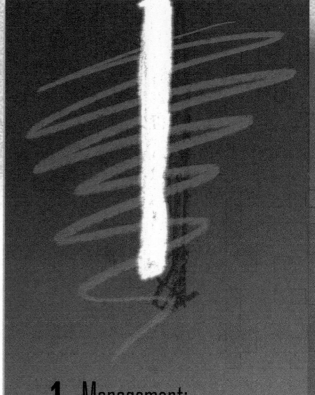

Management: An Overview

LEARNING OBJECTIVES

After reading and discussing this chapter, you should be able to:

- Define the essential terms that appear in the text

- Explain why organizations need managers

- Describe the manager's environment

- Distinguish between the myths and realities of a manager's job

- Identify and explain the three levels of company management

- Identify and explain the five management functions

- Explain how management functions apply to all levels of management

- Describe the manager's roles

- Describe managerial skills in three key categories: technical, human, and conceptual

conceptual skills | efficiency | human skills | middle management
effectiveness | feedback | management | organization
 | first-line management | management hierarchy | role
 | | manager | supervisor
 | | | technical skills
 | | | top management

MANAGEMENT IN ACTION
Southwest Airlines

Great management is not easily defined, but admirers of Dallas-based Southwest Airlines suggest that it thrives at that company. Some industry analysts predict that Southwest will be among the few U.S. airlines to survive the fierce competition that has raged in commercial aviation since 1978, when Congress deregulated America's airline industry. Deregulation meant that, for the first time since 1934, airline routes, fares, and operating practices were not controlled by federal statutes.

Since deregulation, some 169 airline companies have failed, merged, or never left the runway. Meanwhile, Southwest posted profits in each of the past 18 years; in 1990 it was the only carrier to earn a net

Flightplan for success: Southwest's sharply defined business strategy and a people-oriented management philosophy.

profit based solely on operations, and it offered the industry's lowest fares. Moreover, Southwest's aggregate costs ranked lowest among major carriers, and its workers are among the industry's best paid.

Southwest's high performance derives from two sources: a sharply defined business strategy that the company follows faithfully and a management philosophy and culture created and practiced by Chief Executive Officer (CEO) Herbert Kelleher.

The strategy consists of several directives:

- Carve a market niche as the nation's only high-frequency, short-haul, low-fare, point-to-point carrier.

- Provide service where little or no competition exists.

- Offer multiple flights per day to the same destination.

- Standardize the fleet with a single aircraft type (Southwest chose a versatile twin-jet plane, the Boeing 737) to save on training and maintenance costs.

- Maintain a gate turnaround time of 15 minutes.

- Offer a quality service without frills—no meals, no centralized reservation system, no transfer of baggage to other airlines.

But what generates Southwest Airlines' enviable company loyalty and esprit de corps is Herb Kelleher's management philosophy, which is built around three ideas: Have fun, hire people with good attitudes, and treat employees well. Implementing the view that

"You can't teach attitude," Southwest recruits people who are outgoing and positive; the airline hires attitude, then develops skills. Kelleher is called Uncle Herb by some staffers. He's been known to appear on flights, dressed as the Easter Bunny, or at a hangar at 2:00 a.m., dressed as Corporal Klinger of TV's "M*A*S*H," to show his appreciation to mechanics working late. Says Kelleher, "There's no reason that work has to be suffered with seriousness, that professionalism can't be worn lightly. Fun is a stimulant to people. They enjoy their work more, and they work more productively."

Southwest employees are recruited with the customer in mind (frequent flyers even sit in on hiring interviews), and workers are treated well. Once hired, staffers are soon accepted into the extended, although not-too-large, family. (The staffing ratio is low among airlines, as is the age of the average employee, 34.) Nine in 10 Southwest workers belong to labor unions, employees own 11% of the company, the average

> **❝**Fun is a stimulant to people. They enjoy their work more, and they work more productively.**❞**
>
> — **Herbert Kelleher**, CEO, Southwest Airlines

salary of $42,000 ranks among the industry's highest, layoffs are not part of company policy, union negotiations are routinely harmonious, and labor contracts are free of restrictive provisions. Perhaps most important, managers encourage their people to act with initiative: "We can't anticipate [everything]; you handle [problems] the best way possible. Make a judgment, use your discretion; we trust you'll do the right thing. If we think you've done something erroneous, we'll let you know—without criticism, without backbiting."

Some results of Kelleher's philosophy? To speed turnarounds, flight attendants and even pilots pick up cabin trash between flights. Typically, ground crews of six—half the industry average—turn flights around in a snappy 15 minutes (compared with other airlines' more leisurely and costly 60). One gate agent—not two or three, as you'll find at the gates of other airlines—routinely handles passenger check-in.

When fuel costs soared following Iraq's invasion of Kuwait in January 1991, nearly one-third of Southwest's 8,600 employees pitched in to help buy fuel for the fleet. CEO Kelleher learned of the "Fuel from the Heart" scheme only when he received a banner signed by employees who'd pledged voluntary payroll deductions.

Much of Southwest Airlines' success results directly from management's sound strategy and philosophy, along with imagination and respect throughout the organization. ▲

For more about Southwest Airlines, see Wendy Zellner, "Striking Gold in California Skies," *Business Week,* March 30, 1992, p. 48; Edward Welles, "Captain Marvel," *Inc.,* January 1992, pp. 44–48; Charles A. Jaffee, "Moving Fast by Standing Still," *Nation's Business,* October 1991, pp. 57–60; Subrata N. Chakravaty, "Hit 'em Hardest with the Mostest," *Forbes,* September 16, 1991, pp. 48–52.

Why Managers Are Needed

What does a manager do? What skills does an effective manager command? To understand why managers are essential in nearly every human enterprise is to begin to grasp the fundamentals of management theory and practice.

The Organizational Purpose of Managers

Managers, people who direct the activity of others, are necessary because society cannot function without organizations, and organizations cannot function without managers.

From ancient evidence we know that, since the beginning of culture, human beings have worked cooperatively to survive and prosper. Among the most important human inventions is the **organization**, a group of two or more persons that operates to achieve common objectives. While sharing common characteristics, organizations show wide diversity in size, structure, resources, membership, and purpose—from hungry cave dwellers' first hunting bands, to NASA, to the International Red Cross, to the Beatles. Objectives are what organizations strive toward, outcomes to be accomplished through plan and action. Such objectives commonly include creating and providing goods and services to the organization's members or to outsiders.

Without mechanisms to guide and coordinate activities, however, some members of the organization might do work they thought advanced the objectives when, in fact, they were actually undoing the work of other members. Managers prevent such conflict and disorder and coordinate everyone's work toward common objectives. A modern manager may be the owner or operator or founder (or all three) of an organization, or perhaps someone hired to give direction to the entity. In each case, a manager makes decisions and commits the organization's resources (people, capital, information, and equipment) to achieve its objectives.

The Universal Need for Managers

Although they are most often thought of as working in private, for-profit businesses, managers are essential in every kind of organization. The college dean, the local director of the American Heart Association, the school board president, the parish priest, as well as Disney's Michael Eisner and Southwest Airlines' Herb Kelleher, are all managers. For all the range and variety of their individual titles and assignments, managers share fundamental challenges and responsibilities. They exhibit common behaviors and perform similar identifiable functions.

Researchers, scholars, and practitioners in many fields—notably history, economics, mathematics, psychology, sociology, and information theory—have accumulated an imposing body of theoretical and practical knowledge about what managers do. That knowledge is now the sole focus of academic departments, schools, and colleges of business and management, and it grows increasingly useful in solving local, national, and global problems.

In the pages ahead we'll examine what managers do—and how they do it—in sufficient scope and detail to allow the willing student to master the core principles of modern management and its implementation.

What Management Is

Management is the process of setting and achieving goals through five basic functions that acquire and utilize human, financial, material, and information resources. The five basic functions are planning, organizing, staffing, directing, and controlling.

In testing this definition, consider these related ideas, each to be examined in detail in later chapters:

- Managers make conscious decisions about the acquisition and use of resources to achieve objectives.

- Managers accomplish tasks through people. Once managers acquire financial, material, and information resources and set objectives for the organization, they work through the organization's members to reach the stated objectives.

- Managers work with both individuals and groups, not with only one or the other. They work with each subordinate (person) and at the same time develop subordinates into a coordinated work group. Both tasks demand a manager's skill and patience.

The Manager's Universe

The real world of management is complex, exacting, exciting, and filled with pressure. As Apple Computer's CEO John Sculley says, "There's never a dull moment during my days" (Verity, 1992).

Such descriptions appear to accurately reflect the experience of most managers, men and women whose working environments around the world are becoming increasingly complex. Consider only a few examples of significant recent changes in American business:

- Wang Laboratories, the pioneer developer of corporate word processing systems, was forced into bankruptcy after failing to pursue the consumer computer market.

- United Parcel Service, once virtually alone in the private package-delivery business, was suddenly challenged across its markets by innovative competitors—notably, Federal Express.

- American book publishing, long a stable industry, abruptly faced dramatic changes in bookmaking and bookselling technology. The changes spawned a flood of new companies and mergers among the major players.

- U.S. airlines tried to cope with deregulation, computerized sales systems, and shifting global trends. As a result, the skies turned into an economic war zone. In terms of the airline business of 1978, the airline business today is virtually unrecognizable.

Clearly, adjusting to such changes makes day-to-day corporate management exceedingly intricate and exacting. Managers today face multiple demands on their time and resourcefulness. Many demands recur as fairly predictable parts of day-to-day operations. Others are more complex, testing the manager's intelligence, imagination, patience, and commitment. Some challenges arrive swiftly and dramatically. In this category are technological advances that trigger sweeping consumer market shifts (consider the compact disc, the fax machine) and calamities (recall the oil spill involving the Exxon *Valdez* in Alaska [1989] and the toxic gas leak in a Union Carbide facility in Bhopal, India [1984]).

Significant challenges to managers at every level result from natural phenomena, such as the devastating hurricanes Hugo and Andrew in 1992 and the 25-million-gallon spill from the oil tanker *Braer* in the Shetland Islands in 1993. From insurance companies and public utilities to every local firm, managers are needed not only to act immediately and decisively, but to adjust their long-range planning as well.

Other challenges are more subtle and far-reaching. These stem from immensely complex social changes under way around the globe. Among pressing issues directly affecting managers are:

- Immigration patterns. Consider the changing labor market in the southwestern United States or the turmoil in Germany caused by that country's unification and the influx of refugees from disintegrating Yugoslavia.

- Racial tensions. Consider the effects of racial violence in Johannesburg or Los Angeles.

- Health issues. Consider the devastating impact of drug addiction and the HIV, or AIDS, virus.

Even as immediate issues clamor for action, managers cannot ignore emerging trends and developments for which organizations must prepare. Three powerful developments promise to reshape business patterns in the coming century:

- Internationalization

- Consumer commitment to ethical practices by businesses

- Awareness of the relationship between quality and long-term profitability

These trends require thoughtful preparation by managers today.

Globalization is changing the world of business. The manufacturing managers at Honda's plant in Marysville, Ohio, have learned to work together despite their cultural differences.

Internationalization occurs when a transnational firm habitually conducts business worldwide—obtaining raw materials in one country and financing in another, manufacturing components in a third country, assembling final products in several, and selling in dozens more. In a climate of internationalization, borders between countries become practically "transparent." The European Community and the North American Trade Agreement are examples of commitments that foster internationalization. Businesses of every size and kind are affected by internationalization, and the trend is rapidly accelerating.

The second development is the rising recognition among consumers throughout the community that corporations should be held morally and politically responsible for their actions. Issues relating to corporate responsibility are often discussed under the label *ethics,* the moral principles of conduct governing individuals and organizations.

The third is the disarmingly simple discovery that "quality"—defined differently by experts of every persuasion—may be the achievement through which today's corporations will ensure their competitive survival and long-term profitability.

Accommodating and utilizing such developments in the changing business environment will demand a growing portion of every manager's time and focus. So vital will these three trends be in every manager's future that each succeeding chapter will include features that highlights one of them. These features are called *Global Applications, Issues and Ethics,* and *Focus on Quality.*

A final note about the nature of management: Managers must find a way to balance these multiple demands. As a new challenge arises, the manager must attempt to understand its importance and consciously make a place for it among other critical priorities. He or she does this by shifting existing responsibilities.

The Myths and Realities of a Manager's Job

Henry Mintzberg examined the effect of multiple demands on managers by studying how managers actually work (Mintzberg, 1975). His conclusions contrast sharply with myths commonly held about managers.

Myth #1: The manager is a reflective, methodical planner with time to systematically plan and work through a day.

Reality: The typical manager takes on so much and encounters such constant interruption that little time remains for reflection. Events range from trivialities to crises; the average time spent on one activity is 9 minutes.

Myth #2: The effective manager has no regular duties to perform. He establishes others' responsibilities in advance and then relaxes to watch others do the work.

Reality: Although their days may be interrupted by crises, managers have regular duties to perform. They must attend meetings, see to visitors from the community and other parts of the organization, and continuously process information. To perform all their duties, managers often extend the day into the night—recall Herb Kelleher of Southwest Airlines, who entertains mechanics at 2:00 in the morning. One study found that 12-hour days are common for managers (Schares, 1992).

Myth #3: The manager's job is a science; managers work systematically and analytically to determine programs and procedures.

Reality: The manager's job is less a science than an art. Rather than systematic procedures and programs, managers rely heavily on intuition and judgment.

Who Managers Are

Directories of corporate officers display a blizzard of inventive titles for managers. A better way to discover who managers are is to bypass showy labels and examine levels of management and areas of responsibility.

Levels of Management

In comparing managers and their work throughout an organization, similarities and differences abound. Although all managers perform variations of the same functions, different positions in the company require different emphases. In most organizations the management group consists of a **management hierarchy,** a pyramid-shaped arrangement of management levels in three categories: top, middle, and first-line (supervisory). Exhibit 1.1 shows these three levels.

Top management consists of the organization's highest-ranking manager— the chief executive officer or president—and that person's immediate subordinates, who are often called vice presidents. In many U.S. publicly held companies, the CEO, president, and COO (chief operating officer) are appointed by a board of directors. (The titles CEO, president, and COO may be held simultaneously by one or several persons.) The board, in turn, is elected by the corporation's stockholders—the owners to whom all management is presumably accountable.

Such boards traditionally establish the organization's broadest objectives: Management is then charged with meeting those objectives and, if it sees fit,

Exhibit 1.1

The pyramid structure of management hierarchy.

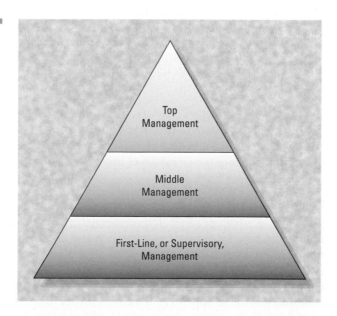

establishing subordinate goals. Methods and goals must be consistent with laws, generally accepted customs, and other broad societal guidelines, as well as the organization's own formal rules and regulations. The degree of control exercised by directors varies widely: Some boards allow top managers a virtually unlimited scope of action so long as objectives are satisfactorily met; others keep managers on leashes of various lengths.

Top management, then, is responsible for the overall management of the organization. With the charter granted by its board, top management establishes company-wide objectives, goals, and operating policies; it directs the company's broad relations with the external environment.

Middle management includes managers below the rank of vice president but above the supervisory level. Some organizations include two or three middle-management levels. Whether labeled by geographic region or group function (such as marketing or production), managers at this level implement top management's objectives and policies; their subordinates are other managers. Typically, planning and sales managers are middle managers.

First-line managers, or **supervisors**, are at the operating level, the lowest level of management. They manage their specific groups and direct the actual work of the organization. Their subordinates are nonmanagement workers—the men and women upon whom all managers depend for execution of their plans. A night manager at a Holiday Inn is a first-line supervisor.

Specific titles of managers depend on the organizations for which they work and on the actual jobs they perform. In government bureaucracies, for example, titles such as administrator, section chief, and director are common; private businesses favor supervisor, manager, or vice president. Outside the specific environment in which they are used, however, management titles convey little meaning. A district manager in one company might be called regional manager in a competing firm. Exhibit 1.2 illustrates the three levels of management in one organization and includes the titles used for managers at each level.

Areas of Management

Managers may be identified by the kind of work, activity, or functions they are responsible for. Common management groupings in large U.S. manufacturing and service corporations include marketing, operations, finance, and human resources.

Marketing Managers. Marketing managers generally direct research and product development, pricing, promotion, and distribution strategy. In Exhibit 1.2, the vice president of marketing is a top-level manager; regional, district, and group managers are midlevel managers; and the branch manager is a first-line supervisor.

Operations Managers. These managers direct activities involved in creating goods and services. For a manufacturing firm, operations managers are responsible for inventory control, plant layout, production control, and quality control. An operations manager in a service setting—a hospital, say, or a restaurant—focuses on maximizing processes to eliminate inefficiency and enhance quality. In Exhibit 1.2, the head of operations is the vice president of manufacturing, a top-level manager; other managers rank below this vice president, in succeeding levels of hierarchy.

Exhibit 1.2

Typical titles in the three levels of management.

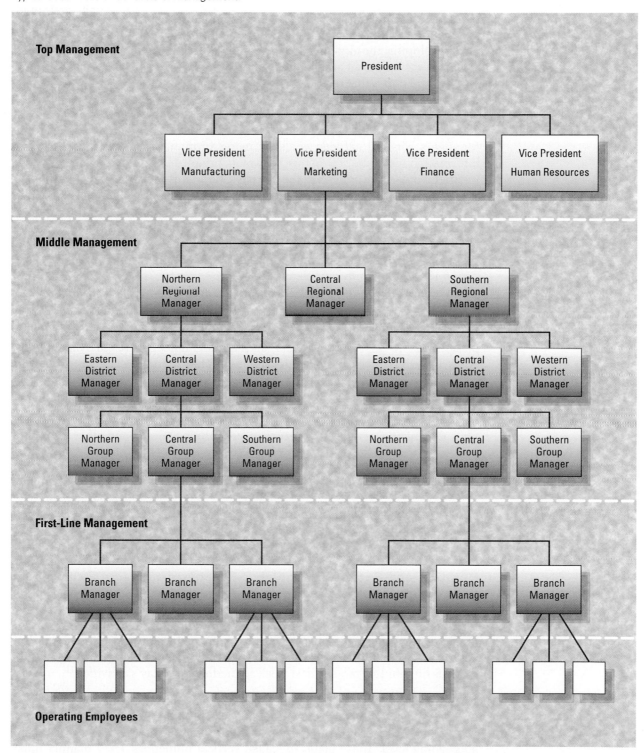

Finance Managers.   Not surprisingly, these people manage an organization's financial assets. Individual managers in this area direct accounting, investments, budgeting, and financial controls.

Human Resource Managers.   These men and women are charged with forecasting staffing needs and recruiting, qualifying, selecting, orienting, training, and developing the organization's people. Human resource managers devise performance appraisal and compensation systems, oversee labor relations, and handle legal issues that relate to employees.

Management Functions

Managers set and achieve goals by using human, financial, material, and information resources. To do this, they plan, organize, staff, direct, and control—in other words, they undertake the five basic functions of management.

The five management functions are inseparable and often simultaneous elements of a continuous, interactive process. Implementing plans, for example, requires acquiring human resources (staffing) and structuring work groups (organizing). Subordinates must be guided to complete the plan (directing), and the plan's progress must be monitored (controlling). Management functions are dynamic and frequently complementary.

Planning

Because it provides the groundwork for the other four management functions, planning is the "first among equals." In planning, managers begin by identifying goals and alternative ways of achieving them. They then project actions that will commit individuals, departments, and the entire organization for days, months, or years to come. Planning initiates each of the other major functions in the management process. These functions are:

- Organizing, or determining how to structure personnel and other resources
- Staffing, obtaining the needed people and training them to accomplish the desired tasks
- Directing, or developing the environment in which work is to be accomplished
- Controlling, or establishing, a standard against which to measure progress toward objectives so that necessary correction can be made

Duration and Scope of Planning.   The proportion of time each manager devotes to planning and the scope of the effort vary according to a manager's level in the organization. Top-level managers routinely plan in five- and ten-year increments, developing long-range plans that address an overall mission. They are also involved in working with managers to develop one-year plans that coordinate with long-range goals. At lower management levels, planning is likely to focus on monthly targets, next week's schedule, or today's activities.

Influences on Planning.   Among immediate internal influences on each manager's plans are the plans of other managers at higher and lower levels in the organization. Each planner must consider the plans laid out at the top and at each succeeding level. These plans are called vertical influences. Each planner must also consider the plans made by other managers on the same level, in the same department and in parallel departments. Plans made by managers on the same level are called horizontal influences.

In addition to influences from inside a company, a manager's plans are constantly subjected to influences from the outside world. Outside influences include laws and regulations as well as more subtle and less predictable pressures such as community attitudes and natural events. Managers must constantly assess and adapt their plans to accommodate the influences of the real world.

Continuity and Flexibility. Planning is not a one-time practice, but a continuous function to be performed throughout an organization's existence. Because outcomes are seldom achieved precisely as planned and because unexpected events so often subvert plans, managers must cultivate flexibility in attitude and performance. In times of rapid change, a company's success depends on management's capacity to adapt effectively to new circumstances.

Evidence of inadequate flexibility fills the daily papers. Giant companies are unable, unwilling, or too slow to adapt to new realities. For example, one firm long pre-eminent in its field, IBM, showed signs of faltering in the early 1990s. After compiling the biggest one-year loss in business history and reducing its staff by more than 100,000 employees, the computer giant faced an uphill battle against smaller competitors in a fast-changing marketplace. Wrote one business commentator, "Big Blue lost control of a market it helped create but never quite understood—and it was out of place in the lean nimble world of 'clone' makers" (Schwartz, 1992). Chapters 4 and 5 will explore planning more closely.

Organizing

In planning, managers establish and determine how to achieve objectives. In organizing, they develop the structures that facilitate the accomplishment of objectives. In fulfilling the organizing function, managers (1) assemble and allocate resources needed to achieve the objectives, (2) establish the organization's authority relationships, and (3) create the structure of the organization.

Managers create the organization structure, a network of interdependent components, by clustering related activities into identifiable working units (divisions, departments, groups, and regions). Organization structures commonly display the branching patterns and hierarchy levels shown in Exhibits 1.2 and 1.3.

Exhibit 1.3

An organization structure.

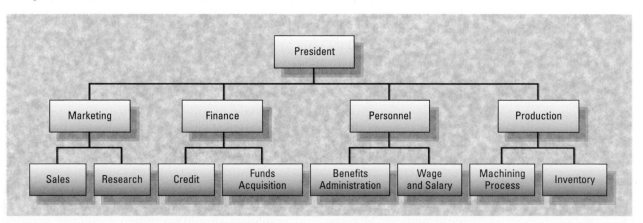

Ideally, for each unit and each person in it, managers establish specific authority, a list of clearly defined duties, and a single person to whom unit members report.

Like the other four management functions, organizing is not done once and then forgotten. As objectives develop and change, a company's managerial and structural relationships should also change. One thing about organizing is certain: Changes within and outside an organization inevitably require new approaches, new plans, and new organizational units.

Staffing

The very definition of *organization*—a group of persons operating to achieve common objectives—informs us that an organization begins with people. Among managers' most important ongoing tasks are attracting, recruiting, training, and retaining qualified employees. These tasks are part of the management function called staffing.

Early in the staffing process, managers analyze and project their organization's personnel needs. They determine what skills and experience their people must possess and how many individuals will be needed to meet objectives. Subsequent actions include attracting suitable job candidates for available positions (through newspaper advertising and other means) and screening applicants to match abilities to job requirements.

After hiring, employees must be oriented to the company environment, trained for a particular job, and continuously developed to ensure that they remain qualified for work assignments. Another staffing duty is to develop and implement systematic performance appraisal, not only to determine appropriate pay and benefits for each job, but to maintain and improve productivity, efficiency, and quality.

In a large contemporary organization, much of the staffing function is handled by the human resources department. Chapter 10 will examine staffing more closely.

Directing

When directing, the manager must provide leadership to the work group. Leadership is a complex phenomenon. Recent research continues to provide revealing data and speculation about it. Leadership demands a manager's focused intelligence, imagination, and empathy; no hard-and-fast rules apply. Effective managers do not simply give orders. Instead, they thoughtfully and systematically develop a personal method to achieve goals through people. In becoming a leader (and many experts concur that most leaders are made, not born) the manager discovers and originates ways to provide guidance, to involve people in decision making, and to coach individual performance. Leaders build cohesive work teams that harness and integrate its members' unique capabilities and inevitable individual differences.

Characteristically, successful leaders create a work environment in which employees are motivated to work toward their personal goals and the goals of the organization simultaneously. To sustain a supportive climate, a manager builds and encourages open communication through easily accessible channels. Such channels allow the manager to transmit performance expectations, actively listen to each employee, respond to employee concerns, and facilitate **feedback** (evaluative or corrective information given to an employee about that employee's performance). Manager and employee should confidently enjoy a genuine

Each person *in the Raleigh Cycle Co. factory takes pride in the work, because everyone at Raleigh is responsible for quality. Managers interact directly with the work force, and call their production employees "craftspeople."*

exchange of ideas, concerns, and actions. The trust Herb Kelleher's team has built at Southwest Airlines was illustrated by the employees' spontaneous support during the fuel crunch in 1991. Chapters 12 through 14 will deal with directing and leading.

Controlling

The wise manager knows that all the fine planning, staffing, and directing the organization undertakes will count for nothing without a mechanism to ensure that everything works as it's supposed to. That essential mechanism is the final management function: controlling.

While controlling, managers at each level strive to promote success and to prevent failure by providing the means to monitor performance of individuals, departments, divisions, and the entire organization. Sound planning, organizing, staffing, and directing are the manager's first line of problem prevention; well-designed and implemented controls ensure that problems (any deviations from the planned norms) can be identified promptly and corrective action initiated swiftly.

Controlling consists of four steps equally applicable to people, objects, and processes. To control, a manager must:

1. Establish standards against which to measure progress toward goals

2. Measure performance against those standards

3. Identify and analyze deviations from standards

4. Take actions needed to correct undesired deviations

Applicable standards differ among organizations. They may include production and sales quotas, timely performance, product or service quality, customer satisfaction levels, and many others. One familiar control device is employed almost universally by managers everywhere: the budget, a projected allocation of resources (costs) against which actual expenditures can be measured. Chapters 15 and 16 will explain controlling in depth.

Applicability by Levels

Regardless of titles, positions, or management levels, managers execute the five management functions and work through and with others to set and achieve the organization's goals. Only the emphasis (and time) devoted to each function differs among managers at the various management levels. Exhibit 1.4 shows typical variations of emphasis by management level. Note the inverse relationship between planning and directing at the top and first-line levels of management.

Top Management.   Top-level managers are concerned with the big picture, not the nitty-gritty. Planning at the top means defining and developing the organization's fundamental purpose, setting the global objectives for the organization, and shaping core policies to be implemented by middle and first-line managers. Organizing deals with the company's all-embracing structure, the framework within which plans will be accomplished and resources acquired. Staffing at the top level entails establishing the corporate attitude toward its people and creating a personnel philosophy. Top managers determine relations with labor unions, staff development and educational assistance, hiring preferences, compliance with equal opportunity statutes and other laws, and company retirement programs. Recruitment of senior managers is often handled at the top as well. Directing focuses on creating the company-wide management philosophy and cultivating a corporate climate for optimal employee performance. Controlling emphasizes the organization's overall performance in the context of its objectives.

Exhibit 1.4

Relative emphasis on each management function at different management levels.

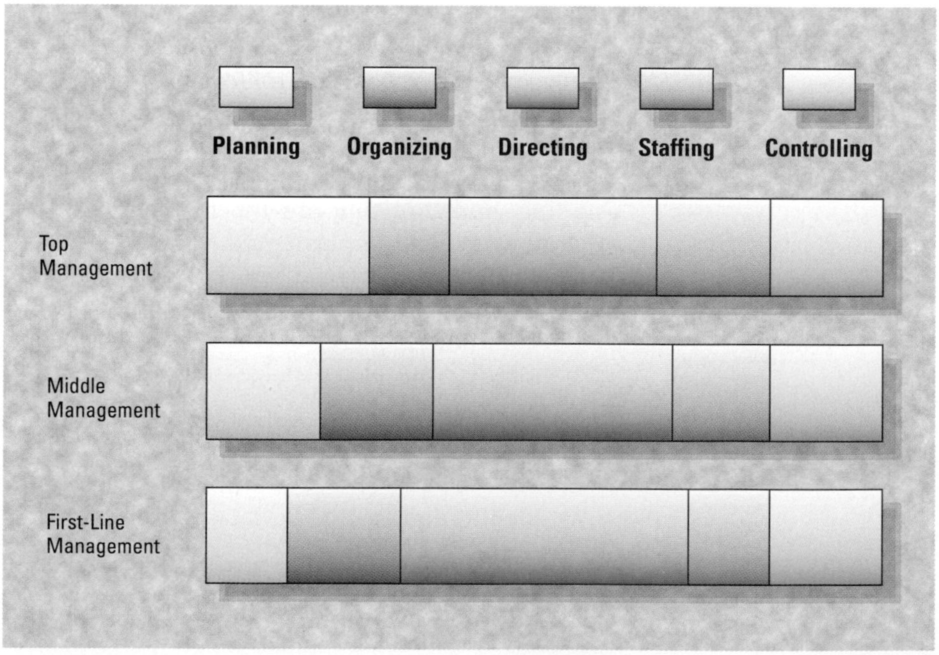

Middle Management.   Middle managers develop strategies to implement top management's broad concepts. The middle managers decide how to attain a desired profit level; whether to pursue new products, customers, or territories; and whether to lower prices to increase market share. Organizing at this level means fine-tuning the structure and allocating the resources acquired by top management. Staffing focuses on implementing equal opportunity policies and employee development programs, negotiating labor contracts, and selecting health care systems. Directing focuses on providing leadership and support for lower-level management. Controlling consists of monitoring the results of plans for specific products, regions, and subunits and refining operations to ensure attainment of objectives.

First-Line Management.   The top manager's big picture and the midlevel manager's implementation of overall plans affect the first-line manager, whose primary concern is supervising the company's day-to-day work. For the first-line manager (also known as the supervisory manager), planning may mean scheduling employees, establishing work priorities, or developing detailed procedures to achieve the goals. Organizing may consist of delegating authority or assigning tasks to specific workers or groups. First-line staffing consists of obtaining authorization for a new position and then hiring and training the new person to perform the job. Directing includes communicating and providing leadership to individual employees. Controlling focuses on ensuring that the group meets its production, sales, or quality objectives.

Management Roles

To plan, organize, staff, direct, and control, a manager must fill various roles at different times. A **role** is a set of expectations for a manager's behavior. As managers perform their duties and interact with various members of the oranization, they must wear different hats. Their role requirements are influenced by their formal job descriptions, which grant certain authority and status, and also by the value and expectations of their superiors, sbuordinates, and peers.

Management writer Henry Mintzberg views management behavior in terms of ten roles grouped into three categories: those primarily concerned with interpersonal relationships, those dealing with transfer of information, and those involved with decision making (Mintzberg, 1975). The ten roles are shown in Exhibit 1.5, along with brief examples of how the work of CEOs demonstrates the roles. An explanation of each category follows.

Interpersonal Roles

A manager's interpersonal roles involve relationships with others and arise directly from a manager's formal position and authority. A manager's roles include:

- Figurehead. As head of a work unit (division, department, or section), a manager routinely performs certain ceremonial duties. Examples of ceremonial duties include entertaining visitors, attending a subordinate's wedding, and officiating at a group luncheon.

Exhibit 1.5

Mintzberg's ten management roles.

Role	Description	Identifiable Activities from Study of Chief Executives
INTERPERSONAL		
Figurehead	Performs symbolic routine duties of legal or social nature	Attending ceremonies or other public, legal, or social functions; officiating
Leader	Motivates subordinates, ensures hiring and training of staff	Interacting with subordinates
Liaison	Maintains self-developed network of contacts and informers who provide favors and information	Acknowledging mail and interacting with outsiders
INFORMATIONAL		
Monitor	Seeks and receives wide variety of special information to develop thorough understanding of the organization and environment	Handling all mail and contacts concerned primarily with receiving information
Disseminator	Transmits information received from outsiders or subordinates to members of the organization (some information is factual, some involves interpretation and integration)	Forwarding mail into the organization for informational purposes, maintaining verbal contacts involving flow to subordinates
Spokesperson	Transmits to outsiders information about organization's plans, policies, actions, results, and so forth; serves as expert on organization's industry	Attending board meetings, handling mail and contacts involving transmission of information to outsiders
DECISIONAL		
Entrepreneur	Searches organization and its environment for opportunities and initiates projects to bring about change	Implementing strategy and review sessions involving improvement
Disturbance Handler	Initiates corrective action when organization faces important, unexpected disturbances	Implementing strategy to resolve disturbances and crises
Resource Allocator	Fulfills responsibility for the allocation of organizational resources of all kinds—in effect, makes or approves all significant decisions	Scheduling, requesting authorization, budgeting, programming of subordinates' work
Negotiator	Represents the organization in major negotiations	Negotiating

Source: Chart from *The Nature of Managerial Work*, by Henry Mintzberg. Copyright 1973 by Henry Mintzberg. Reprinted by permission of HarperCollins Publishers.

- Leader. As a leader, a manager creates the environment, works to improve employees' performances and reduce conflict, provides feedback, and encourages individual growth.

- Liaison. In addition to superiors and subordinates, managers interact with others—peer-level managers in other departments, staff specialists, other departments' employees, and suppliers and clients. In this role, the manager builds contacts.

Informational Roles

Partly as a result of contacts inside and outside the organization, a manager normally has more information than other members of the staff (Mintzberg, 1975). Three key roles derive from the use and dissemination of information.

- Monitor. While constantly monitoring the environment to determine what is going on, the manager collects information both directly (by asking questions) and indirectly (by receiving unsolicited information).

- Disseminator. As a disseminator, a manager passes on to subordinates some information that would not ordinarily be accessible to them.

- Spokesperson. A manager speaks for the work unit to people outside the work unit. Sometimes a spokesperson informs superiors; sometimes he or she communicates with people outside the organization.

Decisional Roles

In playing the four decisional roles, managers make choices, alone or with others, or influence the choices of others. The decisional roles are:

- Entrepreneur. In sharing and initiating new ideas or methods that may improve the work unit's operations, a manager assumes the entrepreneur's role.

- Disturbance handler. As a disturbance handler, a manager deals with schedule problems, equipment failure, strikes, broken contracts, and any other feature of the work environment that decreases productivity.

- Resource allocator. A manager determines who in the work unit gets what resources—money, facilities, equipment, and access to the manager.

- Negotiator. A manager must spend a significant portion of time negotiating, because only a manager has the information and authority required to do so. Items to be negotiated include contracts with suppliers, trade-offs for resources inside the organization, and agreements with labor organizations.

Roles and Managerial Functions

By effectively discharging these multiple roles, managers accomplish their managerial functions. In planning and organizing, a manager performs the resource

Exhibit 1.6

Conflicting role demands on a manager.

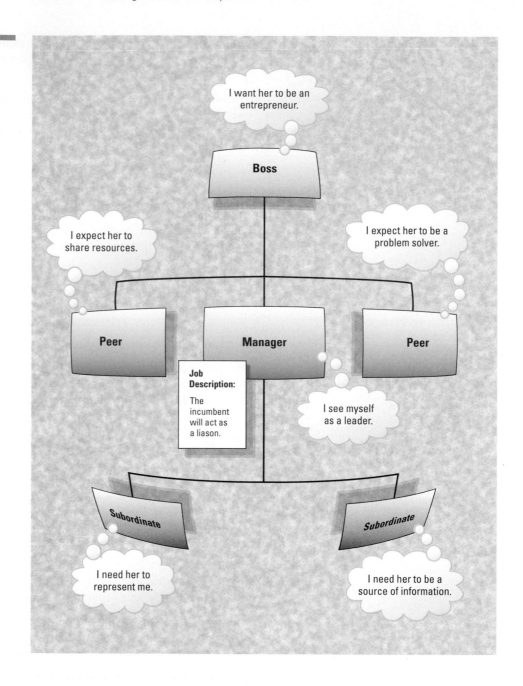

allocator role. In staffing, a manager plays the leadership role by providing subordinates with feedback on performance. In directing, a manager performs as disseminator, entrepreneur, and disturbance handler; in controlling, as monitor.

    Exhibit 1.6 shows how different people within an organization have different expectations of the same manager's role behaviors. The ability to meet these multiple demands separates successful from unsuccessful managers. A work unit whose manager is unable to play many roles will suffer to some extent.

Management Skills

To effectively plan, organize, staff, direct, and control, the manager must master three categories of skills: technical, human, and conceptual (Katz, 1974).

Technical Skills

Technical skills are the abilities to use the processes, practices, techniques, and tools of the specialty area a manager supervises. The manager supervising accountants, for example, must know accounting. Though he or she need not be an expert, the manager must have enough technical knowledge and skill to intelligently direct employees, organize tasks, communicate the work group's needs to others, and solve problems.

Human Skills

Human skills (sometimes called human relations) consist of the abilities to interact and communicate with other persons successfully. These skills include leadership of subordinates and facility in intergroup relationships. A manager must be able to understand, work with, and relate to both individuals and groups to build a team environment. The manager's ability to work effectively as a group member and to build cooperative effort within the group depends upon human skills (Plunkett, 1992).

Conceptual Skills

Conceptual skills—the mental capacity to conceive and manipulate ideas and abstract relationships—allow the manager to view an organization as a whole and to see how its parts relate to and depend upon one another. The conceptually skilled manager can visualize how work units and individuals interrelate, understand the effect of any action throughout the organization, and imaginatively execute the five basic management functions. Also, well-developed conceptual skills equip the manager to identify a problem, develop alternative solutions, select the best alternative, and implement that solution.

Importance of Skills According to Management Level

A manager's level in the organization determines the relative importance of each of the three skills. Technical skills are critical for first-line managers and become less important as the manager moves up in the organization. The supervisor of a word processing department at an airline must possess more technical knowledge about the systems, equipment, and methods of training than the airline's president.

Although human skills enrich all phases of management, they are especially prized for first-line managers, because these managers must interact extensively with many employees.

Because of their comparatively narrow focus on the work group, first-level managers have less need for conceptual skills than top-level managers concerned with broad-based, long-range decisions that affect the entire organization. The

Exhibit 1.7

Proportions of management skills needed by management level.

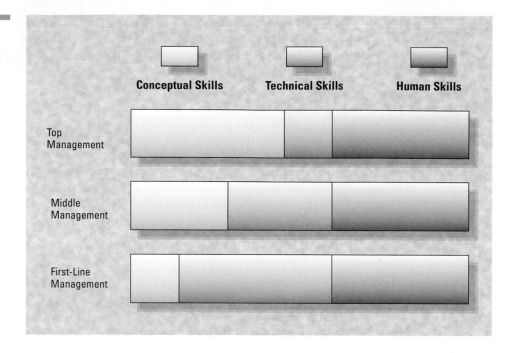

importance of conceptual skills increases as a manager moves up the "pyramid" of management. Exhibit 1.7 illustrates the relative proportions of each kind of skill needed at each management level.

Evaluation of a Manager's Performance

A manager's performance can be measured by two criteria: effectiveness and efficiency.

Referring to a manager's ability to select the right goal and the appropriate means for achieving it, the dean of American management studies, Peter Drucker, defines **effectiveness** as "doing the right thing" (Drucker, 1964).

Efficiency measures the cost of attaining a given goal. Effectiveness is doing the right thing, but efficiency, says Drucker, is doing things right. The manager who incurs the minimum cost to obtain the desired goal is being efficient. Compared with the inefficient manager, the efficient manager achieves the same level of production with fewer resources or increases the production level with the same resources.

Responsible management requires both effectiveness and efficiency; but whereas efficiency is important, effectiveness is indispensable. A manager who does the wrong things (who is ineffective) with minimum use of resources (but is efficient) is not helping the organization. Conversely, the manager who makes the right choices, however clumsily, is helping the organization even if he or she is not very efficient.

Although the criteria for evaluating a manager's performance remain unchanged in the 1990s, the demands placed upon managers to perform effectively and efficiently continue to multiply dramatically. This introduction to management began with a glimpse of who managers are and what they do. Before moving on to

Human skills *are the ability to interact successfully with people on a one-to-one and group basis. These are essential skills for managers.*

consider the history and prospects for management thought, consider the next section, which presents provocative predictions about future trends. The predictions represent the combined expertise of CEOs from Fortune's most admired, best-run companies, the rising stars of the business world and members of the National Business Hall of Fame.

Future Trends

To an increasing degree, managers must:

- Have vision. Challenges will require managers to be very different from the narrowly focused specialists of prior decades.

- Negotiate to solve problems. The traditional hierarchical structure is disappearing. As managers "flatten" organizations by removing management layers and relying on team management, managers will work more closely with people over whom they have no apparent authority. Without authority, they must achieve their aims by balancing the organization's needs with those of team members or the outsiders with whom they are trying to reach agreement. They will be able to do this by thinking empathetically (by seeing the other person's view), by being straightforward in handling disagreements, and by persuading others to agree.

- Think cross-culturally. To work effectively with a work force that includes an increasing number of women and minority groups, managers must open themselves to new ways of thinking. The growing internationalism of business also calls for cross-cultural thinking. Managers should not assume that their way or the American way is necessarily the *best* way.

- Attract and build talent. Managers are as successful as the talent with which they surround themselves. Identifying potential stars and providing them with challenging work will continue to be a key ingredient of productive management. Developing people as quickly as possible is the way to have an exciting organization.

- Go beyond participative management. Managers will need to tap the creative power of every employee. Doing this requires going beyond merely sharing a little information and a bit of decision-making authority. Rather, managers will have to trust employees, listen to them, and encourage experimentation. The winning firms, units, and departments will be brain driven.

- Tap the power of teams. The flatter organizations of the future will require managers to pursue one of two courses of action: (1) to manage them with an increasingly wide span of control, as layers of managers are removed while problems remain, or (2) to create project teams with appropriate authority to tackle the problems.

- Be obsessed with quality. The measure of a company, department, district, or work unit is the quality of its product or service. The manager should incorporate the philosophy of continual improvement: the belief that every employee should try to improve every day and never get discouraged.

C H A P T E R   **S** U M M A R Y

- Managers, people who direct the activities of others, are needed to provide direction and coordination to meet the objectives of every organization.

- Managers and management use human, financial, information, and material resources to perform five functions: planning, organizing, staffing, directing, and controlling.

- Management is complex, demanding, exacting, and pressure-filled. Contributing to the complexity are corporate globalization, intense focus on quality, and the rising demand for the ethical conduct of people and institutions.

- Managers manage both individuals and groups, not one or the other.

- Most organizations operate with the three traditional levels of management: top; middle; and first-line, or supervisory.

- Managers may be described by the kinds of work or activity for which they are responsible. Typical categories are marketing, operations, finance, and human resources.

- Managers at every level perform the same functions. What differs is the time spent on each function and the depth of a manager's involvement.

- Decision making is a separate function of management; it is an activity that takes place within each function.

- To do their jobs, managers must be able to perform certain roles. The roles are influenced by a manager's job description and the expectations held by superiors, subordinates, and peers. The ability to perform multiple roles well is the difference between successful and unsuccessful managers.

- Managers need three basic skills: technical, human, and conceptual. The relative importance of these skills depends upon a manager's level in the organization.

- Managers are evaluated according to two criteria: effectiveness (doing the right thing) and efficiency (doing things right). Of the two, effectiveness is more important.

S K I L L - B U I L D I N G

To answer the following questions, you may apply the contents of this chapter in any of three ways:

Option 1. *If you are a manager, develop your answers from the standpoint of your job.*

Option 2. *If you are a nonmanaging employee, develop your answers by analyzing what your manager does at work.*

Option 3. *If you are not employed, develop your answers by analyzing your family interactions.*

1. In regard to the functions of management:

   a. What plans do you or your manager create?

   b. What departments or work units did you or your manager organize?

   c. What training have you or your manager provided to assist employees in completing tasks?

   d. What types of performance appraisals have you or your manager conducted with employees?

   e. What guidance, encouragement, or problem solving did you or your manager provide to complete these or other tasks?

   f. What control devices did you or your manager establish to make sure plans had been completed?

2. In regard to the roles of management:

   a. What roles were you or your manager required to perform to complete the management functions?

   b. For whom were these roles performed?

   c. Which role was required most frequently? Why?

3. In regard to management skills:

   a. What technical skills did you or your manager use in performing the directing function?

   b. What human skills did you or your manager display in completing the management functions and fulfilling the management roles?

   c. What conceptual skills did you or your manager use in the planning function?

R E V I E W   **Q** U E S T I O N S

1. Can you define this chapter's essential terms? If not, consult the glossary.

2. How do managers assist an organization to achieve its objectives?

3. Why is a manager's universe often described as complex?

4. What three myths are associated with a manager's job?

5. What are the three levels of management in an organization? Whom does each level manage?

6. Identify four general areas of management and the activities associated with each.

7. List and define each of the five major management functions. Why is planning considered the "first" function?

8. How do these functions apply to the three levels of management found in most modern-day organizations? How does the execution of the planning function differ in the three levels of management?

9. What is a management role? List and explain four decisional roles managers are required to perform.

10. Identify the three management skills, and explain how the proportions of the skills needed differ at each management level.

11. Compare effectiveness and efficiency, explaining which is more important and why.

R E C O M M E N D E D   R E A D I N G

Block, Peter. *The Empowered Manager: Positive Political Skills at Work* (San Francisco: Jossey-Bass), 1991.

Dumaine, Briane. "Is Big Still Good?" *Fortune* (April 20, 1992), pp. 50–53.

Horton, Thomas R. *Beyond the Trust Gap: Forging a New Partnership Between Companies and Their Managers* (Homewood, IL: Richard D. Irwin), 1991.

Ireland, R. D. "Self-Confidence and Decisiveness: Prerequisites for Effective Management in the 1990s," *Business Horizons* (January–February 1992), pp. 35–43.

Jamieson, David, and Julie O'Mara. *Managing Workforce Two Thousand: Gaining the Diversity Advantage* (San Francisco: Jossey-Bass), 1991.

Knotts, R. "Rambo Doesn't Work Here Anymore," *Business Horizons* (January–February 1992), pp. 44–46.

Michaels, A. J. "Turmoil in the Executive Suite," *Fortune* (March 23, 1992), p. 13.

Tracy, Diane. *The First Book Of Common-Sense Management* (New York: William Morrow), 1991.

Verespej, M. A. "When Workers Get New Roles," *Industry Week* (February 3, 1992), p. ii.

Walton, Mary. *Deming Management at Work* (New York: Putnam), 1991.

R E F E R E N C E S

Drucker, Peter. *Managing for Results* (New York: Harper & Row), 1964, p. 5.

Katz, Robert L. "Skills of an Effective Administrator," *Harvard Business Review* (September–October 1974), pp. 90–102.

Mintzberg, Henry. "The Manager's Job: Folklore and Fact," *Harvard Business Review* (July–August 1975), pp. 49–61.

Peters, Tom. "Time-Obsessed Competition," *Management Review* (September 1990), pp. 16–20.

Plunkett, W. Richard. *Supervision,* 6th edition (Needham Heights, MA: Allyn and Bacon), 1992, p. 5.

Schares, Gayle. "The New Generation at Siemens," *Business Week* (March 9, 1992), p. 47.

Schwartz, John. "Can the Ailing Giant Remake Itself?" *Newsweek* (December 28, 1992), pp. 46–47.

Verity, John W. "Room at the Top," *Business Week* (March 9, 1992), p. 32.

G L O S S A R Y   O F   T E R M S

conceptual skills   The abilities to (1) view an organization as a whole and see how its parts relate and depend on one another and (2) deal with ideas and abstractions.

effectiveness   Doing the right thing, an indispensable characteristic of a successful manager.

efficiency   The measure of a manager's performance in regard to the cost of attaining a goal.

feedback   Evaluative or corrective information given to the person who performed an action or process.

first-line management   The lowest level of management. A first-line manager's subordinates are nonmanagement workers.

human skills   The abilities to (1) interact and communicate with other people successfully and (2) understand, work with, and relate to individuals and groups.

management   The process of setting and achieving goals through the execution of five basic management functions that use human, financial, material, and information resources.

management hierarchy   The levels of management, which are usually represented by a pyramidal structure.

manager   Someone who directs the activities of others.

middle management   Managers below the rank of vice president but above the supervisory level.

organization   A group of two or more people that exists and operates to achieve common objectives.

role   A set of expectations for a manager's behavior.

supervisor   See first-line management.

technical skills   The abilities to use the processes, practices, techniques, and tools of the specialty area a manager supervises.

top management   Managers responsible for the overall management of an organization. Their tasks include establishing company-wide objectives, goals, and operating policies and directing the company in relationships with the external environment.

C A S E   P R O B L E M
Learning to Be a Manager

In both small and large organizations, individuals are promoted into first-line management positions. The profile of each of these new managers is strikingly similar. The person is a good technician (a good engineer, salesperson, or accountant, for example), probably one of the best in the company. He or she has always wanted to be a manager and is excited and pleased about being promoted to a management position. The company provides the new manager with management training. When the neophyte manager assumes the position, he or she is confident of doing the job well.

For many new managers, the story continues unhappily because being a manager involves more than just learning the basic management functions. The job does require the manager to plan, organize, staff, direct, and control. But it also requires the manager to think like a manager, a process significantly different than thinking like a doer, a technician. Some of the symptoms of nonmanagerial thinking are:

- Doing a job rather than supervising it.

- Being unable or unwilling to make decisions. Managers often become indecisive when they feel uncomfortable with the ambiguity of their role, fear doing something wrong, or fear that they won't be liked if they make an unpopular decision.

- Competing with employees. Managers sometimes feel that they are competing with subordinates for the position of technical guru. Some managers wrongly believe that success as a supervisor is linked to the ability to remain the technical expert in the work group.

- Hiring weak people. Some managers hire people who are technically or interpersonally less skilled than they in order to ensure that the manager outshines others.

- Wanting to be recognized as a powerful person. Some managers make the mistake of forcing employees to acknowledge and respect the manager's power, rewarding those who do and punishing those who don't.

- Being unable or unwilling to delegate decision making. To be sure that the right decisions are made, some managers retain ultimate control over all decisions.

- Needing to be evaluated only on the manager's own performance. Some managers believe that their own personal performance is what counts and that evaluation based on the performance of others is both risky and unrewarding.

- Avoiding rather than dealing with conflict. Some managers are so concerned with being well liked by their employees that they ignore potential threats to the tranquillity of the work group.

- Providing insufficient praise. Managers get lower productivity from their workers if they neglect the need for praise or are not capable of giving it.

Q U E S T I O N S

1. Why do you think a new manager has a tendency to think like a doer and not a manager?

2. How is the ability of a manager to play management roles related to the symptoms described in this case?

3. As a supervisor of a manager displaying one of these symptoms, what would you do to help solve the problem?

For more about learning to be a manager, see Bruce Posner, "The Management Game," *Management Review* (May 1992), pp. 27–33.

Management Thought: Past and Present

L E A R N I N G   O B J E C T I V E S

After reading and discussing this chapter, you should be able to:

- Define the essential terms that appear in the text
- Explain the importance of the evolution of management theories
- Describe these management theories: classical, behavioral, quantitative, systems, and contingency

MANAGEMENT IN ACTION
Sam Walton's Wal-Mart

Never satisfied with the status quo, Samuel M. Walton constantly searched for better ways of doing things in both his business and his personal life. He was not ashamed to learn from competitors or to adopt anything they had that he felt was of value. Walton's approach worked. He built a country store into a giant retail chain based on customer service, discount marketing, and modern technology. In 1992 the editors of Fortune elected Samuel Walton to the National Business Hall of Fame.

In the early 1960s, Walton had watched the emerging discount chains invade large urban centers. As owner of 15 Ben Franklin dime stores, he proposed that he and Franklin jointly begin the discount approach in rural areas. Ben Franklin management declined his offer. Undaunted, in 1962 Walton and his brother James opened the first Wal-Mart Discount City store, in Rogers, Arkansas. By 1992 there were more than 2,000 stores in 42 states, with some 150 new ones opening each year. Most of the stores were in rural locales with populations of about 15,000.

Walton began by focusing on the South and Midwest. Later, Wal-Mart began to penetrate California and the East Coast, with stores, supercenters (Wal-Marts with food), and outlets called Sam's Wholesale Clubs.

Most retail chains buy through distributors. In the beginning, Walton set out to do the same. When he found few that could serve his rural locations, he established his own system. Walton set up about 20 highly automated distribution centers, which were linked to the outlets by a fleet of trucks. Beginning in the 1980s, Wal-Mart computerized nearly every store operation, creating satellite links from stores and distribution centers to corporate headquarters and key suppliers. Suppliers knew the daily status of their inventory and could ship on a day-by-day basis, ensuring that inventories were never depleted. Wal-Mart's distribution centers supply about 80% of what the stores sell; the balance is supplied directly by wholesalers and manufacturers. Wal-Mart works closely with suppliers and suppliers' suppliers to ensure that orders are filled on a timely and cost-efficient basis. The company has invested over $600 million in inventory management equipment and other technologies. Using Wal-Mart's satellite communications system, managers track inventories,

Communication, control, and corporate culture have helped make Wal-Mart one of America's most admired corporations.

process orders, keep records, and handle suggestions from store associates.

In 1988 ill health forced Walton to turn over the tasks of chief executive to David D. Glass. In a *Business Week* interview, Glass described his first meeting with Walton. The meeting took place at the opening of Walton's second discount store, in Harrison, Arkansas. It was a hot July day, just after soaking rains. Walton had a huge pile of watermelons ready as giveaways, and donkeys for the kids to ride. As Glass watched the watermelons burst in the heat and saw mud tracked into the new store, he turned to Walton and advised him to consider another line of work. Of course, Walton didn't listen. As Glass acknowledged: "You can't replace a Sam Walton, but he has prepared the company to run well whether he's here or not." Restating part of the Wal-Mart philosophy, Glass said, "We are agents for our customers. We want to sell them what they want to buy, and the name of the game is who can most

concerns and learn about the competition down the street and across town.

Glass's primary aim now is to keep communication channels open among all Wal-Mart stores. He makes every effort to run the large corporation as a small company. Glass emphasizes cost control and knowing what's happening in each of the more than 2,000 stores that employ, in all, more than 330,000 associates.

His approach has proven effective. In 1990, Wal-Mart was first in sales among U.S. retailers; in 1991, sales reached nearly $44 billion, up 35% from 1990. Profits for 1991 were $1.6 billion, up almost 25% from 1990. During the recession of 1991–1992, the company expanded while its major competitors made massive cutbacks. In 1992, *Business Week* ranked Wal-Mart Stores first among discount and fashion retailers. Wal-Mart earned $400 million more in profits than its closest competitor, Sears, even though Sears had about $14 billion more in sales. In a survey of more than 8,000 senior executives, corporate directors, and

> ❝We are agents for our customers. We want to sell them what they want to buy, and the name of the game is who can most efficiently deliver that merchandise from raw materials to the customer.❞
>
> — **David D. Glass**, CEO, Wal-Mart Stores

efficiently deliver that merchandise from raw materials to the customer."

Walton and Glass shared the same vision: to grow the company while preventing the growth of a large corporate staff and staying close to the customer; their stores; and their sales associates, the employees that breathe life into operations. Like all the managers, Glass visits the company's stores at least two days each week to listen to associates'

financial analysts, *Fortune* rated Wal-Mart the "most admired corporate retailer"; Wal-Mart ranked third on the list of contenders for "most admired corporation." Categories for both classifications were quality of management; quality of products or services; innovativeness; long-term investment value; financial soundness; ability to attract, develop, and retain talented people; responsibility to the community and the environment; and wise use of corporate assets. ▲

For more on Wal-Mart and Sam Walton, see Zina Sawaya, "Cutting Out the Middleman," *Forbes,* January 6, 1992, pp. 169–170; Wendy Zellner, "O.K., So He's Not Sam Walton," *Business Week,* March 16, 1992, pp. 56–58; Patty de Llosa and Jessica Skelly von Brachel, "Samuel M. Walton," *Fortune,* March 23, 1992, pp. 113–114; Kate Ballen, "America's Most Admired Corporations," *Fortune,* February 10, 1992, pp. 40, 61; Sam Walton (with John Huey), *Sam Walton: Made in America* (New York: Doubleday), 1992.

The History and Theory of Management

To understand management today, you must look at its history. The formal academic discipline of management is relatively new, and it has expanded rapidly since being introduced in higher education in the 1920s. Management theories and schools of thought represent differing viewpoints and strategies for managing people, making decisions, and solving problems. Each offers something of value for today's managers.

The Value of History

People ignorant of the past are destined to repeat it. Knowing what has gone before allows us to avoid mistakes and capitalize on successes. Consider what the Japanese learned, for example, by studying the U.S. auto industry. Henry Ford discovered that other firms could produce many parts better and more cheaply than his company could. Getting parts from suppliers was soon standard procedure in Ford manufacturing. Japanese businessmen who studied Ford operations after World War II noted this. In a few years, Japanese car makers expanded Henry Ford's idea by perfecting outsourcing, the use of a network of firms to produce components. Outsourcing is now the model for auto manufacturing and other types of production. To expose you to the lessons of history, this text will explore many management problems and solutions from the past.

Henry Ford was not the first automobile manufacturer, but he was the most daring and innovative in his century. At one time every other car in the world was a Ford.

The Value of Theory

A **theory** is an explanation that helps organize information and knowledge. A theory gives us reasons for doing things one way and not another, and it helps us separate causes from effects. A manager who believes that mathematical formulas will help to determine a course of action will use them. The manager who believes that a solution lies in finding the right person with applicable experience will seek such a person. By knowing both theory and history, managers in every field can avoid past mistakes and forecast, predict, and set sound goals before committing resources to achieving them.

Managers with knowledge of diverse theories can see problems from more than one point of view; this ability increases the number of problem-solving options. Each theory provides tools to help managers make decisions and solve problems.

Ancient History and Practice

Management began when early humans banded into clans and tribes. Community survival depended upon hunting and gathering, devising shelter, and defending against marauders. Such activities needed both individual prowess and cooperative group effort. People soon found that some members were better at some tasks than others. They learned also that by focusing on one function—by specializing—individuals could improve their performance. The groups that planned, organized, and controlled job assignments and other factors were the groups that thrived.

The development of agriculture allowed humankind to turn from life in small nomadic bands to life in large relatively permanent settlements. The expanding communities' need for stability and order led to increasingly complex social structures. Institutions relating to religion, commerce, and government appeared. Specialist groups and classes emerged: Farmers grew the food, craftsmen made goods that merchants traded, soldiers attacked neighboring settlements and defended against them, and shamans and priests led ceremonies of healing and worship. Coordinating all these activities was the job of the administrators.

Graphic records—such as Babylonian clay tablets, Egyptian tomb paintings, and the Bible—vividly tell us how early civilizations managed. Providing testimony that is no less powerful is evidence such as the looming stone circles at Stonehenge, the exquisitely precise and massive pyramids at Giza, and the 1,500-mile Great Wall of China. All these constructions required a high order of planning, organizing, and controlling.

To illuminate the ideas of modern management, Exhibit 2.1 presents a time line that shows the theories we will examine in this chapter.

Classical Management Theory

The **classical management theory** originated during England's Industrial Revolution, which began in the late 1700s with the invention of reliable steam-powered machinery. Steam power freed manufacturers from dependence on running water and wind. For the first time, manufacturers could mass-produce goods in factories that operated year-round. The textile industry was among the first to capitalize on the new technology. Before steam power, cotton or woolen

Exhibit 2.1

The time line of management thought.

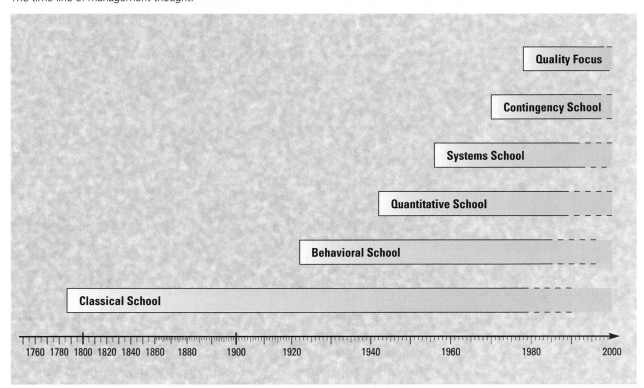

cloth was woven by an individual working on a home loom; after the Industrial Revolution, weaving was done in urban areas by large groups of semi-skilled workers using reliable machines under one roof. The Industrial Revolution allowed manufacturers to make standardized goods for domestic and overseas mass markets.

Early factories depended upon a constant flow of labor and materials. Owners needed to plan, organize, direct, control, and staff many different kinds of operations. Writing of the new managerial skills required of successful industrialists, economic historian P. L. Payne observed, "In many cases, better organization contributed almost as much to increased production as the use of the machines themselves" (Haigh, 1985).

The focus of classical management theory was on finding the "one best way" to perform and manage tasks. As the Industrial Revolution continued, the environment of the early factory gave rise to two separate doctrines of management, two schools of thought linked under the label *classical.*

First came the **classical scientific school**, which focused on the manufacturing environment and getting work done on the factory floor. Then came the **classical administrative school**, which emphasized the flow of information and how organizations should operate. Both schools articulated principles and functions of management discussed throughout this text.

The Classical Scientific School

Among the pioneers of the classical scientific school was British mathematician and inventor Charles Babbage, who in 1832 published *On the Economy of Machinery and Manufactures,* a study that presented the fruit of Babbage's observations of the factory floor. Babbage concluded that definite management principles existed, that they had broad applications, and that they could be determined by experience. He thought that the most important principle was "the division of labor amongst the persons who perform the work." Babbage called for the division of work into discrete processes that could be mastered quickly by one person.

Other pioneers of the classical scientific school also made theoretical contributions that increased labor efficiency and productivity. Frederick W. Taylor, sometimes called the Father of Scientific Management, applied scientific methods to factory problems and urged the proper use of human labor, tools, and time. During a career as executive, consultant, production specialist, and efficiency expert, Taylor pursued four key goals: to develop a science of management, to select workers scientifically, to educate and train workers scientifically, and to create cooperation between management and labor. From his experience at Midvale Steel, Simonds Rolling Machine, and Bethlehem Steel, Taylor developed the core ideas of scientific management. Devising time and motion studies to analyze the movements of workers on the job, he determined the output that individual workers should be able to achieve with specific materials and equipment. From such data he determined the quickest ways to perform tasks. Taylor introduced work breaks and the piece-rate system for worker pay (Merrill, 1970).

Frank and Lillian Gilbreth added to Taylor's findings. The Gilbreths used time and motion studies to analyze workers' activities and remove unnecessary movements and causes of fatigue. One of Frank's first studies involved bricklaying. Frank reduced a ten-step process to five steps, thus doubling productivity. His study of hospital operating room functions saved resources and shortened the time patients spent on operating tables. Lillian assisted her husband and carried on his work after his death.

Henry Metcalf, another thinker of the classical scientific school, emphasized the need for scientific administration. The management system he advocated relied on fixed responsibilities for cost control and an effective flow of information. He urged managers to record their experiences for the benefit of others. Henry Gantt's idea represented a move away from authoritarian management. He advocated a bonus system to reward workers for acceptable and superior work, and he invented the Gantt chart, a graphic means of representing and planning production.

Assessment The theories and principles developed by the early classical scientific thinkers are with us today, although experience and accumulated data have modified the ideas significantly. One of the methods used by the early thinkers, the time and motion study, is still in common use.

Like Babbage and his colleagues, managers today continue to search for a better way; gone, however, is their notion that there is one best way. Influenced by the Japanese philosophy known as **kaizen** (a term that translates roughly as "continual improvement"), modern managers know that they cannot be content, but must constantly seek to improve how people think and act on the job. At

Wal-Mart, Sam Walton exemplified the *kaizen* process, eagerly pursuing better ways to do things and often learning from competitors.

The classical scientific thinkers taught managers to analyze everything, teach effective methods to others, constantly monitor workers, plan responsibly, and organize and control the work and the workers. Their successors—today's managers—realize that, without committed men and women empowered to examine their own output and take responsibility for it, neither productivity nor quality can improve. The idea of specialization, prized in the classical scientific school, has been modified. The aim today is to avoid the physical and psychological hazards of boring, repetitive work, for example. Modern managers emphasize cross-training, which allows workers to perform a variety of tasks, many of which require high literacy and computational skills. Successful modern factories depend on innovation, imagination, and creativity from dedicated workers who are backed by managers. These managers act not as commanders, but as teachers, coaches, and servants.

The Classical Administrative School

As the complexity of organizations grew, managers needed a new theory to help them meet their new challenges. To meet this demand, the classical administrative school grew from classical scientific roots. The administrative branch emphasized efficiency and productivity in running factories and businesses. It provided a theoretical basis for all managers, no matter their area of expertise.

A Frenchman, Henri Fayol, believed that management was not a personal talent that some had by birth and others did not. From practical experience he knew that management required specific skills that could be learned and taught. Fayol developed fourteen principles of management, which are presented in Exhibit 2.2. These principles are the foundation for modern management practice and sound administrative structure (Merrill, 1970). Fayol is the acknowledged leader of the classical administrative school.

Another contributor to the administrative school was American political scientist Mary Parker Follett. Her work in the 1920s focused on how organizations cope with conflict and the importance of goal sharing among managers. She emphasized the human element in organizations and the need to discover and enlist individual and group motivation. Believing that the first principle for both individual and group success is the "capacity for organized thinking," Follett urged managers to prepare themselves for their profession as seriously as candidates for any of the traditional learned professions (Matteson and Ivancevich, 1981).

Another American theorist of the administrative school was Chester Barnard, who was president of New Jersey Bell Telephone Company. In his 1938 work, *The Functions of the Executive,* Barnard argued that managers must gain acceptance for their authority. He advocated the use of basic management principles, and he cautioned managers to issue no order that could not or would not be obeyed. To do so, he believed, destroyed authority, discipline, and morale (Matteson and Ivancevich, 1981).

The German theorist Max Weber (1864–1920) was a professor of law and economics who wrote about social, political, and economic issues. Weber was the first to describe the principles of **bureaucracies**—rational organizations based

Exhibit 2.2

Henri Fayol's general principles of management.

1.	**Division of work**	Specialization allows workers and managers to acquire an ability, sureness, and accuracy that will increase output. More and better work will be produced with the same effort.
2.	**Authority**	The right to give orders and the power to exact obedience are the essence of authority. Its roots are in the person and the position. It cannot be conceived apart from responsibility.
3.	**Discipline**	Discipline comprises obedience, application, energy, behavior, and outward marks of respect between employers and employees. It is essential to any business. Without it, no enterprise can prosper.
4.	**Unity of command**	For any action whatsoever, an employee should receive orders from one superior only. One person, one boss. In no case can a social organization adapt to a duality of command.
5.	**Unity of direction**	One head and one plan should lead a group of activities having the same objective.
6.	**Subordination of the individual to the general interest**	The interest of one person or group in a business should not prevail over that of the organization.
7.	**Remuneration of personnel**	The price of services rendered should be fair and satisfactory to both employees and employer. A level of pay depends on an employee's value to the organization and on factors independent of an employee's worth—cost of living, availability of personnel, and general business conditions, for example.
8.	**Centralization**	Everything that serves to reduce the importance of an individual subordinate's role is centralization. Everything that increases the subordinate's importance is decentralization. All situations call for a balance between these two positions.
9.	**Scalar chain**	The chain formed by managers from the highest to the lowest is called a scalar chain, or chain of command. Managers are the links in the chain. They should communicate to and through the links as they occur in their chains. Links may be skipped only when superiors approve and a real need exists to do so.
10.	**Order**	There should be a place for everyone and everyone in his or her place; a place for everything, and everything in its place. The objective of order is to avoid loss and waste.
11.	**Equity**	Kindliness and justice should be practiced by persons in authority to extract the best that their subordinates have to give.
12.	**Stability of tenure of personnel**	Reducing the turnover of personnel will result in more efficiency and fewer expenses.
13.	**Initiative**	People should be allowed the freedom to propose and execute ideas at all levels of an enterprise. A manager able to permit the exercise of initiative by subordinates is far superior to one unable to do so.
14.	**Esprit de corps**	In unity there is strength. Managers have the duty to promote harmony and to discourage and avoid those things that disturb harmony.

Adapted from *General Principles of Management*, by Henri Fayol. Copyright 1949 by Pitman Learning, Inc., 6 Davis Drive, Belmont, CA 94002. Reprinted with permission.

upon the control of knowledge. Although Weber's milestone work, *The Theory of Social and Economic Organizations,* appeared in Germany early in this century, it was not translated into English until 1947. The book describes how bureaucratic organizations operate and how they lend themselves to the administration of ongoing work and functions.

Weber argued that the bureaucratic organization developed in parallel with the evolving capitalist system. He saw the bureaucratic organization as a superior mechanism for administering businesses, governments, religious orders, universities, and the military. He based his conclusion on his view that bureaucracies are controlled by technically competent individuals who provide stable, strict, intensive, and continuous administration. In the typical bureaucratic hierarchy, he said, clearly defined offices (positions) are occupied by qualified career people selected on the basis of their expertise and experience (often on the basis of standardized examinations). By and large, these workers are promoted according to the judgments of superiors, and the workers are subject to the disciplinary system of the organization. A fine example of a classic bureaucracy is the federal government of the United States. The Agriculture Department, the Federal Bureau of Investigation, the Bureau of Land Management, the Internal Revenue Service, and the many other federal departments are staffed largely by career professionals who hold their positions until retirement age, regardless of political administration.

As Matteson and Ivancevich (1981) report, Weber placed a high value on technical knowledge:

> The primary source of the superiority of bureaucratic administration lies in the role of technical knowledge which, through the development of modern technology and business methods in the production of goods, has become completely indispensable. Capitalism is the most rational economic base for bureaucratic administration and enables it to develop in the most rational form, especially because, from a fiscal point of view, it supplies the necessary money resources.

Assessment   By 1900 industrial leaders began to recognize that a manager did not have to be the one who owned the business. The flow of authority and paperwork could be governed by scientific principles, and people could be trained to be effective managers. Industrial leaders realized that successful organizations needed unity of purpose, command, and direction. An ordered environment; subordination of individual interests to the survival of the organization; and harmony, equity, and stability of tenure for key personnel all became hallmarks of effective organizations.

Management according to the classical administrative school is not without limitations, however. The monumental difficulties experienced by the former Soviet Union—possibly the most rigidly bureaucratic system yet attempted—illustrate the downside. Rigid and unresponsive decision making and a lack of commitment among workers given no autonomy led to a strangled economic system, severely repressive political measures, and pervasive disaffection.

Within the classical administrative school, the work of Mary Parker Follett most directly discussed the disadvantages of bureaucratic theory. She emphasized for the first time the importance of the individual—both manager and worker. Follett believed that scientific methods could be applied to human relationships,

E thics is the branch of philosophy concerned with human values and conduct, moral duty, and obligation. Such concerns have held a central place in the world of ideas from early times, and they continue to challenge academics and other thinkers in many cultures. Philosophers whose work has shaped our modern ideas about ethics include Plato, Kant, Rousseau, Locke, and John Dewey. Theories about the moral awareness of right and wrong have focused on divine will, an innate sense, and individual experience. Among suggested sources for ethical standards have been religion, the state, and the good of the individual or group (Barrett and Kilonski, 1986).

In the management arena, ethics are frequently viewed in two different ways: as an individual's standard of conduct and as a body of social obligations and duties. A. Thomas Young, president and chief operating officer of Martin Marietta Corporation, combined both views in his definition of ethical people: "Ethical people honor their word, follow the law, act honestly, respect other people's property, are loyal and they work hard" (Widder, 1992). Managers make ethical decisions when they decide whether to falsify documents or pad their expense accounts.

Although the core principles of ethics remain unchanged, managers face a constantly shifting array of ethical challenges. Among ethical decisions confronting managers today include decisions about siting workers (in traditional U.S. manufacturing centers or overseas, for example), protecting employee privacy, and interacting with the environment. Although specific issues come and go, the need to make ethical judgments remains.

At the tops of organizations, managers set the ethical tone for a company. For an employee to follow a manager's good example, what a company does must match what it says about ethics. If a company rewards unethical behavior, employees will not act ethically. Ultimately, however, each employee must develop his or her conscience and apply personal values and morals to events. The individual—not the manager—is responsible for ethical conduct.

Imagine being a manager during the classical phase of management, when ethical concerns arose in regard to three practices: (1) the use of piece-rate pay systems, a practice that favored quantity over quality; (2) the establishment of jobs that were so specialized and repetitive that they ignored workers' intelligence, creativity, and physical well-being; and (3) the adherence to rigid hierarchies in which all orders were issued from the top and no feedback was permitted from the bottom. What are the ethical implications of these practices for customers, workers, and their organizations? ▲

and she believed that people could reach their potentials only through groups (Matteson and Ivancevich, 1981). Follett and others defined the social context of work and emphasized reliance on skilled, principled, and professional managers.

The classical administrative school opened the door for the next important school: the behavioral, or human relations, school.

Behavioral Management Theory

The **behavioral school** took management thinking one step further. Its proponents recognized employees as individuals with concrete human needs, as parts of work groups, and as members of a larger society. Enlightened managers were to view their subordinates as assets to be developed, not as nameless robots expected to follow orders blindly.

The first modern author to address the concern for people in the work environment was Robert Owen, considered by many the Father of Modern Personnel Management. In 1813, with the publication of "An Address to the Superintendents of Manufactories," Owen asserted that the quality and quantity of workers' output were influenced by conditions both on and off the job. Owen demonstrated, by referring to the textile mills he managed in Scotland, that devoting attention to the "vital machine" (people) made as much sense as devoting attention to inanimate machines (Merrill, 1970). Owen was far ahead of his time, and not until the work of Mary Parker Follett in the 1920s did the individual worker again receive scholarly attention.

Like Follett, psychologist Elton Mayo emphasized the behavioral aspects of workers. Beginning in 1924, Mayo and the National Academy of Sciences conducted five studies. Each focused on the Western Electric plant in Cicero, Illinois. The studies heightened management's awareness of the social needs of workers and showed how an organization's social environment influenced productivity. He discovered that when employees were treated with dignity, in a way that showed concern for their welfare and individuality, commitment and productivity increased.

Mayo's studies on the effects of piece rates on production led to the discovery that social pressures exerted by co-workers were a significant influence on performance. In the bank-wiring study at Western Electric, workers in teams developed their own production quotas. Mayo found that, rather than release finished pieces, workers kept pieces to help the group meet future quotas, and they pressured co-workers to keep production within the bounds of established quotas (Mayo, 1933). Chapter 12 will examine Mayo's work in more detail.

Abraham Maslow—a humanistic psychologist, teacher, and practicing manager—developed a needs-based theory of motivation. Maslow's theory is now considered central to understanding human motivations and behavior. His work paralleled many of the findings of psychology and sociology, social sciences that were then emerging. These sciences affirmed what artists and historians had always known—that people are extraordinarily complex creatures with many motives for behaviors on and off the job.

In 1943, in an article for *Psychological Review*—"A Theory of Human Motivation"—Maslow identified and analyzed five basic needs, which he believed underlay all human behavior. These needs related to physiology (the needs for food, water, air, and sex), security (safety, the absence of illness), society or affiliation (friendship, interaction, love), esteem (respect and recognition), and self-actualization (the ability to reach one's potentials). Maslow's list of needs provided a radically different perspective for managers; before Maslow, most managers assumed that people were primarily motivated by money. Maslow's work caused many managers to evaluate their own actions, their companies' conduct, and their individual philosophies about people. Chapter 12 will discuss Maslow's hierarchy of needs at length.

In 1960 Douglas McGregor expanded the ideas of his predecessors in management theory by publishing *The Human Side of Enterprise*. In it, McGregor explained his view that all managers operated from one or two basic assumptions about human behavior: Theory X and Theory Y. The first theory, the view traditionally held about labor, portrayed workers in industry as being lazy and needing to be coerced, controlled, and directed. The second described people as

McGregor thought them to be: responsible; willing to learn; and, given the proper incentives, inherently motivated to exercise ingenuity and creativity. McGregor believed that the traditional way of treating people—regarding them as unthinking, uncaring robots—must change. Indeed, McGregor stressed, only by changing these assumptions could managers tap into workers' vast talents. What mattered, he emphasized, was how people were treated and valued in their work settings. McGregor told managers that if they gave employees a chance to contribute and to take control and responsibility, they would do so (McGregor, 1960).

Assessment   The behavioral management school brought the human dimension of work firmly into the mainstream of management thought. The results continue today: Managers work hard to discover what employees want from work; how to enlist their cooperation and commitment; and how to unleash their talents, energy, and creativity. The behaviorists integrated, for the first time, ideas from sociology, anthropology, and psychology with management theory. One result of the behavioral school was the creation of positions for professional human resources managers. Behavioral management theory effectively paved the way for modern-day employee assistance programs, such as substance-abuse interdiction and day care for children, and innovations in communication involving subordinates and peers, individually and collectively.

The major limitation of behavioral management theory is its complexity. It does not yield quick or simple conclusions, and it does not conclusively explain or predict the actions of individuals or groups. Most managers, not being trained social scientists, have a difficult time using the vast amount of information provided by the social sciences, as the behavioral school says managers should do. Behavioral theory becomes even more complicated in light of the facts that people are motivated by more than one need at any given time and that they must constantly reconcile conflicting demands. No simple formulas can always motivate all individuals in the workplace. What's more, peoples' needs change with time, making the same person tough to manage one day and a delight the next. Nevertheless, by considering psychology, managers can prepare themselves to effectively manage their most important and complex resource: people.

Quantitative Management Theory

The next wave of management thought moved from concern for people to the use of quantitative tools to help plan and control nearly everything in the organization. The emphasis in this new school, the **quantitative school** of management theory, was on mathematical approaches to management problems. Such an approach was born in World War II– era research teams that developed radar, information theory, guidance systems, jet engines, and the atomic bomb. Since then, quantitative tools have been applied to every aspect of business (Campbell, 1982).

Management Science

Management science is the study of complex systems of people, money, equipment, and procedures, with the goal of understanding them and improving their effectiveness (Bittel and Ramsey, 1985). Management science is a facet of

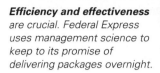

Efficiency and effectiveness are crucial. Federal Express uses management science to keep to its promise of delivering packages overnight.

quantitative management theory. Historians Bittel and Ramsey presented the following explanation of the management science approach:

> Such studies are conducted through the use of the scientific method, utilizing tools and knowledge from the physical, mathematical, and behavioral sciences. Its ultimate purpose is to provide the manager with a sound, scientific, and quantitative basis for decision making.

Management science calls for managers to design specific measures to test the effectiveness of a process. Airlines use the management science approach in scheduling flights, handling passenger reservations, and scheduling aircraft maintenance. In management science, the means of measurement can be statistical tests or some other kind. In an area of management science called **operations research** (**OR**), models, simulations, and games are commonly used as tests. To be effective and valid, these means require the participation and commitment of all the managers and workers involved in the test.

The techniques and tools of management science are frequently used to plan, organize, staff, control, and direct production operations; this aspect of management science is known as operations management. The management science approach is also used to direct facilities, purchasing, investments, marketing, personnel, and research and development. Management science depends on the participation of a variety of experienced researchers and practitioners to gather and process information, analyze operations, and develop and use the appropriate tools and techniques. Regardless of the methods, tools, and personnel used, however, the ultimate test of management science is whether better decisions are made and more effective processes are developed (Bittel and Ramsey, 1985).

Operations Management   The branch of management science that applies to manufacturing or service industries is **operations management**. Some of the most common tools of operations management are:

- Inventory models that determine optimum storage levels and reorder points

- Break-even analyses to determine levels of production and sales at which the organization recaptures the total costs of development and manufacturing

- Queuing theory, whose goal is to minimize waiting time for the users of a product or machine

- Production scheduling, which determines when operations begin and end

- Production routing, which directs the path followed by parts and products during assembly

Chapter 18 will explore operations management in more detail.

Management Information Systems   A key ingredient in management science is the timely and efficient delivery of up-to-date information. Most organizations now utilize a **management information system** (**MIS**), a computer-based system that gives managers the information they need to make decisions. An MIS is maintained by specialists who know what the users of system output need. In using computer links to connect headquarters, suppliers, and outlets, the Wal-Mart chain of retail stores was implementing a management information system. The system allowed Wal-Mart to minimize expenses and the time needed to gather and process information about sales and inventory.

Companies that depend on domestic and foreign suppliers and outlets for their goods and services must know promptly and precisely what is happening in all vital operations. Without such information, managers cannot make timely and appropriate decisions. Chapter 19 will examine management information systems in detail.

Assessment   From the 1950s well into the 1980s, large numbers of American managers became preoccupied with quantitative measurement. The management of business after business was given over to engineers and financial managers dedicated to achieving the lowest possible cost and the highest short-term profits. Symbolic of this view were the substantial bonuses that were paid to managers according to financial performance in each quarter or year. A decision not based on a quantitative tool or technique was considered a poor decision.

This prolonged, intense focus on immediate results generated significant difficulties. Long-term investment was neglected, especially investment in research and development. Companies ignored developing overseas trends and, as a result, lost market share to innovative competitors. Organizations forgot the humanism of the behavioral approach and the lessons learned from behavioral management theory. Companies produced what they wanted to produce in the way they wanted to produce it; they forgot about quality and their customers. The result was disastrous for many firms and whole industries. Perhaps the most dramatic examples of such industries are the American steel and auto manufacturers.

Examples exist in every industry, however. The losers run the gamut, from the makers of small appliances and footwear to the manufacturers of textiles and tires.

In hindsight, the lesson of overemphasizing the quantitative management approach is clear: It's not the tools that are important, but the results they bring to the organization and the community. Management science can help managers analyze, develop, and improve operations, but management science techniques cannot substitute for sound, balanced judgment and management experience. Management science cannot be forgotten or ignored, however. Like all phases of management theory, management science contains positive aspects. The wise manager draws upon the best aspects of each management theory and integrates them with insight and imagination.

Systems Theory

A **system** is a set of interrelated parts that work together to achieve stated goals or function according to a plan or design. Exhibit 2.3 shows an organization as a system, with inputs being processed, through operations, into outputs. Outputs go to users who are either inside or outside the organization. An internal user is the person down the line who receives a part or a project when another worker finishes with it. Anyone in the organization who uses or depends on the output of others in the organization is an internal user, or internal customer. Information, products, or services sent outside go to external users (suppliers, customers, or government agencies).

Exhibit 2.3

The organization as a system.

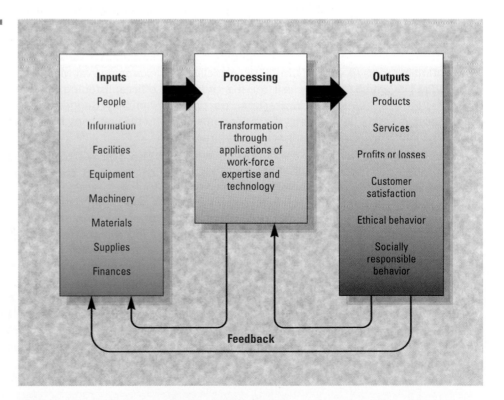

Inputs	Processing	Outputs
People	Transformation through applications of work-force expertise and technology	Products
Information		Services
Facilities		Profits or losses
Equipment		Customer satisfaction
Machinery		Ethical behavior
Materials		Socially responsible behavior
Supplies		
Finances		

Feedback

An organization comprises various parts (subsystems) that must perform tasks necessary for the survival of the whole. Understanding how a system works requires an understanding of how each component functions and what it contributes. Changes in any one subsystem usually affect other subsystems or components. As an example of the interrelationships among subsystems, consider the effects that the subsystems of an airline have on each other. Imagine a Friday afternoon when the reservation staff has oversold all the day's flights by 20 passengers each, the maintenance staff delays three departures by an hour each,

F O C U S   O N   Q U A L I T Y
New Ideas in Quality Assurance

One useful definition of *quality* refers to the characteristics of a product or service that ensure that the needs of product users are met. Organizations strive to ensure that their customers—both inside and outside—receive products and services that meet their needs. Here are a few recent innovations that businesses have used to achieve quality:

Just-in-Time Inventory Control

Timely availability of supplies, raw materials, and finished goods is one key to quality. In traditional inventory management, stockpiles of materials or supplies are kept on hand for long periods before the materials are used. Just-in-time (JIT), or delivery-as-needed, inventory systems call for the ordering and delivery of supplies, materials, parts, or subassemblies only as needed. If components are produced internally, production is scheduled precisely to meet the user's needs. JIT systems eliminate the need to store inventories of all types, and they free the cash formerly tied up in inventory. By linking suppliers, manufacturers, and retailers, response and shipment can be timely enough to prevent shortages. Wal-Mart employs a JIT system for its stores and distribution centers.

Staying Close to the Customer

The term *customer* identifies any user of output. Staying close to the customer means listening to his or her needs. It means sharing key decisions with such people as subordinates, suppliers, and end-users. It means keeping in touch to ensure immediate

availability to customers in need. Increasingly, quality-oriented companies provide 24-hour service to their customers. Repair staff and in-house experts are on call through toll-free numbers, and it's a rare maker of luxury automobiles who does not guarantee round-the-clock road service to buyers nationwide. Timely service is becoming increasingly important. Trumpf, a German manufacturer of machine tools, was asked to design a machine for another German producer, but Trumpf was slow to respond. The customer turned to a Japanese firm, and the need was filled on the customer's timetable, not the manufacturer's.

Contact with customers is another increasingly important means to quality. Two days each week, for example, Wal-Mart managers are away from their offices, listening to customers inside and outside the company. Suggestions from the field are routed directly to the company headquarters.

The Team Concept of Product Development

Chrysler's move to product teams was not unique. Most industrial companies recognize the merits of this approach and use it to bring new products to market effectively and efficiently. Ingersoll-Rand (IR) used teams in the late 1980s to bring its most successful hand tool, an air-powered grinder, to market. IR product team members talked with tool users, then developed a handmade prototype for the intended users to assess and comment on. The lessons learned led to a successful product and a long list of satisfied end-users. ▲

and crew schedulers fail to assign a pilot to one connecting trip. Chapter 3 will explore systems in more detail.

Before managers with a systems approach change the operations they are responsible for, they determine how the change will affect other operations and people. By keeping entire systems and subsystems in mind, they hope to ensure that a positive move in one area does not negatively affect another. In addition, they hope to assess the impact of changes before they take place.

Internal Systems   The subsystems of an organization are its internal systems. A corporation may be structured according to functions—marketing, production, finance, and personnel, for example. Or it may be compartmentalized along product lines, perhaps including a consumer products division and a government contracts division. Within each division the company may be subdivided along functional lines. Each part of the whole is a subsystem that interacts with the others in important and sometimes subtle ways. Unless a mechanism that allows information sharing is in place, subsystems may work at cross purposes, causing confusion and wasting resources.

Imaginative changes in the relations among subsystems can generate dramatic results. Chrysler Corporation provides a case in point. Traditionally, Chrysler auto designers worked in teams composed of experts in only one discipline. When finished, their work went to engineers for approval. After the engineers approved, the design went to production experts. When an insurmountable problem appeared, the design was sent back to the team that had released it last. When the engineers said a part could not be built, for example, the design went back to the designers. Using this system, Chrysler typically took four years to bring a new design to market.

In 1989, Chrysler implemented a radical change in subsystem relations in regard to the design of the Chrysler Viper and the LH line. Instead of subsystems with members from only one discipline, Chrysler organized interdisciplinary teams. Delays dwindled, cooperation thrived, and lead times shrank. Problems were dealt with as they arose, with input from everyone concerned. Changes were negotiated and implemented on the spot. As components were being designed, the men and women who would build them—whether they were internal or external suppliers—participated. The transition to this new approach was not easy: Suppliers were reluctant to share vital information about their costs and operations; old patterns of operation were tough to abandon. But because of the change in subsystem relations, Chrysler is better positioned for competition than it has been for many years. Needless to say, the company will continue to use the interdisciplinary approach.

As Chrysler management saw the need to coordinate operations, Sam Walton of Wal-Mart saw the need to coordinate the subsystems that contributed to his organization. He used innovative technology to link the company's suppliers to stores, distribution centers, and corporate headquarters. As a result, Wal-Mart gained a powerful edge over slower-moving competitors such as Sears and K Mart.

External Systems   Most managers operate in environments that include many subsystems beyond a manager's scope of control. Groups and organizations outside a company dictate to varying degrees what will go on inside the firm. Governments impose restrictions and reporting requirements. The limits of suppliers may constrain a company that uses their products. Stockholders may press management for higher profits and larger dividends. Consumers' tastes and needs change (a hot item one year may gather dust the next), and competitors introduce new products or master new technologies. A manager's family may make demands on his or her time and energy. And market conditions (rising interest rates, inflation increases, recessions, and so on), may require a manager to adapt plans and behavior.

Indeed, the effects of actions taken by outsiders can be as important—sometimes more so—than internal ones. In May 1985, after much media hoopla, the Coca-Cola Company introduced a reformulated, sweeter Coke. The new product was a bomb; loyal consumers and Coca-Cola bottlers besieged the corporate headquarters to demand the return of the old formula. Within six months the company yielded to external pressure: The old product was reinstated as Classic Coke. The process of building a new stadium for the Chicago Bulls and Blackhawks provides another example of outside pressure. Construction was blocked by local protesters who maintained that local and minority workers had not been included in the project. Negotiations followed, and the primary contractor agreed that 25% of the work would go to minority contractors and neighborhood residents.

Outsiders can and do influence management decisions, sometimes under extreme pressure. All businesses are open systems and must interact with forces outside the company.

The Cumulative Energy of Synergy

Synergy is the increased effectiveness that results from combined action or cooperation. It is sometimes described as the $2 + 2 = 5$ effect, because the result of a synergistic partnership is actually more than the sum of the production of each partner alone. A corporate merger often provides an illustration of a synergistic process. When publishing giant Time, Inc. and entertainment goliath Warner Communications merged in 1991, many experts saw enormous synergistic potential. The combined organization, they believed, offered powerful product and marketing potential unavailable to the separate firms. In such mergers, old identities are lost and a new, stronger combination may be formed. Some combinations produce negative effects, however. A merger may lead to a clash of corporate cultures, as described in Chapter 9, and to the loss of jobs and competition.

Synergy may occur when inside or outside groups interact. Chrysler's interdisciplinary team approach, for example, unleashed the talents of those who had been confined to separate internal groups. The result, a shorter time to market, was an example of synergy. Likewise, when Wal-Mart switched to satellite communications to link headquarters, stores, and suppliers, the resulting synergy caused sales to increase dramatically and corporate performance to improve in nearly every category.

Assessment   According to systems theory, the components of an enterprise interact to create synergy that can benefit each component and the whole. The systems approach encourages managers to view their organizations holistically—to envision workers, groups, and tasks as interrelated parts of an organic whole. This integrated approach requires information systems that can provide to managers at every level enough accurate and timely input to facilitate sound decisions. Such a situation brings Henri Fayol's principles—unity of command, unity of direction, and harmony—to mind. Keeping people focused on the objectives to be achieved is the manager's most important task. When all work together toward a goal to which they are committed, synergy results.

The systems view has led managers to think about quality as a concept affected by each action of every employee. The result has been the concept of total quality management (TQM)—a commitment by all employees, beginning at the top, to work to meet the needs of both internal and external customers. Unless all employees work for continuous improvement in every aspect of their jobs, total quality management cannot occur. Companies like Xerox, IBM, Motorola, and Ford have made the commitment to total quality management. Chapter 17 will examine quality issues in more detail.

Fear can beset managers when they consider just how complex and connected their organizations' subsystems are. This fear can lead to paralysis. Managers may become overly cautious and refuse to act until they have contacted every possible source, conducted exhaustive analysis, and asked for reviews from higher-ups. The time constraints and conditions of business seldom allow such luxuries.

Contingency Management Theory

The **contingency school** is based on the premise that managers' preferred actions or approaches depend on the variables of the situations they face. Adherents of the school seek the most effective way to deal with any situation or problem, recognizing that each situation encountered, although possibly similar to others in the past, possesses unique characteristics.

Managers holding the contingency view feel free to draw on all past theories in attempting to analyze and solve problems. The true contingency approach is integrative. During a typical day, a manager may have to use behavioral approaches to soothe a subordinate's hurt feelings, apply management science to program production for a new assembly, and use classical scientific tools to study an assembly operation to determine where it can be improved.

Adherents of the contingency school recognize that a human resources manager at Citibank may need to analyze a job applicant's interview and test results differently than a human resources manager at 1st National of Chicago. Both managers have differing systems, needs, and experiences; the contingency school maintains that their choices should reflect those differences as well as the unique characteristics and histories of the job applicants.

The contingency theory can be summarized as an "it all depends" device. Right and proper conduct under one set of circumstances may fail utterly under another set. Since no two problems possess identical details and circumstances, neither should any two solutions. Several solutions and approaches may be possible and might yield equally good results. Supporters of the contingency theory would acknowledge that many roads lead to a city from several directions; they would also stress that the route that appears the shortest may not be the best choice if it is undergoing repairs.

The contingency theory tells managers to look to their experiences and the past and to consider many options before choosing a course of action. It tells managers to stay flexible and to consider alternatives and fallback positions when defining and attacking problems. The theory also tells them that intelligent choices come only from adequate preliminary research.

GLOBAL APPLICATIONS
Kaizen and Theory Z

With the end of World War II, Japanese policy makers chose to allow government and business to work together to rebuild their nation and its economy. The Japanese created the Ministry for International Trade and Industry (MITI) to work with industrial leaders to determine what direction the country should take. MITI began the rebuilding by concentrating on the creation of a strong infrastructure and the reestablishment of core industries, particularly iron and steel. Next the ministry targeted shipbuilding as the principal industry in which the country should excel. By the 1960s, Japan led the world in building seagoing vessels of nearly every type, including oil tankers and bulk freighters.

Through MITI, Japan's industrial community cooperates and shares resources. National and industry-wide goals are set, and strong commitments are made to achieve them. The Japanese government protects the industries it determines to be vital to the national interest (farming, steel, communications), and industrial trade associations act to protect individual corporate interests.

A strong network of manufacturers and related suppliers dedicated to the survival of the whole is but one reason why foreign corporations find it difficult to do business in Japan. Industries are targeted by Japanese manufacturers, which make long-term efforts to capture market share. America's consumer electronics industry yielded to Japanese competition by bits and pieces; today Zenith is the only American producer of consumer electronics that remains—and it scarcely compares with its giant Japanese rivals.

Similarly, the Japanese targeted the U.S. auto market. They began by offering economy cars to Americans at a time when Detroit companies were not inclined to modify their traditional offerings, big cars. By the early 1990s nearly 30% of all new cars sold in America were Japanese. Today the aggressive and efficient Japanese producers offer upscale cars as well. The Lexus and Infiniti models are making serious inroads into the luxury car market long dominated by European manufacturers.

Japanese management practice differs in many ways from American practice. To a Japanese manager,

decision making involves teamwork and gaining consensus. Once all managers concur about how to proceed, all commit to the enterprise. The Japanese take a long-term view—usually, a 10- to 20-year view. Japanese planners are extremely patient; they willingly await the right opportunities. And Japanese corporations invest heavily and consistently, in good financial years and bad, in the basic research and development essential for creating new products.

Traditionally, employees are dedicated to the *kaizen* philosophy—the continuous search for better ways to do things and a constant devotion to personal growth. Promotions to higher levels in a corporation come only after long apprenticeship in several different positions. Jobs lack narrow definitions; each employee accepts a wide range of duties and spends significant time each year in learning what is new and different. One final contrast between Japanese and U.S. practice is the level of commitment given by each employee to his or her employer. In return for a strong commitment, the Japanese worker in a large firm engaged in international markets may anticipate lifetime employment.

Although the Japanese value group effort, consensual decision making, and sublimation of the individual to the interests of the organization, Americans value privacy and individual effort and achievement. Exhibit 2.4 illustrates the traditional American (Type A) and Japanese (Type J) approaches to managing people. The blending of the two is called Type Z. The term originates from **Theory Z**, a concept created by William G. Ouchi. In his book *Theory Z: How American Business Can Meet the Japanese Challenge* (1981), Ouchi recommends that American business borrow some elements from Japanese management and modify some aspects of the

Exhibit 2.4

American, Japanese, and Type Z approaches to managing human resources.

American	Modified American	Japanese
TYPE A	*TYPE Z*	*TYPE J*
Short-term employment	Long-term employment	Lifetime employment
Specialized careers	Moderately specialized careers	Nonspecialized careers
Limited concern for employees' personal lives and families	Holistic concern	Holistic concern
Individual decision making	Moderate consensual decision making	Consensual decision making
Rapid evaluation and promotion	Slow evaluation and promotion	Slow evaluation and promotion
Individual responsibility	Individual responsibility	Collective responsibility
Explicit formalized controls and mechanisms	Implicit, informal controls using formal and explicit mechanisms	Implicit, informal control mechanisms

Adapted from William G. Ouchi, *Theory Z: How American Business Can Meet the Japanese Challenge* (Reading, MA: Addison-Wesley) 1981, p. 58.

traditional American approach. Of the Japanese elements he recommends for adoption are holistic concern for employees and their families, encouragement of long-term employment, and consensual decision making. He recommends that U.S. companies retain the American practices of rewarding individuals and holding them responsible for their efforts and actions. ▲

Assessment The contingency theory applies to any organization and to managers who face change. The purchase of one company by another is an example of significant change. By using the contingency approach, top managers of the purchasing company may discover that they need to learn or embrace the methods of the purchased company. If the theory works as its supporters predict, they will make the discovery before imposing inappropriate methods on the acquired firm.

The contingency theory tells managers to try the new, to experiment until the right means are found. Such a theory has applications beyond the examples cited here. Contingency theory applies to motivation, performance appraisal, controlling, planning, and almost every area in which a manager may work. Though the contingency school is the most recent school of management thought, it will certainly not be the last.

Future Trends

In 1982, Thomas Peters and Robert Waterman published *In Search of Excellence: Lessons from America's Best-Run Companies* (1982). They profiled successful companies—Disney, Procter & Gamble, McDonald's, and Johnson & Johnson among them—and suggested reasons for the firms' achievements. The companies shared eight characteristics:

- A bias toward action. Peters and Waterman discovered that the best-run companies focus on trying things rather than analyzing problems to death.

- A commitment to staying close to the customer. Staying close means listening, visiting, sharing, and servicing. In the best-run companies, the customer's needs are paramount.

- A capacity to design-in productivity through people. In an effective company, all employees' ideas are valued and disagreements can be aired. Managers in such companies realize that the keys to improving productivity and quality rest in the hands and minds of all employees.

- An ability to foster autonomy and entrepreneurship. In the best-run companies, internal structures and facilities foster access and dialog between and among employees at all levels. Employees are encouraged to take risks and to innovate. Mistakes are tolerated and seen as necessary for growth and improvement.

- A managerial style that is "hands on" and value driven. In successful companies, managers provide a vision and a value system. Leaders are encouraged to get involved in problem solving at all levels.

- A resolve to "stick to their knitting." Successful companies know what they do best and stick to it. They remain focused on one or two lines and keep improving in their areas of expertise.

- A commitment to simple form and lean staff. Excellent corporations have simple structures and few levels of management. Staffs and departments remain small.

- A simultaneous combination of looseness and tightness. Those things that really matter—corporate values, corporate goals, the means of creating high productivity and quality—are closely controlled. In other areas, employees are free to experiment and innovate and encouraged to do so.

C H A P T E R   S U M M A R Y

- Classical management thinkers looked for one best way to do everything. Their tools were time and motion study and a scientific approach to studying work and work flow.

- While some of the classical thinkers' ideas are still with us, several have fallen from favor: narrow job descriptions, the concept of one best way, and piece-rate systems of compensation and production.

- Behaviorists studied the behavior of people in industrial settings. They discovered elements of human motivation that are the foundations for modern understanding of human behavior.

- Behaviorists pointed out how complex human motivation is and how difficult managing unique people with differing needs can be. We now know that when individuals are motivated and committed to give their best, and managers tap into their creativity and enthusiasm, superior performance and quality result.

- Quantitative tools sprang from the quantitative school, which recommended a scientific approach to problem solving and decision making.

- Quantitative tools are not substitutes for experience and intuition gained through years of management; rather, they are aids to experience and intuition.

- Systems thinkers taught managers that they are parts of a whole. They encouraged managers to focus on how each part works and interacts with the whole.

- Contingency theorists reminded managers that no two situations are identical. The urged managers to look for solutions by studying their own experiences and the experiences of others. They stress a manager's need to blend, borrow, and be flexible while solving problems.

S K I L L - B U I L D I N G

State which school of management thought is most likely to lead to the implementation of the innovations listed. Explain your choices.

1. Production teams—that is, teams of workers with either no supervisor or rotating leadership empowered to schedule production, monitor output, hire and discipline members, and make changes.

2. Quality circles, or groups of volunteers from any one department who come together to solve problems relating to the quality of their operations and output.

3. Product teams, or groups assembled to design a product and see it through production. Members come from every area involved in design, and the team often includes suppliers and customers.

4. Management by wandering around, or the practice of regularly getting managers out of their offices so they can communicate with subordinates, customers, suppliers, and other managers within their organizations.

5. Cultural diversity training and workshops. In these seminars, workers improve their understanding of the contributions made by the culture, traditions, and values of their own group or others' groups.

1. Can you define this chapter's essential terms?

2. Identify and explain the central ideas of the major schools of management thought:
   a. The classical school (include the scientific and administrative branches)
   b. The behavioral school
   c. The quantitative school
   d. The systems school
   e. The contingency school

3. Identify at least one significant strength and one weakness of each school.

R E C O M M E N D E D   R E A D I N G

Lawrence, Paul R. "Historical Development of Organizational Behavior," in *Handbook of Organizational Behavior,* Jay W. Lorsch, editor (Englewood Cliffs, NJ: Prentice-Hall), 1987.

Maslow, Abraham. "A Theory of Human Motivation," *Psychological Review* (July 1943), pp. 370–396.

Matteson, Michael T., and John M. Ivancevich, editors. *Management Classics,* 2nd edition (Santa Monica, CA: Goodyear), 1981.

McGregor, Douglas. *The Human Side of Enterprise* (New York: McGraw-Hill), 1960.

Ouchi, William G. *Theory Z: How American Business Can Meet the Japanese Challenge* (Reading, MA: Addison-Wesley), 1981.

Peters, Thomas, and Nancy Austin. *A Passion for Excellence* (New York: Random House), 1985.

Peters, Thomas J., and Robert H. Waterman. *In Search of Excellence: Lessons from America's Best-Run Companies* (New York: Harper & Row), 1982.

Weber, Max. *Theory of Social and Economic Organization* (New York: Free Press), 1947.

Wren, Daniel A. *The Evolution of Management Thought,* 3rd edition (New York: Wiley), 1987.

R E F E R E N C E S

Barrett, Thomas M., and Richard J. Kilonski. *Business Ethics,* 2nd edition (Englewood Cliffs, NJ: Prentice-Hall), 1986.

Bittel, Lester R., and Jackson E. Ramsey, editors. *Handbook for Professional Managers* (New York: McGraw-Hill), 1985, p. 634.

Campbell, Jeremy. *Grammatical Man: Information, Entropy, Language, and Life* (New York: Simon & Schuster), 1982, pp. 15–31.

Haigh, Christopher, editor. *The Cambridge Historical Encyclopedia of Great Britain and Ireland* (Cambridge, England: Cambridge University Press), 1985, p. 269.

Matteson, Michael T., and John M. Ivancevich, editors. *Management Classics* 2nd edition (Santa Monica, CA: Goodyear), 1981, p. 18, 156, 232, 280.

Mayo, Elton. *The Human Problems of an Industrial Civilization* (New York: Macmillan), 1933.

McGregor, Douglas. *The Human Side of Enterprise* (New York: McGraw-Hill), 1960, pp. 33–48.

Merrill, Harwood F., editor. *Classics in Management,* revised edition (New York: American Management Association), 1970, pp. 10, 56, 188.

Ouchi, William G. *Theory Z: How American Business Can Meet the Japanese Challenge* (Reading, MA: Addison-Wesley), 1981.

Peters, Thomas J., and Robert H. Waterman. *In Search of Excellence: Lessons from America's Best-Run Companies* (New York: Harper & Row), 1982.

Widder, Pat. "More Corporations Learning That Ethics Are a Bottom Line Issue," *Chicago Tribune,* June 7, 1992, sec. 7, pp. 1, 6.

G L O S S A R Y O F **T** E R M S

behavioral school   The management theory that focuses on people as individuals with needs and as members of work groups and a larger society. Managers who are adherents of the behavioral school view subordinates as assets to be developed.

bureaucracy   An administrative system marked by diffusion of authority through a hierarchy. The positions in the hierarchy are clearly defined and held by career people subject to rigid rules of operation.

classical administrative school   The branch of classical management theory that emphasized the flow of information in factories and businesses.

classical management theory   The theory of management that originated during the Industrial Revolution. Adherents of this theory pursue the "one best way" to perform tasks. Classical management theory developed into two separate branches: the classical scientific school and the classical administrative school.

classical scientific school   The branch of classical management theory that focused on the manufacturing environment and work on the factory floor; emphasized the division of labor among specialists and the application of scientific methods to management.

contingency school   The branch of management theory based on the premise that managers should make decisions based on the facts and variables of each unique situation. This school suggests that managers draw freely on other schools to seek the most effective solution.

kaizen   A Japanese term used in the business setting to mean incremental, continuous improvement.

management information system (MIS)   The coordinated arrangement of gathering, collating, and distributing information needed for management decision making. The term is often applied to computer systems designed for work units and organizations.

management science   The study of complex systems of people, money, equipment, and procedures, with the aims of understanding how they function and then improving their efficiency and effectiveness.

operations management   The practice of applying management science tools and techniques to all aspects of manufacturing and service industries.

operations research (OR)   The use of models, simulations, games, break-even analyses, queuing theory, and other analytical tools to optimize performance.

quantitative school   The branch of management thought that emphasizes mathematical approaches and measurability.

synergy   The increased effectiveness produced through combined action. When two parties participate in a synergistic relationship, the result of their cooperation is greater than the sum of both individual efforts.

system   A group of interacting, interrelated, or interdependent elements that form a complex whole.

theory   An explanation that helps organize information and knowledge.

Theory Z   The management view that mutual responsibility, loyalty, and regard between companies and their employees yields higher productivity and well-being for all. The theory was introduced by William G. Ouchi in 1981.

CASE PROBLEM
ConAgra Tries Harder

ConAgra is the second largest independent food processor in America (only Philip Morris is larger). In 1991, ConAgra achieved its twelfth consecutive year of record sales and earnings: Sales exceeded $20 billion and net profit was $322 million. In 1992, the participants in a survey published in *Fortune* magazine (more than 8,000 senior executives, outside directors, and financial analysts) rated ConAgra the second most respected company in its industry—a shade behind industry leader, General Mills.

ConAgra owns 60 separate companies. Brand names in the corporate stable include Banquet (frozen foods), Hunt-Wesson, Peter Pan (peanut butter), Country Pride (chicken), and Healthy Choice. Few people have ever heard of ConAgra because it spends its time and money developing its brand names.

Charles M. Harper, CEO and chairman of ConAgra, has primary responsibility for building the company through smart acquisitions. He arranged the purchase of Beatrice Foods for $1.3 billion, for example—the buy that brought Hunt-Wesson into the fold.

Two basic concepts underlie Harper's management philosophy: discipline and decentralization. Managers of the operating divisions enjoy much autonomy in running them. Harper encourages them to innovate and expand their businesses. "It violates our principles to tell a company president what to do," says Phil Fletcher, ConAgra president. "But we do tell him what we think of his plans."

The company's latest entry into the food industry is an extra-lean ground beef. This product represents ConAgra's first effort at transforming a meat product into a value-added consumer item. The company plans to market this new product in packages that will be easier for supermarket butchers to handle than the 80-pound packages that are now standard. The secret to leaner ground beef? Mixing in portions of beef stock, processed oat flour, and a bit of salt.

QUESTIONS

1. To which school(s) of management theory do you think Charles Harper subscribes? Why?

2. ConAgra developed the Healthy Choice line to market taste in dietetic foods. The inspiration for the line was CEO Harper's need to live on dietetic foods after his heart attack in 1985. He realized the foods available at the time were unpalatable, and he saw a niche for good-tasting healthful meals. What parallels do you find between Harper's experience and other events described in this chapter?

3. What effect do you think Harper and Fletcher's free-rein leadership style has on ConAgra managers? Would you like to work in an environment where you were free to innovate and to experiment? Why?

For more about ConAgra, see Ronald Henkoff, "ConAgra: A Giant That Keeps Innovating," *Fortune,* December 16, 1991, pp. 101–102; Kate Ballen, "America's Most Admired Corporations," *Fortune,* February 10, 1992, pp. 40–74.

The Manager's Environments

LEARNING OBJECTIVES

After reading and discussing this chapter, you should be able to:

■ Define this chapter's essential terms

■ Explain why a business is an open system

■ Describe the elements in an organization's internal environment

■ Discuss the directly interactive forces in an organization's external environment

■ Discuss the indirectly interactive forces in an organization's external environment

■ Describe the means available for boundary spanning

■ Discuss how managers can influence their external environments

■ Discuss the obligations a business has to each of its stakeholders

MANAGEMENT IN ACTION
Internationalizing Delta Airlines

The **deregulation** of the U.S. aviation industry resulted in a 14-year dogfight among competing airlines. By early 1992, some 130 carriers had been forced out of business. Several once-proud companies, such as TWA and Continental, wrestled with bankruptcy. Some companies searched frantically for strong international partners to stabilize them. The so-called Big Three of U.S. aviation—American, Delta, and United—coped unevenly with ongoing problems. These problems included diminished passenger loads (attributed to a sluggish economy), rising costs, and depressed yields due largely to irrational price competition. American, Delta, and United undertook massive layoffs and trimmed flight schedules and salaries.

Flying on instruments through the economic night, Delta is setting a course for the future by offering good connections.

Delta's chairman, Ronald Allen, decided to move boldly to minimize the damage of hard times and to position his company for the future. His strategy was to secure Delta's place in the international airline market, the industry's fastest-growing segment. Allen began by acquiring rights to the busiest air route in the United States, the profitable Boston–New York–Washington, D.C., corridor. Next he acquired dozens of routes between New York and Europe; a coveted hub in Frankfurt, Germany; and nearly 50 airplanes.

Allen engineered deals to acquire many of the assets of Pan Am and TWA. These purchases cost Delta $621 million up front and called for Delta to assume $668 million in liabilities. It would seem that Allen placed his company at risk with these expensive acquisitions, but he believed he had little choice. He viewed these purchases as Delta's only means of survival in the decades ahead.

The changes Allen has made were aimed at maximizing Delta's existing strengths. The addition of the European routes now allows Delta to offer closely coordinated connections between overseas and domestic routes. Closely coordinated arrivals and departures provide an immense marketing edge over competitors whose customers must change airlines at gateway cities. Delta, which pioneered the efficient hub-and-spoke system of flight routing, is well positioned in strategic U.S. locations. The airline maintains hubs in six important metropolitan areas: Atlanta, Los Angeles, Salt Lake City, Dallas/Fort Worth, Cincinnati, and Orlando.

Routes and locations are not Delta's only strong suits, however. The airline enjoys a reputation for excellent customer service and employee loyalty. U.S. Department of Transportation records show that for 17 consecutive years, Delta incurred the fewest passenger complaints. The company maintained friendly labor relations as well, and it has only a pilot's union to negotiate with. In addition, Delta paid its employees better than its direct competition.

The smoothness in labor relations may be a result of an informal internal climate. At campuslike Delta headquarters in Atlanta, everyone goes by first names. The company culture includes countless stories about employees who went the extra mile to help customers. The employees take pride in these

▶ Closely coordinated arrivals and departures provide an immense marketing edge over competitors whose customers must change airlines at gateway cities.

stories, and such folklore provides examples for employees to follow.

Will Allen's strategy work? Only time will tell whether the new acquisitions and Delta's ongoing strengths will be tickets to success in the turbulent airline industry. ▲

For more about Delta and the international airline industry, see *Time,* November 23, 1992, p. 38; Kenneth Labich, "Delta Aims for a Higher Altitude," *Fortune,* December 16, 1991, pp. 79–81; John Newhouse, "The Battle of the Bailout," *New Yorker,* January 18, 1993, pp. 45–51.

The Business System: An Overview

Chapter 1 defined *management* and examined the skills and functions associated with it. Chapter 2 reviewed the history of management thought and the theoretical base for managerial action. A familiarity with these ideas allows the exploration of business as a system, the trends and environments within which managers must act, and the responsibilities managers must fulfill.

You already know that a system is a set of interrelated parts that act as a whole to achieve goals or to function according to a plan. You also know that organizations are systems comprising subsystems and that a change in any subsystem affects one or more of the others. In the context of a system, no manager or unit within a company is really independent.

Organizations function as dynamic systems subject to influences from inside and outside. Exhibit 3.1 shows the theoretical flow from input to output in a closed system. Notice that the system includes internal channels that allow feedback. Feedback allows operations and decisions to be modified as needed.

Closed and Open Systems

A **closed system** operates independently of outside influences. For many years businesses were seen as closed systems, as Bittel and Ramsey (1985) described:

> [Classical management theories] dealt with closed systems in the sense that destinies and performance were relatively deterministic and controlled from within.... For a closed system, it is relatively easy to determine components necessary to achieve a given purpose. These components lie within a defined

Exhibit 3.1

The organization as a closed system.

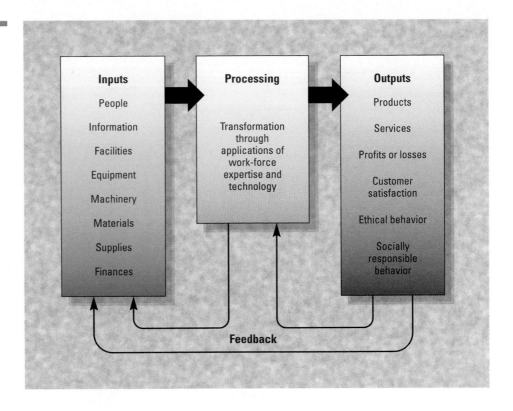

boundary and are under control of the system. All activities outside this boundary and control are classified as the environment.

Classical management theorists had reason to think business systems were closed. During the years when they formed their views, government exerted little control over business, foreign competition was light, and labor was plentiful. Raw materials were readily available, and expanding overseas markets eagerly consumed the output of the burgeoning factory systems of Europe and America. Such conditions vanished long ago. Today, closed systems exist only in textbooks.

Current experts believe that all operating systems are open systems. An **open system** must continuously interact with constantly changing components in the external environment. As Bittel and Ramsey observed:

> The modern concept is to view an organization as an open system with significant interactions with the environment, depending on it for resources and constrained by its influences. The open system usually involves humans as developers, operators, and users who contribute to the uncertainty in function and results.

The diagram of an organization as a closed system, Exhibit 3.1, needs only modest change to reflect the modern view. In Exhibit 3.2, links among system components and the two levels of the external environment have been added. The links span the boundary between the system and its external environment. The next section will begin examining open systems by presenting an overview of the components of the external environment.

Exhibit 3.2

The organization as an open system.

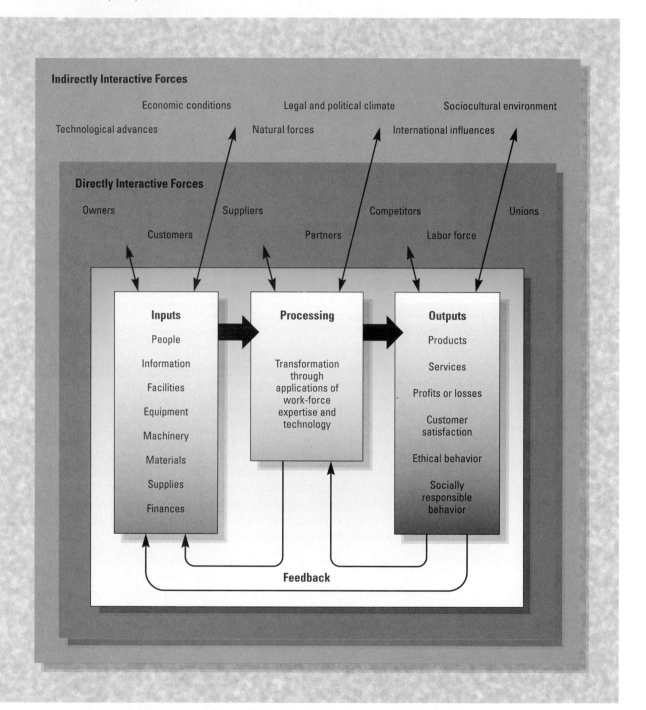

Indirectly Interactive Forces

Economic conditions   Legal and political climate   Sociocultural environment

Technological advances   Natural forces   International influences

Directly Interactive Forces

Owners   Suppliers   Competitors   Unions

Customers   Partners   Labor force

Inputs	**Processing**	**Outputs**
People	Transformation through applications of work-force expertise and technology	Products
Information		Services
Facilities		Profits or losses
Equipment		Customer satisfaction
Machinery		Ethical behavior
Materials		Socially responsible behavior
Supplies		
Finances		

Feedback

The Manager's Environments

The environment within which a manager must operate embraces both internal and external elements. An organization's **internal environment** comprises the elements within its boundaries. These elements are the organization's mission; leadership style; management philosophy; formal structure; policies, culture, and climate; and available resources.

An organization's **external environment** consists of the entire universe beyond an organization's boundaries—all those factors that directly or indirectly influence its people, processes, and systems. The effects of such elements vary from immediate, constant, intense, and measurable to long-range, modest, and conjectural. Among immediate and direct interactive forces are customers and clients; nonmanaging owners; vendors, suppliers, and other partners; competitors; labor unions; and applicable government regulators. The indirect interactive forces are equally powerful but often more difficult to assess. These forces include economic conditions, legal and political climates, sociocultural currents, technological change, events in nature, and international events.

For a business to succeed, it must create an internal environment compatible with the world outside. Its processes must meet the requirements of law, and its outputs must satisfy the expectations of customers. Operations must relate coherently to those of suppliers and competitors. For example, when Ronald Allen of Delta Airlines moved to secure a place for his airline in the global market, he was accommodating to changing external factors. No matter the business or industry, however, understanding the outside world begins by understanding the internal environment.

The Internal Environment

Internal environments consist of elements created by people. To some extent, these elements, or forces, are within management's control. Some are direct forces—an organization's structure, for example, which is devised by management. Others are indirect. Indirect forces develop through formal and social interactions that occur on the job. An example of an indirect force is an organization's climate, which emerges from the daily interactions of people.

Direct and indirect forces and their interaction create the unique character of an organization. The character of an organization is revealed by several tangible and intangible expressions. Let's examine the most important one first.

Organizational Mission

The **mission** of an organization is the explicit expression of its central and common purpose, its reason for existing. (In recent writing about business and politics, the word *vision* is used for *mission,* and it has the advantage of conveying the notion of imaginative commitment.) The mission acts as a unifying force, linking subsystems and dedicating them to the pursuit of common goals.

The language in ineffective mission statements is general, subjective, and idealistic. In ineffective statements, the words *profit, growth, quality, productivity, human need satisfaction,* and *public benefit* are often used. In describing an authentic and effective mission statement, commentator John Naisbitt (1985) wrote:

> A successful corporate vision links a person's job with his or her life purpose and generates alignment—that unparalleled spirit and enthusiasm that energizes people in companies to make the extra effort to do things right and to do the right thing. That is what makes a corporation uncommonly successful.

Chapter 4 will discuss the effective formulation of a mission statement.

The account of the internationalizing of Delta Airlines provides an example of how a vision can mobilize individual and group effort. Ronald Allen acted on his vision to increase Delta's share of international traffic by acquiring assets and routes. He enjoyed strong internal support partly because Delta's people shared that vision.

In an article in *Fortune* (Taylor, 1992), the new vice chairman of Chrysler, Robert J. Eaton, described his vision for his company:

> I see us as a full-line manufacturer with more emphasis on niche areas than other car makers. We're going to have vehicles from subcompact through large, but niches will continue to play an important role: sport utilities, vans, convertibles, et cetera. I want us to be the premier U.S. auto company, with outstanding products, quality, cost, and customer satisfaction, and with the necessary return for the shareholder.

In another *Fortune* article (Schlender, 1992), Chairman Akio Morita of Sony, the Japanese electronics giant, stated his corporate vision: "Our basic concept has always been this—to give new convenience, or new methods, or new benefits, to the general public with our technology." Of Sony's 1,000 new products each year, 80% are enhanced versions of earlier devices, with new features, improved performance, and often a lower price. The remaining 200 products are intended to create new markets.

Philosophy of Management

An employee on the way to work does not leave behind personal beliefs and values. In the work setting those fundamentals continue to govern his or her thinking and conduct, and they contribute to the internal environment. Personal beliefs and values influence what is commonly called the philosophy of management. The manager who believes that people deserve courtesy and personal development, for example, is likely to treat subordinates with respect, show genuine concern for their welfare, and help them succeed and grow. Among significant influences on managers' philosophies are those of other managers. In addition, organizations usually reward managers whose philosophies reflect the organization's values and culture.

Leadership Style

Leadership style depends in part upon the extent to which a manager involves others in problem solving and decision making. Some managers value employee participation and extend authority to those below them in the hierarchy. Such decentralization encourages delegation of authority to the lowest levels possible, to the people best equipped to decide an issue regardless of their status or position.

Judicious decentralization allows organizations to downsize, empower employees, and create self-managing work teams. Just how much authority may be productively shared depends upon circumstances as well as individual leaders and subordinates. Chapter 12 will examine leadership style more closely.

Company Policies

A **policy** is a broad guideline created by top management to help managers and workers deal with ongoing and recurring situations. Company policies, as aspects of the internal environment, ensure uniform treatment in such matters as hiring, disciplining, compensating, promoting, and serving customers. In a company that prefers to hire from within, for instance, a personnel promotion policy might state, "When two otherwise qualified employee candidates for a position possess comparable abilities, the most senior person should be promoted." Such straightforward policy statements help ensure orderly and efficient administration.

In personnel matters, policies help foster a climate of fairness. In other matters, policies give employees a sense of what the organization values, and helps them decide issues and solve problems. Policies are also useful in articulating standards about quality and customer service. In July 1992 McDonald's made a policy statement in a nationwide ad campaign and at each of the chain's 8,800 domestic restaurants (Ryan, 1992). "If you are not satisfied," the statement said, "we will make it right—or your next meal is on us." Such a concrete policy to implement McDonald's mission left little doubt in anyone's mind about the corporate commitment to customer satisfaction.

Formal Structure

The formal structure of a company, a component of the company's internal environment, determines how its activities are conducted. Within each of the three management tiers—top, middle, and first-line—teams may be created to execute such basic tasks as design, production, marketing, finance, and human resource management. The formal structure also determines how authority and communications flow from management to employees. Variations in structure are determined by the tasks a company performs, how management wishes to perform them, and external factors. External determinants include customer demands, competitors' strategies, and government regulations.

For many reasons, the management of a company may choose to change from one type of structure to another. Sometimes restructuring can produce dramatic results. Chapter 2 described how, by implementing a new structure consisting of interdisciplinary teams, Chrysler shortened the time needed to bring a new car to market. In the early 1990s, U.S. business as a whole moved away from centralized hierarchy. The trend was toward "flatter," decentralized organizations based on close communication among internal and outside participants. (Chapters 7 and 8 will explore these issues.)

Corporate Culture

All organizations are dynamic systems of shared values, beliefs, philosophies, experiences, habits, expectations, norms, and behaviors. The combination of all these elements gives an organization its distinctive character. Another term for the distinctive character of an organization is **corporate culture**. Chapter 9 will examine corporate culture in depth. Because corporate culture is such a powerful force in a manager's environment, however, this chapter will consider some of its broad implications now.

Top management provides a primary framework for an organization's culture. Management establishes and articulates the company's values and norms of behavior. Especially in large companies, top management may invest substantially to familiarize employees with these values. McDonald's Hamburger University is an example of such an investment, as are the ritual celebrations for top sellers, sponsored by Mary Kay Cosmetics and Avon Corporation.

A firm's culture is also shaped by employees. They shape the culture by bringing their own values and norms to the organization and by the extent to which they accept the management-defined culture. Delta's culture thrives on the many and often-told stories about co-workers who go to extraordinary lengths to care for customers. Newsletters, inflight magazines, and worldwide advertising emphasize the airline's people, and all these communications reinforce the attitude that management and employees prize.

Moreover, within a company's formal and social subsystems, distinctive minicultures usually flourish. Such subcultures develop spontaneously, and some are encouraged by management. The marketing department may have a unique culture (formed in part by past successes as well as failures), separate from and parallel to the organization's culture. Such a subculture influences the corporate culture. Members of ethnic groups bring their cultures with them and often create, within the workplace, subcultures based on their languages, customs, traditions, values, and beliefs. These subcultures contribute to the corporate culture. Sometimes they blend, sometimes they remain distinct. If management values diversity, it will do more than respect such subcultures; management will seek to derive from them benefits for the entire organization.

Organizational Climate

An outgrowth of a corporation's culture is its organizational climate, or how it feels to work there. Successful companies often have climates that feel "open." They foster the individual's creative energies and take advantage of employees' eagerness to participate. Delta's informal climate is reflected in the ways in which employees address and access each other.

Schlender (1992) reports that Sony of Japan looks for engineering candidates who are "optimistic, open-minded, and wide-ranging in their interests," traits it seeks to develop a particular organizational climate. The firm encourages engineers to move beyond their departments and "to seek out projects elsewhere in the company without notifying their supervisors. If the engineer finds a new position, [the] current boss is expected to let [the employee]... move on." Chapter 9 will further explore the concept of organizational climate.

Resources

The primary resource of any organization is its people, both managers and nonmanagers. Chapter 10 will focus on the management of human resources. An organization needs resources in addition to workers to accomplish its mission and

Participation is a key ingredient of an open corporate culture, where each individual's contributions are recognized and creativity is nurtured.

specific objectives, however. These resources are the inputs to the system—the elements that are processed, transformed, or used—and they influence the internal environment. Such resources include information, facilities and infrastructure, machinery and equipment, materials and supplies, and finances.

Information   The word *information* refers to the facts and knowledge that are vital nourishment for all the operations of an organization. Without accurate, timely, up-to-date information, neither employees nor managers can make daily decisions effectively and efficiently, nor can they plan ahead. Information from insiders and outsiders is needed to coordinate and execute tasks at every level. Keeping others informed of problems and progress is every employee's duty. Chapter 19 will deal with information management in depth.

Facilities and Infrastructure   Facilities consist of the physical structures— the work and office spaces and their layouts—required to accomplish the firm's mission and goals. The location, appearance, and condition of an organization's facilities can significantly influence how employees view their company. The term *infrastructure* refers to the surrounding region or community's permanent framework. The framework might include dams, power stations, roads, railways, harbors, and airports.

In 1992 Nissan built the latest in lean and flexible manufacturing facilities on Kyushu, the southernmost of Japan's five main islands. As Chandler and White (1992) reported, the hospital-clean factory can be used to build a number of different models and types of cars. The key to the flexibility of the plant is that instead of a conveyor belt, the factory uses computer-directed, motor-driven dollies that can move vehicles at various speeds. To make the changes necessary to produce a different kind of car takes minimal retooling.

Infrastructure resources support not only individual companies but the community at large. Such resources are generally built at public expense or with government support of one kind or another. Their extent and quality are basic to most businesses, especially manufacturing. From freeways and airports to sewage systems and power grids, the operation of modern factories depends upon all these and more. BMW, the German auto maker, chose in 1992 to build its first American manufacturing facilities in Spartanburg, South Carolina. According to some observers (Ady, 1992), the aspects of the area that led to the decision were the qualified work force, a favorable tax code, and a local willingness to provide significant support for the company's hiring and training efforts. In addition, South Carolina authorities agreed to provide $40 million in improvements to the Greenville-Spartanburg airport, which is adjacent to the new factory's site.

In 1992 KPMG Peat Marwick, an international accounting firm, surveyed 617 foreign companies with headquarters in Illinois to determine how they decided on a location for their U.S. facilities (Yates, 1992). Most of the firms—which offered a total of 41,439 jobs—chose to locate in the suburbs of Chicago because of "proximity to key industries and markets; [proximity] to air transportation; distribution advantages; living conditions and environment; and quality and cost of [the] work force."

Machinery and Equipment   Nissan's computer-directed dollies and all other hardware used to process inputs are part of an organization's machinery and equipment, the tools used in offices, factories, and other workplaces. Furniture, fixtures, telephones, copiers, fax machines, computers, and robots are but a few examples. The quality of machinery and equipment is a function of its maintainability, efficiency, dependability, and speed of operation. Its compatibility with other equipment influences how effectively and efficiently people work together. Current, reliable, and easy-to-use equipment helps to prevent stress to workers. In addition, high-quality equipment encourages people to do their best, freed from interruptions caused by mechanical breakdowns.

Materials and Supplies   Taken together, the services, raw materials, and parts (components and subassemblies) needed to produce goods or services make up an organization's materials and supplies. The division of General Electric that produces home appliances consumes an astounding amount of goods in this category: miles of wiring; tons of sheet metal, nuts, and bolts; motors; coolants and solvents; plastic; and glass. The division needs all these items to keep production machinery clean and running. At the facility of a service industry—the home office of Aetna Insurance, for example—the materials and supplies list calls for reams of letterhead and multipart forms, printer ribbon cartridges, staples, paper clips, file folders, and cleaning supplies.

Materials and supplies may be acquired outside the company or within. General Motors buys windshields and windows from Pittsburgh Plate Glass and tires from Goodyear. But GM's Chevrolet, Buick, Cadillac, Oldsmobile, and Pontiac divisions build most of their engines and transmissions in their own facilities. GM assembly plants are the customers for GM engine and transmission factories. The quality of materials and supplies greatly affects the quality of the goods and services a company can produce. The same can be said for the other resources discussed so far.

Finances The term *finances* means the money available. Finances can be generated directly from the sale of the organization's goods and services. Finances can be in the form of cash in bank accounts or a line of credit negotiated with a financial institution (usually a commercial bank). Trade credit is the most significant source of short-term finances. Suppliers grant trade credit whenever they agree to provide materials and supplies in exchange for an organization's promise to pay the invoice, plus interest, within a specified number of weeks.

An important financial resource for U.S. corporations is the sale of stocks and bonds on the open market. Such sales are facilitated by investment brokers and public stock exchanges. Another source of cash may be the sale of assets. During the last years of Pan Am, the airline was hard pressed to repay massive bank loans. Pan Am managers repeatedly raised needed cash by selling off valuable assets, including its corporate headquarters building in New York and the worldwide routes it had pioneered during better days.

Money is the basis for all of an organization's operations, from acquiring resources to honoring employee paychecks to compensating investors. Money is the lifeblood of an organization. It flows to all operatives and, in turn, allows work to flow. A company's financial health affects its ability to function at every level.

The External Environment

An organization's external environment includes all the forces outside its boundaries that interact directly or indirectly with it (Bittel, 1989). These forces represent both risks and opportunities for managers. Direct and frequent interaction commonly occurs among the organization's managers, owners, customers, suppliers and other partners, competitors, the community's labor force (including labor unions), government regulators, and society at large. Managers and some other organization members (typically the sales staff, recruiters, planning specialists, buyers, and purchasing agents) maintain regular contacts with members of these groups.

Although seemingly remote and generally beyond the manager's control, other forces in the external environment interact indirectly with the organization and make demands upon it. The manager must be aware and informed about these forces, which can be economic, technological, legal and political, sociocultural, natural, and international. He or she must be able to anticipate and appreciate their possible impact on the organization.

Directly Interactive Forces

As Exhibit 3.2 showed, an organization's external environment includes forces that are both directly and indirectly interactive. The sections that follow will look at these forces in detail.

Owners Owners may actively participate in managing a business (as they normally do in sole proprietorships and some kinds of partnerships). In other cases they may play no active role at all. This is the case with stockholders who do not work for the corporations in which they own stock. Both kinds of owners, however, expect a return on their investments and look to all the employees to preserve and advance their interests. From the owners comes the formal authority

Six Sigma

s part of its policy of customer satisfaction, the Motorola Company developed a company-wide quality program called Six Sigma. The title derives from a statistical measure of deviation from a quality standard. At the one-sigma level, 68% of products are defect-free; at the six-sigma level, 99.997% of products are defect-free. Six sigma represents a level of quality in which there are only 3.4 defects per million (*Business Week,* 1991). A Motorola advertisement asserted that, through Six Sigma, the company could chart "a path to perfection" and that the program was "a daily challenge for each of our employees throughout the world." The Motorola slogan proclaimed: "Quality Means the World to Us." ▲

needed to run the business. In corporations, the board of directors is responsible for protecting the owners' investments and ensuring that management earns an adequate return on them.

Customers   The individuals and groups that use or purchase the outputs of an organization are **customers**. Customers can be either internal or external. Internal customers are employees or work units that receive the work of other employees or units. Internal customers process the work further, use it within their work groups, or deliver it outside. The surgeon anxiously awaiting a biopsy report is the customer for a hospital lab. The Delta passenger-service agent checking the computer screen at the airport is a customer of the reservation department. External customers may be manufacturers, wholesalers, retailers, suppliers, or corporate or individual consumers. Ensuring the satisfaction of both internal and external customers is vital in a highly competitive marketplace.

Suppliers and Partners   Suppliers provide a company with many of the resources it needs. These resources range from expertise and raw materials to money and part-time employees. Suppliers may be separate, autonomous parts of a company or unaffiliated organizations. Suppliers may also be independent companies brought together through a joint venture or temporary partnership. IBM, for instance, maintained 11 partnerships with other companies in 1992. Among them was an agreement with Toshiba to build high-resolution color screens for laptop computers.

Several continuing trends in supplier practices emerged during the 1980s. First, companies increased their use of outsourcing. They selected as suppliers small, efficient businesses that could make resources of higher quality at lower cost than the companies could make.

Second, to enhance the effectiveness of working relationships, companies developed close alliances with outside suppliers. To hasten decision making, suppliers were and continue to be brought into projects early, often at the design stage. Chrysler did this to produce its LH models. Many companies have merged

GLOBAL APPLICATIONS
Keiretsu: The Japanese Connection

apanese manufacturers in Japan and the United States have been in the vanguard of companies that are building increasingly stronger networks between themselves and suppliers. When Hitachi, Toyota, and Mitsubishi built manufacturing plants in the United States, their Japanese suppliers followed. They placed facilities nearby to offer reliable, just-in-time delivery of needed components. This close connection and cooperation, which ties independent companies together through a common concern for each other's welfare and shared goals, is called *keiretsu.* The

practice is an honored tradition among corporations in Japan.

As of September 1991, Japanese companies owned 10% or more of 1,563 manufacturing plants in the United States. A survey by the Japan External Trade Organization reported that the total number of employees in these U.S. factories was about 350,000. Every state but North Dakota, the survey showed, was home to at least one Japanese-affiliated factory, most of them wholly owned by a Japanese company. The states with the largest Japanese presence were California (287 plants), Ohio (121), and Illinois (112). ▲

"Japan's U.S. Plants up 9% in 1991," *Fortune,* April 20, 1992, p. 16; "Learning from Japan," *Business Week,* January 27, 1992, pp. 52–55.

with suppliers or have bought them outright to guarantee a reliable source of quality goods and services. To strengthen its capabilities in electronics and computer systems, for example, General Motors acquired Electronic Data Systems (EDS), Texas entrepreneur Ross Perot's original company.

Third, companies are seeking these "deep" alliances with fewer, more dependable suppliers. And fourth, companies are more willing to procure needed supplies from anywhere in the world, turning more frequently to foreign sources to meet their needs for high quality and low price.

Competitors An organization's **competitors** are those firms that offer similar products and services in the organization's marketplace. Businesses compete on the basis of price, quality, selection, convenience, product features and performance, and customer services. Customer services include delivery, financing, and warranties. Competition is not merely a contest between Toyota and Ford, NBC and CBS, or Delta and Southwest. Instead, competition is an irresistible force at work at every level of commerce in free enterprise systems. Aluminum competes with steel as a manufacturing material, railroads with trucks, network television with cable broadcasters, and long-distance telephone companies with one another.

For most companies, how managers deal with competition determines whether their companies succeed or fail. In 1993 IBM was struggling to recover leadership in its industry. Many experts said the company's decline derived from the failure of IBM's management to counter the competition. The experts said IBM clung too long to mainframe computers and did not pursue the PC market as aggressively as other companies did.

Labor Force and Unions The term **labor force** (sometimes used interchangeably with *labor pool* or *work force*) applies to the people in the community from which an organization can recruit qualified candidates. The key word in the preceding definition is, of course, "qualified."

The needs of businesses are changing. Jobs in the crafts and trades, which traditionally provided work for the members of labor unions, are giving way to jobs that require proficiency in math, verbal communication, and computer sciences. As one business commentator noted (Magnet, 1992): "Though statistics suggest that today's high school student who doesn't go on to college is as literate and numerate as a similar 1950s student, Fifties skills are inadequate to Nineties needs and uncompetitive with the products of foreign school systems."

America's work force is changing, becoming more culturally segmented and diverse. The notion of cultural diversity applies to communities whose members represent distinctly different ethnic and national backgrounds, language, religious beliefs, life-styles, and age groups. Patterns of social change and widespread immigration are the principal agents of this change. In recent decades, women have entered the U.S. labor force in historic numbers and in every calling from medicine to heavy construction. Since 1970, the number of women as a percentage of the total labor force has doubled. In 1992 women accounted for about 48% of all workers. Waves of immigrants from Latin America, Asia, and the Caribbean have altered the character of many U.S. cities, from Miami and New York to Los Angeles and Seattle.

During the next decade, women and people of color are expected to fill 75% of the over 20 million new jobs created in the United States. By the year 2010, white males will account for less than 40% of the total American labor force (Loden and Rosener, 1991). With the increasing emphasis on teams, employee commitment, productivity, innovation, and quality, our newly diverse communities offer unique opportunities and challenges—not only to managers and their organizations, but to every institution in society. Educational institutions must strive especially hard to meet the challenge.

From top management to the workers on office and factory floors, modern business emphasizes the latest technology. It focuses on empowering employees to take on more and diverse tasks and qualifying workers as self-managing individuals and skilled team members. For trade unions especially, changes in U.S. business practices have meant abandoning old assumptions and finding new ways to serve their members. Government agencies have had to adapt too. Several states now offer programs that will train employees; their goal is to encourage employers to remain in or move to the state that offers the training. South Carolina, for example, wooed BMW in the midst of much publicity. The effort paid, though: BMW established its factory there.

Indirectly Interactive Forces

The outer layer of Exhibit 3.2 showed an array of abstract terms whose concrete realities present managers with real challenges and pressures for change.

Economic Forces Conditions in an economy can indirectly influence management decisions and the costs and availability of an organization's resources. These **economic forces** include wages and prices, employment and interest rates, levels of taxation, personal investing and saving, corporate profits, inflation, and business and government spending and investing. Globalization increases the reach of such effects among nations. As a result, a slowdown in the economy of Japan or Germany, say, may generate significant repercussions in Los Angeles and Boston.

National periods of economic growth and decline recur in complex cycles that are difficult to predict and control. In recessions, business and consumer spending fall and unemployment rises; tax revenues to governments decline while demands for public and private services increase. Such was the case in 1991 in America's economy. Amoco Corporation (a major petroleum producer) was just one of several American companies to react to this recession by laying people off and restructuring its assets. In 1992, Amoco cut 8,500 jobs and $430 million in capital spending. It wrote off $800 million in disposing of assets and reducing its work force. All this was in response to declining consumer demand for its products and rising prices for its raw material, imported crude (Solomon, 1992).

Legal and Political Forces   The **legal and political forces** include the general framework of statutes and case law that apply to all segments of communities at large and businesses in particular. Of immediate concern to managers in planning and running a company's operations are the specific regulations imposed by all levels of government. Such regulations are generally part of government efforts to protect society as a whole. In scope they range from defining rights and privileges, to establishing safety standards, to protecting national security.

Laws are often implemented by bureaucratic agencies created by federal, state, or local government. In business, government regulations affect hiring, staffing, and training practices; accounting procedures; wages and hours of work; workplace safety and health; water, air, ground, and noise pollution; transportation

Regulations are established to protect society, from the individual worker to the planet as a whole. Managers must contend with laws governing every aspect of business, from export controls on high-technology products to proper disposal of waste.

and navigation; and international trade. Regulations often dictate business procedures and prescribe actions for managers.

Each year the nation's businesses expend billions of dollars to comply with government regulations. According to Thomas D. Hopkins, an economist with the Rochester Institute of Technology, in 1991 federal regulations cost the U.S. economy more than $400 billion, or $4,200 per household (Warner, 1992). Many observers question the wisdom of such extensive government participation. Brink Lindsey, director of regulatory studies for Cato Institute, a public-policy research group, believes that the "current level of regulation is so high, and so complicated, and so intrusive that it's strangling business and suppressing productivity" (Warner, 1992).

In a poll conducted by *Inc.* magazine in 1992, 83% of responding managers said they believed that most existing regulatory legislation was unnecessary. About one-third felt that "regulators don't understand business," and 25% believed that "regulations don't make much sense." The majority felt that there was too much regulation and that its costs were killing profits and incentives (Caggiano, 1992).

On the other hand, powerful arguments and evidence support the case for much existing regulation. Major improvements in water and air quality have been accomplished through the regulatory process; safety and health regulations unquestionably protect employees and consumers by preventing injuries and deaths. The multibillion-dollar collapse of America's savings and loan industry resulted in large part from the deregulation of the industry in the 1980s. History has repeatedly shown that, when the private sector cannot or will not conduct its affairs in the prevailing public interest, government must act to do so.

In a separate category are the pressures exerted from time to time by politicians to influence managers and companies. These pressures may come in the form of requests for corporate support for political candidates or causes, the encouragement (or discouragement) of a merger, or persuasion to move a plant or service to a particular area.

Sociocultural Forces   **Sociocultural forces** include pressures on managers and their organizations from individuals, groups, and communities. Sensitivity to such forces is generally good business practice as well as simple common sense. Many firms contribute money, equipment, or expertise to worthy causes. Such causes may include neighborhood beautification programs, schools, or community groups. The public spirit and generosity of the business community emerges frequently. When Hurricane Andrew devastated South Florida in 1992, for example, a group of wood products manufacturers donated tons of plywood to assist in rebuilding. Chapter 22 will examine interaction with sociocultural forces more closely.

Technological Forces   Inventors and other creative people are constantly making new discoveries. The resulting deluge of materials, products, systems, opportunities, skills, and problems are **technological forces.** Few businesses are immune from these forces and their effects on products, services, management methods, and organizational resources. Consider only these few examples of modern technology and their impact on management: the airplane, the computer, and the fax machine.

When managers set out to apply new technology in imaginative and productive ways, they are said to be **innovating**—bringing new technologies,

Innovations are brought about by creative people who are given the proper support and encouragement.

knowledge, and methods to bear on the design, production, or application of products and services. As Dumaine (1991) reported:

> The best companies see innovation as a function that needs managing—and then they manage it by basing new products on customers' needs, encouraging employees to use the expertise of the whole company, giving workers incentives for successful innovation, and refusing to punish those whose gambles don't pay off. One key lesson: Good ideas don't go very far unless they are nurtured and developed. Smart managers understand that meeting these challenges is more important than increasing R&D spending or building Taj Mahal–size technical centers.

Natural Forces   Climate, weather, geography, and geology are the **natural forces** that affect organizations. The climate of a region determines a firm's needs for energy for factory processes, heating, and cooling. Storms or flooding can interrupt production. Land forms influence access by rail, road, ship, and air. Some regions are at risk from earthquakes. One major reason why Japanese suppliers choose to locate close to their large corporate customers is to ensure that needed supplies can be delivered without interruption.

The natural resources of an area are significant factors as well. Some locations, such as metropolitan Chicago, offer easy access to large quantities of relatively inexpensive water. Such locations are attractive to businesses that use a lot of water. Conversely, such a user would wish to avoid a region with a chronic water shortage.

Manufacturers require economical transport to bring in raw materials and ship manufactured items. As a result, the management of a manufacturing business would probably favor a factory site adjacent to railways and port facilities. The

A manager's resources will be put to the test when faced by an uncontrollable external threat such as a hurricane.

management of an oil refinery or a grain-shipping company would probably do the same. Likewise, the management of a mining company would place its smelters close to the mines, and an airplane manufacturer would probably prefer a site with good weather year-round. Proximity to the customer base might affect the decision about a manufacturing, production, or headquarters site, however. Such a decision might end up being a compromise between accessibility to materials or special features and accessibility to customers.

International Forces   As the twenty-first century approaches, the world economy is truly global. From the pending Free Trade Agreement of North America (which will remove most trade barriers between Canada, the United States, and Mexico) to the European Community (in which goods and people will soon move unrestricted throughout member states), management decisions in every country increasingly affect organizations and people around the world. The result is the growing influence of **international forces**, the economic, political, sociocultural, technological, and natural factors anywhere in the world that influence managerial decision making and the ability of an organization to fulfill its mission and reach its goals.

When fire shuts down a Hong Kong supplier, the American company takes heat. When Japan enacts trade restrictions that exclude American rice, U.S. farmers have one less market in which to sell their crop. When the oil-producing nations agree to limit production to push oil prices from $18 to $21 per barrel, airline managers in Dallas watch fuel prices climb. Even before the Persian Gulf War ended in 1991, construction firms from nearly every industrialized nation were bidding on contracts to rebuild Kuwait. International forces are so influential in America's economy that Chapter 20 will discuss them exclusively.

Bechtel *has built a business providing technical and management services dedicated to improving the quality of life worldwide. Capping hundreds of flaming oil wells in Kuwait was one of their jobs.*

The Environments and Management

Environmental forces create challenges, risks, opportunities, and changes for every organization. Managers must remain alert to their internal and external environments, sensing changes or shifts, reacting and adapting quickly and imaginatively. They must forecast and plan for the changes they suspect will come and for the changes they wish to initiate. Managers must cultivate a sensible and controlled reactive behavior toward changes that may affect them with little or no warning, and an imaginative program to manage and capitalize on the changes that they can foresee and over which they have some control.

Sensing and Adapting to the Environments

Staying in touch with environments requires that managers monitor events and trends that develop outside their specific areas of influence. The areas could be other departments or divisions within the company, the competition, the economy, and all the other forces that can influence their system or subsystem. This surveillance of outside areas and factors is called **boundary spanning** (Bittel, 1989). Sometimes also called boundary scanning or environmental scanning, the practice requires current information about what is happening or likely to happen. Boundary spanners look for developments that can influence plans, forecasts, decisions, and organizations. Sources of information include feedback from customers and suppliers, competitors' actions, government statistics, professional and trade publications, industry and trade associations, and colleagues and professional associates inside and outside the organization. Through boundary spanning, managers keep up-to-date, establish networks to facilitate the gathering and dissemination of information, and build personal relationships that can lead to increased power and influence over people and events.

Sometimes the challenges posed by the environment are clear to everyone. The key to gaining a competitive advantage is how a firm adapts to the challenges. The intensely competitive field of oil retailing provides an example. In June 1992 Chevron Chemical Company announced the development of a diesel fuel to meet tough new California environmental regulations scheduled to go into effect in October 1993. Chevron was the first company to gain state certification for the fuel. A competitor, Unocal, had dropped out of the California diesel-fuel market after company management decided that the required technology was too costly (Rose, 1992).

Many companies have found that sharing burdens is the best way to go when adapting to their environments. With the help of federal funds ($120 million), Chrysler, General Motors, and Ford joined forces to develop new battery technology for electric cars. In July 1992, IBM, Toshiba, and Siemens AG of Germany announced an international partnership to develop powerful memory chips for computers. Managers and their organizations must stay ahead of change by anticipating it, planning for it, and instituting it—not simply reacting to it.

John Naisbitt, author of *Megatrends: Ten New Directions Transforming Our Lives*, points out 10 internal and external trends that are developing today in America. These trends, shown in Exhibit 3.3, are evident in our daily lives. They mean changes for individuals and organizations.

To cope with these trends, Naisbitt recommends that the corporation be re-invented. In *Re-Inventing the Corporation*, he cites trends in U.S. business and tells how the successful corporation will react to them (see Exhibit 3.4).

Exhibit 3.3

Naisbitt's ten megatrends.

According to John Naisbitt, America is moving:

1. From being an industrial society to being an information, service-based society

2. From forced technology to high-tech, high-touch technology

3. From being a national economy to being a world economy

4. From having a short-term focus to having a long-term focus

5. From centralization to decentralization

6. From getting help from our institutions to relying on self-help

7. From being a representative democracy to being a participatory democracy

8. From having organizations built on hierarchies to having organizations built on networking

9. From having a population and industrial base in the North to having a population and industrial base in the South and West

10. From having an either/or set of choices in our consuming and working lives to having multiple options

Adapted from John Naisbitt, *Megatrends: Ten New Directions Transforming Our Lives* (New York: Warner), 1984.

In the late 1980s the Massachusetts Institute of Technology created the MIT Commission on Industrial Productivity to study the state of American manufacturing. It uncovered weaknesses in the nation's industrial practices, but also many strengths. The commission identified six key similarities among firms responding successfully to their changing environments (Dertouzos, Lester, and Solow, 1989):

- A focus on simultaneous improvements in cost, quality, and delivery
- Closer links to customers
- Closer relationships with suppliers
- The effective use of technology for strategic advantage
- Less hierarchical and less compartmentalized organizations (to provide greater flexibility)
- Human resource policies that promote continuous learning, teamwork, participation, and flexibility

All these characteristics are illustrated throughout this text in nearly every chapter. All represent internal and external environmental changes that have happened and will continue to happen in those companies and industries that wish to survive.

Exhibit 3.4

Ten guidelines for re-inventing America's corporations.

The list that follows presents 10 observations about American business. By responding constructively to each, Naisbitt believes that Americans can radically change and improve U.S. business.

1. The best and brightest people will gravitate toward those corporations that foster personal growth.

2. The manager's new role is that of coach, teacher, and mentor.

3. The best people want ownership—psychic and literal—in a company; the best companies are providing it.

4. Companies will increasingly turn to third-party contractors, shifting from hired labor to contract labor.

5. Authoritarian management is yielding to a networking, people-oriented style of management.

6. Entrepreneurship within the corporation—intrapreneurship—is creating new products and new markets and revitalizing companies inside out.

7. Quality will be paramount.

8. Intuition and creativity are challenging the "it's all in the numbers" philosophy of traditional business schools.

9. Large corporations are emulating the positive and productive qualities of small businesses.

10. The dawn of the information economy has fostered a massive shift from infrastructure to quality of life.

Adapted from John Naisbitt, *Re-Inventing the Corporation* (New York: Warner), 1985.

I S S U E S   A N D   E T H I C S
Under the Influence?

n June 1992, a U.S. subsidiary of a Japanese company and executives at divisions in Tennessee and California agreed to pay more than $18,000 in fines to the Federal Election Commission. The fine was imposed because the subsidiary made illegal corporate donations to several political campaigns in 1988.

An executive (and the exec's wife) were charged with using corporate funds to donate $3,700 to several local political campaigns for federal offices. Federal Election Commission investigators claimed the executive created a system in which the company paid him bonuses to reimburse him for the donations. The executive, through his attorney, claimed he did not understand the federal campaign laws that prohibited corporate contributions to candidates for federal offices.

Various citizen and industry groups, foreign and domestic, have created political action committees (PACs) to sponsor as well as oppose legislators and legislation at the state and federal levels. These groups give millions of dollars each year to political campaigns and to individual politicians. The purpose of the groups is to influence government actions.

What do you think about this issue? Why does the federal government prohibit corporate contributions to candidates for political office? What are the possible dangers of PACs in our society? What are some potential benefits? ▲

Based on "U.S. Charges Toshiba with Contributing Illegally to Campaigns," *Wall Street Journal,* July 1, 1992, p. A10.

Influencing the Environments

Although managers must sense and adapt to environments, they and their organizations can also influence their environments in several ways. In a democratic society, citizens—alone and in groups—have the right to attempt to influence legislation and the rules that determine how the game of business is played. Lobbying allows people to present their points of view to legislators and to push for changes that they see as beneficial. Whether by personal letter to a city alderman or through a paid professional who lobbys legislators, managers and individual citizens' groups will continue to play vital roles in the shaping of our society.

Managers and organizations use the power of the media to influence public opinion and public policy. Their viewpoints and agendas are constantly reported in advertising, public relations announcements, press releases, and in-depth interviews. Industry and trade groups allow businesses to conduct research, build alliances, and raise funds to push their agendas for or against change.

Meeting Responsibilities to Stakeholders

Stakeholders are the groups that are directly or indirectly affected by the ways in which business is conducted and managers conduct themselves. Stakeholders include owners, employees, customers, suppliers, and society—people in local communities, our economy, and the world at large. Members of each of these groups lose or gain depending upon how businesses operate. Chapter 22 will examine in detail the responsibilities that managers and businesses have to these groups. A few introductory concepts are needed here, however.

Owners   To owners, businesses owe a fair return on investment. Managers are obligated to make their best effort to use resources effectively and efficiently. Managers must also give an honest accounting for their stewardship over the owners' assets and interests. Most states require by law that corporations give a financial accounting in quarterly and annual reports to their shareholders.

In most sole proprietorships and small partnerships, owners are the managers. In corporations, however, owners depend upon elected representatives who sit on the board of directors. One of the board's primary duties is to ensure that managers consider owners' interests when they make corporate decisions.

Employees   As the most important asset of a business, employees need a safe and psychologically rewarding environment. Such an environment supports honest and open communication and shows evidence of real concern for employees' values, goals, and welfare. Employees need nurturing environments that help them grow and become more valuable to themselves and their organizations. Because the management of Chrysler Corporation acknowledged the importance of staff in selling the company's new LH line, the company spent $30 million to retrain more than 100,000 employees in Chrysler dealerships (Stertz, 1992).

Employees deserve to know the risks, values, rules, and rewards to which they are exposed. They have the right to ethical treatment, to fairness and equity in their relationships with management. Their legal rights must be granted and respected. Businesses that stay focused on the needs of their employees will attract and hold on to them, thus helping to guarantee future success. To most customers, employees *are* the business in the sense that employees are as important as the product or service in establishing the reputation of the business in the customer's mind.

Customers   One definition of quality is a satisfied customer. In today's economy, serving the customer is why businesses exist and the measure of their success. Customers have rights created by laws. Among these are the right to have safe foods, drugs, cosmetics, and other types of products and services; to have full disclosure of the terms connected with borrowing and investing; and to have the environment relatively free of pollution. Businesses that stay focused and close to their customers will ensure their futures and create the means for continued success. Those that don't will suffer the same fate as those who don't stay focused on employees: They will lose customers to the competition and be unable to meet the needs of their stakeholders.

Suppliers   Suppliers provide the services, materials, and parts needed to carry on the vital operations of business. Quality begins with an understanding of its importance and is designed into products and services from their conception. Most suppliers today are involved in product and service design and determine to a great extent the performance capabilities of the end result. Suppliers need honest and open communication from the managers and organizations they serve. They deserve to be paid for the goods and services rendered and to have the terms of their contracts honored. Reliable sources of dependable supplies are difficult to find; once found, every effort should be made to keep them.

Society   A business's obligations to society begin with its employment base and spread out to the communities in which it does business. A mom-and-pop bakery in Muncie, Indiana, can call the neighborhood in which it operates its piece of society. When the parents in the neighborhood call on the bakery to support a Little League baseball team, the bakery owners are expected to respond with some kind of assistance.

Every business needs to define the portions of society that it must serve. It can serve them in a variety of ways, from following fair employment practices, to donating funds and equipment, to preventing pollution. The United Way charity program is staffed locally by volunteers from businesses whose salaries are donated by their regular employers. Businesses often adopt a school to assist it in a variety of ways. Businesses usually concentrate on serving their communities in ways that enrich both the givers and receivers. In this effort, as in all undertakings, businesses need to be both reactive and proactive. They must sense the needs of their communities and plan to implement the kinds of assistance they are best able to provide.

In 1990 Unocal of California created a program to help clear the air in the Los Angeles Basin, the most polluted area in the nation. It decided to purchase old cars, which produce many times more air pollution than they did when they were new. Unocal bought some 8,000 cars made before 1971. Each cost the company $700. In 1992, two Illinois companies—Clark Oil and Uno-Ven, an oil refiner—followed Unocal's lead, offering to provide the funding to allow the Illinois Environmental Protection Agency to purchase pre-1980 automobiles for $600 to $1,000 each (Swanson, 1992).

Future Trends

Much has been said in this chapter about developing trends in the U.S. economy and business environments. Some key points to remember include:

- It is clear that large corporations will continue to contract out work, opting to outsource and downsize and letting those who can do things better do them.

- The movement toward empowering people through access to information from every level will become even more important than it is today.

- The average worker's job will continue to expand. Narrow job definitions will give way to broad categories of tasks requiring high degrees of literacy and constant training.

- The most distinguished talent will continue to seek employment in those organizations that can best meet their needs for nurturing, challenges, and growth.

- Jobs will continue to move to those regions of the world that can best meet the needs of business for cost competitiveness, a modern infrastructure, and a qualified labor pool.

- Sensing one's environments will become even more time-consuming as warding off surprises from competitors, society, and governments becomes more important.

C H A P T E R   S U M M A R Y

■ Businesses are open systems that interact with internal and external environments.

■ The internal environment is made up of the following elements: mission, philosophy of management, company policies, corporate culture, leadership styles, resources, formal structure, and climate.

■ The external environment consists of directly interactive and indirectly interactive forces.

■ Directly interactive forces include owners, customers, suppliers, competitors, and the labor force.

■ Indirectly affecting the organization are economic, legal and political, sociocultural, technological, natural, and international forces.

■ A business's environments present challenges, opportunities, uncertainties, and change.

■ Managers at every level need to engage in boundary spanning, staying in touch with their environments through a variety of means and activities. Managers also need to learn to adapt to the environmental changes they identify.

■ Managers and their organizations, individually and collectively, can and should attempt to influence their environments, adding their voices and agendas to those of others in society.

S K I L L - B U I L D I N G

In the June 1992 issue, *Nation's Business* presented a list called "Ten Key Threats to Success," shown in Exhibit 3.5. The editors of the publication invited several experts to assemble their own lists of threats. Two of the experts were W. Gibb Dyer, Jr., associate professor of organizational behavior at Brigham Young University in Utah, and Harold P. Welsch, professor at DePaul University in Chicago. As you read the lists, look for similarities and try to relate each point to something specific in the first three chapters of this text. Note that, by rewording them into positive statements, they become key tips for success.

Exhibit 3.5

Ten key threats to success.

THE NATION'S BUSINESS LIST

1. Not knowing how to manage and operate a business
2. Lack of cash
3. Growing too fast
4. Poor interpersonal skills
5. Lack of strategic planning
6. Failure to innovate
7. Trying to go it alone
8. Poor communications
9. Failure to recognize your own strengths and weaknesses
10. Failure to seek and respond to criticism

PROFESSOR DYER'S LIST

1. Inability to think strategically
2. Lack of networking
3. Poor partner relations
4. Inability to cope with stress
5. Lack of balance in one's life
6. Inability to build a team
7. Low commitment and energy
8. Procrastination
9. Unethical or illegal behavior
10. Lack of vision

PROFESSOR WELSCH'S LIST

1. Blaming external causes for failure
2. Lack of planning
3. Inadequate information
4. Lack of a market approach to business
5. Failure to delegate
6. Too many hats to wear
7. Inflexibility
8. Desire for instant gratification
9. Lack of objective feedback
10. Not keeping current

1. Which items appeared on all three lists? Why do you think they are so important?

2. Which items appeared on only one list? Why do you think the other sources did not include them?

3. Which items on the three lists have particular applications to the contents of this chapter?

4. Using your own experience and judgment, construct a list of ten keys to the success of a small business.

R E V I E W **Q** U E S T I O N S

1. Review this chapter's essential terms and look up the meanings of those you cannot define.

2. Why are businesses considered open systems?

3. What are the elements in a business's internal environments? What happens when they interact?

4. Why are some forces in the external environment said to be directly interactive with an organization? Which forces belong in this group?

5. Why are some forces in the external environment said to be indirectly interactive? Which forces belong in this group?

6. When managers engage in boundary spanning, what are they really doing? Why are they doing it?

7. How can managers influence the forces in their external environments?

8. What groups make up an organization's stakeholders? What obligations do businesses have to these groups?

R E C O M M E N D E D **R** E A D I N G

Bleeke, Joel, and David Ernst. "The Way to Win in Cross-Border Alliances," *Harvard Business Review* (November–December 1991), pp. 127–135.

Dertouzos, Michael L.; Richard K. Lester; and Robert M. Solow. *Made in America: Regaining the Productive Edge* (New York: Harper Perennial), 1990.

Dumaine, Brian. "Closing the Innovation Gap," *Fortune* (December 2, 1991), pp. 56–59, 62.

Henkoff, Ronald. "Inside America's Biggest Private Company," *Fortune* (July 13, 1992), pp. 82–90.

Morita, Akio. "Partnering for Competitiveness: The Role of Japanese Business," *Harvard Business Review* (May–June 1992), pp. 76–83.

Naisbitt, John. *Megatrends: Ten New Directions Transforming Our Lives* (New York: Warner), 1984.

Naisbitt, John. *Re-Inventing the Corporation* (New York: Warner), 1985.

Petersen, Donald E., and John Hillkirk. *A Better Idea: Redefining the Way Americans Work* (Boston: Houghton Mifflin), 1991.

Schaffer, Robert H., and Harvey A. Thomson. "Successful Change Programs Begin with Results," *Harvard Business Review* (January–February 1992), pp. 80–89.

Womack, James P.; Daniel T. Jones; and Daniel Roos. *The Machine That Changed the World: The Story of Lean Production* (New York: Harper Perennial), 1991.

R E F E R E N C E S

Ady, Robert M. "Why BMW Cruised into Spartanburg," *Wall Street Journal,* July 6, 1992, p. 8.

Bittel, Lester R. *The McGraw-Hill 36-Hour Management Course* (New York: McGraw-Hill), 1989, pp. 31–33, 34.

Bittel, Lester R., and Jackson E. Ramsey, editors. *Handbook for Professional Managers* (New York: McGraw-Hill, 1985), p. 869.

Business Week, "Questing for the Best," special issue on quality (1991), p. 9.

Caggiano, Christopher. "Results from March: The Inc. FaxPoll," *Inc.* (June 1992), p. 24.

Chandler, Clay, and Joseph B. White. "It's Hello Dollies at Nissan's New 'Dream Factory,'" *Wall Street Journal,* July 6, 1992, p. B11.

Dertouzos, Michael L.; Richard K. Lester; and Robert M. Solow. *Made in America: Regaining the Productive Edge* (New York: HarperCollins), 1989, p. 118.

Dumaine, Briane. "Closing the Innovation Gap," *Fortune* (December 2, 1991), p. 57.

Loden, Marilyn, and Judy B. Rosener. *Workforce America! Managing Employee Diversity as a Vital Resource* (Homewood, IL: Business One Irwin), 1991, p. xvi.

Magnet, Myron. "The Truth About the American Worker," *Fortune* (May 4, 1992), p. 54.

Naisbitt, John. *Re-Inventing the Corporation* (New York: Warner), 1985, pp. 32–33.

Rose, Frederick. "Chevron Develops Diesel-Fuel Formula That Meets California's New Standard," *Wall Street Journal,* June 3, 1992, p. A4.

Ryan, Nancy. "If What You Want Isn't What You Get—It's Free," *Chicago Tribune,* July 10, 1992, sec. 3, p. 1.

Schlender, Brenton R. "How Sony Keeps the Magic Going," *Fortune* (February 24, 1992), pp. 77, 78.

Solomon, Caleb. "Amoco to Cut 8,500 Workers, or 16% of Force," *Wall Street Journal,* July 9, 1992, p. A3.

Stertz, Bradley A. "For LH Models, Chrysler Maps New Way to Sell," *Wall Street Journal,* June 30, 1992, p. B1.

Swanson, Stevenson. "Your Clunker May Actually Pay Dividends," *Chicago Tribune,* September 29, 1992, sec. 2, p. 1.

Taylor III, Alex. "Chrysler's Next Boss Speaks," *Fortune* (July 27, 1992), p. 83.

Time, November 23, 1992, p. 38.

Warner, David. "Regulations' Staggering Costs," *Nation's Business* (June 1992), p. 50.

Yates, Ronald E. "Foreign Firms Flock to Suburbs," *Chicago Tribune,* July 13, 1992, sec. 4, pp. 1, 2.

G L O S S A R Y   O F   T E R M S

boundary spanning A manager's surveillance of external environments to identify current or likely events and determine how those events will influence plans, forecasts, and the organization.

closed system A system in which a person or organization can act without outside interference or concerns.

competitors Firms or individuals that offer similar products or services.

corporate culture The distinctive character of an organization, comprising its shared values, beliefs, philosophies, experiences, habits, expectations, norms, and behaviors.

customers Individuals and groups that use or purchase the various outputs of an organization, whether inside or outside the organization.

economic forces Conditions in an economy that indirectly influence management decisions and the costs and availability of resources.

external environment All the forces, outside an organization's boundaries, that interact directly or indirectly with it.

innovating When managers bring new technologies, knowledge, and methods to bear on the design, production, or application of products and services.

internal environment All the elements, within an organization's boundaries, that help make it unique and that are to some extent under the control of management.

international forces Economic, political, sociocultural, technological, and natural forces anywhere in the world that affect or influence the decision making of managers and the abilities of organizations to fulfill missions and reach goals.

labor force The people from which an organization can recruit qualified candidates for jobs.

legal and political forces   Statutes and case law that apply to all segments of communities at large and businesses in particular; includes specific regulations imposed by all levels of government.

mission   The explicit expression of an organization's central and common purpose, its reason for existing. A mission is sometimes called a vision.

natural forces   The climate, weather, geography, and geology that affect an organization.

open system   A system in which an individual or organization must interact with various and constantly changing components in both the external and internal environments.

policy   A broad guideline created by top management to help managers and workers deal with ongoing and recurring situations.

sociocultural forces   Pressures that individuals, groups, and communities put on managers and organizations.

stakeholders   Groups directly or indirectly affected by the ways in which business is conducted and managers conduct themselves. Stakeholders include owners, employees, customers, suppliers, and society.

suppliers   Individuals and groups that provide the resources an organization needs to produce goods or services inside or outside the organization.

technological forces   The combined effects of scientific discoveries, engineering applications, and inventions that result in new materials, products, systems, opportunities, problems, and challenges for organizations and individuals.

C A S E   P R O B L E M
Tapping Environments to Solve a Problem

n the early 1980s a customer asked the Sara Lee bakery in New Hampton, Iowa, for croissants with tips that curled forward and touched. Making these special items required the assembly workers, who stood on a concrete floor with arms extended over a moving assembly line, to twist their wrists many more times than they did in the traditional croissant-making process. Demand was high for the new croissants. The workers raced each other, often curling nearly one hundred rolls per minute. Their success had dire consequences. Many workers developed carpal tunnel syndrome, a debilitating wrist disorder caused by repeated hand motions.

This problem is one of many cumulative trauma disorders (CTDs) caused by repetitive motion. CTDs make up the fastest-growing, most widespread U.S. occupational hazard, according to the Bureau of Labor Statistics. CTDs affected over 185,000 workers in 1990, more than eight times more people than in 1982.

At Sara Lee, workers began to complain about carpal tunnel syndrome's classic symptoms: numbness and tingling in their fingers, wrist aches, and pain in their forearms. At first, supervisors and many co-workers did not take the worker complaints seriously because there were no outward signs of any injury. "Local doctors couldn't diagnose a problem, and workers felt they were written off as complainers." One worker went for four years to local doctors and the bakery's nurse, only to receive conflicting diagnoses and a prescription for a pain killer. But as worker complaints and days lost to production rose, management decided to take a different approach.

In 1986 Sara Lee hired a hand surgeon who emphasized prevention of the problem rather than treatment of symptoms. He went to the production floor, timed the number of wrist actions per worker per minute, and determined the weight of various doughs and tools being used by workers. "He measured table heights and photographed workers stooping, stretching or flicking their wrists to do their work. He showed the photos to the managers and asked them to suggest ways employees could do the work without using awkward postures."

Management began to make changes. Some workers were asked to increase their pace of work; others were asked to slow down. One worker was added to a production line and others were asked to rotate between hard and easy jobs. Workers were given a slide presentation and told, in technical terms, about the causes of their complaints. Some workers who complained of their CTDs were operated on by the surgeon and then faced weeks of recuperation. Others, fearful that their injuries would lead to the same result, kept their complaints to themselves.

The changes that were implemented were a failure. Workers objected, claiming that the doctor was not a specialist in ergonomics—the study of adapting work environments to people. The bakery management had selected the doctor because "he was the closest thing to an expert in the region." Workers also complained about making the four-hour round trip to the surgeon's office and not being paid for it. They wanted the right to choose their own doctors. These objections, along with those of their union, led to a two-week strike in 1990.

The strike led to additional changes. The bakery agreed to use additional physicians who were closer to the plant, put its CTD policy in writing, and create a CTD committee composed of four managers and four union-selected employees. "If we made any errors in setting up our program, it was not involving our union early on," said the plant's safety manager.

Sara Lee enlisted the cooperation of workers and maintenance staff. The company made dozens of small ergonomic changes. Table heights were modified, conveyors and supplies were moved closer to workers, cushioned mats were provided for workers to stand on, work methods were improved, and new tools were provided that could be fit to each worker's hand. Workers came up with designs for devices they believed could eliminate some problems. New workers now learn proper methods from experienced employees. Members of the CTD committee police the systems now in place, and all workers are checked annually for CTDs.

These changes led to positive results. In 1991 only 13 suspected cases of carpal tunnel syndrome were referred to doctors (in 1987 there had been 34 cases). "And absenteeism related to the disorder has plunged; the eight work days lost through August 1, 1992, present a stark contrast with 1987 when, for the full year, 731 work days were lost."

Q U E S T I O N S

1. What elements from the directly interactive external environment came into play in this case?

2. What elements from the indirectly interactive external environment came into play here?

3. What elements from the internal environment played parts in this case?

4. When and why did things really begin to change at the bakery?

Adapted from Joan E. Rigdon, "The Wrist Watch: How a Plant Handles Occupational Hazard with Common Sense," *Wall Street Journal,* September 28, 1992, pp. Al, A4.

P · A · R · T

Planning and Decision Making

Organizational Planning

LEARNING OBJECTIVES

After reading and discussing this chapter, you should be able to:

- Define this chapter's essential terms

- Explain why planning is crucial to managers and organizational success

- Describe how mission statements, objectives, and plans are related

- Describe the three levels of objectives in an organization

- Discuss the purposes of strategic, tactical, and operational plans

- List and explain the seven basic steps in the formal planning process

- Discuss major barriers to effective planning and how they can be minimized or eliminated

- Discuss aids to effective planning, including communication, information, the involvement of others, and management by objectives

- Identify three tools or techniques used in planning

E S S E N T I A L T E R M S

budget	management by objectives	operational plan	rule
contingency planning	(MBO)	plan	single-use plan
forecasting	mission statement	planning	standing plan
linear programming	objective	policy	strategic objective
	operational objective	procedure	strategic plan
		program	tactical objective
			tactical plan

MANAGEMENT IN ACTION
McDonald's Plan for Global Dominance

f CEO Michael R. Quinlan's plans are successful, the golden arches and Ronald McDonald will be familiar in every country in the world. Quinlan expresses his ambition this way: "I don't know what we will be serving in the year 2000, but we'll be serving more of it than anyone else." His goal is simple and direct: "I want it all. That's all. I want it all."

To realize such an ambition—or even come close—you need a plan, which McDonald's has. Faced with the prospect of limited domestic growth, the world's largest food-service company is training its sights and energies on foreign markets. Today, McDonald's has more than 12,500 restaurants operating in 61 countries. But in preparation for expansion into new territories, it has established 7,000 trademarks in 130 additional nations.

The potential is enormous. Consider this: In the United States there is one McDonald's for every 29,000 Americans; in

Planning for future growth, *McDonald's hopes that one day the golden arches will span the globe.*

Australia, Canada, England, France, Germany, and Japan—referred to by McDonald's as the Big Six countries—there is one set of golden arches for every 134,000 people. In Taiwan, 425,000 people must share a restaurant; in Brazil, the figure is two million. Not only are the potential numbers significant, but the profits abroad are growing nearly three times faster than at home.

McDonald's management plans to open 400 to 500 restaurants a year outside the United States throughout the decade. The company intends to build 1,000 restaurants in Europe in the next five years and add 70 per year for the next 10 years in Japan. Major investments will be made in Mexico, with the YASNY (You Ain't Seen Nothing Yet) development company.

If Michael Quinlan has his way and the plan is successful, perhaps we have not seen anything yet. For starters, Quinlan can add to his 20% share of an estimated $6-billion

95

❝ I want it all. That's all. I want it all. ❞

— **Michael R. Quinlan**, CEO, McDonald's

market in England, a 40% share in France, and a 30% share of a $2-billion market in Australia. The company will focus on the potential of the Big Six countries. Two-thirds of all the new international restaurants will be within their borders. McDonald's will double its presence in the Pacific Rim in five years and triple its sites in Latin America. With these expansion activities the golden arches will indeed span the globe. ▲

For more on McDonald's plans, see Cheryl Hall, "Golden Quest: McDonald's CEO Expects Nothing But Global Dominance in Food Service," *Dallas Morning News,* May 31, 1992, pp. 1H, SH9H.

Why Do You Need to Plan?

If CEO Michael Quinlan's vision of golden arches worldwide is to become a reality, it will be a direct result of a carefully molded plan. A McDonald's will not just "pop up" in Taipei, Guadalajara, or Munich. Rather, a plan will dictate the precise time of the opening and the size and location of the restaurant.

Planning is critical to the success of an organization. Most managers and organizations cannot afford the luxury of trial and error; that approach expends too many resources. Planning helps managers avoid errors, waste, and delays. It is essential if a manager is to be effective and efficient. This is the first of two chapters devoted to planning. It describes how managers look ahead, make informed efforts to predict the future, and then work with that future as it evolves. In this chapter we will examine what planning is, its importance, the types of plans, the processes involved in planning, and barriers and aids to productive planning. In the next chapter we will focus on the foundation of an organization's preparation for the future, the strategic plan.

Planning Defined

Planning is systematic preparation for tomorrow, an orderly process that allows managers to determine what they want and how to get it. In planning, managers assess the future, determine the goals of the organization or work group, and develop the overall strategies to achieve the goals. When managers are planning, they set **objectives**—desired outcomes or targets—and then develop a **plan**, the means of achieving an objective. McDonald's objective is to expand worldwide operations. Opening specific numbers of new outlets in Europe and Japan is the plan to achieve that objective.

At Procter & Gamble, the objective is to be number one in sales in each of its 39 product categories. When Edwin Artzt became CEO, the company was the market leader in 22 product categories. For Artzt, that was not good enough. The new CEO developed a plan to move P&G into an even more dominant position. In quick succession, he reorganized the 4,000-person sales force; placed profit-and-loss responsibility for product lines on the shoulders of brand managers; and eliminated the position of product supply manager, to streamline manufacturing, purchasing, and distributing (Dumaine, 1992). Through his plan, Artzt intends to achieve his objective.

What Plans Do

Plans provide specific answers to six basic questions about an intended activity: what, when, where, who, how, and how much. A plan specifies:

- *What* objectives are to be accomplished

- *When* a long-term objective or the short-term goals that compose it will be achieved

- *Where* the activities pertinent to the objective will take place

- *Who* will perform specific tasks essential to the plan

- *How* actions will be taken to reach the objective

- *How much* management is willing to spend, in terms of resources, to achieve the objective

Exhibit 4.1 shows how the six questions are answered in a plan with the objective of increasing product sales by 10%.

Exhibit 4.1

Six key questions answered through planning.

What?	The target goal: To increase product sales by 10%.
When?	Target date and intermediate dates: By December 31, target goal of 10% increase will be reached. Shorter-term goals: Objectives of 3%, 5%, and 7% increases will be reached on March 31, June 30, and September 30, respectively.
Where?	Geographic location of performance: Targeted areas are the southern and western sales regions.
Who?	The people performing the task: All senior sales representatives.
How?	Methods or activities used to achieve goals: By each rep developing 10 new accounts and boosting reorders from established customers.
How much?	Resources needed: Travel and entertainment allowance increased by 5% for each sales representative.

Ford plans to stay ahead of its competition by anticipating the needs of the market. The '93 Ranger introduces first-time styling features, such as the "flareside," and an improved ride quality.

The Primary Management Function

Planning is the primary management function because it sets the stage for acquiring resources and focusing the energy of the entire organization. Planning provides direction and a common sense of purpose. It helps determine operations and how operations will affect the organization before resources are committed.

To illustrate the point, imagine you are a bank loan officer, and a prospective entrepreneur applies to you for a loan to start a business. The applicant has no mission statement for the business; no specific performance objectives for the first year; no projection of financial needs; no sales forecasts, inventory requirements, or personnel profiles. What will you tell your would-be client? If the applicant has no plan, he or she is likely to have no loan.

All managers engage in planning and in developing plans to meet objectives. As the next section will show, most managers plan in similar ways. What differs are the kinds of plans they develop and the amount of time they spend on planning. Some companies—such as Tenneco, Exxon, and General Motors—maintain departments devoted exclusively to planning. These departments help managers monitor the environment and collect data. In some cases, they develop the plans for presentation to management (Dupuy, 1992). In creating these departments, top management recognizes the critical nature of planning and acts to facilitate the planning process.

The Impact of Planning on Other Management Functions

As you recall, planning is the "first function" among a manager's functions. A manager undertakes planning before organizing, staffing, directing, or controlling. Planning generates objectives and lays the foundation for organizing resources and activities. Even the structure of an organization should be a means to reaching

FOCUS ON QUALITY
BMW Decentralizes Quality Control

At the Bavarian Motor Works (BMW) in Munich, Germany, managers recently received a pointed reminder that quality results from planning. For more than a decade, BMW had enjoyed a comfortable share of the U.S. high-performance luxury-car market. Suddenly, BMWs started losing ground to two elegant Japanese rivals, the Lexus from Toyota and the Infiniti from Nissan. The newcomers soundly thrashed BMW in quality surveys such as the J. D. Power rankings.

BMW plans to change its quality performance—and consumers' perceptions of it. Traditionally, quality at BMW was rooted in the customs of Europe's medieval guilds, in which trades are learned in an apprenticeship of up to three years. The apprenticeship ends only with the creation of a "masterwork," which serves as something like a final exam. But now the company is adopting the principles of quality gurus such as Genichi Taguchi of Japan and J. M. Juran of the United States.

BMW's new plans call for continuous quality improvement. It has created a *Lernstadt* (study city) where supervisors learn the latest quality techniques. In addition, the responsibility for quality is being dispersed throughout the organization rather than being centralized in one department. In 1977 the quality control department employed 1,200 people. Now the payroll lists only 65 people who are specifically dedicated to quality control. In addition, the company has planned for and incorporated its suppliers into the quality program. Rigorous audits of BMW suppliers resulted in the elimination of some four hundred that did not measure up. To build-in quality requires a commitment—and a plan. ▲

For more on BMW's quality plan, see John Templeman, "Grill-to-Grill with Japan," *Business Week*, June 1992, p. 39.

the objective. When the objective changes, so should the structure. Planning influences whether the organization maintains the status quo, expands, or contracts operations; these decisions, in turn, affect human resource planning and the staffing process. Planning provides the guidelines for directing employees and for determining what is communicated to them. Planning establishes the foundation for controlling because, in specifying what is to be accomplished, it suggests standards for measuring progress.

How planning affects management functions became dramatically evident at IBM in 1991. Facing dramatic financial losses for the first time in its history, IBM acknowledged the need to become more competitive. Said one commentator early in 1993, "The world's biggest computer maker [now] resembles nothing so much as a flailing giant unable to extricate itself from the mire of an outdated strategy and culture" (Dobrzynski, 1993).

In the face of global and domestic attacks on its share of the market, IBM began to rework its plans. In 1991 the company was dramatically restructured into 13 independent units. Layers of middle-management positions were eliminated, and management made plans to downsize the work force by 25%, or about 400,000 employees. The impact on the staffing function could hardly be greater, as managers shifted from recruiting and hiring to coping with layoffs and identifying crucial cross-training needs. The directing function found managers urgently trying to reestablish a stable climate and regenerate some sense of security, loyalty, and—ultimately—productivity. Finally, managers responsible for the control function developed standards by which to measure new ways of doing business (Verespej, 1992).

The Ability to Adjust

Planning allows managers the opportunity to adjust the organization to the environment instead of merely reacting to it. The more clearly management can see into the future, and thus develop both long- and short-range plans, the greater the chance that the company will operate smoothly. It is far healthier for managers and employees to adjust plans in response to circumstances on the horizon than to be forced to react abruptly and haphazardly under unanticipated pressure.

Effective planning permits managers to adapt rather than to merely react. The tax preparation office that maintains a list of accountants available for temporary work in March will probably fare better than the one that does not. Planning increases the possibility of survival in business by minimizing the risks inherent in the future.

A Framework for Planning

As we have noted, planning starts with identifying a target or outcome and then creating the means to achieve it. The planning process for all organizations is built on the framework of formal mission and objective statements, which vary by level in the organization.

The Mission

Commerce and business wield enormous influence in modern industrialized societies. Like other powerful institutions, the business world speaks its own language, often coining new words or appropriating old ones into its vocabulary. Two such borrowings much used by managers in recent decades are the words *mission* and *vision*.

Mission and *vision* are labels for the purposes for which an organization is created or presently functions. A mission, or vision, tells why an organization exists. Top executives and boards of directors may devote considerable attention to such a fundamental issue. When they formalize their ideas and commit them to writing, the result becomes the organization's **mission statement**. Its purpose is to guide managers, work units, and individual employees throughout the organization (Want, 1986). A clear mission statement is concise, focused, worthy, imaginative, and realistic. It can serve as a touchstone for nearly everything that an organization undertakes.

In discussing the importance of a mission to the success of an organization, management expert Peter Drucker identifies two central questions which managers must answer: What is our business? and What should it be? (Drucker, 1954).

For companies that have been in the marketplace for some time, customers can answer the question about what the business is. And managers must ask the question continually, not just when the enterprise begins operations. Wise managers pay careful, ongoing attention to customers' perceptions of an organization and to what customers want.

Planning comes before implementation. Outside consultants as well as teams within the company are all resources to be considered.

To answer the second question, What should our business be?, managers must frequently evaluate their mission, to determine if they are still in the "right" business or if they should change direction. For some businesses, competition urges such a change. Some insurance companies, Kemper and Mass Mutual among them, have expanded their lines, offering tax-sheltered retirement accounts (IRAs and Keough plans) as well as insurance. They've moved into real estate development and created mutual funds and money market funds for investors. In other instances, the financial performance of organizations may force them to reassess their missions. Mattel, the toy maker, sharply redefined its mission after two consecutive years of losses that totaled $121 million. In what one writer called the "Toy Town Turnaround," Mattel created a new mission statement: "Become the number one toy maker in the world through disciplined growth." The company is now staging the most dramatic turnaround in the history of the toy business. Mattel managers, unlike many other toy makers, no longer gamble to find one big megahit (Lindstrom, 1991).

Objectives

Once the firm's mission is articulated, managers can begin developing specific mission-related objectives at every managerial level, to reflect the responsibilities applicable to each. (Although some managers define the words *objective* and *goal* differently, this book will use the words interchangeably to mean a target or desired outcome.) The three tiers of objectives—strategic, tactical, and operational—correspond with the top-, middle-, and first-line management levels, as Exhibit 4.2 shows.

Strategic Objectives   Top-level management creates **strategic objectives**, long-term goals that relate to where the organization wants to be in the future. Strategic objectives focus on such issues as profitability, market positioning and share, innovation, productivity, quality, physical and financial resources, managerial performance and development, worker performance and attitude, and public responsibility (Drucker, 1954). One of McDonald's strategic objectives is to increase its market share as measured by percentage of industry sales in targeted regions.

Tactical Objectives   Following logically from strategic objectives are **tactical objectives**. Set by middle managers, these goals set out what the major subunits must do to achieve the strategic objectives. McDonald's regional managers develop

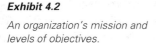

Exhibit 4.2

An organization's mission and levels of objectives.

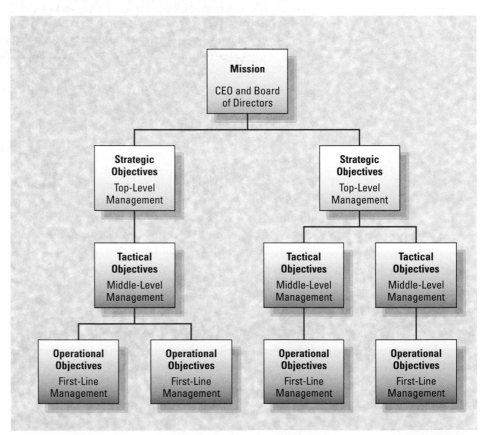

specific sales targets for each of the retail stores in the region, including specific figures for each product category.

Operational Objectives   Top-level managers expect specific results from first-level managers, work groups, and individuals. These results are **operational objectives**. The McDonald's store manager might set daily, weekly, and monthly sales targets for each product category. Objectives at this level frequently address cost controls—overtime or product waste, for example.

At all levels, soundly conceived objectives share some characteristics. As Exhibit 4.3 suggests, effective objectives are specific, reasonable, and relevant, and they define a reward mechanism.

A Unified Hierarchy of Objectives

The results of planning should generate a unified framework for the accomplishment of the organization's purposes. If the managerial pyramid is used as a model for the planning process, the result is a hierarchy of objectives in which the work of each subunit complements that of the next. In Exhibit 4.4 a single objective occupies each subunit; in reality, multiple objectives are the norm. The exhibit shows that top-level management has determined the strategic

Exhibit 4.3

Characteristics of effective objectives.

Characteristic	Explanation
Specific and measurable	Not all objectives can be expressed in numeric terms, but they should be quantified when possible. Specific outcomes are easier to focus on than general ones, and performance can be more easily measured when the task is defined precisely.
Realistic and challenging	Impossibly difficult objectives demotivate people. Objectives should be challenging but attainable, given the resources and skills available. The best goals require people to stretch their abilities.
Focused on key result areas	It is neither possible nor good practice to set objectives for every detail of an employee's job. Goals should focus on key results—sales, profits, production, or quality, for example—that affect overall performance.
Cover a specific period	A measurable objective is stated in terms of the time in which it is to be completed. Sales goals, for example, may cover a day, month, quarter, or year. The period should be both realistic (managers should not require 10 months of work in 5), and productive (a requirement for excessive reporting can be debilitating, for example). Short-term goals should complement long-term goals.
Reward performance	Objectives are meaningless if they are not directly related to rewards for performance. Individuals, work groups, and organizational units should receive prompt rewards for achieving objectives.

objective for the total organization. Middle management has established tactical objectives for the functional areas of marketing and manufacturing. Finally, the first-line management group within the functional areas has devised detailed objectives for the individual work units.

What happens if an individual manager does not plan within this framework? To continue the discussion in the context of Exhibit 4.4, suppose the marketing manager of the shoe company misinterprets the strategic objective. Instead of concentrating on potentially profitable sales sources, the marketing manager asks the operating sales managers to seek out all potential buyers. The sales staff sells to every potential buyer, regardless of the likely size of the order or the cost incurred to service each customer. One likely result is the dilution of the sales effort. The sales staff will waste time on small and bad-credit accounts and, possibly, compromise the overall goal of maximum profitability.

Types and Uses of Plans

After objectives are developed, planning resumes. The fact that an objective has been set does not ensure that it will be reached. Implementation is the job of the plan: It must guide people to the best of all possible ways of achieving the objective.

Within the business setting, three types of plans are common: strategic, tactical, and operational. Each tends to be found at a specific management level, as Exhibit 4.5 shows, and each plays a specific role in achieving the mission.

Exhibit 4.4

Hierarchy of unified objectives.

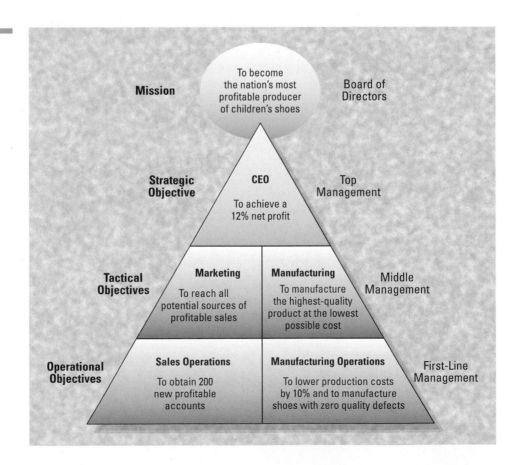

Strategic Plans

A **strategic plan** establishes the steps needed to achieve the company's strategic objectives and shapes the entire organization's direction. Such a plan defines the organizational activities and the allocations of human resources, finances, facilities, and equipment. A strategic plan may look ahead three to five years in an attempt to prepare the organization for success during those years. Just how far into the future a strategic plan should be projected depends upon the characteristics of the firm's industry and management's degree of certainty about the plan. For some industries—heavy manufacturing, transportation, and energy, for example—quality long-term planning used to mean laying a groundwork decades ahead. Now it is not that certain.

McDonald's strategic plan calls for growth targets in individual countries. Achieving the targets will contribute to the overall objective of greater international market share. As Mattel pursues its mission to become the number one toy maker in the world through disciplined growth, its strategic plan includes three components: (1) development of core products (Barbie, Hot Wheels, and the See 'N Say line), (2) expansion into new toy categories, and (3) increased market share wherever the company competes.

Exhibit 4.5

The relationship between objectives and plans in organizational planning.

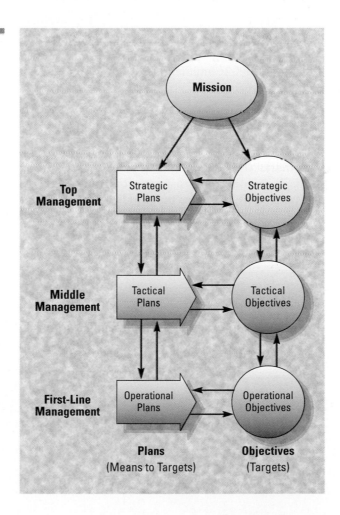

In **times** of economic slowdown, managers may put the heat on subordinates. The message is direct: "Reaching objectives is what matters, and how you get there isn't important." People in such a position may feel threatened and insecure.

Faced with the fear of losing their jobs, some employees may fudge a few sales goals, bad-mouth a competitor, or shortchange the occasional customer. People on the corporate ladder may tell the boss what they believe the boss wants to hear, and outright lying may become a habit. Under sufficient pressure, middle managers may write deceptive status reports on the progress of objectives or inflate budget proposals in the hope of ultimately getting what they really need.

Do such actions serve the company's interests? Why? How might a company support managers to ensure ethical conduct, especially in hard times? What actions could middle-level managers take to ensure that subordinates are not pressured into questionable acts? What actions could top-level managers take? ▲

Strategic plans deal with many hard-to-predict but important future events: Will there be a recession? Will inflation continue at its present rate? How will the industry fare in regard to local, state, and federal regulations? Such matters are difficult enough to predict over a one-year period, let alone for a period of five years or longer.

Tactical Plans

Just as one person's ceiling is another's floor, the completion of one manager's plan marks the beginning of a plan for another manager. Top management's strategic plan becomes a framework that sets the dimensions of the midlevel planning effort, the effort that produces tactical plans. Exhibit 4.6 illustrates how tactical and operational plans evolve from a strategic plan.

Exhibit 4.6

The evolution of tactical and operational plans.

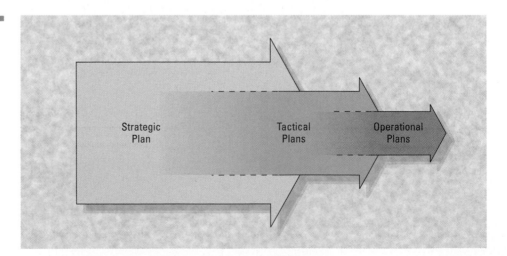

Strategic Plan   Tactical Plans   Operational Plans

A **tactical plan** guides the subunits, setting out what they must do, how they must do it, and who will be responsible for each activity. Tactical planning develops the means needed to activate and implement a strategy. McDonald's tactical plans include research to discover the best areas for new restaurants within each country.

Tactical plans have shorter time frames and narrower scopes than strategic plans. As implementation plans developed by middle management, they usually span one year or less and represent short-term efforts required to reach the strategic objective. Although they may be analyzed separately, strategic and tactical plans are actually almost indivisible. A strategy comprises a series of tactical plans built on each other to achieve the strategic plan.

Mattel's middle managers developed two major tactical plans. As a result:

- The company reduced the number of products offered (from 800 to fewer than 400) and focused on extending existing lines, to keep the brands fresh and selling. For example, Hot Wheels was supercharged with the introduction of Color Racers. The result: a $40-million increase in Hot Wheels sales. The increase represented a 75% jump in sales from the previous year.

- Mattel formed an alliance with the Disney Company. This alliance thrust Mattel to the front ranks in the infant and preschool market, one of the fastest-growing categories in the toy business. The Disney Preschool line generated sales of $55 million.

Shani, a new line of African-American dolls, is Mattel's latest entry in the market-place. Each type of Shani doll will have different skin tones, hairstyles, and facial features which reflect their ethnic diversity.

Each tactical plan was structured as an implementation device for the strategic plan. Together, the two plans brought Mattel increased market share and a 20% increase in financial performance (*Los Angeles Times,* 1993).

Operational Plans

Operational plans are developed by first-line supervisors as the means to achieve operational objectives in support of tactical plans. The operational plan is the first-line supervisor's tool for planning daily, weekly, and monthly activities. Operational plans fall into one of two categories: single-use plans or standing plans.

Single-Use Plans   A one-time activity, one that does not recur, requires a **single-use plan**. Once the activity is accomplished, the plan is no longer needed. The need to move furniture from one site to another requires a single-use plan, for example. When the move is completed, the objective is achieved and the plan has little or no value in the future.

A **program** is a single-use plan for solving a problem or achieving a group of related goals. Like most plans, a program deals with the who, what, where, when, how, and how much of an activity. A college may have programs for updating labs, adding new classrooms, and making the physical plant more accessible for handicapped students. A business may have programs to sponsor a blood-donation drive or to automate its office systems. Once a program's goals are achieved, that program ceases to be. At Mattel, once the tactical plans had been devised, specific promotional programs were developed for each product. Mattel designed a six-month introductory program for Beach Blast Barbie and a separate program for Animal Lovin' Barbie. Each program outlined television and magazine advertising, among other promotional methods.

Another single-use plan is the **budget**. A budget predicts sources and amounts of income and stipulates how income is to be used. Every organization needs a budget for planning and for controlling the use of financial resources. Although budgets may cover any length of time, they are usually prepared for one-year periods. When the specific budget period ends, the value of that budget as a planning and controlling device is exhausted, although the document may be useful as a guide to preparing future budgets. When the promotional programs for the new Barbies were created, a budget was developed to accompany each. The budgets itemized expenses and projected expected revenues. Chapter 16 will discuss budgets and budgeting in depth.

Standing Plans   Unlike budgets, **standing plans** are made once and continue to be useful over the years, though the plans may be revised periodically. Standing plans specify the handling of continuing or recurring activities. Such activities include hiring, granting credit, responding to accidents, and maintaining equipment. Most policies, procedures, and rules are standing plans.

A **policy** provides a broad guideline for workers to follow when dealing with important areas of decision making. Policies are usually general statements about the ways in which managers should attempt to handle routine responsibilities. McDonald's maintains strict policies on quality that all the restaurants in the chain must follow. Policies often represent efforts to comply with laws and regulations. Exhibit 4.7 presents a personnel policy on hiring that was created to

Exhibit 4.7

A human resources policy.

Statement of Policy

There shall be no discrimination for or against any applicant or for or against any current employee because of his or her race, creed, color, national origin, sex, marital status, age, handicap, or membership or lawful participation in the activities of any organization or union, or refusal to join or participate in the activities of any organization or union. Moreover, in each functional division, the company shall adhere to an affirmative action program regarding hiring, promotions, transfers, and other ongoing human resource activities.

comply with Title VII of the U.S. Civil Rights Act of 1964 and regulations of the Equal Employment Opportunity Commission. Note that the policy does not tell managers what to do, how to do it, or whom to hire. It simply states the view the company wants its managers to adopt when performing a repetitive management function. Policies guide people by pointing them in a particular direction.

A **procedure** is a set of step-by-step directions for carrying out activities or tasks. Procedures exist for preparing budgets; paying people; posting month-end balances; culling library collections; preparing business correspondence; and many, many other activities.

Procedures spell out the "how" for a task or function. Like policies, procedures attempt to promote consistency in an organization by establishing unified approaches to problem solving or routine events. When followed, procedures ensure that identical tasks are executed in exactly the same way, no matter where they are performed in the organization.

As an example of a procedure, consider how Mattel sales representatives handle the return of Barbies from retailers. The procedure for returning Barbies to Mattel consists of four steps. The retailer must:

1. Receive the regional representative's approval for the return

2. Identify in writing the invoice number, date, and quantities initially received

3. Identify by stock number, in writing, the items to be returned

4. Package the goods and pay for transportation

If a toy does not sell, Mattel's unambiguous return procedure ensures fairness; because all retailers who return Barbies will be treated equally. In addition, the policy helps the sales reps work effectively with retailers, because the rep can state the return policy as part of the conditions of sale.

A **rule** is an ongoing, specific plan for guiding human behavior and conduct in the workplace. Rules are "do" and "do not" statements that are usually

established to promote employee safety, ensure the uniform treatment of employees, and regulate employees' behavior. Unlike policies, rules tell each employee exactly what to do or not do, or what kind of behavior is expected in a given situation. For example, a rule that prohibits smoking in an office allows a manager no freedom in decision making. Exhibit 4.8 illustrates some commonly imposed rules.

Procedures and rules offer the advantage of standardizing behavior. But the risk remains that rules may stifle creative thought by locking people into specific courses of action or modes of behavior. Rigid rules discourage workers from adjusting to individual situations. Exhibit 4.9 offers additional insights into the advantages of and requirements for policies, programs, procedures, and rules.

Contingency Planning in a Changing Environment

Intelligent planning includes adaptability. In today's turbulent world, a manager's environments change so rapidly that plans may become useless before they have been fully implemented. To prepare themselves to respond effectively to external or internal disturbances, managers practice **contingency planning**. In other words, managers develop plans to be activated if circumstances change so substantially that the original plan becomes infeasible. A phrase often heard among prudent managers is "I'm keeping my options open." The phrase could

Exhibit 4.9

The advantages of and the requirements for policies, programs, procedures, and rules.

Policies	Programs	Procedures	Rules
ADVANTAGES OF			
Promote uniformity	Provide a plan for an operation from beginning to end	Provide the detail for effective performance	Promote safety
Save time		Promote uniformity	Promote acceptable conduct
Outline an approach	Name participants and detail their duties	Save time	Provide security
Set limitations on management conduct	Coordinate efforts of those seeking the same goal	Provide assistance in training	Provide standards for appraising performance and conduct
Promote effectiveness for managers and the organization		Provide security in operations	Save time
		Promote effectiveness and efficiency	Aid in disciplinary situations
REQUIREMENTS FOR			
Should be in writing	Should be in writing in at least an outline format	Should be in writing	Should be in writing
Need to be communicated and understood	Should answer who, when, where, how, and how much	Should be sufficiently detailed	Must be communicated to and understood by all those affected
Should provide some flexibility		Should be revised periodically	Should be reviewed and revised periodically
Should be consistent throughout the organization and consistently applied	Should have clear goals, tactics, and timetables	Should be communicated to and understood by those who need to know them	Should serve needed purposes
Should support the organization's strategy	Need to be communicated to all those affected by them		
Need to be based on the mission			

indicate that the manager has solid contingency plans with which to respond to emergencies and setbacks.

Planning begins with reasonable assumptions about future occurrences. Managers examine available facts, the historical record, and other relevant information, and then they estimate what they think will occur. These estimates form the basis of their planning. In contingency planning, managers project parallel scenarios for the future and construct plans to make the most of them. The wise manager makes contingency plans to accommodate a variety of local, regional, and global factors. Among the factors that often change dramatically and rapidly are the economy, the competition, technology, government, and society.

For example, the maker of novelties for a political convention featuring two potential nominees doesn't manufacture buttons to support the favorite only. The novelty maker produces buttons for both nominees. No matter who's nominated, the vendor has ample merchandise for either contingency.

Contingency planning is a hallmark of high-tech industries. U.S. computer hardware makers—Apple, IBM, Compaq, and Dell—routinely maintain sophisticated contingency plans to respond to products offered by the competition (Kupfer, 1992). The contingency plans of a software developer often involve simultaneously developing the same product for two different hardware systems. The management of these firms knows that one software package may never reach the market. The determining factor is whether the hardware that the software is meant to serve is accepted by the consumer (Fallows, 1993).

TRW, the high-tech aerospace manufacturer, developed contingency plans when its managers considered moving its plant from Hawthorne, California. The company had identified three potential sites for the new plant. As negotiations proceeded with each candidate city, managers prepared contingency plans in regard to assembling personnel, facilities, and equipment at each site. Plans were developed even while advocates of each location jostled for advantage. As one TRW manager explained, "For a while, where we were going to end up depended on what day of the week it was. We created plans for all possible outcomes" (Weintraub, 1992).

The Basic Planning Process

When it comes to formal planning, variations in the process abound. Seven steps are essential, however; Exhibit 4.10 defines each step. Exhibit 4.11 shows how a first-level manager applies the seven steps to create a plan to keep the office staffed during key business hours. The remainder of this section will explain the seven basic steps of the planning process in detail.

Step 1: Setting Objectives

When setting objectives, the manager determines targets for the organization or subunit. These targets will differ by type of organization and its state of development, the overall philosophy of management, and the level in the organization for which objectives are set. The list that follows presents typical objectives. The likely source of the objective is stated in parentheses.

- During the next five years, the company will generate a 10% return on investment. (Top-level management)

- To produce the highest-quality product at the lowest possible cost. (Middle-level production department)

- To reduce personnel turnover by 10%. (First-level management)

- To provide the highest-quality health care available. (Top-level management)

Exhibit 4.10

The seven steps in the basic planning process.

Step 1: *Setting Objectives*
Establishing targets for the short- or long-range future

Step 2: *Analyzing and Evaluating the Environments*
Analyzing the present position, the internal and external environments, and resources available

Step 3: *Identifying the Alternatives*
Constructing a list of possible courses of action that will lead to goals

Step 4: *Evaluating the Alternatives*
Listing and considering the advantages and disadvantages of each possible course of action

Step 5: *Selecting the Best Solution*
Selecting the course of action that possesses the most advantages and the fewest serious disadvantages

Step 6: *Implementing the Plan*
Determining who will be involved, what resources will be assigned, how the plan will be evaluated, and how reporting will be handled

Step 7: *Controlling and Evaluating the Results*
Ensuring that the plan is proceeding according to expectations and making necessary adjustments

- To complete Delta Project by November 15, 1995. (Middle-level management)

As the manager develops objectives, he or she must ensure that they are realistic, specific, and compatible.

Step 2: Analyzing and Evaluating the Environments

Once the objectives are established, the manager must evaluate the internal and external environments. What internal resources do we have or do we lack? What external factors might influence objectives and their accomplishment?

In assessing the internal environment of the organization, the manager might want to examine these elements:

- Capital. What is the availability of capital within the organization? What funds could be acquired from outside?

- Personnel resources. What skills and knowledge are available in the organization? Are they adequate to achieve the objective? Will it be necessary to use personnel resources from outside the organization?

- Managerial attitudes. Is the managerial climate supportive or restrictive? If restrictive, what can be done to change it?

- Company policies, procedures, and rules. Will current policies, procedures, or rules restrict or contribute to accomplishment of objectives?

- Facilities. What facilities are available? Are they adequate?

Exhibit 4.11

*A first-level manager applies
the basic planning process.*

Objective

To ensure that the office is staffed from 8:00 a.m. to 9:00 p.m., Monday through Thursday.
Target date: January 1.

Analysis and Evaluation of the Environment

1. *Present staffing situation.* Office is staffed by two full-time hourly employees. One
   works from 8:00 a.m. to 4:30 p.m. and the other works from 8:00 a.m. to 5:00 p.m.
2. *Financial resources.* Operating budget has sufficient funds to support additional staff
   at a range of $6 to $8 per hour, but benefits are restricted.
3. *Labor supply.* The potential number of part-time applicants is uncertain based on the
   rate of pay available.
4. *Company policy.* (1) Severe limits are placed on the use of overtime and
   compensatory time, and (2) a part-time employee becomes eligible for a limited
   benefit package when he or she works 19 hours per week.

Alternatives

1. Use present office staff by developing a combination package involving overtime and
   compensatory time.
2. Use the present office staff by altering the work hours of one or both.
3. Hire a part-time staff member to work 5:00 p.m. to 9:00 p.m. Monday through
   Thursday.
4. Hire two part-time staff members to work two nights each, from 5:00 p.m. to 9:00 p.m.

Evaluation of Alternatives

Alternative 1   Present staff/combination package. Problems with company pay policy
                   and potential reaction of present staff.

Alternative 2   Present staff/altered work hours. Would provide coverage but would
                   affect daytime productivity. Staff reaction—No!

Alternative 3   One part-time staff member. Would provide office coverage but stretch
                   financial resources because the new employee would be eligible for
                   limited benefits.

Alternative 4   Two part-time staff members/two nights each. Would provide cover-
                   age and not exceed financial resources or benefits restriction
                   (neither will work 19 hours). Only question: Can labor supply produce
                   two qualified applicants?

In assessing the external environment, the manager might want to consider
these factors:

- Economic conditions. What data are available to project the trend of the
  business cycle? Is the economy heading for a period of recession or
  expansion? What is the anticipated rate of inflation?

- Technology. What technology is on the horizon? Will the company's
  present technology remain competitive for three years? Five years?
  Eight years?

- Labor supply. If the company depends on skilled labor, is the supply
  adequate in the immediate area? If not available readily, what can be done

Exhibit 4.11   *(continued)*

Selection of Best Solution

The alternative with the fewest questions and most promise is Alternative 4. The only problem lies in attracting candidates.

Implementation

1. To overcome the potential limitation (supply of qualified candidates), pay the proposed employees the top authorized rate, $8 per hour.
2. Develop advertising by October 1.
3. Advertise the position internally to attract internal referrals.
4. Advertise the position externally, through newspaper advertisements and job placement offices at colleges, private business schools, and high schools.
5. Establish November 1 as the cutoff date for applications.
6. Complete screening and interviews by November 21.
7. Make hiring offers by December 1.

Control and Evaluation

1. Check daily to determine the number of applications.
2. Extend the advertising deadline until a sufficient number (20 to 30) applications are received.
3. If two candidates cannot be found, obtain additional funds and implement Alternative 3.

within company objectives to provide continued access to qualified job candidates?

- Suppliers. Are suppliers of raw materials and components readily available? Have there been or are there potential interruptions in the sources of supply? What alternatives to present sources exist?

- Government controls. What is the future direction of government regulation? Will it affect company operations?

Step 3: Identifying the Alternatives

Alternatives are courses of action to reach a goal. In developing alternatives, a manager should try to create as many roads to the objective as is practical. Alternatives should be genuinely distinctive ways to reach the objective, not merely the same plan with variations. Exhibit 4.11 presented four potential alternatives from which the manager could choose. Each will achieve the objective, but which is best for the circumstances?

Step 4: Evaluating the Alternatives

In this step, the manager must evaluate each alternative to determine which is the best. To do this, he or she constructs lists of advantages (benefits) and disadvantages (costs) for each alternative.

What factors should be considered? The first is resources. What resources, including time, will each alternative require? If possible, the manager should assign a dollar value to each course of action and then relate it to the dollar value of the objective to be achieved. (This sort of evaluation is called a cost-benefit analysis.) If $1,000 is spent to gain an $800 objective, the alternative is unproductive. If resources must be shared with other parts of the organization, how will the sharing affect goals and the mission?

In addition to financial factors, the manager should consider how each alternative is likely to affect organization members, units, and others outside the area of operations. Side effects, both good and bad, may result from the implementation of an alternative.

Step 5: Selecting the Best Solution

Analysis of the benefits and costs of each alternative should permit the manager to rank the alternatives according to merit and determine one superior course of action. If no single alternative emerges as clearly superior, the manager should consider how two or more alternatives could be combined to yield a superior course of action.

The alternative the manager chooses should provide the most advantages, the fewest serious disadvantages, and the greatest benefit at the least cost.

Step 6: Implementing the Plan

After selecting the optimum alternative, the manager develops an action plan to implement it. To do so, he or she must decide many questions. Who will do what? By what date will the tasks be initiated and completed? What human and material resources will be available for the process?

Step 7: Controlling and Evaluating the Results

Having implemented the plan, the manager must monitor its progress, evaluate reported results, and make any needed modifications. Changing environments require timely modification of plans; changes may also improve a plan that wasn't quite perfect when it was implemented. The manager who formulated the alternatives listed in Exhibit 4.11 did more than develop steps to control and evaluate the plan. The manager prepared an alternative as well, just in case the first course of action did not work.

Ways to Make Planning Effective

What can managers do to increase a plan's potential for success? They can identify and work to overcome potential barriers to successful planning and apply the tools and techniques that this section will discuss.

Barriers to Planning

Exhibit 4.12 lists the seven major barriers to effective planning. Each one can inhibit successful planning. The paragraphs that follow will discuss each barrier.

Exhibit 4.12

Barriers to effective planning.

1. Inability to plan
2. Inadequate planning process
3. Lack of commitment to the planning process
4. Inferior information
5. Lack of focus on the future
6. Overreliance on the planning department
7. Overemphasis on controllable variables

The Inability to Plan　Some managers fare poorly in planning because they lack experience. Others may possess little conceptual ability, a more difficult barrier to overcome. Like most skills, however, planning improves with disciplined practice. The more you plan, the more you hone your skill.

Inadequate Planning Process　Some managers have not been exposed sufficiently to the idea of planning as a process, so they do not know how to go about it. Working with experienced planners is perhaps the best remedy. Formal management training can also be helpful.

Lack of Commitment to the Planning Process　Some managers claim they don't have time to plan. Some avoid the process because they are afraid they will fail. One way to overcome this fear is simply to plunge in, to get your feet wet. Planning requires focused, determined effort to succeed—a genuine commitment.

Inferior Information　Computer programmers popularized the acronym GIGO decades ago. It stands for *garbage in, garbage out,* and the abbreviation applies as well to planning as it does to programming. Planning without ample, accurate, and timely information will almost surely be harmful. Inaccurate information about costs, capital, personnel, time frames, historic performance, or potential economic developments can sabotage objectives. To eliminate such barriers, managers should ensure that the information they communicate is reliable. This is usually achieved by establishing an effective information management system. Chapter 19 will examine the role of information in management.

Lack of Focus on the Future　Few mistakes are deadlier to a company than shortsighted planning. When managers concentrate excessively on short-term issues and neglect the organization's long-term needs and prospects, they court disaster. A manager who overemphasizes quarterly profit may work the factory full tilt and fail to fund the development of new technology—the technology that would ensure the factory's ability to compete in the future. Performance evaluations can bring managerial shortsightedness to light. A portion of each manager's performance evaluation should assess the manager's long-term planning ability.

Unless the emphasis on long-term goals comes from the top, however, strategic planning generally takes a backseat to tactical planning.

Overreliance on the Planning Department Some large firms maintain planning departments whose employees study, research, model, and project probable results. Unfortunately, planning specialists may not have a grasp of the realities that face the line managers. Presenting the plans in fancy productions, rather than tailoring plans as means to an objective, often becomes the planners' focus. Managers must translate the planning department's output into concrete programs to achieve specific goals at definite times.

Overemphasis on Controllable Variables Managers may fail to consider factors they cannot influence. They may find little value in devising plans that reflect future technology, economic forecasts, and conjectured government restrictions. But managers cannot ignore future developments. To do so is to risk being surprised by the competition. Managers must make some guesses about the future—but they must make educated guesses, based on sound information. Plans based on guesses must be flexible, and the longer the range of the plan, the greater its need for periodic review.

Aids to Effective Planning

Effective Communication The quality of a plan is proportional to the communication skill of the manager who designs it. As managers establish objectives and flesh out the strategic, tactical, and operational plans to achieve them, they must communicate constantly. Managers must exchange information, ideas, and feedback.

Quality of Information A planner increases the probability of success by starting with information that is current, factual, and verifiable. The manager must develop multiple information sources, and some of the sources should be outside the manager's area of expertise. By acquiring information from experts in accounting, law, and personnel, for example, the manager can incorporate multiple perspectives in his or her plan—even if the manager is not an expert in those fields.

Involvement of Others Opening the planning process to others can result in better plans, a higher level of commitment to the plan, and the long-range development of employees who understand planning as a way of life. Among those who can be involved in planning are employees in a department, consultants from outside the company, and a diverse configuration of teams. (Teams are the subject of Chapter 14.)

Planning Tools and Techniques

Managers can improve the quality of planning by using various tools and techniques. The tools this chapter will address are management by objectives, forecasting, and linear programming.

Involving others in the planning process can lead to better plans, a higher level of commitment, and the long-range development of employees who understand planning as a way of life.

Management by Objectives   One long-established management tool is **management by objectives (MBO)**, which was developed by Peter Drucker in the 1950s. MBO is a management technique that emphasizes collaborative goal setting by managers and their subordinates. MBO focuses on achieving results by offering a systematic way of setting objectives and forcing managers to plan.

The process begins when top management sets objectives for the organization. At each successive level, managers and immediate subordinates collaborate to develop goals that will support the objectives. In pairs consisting of a manager and a subordinate, they discuss the manager's objectives and how the employee can help achieve them. The two then develop a set of verifiable, written objectives for the subordinate and establish a target date for completion.

While the employee is working toward the accomplishment of the goals, his or her manager conducts periodic reviews. During these reviews objectives can be modified, though modification is seldom needed if the goal was carefully developed. On the target date, supervisor and employee hold a review session to evaluate the degree to which the goals have been accomplished and to begin setting new goals for the next period. Employees are rewarded according to how well they have achieved these objectives. In part because rewards are linked to performance, the process results in employees who are committed to accomplishing their objectives.

Forecasting   In **forecasting**, the organization develops predictions about the future. These predictions become the basis for planning. Before plans can be developed, for example, a manager determines, through forecasting, both the anticipated revenues from sales as well as the operating expenses. A manager may also need forecasts about the availability of labor, raw materials, tax rates, capital equipment replacement, space requirements, and other environmental factors.

In developing forecasts, managers rely on both internal information and outside resources. Frito-Lay uses internal information when it develops marketing plans for Doritos; the plans are based on sales forecasts supplied by sales managers. In time-series forecasting, the subject activity is plotted on the basis of a time period of several years. Exhibit 4.13 shows a time-series forecast about sales. Such a forecast can relate to almost any subject, however: demand, expenses, revenue, salmon runs, tree growth, or car rentals, among others. Based on past history the forecaster extends what is called a trend line into the future. In Exhibit 4.13 the number of units sold for the years 1988 through 1992 has been plotted—the time beyond that date is the future. By extending the trend line, the forecaster predicts that 3,500 units will be sold in 1993 and that 4,000 will be sold in 1994.

Forecasters use information from outside sources as well as sources within an organization. Various U.S. agencies regularly generate and publish forecasts concerning many specific and overall economic activities. The forecasts present data for specific states, regions, cities, and other jurisdictions. The subjects of the forecasts are numerous: unemployment, retail sales, consumer spending, interest rates, the growth of individual industries and job categories, and many others. Additionally, thousands of public and private organizations—including universities,

Exhibit 4.13

A time-series forecast.

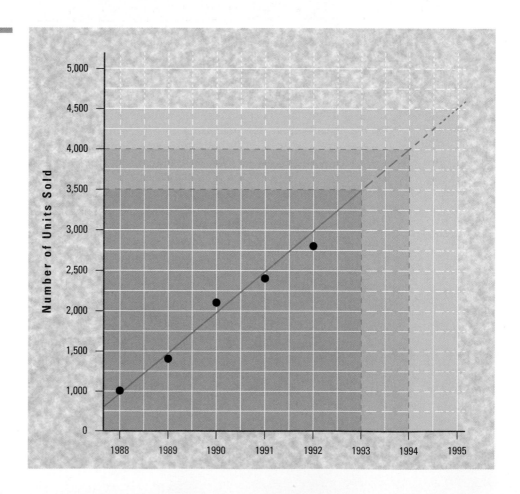

trade associations, private foundations, chambers of commerce, and publishers—offer a wealth of information of every imaginable kind.

Linear Programming   To determine the optimum combination of resources and activities, linear programming can be helpful. Consider, for example, the situation at Armco Products, a small manufacturer of patio chairs, loungers, and footstools. Each product consists of metal frames, fabric webbing, and plastic feet, and each goes through the same production and quality-inspection system. Because of its limited resources, Armco produces only one product at a time. The firm has found that frequent changes from the production of one product to another have been very costly. Armco management needs to know the best way to schedule production. To complicate matters, each product line generates a different profit margin. How many chairs, loungers, and footstools should Armco produce in a given period to optimize resources, satisfy consumer demand, and maximize profit? **Linear programming** can come to the rescue in such a case. It will allow Armco planners to use an equation to quantify profit margins, demand, raw material, and human resources. The results of the equation will tell managers how many units of each product line to produce. (See the Global Applications feature below for an insight into how Nissan Motor Company Ltd. retools to produce different product lines.)

GLOBAL APPLICATIONS
Nissan Plans for "Anywhere"

Japanese managers are famous for taking the long view. Managers at Nissan Motor Co. Ltd. recently faced a long-term planning challenge that was notable even by the Japanese standard. Eight years ago top management at Nissan set the goal of achieving five "anys": any volume, anywhere, any time, anything, anybody. Nissan managers wanted to be able to manufacture any of its models at any of its plants anywhere in the world at any volume level and at any time demanded by local market conditions.

If this goal weren't ambitious enough, planners were given three more goals: (1) Anybody should be able to run the new system, (2) the company should increase its global reach with the least-possible number of assembly plants operating at near-peak capacity, and (3) the smallest-possible number of people should be able to operate the system.

This long-range planning approach sparked the development of what Nissan calls the Intelligent Body Assembly System (IBAS). At the heart of IBAS is a computer-controlled jig, the NC Locator. The jig can be programmed to accommodate any of four different Nissan car models and eight body types. Inside its huge steel framework, 35 robots position the body panels while 16 other robots make the spot welds that hold the panels together.

The first system was installed in 1989 at Nissan's plant in Tochigi, Japan. The system is now up and running at four other plants, including the Nissan plant in Smyrna, Tennessee. IBAS allows Nissan to make model changes simply by changing the computer software that controls body assembly. It can also reduce from 12 months to 3 months the time needed for retooling, and the time savings significantly reduces model changeover costs.

From a planning perspective, IBAS allows Nissan to respond quickly to market fluctuations. Management can adjust production as necessary to build car models that are selling well and cut back on models that are slow sellers. ▲

For more on Nissan's plans, see Brian S. Moskal, "Nissan Heads 'Anywhere,'" *Industry Week,* January 6, 1992, p. 19.

Future Trends

Planning means looking at tomorrow. In the context of this chapter, what could be more appropriate than looking at the future of planning? Based on the present environment, we can make three predictions about the future of planning:

- Strategic plans for organizations will cover a shorter time period. At one time a strategic plan was developed to map out a 10- to 15-year span. In recent years, the time frame for strategic planning was reduced to eight years, then five. With the rapid pace of change, many organizations are reducing the planning window to two years.

- More companies will adopt an almost continuous planning process by making the gaps between implementation and review shorter and shorter. Many organizations are adopting monthly planning cycles, which effectively update a two-year strategic plan on a continuous basis.

- Managers at the lower levels of the management hierarchy will play an increasingly larger role in company-wide planning. Likewise, as companies streamline by removing layers of management, and first-line supervisors and lower-level middle managers acquire greater planning responsibility, management candidates will need greater conceptual ability.

C H A P T E R   S U M M A R Y

- Planning, the management function that precedes and affects all others, sets objectives and selects the means to reach them.

- Planning allows managers to adjust the organization to the environment, not merely to react to it.

- An overall mission provides a framework for related objectives. The objectives vary according to the organization to which they apply.

- An organization's reason for existence and its purposes are expressed in its mission. Building on a mission statement, managers at each level create specific objectives to reflect applicable responsibilities.

- The three levels of objectives—strategic, tactical, and operational—correspond to the three levels of management—top, middle, and first-line.

- Plans answer six basic questions: what, when, where, who, how, and how much.

- All managers engage in planning. Not all make the same types of plans or spend the same amount of time planning, however.

- Plans can be classified as strategic, tactical, or operational. Each type may be a single-use plan or a standing plan.

- The planning process involves seven steps: (1) analyzing the environments, (2) setting objectives, (3) identifying alternatives, (4) evaluating alternatives, (5) selecting the best solution, (6) implementing the plan, and (7) controlling and evaluating results.

- In contingency planning, the manager develops alternative plans. An alternative plan is activated if internal or external circumstances change so drastically that the preferred plan becomes infeasible.

- Among essential aids to planning are accurate, timely, and complete information and clear, concise communication.

- Managers improve planning quality by using sound tools and techniques. Such techniques include management by objectives, forecasting, and linear programming.

S K I L L - B U I L D I N G

In this series of questions, apply the concepts you have studied in this chapter to your present job, a previous job, or any organization you have observed closely.

1. What type of plans—strategic, tactical, or operational—were developed?

2. Who developed each type of plan?

3. What topic categories were included in each type of plan? Consider specific goals, time frames, responsibility, and resource allocation.

4. What part did you play in the development of plans? Were you an active participant or an observer, or did you learn about plans only after they were developed?

5. Focus on one plan and tell when it was implemented. Who implemented it?

6. How was the plan evaluated? Who evaluated it?

7. If you answered question 4 by saying that you were an observer or learned about plans after they were developed, do you believe you should have been included in the planning process? How would you have changed the plan?

R E V I E W   **Q** U E S T I O N S

1. Review this chapter's essential terms and look up the meanings of those you cannot define.

2. How does planning affect the success of a business?

3. How are mission statements, objectives, and plans related?

4. What are the three levels of objectives in an organization? What is the scope of each?

5. What are the purposes of strategic, tactical, and operational plans? In what situation would an organization use each type?

6. List and briefly explain the seven basic steps in the formal planning process.

7. What is the purpose of contingency planning? When would contingency planning not be used?

8. What are the seven barriers to effective planning? How does each interfere with effective planning?

9. How do the three aids to planning help managers make plans?

R E C O M M E N D E D   **R** E A D I N G

Barnum, Paul. "Jury Is Still out on Strategy," *Human Resource Planning* (March 1992), pp. 19–22.

Burkel-Rothfuss, Nancy, and Pam Gray. *Communication and Planning,* 2nd edition (Dubuque, IA: Kendall-Hunt), 1991.

Day, Charles R. "Quality: Make It a Matter of Policy," *Industry Week* (January 6, 1992), p. 46.

Healey, Patsy, and Thomas Hays. *New Dimensions in Planning Practice: Values, Skills, and Ethics,* 2nd edition (Englewood Cliffs, NJ: Prentice-Hall), 1991.

Langler, Gerard H. "The Vision Trap," *Harvard Business Review* (March–April, 1992), pp. 46–55.

Miller, Danny. "The Icarus Paradox: How Exceptional Companies Bring About Their Own Downfall," *Business Horizons* (January–February 1992), pp. 24–36.

Pollock, Thomas. "How to Be a Better Planner," *Supervision* (January 1992), p. 23.

Steiner, George. *Planning: What Every Manager Should Know* (Los Angeles: Roxbury), 1991.

Telling, A. E. *Planning and Procedure,* 7th edition (San Francisco: Jossey-Bass), 1991.

Woods, William. *Applied Planning Techniques* (Lincolnwood, IL: National Textbook), 1991.

R E F E R E N C E S

Dobrzynski, Judith H. "IBM's Board Should Clean Out the Corner Office," *Business Week* (February 1, 1993), p. 27.

Drucker, Peter F. *The Practice of Management* (New York: Harper & Row), 1954, pp. 49–61, 55–83.

Dumaine, Brianc. "Procter & Gamble Shoots for the Top," *Industry Week* (January 6, 1992), pp. 24–25.

Dupuy, John. "Learning to Manage World-Class Strategy," *Management Review* (March 1992), pp. 40–43.

Fallows, James. "Computers: Crash-Worthy Speedster," *Atlantic* (February 1993), pp. 103–108.

Kupfer, Andrew. "Apple's Plan to Survive and Grow," *Fortune* (May 4, 1992), p. 69.

Lindstrom, Robert. "Toy Town Turnaround," *California Business* (December 1991), pp. 30–35.

Los Angeles Times, February 5, 1993, p. D3.

Verespej, Michael A. "John Akers' Mission: A New IBM," *Industry Week* (February 17, 1992), pp. 23–24.

Want, Jerome H. "Corporate Mission: The Intangible Contributor to Performance," *Management Review* (August 1986), p. 47.

Weintraub, Pamela. "Challenge and Response: Business Management in the 21st Century," *Omni* (January 1992), p. 36.

G L O S S A R Y   O F   **T** E R M S

budget A single-use plan for predicting sources and amounts of income and how it is to be used.

contingency planning Developing plans that are activated if changes in circumstance cause the preferred plan to become infeasible.

forecasting A planning technique used to develop predictions about the future, which become the basis of plans.

linear programming A planning technique that uses an equation to determine the optimum combination of resources and activities.

management by objectives (MBO) A planning technique that emphasizes collaborative goal setting by managers and their subordinates.

mission statement The formal written statement of an organization's purpose.

objective The desired outcome or target that an individual or an organization intends to achieve through planning.

operational objective The specific result expected from first-level managers, work groups, and individuals.

operational plan A plan developed by a first-level supervisor as the means to achieve operational objectives and in support of tactical plans.

plan The means to achieving an objective.

planning Determining the objectives of an organization or work group and developing the overall strategies to achieve them.

policy A broad guideline to aid workers in making decisions about recurring situations or functions.

procedure The set of step-by-step directions that describes how to carry out an activity or task.

program A single-use plan for solving a problem or accomplishing a group of related activities needed to reach a goal.

rule A plan that aims to control human behavior or conduct at work.

single-use plan A plan that applies to activities that do not recur.

standing plan A plan that is usually made once and retained over the years. A standing plan may be revised.

strategic objective A long-term goal that relates to the future role or position of an organization. Strategic objectives are set by top-level management.

strategic plan The steps by which an organization intends to achieve its strategic objectives.

tactical objective A goal that states what a subunit must do to achieve a strategic objective. Tactical objectives are set by midlevel managers.

tactical plan The steps by which the major units in an organization will achieve tactical objectives.

C A S E   P R O B L E M
Macy's Motto: More *Was* Better

n the 1980s, after years of profit growth, retailer R. H. Macy and Company began to stumble. An executive-led leveraged buyout of the company plus the acquisition of regional department-store chains (Bullock's and I. Magnin) created a debt load of $4.5 billion. Losses, which were only $14 million in 1987, shot to $1.25 billion in 1992.

Debt, of course, is not the only problem plaguing the giant retailer. Intense competition and a lingering recession have also had an impact. In addition, Macy's found itself hampered by its traditional way of doing business. For decades, Macy's motto was "More is better." The chain loaded up on inventory to ensure that customers would have all the choices they wanted. The result: Much of the inventory didn't sell. In 1992, Macy's management unveiled a new five-year plan that relied upon a new operational approach aimed at bringing the company back to financial health.

The keystone of this new plan is a new position, the position of planner. The planner works with both the merchandise buyers and the managers of individual stores. By poring over computer printouts that register how well individual items sell, the planner can target the hot sellers, get the customer to buy more, and tell the store manager what to stock.

Before adopting the planner's recommendations company-wide, Macy's tested the new planning system for a year in the Men's Department. The results were dramatic. A sale of men's shirts in 1992 yielded 30% more revenue than a shirt sale the year before. What was the difference? In preparation for the 1992 sale, the planner reviewed the results of the prior year's sale and stocked up on the styles and colors that moved. The store enjoyed similar success with the Hanes line of hosiery. Although Macy's carried 25% less inventory of the brand, revenue from Hanes sales rose 15%.

Another aspect of Macy's new plan is the increased use of up-to-the-minute information. Macy's has installed a new computerized inventory management system. With information from the new computer system and from newly installed point-of-sale terminals, management can respond quickly to sales trends.

Macy's management projects that by 1998, cash flow will have increased by 400% in terms of what cash flow would have been without the new data systems. The managers hope that with all that new cash flowing, the company can reduce its debt. All it takes is a little planning.

Q U E S T I O N S

1. Which type of planning—strategic, tactical, or operational—is Macy's engaged in?

2. What key factor do Macy's new systems make use of? How is that factor used? How was it used before the changes were made?

3. How does this scenario relate to the need for flexibility in planning?

For more about planning at Macy's, see Stephanie Strom, "A Key for a Macy's Comeback," *New York Times,* November 1, 1992, p. F4.

Strategic Planning and Strategic Management

L E A R N I N G   O B J E C T I V E S

After reading and discussing this chapter, you should be able to:

- Define this chapter's essential terms
- Describe the nature of strategic planning and strategic management
- Distinguish between strategy formulation and strategy implementation
- Discuss the steps in the strategic planning process
- Discuss the importance of assessing the internal and external environments as a basis for strategic planning
- Identify the sources and kinds of information required in the strategic planning process
- Discuss the major approaches to corporate-level strategy, business-level strategy, and functional-level strategy
- Describe the factors involved in strategy implementation

M A N A G E M E N T   I N   A C T I O N
Planning for Survival and Growth at Apple

Apple Computer, under the direction of CEO John Sculley, has been forced by an ever-changing marketplace to re-evaluate its corporate goals and formulate a grand plan that will take the company into the next century. As Sculley explains:

> We looked at ourselves in the mirror and wondered if we had a justifiable business strategy for the 1990s. Our model was one of high margins with huge product differentiation. But, growth was slowing. Computers were becoming more of a commodity. And we lost differentiation because of Microsoft's Windows.

The result of this assessment was a three-pronged strategy to propel Apple upward and onward.

After more than a decade of making high-priced personal computers, Apple has trimmed profit margins and is driving hard for market share. With the strategy

The personal digital assistant (PDA) is a pocket-sized, pen-based technology that Apple is hoping will replace the notepad.

of establishing itself in the consumer market, Apple is bringing out a cut-price version of its main machine, the Macintosh, to increase Apple's impact in the home computer market. The strategy even calls for selling Macs at Sears.

The second element of the strategic plan is the development of an alliance with former archrival, IBM. Heralded by many at Apple as the deal of the century, the alliance calls for the two firms to work together on several significant new ventures. One venture involves development of the Power PC, a new kind of Mac that uses superfast processors originally developed by IBM. Another project, Taligent, involves a new operating system that will enable programmers to write software more easily. A project called Kaleida will merge sound, data, graphics, and video in one new supergadget. Yet another venture will enable Apple and IBM machines to work better together—thus helping Apple attract more business customers.

The final element of the new strategic direction calls for Apple to position itself for an assault on what could be a $3-trillion market 10 years from now. This huge market will emerge out of a combination of telecommunications, office equipment, computers, consumer electronics, media, and publishing. Starting within a year, Apple will launch a host of new high-tech machines that represent an intersection of all these fields. Such products will include electronic books, electronic organizers, electronic note takers, display telephones, and personal communicators.

129

66 The PC industry is dead and the only thing you can do is aggressively cross the chasm into the next world. **99**

— **Paul Safflo**, Consultant, Institute for the Future

The strategy has barriers to overcome. Apple must generate enough profits from the computer business to fund the new ventures, find ways of reaching new customers and markets, and effectively manage the strategic alliances. To make this plan a reality, Sculley is betting on two of Apple's strengths: software and "Apple Magic." Software has always been Apple's number one asset. Apple Magic—the quality, empowerment, and innovativeness of its employees—has pushed the company to success in the past.

"What they're doing is unbelievably gutsy," said Paul Safflo, a consultant at the Institute for the Future in Menlo Park, California. "The PC industry is dead and the only thing you can do is aggressively cross the chasm into the next world. But Apple could have the right vision and still fail." ▲

For more on Apple's planning for survival and growth, see Andrew Kupfer, "Apple's Plan to Survive and Grow," *Fortune,* May 4, 1992, pp. 68–72; Rory O'Connor, "Now, Hand-Held Computers," *Philadelphia Inquirer,* September 6, 1992, pp. C1–C2; and John Markoff, "Beyond the PC: Apple's Promised Land, *New York Times,* November 15, 1992, sec. 3, pp. 1, 10.

The Nature of Strategic Planning and Management

Chapter 4 introduced the basics of planning, examined the types of objectives, and differentiated the types of plans created to carry them out: strategic, tactical, and operational. This chapter will focus on **strategic planning**—the decision-making and planning processes that chart an organization's long-term course.

Companies engage in strategic planning as an element of strategic management. **Strategic management** is top-level management's responsibility to define the firm's position, formulate strategies, and guide long-term organizational activities. The ultimate purpose of strategic planning and strategic management is to help position the organization to achieve a superior competitive fit between the organization and its environment. Only by being able to compete in its external environment can an organization reach its objectives (Prescott, 1986).

Companies large and small undertake strategic planning to respond to competitors, cope with a rapidly changing environment, and effectively manage their resources—all within the goal of fulfilling their missions (Holt, 1990). With a sharp strategic focus, a company can accomplish all its objectives. A curtain-rod maker from Freeport, Illinois—Dan Ferguson—recognized this fact and applied it to his firm, Newell Company. Through strategic planning and management, Ferguson shifted the company's focus from selling one line of products to many customers to selling several different kinds of products to the inner circle of dominant national mass merchandisers. The result: Newell Company's profits have shot up at a compound annual rate of 40% (Magness, 1992).

The Elements of Strategic Planning

Strategic planning is designed to help managers answer critical questions. These questions include:

- What is the organization's position in the marketplace?
- What should the organization's position be?
- What trends and changes are occurring in the marketplace?
- What are the best alternatives to help achieve the objectives?

The strategic planning process generates answers to these questions. Designed to guide a company in achieving its comprehensive objectives, strategy relies upon four elements: scope, resource deployment, distinctive competitive advantage, and synergy (Hill and Jones, 1989).

Scope   The notion of **scope** refers to the area, range, or size the firm chooses to develop or maintain within its environment. Included are the markets in which it elects to compete as well as the products and services it will offer. Apple Computer's future plans call for increasing both its scope of products and its markets. General Motors, in contrast, has chosen to limit its scope by eliminating products (Taylor, January 13, 1992).

Resource Deployment   **Resource deployment** denotes how the company intends to allocate its resources—human, physical, and financial—to achieve its strategic objectives. To achieve its new strategy, Apple is deploying more resources to new product development and to the forming of alliances. McDonald's, as Chapter 4 reported, is deploying resources for global expansion. Another fast-food restaurant, Taco Bell, is allocating millions to remodel old restaurants, bring out new products, and push for increased market share (Hall, 1992).

Distinctive Competitive Advantage   The term **distinctive competitive advantage** refers to the benefits of an organization's unique position in relation to its competition. John Sculley hopes that Apple's distinctive advantage—its reputation for high-quality, easy-to-use software—will help the firm meet its strategic goals. Southwest Airlines' competitive advantages lie in low fares and frequent flights—advantages that the firm has parlayed to become the leading short-haul carrier in the United States (Welles, 1992).

Synergy   **Synergy** occurs when two forces, working together, create an effort that is greater than the sum of what either force could produce alone. In the business world, two parts of one organization may create synergy by working together. The result may be an advantage in market share, technology, cost, or management skill (Daft, 1991). The management of Sony sought synergy by

F O C U S   O N   Q U A L I T Y
Jaguar Bounces Back

or **Mike Dale,** president of Jaguar Cars, Inc., 1988 was the kind of year to have nightmares about. "Jaguar executives remember 1988 as the year product reliability went bonkers. Engine assembly and quality controls were so sloppy that variances among factory-fresh, in-line sixes wavered by as much as 40 horsepower, 18 percent of potential power."

These days, Dale can sleep soundly. Tighter manufacturing methods have resulted in significant improvements in the last 18 months. "You know," he says with a sly smile, "I just can't get used to how the chrome lines up straight."

How did Jaguar achieve such a turnaround? Recovery began when Ford Motor Company of Dearborn, Michigan, purchased Jaguar Cars of Coventry, England, for $2.5 billion. Ford bought Jaguar to enter the lucrative segment of the luxury-car market. Ford management wanted Jaguars to hold their own against BMWs and the Infiniti and Lexus. First, however, Ford had to solve Jaguar's quality problem.

In July 1990, Ford appointed Bill Hayden, former director of manufacturing for Ford of Europe, to head up Jaguar. Hayden was known in the auto industry for being ruthless in pursuit of quality. He introduced a quality-control measurement method called the Uniform Product Assessment System. He not only overhauled 30-year-old manufacturing processes, but quickly tackled a crippling labor situation.

"The working practices were out of the Industrial Revolution era," says a Jag spokesman. "Hayden went direct to the work force and said, 'If we don't change these practices, bring them up to date, this company will not survive. You have the future of the company on your hands. You can vote to save it or vote to continue these practices and kill it.'"

The union group voted 69% to overturn established work practices. As a result, beginning in August 1990, Jaguar's quality position improved remarkably. Manufacturing efficiency did too. From August 1990 until September 1992, manufacturing efficiency increased 1.5% per month, and the rise has continued. Most auto industry observers call that rate "staggering, especially for a British car company." Faults per 100 cars were reduced by 80% over the same period, and the number continues to fall month by month.

In 12 months Jaguar moved from 25th to 10th place in the J. D. Power customer satisfaction index. The rating for vehicle reliability shot up by 21% in same period. Recent sales are also much improved. In December 1991, Jaguar sold only 693 cars in the United States; the December 1992 total was 1,072. To prove its own faith in the new cars, Jaguar recently offered an unprecedented 30-day, money-back guarantee on cars sold in selected test markets. To date, 400 Jaguars have been sold in those markets. Only four have been returned. ▲

For more about Jaguar, see Paul Dean, "Scratching Back," *Los Angeles Times,* February 5, 1993, pp. E1, E5.

acquiring Columbia Pictures and CBS Records. The aim was to create a smooth union of entertainment products (CDs and videotapes) with technology (CD players and VCRs).

Responsibility for Strategic Planning

Which manager is responsible for strategic planning depends on the organization. Some, like General Foods, hire strategic planning experts and maintain strategic planning groups. But in most organizations, top-level managers delegate the responsibility to line managers.

The core group of strategic managers includes the senior executives—chief executive officer, chief operating officer, and chief financial officer. But in more and more large organizations—Marriott Corporation, General Electric, and Procter & Gamble among them—middle-level and line managers are expected to think and act strategically. Senior executives encourage these managers to take the long-term view about where the organization is going, what major changes are likely to occur, and which decisions will have to be made now to achieve their organization's long-term objectives. By encouraging lower-level managers to think and act strategically, the company not only develops a unified plan, but develops its managers. According to Wrapp (1967), successful strategic managers are:

- Well informed. They use a wide range of information sources to keep in touch with activities throughout the organization, and they use information to make effective decisions.

- Skilled at focusing their time and energy. They delegate effectively and can protect their time, but they know when to make a decision or take action themselves.

- Good at playing the power game. They are sensitive to relationships in the organization's hierarchy, and they know how to build consensus for their ideas and form coalitions to get their plans accomplished.

- Good at being flexible. They know how to adapt their goals to changing conditions and avoid committing publicly to detailed plans that may require substantive change.

- Accomplished at "muddling with a purpose." They recognize the difficulty in trying to accomplish complex goals, so they push their programs through piecemeal, dividing objectives into smaller, more easily accomplished parts.

Strategy Formulation Versus Strategy Implementation

Another important element in understanding the nature of strategic planning is recognizing the difference between formulation and implementation. **Strategy formulation** includes the planning and decision making that goes into developing the company's strategic objectives and strategic plans. It includes assessing the environments, analyzing the internal and external situations, and creating objectives and plans. On the other hand, **strategy implementation** refers to the means associated with executing the strategic plan. These means may include communication, incentives, structural changes, or new technology. Both aspects will be discussed in detail later in the chapter.

The Levels of Strategy

Managers think in terms of three levels of strategy: corporate, business, and functional. Exhibit 5.1 shows how the three levels relate.

Exhibit 5.1

The three levels of strategy.

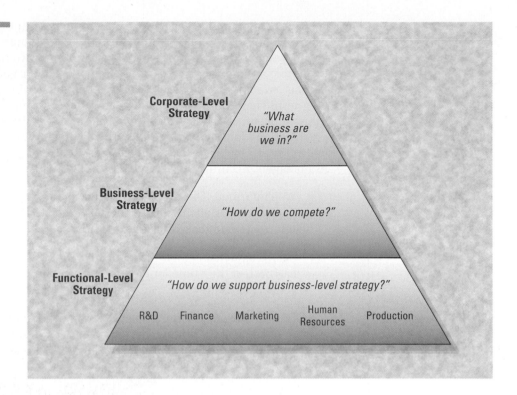

Corporate-Level Strategy   The purpose of **corporate-level strategy** is to answer the questions, "What business are we in?" and "What business should we be in?" The answers chart the course of business for the entire organization. Apple Computer answered its questions by deciding not to continue being a maker of high-priced personal computers. Rather, it chose to focus strategically on being a leader in market share, in developing new types of computer software, and in developing new electronic gadgetry that could take the company's products into the everyday lives of consumers. The management of Veda International, a firm that makes flight simulators, decided to branch into the consumer market by developing a simulator that could be sold to amusement parks (Gnoffo, 1992).

Business-Level Strategy   A **business-level strategy** answers the question, "How do we compete?" It focuses on how each product line or business unit within an organization competes for the customer. The decisions at this level determine how much is spent on advertising, product development, and research and development; what equipment and facilities to use; and whether to expand or contract product lines. For example, the managers of Mattel made a business-level strategy when they decided to reduce the number of marginal products but extend existing successful lines. This strategy was a means to achieving the corporate-level strategy of increasing market share. Mattel also developed an alliance with Disney. This alliance, another business-level strategy, was designed to achieve the corporate strategy of developing new products (Jacob, 1992).

Functional-Level Strategy   The strategy for the major functional departments answers the question, "How can we support the business-level strategy?" **Functional-level strategy** focuses on the major functions of the company: human resources, research and development, marketing, finance, and production. For American Airlines to compete successfully, its functional-level strategy in marketing called for a pricing structure that met consumer needs and controlled competition. For a brief period, the result was a simplified pricing structure for the consumer that forced competition to lower prices (Mitchell and Tiles, 1992). Häagen-Dazs, a maker of premium ice cream, provides another example. Its functional-level strategy for research and development cut the testing time for new products by 25%, an achievement that allowed the company to compete more effectively with other brands (Lii, 1992).

The Strategic Planning Process

At all levels of an organization, the strategic planning process can be divided into six steps, as Exhibit 5.2 shows. Strategic planning requires managers to (1) evaluate the organization's current mission, objectives, and strategies; (2) analyze the internal and external environments; (3) reassess the organization's mission and objectives; (4) formulate strategies to accomplish the objectives; (5) implement the strategies; and (6) monitor and evaluate the results. As you review these steps

Exhibit 5.2

The strategic planning process.

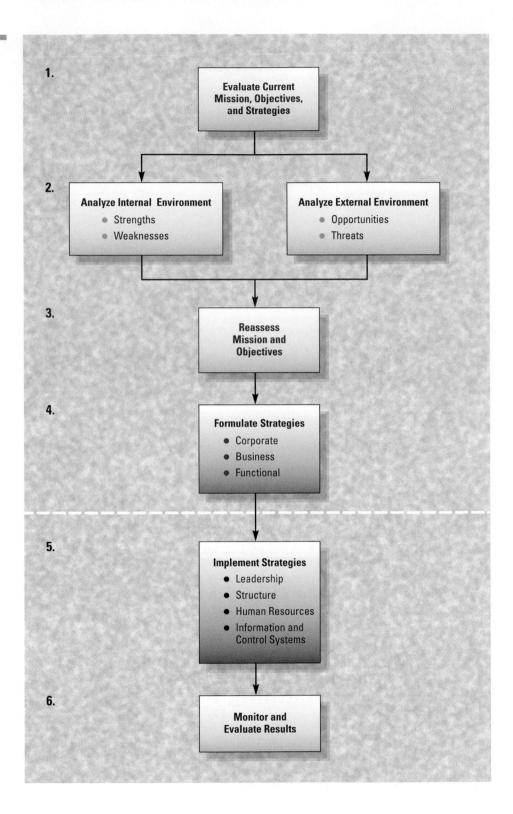

in detail, keep in mind a company that interests you and imagine how you might apply the process to its operation.

Evaluate Current Mission, Objectives, and Strategies

The first step in strategic planning is to evaluate the status and effectiveness of the organization's current mission, objectives, and strategies. The step is critical because to succeed, a company must never lose focus on its purpose. Management must constantly redetermine if the firm's activities are aimed at its mission and whether that mission is still appropriate. As the Management in Action feature in this chapter explained, the management of Apple Computer determined that the company's mission, supporting objectives, and strategies were not viable for the 1990s. This realization prompted Apple management to declare a new mission. The presidential campaign of 1992 provided an example of a focused mission. A sign on the wall behind the democratic campaign manager's desk brought everyone forcibly back to the point. The sign said, "The Economy, Stupid!"

Analyze the Environments

Once the mission statement has been evaluated, the environments—external and internal—must be assessed and analyzed. In completing this phase, the managers perform a **situation analysis**—a search for strengths, weaknesses, opportunities, and threats (SWOT).

Sources of Information   Strategic planners can acquire information about internal strengths and weaknesses by tapping an array of potential sources—profit and loss statements, ratio analyses, employee morale surveys, and budget printouts. Simply by being in the environment, talking to other managers, and observing, a strategic planner can build a sound assessment of the organization's strengths and weaknesses. To complete this assessment, the organization's managers must have information from external as well as internal sources. External information—about threats and opportunities—can be gathered from government reports, professional journals and meetings, consultants, customers, and suppliers. The expertise of consultants can help managers obtain and analyze internal as well as external information.

Internal Strengths and Weaknesses   An organization's internal strengths are factors the company can build on to reach its objectives. Weaknesses inhibit performance and should be either compensated for or eliminated. In assessing strengths and weaknesses, strategists should examine:

- Management, including management structure and managers' abilities

- Marketing factors, including distribution channels, market share, service reputation, and customer satisfaction

- Production factors, including manufacturing efficiency, obsolescence of equipment, and quality control

- Research factors, including research and development capabilities, new product development, and the prospect of technological innovation

- Human resource factors, including the quality and depth of employee talent, degree of employee job satisfaction and morale, turnover rate, and union status

- Financial factors, including profit margin, return on investment, and debt-equity ratio

Apple's strategic plan of 1993 was shaped by the company's strengths, which include the ability to develop software, and the employee power John Sculley calls Apple Magic.

External Threats and Opportunities   In an external assessment, management focuses on two areas: threats and opportunities. Threats are factors that can prevent the organization from achieving its objectives. Opportunities are the opposite— they can help the organization achieve its objectives. An external assessment should examine the threat or opportunity posed by:

- New competitors

- Substitute products

- Changes in the strategy of major competitors

- Potential actions and profitability of customers

- Actions of suppliers

- New or abandoned government regulations

- New technology

- Changes in the economy

To realize Apple's need for a new mission, John Sculley performed the assessment process. He rightly assessed that his company had lost product differentiation, the basis of Apple's traditional competitive advantage.

Reassess Mission and Objectives

Analysis of internal strengths and weaknesses and external opportunities and threats urges managers to consider one of two possible courses: to reestablish the current mission, objectives, and strategies or to define a new mission and supporting objectives. At Apple, the analysis of the environment brought a major shift in strategy: The new mission consists of developing innovative, low-priced electronic gadgetry and forming alliances with former archrival, IBM.

Formulate Strategies

Once the mission and objectives are reestablished or re-defined, strategies at the corporate, business, and functional levels can be formulated. At Apple, the new strategies focused on developing a greater consumer market share for the Macintosh (by cutting prices and opening new distribution channels) and on accelerating the development of new products.

Implement Strategies

Once strategies are formulated, they must be implemented. Strategy formulation and strategy implementation are two distinct tasks—a fact that Exhibit 5.2 illustrates by means of the dotted line after step 4. The last section of this chapter will explore the implementation phase in depth.

Monitor and Evaluate Results

Once the strategy is implemented, managers must monitor and evaluate the results. If necessary, they will have to make modifications. Now that you understand the strategic process as a whole, the next section will show how it operates at each level of an organization.

Formulating Corporate-Level Strategy

Recall that corporate-level strategy involves determining what business or businesses the firm expects to compete in. For companies with a single market or a few closely related markets, developing corporate-level strategy involves making a grand, organization-wide strategy. Large corporations, on the other hand, may consist of discrete business divisions. Each division has different products, markets, and competitors. In the case of a corporation with diverse holdings, developing corporate-level strategy involves making decisions about divisions and product lines. The sections that follow will examine each type of corporate-level strategy.

Grand Strategy

A **grand strategy** is the overall framework, or plan of action, developed at the corporate level to achieve an organization's objectives. The five types of grand strategies are growth, integration, diversification, retrenchment, and stability.

Growth Strategy   An organization adopts a **growth strategy** when it expands significantly in one or more of its areas of operations or business units. Growth can be achieved internally by investment. Organizations achieve external growth by acquiring business units. McDonald's has embarked on an ambitious program of internal expansion by targeting the international arena for future restaurant sites (Hall, 1992). On the other hand, PepsiCo's recent expansion in the pizza business is being achieved through a 70% stake in California Pizza Kitchen—in other words, through external growth.

Integration Strategy   An organization adopts an **integration strategy** when its managers see the need (1) to stabilize supply lines or reduce costs, or (2) to consolidate competition. In the first situation the company creates a strategy of **vertical integration**. In other words, the firm gains ownership of the resources, suppliers, or distribution systems on which it relies. The merger of Time, Inc. with Warner illustrates this strategy. The strategy of **horizontal integration**, in contrast, acts to consolidate competition by acquiring similar products or services. The purchase of Flying Tiger by Federal Express provides an example of this strategy.

Motorola moves *into new markets and product lines when it perceives a need it can meet. The KDT 840 is a mobile data communications terminal that assists maintenance personnel in transmitting repair information at the work site.*

Diversification Strategy   An organization adopts a **diversification strategy** if its managers opt to offer new types of products or enter new markets. Managers usually pursue diversification by acquiring other businesses. Both R. J. Reynolds and Philip Morris have diversified through the purchase of food companies.

Retrenchment Strategy   Managers choose a **retrenchment strategy** to reduce the size or scope of a firm's activities. Such strategies call for cutbacks in some areas or the elimination of entire businesses. Sears and Xerox have pursued retrenchment strategies in the early 1990s. Sears eliminated virtually all its nonretail businesses—it even abandoned its catalogue operation. Xerox initiated an identical strategy when it chose to divest itself of its real-estate ventures.

Stability Strategy   When managers decide that an organization should stay the same, they adopt a **stability strategy**. The reason for choosing such a strategy could be to allow the organization to grow slowly. A strategy of stability might also be appropriate if an organization needs time to recover after a period of sharp growth or retrenchment. Nation's Bank, formerly North Carolina National Bank, adopted a strategy of stability after a five-year growth period in which the organization expanded into Texas and acquired banks in Florida and Ohio.

Portfolio Strategy

Once the managers of a large diversified organization decide on a grand strategy, they develop a portfolio strategy. A **portfolio strategy** focuses on the strategic business unit, and it involves determining the proper mix of business units and product lines to provide a maximum competitive advantage.

Developing a portfolio strategy begins by identifying **strategic business units** (**SBUs**). The concept of the SBU was developed at General Electric in 1971 to provide managers with a framework for directing GE's many different businesses. An SBU has its own competitors, its own market, and its own product line.

In trying to manage a portfolio of business units, which is much like managing a portfolio of stocks, corporations often employ a device called the **Boston Consulting Group (BCG) matrix**. Exhibit 5.3 shows a BCG matrix.

Exhibit 5.3

A BCG matrix.

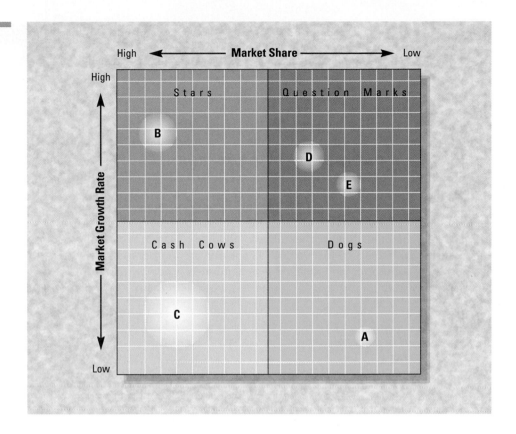

The matrix, designed at the Boston Consulting Group in the late 1960s, aids managers by grouping SBUs into meaningful categories. The matrix classifies the SBUs along two axes: market growth rate on the vertical and market share on the horizontal. Market growth rate is the rate of increased purchasing for the entire industry. Market share is the SBU's position relative to competitors. Exhibit 5.3 plots the location of five businesses (A through E) in the grid. The size of each circle represents the sales revenue produced by each SBU in relation to the organization's other SBUs. The matrix identifies four types of businesses:

1. Stars. Business B is a star because it has a large market share in a rapidly growing industry. A star has the potential to grow and will generate profits.

2. Cash cows. The cash cow, Business C, claims a large market share in a stable, slow-growth industry. Because the industry is in slow growth, the business unit can maintain its position with little or no investment. It is in a position to generate cash for investment in other businesses— the question marks.

3. Question marks. The question marks, Businesses D and E, hold small shares of the market in rapidly expanding industries. Question marks are risky. A business in this category could become a star, but it could also fail.

4. Dogs. The dog, Business A, is a business with small market shares in a low-growth industry. Notice that A also earns the smallest revenue relative to any of the other businesses in the portfolio.

or managers responsible for formulating corporate-level strategy, analysis of the external environment is now more complicated than ever. Managers in the tobacco industry, for instance, must acknowledge a profound shift in the American attitude toward tobacco products.

Traditionally, strategists who evaluated expansion options were concerned with dollars, market share, and market potential. But in the tobacco industry, they must now factor in the values of society. In recent years, cigarette companies have generated extraordinary public protest for targeting young people, women, African-Americans, and other groups. The tobacco companies' prodigious efforts to sell their products to Third World countries has been called cynical exploitation. Does a puffing cartoon camel that appears in U.S. ads have an insidious influence on children? The question was argued vigorously in the press.

Are there ethical questions involved in the promotion of certain types of businesses, to certain target markets? Why? If you were a strategic planner, how would you address the ethics questions in the case of the tobacco industry? ▲

The BCG matrix provides a valuable tool to corporate-level strategists because it indicates where expansion should and can take place. It also indicates which business units should be sold.

Formulating Business-Level Strategy

A business strategy is that which managers formulate, within each SBU (or within the firm itself for a single-product business), to define how they choose to compete. The many possible approaches can be grouped as either adaptive strategies or competitive strategies.

Adaptive Strategies

The philosophy behind adaptive strategies—a typology developed by Raymond E. Miles and Charles C. Snow in the late 1970s—is that a firm's strategy should suit its internal characteristics and the external environment. The four adaptive strategies are prospector, defender, analyzer, and reactor (Miles and Snow, 1978). Exhibit 5.4 shows what kinds of environments and organizations are suitable for each strategy.

Prospector Strategy   The **prospector strategy** calls for innovation, risks, the pursuit of opportunities, and expansion. For a flexible, innovative, and creative organization in a dynamic climate, this strategy is appropriate. A model prospector may be the 3M Company, regularly included among *Fortune*'s Most Admired Corporations and noted for constantly re-inventing itself with cutting-edge products, new applications for technology, and entrepreneurship.

Defender Strategy   The **defender strategy** is the reverse of the prospector strategy. It calls for retaining current market share or even retrenching. Companies

Exhibit 5.4

The relationship between adaptive strategies, organizational characteristics, and the external environment.

Strategies	External Environment	Organizational Characteristics
Prospector: Innovate. Find new market opportunities. Grow. Take risks.	Dynamic, growing	Creativity, innovation, flexibility, decentralization
Defender: Protect turf. Hold current market. Retrench.	Stable	Tight control, centralization, product efficiency, low overhead
Analyzer: Maintain current market. Innovate moderately.	Moderate change	Tight control, flexibility, efficient production, creativity
Reactor: No clear strategy. React to specific conditions. Drift.	Any condition	No clear organizational approach, depends on current needs

Source: Based on Raymond E. Miles, Charles C. Snow, Alan D. Meyer, and Henry L. Coleman, Jr., "Organizational Strategy, Structure, and Process," *Academy of Management Review* 3 (1978): 546–562.

using the defender strategy do not seek to grow. The approach is appropriate in a stable environment for companies concerned with internal efficiency and producing reliable products for regular customers. In the early 1990s Exxon, Mobil, and Shell Oil Company adopted the defender strategy.

Analyzer Strategy   Managers who adopt the **analyzer strategy** seek to maintain current market share while innovating in some markets. This strategy calls for a balancing act, maintaining position in some markets while aggressively pursuing opportunities in others. The strategy suits an environment where growth is possible and the firm is both efficient and creative. Examples of analyzers include Frito-Lay and Anheuser-Busch. Each retains a consistently reliable product base yet innovatively brings new products to the market.

Reactor Strategy   An organization whose managers have adopted the **reactor strategy** may be said to employ no strategy at all. Rather than formulate a plan to fit a specific environment, reactors respond to environmental threats randomly. With no clear sense of internal direction, a reactor organization is doomed to chance until its management develops some strategy. A common outcome of nonstrategy is slow demise or abrupt failure. As it floundered in the midst of financial and managerial reorganization, Zales Corporation illustrated the difficulties of merely reacting.

Competitive Strategies

The second set of business-level strategies that an organization can initiate—the competitive strategies—were defined by management strategist Michael Porter. Whereas adaptive strategies are based on a fit between an organization and its

Strategy	Commonly Required Skills and Resources	Common Organizational Requirements
Differentiation	Strong marketing abilities. Product engineering. Creative flair. Strong capability in basic research. Corporate reputation for quality or technological leadership.	Strong coordination among functions in R&D, product development, and marketing. Subjective measurement and incentives instead of quantitative measures. Amenities to attract highly skilled labor, scientists, or creative people.
Cost-Leadership	Sustained capital investment and access to capital. Process-engineering skills. Intense supervision of labor. Products designed for ease in manufacture. Low-cost distribution system.	Tight cost control. Frequent, detailed control reports. Structured organization and responsibilities. Incentives based on meeting strict quantitative targets.
Focus	Combination of the above policies directed at a particular strategic target.	Combination of the above policies directed at a particular strategic target.

Source: Reprinted with permission of The Free Press, a division of Macmillan, Inc., from *Competitive Strategy: Techniques for Analyzing Industries and Competitors* by Michael E. Porter. Copyright 1980 by The Free Press.

environment, competitive strategies are dictated by how the organization can best compete. The ability to compete is based on internal skills, resources, and philosophy. The three competitive strategies are differentiation, cost-leadership, and focus (Porter, 1980). Exhibit 5.5 relates these strategies to compatible organizational characteristics.

Differentiation Strategy   A **differentiation strategy** attempts to set an organization's products or services apart from those of other companies. This can be accomplished by focusing on customer service, product design, technology, or quality. Rolls-Royce and Rolex rely on quality; UPS and Maytag differentiate by service.

Cost-Leadership Strategy   A **cost-leadership strategy** focuses on keeping costs as low as possible. The means to low cost are efficient operations and tight controls. The company that is successful in maintaining low costs can charge low prices. Low price becomes the organization's distinguishing characteristic. Price Club, Pace, and Sam's Wholesale Clubs apply the cost-leadership strategy to retailing. In the motel business, Scottish Inns and Motel 6 provide travelers with low-cost alternatives.

Focus Strategy   When the managers of a firm target a specific market—a particular region or group of buyers—they are applying **focus strategy**. Some companies manufacture products for certain buyers. Pro-Line Corporation

Nike held on to a large share of the sneaker market by strategically focusing its product on female athletes.

produces health and beauty aids for the African-American market. R. J. Reynolds and other tobacco companies target young women. Mazda upgraded its sporty RX-7 coupe to target buyers of Nissan's 300ZX and low-end Porsches.

Formulating Functional-Level Strategy

The final level of strategy in the organization is that developed by the major functional departments. These action plans support the accomplishment of the business-level strategies for marketing, production, human resources, finance, and research and development.

Marketing Strategy

Marketing strategy applies to the functional level of a company's products or services and focuses on pricing, promotion, packaging, and distribution. The decisions in each area, taken as a whole, become a firm's marketing strategy. At the center of the Nike Shoe Company's marketing strategy is imaginative advertising built around sports superstars such as basketball hero Michael Jordan. Doritos, from Frito-Lay, can be found in six different-sized packages. Celestial

Seasonings Tea has multiple distribution channels—grocery-store chains, wholesalers, and health food stores. For years, Compaq Computers followed a strategy for a quality image. Many makers of personal computer clones build market volume with low prices.

Kroger Grocery and the Pavilions subsidiary of Safeway introduced telephone ordering and home delivery of groceries. The aim was to appeal to working families. The SuperCuts hair styling and barbershop franchises promote low prices. Banks place automated-teller machines in all sorts of locations, from supermarkets to college campuses, to use convenience to attract customers.

Production Strategy

Functional-level production strategy involves manufacturing goods or providing services. Decisions in this area influence how the organization will compete. Such decisions include choices about plant location, inventory control method (traditional in-plant stock or just-in-time), robotics and automation, the commitment to quality and productivity, and the use of fabricators or subcontractors.

Human Resources Strategy

Many experts believe that human resources is the key functional area of an organization. Human resources strategies must address such issues as staffing, internal training and development, replacement schedules, compensation, and recruiting. Human resources strategy is certain to assume greater significance in years to come, as the nation's work force becomes increasingly diverse. From the efficient utilization of foreign-trained physicians and engineers to the transformation of trade unionism, intelligent and innovative human resources strategists can truly benefit their organizations and society as a whole as they face this era's crucial people-oriented challenges.

Financial Strategy

The financial strategy of a firm involves decisions about the actions to be taken with profits. Will the organization pay dividends to stockholders or retain earnings, for example? Other aspects of financial strategy include capital investment in the firm, how additional funds will be raised, and how debt will be handled. As the debt burden approaches a level unprecedented in commercial history, debt handling will assume increasing significance.

Research and Development Strategy

The functional-level strategy for research and development involves the invention and development of new products and services. In the tire industry, Goodyear and Michelin have invested hundreds of millions of dollars in research and development. Others, such as Cooper Tire and Rubber, choose to let others take the lead and to minimize investments in R&D (Taylor, April 6, 1992).

For functional-level strategies to succeed, the planning efforts in individual areas must be integrated. The development of Chrysler's K cars would not have been possible without total integration of finance (funds), human resources (engineering talent), production (manufacturing capability), and marketing (promotional ideas and timing).

Strategy Implementation and Corporate Culture

After the strategy is developed, the challenge facing management is implementation. Many experts argue that strategy implementation is the most difficult and important element of the strategic process. No matter how creative and well formulated the strategy, the organization receives no benefit unless it is implemented—and implemented correctly. Implementation depends mightily upon the fit between the two central organizational foundations: strategy and culture. The implementation of strategy may require changes in the organization's behavior and culture. Chapter 9 will consider corporate culture in detail. For now, look again at Exhibit 5.2 to review the steps of the strategic planning process. Note that step 5, the step in which strategy is implemented, calls for the union of the key elements of an organization's culture: leadership, structure, people, and information (Galbraith and Kazanjian, 1986).

Leadership

When implementing strategy, leadership involves the ability to persuade others in the organization to adopt the behaviors needed to put the strategy into action. Top-level managers face the challenge of convincing people in the organization to accept new values and new ways. To accomplish this, they might choose to involve middle- and low-level managers in the strategy formulation process—that is, they

American workers rate "important and meaningful work" above high income and job security. American business must learn to involve workers so that jobs fulfill these personal needs.

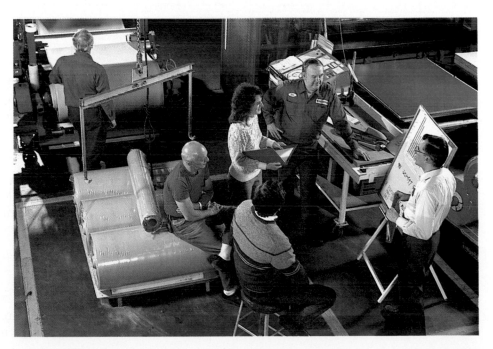

GLOBAL APPLICATIONS
Arvin Achieves World-Class Performance

o global—that's the cry heard by managers and executives across the country. But saying and doing are two different things. Managers who wish to expand markets to capture a share of the international pie need to plan effective strategies at all levels. Just ask James Baker, chairman of Arvin Industries, an auto parts manufacturer headquartered in Columbus, Indiana.

Back in the early 1980s, Arvin was a loose collection of unrelated industries—consumer electronics here, portable heaters there, and laminated panels elsewhere. The biggest share of the business was parts for auto exhaust systems—mufflers and catalytic converters. The auto exhaust business generated 60% of the company's sales. But Arvin faced danger. Arvin sold its auto parts to GM, Ford, and Chrysler, and all those companies were watching their market shares plummet. Baker and other executives developed a plan: Focus on auto parts and expand Arvin's reach by selling to international markets. They tailored their approach to suit each market. In Latin America, they acquired existing plants. In Europe, they bought four different companies and built their own factories in Britain and the Netherlands. In Japan, Baker cultivated personal relationships—a hallmark of Japanese style.

To fund these moves, the company had to take on debt, which lowered short-term profits and dividends. Wages for domestic workers decreased. Baker cut the hourly rate from $11 to $8 to help reduce costs and give the company competitive prices. As he put it, "We had to globalize the wage structure."

But Baker's plans should pay off in the long run. About 33% of the company's sales now come from overseas, and the company is well positioned to take advantage of an expected boom in catalytic converters in Europe, where new environmental regulations may force auto makers to install the devices. As a result of Arvin's moves, one securities analyst predicts that the company's earnings will rise 20% per year in the first half of the 1990s. That's world-class performance. ▲

For more on Arvin's global strategy, see Peter Nulty, "A Quick Course in Going Global," *Fortune,* January 13, 1992, p. 64.

---

might build coalitions to persuade them to support the change. The relations between the U.S. President and Congress in recent decades vividly illustrate the importance of enlisting the support of all elements in an organization before change—or even day-to-day business—can be conducted effectively.

Organizational Structure

The implementation of strategy can be assisted by changes in the structure of the organization as reflected in its organizational chart. Managers can facilitate new strategies by changing reporting relationships, creating new departments or work units, and providing the opportunity for independent decision making. Chapter 8 will focus on organizational structure.

Human Resources

An organization's human resources are its people. To achieve the company's strategic objectives, the human resource function recruits, selects, trains, transfers, promotes, lays off, and fires people. To implement its new strategies, Apple is relying heavily on Apple Magic—the long-proven ability of its people to adapt, perform, and enjoy a challenge. Chapter 10 will explore human resources.

Information and Control Systems

Management must create a proper blend of reward systems, policies, procedures, rules, incentives, information systems, and budgets to support strategy implementation. All these elements constitute information and control systems. The members of an organization must receive rewards for adhering to a new system and making it successful (Gupta and Govindarajan, 1984). Chapter 19 will explore information systems; Chapter 16 will discuss control techniques.

Future Trends

Probably the greatest business challenge of the 1990s will not be developing a global strategic plan but finding the tools to implement it. The best strategy in the world, once formulated and written down, becomes little more than a blueprint in the file cabinet if the organization isn't structured to achieve it.

By following six suggestions, managers can create organizations that implement new strategic plans effectively (Dupuy, 1992):

- Build a fluid, dynamic organization. Organizations must be able to respond to the need for geographical flexibility. Central guidance, along with localized decision making, supports the strategic plan.

- Create mechanisms to respond to revolutionary change. Typically, organizations are structured to handle routine and evolutionary situations and have a hard time coping with unforeseen competition. Businesses can succeed by opening themselves to major changes and capitalizing on them.

- Keep specialization to a minimum. Overspecialization has caused many problems in American and European companies, including organizational inflexibility, lost identity of the end product, and underutilization of the capabilities of the individual. Most people value diversity; companies must find ways to provide it, to maximize creativity and productivity.

- Draft the best player. When hiring, select the best all-around candidate— not necessarily the person who fits the current job requirement. Hire long-term potential. Toyota follows this principle. Applicants selected after undergoing Toyota's rigorous selection process receive extensive training and then work in many jobs during their lifelong career with the company.

- Develop from within; stimulate from without. Filling positions from within the organization produces high morale and reinforces company culture. Hiring from outside can be an effective way of dramatically changing the internal environment. New people can help bring about an outcome that is totally new to the company.

- Encourage everyone to take full responsibility. Individual goals should be linked to functional areas. U.S. and European firms have failed to link the goals of the individual with the goals of the organization. In worldwide competition, everyone must act as if he or she is responsible for everything.

C H A P T E R   S U M M A R Y

- Strategic planning is the set of processes and actions that chart an organization's long-term course to achieve a superior competitive fit in the environment.

- A strategy, or plan of action, has four elements: scope, resource deployment, distinctive competitive advantage, and synergy.

- The responsibility for strategic planning depends on the organization. Some corporations have strategic planning groups, but most often strategic management is delegated to line managers.

- Strategy formulation involves developing the company's strategic plans; strategy implementation involves executing them.

- Strategic planning involves three levels of strategy: corporate, business, and functional.

- The strategic planning process involves six steps: (1) a manager's evaluation of the organization's current mission, objectives, and strategies; (2) an analysis of the internal and external environments; (3) the reassessment of the organization's mission and objectives; (4) the formulation of strategies to accomplish the objectives; (5) implementation of the strategies; and (6) the monitoring and evaluation of the results.

- Corporate-level strategies involve defining an overall strategic direction and then balancing strategic business units in a portfolio strategy. There are five basic grand strategies: growth, integration, diversification, retrenchment, and stability.

- A strategic business unit (SBU) has its own mission, its own market, its own competitors, and its own product line. The BCG matrix helps managers chart SBUs by classifying them along two axes: market growth rate and market share.

- Business-level strategies are formed within each business unit and for single-product firms that are not broken down by SBUs. The focus of these strategies is on how to compete.

- Adaptive strategies—prospector, defender, analyzer, and reactor— try to match organizational assets to the external environment.

- Competitive strategies—differentiation, cost-leadership, and focus—suggest how to compete.

- Functional-level strategy involves the plans of action developed by the major functional departments: marketing, production, human resources, finance, and research and development.

- The implementation of strategy is the most difficult and important part of the strategic planning process. Implementation is achieved by changing management's leadership approach, organizational structure, human resources, and information and control systems.

S K I L L - **B** U I L D I N G

The following activities are designed to let you apply the concepts of strategic planning. As you answer the questions, consider a company for which you work now or worked previously or the college you are attending. If you prefer, select another organization about which you have enough information to make reasonable speculations. Complete the activities in sequence.

1. Draft a statement defining the mission of the company.

2. Assess the environment by performing a SWOT analysis for the business.

3. Draft a statement defining the business's current grand strategy.

4. Draft a statement that defines an objective you would like the company to achieve in the next two years. Write a strategy for achieving it.

5. Draft a statement describing how to implement the strategy you developed in exercise 4. List any changes that implementation will require.

R E V I E W   **Q** U E S T I O N S

1. Review this chapter's essential terms and look up the meanings of those you cannot define.

2. What is the purpose of strategic planning?

3. On what issues does strategy formulation focus? On what issues does strategy implementation focus?

4. What steps are involved in the strategic planning process?

5. Why is it important to assess the internal and external environments in strategic planning? What four factors are assessed?

6. What kinds of information are helpful in the strategic planning process?

7. What is the difference between corporate-level strategies for growth, retrenchment, and stability?

8. What is the purpose of the BCG matrix in the development of business-level plans? What factors are considered?

9. What are three of the five functional-level areas of planning?

10. What four factors do managers manipulate to implement strategy?

R E C O M M E N D E D   R E A D I N G

Altier, William. "Strategic Thinking for Today's Corporate Battles," *Management Review* (February 1992), pp. 20–21.

Bangs, David H. *Managing by the Numbers: Financial Essentials for the Growing Business* (Dover, NH: Upstart), 1991.

Beddow, John W. *Management Strategies & Tactics* (Iowa City, IA: Shape Tech Ltd.), 1991.

Graham, Pauline. *Integrative Management: Creating Unity from Diversity* (Cambridge, MA: Blackwell, Basil), 1991.

Holbrook, Stephen F. *Effective Planning,* 6th edition (Bellemead, NJ: Princeton Management Association), 1991.

Kanter, Rosabeth Moss. "Six Certainties for CEOs," *Harvard Business Review* (March–April 1992), pp. 7–8.

McGregor, Eugene. *Strategic Management of Human Knowledge, Skills, & Abilities* (San Francisco: Jossey-Bass), 1991.

Reimann, B. C. "Challenging Conventional Wisdom: Corporate Strategies That Work," *Planning Review* (January–February 1992), pp. 38–45.

Seiger, Joseph M. "Manage Your Numbers to Match Your Strategy," *Management Review* (February 1992), pp. 46–47.

Stalk, George; Philip Evans; and Lawrence Shuman. "Competing on Capabilities: The New Rules of Corporate Strategy," *Harvard Business Review* (March–April 1992), pp. 57–69.

R E F E R E N C E S

Daft, Richard L. *Management,* 2nd edition (Homewood, IL: Dryden Press), 1991, p. 154.

Dupuy, John. "Learning to Manage World-Class Strategy," *Management Review* (June 1992), pp. 40–42.

Galbraith, Jay R., and Robert Kazanjian. *Strategy Implementation: Structure Systems and Process,* 2nd edition (St. Paul, MN: West), 1986.

Gnoffo, Anthony Jr. "Taking Flight Simulators for a Ride," *Philadelphia Inquirer,* August 30, 1992, pp. DI, D7.

Gupta, Anil K., and V. Govindarajan. "Business Unit Strategy, Managerial Characteristics, and Business Unit Effectiveness at Strategy Implementation," *Academy of Management Journal* 29 (March 1984), pp. 25–41; and Bourgeois III, L. J., and David R. Brodwin. "Strategic Implementation: Five Approaches to an Elusive Phenomenon," *Strategic Management Journal* 5 (October–December 1984), pp. 241–264.

Hall, Cheryl. "Golden Quest," *Dallas Morning News,* May 31, 1992, pp. 1H, 8H.

Hill, Charles W. L., and Gareth R. Jones. *Strategic Management: An Analytical Approach* (Boston: Houghton Mifflin), 1989 [a review].

Holt, David H. *Management: Principles and Practices,* 2nd edition (Englewood Cliffs, NJ: Prentice-Hall), 1990, p. 174.

Jacob, Rahul. "What Selling Will Be Like in the 90s," *Fortune* (January 13, 1992), p. 63.

Lii, Jane H. "In the Cut-Throat World of Ice Cream, Flavormania," *New York Times,* August 7, 1992, p. F7.

Magness, Myron. "Meet the New Revolutionaries," *Fortune* (February 24, 1992), p. 97.

Miles, Raymond E., and Charles C. Snow. *Organizational Strategy, Structure, and Process* (New York: McGraw-Hill), 1978.

Mitchell, Jim, and Jennifer Tiles. "Challenging the Imagination," *Dallas Morning News,* May 17, 1992, p. K3.

Porter, Michael E. *Competitive Strategy: Techniques for Analyzing Industries and Competitors* (New York: Free Press), 1980, pp. 36–46.

Prescott, John E. "Environment: As the Moderator of the Relationship Between Strategy and Performance," *Academy of Management Journal* 29 (1986), pp. 329–346.

Taylor, Alex. "Can GM Remodel," *Fortune* (January 13, 1992), p. 27.

Taylor, Alex. "Now Hear This, Jack Welch," *Fortune* (April 6, 1992), pp. 94–95.

Welles, Edward O. "Captain Marvel," *Inc.* (January 1992), pp. 44–46.

Wrapp, Edward. "Good Managers Don't Make Policy Decisions," *Harvard Business Review* (September–October 1967).

GLOSSARY OF TERMS

analyzer strategy A business-level strategy based on maintaining the current market share while innovating in some markets.

Boston Consulting Group (BCG) matrix A planning tool that groups strategic business units into categories based on market growth rate and market share.

business-level strategy The kind of plan that focuses on how each product line or business unit within an organization competes.

corporate-level strategy The kind of plan that charts the course of business for the entire organization.

cost-leadership strategy A business-level strategy that focuses on keeping costs as low as possible through efficient operations and tight controls.

defender strategy A business-level strategy based on holding the current market share or even retrenching.

differentiation strategy   A business-level strategy that attempts to set the organization's products or services apart from those of other companies.

distinctive competitive advantage   An element of strategy that identifies the unique position the organization has in relationship to its competition.

diversification strategy   A corporate-level strategy that allows the company to move into new products or markets.

focus strategy   A business-level strategy in which an organization targets a specific market.

functional-level strategy   The kind of plan that details the activities of the organization's major functional departments.

grand strategy   The overall plan of action developed at the corporate level to achieve an organization's objectives.

growth strategy   A corporate-level strategy adopted when managers of an organization want to create high levels of growth.

horizontal integration   A strategy to consolidate competition by acquiring similar products or services.

integration strategy   A corporate-level strategy adopted when managers see a need to stabilize supply lines, reduce costs, or consolidate competition.

portfolio strategy   A strategy focused on determining the proper mix of business units and product lines that fit together to provide a maximum competitive advantage.

prospector strategy   A business-level strategy based on innovation, risk, the pursuit of opportunities, and expansion.

reactor strategy   A business-level approach in which a business does not adopt a strategy, but responds to environmental threats randomly.

resource deployment   An element of strategy that defines how managers of a company intend to allocate its resources to achieve objectives.

retrenchment strategy   A corporate-level strategy adopted when managers of an organization want to reduce the size or scope of activities.

scope   An element of strategy that specifies the size or position managers want a firm to have in the environment.

situation analysis   A search for an organization's strengths, weaknesses, opportunities, and threats (SWOT). The search forms part of the strategic planning process.

stability strategy   A corporate-level strategy adopted when managers of an organization want it to remain the same.

strategic business unit (SBU)   An autonomous business division operating within a corporation. An SBU has its own competitors, market, and product line.

strategic management   Top-level management's responsibility for defining the firm's position, formulating strategies, and guiding long-term organizational activities.

strategic planning The decision-making and planning processes that chart an organization's long-term course of action.

strategy formulation The processes associated with the planning and decision making that go into developing a company's strategic objectives and strategic plans.

strategy implementation The processes associated with executing the strategic plan.

synergy When two forces, working together, create an effort that is greater than the sum of what either force could produce alone.

vertical integration A strategy focused on gaining ownership of resources, supplies, or distributive systems that relate to a company's business.

C A S E P R O B L E M
The Strategic Trap

Mentor Graphics Corporation of Wilsonville, Oregon, was the brainchild of a group of engineer-MBAs. Founded in April 1981, the company defined its mission as the development of computer-aided products. These products included computer-aided engineering (CAE) devices, tools that automated the production of schematic drawings for engineers who designed complex integrated circuits and printed circuit boards.

With enthusiasm Mentor Graphics sped off in pursuit of its vision—to become the leader in six businesses: computer-aided engineering, computer-aided design, computer-aided software engineering, computer-aided publishing, computer-aided electronic packaging, and computer-aided circuit testing. What Mentor Graphics did not do in the pursuit of the vision was to figure exactly how these outcomes were to be achieved. Where would the technology, the people, the skills, and the talent come from? Where would Mentor find the capital to invest in all these businesses? Which business would be the primary target initially?

The founders understood the vision, shared it, and admired it, but they soon found out that the vision created unmistakable hurdles. Each business had an appetite for financial resources that had to

be satisfied. The team found itself making decisions to satiate these appetites rather than to satisfy the company's business requirements. Resources were allocated according to the squeaky-wheel concept rather than an analysis of potential. Under this strain, the business began to deteriorate. Worse, it degenerated from the bottom up, as middle managers came to understand that the resources needed to lift their business into leadership were not in place and never would be. Middle managers and their subordinates began to leave the company.

Q U E S T I O N S

1. What does the case of Mentor Graphics tell about the importance of strategic planning?

2. Judging from the history of Mentor Graphics, what step or steps in the strategic planning process were completed?

3. What plan of action would you have recommended for the founders of Mentor Graphics?

For more on the strategic trap, see Gerard H. Langeler, "The Vision Trap," *Harvard Business Review* (March–April, 1992) pp. 46–55.

6 Making Decisions

LEARNING OBJECTIVES

After reading and discussing this chapter, you should be able to:

- Define the chapter's essential terms

- Recognize elements of decision making at all management levels

- Distinguish between formal and informal approaches to decision making

- Describe the steps in the decision-making process

- Describe the factors that influence decision making

- Identify and describe the personal attributes that influence decision making

- Discuss the value of group decision making and identify three techniques of group decision making

- Explain three quantitative techniques for decision making and describe the situations in which each is appropriate

- Describe strategies a manager can use to create a more effective decision-making environment

MANAGEMENT IN ACTION
The Right Decisions at Cooper Tire & Rubber

Although close to forty U.S. tire plants have closed since the 1970s, Cooper Tire & Rubber of Findlay, Ohio, keeps rolling. Its operations are so well managed that since 1985 it has taken on no new private-brand customers, as other major tire producers have had to do. (These private-brand customers provide the tire producers with additional revenue.) Furthermore, all seven of the quality-conscious Japanese car manufacturers that produce cars in the United States buy Cooper rubber products.

The company's stockholders have been winners too. Among Fortune 500 industrial companies, Cooper ranks 28th in total return to investors since 1980. (General Electric ranks 104th.)

The consistent success of Cooper Tire & Rubber stems from the ability of CEO Ivan Gorr to make the right decisions in all facets of the

Making all the right decisions, the management of Cooper Tire & Rubber sells smart and keeps its plants running at full capacity.

operation—marketing, manufacturing, and research and development. Unlike other major tire manufacturers, Gorr refuses to compete for low-profit sales. This means that he does not try to convince auto makers to use Cooper tires as original equipment on new cars. Instead, Gorr decided to concentrate on the replacement market (often called the aftermarket). The aftermarket for tires is three times larger than the original-equipment market. And, because cars are more durable now than in the past, the aftermarket is growing faster than the original-equipment market because people are keeping their cars longer.

Gorr made another decision: not to establish a company retail chain, as Goodyear and Bridgestone/Firestone have. Instead, Cooper distributes half its production as private-label merchandise. The other half goes to independent dealers, who account for 67% of replacement-tire sales.

In manufacturing, top-level managers made two significant decisions. First, Cooper's plants run at 100% capacity. (Those of other tire makers operate at 80% capacity.) Second, when Cooper needs to add capacity, it does so cheaply by buying old plants and refurbishing them. Refurbishing old factories costs less than building new ones.

In regard to research and development, Gorr and his senior advisors have decided to chart a safe course.

▶ The consistent success of Cooper Tire & Rubber stems from the ability of CEO Ivan Gorr to make the right decisions in all facets of the operation.

Instead of pioneering its own designs, Cooper managers often wait to see which new designs sell well as original equipment. Because new tires last up to four years, Cooper has time to produce its own version for the aftermarket.

For Ivan Gorr and Cooper Tire & Rubber, the challenge is to keep making the right decisions. ▲

For more on Cooper Tire & Rubber, see Alex Taylor, "Now Hear This, Jack Welch," *Fortune,* April 6, 1992, pp. 94–95.

What You Need to Know About Decisions

For each of us, the complex business of living that constitutes a unique life results from countless decisions—our own and those of others. Decisions range from routine and trivial to profound and historic. Should I take my umbrella? Is the defendant guilty or not guilty? Should we drop an atomic bomb?

Regardless of significance or complexity, a **decision** is a judgment reached after consideration, a choice made from available alternatives (Daft, 1991). An **alternative** is a potential course of action that is likely to eliminate or correct a problem or maximize an opportunity.

Managers face an array of decisions. But unlike most individual choices, the decisions that managers face can profoundly influence the lives of thousands of people. Consider the decision of whether to create an automobile division. Managers at General Motors faced this question in the early '80s, when they considered whether to create the Saturn division in Spring Hill, Tennessee. They decided to go ahead with the project. By 1991 some 6,000 people were earning almost $310 million there, and the company's supply purchases in Michigan and Tennessee exceeded $1.5 billion (LeFauve, 1992). Conversely, managers at IBM, Sears, General Motors, and Pratt & Whitney recently had to decide whether to downsize operations. Personnel layoffs in the early 1990s put hundreds of thousands of people out of work, thus ending career plans and disrupting families and communities nationwide.

This chapter will examine the decision-making process, the nature of the decision-making environment, influences on decision making, decision-making techniques, and how managers can create an environment for effective decision making. Fearful of making mistakes, many people avoid and delay decisions. But as you discover that making decisions is a rational process that can be learned and mastered, you acquire two keys to management success: decision-making skills and the confidence to use them.

What Decision Making Is

Decision making is the process of identifying problems and opportunities, developing alternative solutions, choosing a preferred alternative, and then implementing it (Holt, 1990). Decision making is a process—decisions don't come out of nowhere, like lightning bolts. In making a decision, the manager reaches a conclusion based on the evaluation of options or alternatives. In ordinary usage, a **problem** is any issue raised for the purpose of inquiry, consideration, solution, or decision making. Managers often use the word to refer to a current condition that is not a desired or preferred condition. Keep in mind that in business, as in life, one person's problem may be another's eagerly sought outcome.

In management the terms *decision making* and *problem solving* are often used interchangeably because managers constantly make decisions to solve problems. For example, when an account representative resigns at MCI Communications, the sales manager faces a problem. The vacancy calls for the manager to decide which of several alternatives to choose: The manager could reassign the rep's clients or replace the rep by promoting from within, hiring an experienced sales rep, or recruiting an inexperienced college graduate. Each alternative could solve the problem.

Problem Solving and Opportunity Management

Not all decision making is aimed at solving problems. Many decisions are made to seize opportunities. An **opportunity** is a chance for progress or advancement whose realization requires that a decision be made. The history of business is filled with examples of managers who saw opportunity and seized it. At the beginning of the twentieth century, managers at Sears, Roebuck saw the opportunity presented by the lack of rural retail stores. They seized the opportunity by developing catalogue sales. In 1954, the Boeing Company and Pan American World Airways saw the opportunity presented by available technology and a waiting market. They introduced the Boeing 707, the tremendously successful passenger jetliner. Managers at Toyota, Datsun, and Honda saw the energy-crisis years of the early 1970s as an opportunity. By manufacturing small, fuel-efficient cars, these foreign auto makers captured large chunks of the U.S. market.

The Universality of Decision Making

Recall from Chapter 1 that decision making is a part of all managers' jobs. A manager makes decisions constantly while planning, organizing, staffing, directing, and controlling. Decision making is not a separate, isolated function of management but a core activity common to the other functions.

Managers at all levels engage in decision making. The decisions made by top managers deal with the mission of the organization and strategies for achieving it. The decisions of top managers affect the whole organization. Middle-level managers focus their decision making on implementing the strategies and on budget and resource allocations. To first-level managers fall the continual decisions about day-to-day operations.

Managers make decisions large and small every day. Although the process of decision making is often so routine that managers do not notice it, decision making is a definable process.

Approaches to Decision Making

Because problems and opportunities are seldom identical, a manager's approach to decision making varies. A manager can resolve relatively simple problems and recurring problems by following prior patterns. Complex or uncertain problems benefit from formal decision-making processes. Circumstances determine the appropriate technique, or whether the decision should be a programmed or a nonprogrammed one.

Programmed Decisions   **Programmed decisions** apply to problems and situations that occur so often that the circumstances and solutions are predictable. Programmed decisions are made in response to recurring organizational activities. When the need for a programmed decision arises, managers often turn to formal procedures that outline the appropriate response. The decision, in these cases, is to follow standard procedure. Inventory reordering at Wal-Mart, handling blizzard-delayed flights at O'Hare Airport, processing student-aid applications in a college admissions office, and inaugurating a President are examples of activities that result from programmed decisions. Exhibit 6.1 models a programmed decision for processing a payroll.

Nonprogrammed Decisions   **Nonprogrammed decisions** are made in response to problems and opportunities that present unique circumstances and have unpredictable results and important consequences. Managers make nonprogrammed decisions in situations that are unprecedented and partially defined. To make such complex and significant choices effectively, managers follow a rigorous decision-making process.

The Seven-Step Decision-Making Process

In the first year of law school, aspiring attorneys learn to manipulate the elements of the legal environment and think like lawyers. Physicians in the making begin to think like doctors in their clinical residencies. The training for managers is more varied than training for lawyers or doctors. Few experts would, however, dispute the need for serious management candidates to learn to think like managers.

At the core of such thinking lies mastery of the decision-making process. If you master the habits of mind represented in the seven steps of Exhibit 6.2, you will be equipped to contribute meaningfully to any organization. Beyond the workplace, the process can enrich every aspect of daily life by imparting balance and order. The sections that follow will discuss each step of the decision-making process.

Exhibit 6.1

A programmed-decision outline for completing a routine payroll.

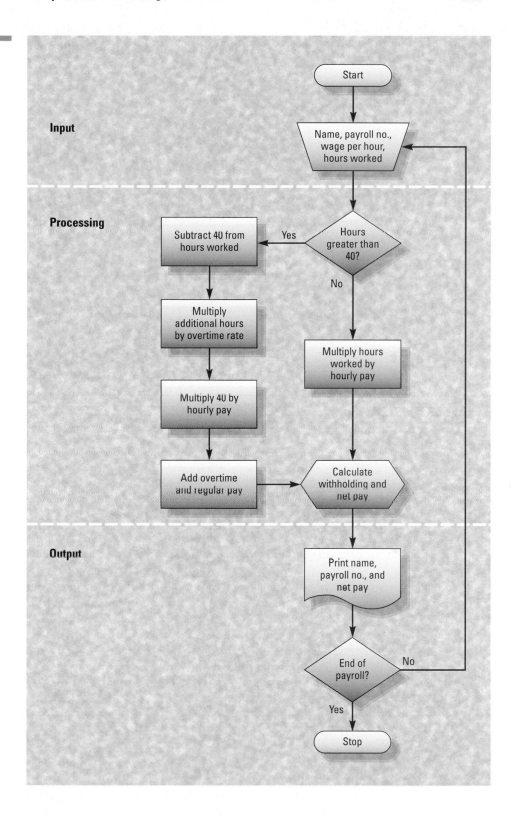

Exhibit 6.2

The decision-making process.

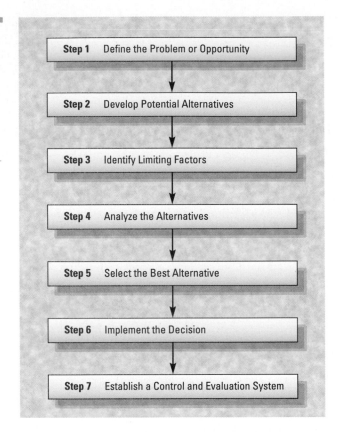

Step 1	Define the Problem or Opportunity
Step 2	Develop Potential Alternatives
Step 3	Identify Limiting Factors
Step 4	Analyze the Alternatives
Step 5	Select the Best Alternative
Step 6	Implement the Decision
Step 7	Establish a Control and Evaluation System

Define the Problem or Opportunity

Recognize at the outset that six of the seven steps in decision making are analytical. They require the separation of the whole matter into its constituent parts for individual study. Before the relationships among parts and how they affect one another can be determined, they must themselves be clearly understood.

Understanding requires adequate definition of the facts and substance that make up the problem or opportunity. Adequate definition depends upon a clear, distinct, and precise determination and statement of the problem's nature and limits. This means that even before beginning the decision-making process, a manager must gather the necessary information. As with most sequential endeavors, this initial step determines the effectiveness of each step that follows it and influences the quality of the decision.

The wise manager carefully discards false or misleading definitions. If the company's dwindling market share is caused by low product quality, for example, hiring more sales representatives will probably compound the problem. The manager must also differentiate between symptom and problem. In the case of dwindling market share, the symptom is decreasing market and the problem is poor quality. **Symptoms** alert the manager to the need to seek the cause, the actual problem.

To isolate and define the problem, a manager will observe keenly and ask the right questions. According to Peter Drucker, "The most common source of mistakes

Exhibit 6.3

The funnel approach to defining a problem.

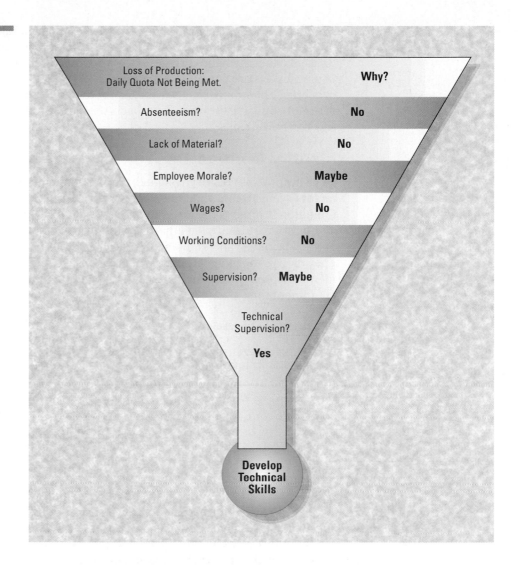

in management decisions is the emphasis on finding the right answer rather than the right questions" (Drucker, 1954). In the process of asking questions, the manager gathers relevant and timely data about the problem. Wise managers are attuned to the work environment—to what is happening on the factory floor and in the offices and with the field representatives and sales staff. Management expert Tom Peters suggests that a manager's most relevant and accurate information source is the people in the workplace (Peters, 1990).

To assist in defining the problem, the focus of managers' questions should narrow from the most general to the most targeted. The process is called the funnel approach, and Exhibit 6.3 illustrates it in terms of a problem of unmet production quotas.

A manager begins the funnel approach by asking questions to identify the real problem, not just the symptom. Are hours worked decreasing? No, degree of absenteeism is normal. Is the material needed for operations unavailable? No, material is flowing at a normal pace. How is employee morale? Are there complaints or concerns? Well, as a matter of fact, there are some rumors of discontent. Are workers concerned about wages? No. Working conditions? No. Is it supervision? Some workers are concerned about the supervision they receive. What are their concerns? The supervisor does not answer their questions about technical aspects of the job. By using the funnel approach, the manager discovers that the supervisor lacks technical skills.

Identify Limiting Factors

Once the problem has been defined, the manager must identify applicable **limiting factors**—constraints that rule out certain alternative solutions. One common limitation is time. If a new product must be on dealers' shelves in one month, an alternative requiring longer than one month is eliminated. Resources—personnel, money, facilities, and equipment, as well as time—are common limiting factors. They narrow the range of possible alternatives. At Cooper Tire & Rubber, Ivan Gorr identified profitability goals as a limiting factor in his decision not to sell original-equipment tires to auto makers.

Develop Potential Alternatives

Now the manager searches out, identifies, develops, and lists as many potential alternatives as possible. Each alternative should eliminate, correct, or neutralize the problem or maximize the opportunity. Alternative solutions for a manager faced with the problem of maintaining a production schedule may be to add an extra work shift, to regularly schedule overtime, to increase the size of the present work force by hiring employees, or to do nothing. Doing nothing about a problem is sometimes the proper alternative, at least until the situation has been thoroughly analyzed. Occasionally the passing of time provides a cure. Deep-seated or long-term problems, however, are unlikely to solve themselves.

Sources for alternatives include the manager's experience, other persons whose opinions and judgments the decision maker respects, the practice of successful managers (both inside and outside the firm), and group opinions obtained through the use of task forces, committees, and focus groups. (This chapter will discuss group decision making later.)

***Alternatives** must be explored before a final decision is made. Group opinions formed by task forces, committees, and focus groups can augment the manager's own experience.*

While building the list of alternatives, the manager avoids being critical or judgmental about any ideas that arise. Censorship needlessly limits the number and variety of alternatives developed. Initially, each projected alternative should offer a distinct and separate solution to the problem or strategy to seize the opportunity. Insufficiently differentiated alternatives only blur analysis. After the initial brainstorming process (which will be outlined later in this chapter), variations of the listed ideas will begin to crystalize and combinations will emerge.

In developing alternatives, the goal is to be as creative and wide ranging as possible. Any action for which only one alternative can be devised is by definition not a decision. With only one choice, a bad decision is likely.

Analyze the Alternatives

By evaluating the relative merits of each alternative, the manager is able to identify the advantages and disadvantages of each. The manager should pose two questions: Does the alternative fit within the limiting factors? and What are the consequences of using this alternative?

Any alternative inconsistent with the established limiting factors must be discarded or revised. For example, suppose a department must produce 1,000 motors by the end of the month—500 more than the normal quota—and it must do so with no more than a $10,000 increase for employee wages. One alternative is to schedule overtime at night and on Saturdays. On evaluation, however, the manager calculates that overtime will yield the 1,000 units, but at a cost of $17,000. The alternative exceeds the limiting factor, cost. Therefore, the manager must reject that alternative or combine it with another. Note the fates of Alternatives 1 and 2 in Exhibit 6.4.

Second, the manager must consider the consequences of implementation. Some alternatives may fall within the guidelines set by the limiting factors but

Exhibit 6.4

Analyzing alternatives.

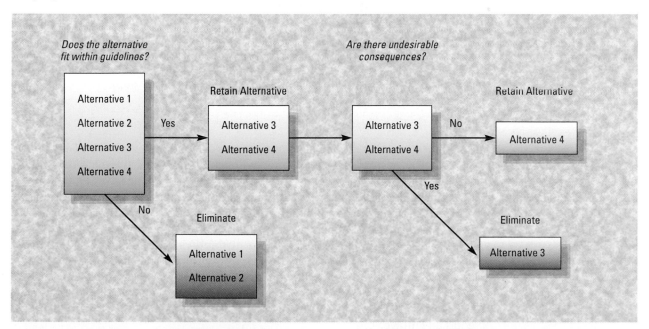

generate undesirable consequences. One alternative to increase output may be to invest in a new computer system; the money to fund the system, however, must come from other departments. Even though the alternative solves the problem, the political difficulties it raises and the morale problems it causes may require the manager to eliminate it.

Depending on the type of problem, the manager's analysis of the alternatives can utilize one or more tools: nonquantitative methods, such as experience and intuition; and quantitative methods, such as payback analysis, decision trees, and simulations. This chapter will discuss each of these in detail.

Select the Best Alternative

By this point, the alternatives have been listed with their corresponding advantages and disadvantages. The best choice offers the fewest serious disadvantages and the most advantages. Sometimes that choice combines the best elements of several alternatives. Consider Richard Stegemeier's decisive actions in 1990, when he was named president and CEO of Unocal, the Los Angeles–based petroleum company. To solve the problem of Unocal's crippling $6.1-billion debt, Stegemeier (1) sold nonessential real estate, including the company headquarters; (2) disposed of Canadian mining operations; (3) closed unprofitable service stations; (4) suspended operations at the money-losing Beaumont Refinery in Texas; and (5) signed an agreement to transfer the Chicago refining operations and related marketing assets to a joint venture with the national petroleum company of Venezuela (Murray, 1991).

Implement the Decision

Although managers are paid to make decisions, they are also paid to get results. A decision that just sits there, without implementation, may as well never have been made. For implementation to be successful, everyone involved must know what to do, how to do it, why, and when. For success, implementation must be as sound as the decision itself. Rather than solving problems, a good alternative halfheartedly implemented often creates them. Those involved in implementing decisions must be convinced of the importance of their roles. In addition, managers must establish programs, procedures, rules, and policies that effectively support the decision.

Establish a Control and Evaluation System

The final step in the decision-making process is to create a control and evaluation system. This system should provide feedback on how well the decision is being implemented, what the positive and negative results are, and what adjustments are necessary to obtain the results desired. The implementation of a decision often generates new problems or opportunities that require new decisions. An evaluation system can help identify those outcomes.

Because the process mandates care in identifying and evaluating alternatives, following the process tends to produce quality choices. The orderly steps allow the decision maker to proceed with confidence, knowing that important points have not been overlooked. The creation of a control system helps ensure that the decision is effectively implemented and that subsequent outcomes are turned to good advantage.

Evaluation of management decisions is the final step in the process and often reveals new problems or opportunities that require a new cycle of decisions.

To make successful decisions, the manager must understand thoroughly the environment in which decision making is undertaken.

Environmental Influences on Decision Making

Decision making, like planning, cannot be separated from other management functions. Many factors in the environment affect the process.

The Degree of Certainty

In some situations, the manager has nearly perfect knowledge of what to do and what the consequences of the action will be. In others, no such knowledge exists. Decisions are made under three conditions, each requiring different responses: certainty, risk, and uncertainty.

In conditions of certainty, the manager enjoys what is called perfect knowledge: the circumstances have been encountered before, the alternatives are known, and the consequences of each are predictable and fully understood. In such situations the manager simply chooses the alternative known to achieve the best results; the manager can rely on a policy or standing plan. Under conditions of certainty, decisions—typical programmed decisions—are a matter of routine.

Risk generates a more complex environment in which the manager knows the problem and the alternatives but cannot be certain of the consequences of each. In other words, risk accompanies each alternative. Suppose, for example, that a manager must choose one person from among three candidates for a position. All come from inside the company and their performance history is known. All three worked in unrelated jobs, however, so their performance capacity in the new position is unknown. After extensive interviewing, the manager must make a decision. A dilemma arises because each candidate displays strengths but none appears perfectly matched to the job. Although successful performance in the new position seems probable for each candidate, a degree of risk pertains to each as well. Candidate B, for example, has a good track record but has alienated fellow workers to achieve goals. The manager gives a success probability of 65% to this candidate.

Uncertainty creates the most difficult decision-making conditions for a manager. In conditions of uncertainty, a manager becomes something of a pioneer charting unknown territory. The manager cannot determine exact outcomes because too many variables exist, too few facts are known, or both. Uncertainty deepens if the manager cannot identify all the possible alternatives to be considered.

To illustrate, picture a person who has just been promoted into a management position. On the first day an employee reports that a shipment to a highly valued customer has not arrived. The customer needs the goods—now! The manager can identify two alternatives: Send another shipment (but delivery will take three days) or wait to see if the goods arrive today. Unfortunately, the probability that either alternative will satisfy the customer is uncertain, and there may be other alternatives the manager has not considered. What can be done? Reliance on experience and judgment—one's own and others'—can help the manager identify alternatives and assess their merits.

Imperfect Resources

Managers would like to make perfect decisions. To accomplish that lofty goal they need limitless information, time, personnel, equipment, and supplies. But managers operate in an imperfect environment that seldom provides ideal resources.

Real-world managers do not always have, for example, the time they need to collect all the information they desire about a problem. They do not always have the capital to fund the perfect fleet, the ultimate CAD system, or the most lavishly equipped headquarters. Faced with limits, managers choose to do something realistic, to satisfice. To **satisfice** is to make a decision based upon a minimum level of acceptability, given the information, time, and other resources available. If a manager tries always to maximize decisions, the result may be a great deal of time spent gathering information and not making the decision.

The Internal Environment

Decisions cannot solve problems or seize opportunities unless they are accepted and supported. A manager's decision-making environment is profoundly shaped by support from superiors, subordinates, and organizational systems. Likewise, lack of support can be a profound influence in the internal environment.

Superiors   Among the major factors in the manager's decision-making environment, few outrank the boss. Does the manager's superior display confidence in subordinates, want to be informed about their progress, and support logical decisions after receiving the relevant information? If so, the boss can help foster a supportive decision-making environment for subordinate managers by providing guidance and ongoing feedback.

G L O B A L   A P P L I C A T I O N S
Think Globally, Act Locally

How important can a decision be? Daniel Gill, CEO of Bausch & Lomb, made one decision that resulted in a 21% increase in total revenues and a doubling of the profit margins for his company's international business. What was this key decision? Gill decided to let local managers in foreign markets—Japan, China, India—make their own decisions.

Until the "big decision," production and marketing policies came from headquarters, in Rochester, New York. The foreign subsidiaries were treated as sales adjuncts to the U.S. division. Local managers who understood the decision-making environment were not involved in decisions in their own markets.

Under the new arrangement, the company sets the strategic goals and then lets local managers determine how to achieve those goals in their market. Turning the local managers loose has made quite a significant difference.

- In Japan, Bausch & Lomb gas-permeable contact lenses were going nowhere because Japanese ophthalmologists insisted on a lens surface manufacturered to tolerances well beyond clinical requirements. Instead of fighting these demands, the local leadership persuaded the company to build a new plant in South Korea and develop a process to manufacture lenses that met the Japanese requirements. By 1992 Bausch & Lomb had garnered 11% of the Japanese market.

- In the international market, Bausch & Lomb had failed to capitalize on the immense appeal of the firm's Ray-Ban sunglasses. Of the 25 new designs created in 1986, only one was developed for a foreign market. When local managers received additional authority, they saw to it that more than half of Ray-Ban's new products were developed for international sale in one year. Today Ray-Ban controls 40% of the world market for premium-priced ($40 to $250) sunglasses.

- In China, at the urging of local executives, Bausch & Lomb priced its contact lenses lower than anywhere else in the world. The strategy: Make money on volume. Five years later, China ranks behind only the U.S. and Japan in unit sales of Bausch & Lomb lenses. B & L's operation in China turned a profit in its second year and repaid its investment in its fourth. ▲

For more on Bausch & Lomb's international decision making, see Rahul Jacob, "Corporate Performance: Bausch & Lomb—Trust the Locals, Win Worldwide," *Fortune,* May 4, 1992, pp. 76–77.

On the other hand, insecure bosses may fear successful subordinates and jealously hoard knowledge that might help them make sound decisions. In addition, some superiors are so afraid of being held accountable for their subordinates' failures that they are reluctant to let subordinates make any decisions of consequence. In such an environment, the subordinate manager faces tough alternatives. He or she can make a long-term commitment to create a climate of mutual trust in which bosses and subordinate managers trust each other. The manager can choose to live with frustration and be ineffective as a decision maker. Or, the manager can find a more acceptable situation in another environment.

Subordinates   Subordinates affect a manager's decision-making environment in important ways. Without their subordinates' support, input, and understanding of decisions, managers cannot work effectively. The manager must evaluate the

Exhibit 6.5

Five styles of subordinate involvement.

1. The manager makes the decision with no input or assistance from subordinates, using only information available at that time.

2. The manager obtains the necessary information from subordinates and then makes the decision. While obtaining the information, the manager may or may not reveal the problem under consideration. The subordinate merely provides information; he or she does not generate or evaluate alternatives.

3. The manager discusses the situation with relevant subordinates individually, solicits input without bringing them together as a group, and then makes a decision which may or may not reflect subordinates' influence.

4. The manager involves subordinates as a group; collectively obtains their ideas and suggestions; and then makes a decision, which may or may not reflect the subordinates' influence.

5. The manager reviews the situation with the subordinates as a group. Together they generate and evaluate alternatives and attempt to reach agreement (consensus) on a solution. The manager functions as the leader of a committee; he or she does not try to influence the group to adopt a particular solution. The manager accepts and implements any reasonable solution that receives the support of the entire group.

Source: Victor H. Vroom, "A New Look at Managerial Decision Making," *Organizational Dynamics*, Spring 1973, p. 67.

level of the subordinates' involvement, which can range from zero input to full responsibility. Victor Vroom (1973) described five levels, or styles, of involvement. Exhibit 6.5 shows these styles.

Which approach should a manager use? Two criteria offered by Norman Maier (1963) influence the choice: (1) the objective quality of the decision needed and (2) the degree to which subordinate acceptance determines the decision's success. A decision has a high degree of objective quality when it was reached as the result of a logical, rational, incremental system. A decision made through the formal process illustrated in Exhibit 6.2 meets the objective quality criteria Maier suggested. Decisions whose success depends on the understanding and support of those affected by them must meet the acceptance criteria. One effective way to secure acceptance is to first solicit the input of those who would be affected. Examples include decisions about changing procedures, altering the work environment, or scheduling vacations.

How can a manager know which factors are most important in a given decision, especially when both acceptance and quality criteria apply to the same decision? Victor Vroom and Phillip Yetton have provided managers with a series of questions that guide the manager to the appropriate style. The model is the **Vroom and Yetton decision tree**, which Exhibit 6.6 illustrates. As each question is asked and answered, the manager learns more about the nature of the decision. The circled number at the end of the relevant series of questions designates the most effective decision-making method and corresponds to the numbers in Vroom's subordinate-involvement styles (see Exhibit 6.5).

As an example of how the Vroom and Yetton guide works, consider Emil, a department manager who is developing work schedules. Emil begins by asking these questions:

Exhibit 6.6

Applying the Vroom and Yetton decision tree for choosing a decision-making style.

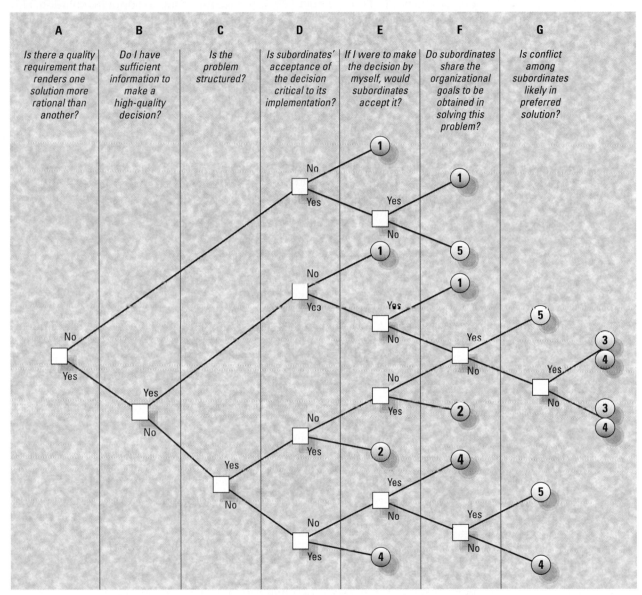

A. Is there a quality requirement that might make one solution more rational than another? Since the answer is no, Emil moves to D.

D. Is acceptance of the decision by subordinates critical to effective implementation? Since the answer is yes, Emil moves to E.

E. If Emil makes the decision alone, will subordinates be likely to accept it? Since the answer is no, Emil should use style number 5.

In other words, by applying the Vroom and Yetton decision tree, Emil learns that he should share the problem with the subordinates as a group. Together they will generate and evaluate alternatives and attempt to reach agreement (consensus) on a solution. Emil should not try to influence the group to adopt his solution, and he must be willing to accept and implement any solution that has the support of the entire group, so long as it fits within company policies. In this, as in most work environment situations, managers must collaborate with and cultivate the support of employees for decisions. Even the highest-quality decisions will not be effectively implemented if subordinates do not support them.

Organizational Systems   In the internal environment, the organizational system is another element that affects decision making. An organization's policies, procedures, programs, and rules serve as boundaries for a manager's alternatives. When these rules become obsolete or cause unreasonable delay, they are known as red tape. Outmoded systems can act as barriers to action and create problems. If such barriers exist, a manager may wisely delay a decision until the system is modified.

The External Environment

Chapter 3 observed how powerful the external environment can be in influencing a manager's actions. The external environment can be an especially powerful force in decision making. Beyond the company's own boundaries, customers, competitors, government agencies, and society at large behave with little regard to one firm's needs or wants. In 1992 the external environment had a profound impact on the decisions of John McDonnell, president of McDonnell Douglas Corporation. To strengthen his financially troubled aerospace company, McDonnell had been seeking an alliance with an overseas firm. Months of negotiations had produced a tentative agreement in which Taiwan Aerosapce Corporation would buy 40% of McDonnell Douglas. McDonnell Douglas would receive $2 billiion to develop new planes. Several U.S. senators raised questions about the effect of the alliance on national security, however, and the decision to sell to Taiwan Aerospace was derailed (Verespej, 1992).

The Influence of Managerial Style on Decision Making

In addition to the environment in which decisions take place, other factors influence managerial decision making. Singularly important among these factors is a complex phenomenon commonly called managerial style. **Managerial style** is the way a manager goes about managing. A manager's style derives from personal attributes and attitudes, decision-making approach and ability, timing, scope of vision, prior commitments, and creativity.

Personal Decision-Making Approaches

Different managers approach decisions in diverse ways. Many select one of the following three approaches:

- The rational/logical decision model. This process, which Exhibit 6.2 illustrated, focuses on facts and logic and minimizes intuitive judgments. The manager who uses this method systematically and thoroughly examines a situation or problem and relies on process and quantitative decision-making tools such as payback analysis, decision trees, and simulations. (These tools will be discussed later in this chapter.)

- The nonrational/intuitive model. Managers who use this approach prefer to avoid statistical analysis and logical processes in reaching a decision. These decision makers rely on hunches and feelings about the situation. Completely eliminating intuition from decision making is difficult. Nevertheless, the manager who makes long-range decisions by relying on gut feelings alone may court disaster. The best decisions often result when intuition (derived from experience and hindsight) and rational process are imaginatively combined.

- Predisposed decision model. This approach is exemplified by a manager who decides on a solution and then gathers the material to support the decision. A manager with this tendency is likely to ignore critical information. Such managers may face the same decisions repeatedly. A manager who influences the solution by favoring specific alternatives is employing a variation of the predisposed decision model. Such a manager is likely to distort the value of a pre-selected alternative.

In a recent survey of management executives, 75% of respondents preferred the rational/logical decision model. The executives reported that when making tough decisions, they asked staff members for their recommendations and used statistics and consultants. The remaining 25% said they relied on gut feelings (McDermott, 1992).

A manager must know and acknowledge his or her own decision-making tendencies and deliberately strive to use the rational model. Serious problems may arise for the manager who believes that he or she is using one approach but in reality is using another.

The Ability to Prioritize Decisions

On each box of Morton Salt, beneath the waif with her dripping umbrella, is the slogan "When it rains it pours." Many managers believe the cliché because it so aptly describes the nature of problems: They tend to happen in clusters. As a result, a manager's success at decision making may depend on his or her ability to establish priorities—to rank problems in a sequence of diminishing urgency. Managers have different criteria when it comes to setting priorities. Some assign top priority to the problem that has the greatest impact on the organization's goals. Others may assign priorities based upon what they believe their bosses value. A third group may make decisions based on personal preferences. No matter what criteria they use, managers must assign priorities and be aware of the criteria they use to do so.

For some managers the ability to set priorities may be limited by the tendency to procrastinate, or put off, difficult decisions. Avoiding difficult decisions creates an arbitrary priority system—simple decisions come first, difficult ones later. Such a practice is dangerous. Tough decisions are often the ones that cannot be delayed.

The Timing of Decisions

After a decision is made, it must be translated into action. Good timing often determines a decision's success; bad timing can render the best decision useless. The wise manager regards timing as an important factor in its own right, not a coincidental trifle. Toy manufacturers move swiftly to take advantage of fads and trends, knowing this year's hit is next year's bomb.

H. Wayne Huezenga, chairman of Blockbuster Entertainment Corporation, is timing his company's growth carefully. Having reached a dominant position in the video-rental industry, he knows the first wave of VCR sales growth is tapering off. Competition from cable companies offering pay-for-view movies is on the horizon. With these facts in mind, Huezenga has propelled Blockbuster into the field of music retailing. In addition, his company is creating mini-amusement parks with rides in which computer simulators produce the effects. According to Huezenga, "The time to move into these markets is now. If we wait we'll lose our advantage" (DeGeorge, 1992).

Tunnel Vision

A manager who approaches a problem with the restricted viewpoint called tunnel vision seldom develops the full range of alternatives that nourish good decisions (Mondy, Sharplin, and Premeaux, 1991). Tunnel vision arises from many causes. Among them are ignorance, prejudice, bias, limited experience, and greed. Among the contemporary business problems that some attribute to tunnel vision are the "glass ceiling," a barrier that prevents women from rising in corporate management (Ettorre, 1992); the poor quality of much commercial television programming; the practice of redlining in the real-estate and insurance industries; and discrimination against persons with AIDS.

Commitment to Previous Decisions

Managers must frequently make decisions that relate to previous decisions. Consider the CEO who has committed substantial financial resources to the development of a product that could revolutionize the marketplace. He or she may be strongly influenced to commit additional resources even if the decision seems not to be working. It is difficult to undo a decision, especially with reputations and personal pride at stake. In such instances, the implementation of a control mechanism, with benchmarks for follow-up actions, may be helpful.

Creativity

The elements of creativity—imagination and innovation—benefit decision making. Circumstances in the workplace often make being creative difficult, however. Consider the shift manager at a McDonald's restaurant. His or her day speeds by in rigid patterns set by policies, procedures, and systems that dictate how and when tasks will be completed. Furthermore, at mealtimes this manager's environment is so chaotic that there is no time for the reflection that nourishes creativity (Hall, 1992).

I S S U E S   A N D   E T H I C S
Worker Layoffs and Executive Bonuses

The new chairman of the board and CEO of a major manufacturing company decided to restructure the firm. As a result, 12,000 workers were laid off in the first year; more were scheduled to lose their jobs soon afterward. The CEO cut the firm's research and development budget and capital spending in half. In addition, the CEO established an executive incentive plan that during a nine-month period paid bonuses of $18 million to top executives. The CEO personally received incentives worth $2 million—2½ times his annual salary.

Can you think of three reasons why this manager might decide to lay off thousands of workers, reduce the firm's long-range prospects, and simultaneously provide substantial benefits to top managers? If you sat on this company's board as an outside director, what action would you take in response to these decisions? Why? ▲

Group Decision Making

Recall how subordinates influence a manager's decision-making process. You have learned that workers who participate in decisions are likelier to support them. As more managers accept that fact, the concept of group decision making will become an increasingly important part of the work environment. For companies to compete in today's world, such experts as Tom Peters argue, their frontline employees must become partners with the manager in the decision-making process (Peters, 1990). Such partnerships are a primary goal of team management, the theme of Chapter 14. The following sections will examine three proven devices that facilitate group involvement in decision making: brainstorming, the nominal group technique, and the Delphi technique.

Brainstorming

Brainstorming is a method of shared problem solving in which all members of a group spontaneously contribute ideas focused on the subject problem or opportunity. First formalized by advertising executive Alex Osborn in the late 1940s, the technique works most effectively when basic guidelines are followed (Detz, 1987). First, brainstorming sessions should be held in a comfortable setting for a specified time and free from outside interruptions. Second, participants must know they may speak openly, free from constraints of rank or position. Third, group members must understand that no idea or suggestion is too farfetched to be voiced. And fourth, everyone should be encouraged to build upon the contributions of others, until all opinions have been presented. During the session, ideas are recorded on a chalkboard or flip chart. Later, ideas are sorted and the best examined in detail, either by the manager or another group.

Brainstorming generates enthusiasm and stimulates participants to think creatively. What may seem absurd to one person may stimulate someone else to make a suggestion. Osborn wrote that "The proof of a good brainstorming session is the number of ideas produced and the way participants feel afterwards."

Brainstorming works well when the problem is straightforward and well defined and the atmosphere is supportive. Issues appropriate for brainstorming include product demand, expansion opportunities, and internal barriers to growth and development (Hawken, 1987).

At Levi Strauss, brainstorming helped to solve a growth and development problem. A small group of minority and women managers asked the CEO to solve the problem of barriers to their advancement in the company. After a series of brainstorming sessions, the company developed separate career programs for women, African-Americans, Hispanics, and Asians. In addition, it created a company-wide task force to recommend new policies to support a better balance between work and family (Howard, 1990).

The Nominal Group Technique

Group discussion sessions can be ineffective when a few people dominate the conversation. The **nominal group technique** helps eliminate this problem by creating a structure that encourages equal participation by all members (Fox, 1989). Exhibit 6.7 shows the steps in the nominal group technique.

In addition to providing a structure for equal participation, the nominal group technique encourages individual creativity. In the structured environment, ideas may be developed and presented without interference. The technique does require a fair amount of time.

The Delphi Technique

Developed by the RAND Corporation to forecast the effects of a nuclear attack on the United States, the **Delphi technique** provides structure to group discussion, leads to consensus, and emphasizes equal participation. Unlike other group

---

Exhibit 6.7

The steps in the nominal group technique.

1. *Problem definition.* When the group is assembled, the group leader defines the problem. Questions to clarify the problem are permitted, but no discussion.

2. *Development of ideas.* Each member writes down his or her ideas about the problem, with no discussion.

3. *Round-robin presentation.* Members individually present their ideas to the group. The leader records the ideas on a flip chart or chalkboard. The process continues without discussion until all ideas are recorded.

4. *Clarification of ideas.* The group conducts an open discussion of the ideas (solutions), with members explaining their ideas as needed.

5. *Initial voting.* By secret ballot, members individually rank the recorded solutions. The solutions with the lowest average rankings are eliminated.

6. *Evaluation of revised list.* Members question each other about the remaining solutions.

7. *Final voting.* In another secret ballot, all ideas are ranked. The idea that receives the highest vote total is adopted.

decision-making techniques, Delphi participants do not assemble. Instead, decision making is conducted by a group leader through written questionnaires. The Delphi technique includes five steps:

1. A questionnaire puts a problem before a group of experts who do not interact. Each person is asked to provide solutions.

2. Each participant completes and returns his or her questionnaire.

3. A summary of opinions is developed from the answers received. This summary is distributed along with a second questionnaire.

4. Experts complete the second questionnaire. In this stage participants have the benefit of others' opinions and may change their suggestions to reflect them.

5. The process continues until the experts reach consensus.

Although expensive and time-consuming, the Delphi technique works especially well for solving ambiguous problems (*Small Business Reports,* 1988).

The Advantages and Disadvantages of Group Decision Making

Managers should recognize the distinct advantages and disadvantages inherent in group decision making.

Advantages A group of problem solvers can bring more perspectives to a problem than a single person can. Moreover, when people participate in making a decision, they are more likely to be satisfied with it and support it. Group

Smart managers recognize the importance of seeking out other perspectives. Many important decisions are best put to the group.

decision making may also reduce uncertainty for decision makers who are unwilling to take risks alone.

Disadvantages   One of the major disadvantages of group decision making is obvious: involving everyone and seeking consensus takes time. Another disadvantage is less obvious but just as serious. Groups may favor unsuitable compromise, particularly when influenced by a curious phenomenon called groupthink. When infected with **groupthink**, members grow so committed to the group that they become reluctant to disagree with other members. Groupthink degrades decision making. Perhaps the gravest disadvantage in group decision making lies in its dispersed accountability: No one person bears responsibility for the decision.

Quantitative Decision-Making Tools

Some managers use quantitative tools to improve the quality of their decisions. These tools include decision trees, payback analysis, and simulations. The type of problem determines which tool is most appropriate.

Decision Trees

This chapter has already presented one example of a decision tree, Exhibit 6.6. Exhibit 6.8 shows another example. As you can see, a **decision tree** displays alternative decision paths, allowing a manager to observe potential outcomes and their relationships to future events.

Exhibit 6.8 shows the situation that confronts Lisa, a marketing manager. Lisa must decide whether to spend money test-marketing in a new market or spend money improving the company's marketing performance in an existing market. (Companies such as J.C. Penney, RJR-Nabisco, and John Hancock frequently face such situations.) If the venture into the new market succeeds, Lisa's company will gain a competitive edge. If the venture fails, the competition may enter the market and gain so much momentum that Lisa's firm could lose its overall position. The danger stems from the simultaneous lack of success in the new market and the vulnerability created in the old market when funds and attention are diverted.

The decision tree comprises branches from decision points (squares) and chance or competitive moves (circles). In Exhibit 6.8, the decision path starts with the initial decision at point A. The outcomes are shown to the right of the tree's branches.

If Lisa decides to authorize the project, point B represents the second point for a decision. At point B, the test marketing has been successful. Now Lisa must decide between entering the market with a full-scale promotional program and product distribution, and waiting until a later date.

Decision trees require the manager to include only those decisions and events or results that produce consequences that can be compared. The decision tree in Exhibit 6.8 projects an outcome for Lisa's possible choice not to begin test marketing at all.

Exhibit 6.8

A decision tree with chains of activities and events.

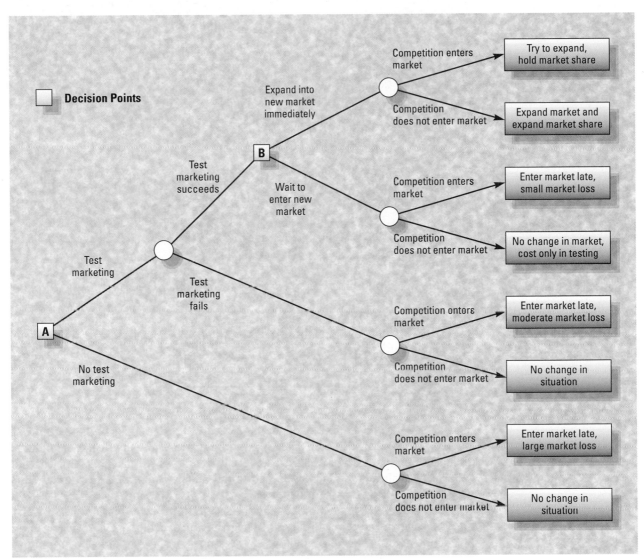

Payback Analysis

To evaluate capital purchasing alternatives, the manager may wish to employ **payback analysis**, a procedure that ranks alternatives according to how long each takes to pay back its initial cost. The strategy is to choose the alternative that has the quickest payback. Exhibit 6.9 shows an example of a payback analysis.

Copy center owner Tim Collins plans to purchase a computerized printing system. Three vendors have given him prices for three different systems. Each system offers unique features that will affect the revenue to be earned. In

Exhibit 6.9

*An example of a payback
analysis.*

		Computerized Printing System		
		A	B	C
Initial Cost		$ 14,000	$ 12,000	$ 17,000
Revenues	Year 1	0	500	2,000
	Year 2	1,000	1,000	3,000
	Year 3	1,500	1,500	5,000
	Year 4	2,000	2,500	7,000
	Year 5	2,500	3,000	
	Year 6	3,000	3,500	
	Year 7	4.000		
Payback Period		$\dfrac{\$14{,}000}{\$2{,}000} = 7.0$	$\dfrac{\$12{,}000}{\$2{,}000} = 6.0$	$\dfrac{\$17{,}000}{\$4{,}250} = 4.0$

preparing a payback analysis to compare the systems, Tim lists the initial cost of each system and the annual anticipated revenues until that cost is paid back. As Exhibit 6.9 shows, System A will take seven years to recover Tim's investment. System B will take six years. In this case, System C's four-year payback makes it the best investment.

Simulations

The philosophy of management science, the school of management thought that focuses on the development of mathematical and statistical tools to improve efficiency, has contributed to the development of several analytical tools that aid in decision making. These tools are generally known as simulations. This chapter will examine simulations in general and then discuss queuing and game theory.

A **simulation** is a model of a real activity or process (Fourre, 1970). Sophisticated modeling techniques have been applied to a wide variety of problems, from weather forecasting to aircraft design, from beach erosion to war games. Among principal users of modeling are the U.S. government, large corporations, and research facilities. Models range in fidelity from near-perfect to nearly useless. Computer modeling of economic phenomena can provide broad-brush guidelines for evaluating the effects of tax schedules, interest rate changes, and tariffs, for example. Academic economists and government planners cannot yet produce accurate models of large-scale economic behavior, however.

Models can be abstract or physical. Computer models are in the abstract class, as are architect's plans, mathematical formulas, and chemical equations. Physical models—with their hands-on three-dimensional appeal—run the gamut from one-of-a-kind, hand-built prototypes of airliners to elegant miniature skyscrapers to sexy Detroit concept cars. In 1990 Chrysler's prototype of the Viper sports coupe caused such a sensation at auto shows that Chrysler decided to bring

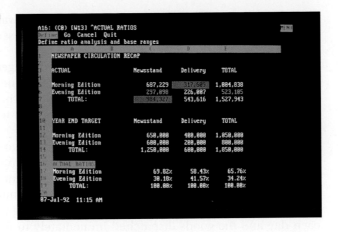

"What-if" programs such as Instant Analyst reveal hidden trends and relationships in raw data, helping managers to test different scenarios before making a decision.

the model to market and create a stretch version with four doors for exhibition throughout 1991 (Matega, 1992).

To instruct a model maker to build a model, managers must know and understand the process they wish to simulate and the interrelationships of its variables. Invalid simulation provides no helpful guidance; indeed, it can be extremely misleading.

A properly constructed model or simulation offers many advantages:

- It allows managers to perform experiments away from the demands and interruptions of a real-life business operation.

- It avoids the time loss and expense associated with experimenting with actual company assets.

- It allows experimentation or training without annoying the customers and taking facilities out of service.

- It allows an observer to see results much more quickly than an observer would see them in the real world. This is especially true of computer simulations.

Aircraft flight simulators are among the most dramatic simulations. The simulators are sophisticated replicas of airliner cockpits. Student pilots use them in flight training, and experienced pilots use them to maintain their qualifications. The simulators, which are elaborately computerized, are mounted on hydraulic struts. The struts allow the simulator to move according to the instructions given by the student at the controls. The result for the student is the sensation of real flight. Instructors outside the simulator can test the student's knowledge and build the student's skill by replicating every imaginable flight condition, including emergencies. The model can simulate crashes so vividly that shaken students teeter from the trainer, drenched in sweat. All this can take place in absolute safety and for a fraction of the cost of real training flights. By using simulators, airline managers help ensure that pilots operate at the peak of proficiency.

Managers use **queuing models**, or **waiting-line models**, to help decide the optimum length of a waiting line, or queue. At K Mart, McDonald's, and supermarkets everywhere, managers have a continuing concern about the length of the line at the cash register. Customers forced to wait too long may take their business somewhere else. Managers must weigh the cost of opening other checkout areas against the risk of losing customers.

To help them achieve the proper balance, managers can create a model that simulates the bottleneck that is a checkout line. In the neighborhood supermarket, additional checkout counters are opened after two to three customers are in a line. Theaters routinely maintain a separate ticket window where advance tickets may be purchased hours, even days before a show.

Queues also form in manufacturing plants as goods are funneled through a production run. To help solve the problem, companies have devised the just-in-time inventory approach. At Texas Instruments, just-in-time delivery of raw materials or other kinds of inventories has eliminated the need to warehouse items. Delivery of parts used in manufacturing can be made several times each day and the goods dispatched immediately to the proper spot and at the appropriate time.

Game theory attempts to predict how people or organizations will behave in competitive situations. It allows managers to devise strategies to counter the behavior of competitors. Managers apply game theory in situations in which organizations compete against one another in regard to price, product development, advertising, and distribution systems. If managers at Procter & Gamble were able to predict with a degree of accuracy whether and within what time frame Lever Brothers would initiate a price decrease, the managers at Procter & Gamble could decide whether or not to decrease its own price.

F O C U S   O N   Q U A L I T Y

"Thomas Time" Leads to Quality Decisions

The managers of today are learning that they must incorporate the concern for quality into all phases of an operation. Nowhere is quality more critical than in an organization's decision-making processes. Nevertheless, the crush of business often brings messages that subvert quality: "The customer needs it now," "We're behind schedule," "We haven't got the time," and "Let's go with it." In the midst of real-world pressures, the making of a decision—not its quality—often seems to be the top priority.

This distorted emphasis plagues small businesses especially. For a small business, competition often drives hasty decision making.

Managers at Thomas Interior Systems, a Chicago-area firm that designs and sells office furnishings, are trying to counter the pressures that subvert quality decision making.

The firm's top managers make their decisions on "Thomas Time"—in other words, in slow motion. The objective of this quality commitment is to work toward consensus.

If a decision requires managerial discussion and re-discussion to ensure that the final result is a quality decision, then that discussion and re-discussion takes place. Only when the managers reach final consensus do they act. ▲

For more on quality in decision making, see "Entrepreneurs Are Learning That Total Quality Management Can Be Critical to Survival," *Nation's Business,* May 1992, p. 24.

Creating an Environment for Effective Decision Making

Because managers in today's organizations face complex and stressful decision-making challenges, they must create an effective decision-making environment for themselves. To create such an environment, experts such as Ireland, Hill, and Williams (1992) recommend that managers:

1. Provide time for decisions to be made. Don't be pushed—or push others—into making a decision too rapidly. If necessary, negotiate for more time to make a quality decision.

2. Have confidence. Courage and self-confidence are required for a manager to make the risk-laden decisions called for in today's rapidly changing business environment.

3. Encourage others to make decisions. Trust subordinates and allow them the freedom to act.

4. Learn from past decisions. Another way to gain confidence is to study and learn from the past mistakes of others. Don't make the same mistakes. Also, study successful decisions to see why they worked.

Haste makes waste.
Managers who shoot from the hip by making a decision without sufficient time to consider the consequences risk missing the target—or, worse yet, hitting themselves in the foot.

5. Recognize the differences in decision-making situations. All decisions do not have the same degree of risk or priority; therefore, all decisions should not be approached in the same way.

6. Recognize the importance of quality information. Assume that quality information is available and insist that subordinates support their decisions with data.

7. Make the tough decisions. Don't procrastinate or avoid dealing with decisions that could be unpopular. Once the decision is made—whether yes or no—provide an explanation to everyone.

8. Know when to hold off. Recognize that sometimes the best decision is no decision; it may be necessary for events to play themselves out or for more information to be gathered.

9. Be ready to try things. Tom Peters and Robert Waterman argue that the excellent companies are those that act—that try things. Rather than debating a new product idea, they test-market it. Managers who change the status quo, even on a small scale, can learn more about their market or work force by watching the effects of those changes than can those who simply observe the status quo.

10. Be willing to ask for help. Everyone needs help at some time or another; it isn't a sign of weakness to ask for assistance. In fact, knowing when to ask for help is an indication of wisdom.

Future Trends

In terms of decision making and the decision-making environment, several trends are noteworthy:

- Managers at all levels will depend more heavily on the rational decision-making style in matters relating to finance, marketing strategy, facilities, production, and expansion. With more competition and fewer resources available, decision makers will have a smaller margin for error. They will need the rational approach to make sound decisions.

- The increasing use and sophistication of computers will make information for decision making more accessible than ever before. Computer systems and high-tech communication devices are capable of storing and transmitting vast quantities of information immediately. As a result, a premium will be placed on a manager's ability to assimilate an enormous amount of relevant information and extract only the most pertinent.

- To an increasing degree, computers will be valued for their ability to produce simulations. Managers at all levels will be able to work with computers to examine alternatives.

- More and more decisions will be channeled down the organization to be made by those who have firsthand knowledge, especially those working in teams. The result will be decisions that are closer to the issues, and employees who are more committed to the decisions.

- With the growing emphasis on workers' attitudes and job satisfaction, an increasing number of decisions will address nonquantitative issues. These decisions will put great demands on managers' human skills and their abilities to decide in situations of uncertainty.

C H A P T E R   **S** U M M A R Y

- A decision is a choice made from available alternatives. The purpose of a decision is to solve a problem or seize an opportunity. All managers make decisions.

- Decisions can be viewed as either programmed or non-programmed. Programmed decisions involve situations that have occurred often enough that both the circumstances and solutions are predictable. Nonprogrammed decisions are made in response to situations that have unique circumstances and unpredictable results. Nonprogrammed decisions often have important consequences for an organization.

- The formal decision-making process consists of seven steps: defining the problem or opportunity, developing alternatives, identifying limiting factors, analyzing alternatives, selecting the best alternative, implementing the decision, and establishing a control and evaluation system. Using this process is critical to success in decision making.

- In making decisions a manager should consider the degree of certainty, the problem of limited resources, and the internal and external environments.

- Personal influences on a manager's decision making include personal attributes and attitudes, decision-making approach and ability, timing, scope of vision, prior commitments, and creativity.

- The quality of decision making can be enhanced by involving people other than the manager. Group decision-making techniques include brainstorming, the nominal group technique, and the Delphi technique.

- A manager can improve the quality of decision making by applying several quantitative tools, including decision trees, payback analysis, and simulations.

- Managers in today's organizations face complex, challenging, and stressful decision-making demands. In recognition of these realities, managers must create an effective decision-making environment for themselves.

S K I L L - B U I L D I N G

This series of questions is designed to place you in a manager's decision-making environment and test your decision-making skills.

1. Read the scenario that follows.

   It is Tuesday afternoon. You have been gone from work all morning at meetings and have just arrived at your office. When you enter, you are greeted by the following situations:

   - A preliminary report of test results on the new product has just been delivered. The lab cannot proceed with further tests until you respond to this report. Anticipated time for you to review the report and respond: 30 minutes.

   - A fax from your sales representative in Chicago requests approval for priority processing of a large order. Anticipated time to consider the request and answer it: 15 minutes.

   - A note says your boss wants to see you as soon as you arrive. Such meetings always take 30 to 60 minutes, regardless of the topic.

   - Your telephone is ringing. It may be Chicago.

   - Your production foreman wants to talk to you immediately about rumors of a work slowdown to begin tonight on the third shift. Estimated time: 60 minutes minimum.

   - A note from a peer manager requests 15 minutes of your time as soon as possible to discuss something of vital concern to both of you. The note does not specify the topic.

   - Your secretary became ill at lunch and is resting in the company infirmary. Stopping by to express concern will take 10 minutes.

   - Three persons are seated in your outer office. Two appear to be sales representatives and one is a job applicant. It will take 10 minutes just to find out who they are.

   - You just remembered a purchase order that has to be processed today to keep your production schedule on target. Estimated time to complete the purchase order: 15 minutes.

2. Number the situations in the order you would deal with them. The first situation to be resolved would be number 1 and the last would be number 9.

3. Explain why you established the priorities you did.

R E V I E W   Q U E S T I O N S

1. Review this chapter's essential terms and look up the meanings of those you cannot define.

2. For each management level, provide examples of the kinds of decisions that managers at that level would make.

3. What factors influence whether a manager should use a formal or informal approach to decision making?

4. Identify each step in the decision-making process and describe briefly what should happen in each step.

5. What four factors in the decision-making environment influence the decision-making process and the decision maker?

6. What are the three personal decision-making approaches a manager can use? What are the characteristics of each?

7. What are three group decision-making techniques? What is the value of each?

8. Under what circumstances would you use payback analysis? What purpose does payback analysis serve?

9. What are three strategies a manager can use to create a more effective decision-making environment?

R E C O M M E N D E D   R E A D I N G

Alstadt, Donald M. "Redefining the U.S. Corporation," *Design News* (January 6, 1992), p. 117.

Gibbons, Kent. "Lessons for Tough Times," *Nation's Business* (January 1992), p. 16.

Holbrook, Stephen F. *Effective Decision Making,* 14th revised edition (Bellemead, NJ: Princeton Management Association), 1991.

Kiechel, W. "When Management Regresses," *Fortune* (March 9, 1992), pp. 157–165.

Lammers, Terry. "The Troubleshooter's Guide," *Inc.* (January 1992), pp. 65–68.

Maroun, Jack. *Decision Making in Business,* 2nd edition (Los Angeles: Roxbury), 1991.

Morton, Adam. *Disasters & Dilemmas: Decisions Without Tradeoffs* (Cambridge, MA: Blackwell, Basil), 1991.

O'Dell, William. *Effective Business Decision Making: And the Educated Guess* (Lincolnwood, IL: National Textbook), 1991.

Roman, Monica. "A Portrait of the Boss," *Business Week* (November 25, 1991), pp. 180–183.

Zeckhauser, Richard. *The Strategy of Choice* (San Francisco: Jossey-Bass), 1991.

R E F E R E N C E S

Daft, Richard L. *Management,* 2nd edition (Chicago: Dryden Press), 1991, p. 180.

DeGeorge, Gail. "They Don't Call It Blockbuster for Nothing," *Business Week* (October 19, 1992), pp. 113–114.

Detz, Joan. "The Adaptive Leader," *Success* (June 1987), p. 46.

Drucker, Peter F. *The Practice of Management* (New York: Harper & Row), 1954, p. 351.

Ettorre, Barbara. "Breaking the Glass . . . Or Just Window Dressing," *Management Review* (March 1992), p. 16.

Fourre, James P. *Quantitative Business Planning Techniques* (New York: American Management Association), 1970, p. 55.

Fox, William M. "Anonymity and Other Keys to Successful Problem-Solving Meetings," *National Productivity Review* (Spring 1989), pp. 145–146.

Hall, Cheryl. "Golden Quest," *Dallas Morning News,* May 31, 1992, p. 8H.

Hawken, Paul. "Problems, Problems," *Inc.* (September 1987), pp. 24–25.

Holt, David H. *Management: Principles and Practices,* 2nd edition (Englewood Cliffs, NJ: Prentice-Hall), 1990, p. 100.

Howard, Robert. "Values Make the Company: An Interview with Robert Haas, *Harvard Business Review* (September–October 1990), p. 140.

Ireland, R. Duane; Michael A. Hill; and J. Clifton Williams. "Self-Confidence and Decisiveness: Prerequisite for Effective Management in the 1990s," *Business Horizons* (January–February 1992), pp. 36–42.

LeFauve, Richard G. "The Saturn Corporation: A Balance of People, Technology, and Business Systems," *Looking Ahead* (the journal of the National Planning Association), vol. XIII, no. 4 (April 1992), pp. 14–23a.

Maier, Norman R. F. *Problem Solving Discussions and Conferences: Leadership Methods and Skills* (New York: McGraw-Hill), 1963, pp. 95–110.

Matega, Jim. "Chrysler Future Bright in Concept," *Chicago Tribune,* January 6, 1992, sec. 17, pp. 1, 5.

McDermott, Peter. "Tough Decisions," *USA Today,* April 1992, p. 8B.

Mondy, R. Wayne; Arthur Sharplin; and Shane R. Premeaux. *Management: Concepts, Practices, and Skills,* 5th edition (Boston: Allyn and Bacon), 1991, p. 116.

Murray, Kathleen. "Unocal's New Man: Stegemeier Pares Debt, Refines Look of Company," *Orange County Register,* January 28, 1991, p. Kl.

Peters, Tom. "Time-Obsessed Competition," *Management Review* (September 1990), pp. 17, 18.

Small Business Reports, "Group Decision Making: Approaches to Problem Solving" (July 1988), pp. 30–33.

Verespej, Michael A. "Tough Times, Tough Decisions," *Industry Week* (February 17, 1992), pp. 27–28.

Vroom, Victor H. "A New Look at Managerial Decision Making," *Organizational Dynamics* (Spring 1973), p. 67.

G L O S S A R Y O F **T** E R M S

alternative   A potential course of action that is likely to eliminate, correct, or neutralize the cause of a problem or maximize an opportunity.

brainstorming   A method of shared problem solving in which all members of a group spontaneously contribute ideas focused on the subject problem or opportunity.

decision   A judgment reached after consideration; a choice made from among available alternatives.

decision making   The process of identifying problems and opportunities, developing alternative solutions, choosing an alternative, and implementing it.

decision tree   A graphical representation of the actions a manager can take and how these actions relate to other events.

Delphi technique   A group decision-making technique in which equal participation is structured by the use of written questionnaires.

game theory   A mathematical simulation model in which a competitive situation is analyzed to determine the optimal course of action to counter a competitor's behavior.

groupthink   In group decision making, a phenomenon in which members are so committed to the group that they become reluctant to disagree with other members. Groupthink can seriously compromise decision making.

limiting factors   Constraints that rule out potential alternatives.

managerial style   The individual way in which a manager goes about managing. Managerial style includes personal attributes and decision-making approach.

nominal group technique   A group decision-making technique that creates a structure to allow equal participation by all members.

nonprogrammed decision   A decision made in response to a situation involving unique circumstances, unpredictable results, and important consequences.

opportunity   A good chance for progress or advancement whose realization requires that a decision be made.

payback analysis   A procedure that ranks alternatives according to how long each takes to pay back its initial cost.

problem   Any question raised for the purpose of solution, answer, or decision. A current condition that is not a desired or preferred condition.

programmed decision   A decision about a problem or situation that has occurred so often that the situation, solution, and outcome are predictable.

queuing model   A simulation used to help managers decide what length of waiting line, or queue, is preferable.

satisfice   To make the best possible decision with the time, resources, and information available. A satisficing decision contrasts with an ideal one.

simulation   A model of a real activity or process.

symptom   A signal that indicates a problem is present.

Vroom and Yetton decision tree   A series of questions, in the context of a decision tree, that guide managers to a decision-making style appropriate for a specific situation.

waiting-line model   *See* queuing model.

C A S E   P R O B L E M
Deal With Us Direct—or Don't Bother

EO David Glass made his message clear. He firmly and politely told suppliers of Wal-Mart Stores, Incorporated, that if they wanted to continue to do business with Wal-Mart, they would have to deal directly with the company. In other words, if the supplier sent anyone else—a distributor, a manufacturer's representative, or an independent sales representative—to Wal-Mart headquarters, that individual would not be welcome.

The decision was based on two factors. First, Wal-Mart's computer system gives suppliers access to its store and warehouse inventory records. Glass wanted to place some degree of control on that access. Second, Glass wanted to improve the efficiency, cost control, and competitiveness of Wal-Mart. Eliminating the go-betweens would reduce prices for Wal-Mart by squeezing out the 2% to 3% that went to the commissioned brokers.

This hard decision was not without a degree of risk. Alienated suppliers could sue. Or, a supplier could rush to Wal-Mart's competitors with their goods—and their information.

Q U E S T I O N S

1. Do you think Glass's decision was a programmed or nonprogrammed decision? Why?

2. What characteristics were present in Glass's decision-making environment? Certainty? Risk? Uncertainty? Explain your answer.

3. What internal and external factors might influence the success of this decision?

For more on Wal-Mart's decision making, see Michael A. Verespej, "Tough Times, Tough Decisions," *Industry Week,* February 17, 1992, p. 23.

P·A·R·T

Organizing

Organizing Principles

LEARNING OBJECTIVES

After reading and discussing this chapter, you should be able to:

- Define the essential terms that appear in the text

- Explain the relationship between planning and organizing

- Explain the importance of the organizing process

- List and discuss the five steps in the organizing process

- Describe and give an example of the four approaches to departmentalization

- Define authority and explain how line, staff, and functional authority differ

- Explain the concept of power and its sources

- Discuss the major organizing concepts and how they influence organizing decisions

- Explain the term *informal organization*

- Compare an informal organization to a formal organization

ESSENTIAL TERMS

accountability
authority
centralization
chain of command
cohesion
customer departmentalization

decentralization
delegation
departmentalization
division of labor
formal organization
functional authority
functional definition

functional departmentalization
geographical
   departmentalization
informal organization
interaction chart
line authority
line department
norm
organization chart

organizing
power
product departmentalization
responsibility
sanction
span of control
specialization of labor
staff authority
staff department
unity of command
unity of direction

MANAGEMENT IN ACTION
Coping at Mrs. Fields Incorporated

Debra Fields started her bakery business in 1977, in Palo Alto, California. By early 1993 the business was faced with tough problems. Mrs. Fields, Inc., owned about 400 stores. Franchisees operated another 380, and licensees (including 45 overseas) operated more.

But the costs of expansion during the slowdown in the U.S. economy in the early 1990s saddled the firm with heavy debt—more than $96 million—and large losses in 1991 and 1992. In February 1993, Mrs. Fields surrendered 80% of the company in exchange for $46 million in loan relief. Debra Fields continued as board chair but gave up the posts of president

Rolling in dough but strapped for cash, *Mrs. Fields, Inc., has been forced to write a new recipe for the delegation of power.*

and CEO, thus relinquishing daily management of the company.

For over a decade Debra Fields had practiced hands-on management, popping into stores to quiz workers on cookie dough or to show them how to mop the floor correctly. Though this approach allowed her to create an international chain, it didn't allow her time to take on new directions or introduce a wider range of products.

Debra Fields acknowledges that she needed to learn the art—and the power—of delegation. "I used to ask managers what they needed, and then I did it for them. 'Your ice machine is broken? Your milk delivery is off? I'll take care of it.'

If I saw something I didn't like, I'd fix it myself, right then and there. Those days are over."

To turn the company around, Fields realized that "we needed to develop our people so that the business would not be solely dependent on us."

operating officer. Fields's goal was to turn over most of her activities to the operating officer. After long trips, visits to the stores, and hours of watching Fields function, the new COO Paul Baird took charge. Duties were reassigned and authority delegated.

> **❝ If I saw something I didn't like, I'd fix it myself, right then and there. Those days are over. ❞**
>
> — **Debra Fields**, Chairman of the Board, Mrs. Fields, Inc.

With the decision came action. Immediately, Fields developed a new level of management that included a senior vice president in charge of expansion plans, a chief financial officer, and a chief

Along with the restructuring in 1993, plans called for establishing stores, kiosks, and counters at supermarkets, airports, and university campuses—areas that are relatively unaffected by business cycles. ▲

For more about the art of delegation, see Alan Pendergast, "Learning to Let Go," *Working Woman,* January 1992, pp. 42–45. For details of the restructuring at Mrs. Fields Incorporated, see George White, "Creditors Put Bite on Mrs. Fields Cookies," *Los Angeles Times,* February 17, 1993, p. D1.

The Formal Organization

"You can't tell me what to do; only Larry can—he's my boss!" "When did the research and development department start reporting to marketing? I thought it was part of the production group." "All I want is a decision on this engineering drawing. Can't anyone make a decision? Who's in charge here, anyway?"

If these words sound familiar, you have had practical experience with problems relating to the second managerial function—organizing. Chapters 4 and 5 observed that an organization's success begins with imaginative and thorough planning. Recall that the very foundations of planning consist of using the process called organizing to purposefully deploy people, ideas, and resources.

Planning, as Chapters 4 and 5 discussed, provides the necessary beginning. Organizing converts plans into reality—it makes things happen. A company that has invested the time, energy, and money to develop quality plans must organize its employees to attain the planned objectives. Its managers must understand the importance of organizing. The organizing process, like planning, must be thoughtfully worked out and applied.

In organizing, a manager determines what work is needed. He or she assigns tasks and arranges them into a decision-making framework—an organizational structure. This framework clearly establishes who is responsible for what tasks and who reports to whom. An organization without structure generates confusion, frustration, inefficiency, and failure.

Owners and managers create a business organization to achieve a specific objective: to provide a product or service at a profit. (Not-for-profit organizations also require structure and objectives; these groups differ from for-profit organizations in terms of their goals and details.) When managers build an organization, they are developing a framework in which to create the desired product or service and generate the profit. The framework establishes operating relationships among people: who supervises whom, who reports to whom in work units, and what kind of work is to be done in each unit. Such a framework is known as a **formal organization**—the official organizational structure that top management conceives and builds. A formal organization does not just happen. Managers develop it through the organizing function of management.

The Organizing Process

Organizing is establishing the orderly use of resources by assigning tasks that establish relationships between activity and authority. Organizing includes five steps, which you will study later in this chapter. The result of the organizing process is an organization—a whole consisting of unified parts acting in harmony to execute tasks that achieve goals effectively and efficiently.

The Relationship Between Planning and Organizing

The managerial functions of planning and organizing are intimately related. Organizing begins with and is governed by plans, which state where the organization is going and how it will get there. An organization must be built, or an existing one modified, to ensure that plans are executed and goals reached. The organization must be able to concentrate its resources in a unified way to translate plans from intentions into realities.

Examples of the relationship between planning and organizing—specifically, how changes in plans affect an organization—can be seen in the changes constantly under way throughout business and industry.

- Hughes Aircraft realigned its divisions into units aimed at market segments—transportation and communications—instead of technology units. The new plans for Hughes call for the long-range development and application of military technology to peacetime use. The new structure will facilitate these plans (Healey, 1992).

- CEO Paul Stern of Northern Telecom dismantled an organizational structure that divided the firm into units based on geographical boundaries. He created a new structure based on product groups for research, manufacturing, and engineering. The revised structure will help Northern Telecom employees achieve their new objectives: to make the firm a world leader, not just a Canadian leader, and to help Northern Telecom create global, not regional, products (Verespej, 1992).

- The managers of United Technologies reorganized the divisions of the company to incorporate separate operating groups in the design and manufacture of commercial and military aircraft engines. Now the divisions—Pratt & Whitney, Sikorsky Helicopter, and Hamilton Standard— should be able to capitalize on the synergies that working together can produce (Velocci, 1992). The reorganization should help United Technologies improve its profitability and competitiveness.

With the relationship between planning and organizing in mind, the benefits of the organizing process emerge clearly.

The Five-Step Organizing Process

Exhibit 7.1 models the organizing process at the Excelsior Table Saw Corporation. At Excelsior—as in all organizations—organizing involves five steps:

1. Reviewing plans and goals

2. Determining activities

3. Classifying and grouping activities

4. Assigning the work and delegating authority

5. Designing a hierarchy of relationships

The paragraphs that follow will discuss each step in turn.

Reviewing Plans and Goals   A company's objectives and its plans to achieve them determine its activities. Excelsior Table Saw plans to make and sell a quality table saw; this objective will shape every action.

Some purposes and activities are likely to remain fairly constant once a business is established. The business will continue to seek a profit, for example. In addition, it will continue to employ people and other resources. As time passes and plans change, however, the ways in which basic activities are carried out will change. New departments may be created; old ones may be given additional responsibilities. Some departments may cease to exist. New relationships between groups of decision makers may come into being. These changes will come about through the process of organizing.

This chapter has already illustrated organizational restructuring at Mrs. Fields, Hughes Aircraft, Northern Telecom, and United Technologies. Business organizations are continually adjusting their organizational structures in response to new plans. Business magazines and daily newspapers frequently carry announcements about structural changes at firms as diverse as IBM, Apple Computer, AT&T, Coca-Cola, Sears, and Boeing. The firms that publish the magazines and newspapers themselves are not immune to change. Their managers try to solve problems and seize opportunities by adapting the organizations to compete in the world economy (Loomis, 1991).

Determining Activities   In the second step, managers list and analyze the activities needed to accomplish the objectives. The list should include tasks common to every business (such as hiring, training, keeping records) and those peculiar to the specific firm (assembling, machining, shipping, and storing are activities at Excelsior Table Saw). All necessary activities must be identified.

An important concept that applies to specifying tasks is **specialization of labor**, or **division of labor**. Both terms refer to the degree to which tasks are subdivided into separate jobs (Daft, 1991). When organizing according to the concept of specialization of labor, a manager breaks a complex job into simpler

Exhibit 7.1

The organizing process in action.

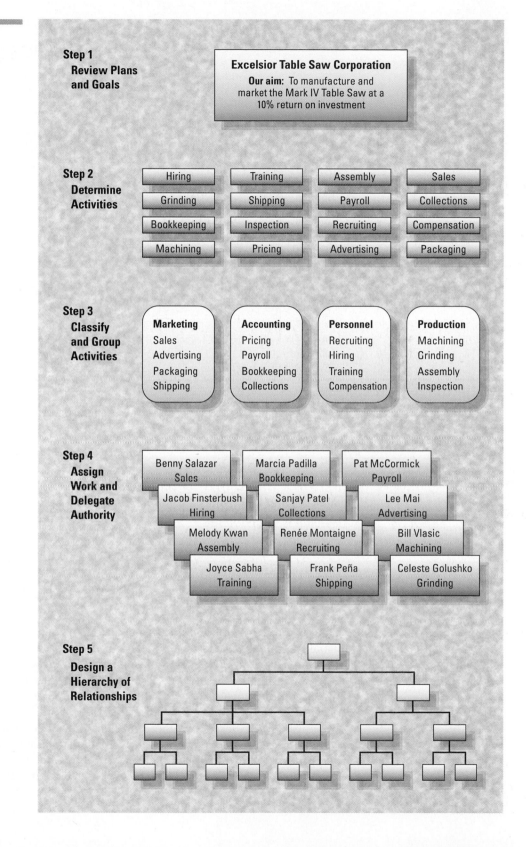

Step 1
Review Plans and Goals

Excelsior Table Saw Corporation
Our aim: To manufacture and market the Mark IV Table Saw at a 10% return on investment

Step 2
Determine Activities

Hiring | Training | Assembly | Sales
Grinding | Shipping | Payroll | Collections
Bookkeeping | Inspection | Recruiting | Compensation
Machining | Pricing | Advertising | Packaging

Step 3
Classify and Group Activities

Marketing
Sales
Advertising
Packaging
Shipping

Accounting
Pricing
Payroll
Bookkeeping
Collections

Personnel
Recruiting
Hiring
Training
Compensation

Production
Machining
Grinding
Assembly
Inspection

Step 4
Assign Work and Delegate Authority

Benny Salazar — Sales
Marcia Padilla — Bookkeeping
Pat McCormick — Payroll
Jacob Finsterbush — Hiring
Sanjay Patel — Collections
Lee Mai — Advertising
Melody Kwan — Assembly
Renée Montaigne — Recruiting
Bill Vlasic — Machining
Joyce Sabha — Training
Frank Peña — Shipping
Celeste Golushko — Grinding

Step 5
Design a Hierarchy of Relationships

Exhibit 7.2

Degrees of specialization in producing a VCR.

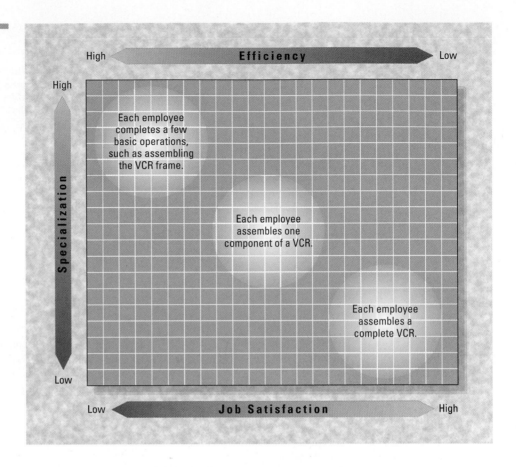

tasks or activities. One person or group may complete only that activity or a related group of activities. Exhibit 7.2 displays three different levels of specialization in the job of producing a videocassette recorder (VCR). The shaded bars at the side, top, and bottom of the exhibit show how specialization, efficiency, and job satisfaction usually relate.

Usually, the efficiency of workers increases in proportion to their specialization (Smith, 1937). When employees specialize, they may gain skill and expertise. Specialization facilitates employee selection and decreases training requirements. Specialized work can be evaluated according to just a few criteria. What is more, quality or performance problems relating to specialized work are usually easy for managers to detect. These two facts allow the managers of specialized workers to manage more employees than those who manage generalists.

Despite its advantages, specialization can create problems. When specialization is overdone and jobs are oversimplified, workers quickly become bored and tired. Imagine how you would feel, entering data eight hours a day, five days a week. Serious medical problems have been traced to such repetitive work. Carpal tunnel syndrome is just one malady associated with long hours at computer display terminals. Some companies have tried to overcome such difficulties by job redesign. Others have developed teams responsible for an entire product (see Chapter 14).

The diverse range of activities at American Iron and Steel are logically grouped by their functional similarities. The pouring of molten steel bears little practical resemblance to the activities of the R&D department— yet all this activity is part of running one company.

The specialization of labor is no mere theory. Specialization leads directly to the analysis and design of real positions. It allows managers to outline the qualifications people need to fill those positions. Managers state this information in job descriptions and job specifications. The U.S. Department of Labor maintains a massive document, *The Dictionary of Occupational Titles*, which provides details about thousands of positions. This dictionary and others like it serve as the basis for staffing an organization (see Chapter 10).

Classifying and Grouping Activities   Once managers know what tasks must be done, they classify and group activities into manageable work units. Refer back to Exhibit 7.1 to see how this step arranges the jumble of necessary tasks into four coherent groups of like activities. When managers group tasks according to process and skill, they are grouping them according to the principle of functional similarity, or similarity of activity. Functional similarity forms a logical basis for establishing work units.

Managers apply the principle in three sequential steps:

1. They examine each activity to determine its general nature. Labels such as *marketing, production, finance,* and *personnel* often apply at this stage.

2. They group the activities into related categories.

3. They establish a basic departmental design for the organizational structure.

In practice, the first two steps in the process occur simultaneously. As the tasks are classified and grouped into related work units, the third step, **departmentalization**, comes into play. Decisions about the basic organization, or departmental structure, of the company emerge. Groups, departments, and divisions are formed on the basis of the organization's objectives, and management may then choose from among four proven departmental models. Although Chapter 8 will discuss these models in detail, an overview of department types will be helpful at this point.

Functional departmentalization involves creating departments on the basis of the specialized activities of the business—marketing, accounting, personnel, and production, for example. This is the type of departmentalization the managers at Excelsior Table Saw used. For most businesses, the functional approach offers a logical way to organize departments. The approach is simple, it groups same or similar activities, it simplifies training, and it allows for specialization (Daft, 1983).

G L O B A L   A P P L I C A T I O N S
Delegation and Decentralization at Siemens

At Siemens AG, a $45.6-billion electronics giant, the organizational philosophy is changing rapidly. The change is due to the need to gird up for intense competition from the Japanese in Europe. Rigid hierarchy is out, and entrepreneurial drive is in. The old management structure—which required young candidates to wait years to move up the ranks—is being disassembled. In its place, smaller, nimbler operating units headed by entrepreneurial managers are being developed.

Installing the new philosophy is not an easy task. Thousands of midlevel managers refuse to take personal initiative; worse, they undermine those who do. As one young manager says, "They are used to tight structures. They can only take orders and execute them." If managers are unable to change, they will be quietly pushed aside and told to seek employment elsewhere.

This new organizational philosophy comes from CEO Heinrich Von Pierer, a 51-year-old lawyer, economist, and former tennis champion. Only the second nonengineer to run Siemens in its 150-year history, experts rate Von Pierer as an excellent strategist, negotiator, and entrepreneur. Renowned in his early years for breaking rules and working around the chain of command—behavior unheard of in a German company—many think Von Pierer is the ideal person to decentralize, delegate, and hold managers accountable. The future of Siemens could depend on his success.

For more about delegation and decentralization, see Gayle Schares, "The New Generation at Siemens," *Business Week*, March 9, 1992, pp. 46–48.

Geographical departmentalization involves grouping activities and responsibilities according to territory. To be near customers, expanding companies often place production plants, sales offices, and repair facilities in several market areas. Geographical departmentalization allows the companies to serve customers quickly and efficiently. The Disney Company—with theme parks in California, Florida, France, and Japan—uses geographical departmentalization in that aspect of its business.

Product departmentalization involves grouping activities by product. This option is adopted when each product of a company requires a unique marketing strategy, production process, distribution system, or financial resources. Marketing-oriented companies that have many product categories—Mattel is an example—often capitalize on this approach.

Customer departmentalization involves grouping activities and responsibilities in departments organized to meet the needs of specific customer groups. A company that markets products to different customer groups faces a difficult task. Because each type of customer poses different demands, needs, and preferences, the company must use tailored strategies that are not necessarily compatible. High-tech firms such as Boeing, IBM, and Raytheon—which do substantial business with the private sector and the U.S. government—often departmentalize so they can tailor service to each type of customer. (Indeed, managers throughout the defense industry commonly refer to the Pentagon as The Customer.) Department stores favor this mode of organization, as the term *department store* indicates. A manager in the men's department works in a universe that is distinct from that of a manager in the teens' department.

The John Deere Company is more than just reapers and threshers; it is also earth-moving equipment and lawn mowers. The needs of agriculture, industry, and the private homeowner are about as different as any three markets could be.

Although the three types of departmentalization have been presented as if each were used by itself, most companies combine the types to suit their needs. Large companies—such as General Motors, AT&T, and Digital Equipment—incorporate departments arranged by function, geography, product, and customer.

Assigning Work and Delegating Authority   After identifying the activities necessary to achieve objectives, and classifying and grouping them departmentally, managers must assign the activities to individuals and give them the appropriate authority to accomplish their tasks. This step is critical to organizing and is based on the principle of **functional definition**—in establishing a department, its nature, purpose, tasks, and performance must first be determined as a basis for authority. This essentially means that the activities to be performed should determine the type and quantity of authority necessary.

The step of assigning work and delegating authority is as necessary in a reorganization as it is in a start-up operation. When Procter & Gamble inserted a new level into its management structure, additional activities were created, departmentalized, and assigned to an appropriate manager (Dumaine, 1992). At Apple Computer, top managers reassigned marketing activities (those relative to software, hardware, enterprise solutions, and new personal electronics devices) according to product. As a result, the senior vice president at Apple USA is no longer in charge of product marketing (Quinlan, 1992).

Designing a Hierarchy of Relationships   The last step in the organizing process requires managers to determine the vertical and horizontal operating relationships of the organization as a whole. In this step, in effect, managers assemble all the parts of the organizing puzzle.

The vertical structure of an organization is a decision-making hierarchy. A diagram of the hierarchy shows who is in charge of each task, each specialty area, and the organization as a whole. The vertical structure defines levels of management throughout an organization. These levels create the hierarchy of decision-making levels. (As this chapter will discuss later, this hierarchy is known as the chain of command.) Creating the hierarchy also delineates the **span of control**—the number of subordinates under the direction of each manager.

Horizontal structuring defines the working relationships between operating departments.

From this final step should emerge a complete organizational structure that can be displayed in graphic form. A diagram of organizational structure is called an **organization chart**. Organization charts are disarmingly simple—so much so that many people mistakenly dismiss them as old-fashioned. A properly prepared organization chart provides managers with a powerful, effective, and convenient tool. Few models compress so much useful information into such an easy-to-read format. Look closely at Exhibit 7.3 and see what you can learn about Excelsior Table Saw by studying its organization chart.

An organization chart records:

1. Who reports to whom (the chain of command).

2. How many subordinates work for each manager (the span of control).

3. Channels of formal communication (the solid lines that connect each position represent these channels).

Exhibit 7.3

The organization chart of Excelsior Table Saw Corporation.

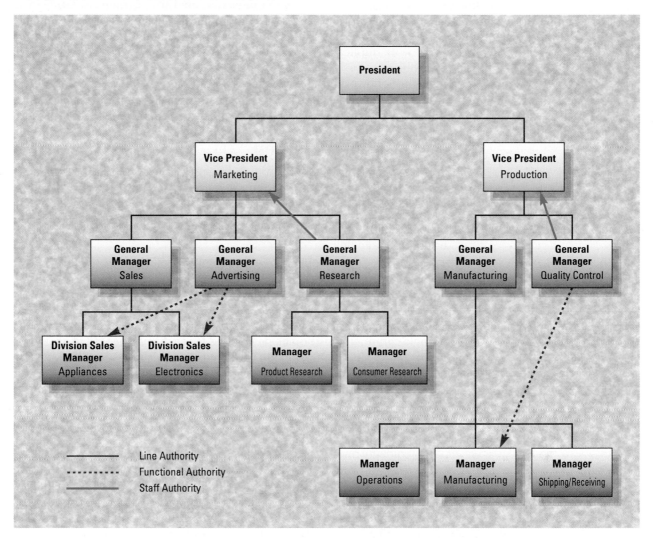

4. How the company is departmentalized—by function, customer, or product, for example.

5. The work being done by the people in each position (the titles in the boxes describe each person's activities).

6. The hierarchy of decision making.

7. The types of authority relationships (the lines between boxes show different types of authority). The next section in this chapter will describe each type.

Some managers use organization charts in much the same way that architects and engineers use drawings and blueprints—to design and construct and to maintain and troubleshoot. In the planning and design (or redesign) stage, managers can easily display alternative organizational arrangements to study their effectiveness and spot difficulties. In the operational stage, a review of the chart could suggest the presence of a bottleneck. Or, by studying the chart a manager might spot work duplications, personality clashes, obstacles to communication, or other problems.

Recognize, however, that such charts do not reveal some subtle but crucial organizational elements: degrees of authority, informal communication channels, and informal relationships. All these aspects will be considered later in this chapter.

The Benefits of Organizing

While propelling the firm toward its core purpose, the properly implemented organizing process:

- Clarifies the work environment. When a firm is properly organized, everyone knows what to do and what each unit's job is. Authority is established and delimited.

- Creates a coordinated environment. Unambiguous interrelationships among work units and sensible guidelines for interaction prevent confusion and preclude obstacles to performance.

- Achieves unity of direction. The principle of **unity of direction** states that a single command position be designated for each specific task of an organization and that the person who holds that position should have sole authority to coordinate all plans concerning the task.

- Establishes the chain of command. The **chain of command** is the formal decision-making structure. It establishes an orderly way for communication to proceed up and down the hierarchy.

The organizing process, like all managerial functions, is ongoing. The process enables managers in a new organization to construct an organizational structure and organization chart. As the firm begins its systematic pursuit of goals, managers monitor and control the structure. The organizing process can help managers make necessary changes and reassignments. Organizing is among managers' most useful tools. It allows them a pattern by which to continuously make changes to improve the chances of success for their organizations.

The Concepts of Organizing

The organizing process draws its force from tested organizational concepts that managers use to develop powerful systems. To organize effectively, managers must master these concepts: authority, unity of command, power, delegation, span of control, and centralization/decentralization.

Authority

Because authority plays so central a role in organizations, managers should fully understand its nature, sources, importance, variations, and relationship to power.

Nature, Sources, and Importance of Authority   Managers possess authority in different degrees, according to the management level they occupy. **Authority** is the formal and legitimate right of a manager to make decisions, give orders, and allocate resources. Authority binds an organization together because it provides the means of command.

Authority arises from the position a person occupies in an organization. It is specified and defined in the job description, or job charter. The person is vested with the authority of a position while he or she occupies that position. As the job changes in scope and complexity (in young organizations such change is common), so does the amount and type of formal authority that accompanies it. Albert Bersticker, the CEO of Ferro Corporation, noted: "The Ivory Tower isn't dictating all corporate moves. What I stress from my management team is that they make the decisions. I won't tell a divisional manager what to do—I want him to decide how to fix it, tweak it, or get rid of it. The authority for decisions is theirs—that's what their job is" (Moskal, 1992).

Types of Authority   The relationships between individuals and departments give rise to three different types of authority: line authority, staff authority, and functional authority.

Line authority defines the relationship between superior and subordinate. Managers who supervise operating employees—or other managers—possess line authority and may give direct orders to those subordinates, evaluate their actions, and reward or punish them. At a Mrs. Fields store, each store manager holds line authority over the employees. Line authority flows downward from superior to subordinate, as Exhibit 7.4 illustrates. In organization charts, solid lines usually represent line authority.

Managers who provide advice or technical assistance and who serve in an advisory capacity have **staff authority**. Staff authority (which is sometimes called advisory authority) provides no basis for direct control over subordinates or activities. Within the advisor's department, the staff manager is vested with line authority over subordinates. Staff authority—in the form of advice, assistance, or

Exhibit 7.4

Line authority: the relationship between superior and subordinate.

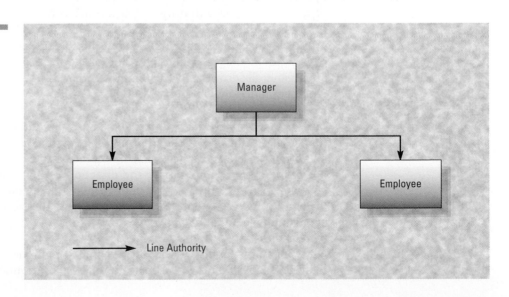

Exhibit 7.5

Staff authority: advice and information flow upward and laterally.

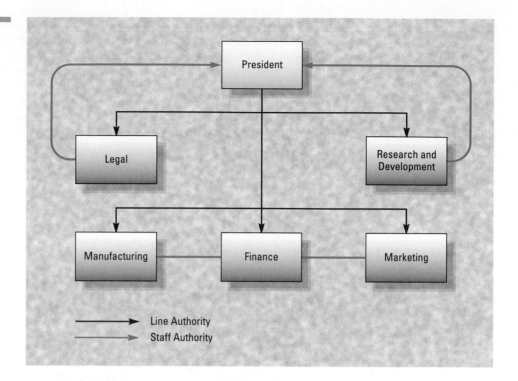

service—routinely flows upward and laterally. In organization charts, as Exhibit 7.5 shows, dotted lines usually represent staff authority.

Functional authority permits staff managers to make decisions about specific activities performed by personnel within other departments. Staff departments often utilize functional authority to control procedures in other departments. Exhibit 7.6 shows how the personnel manager monitors and reviews recruiting, selection, and evaluation systems in the operating departments. Functional authority is restricted and precise: For example, the personnel manager does not have the authority to tell the marketing manager which products to promote or the manufacturing manager which products to make. For budgeting purposes, the chief financial officer at Mrs. Fields exercises functional authority over all the managers. Functional authority routinely flows across departmental lines, generally downward or laterally. In organization charts, broken lines usually represent functional authority.

Line and Staff Departments   Line and staff authority describe that granted to managers; line and staff departments are terms for different roles or positions for various functions in the organizational structure.

Line departments, under the direction of line managers, accomplish the core work of a firm. Such work includes production (goods and services), marketing (sales, purchasing, advertising, and physical distribution), and finance (the acquisition of capital resources). Line departments directly influence the success of a business.

Staff departments, under the direction of staff managers, provide assistance to the line departments and to each other. Their contribution to the firm's objectives

Exhibit 7.6

Functional authority: managers make decisions about personnel in other departments.

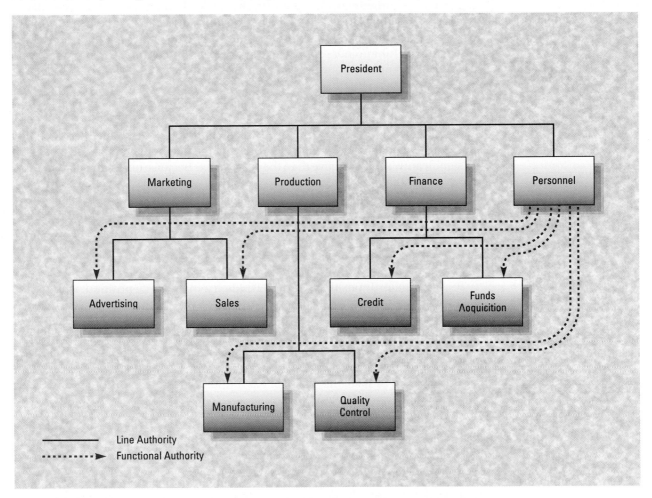

Line Authority

Functional Authority

may be characterized as indirect. Staff departments advise, serve, and assist. Traditional examples of staff departments include legal services, human resources, computer services, public relations, and medical services.

Managers must carefully monitor interactions between line and staff departments. Because staff people must "sell" their ideas, line personnel may view them as pushy or, occasionally, as actually undermining the line managers. To maintain credibility, staffers must perform their roles with tact and diligence. Unsound or arrogantly presented advice quickly generates resistance from line people.

Unity of Command

Another major organizational concept is the principle of **unity of command**. According to this principle, each person in an organization should take orders from and report to only one person.

Situations that lead to violations of the principle tend to arise inadvertently. They may continue for some time before they cause difficulty, depending upon circumstances and personalities. Operating relationships developed through staff departments sometimes interfere with the unity of command. On a given day, a worker may be asked to accept guidance from human resources about employment practices, from finance about the budget, and from data processing about computer procedures. Unhappiness may result. By respecting command unity, managers can help prevent or minimize such problems.

Power

Two managers with comparable technical skills and experience may occupy positions of equal formal authority. Nevertheless, one manager may be perceived as significantly more effective than the other. Why? Because one manager possesses more power than the other.

Power is the ability to exert influence in an organization. Possessing power multiplies a manager's effectiveness beyond the result attainable through formal authority alone. Authority is positional. It remains when the incumbent leaves. Power is personal. It exists because of the person who has it. Among the types of power are:

- Legitimate, or positional power. Holding a managerial position, with its accompanying formal authority, provides a manager with a power base. The manager has the right to use power because of the position. The higher a manager's place in the organization hierarchy, the greater the "perceived power"—the power that subordinates think exists, regardless of whether it actually does. Positional power also includes the power to reward or punish; the manager has authority over raises, promotions, and preferential treatment.

- Referent power. This power derives from an individual's personality or charisma and how others perceive it. A manager admired by others, who may strive to identify with or emulate him or her, has this type of power, which can be used to motivate and lead others.

- Expert power. Those who demonstrate superior skills and knowledge have expert power. Others hope to stay on an expert's good side so they will benefit from his or her expertise.

Chapter 13 will discuss power in detail.

Delegation

Delegation occurs as a company grows and additional demands are placed on a manager, or because a manager wishes to develop the managerial skills of subordinates. **Delegation** is the downward transfer of formal authority from one person to another (Plunkett, 1992). Superiors delegate authority to subordinates to facilitate the accomplishment of work.

The Importance of Delegation   As Debra Fields discovered, no one person can do it all. To allow themselves to focus on critical concerns, managers should delegate tasks. Capable subordinates can multiply a manager's ability; thoughtful delegation allows subordinates to acquire experience and confidence.

The Fear of Delegation   "When you fail to delegate, the monkey on your back gets fatter and fatter until it squashes you," says Paul Maguire, a senior partner of a management consulting firm (Ayers-Williams, 1992). Even knowing this, some managers resist delegating. Some fear giving up authority, or lack confidence in subordinates. Others worry that employees will outperform them, or are too impatient or detail-oriented to give up their task focus. Some managers simply do not know how to delegate. Learning how to entrust power to others has been compared to learning to ride a bicycle—you have to learn to let go (Hellman, 1992).

Delegation ranks high among the factors that determine a manager's success or failure (Taylor, 1992). The delegating process embraces two central management precepts: responsibility and accountability.

The Delegation Process   When managers delegate, they set a four-step sequence of events in motion. The steps include:

1. Assignment of tasks. The manager identifies specific tasks or duties and assigns them to the subordinate. At Grimpen Advertising, Sharon's manager assigns to her the task of creating a campaign for the agency's new account, a styling salon called The Hair Connection.

2. Delegation of decision-making authority. To accomplish the assigned tasks or duties, a subordinate must possess the necessary authority to make decisions, which the manager should delegate along with the assignment. The subordinate should understand precisely what amount of authority the manager is delegating. The authority should be sufficient to accomplish the assignment—no more, no less. In Sharon's case, she receives the authority to spend $10,000 on the campaign and to hire the graphic designer who will help create it.

3. Acceptance of responsibility. **Responsibility** is the obligation to carry out one's assigned duties to the best of one's ability. Responsibility is not delegated by a manager to an employee; rather, the employee's acceptance of an assignment creates an obligation to do his or her best. When Sharon accepts The Hair Connection account and agrees to prepare the campaign by the deadline and within the budget, she becomes responsible to her boss for the project.

4. Creation of accountability. Being answerable to someone for your actions creates **accountability**, an obligation to accept the consequences—either credit or blame. A subordinate, in accepting an assignment and the requisite authority, becomes accountable to the manager.

Delegation does not relieve a manager of responsibility and accountability. A manager remains responsible and accountable for the use of his or her authority, and for personal performance as well as the performance of subordinates. If Sharon misses her deadline, exceeds the budget, or produces an unacceptable campaign, she must answer to her manager. For having assigned the account to an incompetent, her manager must answer to the vice president. On the other

---

F O C U S   O N   Q U A L I T Y

The Power of Empowerment

As the quest for quality picks up momentum in American industry, old methods to achieve results are being rediscovered and renamed. At the core of quality philosophy, programs, and training—whatever their names—lies employee empowerment. Empowering employees means allowing them the freedom to make decisions.

At Alphatronix—a small, high-tech company in Research Triangle Park, North Carolina—CEO Robert Freese attributes some of the recent achievements of his firm to his long-practiced philosophy of delegating authority. "Wise business people have known for years that it pays to delegate, because it unleashes subordinates' energies, and frees managers to deal with broader issues."

Through delegation at Alphatronix, Freese has freed himself up to do a "great deal of strategic planning." At the same time, the employees have taken hold of the quality program. As Freese says, "That's the ideal situation, where management doesn't have to spend all of its time making things happen."

Employees have become the problem solvers at Alphatronix. When the company suffered from cash-flow problems, a team of employees identified part of the cause: a backlog of supplies in inventory. Inventories grew because suppliers shipped only once a month. On the recommendation of the employee team, Alphatronix switched to once-a-week deliveries. Shipping costs went up, but inventories went way down. Cash flow improved accordingly. Comparable success came in the production department, where employees were empowered to make quality decisions. When a product series began to come off the assembly line scratched, the employee team members devised a permanent solution—they recommended giving the product a scratchproof surface.

For more about delegation and quality, see Michael Barrier, "Small Firms Put Quality First," *Nation's Business,* May 1992, pp. 22–30.

---

hand, if Sharon creates a dazzling campaign a week ahead of schedule for 20% below budget, Sharon gets the credit and maybe a raise; her manager becomes creative director.

By following the four steps of delegation, the manager and the subordinate should gain a clear understanding of the task and how it is to be accomplished.

Span of Control

As managers design the organizational structure, they are concerned with the span of control—the number of subordinates a manager directly supervises.

Wide and Narrow Spans of Control   As a general rule, the more complex the jobs of a manager's subordinates, the fewer subordinates the manager should supervise. The more routine the work of subordinates, the greater the number of workers the manager can direct and control effectively. These facts explain why organizations usually incorporate narrow spans at their tops and wider spans at lower levels. The higher the manager's position, the smaller the number of subordinates that report to him or her. In a word processing department or on the factory floor, a production manager who supervises 15 or more subordinates

Exhibit 7.7

Narrow and wide spans of control.

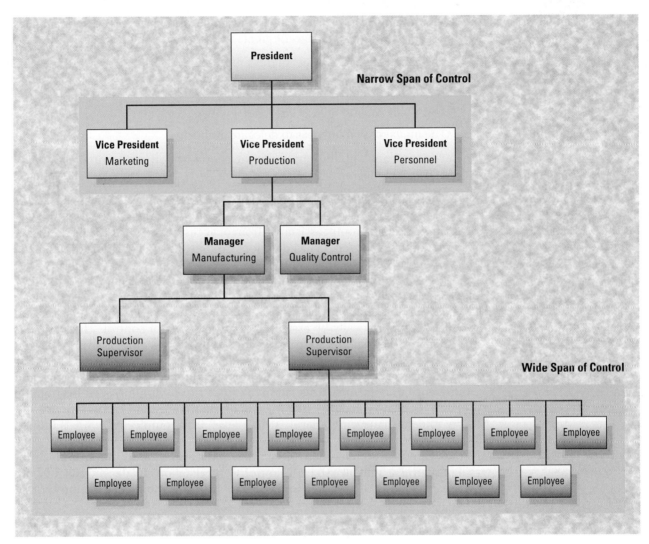

is not uncommon. These realities often result in organization charts that resemble Exhibit 7.7.

Workers who can be well trained to follow procedures will, once they master their tasks, require little of their supervisor's time and energy. They will know what they must do and exactly how to do it to meet performance standards.

Conversely, it is rare for more than a handful of subordinates to report to a corporate vice president. Because they encounter complex problems that are seldom routine, middle and upper managers must apply ingenuity and creativity. These managers require more time to plan and organize their efforts. When they turn to their bosses for help, the bosses must have the time available to assist them. The way to make that time available is to limit the number of people who will normally need it. Hence, narrow spans of control are typical in the high levels of an organization.

The Proper Span of Control   Given these facts, how many subordinates should report to any one manager? A great many variables influence each situation:

- The complexity and variety of the subordinates' work

- The competence and ability of the manager

- The ability and training of the subordinates

- The manager's willingness to delegate authority

- The company's philosophy about the centralization or decentralization of decision making

The span of control has a crucial influence on a manager's effectiveness. If a manager must supervise too many people, the subordinates will be frustrated by the inability to gain prompt assistance from or access to their boss. Time and other resources may be wasted. Plans, decisions, and actions may be delayed or made without proper controls or safeguards.

If a manager supervises too few people, the subordinates may be overworked or oversupervised. They may become frustrated and dissatisfied.

Two managers who hold positions at the same level in the organization should not automatically be assigned identical spans of control. Their abilities and those of their subordinates may differ, and their spans of control should reflect those differences.

In general, control spans can be widened with the growth in experience and competence of personnel. This fact underlines the continuing need for training and development. Of course, training and development can widen spans only up to the middle-management level. At that level, task complexity compels limited spans of control.

A company's preference for centralization or decentralization in decision making can also influence span of control. Centralization and decentralization are factors of growing significance in the 1990s, as this chapter will describe shortly.

Centralization Versus Decentralization

The terms **centralization** and **decentralization** refer to a philosophy of organization and management that focuses on either the selective concentration (centralization) or the dispersal (decentralization) of authority within an organizational structure (Kountz and O'Donnel, 1976). A management operating philosophy determines where an organization's authority resides. Managers decide whether to concentrate authority for decision making in the hands of one or a few or to force it down the organization structure into the hands of many.

Centralization and decentralization are relative concepts when applied to organizations. Top managers may decide to centralize all decision making—that is, all decision making about purchasing, staffing, operations, and the like. Or they may decide to partially decentralize. In this case top managers set limits (in terms of dollar amounts) on what can be purchased at each level. They give first-level

I S S U E S   A N D   E T H I C S
Ethics Violations Make Banner Headlines

Did television networks rig crash tests to embarrass auto makers? Do drug manufacturers price vaccines so high that American children remain vulnerable to preventable diseases? Do professional weight-loss centers operate on empty promises? Issues of corporate ethics have become banner headlines. In recent months, managers have been accused of:

- Passing off sugar-water as apple juice for babies

- Spending lavishly while the organization's revenues fall

- Introducing a product with erroneous and outdated information about its abilities

- Peddling influence and falsifying documents and test results

- Defrauding fixed-income investors of millions of dollars

- Dumping deadly toxic wastes into rivers and lakes

- Transporting milk in unwashed tank trucks whose prior loads were carcinogenic pesticides

The individuals involved in these cases, following lengthy civil or criminal litigation, were censured or jailed. Their companies were fined or shut down.

How can middle-level managers ensure that subordinates act ethically? Who is responsible for corporate acts of the kind cited in the preceding list? Who should be held accountable? If you were the president of a corporation accused of any of the cited acts but did not know about them until they were publicly disclosed, would you feel responsible? How would you respond when you were informed? ▲

managers authority to hire clerical workers and to make operational decisions when appropriate.

Decisions at Honda Motor Company of Japan illustrate how a company's preference for centralization or decentralization can change. In March 1991, Honda President Nobuhiko Kawamoto abruptly reversed the firm's long tradition of consensus management. At Kawamoto's direction, top executives began making more decisions. In June 1992, Kawamoto launched a company-wide reorganization that decentralized authority, sending it to lower levels of management.

Kawamoto said the decision of March 1991 was an interim move required during an analysis of the company's overall direction and operations. He said the decision of June 1992 was designed to give more decision-making authority to middle management. As Kawamoto noted, "I'm moving out of the day-to-day management. I have to take a broader view" (Chandler, 1992).

Why Decentralize?   To be effective, authority should be decentralized to the management level best suited to the decision in question. A company president should not decide when to overhaul the engine in a forklift. Authority for that decision should be decentralized to the lowest possible level—in this case, the plant maintenance manager.

More and more organizations see decentralization as a means to achieve greater productivity and a way of rebuilding themselves. Decentralization allows managers to be closer to the action. As more organizations move toward "flat" organizational structures, with few levels of management, *decentralization* and *accountability* are becoming watchwords for management success (Spertus, 1992). Major corporations—such as Mattel, General Foods, and Intercraft Industries—are moving to a more decentralized philosophy of management (Straub and Attner, 1991).

Guidelines for Judging Decentralization   Research and experience have produced guidelines for determining the degree to which a company is decentralized:

- The greater the number of decisions made at the lower levels of management, the more the company is decentralized.

- The more important the decisions made at lower levels, the greater the decentralization. Purchasing decisions are a good measure. A company with a purchasing limit of $100,000 at the first level is more decentralized than a company in the same industry with a first-level limit of $1,000.

- The more flexible the interpretation of company policy at the lower levels, the greater the degree of decentralization.

- The more widely dispersed the operations of the company geographically, the greater the degree of decentralization.

- The less a subordinate must refer to a manager prior to making a decision, the greater the decentralization.

Relationship Between Centralization and Span of Control   A company's philosophy of centralization or decentralization in decision making can influence the span of control of lower and middle managers. It can also influence the number of levels in an organization. Centralized decision making produces narrow spans of control and more levels of management. With centralized management, top-level managers delegate little authority and must closely supervise those who report to them.

Recall that, if a manager must supervise subordinates closely, he or she must commit time to a limited few. Given the philosophy of centralization, successive levels of managers will follow the same practice. Therefore, there will always be narrow spans of control and the company will need many levels of management to reach first-line supervisors. This condition is common to large, mature companies like General Motors and IBM. Exhibit 7.8 presents the organization chart of a centralized organization.

Conversely, a philosophy of decentralized decision making generally leads to a company with wider spans of control and fewer levels of management. Such firms delegate authority and decision making to lower levels of management, which allows managers to spend time with subordinates. As managers at each successive level follow this philosophy, the results are wide spans of control. Fewer management levels are needed to do the same job, because people operate relatively independently. See Exhibit 7.8 to study the organization chart of a decentralized organization.

Despite the logic of the interrelationship of decision making and span of control, it does not always hold true in practice. Managers with wide spans of control may choose not to delegate authority, and many times they are not as

Exhibit 7.8

The structures of centralized and decentralized organizations.

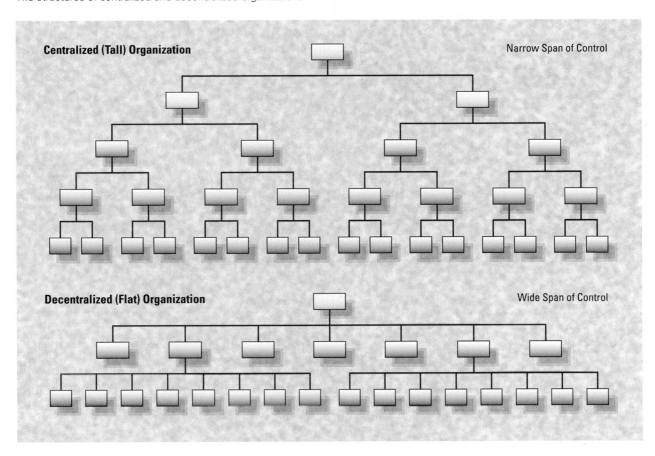

Centralized (Tall) Organization   Narrow Span of Control

Decentralized (Flat) Organization   Wide Span of Control

effective as they could be if they did delegate. In addition, other factors (such as those noted in the discussion about span of control) can influence how many subordinates report to any one manager.

The Informal Organization

Within the formal organization designed by management—the organization of departmental structure, designated leaders (managers), decision-making guidelines, policies, procedures, and rules—is another system of social relationships. These relationships constitute the informal organization. Managers must understand this informal organization because it influences the productivity and job satisfaction of all members of the organization, managers as well as nonmanagers. Managers soon find through experience that not everything in an organization takes place within the squares of the organization chart. People by nature refuse to "stay in the boxes." They choose to operate within the confines of and with the support of the informal organization.

The Informal Organization Defined

The **informal organization** is a network of personal and social relationships that arise spontaneously as people associate in a work environment (Davis and Newstrom, 1989). It consists of all the informal groupings of people within a formal organization, and memberships shift fluidly over time. Members join because of the need for and enjoyment of one another's company. They find membership beneficial in one or several ways.

The informal organization challenges a manager because it consists of actual relationships that have real consequences on workers' behavior but that are not prescribed by the formal organization. Obviously, these relationships do not appear on the company's organization chart.

The informal organization knows no boundaries. It cuts across the organization because it is the result of personal and social relationships, not prescribed roles. The informal organization is two workers who, at work or after work, share their perceptions of company affairs and colleagues. It is one employee assisting someone in another department to solve a work problem. The informal organization is not the domain of workers only. Managers often form informal groups that cut across departmental lines. In addition, they actively participate in other groups with nonmanagers. The informal organization thrives everywhere.

Informal and Formal Organizations Compared

In the informal organization, the emphasis is on people and their relationships; in the formal organization, the emphasis is on official organizational positions. The leverage, or clout, in the informal organization is informal power—it is attached to an individual. On the other hand, in the formal organization formal authority comes directly from the position. An individual retains formal authority only so long as he or she occupies the position. Informal power is personal; authority is organizational. Exhibit 7.9 makes these distinctions apparent.

Exhibit 7.9

A comparison of informal and formal organizations.

Informal Organization	Formal Organization
Unofficial organization created by relationships	Official organization created by management
Primary area of emphasis is on people and their relationships	Primary area of emphasis is official organization positions
Leverage is provided by power	Leverage is provided by authority
Source of power: given by the group	Source of authority: delegated by management
Functions with power and politics	Functions with authority and responsibility
Behavior guidelines provided by group norms	Behavior guidelines provided by rules, policies, and procedures
Sources of control over the individual are positive or negative sanctions	Sources of control over the individual are rewards and penalties

The members of an informal group allow certain people to exercise informal power. Informal power does not come from within a person; rather, it is given by group members. Authority, in contrast, is delegated by management and creates a chain of command. Informal power does not follow the official chain of command. Workers may grant power to a co-worker at the same level or to someone in another department. Power is far less stable than authority; it comes from how people feel about each other and may change rapidly.

A manager probably possesses some informal power along with his or her formal authority. The manager does not necessarily have more informal power than anyone else in the group, however. The manager and the informal leader can be—and often are—two different people.

Formal organizations may grow to be extremely large. Informal organizations tend to remain small because they are based on personal relationships. As a result, large corporations usually contain hundreds of informal organizations (Davis and Newstrom, 1989).

How the Informal Organization Emerges

Informal organizations may affect workers' behavior. Because of the relationships and alliances in the informal group, workers may not adhere to the reporting relationships, procedures, and rules established in the formal organization. Four factors cause this:

- Because employees are not robots, they sometimes act differently than anticipated. They may work faster or slower than expected or modify a work procedure based on their experience and knowledge.

- Employees may interact with people other than those the formal organization specifies or interact with specified people more or less often than their jobs require. Gene may seek advice from Joy instead of Larry, for example. Or Cindy may spend more time helping Buddy than Maceo.

The informal organization is composed of spontaneous relationships, such as those formed by a sports team. Managers need to realize that such associations exist and can both help and hinder the formal structure.

- Workers may adopt a whole set of beliefs and attitudes that differ from those the organization expects of them. The company may expect loyalty, commitment, and enthusiasm, but some employees may become totally unenthusiastic while others are openly rebellious and alienated. Values or attitudes that employees as a group accept as standards of behavior are known as **norms**. A norm serves as a guideline for behavior and an internal control device on members.

- The groups of workers that form may begin to display cohesion. **Cohesion** is a strong attachment to the group and a closeness measured by a single-ness of purpose and a high degree of cooperation. As a result, a manager has dual sets of behavior to monitor—the activities, interactions, and beliefs required by the formal organization and the ones that develop as people interact (Davis and Newstrom, 1989).

The Structure of the Informal Organization

Because individuals are constantly entering and exiting an informal organization, it is constantly changing. Its structure can be identified through the communication and contact developed throughout the group. An **interaction chart** identifies the informal organization structure according to the interactions of its members. Exhibit 7.10 presents an example of an interaction chart. Notice that the contacts represented in the interaction chart can short-circuit the chain of command shown in the organization chart.

Leadership of the Group   As in a formal organization, the informal group develops leader-follower relationships. Because of the number of informal groups in an organization, a person may lead in one group and be a follower in another.

Exhibit 7.10

The interaction of informal communication.

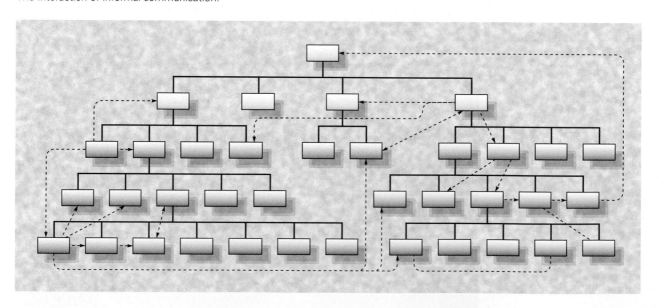

Each group member exhibits identifiable characteristics that distinguish him or her from other members. Some of these characteristics are age, seniority, earnings, and technical ability. Each characteristic can confer status on its holder—the nature of the status is based on what the group members value. The employee with the most status in the informal organization emerges as its informal leader. This person possesses great informal power. In some groups, charismatic leadership is common. In others, the leader may be the most senior person or the person holding the highest position in the formal organization.

A group may include several leaders of varying importance. Each one performs different functions. The group may look to one person as the expert on organizational matters and to another as its social leader. A third may be required to answer technical questions. But even in a multileader situation, one leader usually exerts more influence on the group than the others.

Nonleader Roles for Members   Members of an informal group play other roles besides leader. As Exhibit 7.11 suggests, informal groups normally develop an inner core, or primary group; a fringe group, which functions inside and outside

Exhibit 7.11

The composition of an informal group.

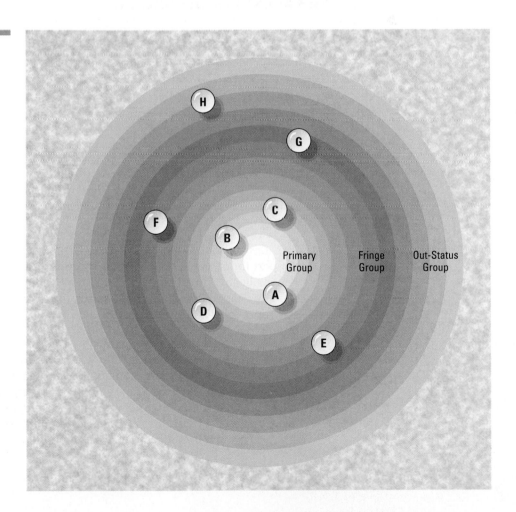

the group; and an out-status group, which though identified with the group, does not actively participate in group activities (Harmon and Scott, 1970).

How to Work with the Informal Organization   Recognizing the existence of informal groups is the first step for the manager who wants to work with them. The second step is to identify the roles members play within each. The third step is to use the information to work with the informal groups.

Managers should understand the personality, values, and culture of each group and how the groups' values and norms differ from those of the formal organization (if they do). Ideally, the manager will be able to identify the leaders of these groups and work with them to influence the total group. Subtle distinctions are important: Trying to influence a group by appealing to a fringe member will fail. The leaders, at the core of decision making, are the ones to approach.

Managers can use the communication network of an informal organization to spread the word about a new company policy or to learn about how workers perceive a new company head.

The Impact of the Informal Organization

Because the informal organization can affect the formal organization so significantly, Exhibit 7.12 bears close examination. It presents the positive and negative potentials of informal organizations.

Positive Impact   As Davis and Newstrom (1989) reported, an informal organization may be helpful to managers in a number of ways. An informal organization:

- Makes the total system effective. If the informal organization blends well with the formal system, the organization can function more effectively. The ability of the informal group to provide flexibility and instantaneous reactions can enhance the plans and procedures developed through the formal organization.

- Provides support to management. The informal organization can provide support to individual managers. It can fill in gaps in the manager's knowledge by providing advice or actually doing the needed work. When the group performs effectively and positively, it builds a cooperative environment. This, in turn, can lead the manager to delegate more tasks to employees.

- Provides stability in the environment. The informal organization provides acceptance and a sense of belonging. These feelings of being wanted and part of the group can encourage employees to remain in the environment, reducing turnover. Additionally, the informal organization provides a place for people to vent frustrations. Being able to discuss difficulties in a supportive environment can relieve emotional pressure.

Exhibit 7.12

The positive and negative potential of informal organizations.

Positives	Negatives
+ Makes the total system effective	− Develops pressure for conformity
+ Provides support to management	− Creates conflicts
+ Provides stability in the workplace	− Resists change
+ Provides a useful communication channel	− Initiates rumors and processes false information
+ Encourages better management	− Exposes weak management

- Provides a useful communication channel. The informal organization provides employees with opportunities for social interaction and discussion about work that helps members understand the work environment.

- Encourages better management. Managers should be aware of the power of the informal organization; it can be, in effect, part of a check-and-balance system. Planned changes should be made with an awareness of the ability of the informal group to make the plan successful or unsuccessful.

Negative Impact   Davis and Newstrom (1989) have also identified the potential problems of an informal organization. An informal organization may present:

- Pressure to conform. The norms of informal groups strongly pressure group members to conform. The more cohesive the group, the stronger the acceptance of behavioral standards. An informal group often uses rewards or penalties, called **sanctions**, to persuade its members to conform to its norms. Nonconforming can result in little more than gentle verbal reminders. On the other hand, group members might resort to harassment or ostracism. They might hide tools, or rearrange the work area in an effort to enforce norms.

- Conflict. The informal group can be, in effect, a second master for an employee. In an attempt to satisfy the informal group, the employee may come into conflict with the formal organization. Suppose, for example, that an office "lunch bunch" enjoys eating a leisurely meal and analyzing the company. The group takes a 60-minute break though management has authorized only a 30-minute break. The employees' social satisfaction conflicts with the employer's need for productivity.

- Resistance to change. To protect its values and beliefs, the informal group can place roadblocks in the path of modifications. If a proposed four-day workweek or the hiring of younger workers infringes on the values of the informal group, the result can be the group's resistance to change.

- Rumor. The informal communication system—the grapevine—can create and process false information, or rumors. Rumors can upset the balance of the work environment.

- Exposure for weak managers. Although skilled managers can see and use the relationships of informal organizations, other managers may be stymied by them. The result may be a work group that does not perform and a manager who does not last.

Future Trends

Based on the current environment, three predictions relate to core organizational concepts in the future:

- Decentralization of decision-making authority will continue to be a driving force within organizations. As companies try to deal with fierce competition and a lagging economy, the ability to respond quickly is vital. The best way to cultivate that ability is to force decision making down the structure.

- Delegation of authority will become a key to quality efforts and employee commitment. As a key ingredient in employee empowerment, delegation can serve as an aid in productivity, commitment, and growth.

- Accountability will become increasingly prominent in the organizational environment. In a climate that encourages delegation, accountability for actions, decisions, and results will become ever more important.

C H A P T E R   **S** U M M A R Y

- Planning alone cannot ensure an organization's success. Having taken the time, energy, and money to develop plans, the firm needs to organize its employees to implement those plans.

- The organizing process is continuous. New plans and goals may require changes in an organization's structure or in the number and kinds of subdivisions needed to execute plans.

- In the organizing process, the company reviews plans and goals, determines the work activities necessary to accomplish them, classifies and groups activities, assigns work and delegates appropriate authority, and designs a hierarchy of relationships.

- Organizations may choose to divide their personnel and other resources along various departmental lines. The most popular approaches concentrate on function, geography, product line, or customer type.

- The three types of authority—line, staff, and functional—derive from the position a manager holds.

- Organizations operate with line and staff departments. Line departments meet the major objectives of an organization and directly influence its success. Staff departments contribute indirectly, by providing advice, service, and assistance.

- According to the principle of unity of command, each person within an organization should take orders and report to only one person.

- Power is a management tool. A personal phenomenon, power comes from charisma, skill, and knowledge, and the position a person holds in the company.

- Delegation is the downward transfer of formal authority from one person to another. It involves assignment of tasks, delegation of decision-making authority, acceptance of responsibility, and creation of accountability.

- Span of control refers to the number of employees a manager supervises. There is no correct number for the span of control, but it is normally more narrow at the top of the organization than at the bottom.

- Centralization and decentralization focus on either the concentration (centralization) or dispersal (decentralization) of authority within the organization.

- Functioning within the formal organization is a system of social relationships. These relationships constitute the informal organization, which has its own leaders and followers. Managers need to work with the informal organization to be effective.

- The informal organization can affect the formal organization positively by making the total system effective, providing support to management, providing stability in the environment, providing a useful communication channel, and encouraging better management.

- The informal organization can affect the formal organization negatively by pressuring for conformity, creating conflict, resisting change, initiating rumor, and exposing weak management.

S K I L L - B U I L D I N G

This series of questions invites you to apply your knowledge of organizing principles. In developing your thoughts, consider the organizational structure in place at your present job, at another company where you worked before, or at another organization with which you are sufficiently familiar.

1. Identify and briefly describe the department where you work.

2. Was the department created on the basis of function, geography, product line, or customer? Explain.

3. Do you consider the department a line or staff unit? Explain.

4. Does your manager have line, staff, or functional authority, or a combination of all three types? Explain your answer.

5. Is your department organized according to the principle of unity of command? Explain.

6. What are the sources of your manager's power?

7. What is your manager's span of control?

8. Does your manager delegate authority? Cite examples.

R E V I E W   Q U E S T I O N S

1. Review this chapter's essential terms and look up the meanings of those you cannot define.

2. How do the functions of planning and organizing relate to each other (a) in the initial development of a company and (b) during the modifications of a company's structure?

3. Identify three important benefits of the organizing process.

4. List the five steps in the organizing process and draft a one-sentence description of each.

5. Identify the four popular approaches to departmentalizing. Specify which approach you would recommend for each of the following organizations, and defend your choices.

   a. A retail hardware store

   b. A company that makes and markets one product

   c. A company with sales offices in 40 states

   d. A retail department store

6. Identify and characterize the three types of authority.

7. What is power? What are its sources? How does it differ from authority?

8. Explain the importance to managers of each of these organizing concepts or principles:
   a. Unity of direction
   b. Unity of command
   c. Chain of command
   d. Delegation of authority
   e. Span of control
   f. Centralization/decentralization
   g. Line and staff departments
   h. Responsibility
   i. Accountability

9. What does the term *informal organization* mean? Of what does the informal organization consist?

10. How does a formal organization differ from an informal organization?

R E C O M M E N D E D **R** E A D I N G

Berger, Joseph. *Status, Rewards, and Influence* (San Francisco: Jossey-Bass), 1991.

Brislin, Richard W. *The Art of Getting Things Done: A Practical Guide to the Use of Power* (Westport, CT: Greenwood), 1991.

Bubler, O. M. "The Keys to Shaping Organizations," *Supervision* (January 1992), pp. 18–20.

Dankbaar, Ben. *Perspective in Industrial Organization* (Norwell, MA: Kluwer Academic Publishing), 1991.

DiPorto, Amy. "The Jobs That Lead to Better Jobs," *Executive Female* (January–February 1992), pp. 38–41.

Dowding, Keith. *Rational Choice and Power* (Brookfield, VT: Gower), 1991.

Marsh, R. M. "The Difference Between Participation and Power in Japanese Factories," *Industrial Labor Relations Review* (January 1992), pp. 29–31.

Sondak, Allen. "Upward Delegation—It's Alive and Well," *Supervisory Management* (January 1992), p. 36.

Yovovich, B. G. "Vertical No More," *Business Marketing* (January 1992), pp. 20–21.

Zuker, Elaina. *Seven Secrets of Influence* (New York: McGraw-Hill), 1991.

R E F E R E N C E S

Ayers-Williams, Roz. "Mastering the Fine Art of Delegation," *Black Enterprise* (April 1992), pp. 91–93.

Chandler, Clay. "Honda's Middle Managers Will Regain Authority in New Overhead of Company," *Wall Street Journal,* June 15, 1992, p. 173.

Daft, Richard L. *Management,* 2nd edition (Hinsdale, IL: Dryden Press), 1991, p. 246.

Daft, Richard L. *Organization Theory and Design* (St. Paul, MN: West), 1983, p. 227.

Davis, Keith, and John Newstrom. *Human Behavior at Work: Organizational Behavior,* 8th edition (New York: McGraw-Hill), 1989, pp. 262, 362–363, 364, 366–367.

Dumaine, Briane. "Procter & Gamble Shoots for the Top," *Industry Week* (January 6, 1992), pp. 24–25.

Harmon, Theo, and William B. Scott. *Management in the Modern Organization* (Boston: Houghton Mifflin), 1970, p. 452.

Healey, James R. "Hughes Aircraft to Lay Off 9,000," *USA Today,* July 1, 1992, p. 1B.

Hellman, Paul. "Delegating Is Easy, Deputizing a Posse Is Tough," *Management Review* (June 1992), p. 58.

Kountz, Harold, and Cyril O'Donnel. *Management* (New York: McGraw-Hill), 1976, p. 375.

Loomis, Carol J. "What If They Had Broken Up IBM Like AT&T," *Fortune* (July 27, 1991), p. 52.

Moskal, Brian S. "The Buck Doesn't Stop Here," *Industry Week* (July 15, 1992), pp. 29–30.

Plunkett, W. Richard. *Supervision,* 6th edition (Needham Heights, MA: Allyn and Bacon), 1992, p. 70.

Quinlan, Tom. "Apple Shakes Up Marketing Division," *Info World* (March 16, 1992), pp. 1, 8.

Smith, Adam. *The Wealth of Nations* (New York: Modern Library), 1937.

Spertus, Philip. "It's Easy to Fool the Boss," *Management Review* (May 1992), p. 28.

Straub, Joseph, and Raymond Attner. *Introduction to Business* (Boston: PWS-Kent), 1991, pp. 124–125.

Taylor, Alex. "Chrysler's Next Boss Speaks," *Fortune* (July 27, 1992), pp. 82–83.

Velocci, Anthony L. "United Technologies Restructures in Bid to Boost Profitability, Competitiveness," *Aviation Week and Space Technology* (January 27, 1992), p. 35.

Verespej, Michael A. "Stern Hand," *Industry Week* (February 17, 1992), p. 25.

G L O S S A R Y   O F   T E R M S

accountability   The need to answer for the results of one's actions.

authority   The formal legitimate right of a manager to make decisions, give orders, and allocate resources.

centralization   A philosophy of organizing that concentrates authority within a selected portion of an organizational structure.

chain of command   The unbroken line of reporting relationships, from the bottom to the top of an organization, that defines the formal decision-making structure.

cohesion   The measure of a group's solidarity—the degree to which the members cooperate and share the group's ideas.

customer departmentalization   Creating departments in response to the needs of specific customer groups.

decentralization   A philosophy of organizing and management that disperses authority within an organizational structure.

delegation   The downward transfer of formal authority from one person to another.

departmentalization   Creating groups, subdivisions, or departments that execute and oversee the various tasks that management considers essential.

division of labor   *See* specialization of labor.

formal organization   The official organizational structure that top management conceives and builds.

functional authority   The authority to make decisions about specific activities that are undertaken by personnel in other departments.

functional definition   A principle that maintains that the nature, purpose, tasks, and performance of a department must determine its authority.

functional departmentalization   Creating departments on the basis of the specialized activities of the business.

geographical departmentalization   Creating departments according to territory.

informal organization   A network of personal and social relationships that arises spontaneously as people associate with one another in the work environment.

interaction chart   A diagram that shows the informal organization.

line authority   Direct supervisory authority from superior to subordinate.

line department   A core work unit established to meet the major objectives of an organization and directly influence its success.

norm   Any standard of conduct, code, or pattern of behavior perceived by a group to be important for its members.

organization chart   A visual representation of the structure of an organization and how its parts fit together.

organizing   Establishing an orderly use of resources by assigning and coordinating tasks.

power   A person's ability to exert influence.

product departmentalization   Creating departments according to product.

responsibility   The obligation to carry out one's assigned duties to the best of one's ability.

sanction   A reward or penalty used by informal groups to persuade members to conform to norms.

span of control   The principle of organizing concerned with the number of subordinates each manager directs.

specialization of labor   The degree to which organizational tasks are subdivided into separate jobs.

staff authority   Authority to serve in an advisory capacity.

staff department   A work unit that, by providing advice or technical assistance, helps all departments meet the objectives of the organization.

unity of command   The organizing principle that states that each person in an organization should take orders from and report to only one person.

unity of direction   The organizing principle that states that each task be directed by a single command position and that the person in that position have the authority to perform the task.

C A S E   P R O B L E M

Crises at GM

he future of General Motors is in the hands of President John Jack Smith—and he has his work cut out for him. The company continues to flounder. It lags behind its major competitors in almost every measure of efficiency. By some key standards—how many worker hours it takes to assemble a car, for example—GM is 40% less productive than Ford. In 1991 GM lost, on average, $1,500 on every one of the more than 3.5 million cars and trucks it made in North America. It ended 1991 with about 35% of the U.S. market; the company had sold fewer than 13 million new cars and light trucks that year. In comparison, in 1979 GM had commanded 46% of the market.

Salvaging GM, in the opinion of both insiders and outside observers, will require a radical restructuring. The company has a long tradition of being highly centralized and insulated from the rest of the industry. The current structure still reflects a time when the company had abundant time to work on any problem.

The organizational problems that Smith faces include:

- The existence of separate marketing operations for each of its six car divisions—Chevrolet, Pontiac, Oldsmobile, Buick, Cadillac, and Saturn.

- The fact that GM, unlike any other auto company in the world, has a chief of design and a head of research who do not report to the auto-making side of the business. Instead, both report to the head of R&D, who in turn reports to another executive—a top-level manager who runs the aerospace divisions. This arrangement penalizes GM in two ways. Because designers do not work closely with vehicle engineers, development is long and costly. Second, scientists do not work with the engineers, so GM is slow to apply new technologies—even when GM developed them.

- A past history of poor managerial performance without accountability. Fewer than 100 salaried workers out of well over 100,000 were dismissed annually for poor performance between 1977 and 1983.

- A nonfunctioning decision-making structure. Middle managers—sometimes referred to as the "frozen middle"—have often been unable or unwilling to make decisions.

Q U E S T I O N S

1. For each of the four situations noted, what organizational concepts apply? Explain.

2. As an advisor to President John Jack Smith, how would you resolve each situation?

For more about the crises at GM, see Alex Taylor, "Can GM Remodel," *Fortune,* January 13, 1992, pp. 26–29, 32–34.

Organizational Design

LEARNING OBJECTIVES

After reading and discussing this chapter, you should be able to:

- Define this chapter's essential terms

- Explain the meaning of *organizational design*

- Describe the four objectives of organizational design

- Distinguish between mechanistic and organic organizational structures

- Discuss the influence that contingency factors—strategy, technology, organizational age and size, and environment— have on organizational design

- Describe the characteristics, advantages, and disadvantages of functional, divisional, matrix, team, and network structural designs

ESSENTIAL TERMS

continuous-process production

divisional structure
functional structure
large-batch technology

mass-production technology
matrix structure
mechanistic structure
network structure

organic structure
organizational design
organizational life cycle
small-batch technology
team structure
technology
unit production technology

MANAGEMENT IN ACTION
Johnson & Johnson, Structure That Works

Johnson & Johnson's 166 separately chartered operating companies are among the most aggressive and successful marketers in America. Their independence and aggressiveness came about by design, not by accident. At Johnson & Johnson, the presidents of the business units are expected to act independently. The result: In 1991, while so many American businesses barely scraped by, J & J boosted earnings 15%, to $1.5 billion.

Long before the rest of corporate America made *empowerment* a management buzzword, J & J was practicing it. In the 1930s, long-time Chairman Robert Wood Johnson advocated decentralization and set up business units that would operate independently. He believed that small, self-governing operating companies were more manageable and reactive than business units that were tightly tied to head-quarters bureaucracy.

Many other companies are following J & J's lead. Desperate to make International Business Machines more competitive, top managers at IBM broke the company into smaller operating units. Du Pont has

Young consumers of J & J products piece together a puzzle just as managers look for a good fit in designing organizations.

been gutting its middle-management ranks and giving survivors more responsibility. The goal is to cut costs and decrease the time Du Pont takes to get products to market. Top managers at PepsiCo are pushing decision making down to the lowest levels.

But J & J is not just a model of how to implement decentralization. The company also shows how to maintain it. At J & J, the system is not static. Top managers have, over the years, fine-tuned their approach and achieved a balance between entrepreneurial spirit and corporate structure. In the thick of this fine tuning is CEO Ralph Larsen, who is now seeking ways to cut corporate redundancies. Says Larsen, "We are working hard on integration. Even if we want to maintain the identity and autonomy of units that have built up a franchise over long periods, we are focusing on integration. It's a tremendously tough balancing act."

The integration efforts focus on back-office functions: payroll processing, computer services, purchasing, distribution, accounts payable, and benefits. Larsen's thrust has resulted in less redundancy in performing credit reviews, for example. Four separate departments used to do credit reviews (sometimes on the same customers); now one does the job. With Larsen intent on integrating and streamlining, Johnson & Johnson employees can expect more refinement in the future. ▲

> ❝ We are working hard on integration. Even if we want to maintain the identity and autonomy of units that have built up a franchise over long periods, we are focusing on integration. It's a tremendously tough balancing act. ❞
>
> — **Ralph Larsen**, CEO, Johnson & Johnson

For more about structure that works, see "A Big Company That Works," *Business Week,* May 4, 1992, pp. 124–132.

Designing Organizational Structures

Ralph Larsen and his team of managers continually refine the structure of Johnson & Johnson to boost the competitiveness of the company. Although this continual effort does not grab the headlines—as does recent dramatic restructuring of IBM and General Motors—it is representative of the practice of managers who have realized the importance of re-evaluating structure. These managers reorganize their companies as necessary to counter conditions in the environment, to incorporate new technology, or to accommodate organizational growth.

Chapter 7 examined the concepts and process of organizing. This chapter will focus on organizational structure as a tool. It will examine how managers integrate departmentalization, decentralization, and chain of command into an organizational design that will help them achieve specific objectives. Recently, many organizations—including Honda, Digital Equipment, Apple Computer, and GM—have restructured or are restructuring as a way to attain new strategic objectives (Verespej, 1992, p. 21). Structure is a powerful tool for attaining management objectives.

Organizational Design Defined

Organizational design is the creation of or change to an organization's structure. It includes developing the overall configuration of the positions and departments as well and the interrelationships among them (Robbins, 1991).

For an organizational designer like Johnson & Johnson's Ralph Larsen, organizational design is like putting together a jigsaw puzzle. But there are two differences. When a manager puts together an organization, there is no picture to tell him or her what the final result should be. And, in contrast to putting together puzzle pieces, assembling the elements of an organization can cost billions of dollars.

Organizations contain common elements: They operate with authority, they contain departments, and they utilize line and staff positions and departments. But, as alike as they may seem, no two organizations are exactly the same. Some, such as PPG Industries, rely on functional departmentalization. Others, such as Northern Telecom, are organized into product groups (Verespej, 1992, p. 25). Sears provides a model for centralized decision making; Honda has decentralized. Managers at Digital Equipment Corporation have narrow spans of control; the spans of control at American Airlines are wide. Ideally, organizations evolve to suit their operational requirements.

Objectives of Organizational Design

Managers responsible for organizational design must respond to change, integrate new elements, ensure coordination, and encourage flexibility.

Responding to Change   If organizational designers had a motto, it might be "Nothing lasts forever." For a firm to remain competitive, it must respond to changes in the environment as well as to changes that emerge from the company's evolutionary development. Ideally, changes should be undramatic and continual. (Just as frequent small earthquakes tend to be less devastating than infrequent big ones, organizations recover more quickly from frequent fine tuning than from major overhauls.) A company that remains static in the face of warning signals in the external environment courts disaster. By 1992, General Motors a bloated, slow-moving bureaucracy marked by overcentralization and a cultural disdain for ideas from anywhere else—lost more than $7 billion in three years (Reese, 1992). Auto industry experts summarized GM's circumstances curtly: "The company has lived in a dream world for years. . . . Change may be hard, but not changing could be fatal" (*Newsweek*, 1992).

Integrating New Elements   As organizations grow, evolve, and respond to changes, new positions and new departments are added to deal with factors in the external environment or with new strategic needs (Daft, 1989). This may mean adding a department to one level of an organization or virtually restructuring the whole company. The objective of organizational design is "seamlessness"— complete integration of new elements into the fabric of the organization. CEO Eckhard Pfeiffer of Compaq Computer added a new division to lead his company into the highly profitable PC printer business. Compaq introduced the fastest printer designed to serve a network of PCs (Schneidawind, 1992).

Ensuring Collaboration   Simply placing a department in a structure is not enough. Managers must find a way to ensure collaboration among departments. Without accomplishing this objective, the departments may not work together. Whether through reporting relationships, teams, or task forces, departments must collaborate to avoid conflict and problems. After reducing the number of partners by 15%, top managers at accounting giant Peat Marwick introduced a new layer of management and instituted consulting teams. CEO of Peat Marwick, John Madonna, has carefully orchestrated this makeover. Under his direction, profit per partner has increased 12% (Stodghill, 1992).

Fire Fighting? Or Fire Prevention?

Managers at Pooler Industries—a small producer of precision auto parts and components for other products—decided to change Pooler's approach to quality control. They decided to do things right the first time rather than correct errors after they happened. To use a metaphor, managers at Pooler decided to prevent fires rather than fight them.

To realize this goal, managers restructured the company. The quality-assurance department was eliminated, and the product inspectors that department had employed were assigned to "minifactories"—self-contained units of 15 persons.

In their new settings, the inspectors do not monitor product quality. Rather, they create and monitor quality systems, set training standards, and perform audits. They now emphasize process control rather than production control, and the new structure enables them to do it. The new structure prevents fires by allowing inspectors to monitor the process so errors do not occur. ▲

For more about "fire prevention," see Michael Barrier, "Entrepreneurs Are Learning That Total Quality Management Can Be Critical to Survival," *Nation's Business,* May 1992, pp. 22–23.

Encouraging Flexibility   Organizational designers aspire to build flexibility into the structures they create. Flexible structures allow managers to make timely decisions, re-direct energies, and spotlight available talent. The goal of structural flexibility is different from that of organizational responsiveness. The goal of flexibility involves institutionalizing the capacity to respond to change. One significant reason for Dell Computer's success is its flexibility and responsiveness to change. Top managers have been able to institutionalize these capabilities.

The Range of Organizational Design Outcomes

The elements that an organizational designer has to work with are chain of command, the degree of centralization, formal authority, and the like. The way the designer balances these elements determines whether the result will be a tight, mechanistic organization or a flexible, organic one.

Mechanistic Organizational Structures

A tight structure, or **mechanistic structure**, is characterized by rigidly defined tasks, formalization, many rules and regulations, and centralized decision making. Exhibit 8.1 shows the characteristics of a mechanistic structure. In mechanistic organizations, the vertical structure is tight and the emphasis is on control from top levels. Tasks are broken down into routine jobs and are rigidly defined. Many rules exist, and the hierarchy of authority is the major form of control. Decision making is centralized. Communication is vertical—that is, it follows the chain of command (Burns and Stalker, 1961). The U.S. Army maintains a classic mechanistic structure. Sears, Roebuck & Company—with its tight controls, rigidly

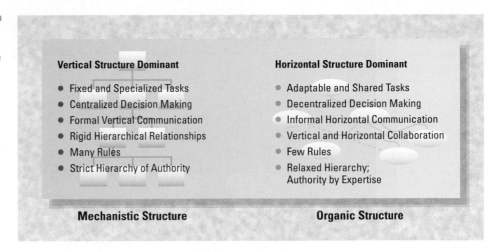

Vertical Structure Dominant

- Fixed and Specialized Tasks
- Centralized Decision Making
- Formal Vertical Communication
- Rigid Hierarchical Relationships
- Many Rules
- Strict Hierarchy of Authority

Mechanistic Structure

Horizontal Structure Dominant

- Adaptable and Shared Tasks
- Decentralized Decision Making
- Informal Horizontal Communication
- Vertical and Horizontal Collaboration
- Few Rules
- Relaxed Hierarchy; Authority by Expertise

Organic Structure

defined tasks, and numerous rules and regulations—typifies a private-sector mechanistic system.

Organic Organizational Structures

A flexible structure, or **organic structure**, is free flowing, has few rules and regulations, and decentralizes decision making right down to the employees performing the jobs. Organic structures freely adapt to shifting conditions and are as loose and accommodating as mechanistic organization structures are tight and rigid. Rather than depend upon standardized jobs and regulations, the organic structure allows change whenever it is needed. Organic structures incorporate division of labor, but jobs are not standardized. Tasks may be frequently re-defined to fit employee and environmental needs (Robbins, 1991). Few rules intrude, and authority derives from expert knowledge rather than hierarchical position.

Organic structures thrive on decentralized decision making and communication across the network rather than up and down the vertical chain of command. At Atmosphere Processing Inc., a small company that heat-treats auto parts, managers developed a free-flowing structure with few rules and decentralized decision making. The flexible structure lets the company adapt swiftly to rapid changes in its marketplace (Lammers, 1992). Exhibit 8.1 contrasts the characteristics of organic organizations with those of mechanistic structures.

An organization exhibits a tendency toward mechanistic or organic form depending upon how its designers have integrated contingency factors. The next section will explain what the contingency factors are.

Contingency Factors Affecting Organizational Design

A manager who designs or re-designs an organization must decide how mechanistic or organic to make it, for either may be successful or unsuccessful. The appropriate solution lies in correctly assessing the relevant contingency factors: the organization's strategy, size, age, environment, and technology. As

Exhibit 8.2

Contingency factors that
affect organizational design.

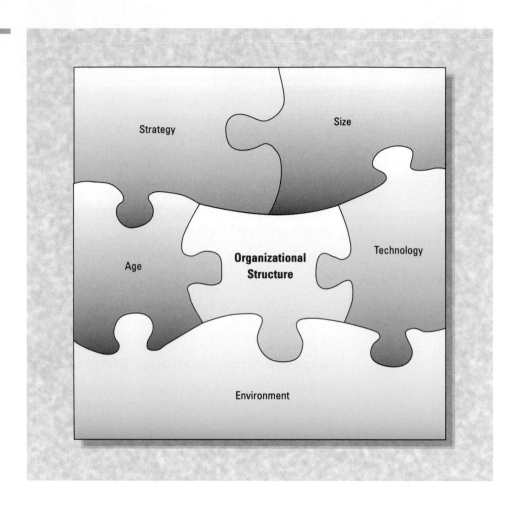

Exhibit 8.2 shows, the organizational design must accommodate the contingency factors (Lammers, 1992).

Strategy

Because managers build organizational structures to achieve objectives, logic requires that structure follow strategy. When strategy changes, structure must change as well.

Chapter 5 discussed the different strategies that companies can pursue to achieve their goals. If top managers at Dell Computer pursue a prospector strategy, they must innovate, seek new markets, grow, and take risks—activities for which an organic structure is well suited (Simnacher, 1992). On the other hand, if top managers at Exxon adopt a defender strategy to hold the company's current market, they need a structure that provides tight control, stability, efficiency, and centralization. For Exxon in this situation, a mechanistic structure would be best (Miles and Snow, 1978).

Competitive strategies include differentiation and cost-leadership (Porter, 1980). Managers choose a differentiation strategy to develop new products for the market. Internally, such innovation calls for coordination, flexibility, and

Exhibit 8.3

The influence of strategy on structure.

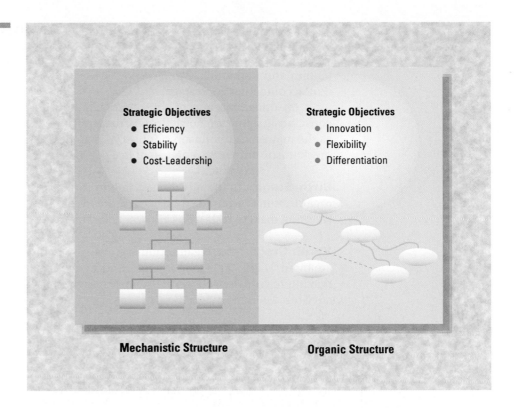

Strategic Objectives
- Efficiency
- Stability
- Cost-Leadership

Strategic Objectives
- Innovation
- Flexibility
- Differentiation

Mechanistic Structure

Organic Structure

communication—characteristics that mark an organic structure such as the one at Johnson & Johnson. The strategy of cost-leadership, which is the strategy used by Price Club, requires internal efficiency and rigorous accountability—characteristics that a mechanistic structure promotes. Exhibit 8.3 shows the relationship between an organization's strategic objectives and its structure.

The Size of the Organization

Small organizations are structured differently than large ones, and the principal measure of size is the number of employees. Small businesses with few employees, such as Mom & Pop Grocery, Cobbler's Shoe Repair, or Ace Dry Cleaner, are characterized by little division of labor and few rules and regulations. The organization is loose—just the condition usually associated with organic systems. At Ford, GE, and Mobil, there are lots of people—tens of thousands. Most of them are specialists. Everyone must comply with precise rules and detailed regulations. The organization is tight—just the condition usually associated with mechanistic systems (Astley, 1985). In the 1990s many large organizations began to recognize the limitations of mechanistic structures and moved toward organic structures.

The Age of the Organization

The longer an organization operates, the more formalized it tends to become. Longevity breeds standardized systems, procedures, and regulations. Consequently, older companies tend to acquire characteristics of mechanistic structures.

Like people, organizations evolve through stages of a life cycle. The predictable pattern of business growth is called the **organizational life cycle**. Exhibit 8.4 presents the four stages of the cycle: birth, youth, midlife, and maturity (Quinn and Cameron, 1983). The sections that follow will discuss the structure that accompanies each stage.

An understanding of the organizational life cycle permits managers to consciously shape their own firm's structural development. Alert managers—such as the managers at Johnson & Johnson—can prevent or eliminate the excessively mechanistic outcome so prevalent in a company's maturity stage.

Birth Stage   In the birth stage, an entrepreneur creates the organization. The organization is informal; there is no professional staff, and no rules or regulations. Decision making rests with the owner, and tasks are not specialized.

Youth Stage   The organization is growing—products succeed, more employees are hired. Division of labor emerges, and so do formal rules and policies. Decision making remains largely centralized, although it is shared with an inner circle of advisors.

Exhibit 8.4

Relationship between organizational life cycle and structural characteristics.

Structural Characteristics	Birth Stage	Youth Stage	Midlife Stage	Maturity Stage
Division of labor	Overlapping tasks	Some departments	Many departments, well-defined tasks, organization chart	Extensive—small jobs, written job descriptions
Centralization	One-person rule	Top leaders rule	Decentralization to department heads	Enforced decentralization (top management overloaded)
Degree of formal control	No written rules	Few rules	Policy and procedures manuals	Extensive—most activities covered by written manuals
Administrative staff	Secretary, no professional staff	Increasing clerical and maintenance, few professional staff members	Increasing size of professional support staff	Large—multiple professional and clerical staff departments
Internal systems (information, budget, planning, performance)	Nonexistent	Crude budget and information system	Control systems in place—budget, performance, operational reports	Extensive—planning, financial, and personnel systems added

Source: Based on Robert E. Quinn and Kim Cameron, "Organizational Life Cycles and Some Shifting Criteria of Effectiveness: Some Preliminary Evidence, *Management Science* 29 (1983), 31–51.

Midlife Stage The company prospers and grows large; extensive rules, regulations, policies, and systems guide a growing force of increasingly specialized workers. Control systems are set into place. Professional and clerical staff are hired to undertake expert support activities. Top managers delegate many responsibilities to functional departments. The result is the loss of some flexibility and innovation.

Maturity Stage The organization is large and indisputably mechanistic. The vertical control structure becomes overwhelming. Rules, regulations, specialized staffs, budgets, refined division of labor, and control systems are in place. The company—as with IBM and GM—faces stagnation. Innovation and aggressiveness can come only with moves to decentralization and flexibility, as seen with IBM's reorganization (Verity, 1992).

The Environment

Just as the environment profoundly influences decision making in an organization, the environment has a significant effect on organizational structure (Robbins, 1990). Exhibit 8.5 shows the relationship between environment and structure.

When the environment is stable and predictable, a reasonably mechanistic design may prove effective: Centralized decision making, wide spans of control,

Exhibit 8.5

The relationship between environment and structure.

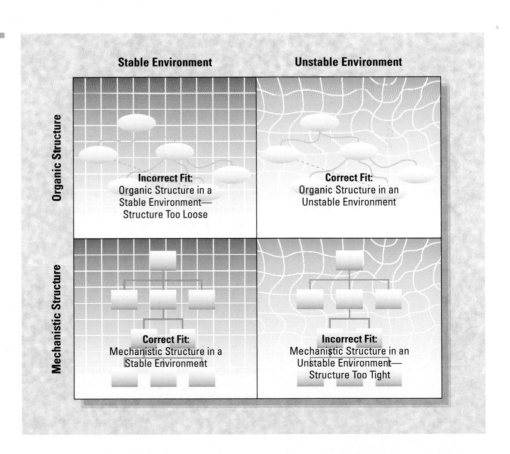

and specialization suit such an atmosphere. An uncertain environment calls for an organic structure, which promotes flexibility, coordination, and informal procedures (Lawrence and Lorsch, 1969).

In an unpredictable environment, managers should strive for organizational flexibility so that they can respond to change. Under these circumstances, top managers must remember that departments tend to work autonomously; therefore, top managers must not let department managers create independent goals or ignore one another. Unpredictable environments call for close co-ordination among departments.

The U.S. auto industry offers an instructive example of the influence of environment. In 1955 General Motors, Ford, and Chrysler—with their mechanistic structures—thrived in a stable environment. More than seven million cars were sold in the U.S. and 95% of them came from one of the Big Three manufacturers. The United States made more than 67% of all the world's vehicles that year. American cars commanded the market regardless of styling, reliability, or fuel economy. By 1990 the U.S. made only about 20% of the world's vehicles. Japanese manufacturers claimed about 25% of the U.S. market (Womack, Jones, and Roos, 1991).

In the 1990s GM is being rocked by an unstable environment. Competition continues to get tougher. The Japanese will not quit, and GM must now deal with the resurgence of Ford and Chrysler-AMC as well as manufacturers in Germany, Sweden, and South Korea. As the rumblings from GM will attest, the mechanistic structure of U.S. firms is not functioning (Taylor, 1992). To help turn around the fortunes of General Motors, President John Smith is taking steps to make the structure of the company less mechanistic. His plans focus on slashing 10,000 of 13,500 corporate staffers. Smith hopes the cut will "oust GM's hierarchical and fiefdom clogged bureaucracy" (Kurwin and Treece, 1992).

I S S U E S   A N D   E T H I C S
When Are Layoffs Justified?

Today, the word *layoff* is familiar to anyone who reads the daily newspaper. Beset by economic uncertainty, competitive pressures, and lagging profits, managers have resorted to layoffs as a means of increasing efficiency. Layers of management, departments, and even entire operating units have been lost to the strategy of reorganizing by reduction.

Many of the layoffs have occurred for compelling reasons. Some managers, however, have axed employees just for the purpose of pumping up short-term profits. (An increase in short-term profits usually impresses the tape readers on Wall Street.) Furthermore, layoffs do not always increase cost-effectiveness. If work load remains though many employees do not, managers pressure the remaining employees to work overtime. The increase in overtime costs can actually offset the effect of the reduction in force.

Do you think layoffs used as a management tool are a matter of ethical concern? Do managers owe a greater duty to stockholders than to employees? Is it ethical for a company to lay off people for short-term gain or to impress the financial community? Should ethical guidelines apply to performance demands placed on the survivors of a layoff? What might these guidelines be? ▲

Technology

Every organization uses some form of technology to convert its efforts into outcomes. **Technology** is the knowledge, machinery, work procedures, and materials that transform inputs into outputs (Daft, 1991). The technology that Mobil Oil uses to produce petroleum products differs markedly from the technology that Nike employs to produce shoes. Nevertheless, both firms use some kind of technology. Production technology is important because it directly influences organizational structure. The structure must fit the technology just as it must fit the organization's age, strategy, size, and external environment.

British industrial sociologist Joan Woodward related the three basic types of work-flow technology (small batch, mass production, and continuous process) to elements of structure (Woodward, 1965). Firms that produce goods in small quantities to customer specifications use **small-batch technology**, or **unit-production technology**. Human labor plays a large part in small-batch technology. The making of custom clothing, space satellites, or leather-bound books requires small-batch technology.

When a company produces a large volume of standardized products, it employs **large-batch technology**, or **mass-production technology**. Such technology makes greater use of machines than does small-batch production. Some auto makers' assembly lines use mass production. In **continuous-process production**, the entire conversion process is completed through a series of mechanical or chemical processes. Employees are not a part of actual production; they maintain equipment and oversee the process. An Exxon refinery or Coors brewery employs continuous-process production.

The dominant technology should influence organizational structure. Exhibit 8.6 shows the appropriate correlations. Organizations that rely on small-batch technology should employ an organic structure. Organizations that use mass-production technology function best when they have a mechanistic structure, with centralized decision making and well-defined rules (Nemetz and Fry, 1988).

Exhibit 8.6

The relationship between production technology and organizational structure.

Elements of Structure	Production Technology		
	Small Batch	Mass Production	Continuous Process
Complexity of technology	Low	Medium	High
Organizational structure:			
Degree of formal control	Low	High	Low
Centralization	Low	High	Low
Typical span of control	23	48	15
Overall structure	Organic	Mechanistic	Organic

Source: Based on Joan Woodward, *Industrial Organization: Theory and Practice* (London: Oxford University Press), 1965.

Since Woodward conducted her studies thirty years ago, manufacturing technology has changed dramatically. With a sophisticated computer system, every manufacturing phase—from the design of the product to inventory delivery and performance analysis—can be automated and integrated. Production technology that employs such a system is known as flexible manufacturing. (Chapter 18 will discuss flexible manufacturing in detail.) Flexible manufacturing is revolutionizing the traditional perception of mass-production technology and small-batch technology. Now both can be done simultaneously in the same facility.

The technology associated with flexible manufacturing places this system in a higher position of complexity than any of the three technologies Woodward studied. Such complexity accommodates an organic structure that involves low formal control, high decentralization of decision making, and a very narrow span of control (Womack, Jones, and Roos, 1991).

Structural Options in Organizational Design

Because no single organizational design suits all circumstances, managers must carefully consider their company's strategy, age, size, environment, and technology before designing a structure for it. Happily, managers have a range of design options to choose from. Managers can select a structure depending on the contingency factors. Exhibit 8.7 shows the five structural design options: functional, divisional, matrix, team, and network. Note that most combine mechanistic and organic characteristics.

Exhibit 8.7

Structural options on the mechanistic-organic continuum.

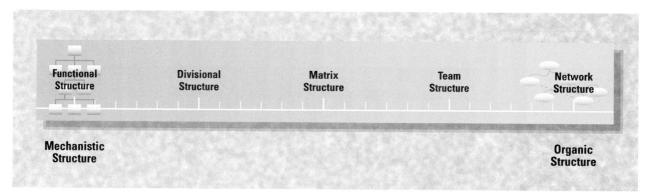

The Functional Structure

The **functional structure** groups positions into departments based on similar skills, expertise, and resources. Functional structure is an expanded version of functional departmentalization, which Chapter 7 introduced. In an organization with functional structure, activities are grouped under headings common to nearly every business—headings such as finance, production, marketing, and human resources. The entire organization is then divided into areas such as the ones

Exhibit 8.8

A functional organizational structure.

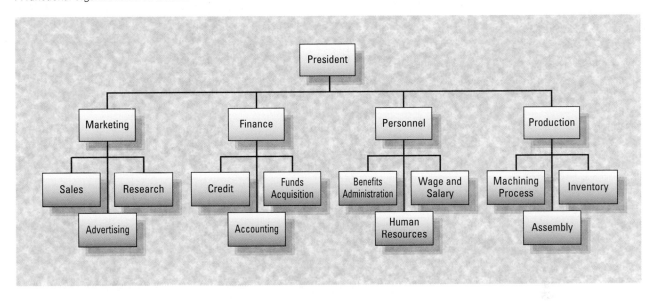

shown in Exhibit 8.8. American Airlines, PPG, and USX use this type of structure (Mitchell and Files, 1992).

Advantages of Functional Structure   Putting specialties together results in economies of scale and minimizes duplication of personnel and equipment. Employees tend to feel comfortable in a functional structure, because it gives them the opportunity to talk the same language with their peers. Because the structure acknowledges occupational specialization, it also simplifies training.

Organizationally, the functional structure offers a way to centralize decision making and provide unified direction from the top. Within each department communication and coordination are excellent. Finally, the functional structure increases the quality of technical problem solving because it gives workers quick access to those with technical expertise.

Disadvantages of Functional Structure   Because functions are separate from one another, workers may have little understanding of or concern for departments that are outside their own functional area. Such a narrow perspective can lead to barriers in communication, cooperation, and coordination. Each department may develop a department focus rather than a company focus. Because a functional structure contains separate chains of command, it may contribute to slow response time in the face of environmental changes. A functional structure can make identifying profit centers difficult.

Managers in a functional structure are susceptible to the same narrow focus as employees. They may not maintain a broad perspective on the company or other functional areas. A broad perspective is crucial for future chief executives.

Exhibit 8.9

A divisional organizational structure.

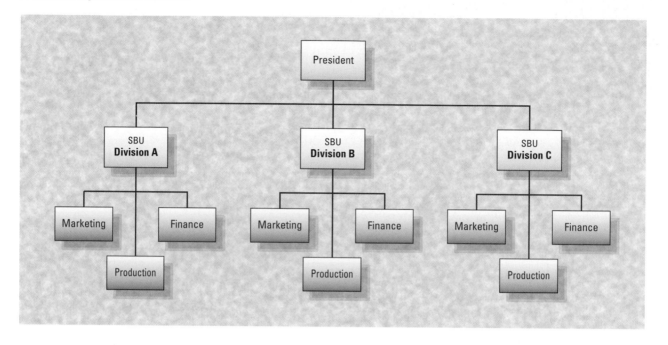

The Divisional Structure

An alternative to the functional structure is the **divisional structure**, in which departments are grouped according to organizational outputs.

As Exhibit 8.9 shows, divisions are self-contained strategic business units (SBUs) that produce a single product. (Chapter 5 discussed SBUs.) In the businesses the exhibit describes, each division is responsible for the management of a given product or product family. Within each division, diverse departments accomplish the division's objectives.

The divisional structure creates a set of autonomous minicompanies. In a large company such as General Foods or PepsiCo, each division has its own market, competitors, and technologies. At PepsiCo, the divisions include Frito-Lay, Pizza Hut, Taco Bell, and Kentucky Fried Chicken.

The term *divisional structure* can also apply to a company organized by customer or geography. A divisional structure arranged according to customer is called for when customers are distinct enough in their demands, preferences, and needs to justify it. When a particular customer creates a large demand for a certain line of products, the company can group all the skills necessary and establish a division to serve the customer full-time. (Frequently, companies that serve commercial and government customers display divisional structure arranged according to each type of customer.) Such a structure provides a company focus for employees. Customer divisions are found at Shearson Lehman Brothers, where one division targets individual investors and the other serves corporate and institutional accounts.

Overseas offices are
established to meet the
unique needs of a particular
geographic community and to
better anticipate problems
that may arise from cross-
cultural exchanges.

Managers create geographic divisions when their company needs to group functional skills for a specific region—international, national, or regional. Divisional structure based on geography is an attempt to respond to situations in which laws, currencies, languages, and taxation differ by geography. Department stores such as J.C. Penney and Sears have created regional divisions, as has the Carnation Company. On an international scale, McDonald's has structured geographically by continent. The corporation contains the European, North American, and Asian divisions (Hall, 1992).

Advantages of Divisional Structure The divisional structure focuses the attention of employees and managers on results—for the product, customer, or geographic area. Divisional structure is flexible and responsive to change, because each unit focuses on its own environment. Coordination among different functions within the division benefits from singleness of purpose. Because each division is a self-contained unit, responsibility and accountability for performance is easier to target.

Finally, divisional structure offers an excellent vehicle for developing senior executives. Division managers gain a broad range of experience in running their autonomous units. An organization with several divisions is developing a number of generalists for the company's top positions.

Disadvantages of Divisional Structure The major disadvantage of divisional structure is duplication of activities and resources. Instead of a single marketing or research department, each division maintains its own. The structure loses efficiency and economies of scale, and a lack of technical specialization, expertise, and training can result. Interdivisional coordination may suffer, and employees in different divisions may feel they are in competition with one another—a mixed blessing.

General Motors illustrates all these limitations. Among the early U.S. companies to adopt the divisional structure (it acquired most of its divisions as ongoing concerns), GM has long been limited by inefficient, overcompetitive, internally uncooperative, and duplicative divisions. Furthermore, its many layers of middle management have limited its responsiveness (Keller, 1989).

In 1992, IBM reorganized into 13 divisions. Nine are product-based, focusing on product lines and manufacturing processes. The remaining four are geographically organized marketing and services divisions that sell what the other divisions make (Kirkpatrick, 1992). Exhibit 8.10 shows the new structure.

Exhibit 8.10

IBM's divisional structure is based both on product lines and on geographic region.

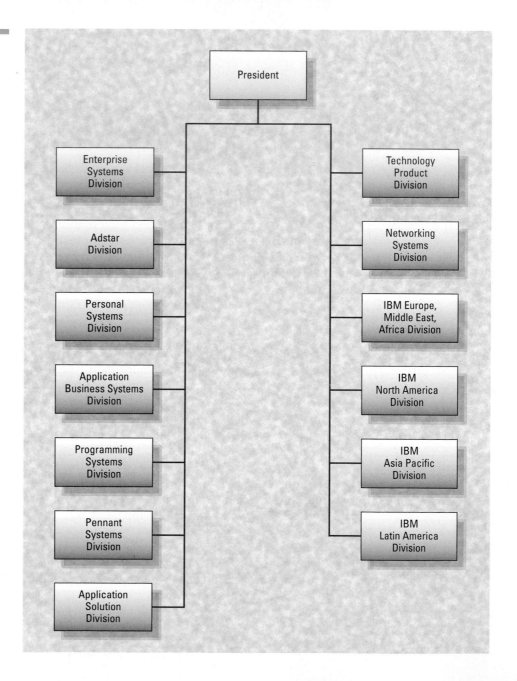

The Matrix Structure

The **matrix structure** combines the advantages of functional specialization with the focus and accountability of the divisional structure. A matrix utilizes functional and divisional chains of command simultaneously in the same part of the organization (Burns, 1989).

To achieve this combination, the matrix structure employs dual lines of authority. As Exhibit 8.11 shows, the functional hierarchy of authority runs vertically from the functional departments—production, materials, personnel, and so on—while project authority runs laterally from group to group. This

---

Exhibit 8.11

A matrix organizational structure.

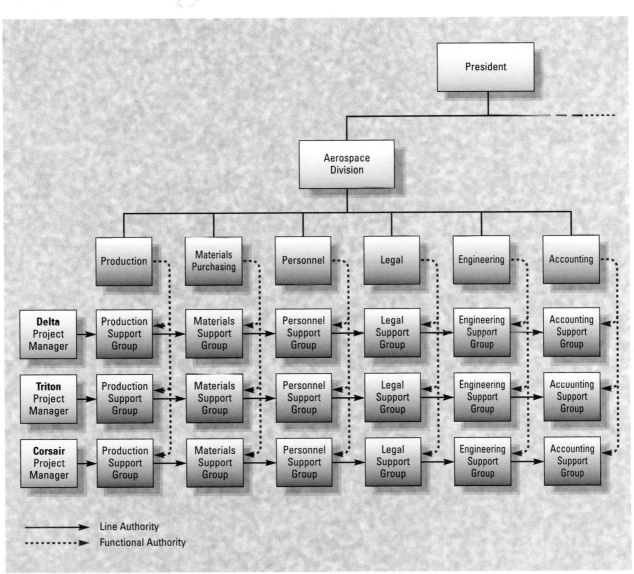

combination of function and project authority composes a grid, or matrix. The result is that each employee has two bosses, a dual chain of command based on both the department and individual projects (Koloday, 1981).

A matrix structure can be created by combining any divisions established for a specific product, program, or project with a functional structure. In general, a matrix design is most likely to be used in one of two situations (Van Fleet, 1991). First, it is used when a firm offers a diverse set of products, has a complex environment, and requires functional expertise. With a matrix, the company can bring important functional skills to bear on each product while simultaneously responding to the changing environment.

The second situation in which the matrix organization is used is when managers want to maximize economies of scale and shared resources. Resource duplication is minimized by having employees work for more than one division or by transferring employees among divisions as requirements change. The manager in charge of the engineering department shown in Exhibit 8.11 can reassign engineers as the needs of each project demand.

Advantages of Matrix Structure   The matrix structure has been used successfully by the Allison Gas Turbine Division at General Motors, Monsanto, NCR, Dow Chemical, and Asea–Brown Boveri (ABB). The structure has proven

---

GLOBAL APPLICATIONS
ABB Designed for Action

A **senior executive** at Mitsubishi Heavy Industry described ABB, a global electrical equipment manufacturer, in these words: "They are as aggressive as we are. I mean this as a compliment. They are sort of super-Japanese." This aggressiveness has been designed into ABB by CEO Percy Barnevik.

In four years, Barnevik has welded ASEA, a Swedish engineering group, to Brown Boveri, a Swiss competitor; bolted on 70 more companies in Europe and the United States; and created a company that can go head-to-head with General Electric. Barnevik has a formula and a working organizational design.

Regardless of the business Asea–Brown Boveri acquires, Barnevik's first step is to cut headquarters staff and decentralize. Barnevik's philosophy: "Ideally you should have a minimum of staff to disturb the operating people and prevent them from doing their jobs." Barnevik cuts headquarters staff by one-third.

He assigns another third to new companies and the remaining third to operating units. Headquarters personnel become coaches, not decision makers: Decisions are made on the line by managers, not bureaucrats.

Barnevik has installed a matrix management structure that gives all employees two managers, a country manager and a business-sector manager. The country managers run traditional national companies. The business-sector managers provide leadership to employees in a specific business. This matrix allows the transfer of technology and products between countries. In addition, it allows business segments the opportunity for global coordination. Every month, for example, the business-segment headquarters issues reports that tell how all the factories in all the countries are doing. If one factory is lagging, managers in different countries can discuss solutions to common problems. ▲

For more about ABB's structural design, see Carla Rapaport, "A Tough Swede Invades the U.S.," *Fortune,* June 29, 1992, pp. 26–29.

flexible—teams can be created, changed, and dissolved without major difficulty. The matrix structure facilitates communication and coordination.

The matrix structure increases the motivation of individual employees. The achievement of goals can bring a sense of commitment and satisfaction. The structure also provides training in functional and general management skills. People within functional departments receive technical training, and team coordination provides the opportunity to develop a general perspective.

Disadvantages of Matrix Structure   The dual chain of command of the matrix structure provides the potential for conflict, confusion, and frustration. Employees may not know whether to take orders from the functional manager or the project manager. Similarly, the matrix often pits divisional objectives against functional objectives, and the result can be conflict. Another disadvantage is directly related: Productive time is lost to meetings and discussions to resolve conflict. Working for two bosses requires well-developed interpersonal and conflict-resolution skills. Finally, the matrix structure may create a problem of balance of power between the functional and divisional sides of the matrix. If one side has more power, the advantages of the matrix—coordination and cooperation—are lost.

The Team Structure

The **team structure** is the newest and potentially most powerful approach to organizational structure. This structure involves organizing separate functions into a group based on one overall objective. The team structure, in effect, takes direct aim at traditional organizational hierarchy—whether functional, divisional, or matrix—and flattens it. Although the vertical chain of command is a powerful

Teamwork is the key to an organizational structure that is more responsive to change, and businesses such as Domino's Pizza prove that it pays to "flatten out."

control device, proposed decisions must move up the hierarchy for approval—a process that often takes too long. Such an approach also keeps decision making and responsibility at the top. Throughout the business sector, a significant trend in the 1990s is delegation, pushing authority and accountability down to lower levels and creating teams of workers who take credit for their work.

In a team structure, departments are based on teams rather than functional specialty. Team members representing different functions are grouped together. Several such teams report to the same supervisor. Although there are variations of the team concept—some teams are responsible for a product, others for a process—the result is the same. The traditional functions are reorganized, layers of management are removed, and the company becomes decentralized. Exhibit 8.12 shows how a vertical functional structure looks after it is converted to a horizontal team structure.

Although Procter & Gamble, Quaker Oats, and General Foods have tried teams, the team structure at the General Electric factory at Bayamón, Puerto Rico, illustrates the concept especially well. The facility employs a factory manager, 172 hourly workers, and just 15 salaried supervisors who act as advisors. (A conventional plant would require twice as many salaried workers.) That translates to three

Exhibit 8.12

The development of a team structure.

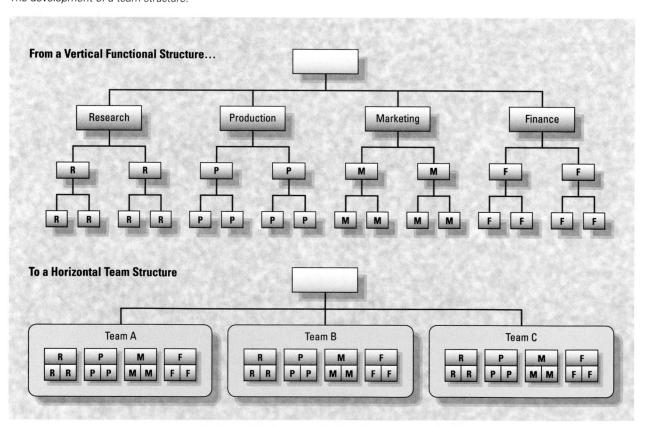

layers of organization. Each hourly worker is on a 10-person team. The team is responsible for part of the factory's overall work—assembly, shipping and receiving, and so on. But team members come from all areas of the plant, so that each group has representation from operations in the process. A supervisor-advisor sits in the back of the room and speaks up only if the team needs help (Stewart, 1992). Chapter 14 will discuss teams in detail.

Advantages of Team Structure The team concept breaks down barriers across departments because people who know one another are more likely than strangers to compromise. The team structure also speeds up decision making and response time. Decisions no longer need to go to the top of a hierarchy for approval. Employees are strongly motivated. They take responsibility for a project rather than for a narrowly defined task, and the result is enthusiasm and commitment. Decentralization of authority is accompanied by the elimination of levels of managers, and the result is lower administrative costs. Finally, team structure is an improvement over the matrix structure in that it does not involve the problem of double reporting. Each worker believes he or she is a part of a team rather than an individual who performs a designated function.

Disadvantages of Team Structure Team structure depends on employees who learn and train for success. If the company is unwilling to provide training, performance suffers. Also, those in a team structure spend much time in meetings.

The Network Structure

An organization arranged in **network structure** relies on other organizations to perform critical functions on a contract basis. These functions include manufacturing, marketing, and engineering (Miles, 1989). Nike and Esprit Apparel use network structures to run booming businesses even though they own no manufacturing facilities and employ only a few hundred people. Rather than perform the functions internally, these companies connect independent designers, manufacturers, and sales representatives to perform them on a contract basis (Rammrath, 1992).

Advantages of Network Structure The network structure provides flexibility because only the specific services needed are purchased. Administrative overhead remains low because large teams of staff specialists and other administrative personnel are not needed.

Disadvantages of Network Structure The major shortcoming of this type of structure is lack of control. The management core must rely on contractors. This limitation can be minimized if management is willing and able to work closely with the suppliers. But the reliability of supply is less predictable than it would be if the company owned the means of supply. If a supplier fails to deliver, goes out of business, or suffers a plant breakdown, the central hub of the network is endangered. Also, if an organization relies on contract work, central managers may lack technical expertise to resolve problems effectively.

Future Trends

According to management guru Tom Peters, a company "can't survive, let alone thrive, in a time-competitive world with a six- to eight-layer organization structure." Consequently, several certainties loom in the future for organizational design:

- More companies will follow the lead of Wal-Mart, The Limited, Federal Express, MCI, Domino's Pizza, and Cypress Semiconductor; they will flatten their organizations. Time will become more critical in the competitive environment. This, in turn, means less time to call meetings, less time to pass memos up and down the structure, and less time for managers in the middle of the structure to hoard information.

- Because of increasing structural flatness and the philosophical change that accompanies it, decentralization will become more common. Front-line employees will be empowered to make decisions where the action is taking place.

- In some companies an organizational revolution will take place. The resulting organization charts will not only show a flatter structure, they will include a series of circles that indicate networks. Such a structure resembles a spiderweb with all strands in constant contact with each other. This type of structure will minimize barriers among functions.

- As structures change and layers of management are eliminated, the manager of the future will bear little resemblance to the corporate manager of the past. Consider these comparisons:

  Past: Managers adhered strictly to boss-subordinate relationships.
  Future: Managers will adhere less strictly to hierarchical relationships; functional and peer relationships will be crucial.

  Past: Managers accomplished tasks because they were ordered to accomplish them.
  Future: Managers will accomplish tasks through negotiation.

  Past: Managers carried messages up and down the chain of command.
  Future: Managers will solve problems and make decisions.

  Past: Managers had a narrow functional focus.
  Future: Managers will practice broad cross-functional collaboration.

  Past: Managers went through channels.
  Future: Managers will emphasize speed and flexibility.

  Past: Managers controlled subordinates.
  Future: Managers will coach their people.

  Past: Managers performed a prescribed set of tasks according to a job description.
  Future: Managers will create their jobs by developing entrepreneurial projects.

C H A P T E R   **S** U M M A R Y

- Organizational design is the creation of or change to an organization's structure. It determines the overall configuration and establishes the interrelationships of positions and departments.

- The managers responsible for organizational design create structures to respond to change, integrate new elements into the organization, ensure collaboration, and encourage flexibility.

- Depending on how organizational concepts are balanced, the design produced can be a tight, or mechanistic, structure or a flexible, or organic, structure.

- A mechanistic structure is characterized by rigidly defined tasks, formalization, many rules and regulations, and centralized decision making.

- An organic structure has few rules and regulations. In an organic structure, decision making is decentralized—the employees performing the job often make the decisions.

- Five contingency factors determine whether an organization will be mechanistic or organic. The factors are strategy, size, age, the environment, and technology.

- Organizational design alternatives include these structure types: functional, divisional, matrix, team, and network. Divisional structure can be organized on the basis of product or project, customer, or geographical area.

- Functional structure can maximize economies of scale, minimize duplication of personnel and equipment, make employees comfortable, and simplify training. Disadvantages include lack of understanding of and concern for other specialty areas, communication barriers, lack of cooperation and coordination, slow response to changes in the environment, and difficulty in determining profit centers.

- Whether a divisional structure is arranged according to product, customer, or geography, it allows employees and managers to focus on results. Divisional structure is flexible and responsive to change. It makes performance easier to target and aids in developing senior executives. Disadvantages include duplication of activities and resources; lack of technical specialization, expertise, and training; lack of coordination across positions; and competition among divisions.

- The matrix organization is flexible. It facilitates communication and coordination. Employees who work in a matrix organization tend to be highly motivated, and the structure facilitates technical training for functional and general management skills. The primary disadvantage—the high potential for conflict, confusion, and frustration—stems from the dual chain of command. A matrix organization can have a tendency to pit divisional objectives against functional objectives. This results in lost time as employees and managers try to resolve conflicts. If functional and divisional elements of the matrix do not have equal power, the matrix structure may fail.

- The team concept breaks down barriers across departments, speeds up decision making and response time, motivates employees by developing employee responsibility, lowers administrative costs by eliminating levels of managers, and eliminates the double-reporting problem associated with the matrix structure. Disadvantages include dependence on employee learning and training and the large amount of time required for meetings.

- The network structure provides flexibility and reduces administrative overhead. Disadvantages include lack of control and internal managerial technical expertise, and unpredictability of supply.

S K I L L - **B** U I L D I N G

You work for a company involved in the design, development, and marketing of satellite and communications technology. Although currently structured functionally, top managers of the firm are considering other organizational design alternatives to shift the focus from national to global interests. As part of an executive analysis team, you have been asked to create and present design options for senior managers to review. To complete the assignment, design a functional structure, a divisional structure, a matrix structure, a team structure, and a network structure that will accommodate the following functions:

Accounting	Personnel
Contracts administration	Production
Design & engineering	Purchasing
Marketing	Research

R E V I E W   Q U E S T I O N S

1. Review this chapter's essential terms and look up the meanings of those you cannot define.

2. With what elements of an organization does an organizational designer work?

3. Identify the four major objectives of organizational design.

4. What are the characteristics of a mechanistic organization? What are the characteristics of an organic organization?

5. What five factors influence organizational design?

6. How does an organization's strategy influence organizational design? Support your answer with an example.

7. What two organizational design needs result from a volatile environment?

8. Describe the characteristics of a functional organizational design.

9. What are the advantages and disadvantages of the divisional structure?

10. What are the characteristics of a matrix organizational structure?

11. What are the characteristics of teams?

12. What are the advantages and disadvantages of the network structure?

R E C O M M E N D E D   R E A D I N G

Bedrian, Arthur G., and Raymond F. Zammuto. *Organization Theory and Design* (Homewood, IL: Dryden Press), 1991.

Cook, William J. "Rebuilding Big Blue," *U.S. News and World Report* (January 7, 1992), pp. 48–50.

Dealy, Michael F. "Changing Organizational Structures," *Fortune* (July 13, 1992), pp. 50–51.

Gibson, James L. *Organizational Behavior, Structures, Processes* (Homewood, IL: Richard D. Irwin), 1991.

Kuhn, Alfred, and Robert Beam. *The Logic of Organization* (San Francisco: Jossey-Bass), 1991.

Mills, Quinn D. *Rebirth of the Organization: Managing Companies for the 1990's* (New York: Wiley), 1991.

Ollins, Wally. *Corporate Identity: Making Business Strategy Visible Through Design* (Boston: Harvard Business School Press), 1991.

Sellers, Patricia. "Can He Keep Philip Morris Growing?" *Fortune* (April 6, 1992), pp. 86–92.

Taylor, Alex. "A U.S.-Style Shakeup at Honda," *Fortune* (January 31, 1992), pp. 115–120.

Verespej, Michael A. "Motorola Stays Home to Compete with Japan," *Industry Week* (February 17, 1992), pp. 21–22.

R E F E R E N C E S

Astley, W. Graham. "Organization Size and Bureaucratic Structure," *Organization Studies* 6 (1985), pp. 201–228.

Burns, Lawton R. "Matrix Management in Hospitals: Testing Theories of Matrix Structure and Development," *Administrative Science Quarterly* 34 (1989), pp. 349–368.

Burns, Tom, and G. M. Stalker. *The Management of Innovation* (London: Taristock), 1961.

Daft, Richard L. *Management,* 2nd edition (Hinsdale, IL: Dryden Press), 1991, p. 292.

Daft, Richard L. *Organization Theory and Design,* 3rd edition (St. Paul, MN: West), 1989.

Hall, Cheryl. "Golden Quest," *Dallas Morning News,* May 31, 1992, pp. 1H, 8H.

Keller, Maryann. *Rude Awakening: The Rise, Fall, and Struggle for Recovery at General Motors* (New York: William Morrow), 1989.

Kirkpatrick, David. "Breaking Up IBM," *Fortune* (July 27, 1992), pp. 44–45.

Koloday, Harvey F. "Managing in a Matrix," *Business Horizons* (March–April 1981), pp. 17–24.

Kurwin, Kathleen, and James B. Treece. "GM Is Meaner But Hardly Leaner," *Business Week* (October 19, 1992), pp. 30–31.

Lammers, Terry. "The New Improved Organization Chart," *Inc.* (October 1992), pp. 147–149.

Lawrence, Paul R., and Jay W. Lorsch. *Organization and Environment* (Homewood, IL: Richard D. Irwin), 1969.

Miles, Raymond E. "Adapting to Technology and Competition: A New Industrial Relation System for the 21st Century," *California Management Review* (Winter 1989), pp. 9–28.

Miles, Raymond E., and Charles C. Snow. *Organizational Strategy, Structure, and Process* (New York: McGraw-Hill), 1978.

Mitchell, Jim, and Jennifer Files. "Challenging the Imaginative," *Dallas Morning News,* May 17, 1992, p. 18K.

Nemetz, Patricia L., and Louis W. Fry. "Flexible Manufacturing Organizations: Implications for Strategy Formulation and Organization Design," *Academy of Management Review* (October 1988), pp. 627–638.

Newsweek (November 9, 1992), pp. 54–57.

Porter, Michael E. *Competitive Strategy: Techniques for Analyzing Industries and Competitors* (New York: Free Press), 1980, pp. 36–46.

Quinn, Robert E., and Kim Cameron. "Organizational Life Cycles and Some Shifting Criteria of Effectiveness: Some Preliminary Evidence," *Management Science* 29 (1983), pp. 31–51.

Rammrath, Herbert G. "Globalization Isn't for Whiners," *Wall Street Journal,* April 6, 1992, p. C27.

Reese, Jennifer. "The Big and the Bloated," *Fortune* (July 27, 1992), p. 49.

Robbins, Stephen P. *Management,* 3rd edition (Englewood Cliffs, NJ: Prentice-Hall), 1991, pp. 286, 301.

Robbins, Stephen P. *Organization Theory: Structure, Design, and Applications,* 3rd edition (Englewood Cliffs, NJ: Prentice-Hall), 1990, pp. 210–232.

Schneidawind, John. "Four-Pronged Plan Saves PC Maker," *USA Today,* September 24, 1992, pp. 131–132.

Simnacher, Joe. "Boardroom Rumblings," *Dallas Morning News,* April 8, 1992, pp. 18–20.

Stewart, Thomas A. "The Search for the Organization of Tomorrow," *Fortune* (May 18, 1992), pp. 93–94.

Stodghill, Ron. "Who Says Accountants Can't Jump?" *Business Week* (October 26, 1992), pp. 98–100.

Taylor, Alex. "Can GM Remodel," *Fortune* (January 13, 1992), pp. 26–28.

Van Fleet, David D. *Contemporary Management,* 2nd edition (Boston: Houghton Mifflin), 1991, p. 250.

Verespej, Michael A. "Stern Hand," *Industry Week* (February 17, 1992), p. 25.

Verespej, Michael A. "Tough Times, Tough Decisions," *Industry Week* (February 17, 1992), p. 21.

Verity, John W. "Out of One Big Blue, Many Little Blues," *Business Week* (January 12, 1992), p. 33.

Womack, James P.; Daniel T. Jones; and Daniel Roos. *The Machine That Changed the World: The Story of Lean Production* (New York: Harper Perennial), 1991, pp. 43–45.

Woodward, Joan. *Industrial Organization: Theory and Practice* (London: Oxford University Press), 1965.

G L O S S A R Y   O F   **T** E R M S

continuous-process production   A technology in which the entire conversion process is completed through a series of mechanical or chemical processes. Employees are not a part of the actual production.

divisional structure   An organizational design in which people are grouped according to products, geography, or customers.

functional structure   An organizational design that groups positions into departments according to similar skills, expertise, and resources.

large-batch technology   *See* mass-production technology.

mass-production technology   A type of technology that produces a large volume of standardized products.

matrix structure   An organizational design that utilizes the functional and divisional chains of command simultaneously in the same part of an organization.

mechanistic structure   A tight organizational structure characterized by rigidly defined tasks, formalization, many rules and regulations, and centralized decision making.

network structure   An organizational design option in which a small central organization relies on other organizations to perform manufacturing, engineering, or other critical functions on a contract basis.

organic structure   A flexible, free-flowing organizational structure that has few rules and regulations. An organic structure is characterized by decentralization—many decisions are made by on-the-job employees.

organizational design   The creation of or change to an organization's structure.

organizational life cycle   The observable and predictable stages of an organization's evolution.

small-batch technology   A type of technology that produces goods in small amounts designed to customer specification.

team structure   An organizational design that places separate functions into a group according to one overall objective.

technology   The knowledge, machinery, work procedures, and materials that transform inputs into outputs.

unit-production technology   *See* small-batch technology.

C A S E   P R O B L E M
Restructuring the Organization

Most people prefer the predictable, the familiar. Predicting what a company's organization chart would look like used to be easy: It would look like a pyramid, with the label "President" at the top. Because the company was shaped like a pyramid, each successive level of management from the president on down had a wider span of control. The president might have a span of control of three to six individuals. Down where the work was done, however—at the first level—a manager would supervise from 16 to 25 employees. Also, decision-making authority and money were controlled at the top. Only when the man (and it was a man) at the top decided, would authority and budget money trickle down the pyramid. This was the case at J.C. Penney, Sears, IBM, Kodak, United States Steel, Bell Telephone...

The predictable is no longer predictable. For most managers, the pyramid structure is vanishing. It is being replaced by flatter organizational structures with wider spans of control and decentralized decision-making authority. The number of layers of management between top-level executives and first-level managers has been reduced.

From a management perspective, the managers are closer to the action. This change encourages autonomy and entrepreneurship. Managers can be freer to innovate and experiment.

That is the positive side. The potential negative is an ever-widening span of control. When layers of management are removed from an organization, the work must still be done somewhere. The "somewhere" is in the levels of management that remain. And the problem lies in choosing what to decentralize. Specifically, will managers at lower levels in the organization be making decisions on strategy, human resource policy, and productivity? How will decentralization change the predictable picture of an organization?

Q U E S T I O N S

1. How does the described restructuring relate to the concepts of mechanistic and organic organizational structures?

2. What contingency factors influence such restructuring?

3. What should a manager in a decentralized organizational structure do to work with a potentially larger span of control?

4. What activities and decisions should be decentralized in the restructuring? Which should remain centralized? Why?

For more about restructuring an organization, see William E. Schiemann, "Organizational Change: Lessons from a Turnaround," *Management Review,* April 1992, pp. 34–37.

Organizational Culture and Change

LEARNING OBJECTIVES

After reading and discussing this chapter, you should be able to:

- Define this chapter's essential terms
- Define corporate culture and the seven factors that influence it
- List and describe the ways that culture is manifested
- Explain what factors make a culture effective
- Define change and identify the four kinds of change that can occur in an organization
- Distinguish between planned and unplanned change
- Explain the steps that managers can follow to implement planned change
- Identify the organizational traits that promote change
- Explain why people resist change and what managers can do to overcome that resistance
- Explain why change efforts fail
- Explain the purpose of an organizational development program

change

change agent
force-field analysis

management by reaction
mutual trust
organizational climate
organizational culture

organizational development
   (OD)
organizational learning
planned change
subculture
three-step approach

MANAGEMENT IN ACTION
Schneider National's Cultural Revolution

When your business environment changes radically, you can change with it or perish. The trucking industry—and Schneider National, a trucking company—had to react to two changes. The first change was federal deregulation of interstate trucking. The government would no longer determine what kind of freight a company could carry and where it could be carried. At the same time, major customers—big retailers and manufacturers— were in the midst of their own change. They were incorporating just-in-time inventory systems that allowed them to slash inventory costs. Because these customers no longer had warehouses bulging with goods, they demanded a new commitment from the shipping companies they used. Under the just-in-time system, when the customers needed goods, they needed them now.

Schneider National CEO Don Schneider responded to these changes with a two-part strategy. First, he brought about a sweeping cultural change by motivating his employees to trade a passive mentality based on regulation for one that prized swift, reliable responses to customers' needs. He quickly changed the organization. He flattened the structure, renamed all employees *associates,* and banished status symbols. His purpose: to emphasize the ability and importance of each person. In regard to suggestions about improving performance, all employees—including drivers—were encouraged to speak their minds to anyone in the company. To encourage "a culture that allows people to hustle," Schneider gave his 8,500 drivers a fifth paycheck each month— a check based solely on performance. The cultural changes and the new incentive plan produced an involved, creative work force.

The second part of Schneider's strategy involved using the latest information technology. Initially, this included adding a computer system that was updated constantly to allow the most efficient assignment of trucks. Later, each truck was outfitted with a computer and a rotating antenna. Now a satellite tracks each rig, making sure it is on schedule—and more important— expediting orders from customers. When a customer calls in a new order, Schneider National's dispatchers know exactly which truck is closest to the customer and when it will be empty and available.

On the move, *Schneider National has responded to change by involving and motivating its associates.*

The culture has changed at Schneider National and, with it, the company's fortunes. No longer is the company struggling to cope with a deregulated environment. Now it is focused on responding to customer needs and maintaining its newly achieved

▼

When a customer calls in a new order, Schneider National's dispatchers know exactly which truck is closest to the customer and when it will be empty and available.

position as the continent's largest carrier of full-truckload cargoes. The company has also become an industry leader in the use of technology. Competitors who initially responded to deregulation by merely lowering rates are imitating Schneider—their trucks are sprouting little antennae too. ▲

For more about Schneider National, see Myron Magnet, "Meet the New Revolutionaries," *Fortune*, February 24, 1992, pp. 94–101.

Organizational Culture

An organization is a collection of humans. As such, it exhibits the characteristics of a society. Like a society, each organization embraces a system of shared beliefs, values, and norms unique to it. That system, the **organizational culture**, defines what is important to the organization, how people should behave, how they should interact with one another, and what they should be striving for. Employees who share these beliefs, values, and norms tend to develop a sense of group identity and pride, important elements of organizational effectiveness.

Each organization's specific beliefs, values, and norms create a unique culture with identifiable manifestations. At Nordstrom, the department-store chain, the organizational culture makes a crusade of customer service. Procter & Gamble's culture stresses quality and competitive marketing. Organizational culture may seem suspiciously like a company's mission, but there is more to it than that. The organizational culture provides a means through which each employee can adopt the core tenets of the firm's mission as his or her own guiding passion.

Management writers Tom Peters and Robert Waterman (1982) related the words of a business executive who had worked at McDonald's as a seventeen-year-old. In describing his experience at McDonald's, the exec pointed out the importance of the company credo of quality: "If french fries were overdone, we threw them out ... if we punched holes in the buns with our thumbs (a frequent occurrence for those new at the tough job of handling thousands of buns), we threw them out." Though they were young, inexperienced workers on the burger assembly line, he and his co-workers had absorbed the company's chief value—quality—and the norms for defect handling.

The young workers absorbed those values and norms because McDonald's culture was strong. The more a culture's values permeate the organization, the stronger the culture. McDonald's culture is also highly functional: The factors that influence culture are consistent with and supportive of the organization's strategy.

Factors That Shape Culture

Although each company's special blend of elements develops a unique culture, a comparison of many organizations identifies seven culture-shaping factors:

- Key organizational processes
- Employees and other tangible assets
- Formal organizational arrangements
- The dominant coalition
- The social system
- Technology
- The external environment

Each of these factors is in itself a complex of phenomena. None is independent of the others. Their dynamic interaction shapes organizational culture and so deserves close examination. Begin by studying Exhibit 9.1 (Kotter, 1978).

Key Organizational Processes   At the core of every organization, and fundamental to it, are the processes people follow to gather information, communicate, make decisions, manage work flow, and produce a good or service. How managers communicate to employees, how they share decision making, and how they structure the flow of work define the organization. These processes affect and are affected by the other six factors that influence organizational culture.

Employees and Other Tangible Assets   An organization's employee population, plant and offices, equipment, tools, land, inventory, and money are the resources the organization uses to carry out its activities. These assets are the most visible and complex of the factors that influence culture. Their quantity and quality determine much of an organization's culture and performance. The quality, empowerment, and innovativeness of employees at Apple Computer contribute to what Apple insiders call Apple Magic, a quality that has made the adaptation of technology a means to success for the company (Kupfer, 1992). Likewise, a lack of

Exhibit 9.1

Factors that shape organizational culture.

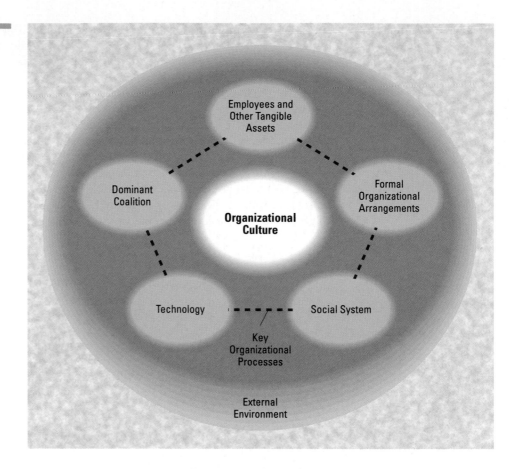

resources has a profound effect on an organization. In a cash-poor company, decision making will reflect a concern for guarding the firm's resources.

Formal Organizational Arrangements   The formal arrangements that organize tasks and individuals constitute another factor that affects organizational culture. These arrangements include the structure of the organization and its procedures and rules. Specific mandated behaviors are also a part of organizational arrangements. A firm called Atmospheric Processing, for example, invests its major efforts not in manufacturing but in heat-treating auto parts. For this organization, the prime challenge is rapid response to marketplace changes. The firm's skilled and creative employees function better with no traditional formal hierarchy, few rules, and decentralized decision making (Lammers, 1992).

The Dominant Coalition   An organization's culture is very much affected by the objectives, strategies, personal characteristics, and interrelationships of its managers, who form the dominant coalition. Managers' leadership style determines how employees are treated and how they feel about themselves and their work. The dynamic energy and vision of Bill Gates at Microsoft have made his company the world leader in computer software. Herb Kelleher of Southwest Airlines created a culture that values having fun at work and that stresses the importance of the contribution of each employee.

I S S U E S   A N D   E T H I C S
Grabbing the Buck Before Getting the Boot

The American business environment continues to be characterized by corporate shakeups—mergers, acquisitions, hostile takeovers, downsizings, and collapses. These actions push managers from job to job. No longer can workers or executives anticipate 40 years of loyal service and a gold watch. Some move to a new company when they see trouble brewing, others are forced out in early retirement. Business analysts warn that these trends can lower corporate loyalty and lure executives to seek a quick, underhanded buck, to make a financial killing before they are booted out.

In such an atmosphere, can a corporate culture that values strong commitment to ethical practices be effective? Does the current trend undermine ethical behavior among executives? As the corporate CEO, the person most responsible and accountable for corporate ethics, how could you influence the culture of your large company to reinforce ethics in this volatile environment? ▲

The Social System   The social system contributes norms and values to organizational culture. One component of the social system is the set of employee relationships that relate to power, affiliation, and trust. The grapevine and the informal organization are also parts of the social system, and they help render it one of the most important factors of organizational culture. Because people *are* the organization, their relationships define the organization's character. In the armed services, rigid hierarchy creates formal social interactions; subordinates must behave toward superiors in certain ways. On the other hand, the dangers soldiers face can mitigate the formal structure, leaving room for informal interaction that exists alongside the rigid behavior patterns required by hierarchy. Therefore, formality and informality are part of the culture.

Technology   The principal technological processes and equipment that employees use also affect organizational culture. The uses to which technology is put plays a role, for example. Is a machine or process intended to replace human labor or enable employees to enhance their skills and productivity? The answer sends a message about the value of employees in the organization. Assembly-line technology promotes an impersonal, uninvolved culture. Many years ago, Volvo of Sweden embraced quality and worker satisfaction as corporate values. As a result, Volvo managers adopted team organization and unconventional layouts in Volvo facilities. These changes helped shift the organizational culture away from the mechanistic values of the assembly line.

The External Environment   Recall the discussion of the external environment in Chapter 3. The discussion showed how suppliers, markets, competitors, regulators, and other elements outside an organization affected its goals, resources, and processes. Clearly these elements shape a firm's culture in many ways. Consider the corporate culture that was likely to develop in the Soviet Union from 1917 to 1991. Contrast that culture with the one likely to develop in Russia in 1993. How do the corporate cultures at the Rolls-Royce automobile factory in England and the Hyundai automobile factory in Korea reflect their external environments?

Government regulation can have a profound effect on corporate culture. In the 1940s and '50s federal regulations protected Pan American World Airways from competition. As a result, the Pan Am culture glowed with confidence bordering on arrogance. All that changed swiftly in 1977, when U.S. airlines were deregulated and Pan Am became just another naked competitor among hundreds of hungry fledgling airlines (Bender and Altschul, 1982).

Manifestations of Culture

An organization's culture is nurtured and becomes apparent to its members in various ways. Some aspects of culture are explicit; some must be inferred. The chief evidences of culture are statements of principle, stories, slogans, heroes, ceremonies, symbols, climate, and the physical environment.

Statements of Principle

Some corporations have developed written expressions of basic principles that are central to organizational culture. Many years ago Forrest Mars developed the "Five Principles of Mars," which established fundamental beliefs for the company (Brenner, 1992). Mars's principles, which still guide the company today, are:

- Quality. No one at Mars has the word *quality* in his or her job title; quality control is everywhere and everyone is responsible for it.

Quality control at Harley-Davidson factories increased significantly after the employees received a stock ownership plan. Being personally invested in the company improved their work performance.

- Responsibility. All employees are expected to take on direct and total responsibility for results, exercising initiative, and making decisions.

- Mutuality. In all dealings—with the consumer, other employees, a supplier or distributor, or the community at large—employees are to act so that everyone can win.

- Efficiency. Almost all of the company's 41 factories operate 24 hours a day, 7 days a week. As a whole, the company uses 30% fewer employees than its competitors do.

- Freedom. The company provides freedom to allow employees to shape their futures, and profits that allow employees to remain free.

Stories

Shared stories illustrate the culture. Telling them is a way to acquaint new employees with the values of the culture and to reaffirm those values for existing employees. For example, all employees of Stew Leonard learn how its founder became known as the King of Customer Service.

The story recounts how, a week after opening his small store, Leonard received a customer who angrily complained that the eggnog she had bought was sour. Leonard tasted the eggnog, thought it was fine, and told her she was wrong. He added that he had sold 300 half gallons of eggnog that week and that she was the only customer to have complained about it. By then the customer was boiling mad and asked for her money back. When Leonard complied, she left the store—but not without taking a parting shot. She proclaimed: "I'm never coming back to this store again." From that day on, the customer has always been right at Stew Leonard's, and his little store is now a 100,000-square-foot operation with annual sales approaching $100 million (Richman, 1990).

Slogans

A slogan is a phrase or saying that clearly expresses a key organizational value. The late Sam Walton's slogan, "The customer is the boss," keeps the culture of Wal-Mart focused on providing high-quality customer service. But a slogan should not be confused with a company's advertising campaign, as two experts on corporate culture point out, unless the slogan is genuinely backed by the actions of the company and becomes a company value. In discussing Dana Corporation, with its slogan "productivity through people," Terrence Deal and Allan Kennedy (1982) explained how a slogan that expresses an important cultural value can be made to live in the organization.

> [Dana] has virtually doubled its productivity over the past seven years, a period when the overall growth of American productivity has been slowing.... [To achieve this growth, Dana] relied on its people, right down to the shop-floor level.... It put this value into action by creating a multitude of task forces and other special activities; by giving its people practical opportunities to generate productivity; by listening to ideas and then implementing them; and by consistently, visibly, and frequently rewarding success.

Heroes

A hero is a person in the organization who exemplifies the values of the culture. The hero of an organization is often the company's founder or an executive who spurred the organization's initial success. James Allison of the Allison Division of General Motors was revered for his devotion to quality in the firm's earliest days. "Whatever leaves this shop over my name must be the finest work possible," Allison said in 1917, and the firm's devoted engineers are still quoting him, 75 years later (Sonnenburg and Schoneberger, 1990). An organization can benefit when heroes are drawn from employees at all levels. One way of doing that is through ceremonies.

Ceremonies

Managers hold ceremonies to exemplify and reinforce company values. Awards ceremonies for outstanding service, top producers, or high-performance teams promote the values of the culture and allow recipients and colleagues to share the experience of achievement. Awards ceremonies at Mary Kay Cosmetics are legendary in the cosmetics industry. They are lavish affairs at which high-achieving sales representatives receive furs, pins, and cars. Many companies use ceremonies to mark the advancement of a new hire from trainee to full-fledged employee. Ceremonies also include rituals that honor promotions. These events strengthen employee identification with the organization's values.

Symbols

An object that conveys meaning to others is a symbol. Some organizations use symbols to embody their core values. At Stew Leonard's the employees are reminded of the value of customer service by a rock positioned next to the front door of the store. On it are chiseled the words "Our Policy" followed by the company's two rules: "Rule 1: The customer is always right. Rule 2: If the customer is ever wrong, re-read Rule 1" (Deal and Kennedy, 1982).

Symbols may include job titles and features of the office environment, such as a reserved parking space, the size or location of an office, or the size of a desk.

Climate

The **organizational climate** is the quality of the work environment as experienced by employees. Climate is largely a function of how workers feel about their organization. Do they work hard and apply themselves to the task, cooperating with management goals and directives? Do they drag their feet, resenting management instructions and resisting demands for output? Cooperative employees who work hard probably work in an organization that takes employees' needs into account. These employees enjoy a positive corporate climate because they have a positive view of their organization. Resentful employees are likely to work in an enterprise in which managers and employees hold different values or pursue widely divergent goals. For these employees, the corporate climate is negative.

Physical Environment

Last but not least in the discussion of culture-shaping factors is a simple but powerful force: the physical environment of an organization. It is no coincidence that Sears & Roebuck, a hierarchical organization, built the world's tallest building. The Sears Tower dominates the Chicago skyline and reflects the multi-layered structure and centralized culture of the organization that built it. A software developer or computer maker, on the other hand, may create a campuslike environment to promote the free exchange of ideas. Such enclaves are common in California's Silicon Valley.

The Creation of Culture

The efforts of managers and employees create culture. Some of the efforts are intentional: Managers like Stew Leonard deliberately set out to instill certain values. In other cases, culture simply emerges from a pattern of behaviors that are not consciously planned.

The Role of Managers and the Dominant Coalition

Managers at all levels in an organization help develop the culture. Quite simply, supervisors set the tone, manage the resources, and control the means to influence the results. Managers help create culture by:

- Identifying underlying values

- Clearly defining the company's mission and goals

- Determining the amount of individual autonomy and the degree to which people work separately or in groups

- Structuring work to achieve goals in accordance with the corporation's values

- Developing reward systems that reinforce values and goals

- Creating methods of socialization that will bring new workers inside the culture and reinforce the culture for existing workers

Methods of socialization are an extremely important aspect of corporate culture. Unless managers actively develop and nurture ways of passing the culture along, they cannot be certain that employees will adopt it. (Chapter 21 will examine socialization in detail.)

The task of defining the culture often begins with the organization's founder. Stew Leonard and Sam Walton are but two examples of entrepreneurs who created and put their stamp on strong organizational cultures. Sometimes, though, managers in charge of existing organizations find that they wish to change the culture. Jack Welch, CEO of General Electric, set out to change the culture of his company. He realized that the change would depend on a new relationship between workers and management. "We agreed on a set of values we will need to take this company forward, rapidly, through the 1990s and beyond. The values are built on trust and respect between workers and managers" (Holusha, 1992).

Organizational culture significantly affects managers—and, indeed, all employees—by determining to a large degree how managers perceive events and how they will respond (Robbins, 1991). Perceptions are influenced by values. Values channel attention and create a frame of reference for interpreting the world. In a culture that values customer service, most problems will be defined in terms of how they affect customers. More important, perhaps, problems that have nothing to do with customer service will be overlooked because they involve issues that are not valued. They will simply go unnoticed.

The Role of Employees

Employees contribute to organizational culture to the extent that they accept and adopt the culture—by how well the socialization takes. Workers at Disney theme parks are renowned for their sunny dispositions and friendliness to patrons. The training they receive after hiring clearly succeeds in making them see themselves as performers whose task it is to give enjoyment.

Another way that workers contribute to organizational culture is by helping to shape the values it embodies. Employees who shirk the tasks at hand—and influence newcomers to do the same—have a significant effect on quality, regardless of what top managers may say about quality as a value. Employees who give each other a hand to meet a deadline create a feeling of teamwork that exists regardless of management's decisions about structuring work.

Finally, workers play a role in influencing organizational culture by forming subcultures. **Subcultures** are units within an organization that are based on the shared values, norms, and beliefs of their members. The values of the subculture may or may not complement those of the dominant organizational culture. Unionized employees constitute a subculture. Groups of workers who share a common background or interest or who work in the same department may also form subcultures. When workers form a subculture, their shared experiences take on a deeper meaning because they also share values, norms, and beliefs. Because subcultures influence their members' behavior, they are important factors for managers to consider. If a subculture's values and norms conflict with those of the dominant culture, managers must take action.

Factors That Contribute to the Effectiveness of Culture

Understanding organizational culture is important because culture affects performance. In a recent study of hundreds of firms, Kotter and Heskett (1992) found a dramatic difference between effective and ineffective cultures.

> We found that firms with cultures that emphasized all the key managerial constituencies (customers, stockholders, and employees) and leadership from managers at all levels outperformed firms that did not have those cultural traits by a huge margin. Over an eleven-year period, the former increased revenues by an average of 682 percent versus 166 percent for the latter, expanded their work forces by 282 percent versus 36 percent, grew their stock prices by 901 percent versus 74 percent, and improved their net incomes by 756 percent versus 1 percent.

Kotter and Heskett went on to warn that managers must do more than promote an effective culture; they must be constantly on the lookout for the signs of an ineffective culture.

> Corporate cultures that inhibit strong long-term financial performance are not rare; they develop easily, even in firms that are full of reasonable and intelligent people. Cultures that encourage inappropriate behavior and inhibit change to more appropriate strategies tend to emerge slowly and quietly over a period of years, usually when firms are performing well.

Three factors help determine how effective an organizational culture is; they are coherence, pervasiveness and depth, and adaptability to environment.

Coherence   In discussions of organizational culture, *coherence* refers to how well the culture fits the mission and other organizational elements. A culture like the one at Wal-Mart, which values customer service and a low-cost strategy, must train employees to recognize customer needs. It must also empower them to make decisions to meet those needs, create processes and structures that will achieve the goals of low inventory cost and low overhead, and employ technology to meet those goals. If decision-making authority at Wal-Mart were centralized, the culture would be less coherent, because such a design does not mesh with other aspects of the culture.

Pervasiveness and Depth   The phrase *pervasiveness and depth* refers to the extent to which employees adopt the culture of an organization. The greater the acceptance of and commitment to organizational values, the stronger the culture (Dubrin, 1974). By insisting that all employees take responsibility for quality, Mars ensures that quality, as a value, is pervasive. By training theme-park employees extensively, Disney helps guarantee that its values are deeply held.

Adaptability to the External Environment   If organizational culture fits the external environment, managers and employees have the mindset they need to compete. For decades American Telephone & Telegraph (AT&T) enjoyed a monopoly on long-distance telephone service. In the 1980s, when long-distance service was deregulated, AT&T employees found they did not have the mindset to compete in their new environment; their organizational culture had a poor degree of fit in terms of the real world. The new external environment had created new demands, and it required a new way of thinking—a new culture.

Of the three factors that determine the effectiveness of organizational culture, the degree of fit with the external environment is perhaps the most critical. Its importance lies in the fact that the environment changes. Just ask managers at Sears, IBM, or General Motors about the importance of change in the external environment. These three organizations have fallen on hard times because they were not adaptable enough. Each organization possessed an effective culture. Indeed, IBM provided a model of strong corporate culture. The true measure of the effectiveness of a culture, then, is its ability to adapt. Managers must achieve the difficult task of building a culture that is strong enough to compel commitment and unwavering support but flexible enough to allow change in the face of emerging external demands.

FOCUS ON QUALITY

Quality as a Cultural Value

Quality. Perhaps the most important (certainly the most ballyhooed) business concept of the decade. As a topic, quality shows up on the agenda of every top-management conference. Quality has become the basis of a new school of management focus. And a prize for quality—the Malcolm Baldridge Award—quickly became an item of great prestige, the Oscar of managerial excellence. Quality is no luxury: It's the way business is going to be done from now on.

With this in mind, the nation's CEOs are concentrating not only on implementing quality programs, but also on making quality a core value of the corporate culture. Perhaps McDonald's was the inspiration—the fast-food franchiser has thrived for decades with its emphasis on QSC&V (quality, service, cleanliness, and value). Some organizations have made a senior executive responsible for quality; others have taken a more decentralized approach by placing a quality chief in each business unit throughout the organization. Either way, the goal is to make quality a concern of all employees.

No matter what approach managers take to promote quality in the culture, they must follow some basic principles. First, they must change each element of the organizational culture in a way that supports the new emphasis. Processes must be revamped to emphasize quality, not just productivity. Training must teach personnel to think in terms of doing the job right rather than doing it quickly. Managers must work in the external environment to ensure, for example, that suppliers deliver quality materials. The second requirement of a cultural change is the development of cultural expressions that emphasize the new cultural value. The creation of in-house quality awards and the writing of quality-oriented slogans are just two ways to reinforce the new emphasis. Third, managers must be aware of why individuals and groups resist change and how they can overcome that resistance.

Managers need to remember something else, too: You can't institute a program of quality-consciousness overnight. It can take six to nine years for the new value to become embedded in corporate culture. ▲

For more about creating a culture that values quality, see "Executive Insights: The Quality Dilemma," *Management Review*, November 1991, pp. 30–34.

Meeting that challenge is likely to become even more important to business survival in the future. In the volatile world of today, environmental change is a constant. This chapter will now turn to the vital matter of understanding change and learning how to manage it.

The Nature of Change

Not since the Industrial Revolution has U.S. business experienced so much change. In the past decade, almost every industry has been rocked by it. Telecommunications has been changed by divestitures. Pharmaceuticals and banking have undergone consolidation. Banking and transportation have had to adjust to deregulation as investment brokers and health care providers have had to adjust to increasing regulation. Manufacturers are battling an increase in foreign competition, and the computer industry must constantly accommodate technological innovation. Managers are assaulted by change. And they are often frustrated to find that as soon as they adjust to one change, they must readjust to accommodate another.

Change is any alteration in the work environment. The shift may be in the way things are perceived or in how they are organized, processed, created, or maintained. Every individual and organization experiences change. Sometimes change is the result of external events beyond the control of a person or an organization. Schneider National, the trucking company that was suddenly confronted with a deregulated environment, experienced change that was beyond its control. Sometimes the change is the result of planning. When a company lowers prices to increase market penetration, for example, the change in price is purposeful.

The example about lowering prices indicates how complex a change can be. Lowering prices may seem to be a simple matter, but it involves more than just printing a new price list. A company lowers prices to increase sales. If sales increase, the company may need additional staff or equipment (phone lines or computers) to handle the volume of orders. It may need more production capacity to fill the orders, a more efficient technology to meet the needs, and so on. Furthermore, the information system must communicate the new price throughout the organization, and employees must receive briefings so they will know how to handle the increase. Even an apparently mechanical change calls for adjustments throughout an organization. Change is not easy.

This section will explore change by discussing its sources and types. The sections that follow will examine the kinds of changes that confront an organization during a typical life span and how change affects managers at each level.

Sources of Change

Change originates in either the external or the internal environments of the organization.

External Sources of Change   Change may come from the political, social, technological, or economic environment. Externally motivated change may involve government action, technology, competition, social values, and economic variables. Developments in the external environment require managers to make adjustments. New government regulations can require that a manufacturer install pollution-control devices or that a restaurant raise the wages of its workers to meet a new minimum. The actions of competitors certainly put demands on a business. When one U.S. airline launches new low fares, other domestic airlines in the same markets feel compelled to follow suit.

Internal Sources of Change   Internal sources of change include managerial policies or styles, systems and procedures, technology, and employee attitudes. When a manager changes the standards by which job performance is measured, or when a new manager takes over a department, employees must adapt their behavior to fit the new situation. Schneider National, by adopting new information technology, changed vehicle routing, response time, and the way drivers worked.

New conditions in the external environment can bring about change within an organization; it is also true that internal change can cause external change. Whether internal change affects the external environment depends on the extent of the internal change and on whether the change affects a part of the organization that has impact on the environment. New internal policies about reporting travel and entertainment expenses are unlikely to affect the external environment. The changes instituted at Schneider National, however, had a major effect on other companies in the industry. These companies had to adopt Schneider National's new methods to remain competitive.

Types of Change

Change can also be understood on the basis of its focus, which can be strategic, structural, process-oriented, or people-centered. Such changes can produce dramatic impact on the organizational culture.

Strategic Change   Sometimes managers find it necessary to change the strategy or the mission of their organizations. Managers who decide to focus on a single mission may find it necessary to divest themselves of unrelated businesses, as Beatrice Foods has recently done. Managers who want to expand operations to new areas may move to acquire another company, as British Airways did when it tried to purchase part of USAir in 1992.

Achieving strategic changes can require, in turn, a change in organizational culture or other elements. When Ford adopted quality as a key to its competitive strategy, it had to adopt quality work as a corporate value.

Structural Change   Managers often find it necessary to change the structure of their organizations. This has certainly been the case in recent years, when team building and downsizing have been so prevalent. The purpose of these changes is usually to make operations run more smoothly, improve overall coordination and control, or empower individuals to make their own decisions. Because structural change has a major impact on an organization's social system and climate, it greatly affects organizational culture.

Process-Oriented Change   Many changes relate to processes. These changes include adopting new technology, as at Schneider National; shifting from human to mechanical labor, as has been done in plants that use robotics; or adopting new procedures. Since an organization's processes are an important component of its culture, changes in processes significantly affect that culture.

People-Centered Change   Many changes are directed at the attitudes, behaviors, skills, or performance of employees. These changes can be achieved through retraining, replacing current employees, or increasing the performance expectations of new employees. The task of changing attitudes and behaviors falls into the domain of behavioral training. As an aspect of organizational development, behavioral training will be discussed later in this chapter.

Management and Change

Each level of management faces change in a different way. Top-level managers are involved in change in terms of the organization as a whole. They tend not to address minute details; instead, they focus on the broad outlines of the desired change. Top-level managers are likely to be involved in changes of strategy,

Procedures change with changing technology. At Martin Marietta Astronautics, the manager of manufacturing uses an Electronic Shop Floor Traveler to examine vital documents.

structure, and process. Because such changes have a major impact on culture and the way an organization does business, the effects of change decisions made by top managers ripple throughout an organization. Top managers must be sensitive to the external environment, which means that they need to stay attuned to changes in that environment. By scanning the external environment, they may be able to see when internal changes are needed to fit new circumstances and meet new opportunities.

Middle managers are likely to face structural, process-oriented, or people-centered changes, though they may well have some input into decisions about strategic change. To achieve greater efficiency or higher quality, they may reorganize staff or work flow. They may develop training programs to introduce new technology. In any case, the changes implemented by middle managers are likely to have a wide impact. They may affect all members of a division.

Though first-line managers may participate in discussions about strategic or structural changes, they are unlikely to make decisions about these issues. First-line managers institute process-oriented and people-centered change. They are the managers who implement all types of changes developed higher in the hierarchy. Because they come into close contact with their employees, it is especially important for these managers to understand how to manage change.

How to Manage Change

One way a company can deal with change is to try to anticipate the need for it and plan for it. A company and its managers can adopt a philosophy of **planned change**, which involves trying to anticipate what changes will occur in both the external and internal environments and then developing a response that will maximize success. When managers plan for change, they are more likely to be able to predict the results and thereby control events. Dan Schneider instituted planned change at Schneider National, and his company has thrived. The alternative—**management by reaction**—can invite disaster. The reactions of many of Schneider National's competitors illustrated this kind of management. Their response to deregulation was to lower their prices. When that was ineffective, they continued to lower prices and eventually went bankrupt. Their failure can be partially attributed to the fact that they had no long-range plan for change.

The person who implements planned change is the **change agent**. This could be the manager who conceived of the need to change. (Dan Schneider was the change agent for Schneider National.) It could be another manager, to whom the task is delegated. Or it could be an outsider, a consultant brought in to help an organization adopt a new way of doing things.

The next sections will examine planned change by looking at the kinds of changes that managers can expect throughout the life of an organization, the steps involved in planning change, and the attitudes that underlie an effective approach to change.

The Need for Change: Diagnosing and Predicting It

Managers can diagnose and predict the need for organizational change by studying the typical phases of change. Recall the organizational life cycle of birth, youth, midlife, and maturity (see Chapter 8) and some of the crises commonly experienced by organizations at each stage. Management consultant Larry Greiner (1972) has graphed these predictable phases of organizational evolution (see Exhibit 9.2). Anticipating these phases can help managers prepare for change and not simply react to it. Greiner has identified five phases of growth:

Phase 1: Creativity   This birth stage of the organization is marked by concerns for product and market, by an informal social system, and by an entrepreneurial style of management. Soon the need for capital, new products, new markets, and new employees forces the organization to change. A crisis of leadership occurs when management becomes incapable of reacting to the growing organization's need for structure. The organization enters a new phase.

Phase 2: Direction   The second phase is characterized by the implementation of rules, regulations, and procedures. A functional organizational structure is introduced; an accounting system is created; incentives, budgets, and work standards are established; and formal, impersonal communication begins. Eventually, lower-level managers demand greater decision-making authority, which brings on another crisis and launches the organization into the next phase.

Phase 3: Delegation   Decentralization is the key to the third phase, in which top management creates profit centers under territorial managers who are given leeway to act and who are held accountable for the results. Communication from the top becomes less frequent. Eventually, top managers sense that they have lost control of the organization. This realization brings on another crisis and another major change.

Exhibit 9.2

A model of organizational growth and change.

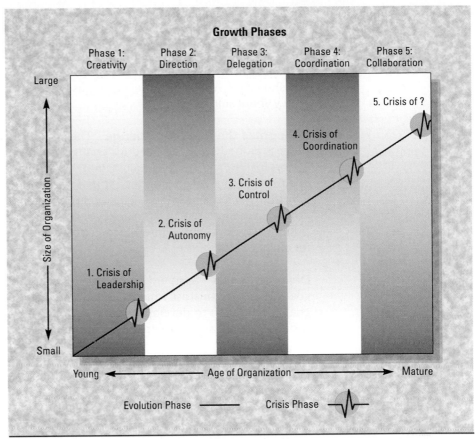

Growth Phases

| Phase 1: Creativity | Phase 2: Direction | Phase 3: Delegation | Phase 4: Coordination | Phase 5: Collaboration |

Size of Organization — Large ... Small

5. Crisis of ?

4. Crisis of Coordination

3. Crisis of Control

2. Crisis of Autonomy

1. Crisis of Leadership

Young ← Age of Organization → Mature

Evolution Phase ——— Crisis Phase

Source: Adapted from "Evolution and Revolution as Organizations Grow," by Larry E. Greiner, *Harvard Business Review*, July–August 1972, pp 55–64 Copyright 1972 by the President and Fellows of Harvard College.

Phase 4: Coordination Responding to their sense of loss of control, managers attempt to seize control by emphasizing coordination. Decentralized work units are merged, formal organization-wide planning is introduced, capital expenditures are restricted, and staff personnel begin to wield greater power. The price of this phase is red tape and interpersonal distance, which develops between line and staff and between headquarters and field. A new crisis takes place.

Phase 5: Collaboration The final phase introduces a new people-oriented and flexible system, and managers exhibit more spontaneity. Characteristics of this phase include problem solving by teams, reductions in headquarters staff, simplification of formal systems, and encouragement of an attitude of risk taking and innovation.

At the heart of Greiner's model is a key point about change: The solution to one set of problems eventually creates another set of problems that require solving. In other words, the need for change is constant.

The Steps in Planned Change

Once a manager or organization commits to planned change, it is necessary to create a step-by-step approach to achieve it. Exhibit 9.3 presents the steps that a manager can use to implement change (Greiner, 1967). The paragraphs that follow will show how Wendy, a manager, can use this process to change her company's policy about smoking.

Recognize the Need for Change   The first step in the change-implementation process is to identify the need for change. Recognition can come as a result of factors inside or outside an organization. In Wendy's case, suppose the company's health-insurance carrier notifies her that it will conduct a rate-structure review in light of research about the effects of smoking. Meanwhile, an internal force, a group of employees, requests a policy statement about smoking in the workplace. In this case, external and internal forces contribute to the recognition of the need for change.

Develop Goals   As in any planning process, a key step is the identification of goals. Managers must ask what they wish to achieve. In Wendy's case, the manager's goals become (1) to develop a smoking policy for the organization that will be widely accepted and (2) to prevent insurance costs from rising.

Select a Change Agent   With goals in mind, the next issue is to determine who will manage the change. Wendy asks the leader of the group concerned about smoking to assist her as a change agent.

Diagnose the Problem   This step calls for the manager to gather data about the problem and then analyze it to identify the key issues. The two change agents in the current example find that other companies are able to control health-

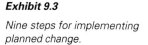

Exhibit 9.3

Nine steps for implementing planned change.

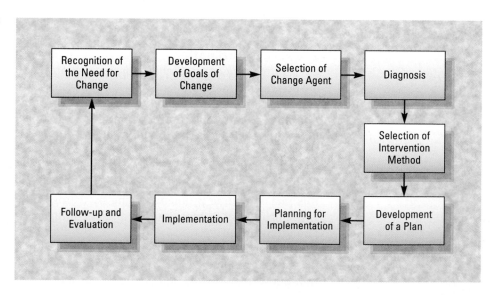

insurance costs by instituting smoking restrictions. They also learn that whether employees are for or against smoking, smoking is an emotional issue.

Select the Intervention Method   In the fifth step, the manager must decide how to achieve the change. Because smoking is such an emotionally charged issue, the change agents in the current example decide not to create the needed policy themselves. Instead, they form a task force that includes representatives from all departments. They believe that large-scale participation will help ensure that the change can be facilitated.

Develop a Plan   This step involves actually putting together the "what" of the change. The task force must decide if the company will have a no-smoking policy or will designate areas in which smoking is permitted.

Plan for Implementation   In this phase, the decision maker must decide the "when," "where," and "how" of the plan. The task force in Wendy's case must decide when the policy will go into effect, how it will be communicated, and how its impact will be monitored and evaluated.

Implement the Plan   After a plan is created, it must be put into effect. This requires notifying the employees who will be affected by the change. Notification may consist of written messages, briefings, or training sessions. The choice depends on the depth of the change and the impact it will have on people. With a major change, such as the adoption of work teams, training may need to go on for some time. In Wendy's case, the task force decides to settle the smoking issue by announcing the plan and holding briefings.

Follow Up and Evaluate   Once a change has been implemented, the manager must follow up by evaluating it. Evaluation consists of comparing actual results to goals. If the new smoking policy receives widespread employee acceptance and holds the line on insurance costs, then the change was worthwhile.

Traits That Promote Change

Managers can help create a climate that promotes change by developing a philosophy toward change that includes three elements: (1) mutual trust, (2) organizational learning, and (3) adaptability.

Mutual Trust

Creating an environment of mutual trust between managers and employees is vital for managers who wish to implement change. Many research studies indicate that trust is the most important factor in creating an effective, well-run organization (Barnes, 1981). In this context, **mutual trust** is the ability to rely on someone based on his or her character, ability, and truthfulness. In a period of uncertainty and hard times, mutual trust allows individuals to continue to function while maintaining a hope that things will improve.

Mutual trust can lessen fear of change in a period of uncertainty and hard times.

The two essential ingredients of mutual trust are a sense of adequacy and personal security. Adequacy means that each employee feels that he or she counts for something in the organization and that his or her presence makes a difference in the overall performance of the firm. Personal security is the degree to which each person feels safe when speaking honestly and candidly.

Mutual trust can lessen fear of change, and this can help managers implement change. When trust is present, employees will feel comfortable as the organization moves through change, even though change is threatening.

Organizational Learning

The term **organizational learning** refers to the ability to integrate new ideas into established systems to produce better ways of doing things. A manager can view organizational learning as either single-looped or double-looped (Argyris and Schon, 1978).

A single-looped learning situation is one in which only one way of making adjustments exists. An organization with single-looped learning has a prescribed method of doing things. When actions do not follow the prescription, the actions are adjusted to meet the standards. An organization with this belief is inflexible; it does not change its attitude, only its responses.

Double-looped learning, on the other hand, is based on the realization that more than one alternative exists. Double-looped learning facilitates change because its premise is that there is more than one way to do something. If a manager believes there are numerous ways of reaching a goal, each employee is free to share ideas and the assumptions underlying them. Double-looped learning allows for change in attitude and behavior.

Adaptability

Managers can either plan for change or react to it. Being adaptive takes energy, commitment, and caring, but the wear and tear of the reactive approach are far worse. Adaptiveness means being open to new and different ways of doing things; it means being flexible rather than rigid.

The Implementation of Change

To implement a program of change, a manager must be aware of why people resist change, why change efforts fail, and what techniques can be used to successfully modify behavior.

Resistance to Change

One of the greatest difficulties faced by managers trying to institute change is overcoming the resistance of those who must adapt. But overcome it they must, or the change cannot take place.

Sources of Resistance   People resist change for many reasons. The list that follows presents some of them.

- Loss of security. Change scares people. Individuals tend to find security in traditional methods—the familiar is comfortable. New technology, new systems, new procedures, and new managers can threaten that security and thus cause resistance.

- Fear of economic loss. Sometimes people resist change because they foresee, or fear, an economic loss. Workers may disapprove of new processes because they feel that the result will be layoffs or reduced wages.

- Loss of power and control. Change often poses problems of power and control. An employee may ask, "Will my influence still exist?" "Where will I end up in the pecking order?" These questions reflect the anxiety caused by change (Nadler, 1987). Some reorganizations clearly indicate that specific people will lose power. These people are likely to wish to preserve the status quo.

- Reluctance to change old habits. Habits provide a programmed method for decision making and performing. Someone who needs no initiative to solve problems may think, "I can do this job blindfolded." Learning new processes requires rethinking or learning to think again; it's hard work.

- Selective perception. A person who has a biased interpretation of reality is guilty of selective perception. To someone with selective perception, reality is what the person thinks it is. Employees prone to selective perception tend to think in terms of stereotypes, and these stereotypes can permeate their logic. Faced with a change at work, a person with selective perception might think, "It's a management plot to do away with us." An employee with such an attitude is difficult for a manager to deal with. If the employee's views are extreme, he or she regards all actions of management as suspect.

- Awareness of weaknesses in the proposed change. Sometimes employees resist change because they see that the change may cause problems. This type of resistance can be constructive. By listening to the objections of these employees, managers can help the organization avoid problems and save time, money, and energy. For employees to have a constructive effect, however, they must communicate their concerns effectively and early.

Techniques for Overcoming Resistance   Managers can use five techniques to overcome resistance to change:

- Participation. A person who is involved in the process of change is more strongly committed to the change than someone who did not participate. Organizations have recognized this and have responded by implementing cross-functional teams, which Chapter 14 will discuss.

- Open communication. Uncertainty breeds fear, which creates rumors, which cause more uncertainty. Managers can reduce the likelihood of this unsettling cycle by providing timely, complete, and accurate information. Holding back information destroys trust.

- Advance warning. Sudden change is revolutionary—like an earthquake. People adapt better to change if they are prepared for it. As a manager senses a need for change or knows that change is imminent, he or she is well advised to make it known to the employees who will be affected. Another tool to help people prepare for change is continuous education and training. Continuous learning seems to enhance adaptability.

- Sensitivity. When implementing change, managers must work with those affected to learn each employee's concerns and respond to them. In other words, managers must be sensitive to the effects the change has on each person. Sensitivity minimizes resistance to change.

- Security. People are much more willing to accept change if the fear of dire consequences can be removed. In many cases, managers can reassure workers simply by explaining that the change will not affect income and job security. Of course such a commitment is meaningful only if it is true. When managers break promises, they are taking the first step toward employee discontent.

Why Change Efforts Fail

Not all change efforts are successful. Even when managers undertake change for the best of reasons, they cannot always bring it about. The paragraphs that follow present the typical causes for failure.

Faulty Thinking   Managers can fail to achieve change by not analyzing the situation properly. If Dan Schneider had not perceived the need to promote a new culture in which workers hustled, all the new technology he installed may well have been worthless.

Inadequate Process   Sometimes change efforts fail because of the process used to bring them about. A change may fail because the manager did not follow the steps for change shown in Exhibit 9.3 or because he or she did not follow the steps properly. Perhaps the manager chose an inappropriate change agent or neglected a step in the process. In any case, an incomplete approach usually leads to failure.

Lack of Resources   Some changes require a significant expenditure of time and money. If those resources aren't available, the change effort may be doomed from the beginning.

Lack of Acceptance and Commitment   If individuals, both managers and employees, do not accept the need for change and commit to it, change will not occur. Lack of commitment is typical in an organization whose managers frequently announce change but do not follow through to implement it. In such an organization, employees view each new announcement of change as "the program of the month"—entertaining perhaps, but not to be taken seriously.

Lack of Time and Poor Timing   In some situations, not enough time is allowed for people to think about the change, accept it, and implement it. In other instances the timing is poor—an economic downturn may lower revenue, employees may be occupied with other commitments, or a competitor may release a new product. A company may invest years and millions of dollars into a change only to find that the environment has evolved so much that the plan devised for success no longer applies.

A Resistant Culture   In some cases, the cultural climate of an organization needs to be changed before anything else can be.

Methods of Effecting Change

This section will explore how to change behavior on the individual level. This is the kind of change that most first-line managers need to understand, for their change efforts will be directed at modifying or altering their subordinates' behavior. Change in individuals usually relates to a change in skills, knowledge, or attitude. The paragraphs that follow explore two approaches: the three-step approach and force-field analysis.

The Three-Step Approach   Many psychologists and educators have observed that different people react differently to pressures to change. Most will accept the need to learn new skills and update their knowledge, but most resent efforts to change their attitudes. Accordingly, workplace efforts to change attitudes meet the least success of any change efforts. Yet if attitudes are not changed, the behaviors that grow out of attitudes cannot change. Kurt Lewin (1947) provided a useful approach to changing attitudes in a lasting way. His method, called the **three-step approach**, consists of three phases: unfreezing, change, and refreezing.

Unfreezing *a subordinate's attitude is the first step in correcting unwanted behavior. Then the desired values are instilled. In step 3, refreezing, the manager recognizes and rewards new and approved attitudes and behaviors.*

In unfreezing, the first step, managers who spot deficiencies in a subordinate's behavior must identify the causes of that behavior. They confront the individual with the behavior and the problem it causes, and then begin trying to convince him or her to change by suggesting methods and offering incentives. This step may include pressure on the individual that makes him or her uncomfortable and dissatisfied. When the person is upset enough, step 2 may begin.

For example, say that Jessica wants to improve the productivity of Jane, a staff member in the Information Center. By taking too much time on her work, Jane is increasing the work load of others in the department. To resolve the problem, Jessica must first explain to Jane that her work is inadequate and that her co-workers are being required, unfairly, to carry her burden. She may mention that the others are starting to complain about Jane. Having reviewed Jane's work, Jessica thinks that the basic problem is lack of training. As a result, she suggests that Jane undertake a special week-long training course offered by the company. She could offer an incentive, too, pointing out that the higher productivity could mean a better chance at a salary increase.

In change, the second step, the individual's discomfort level rises. When it rises high enough, he or she will look for ways to reduce the tension. This leads the employee to question his or her motives for current behavior, and this questioning provides the manager with the opening to present new role models that promote the desired behavior. As the individual adopts that behavior, performance will improve—but the manager must support and reinforce that behavior if it is to last.

In this example, Jane might begin to notice the disapproving looks or whispered comments from co-workers. Uncomfortable in this unfriendly atmosphere, she might decide that she is willing to undertake the needed training.

In step 3, refreezing, the manager recognizes and rewards new and approved attitudes and behaviors. If any new problems arise, the manager must identify and discourage them; in other words, the process begins again. After Jane takes the training, Jessica should closely monitor her productivity. When she sees output

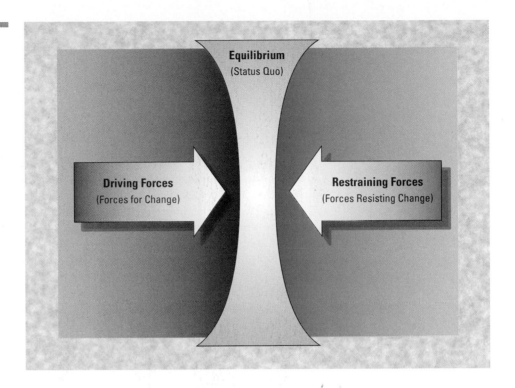

increase, she must be sure to congratulate Jane on the improvement. For the desired behavior to continue, positive reinforcement should come fairly frequently especially at first. If a salary increase was promised, that promise must be kept.

A key point to bear in mind is that the three-step process is continuous. Managers must watch that the new behaviors do not become counterproductive. If they do, the behaviors must be unfrozen and replaced by a new, more desirable behavior.

Force-Field Analysis   Another useful tool for managing change is **force-field analysis**, which was also developed by Kurt Lewin. As Exhibit 9.4 shows, to achieve change a manager must overcome the status quo. Lewin views the proclivity toward change as a balance between forces that favor change and forces that resist it. The change forces are known as driving forces, and the resisting forces are known as restraining forces. Managers who are trying to implement a change must analyze the balance of driving and restraining forces, then attempt to tip that balance by selectively removing or weakening the restraining forces. The driving forces will then become strong enough to enable the change to be made.

To see how force-field analysis works, return to the example of Jane, the worker in the Information Center. To convince Jane to change, Jessica must first identify the driving forces: self-esteem, the regard of peers, and increased monetary compensation. The key restraining forces might be Jane's lack of desire to expend the effort to improve and discomfort with the computer. Jessica can weaken the restrainers by having one of Jane's co-workers tell Jane how helpful the training program was. This may strengthen the driving forces and alter the balance of the forces, leading Jane to accept the change.

Organizational Development

Managing change is an ongoing process. If a manager does it well, he or she can maintain a positive organizational climate. Some organizations make thorough analyses of their problems and then implement long-term solutions to solve them. Such an approach is called **organizational development (OD)**.

The Purposes of Organizational Development

The main purpose of OD, according to one management writer, is "to bring about a system of organizational renewal that can effectively cope with environmental changes. In doing so, OD strives to maximize organizational effectiveness as well as individual work satisfaction" (Burton, 1976). Organizational development is the most comprehensive strategy for intervention. It involves all the activities and levels of management in ongoing problems that respond to external and internal sources. The OD process is cyclical, as Exhibit 9.5 shows.

Exhibit 9.5

A model of the organizational development process.

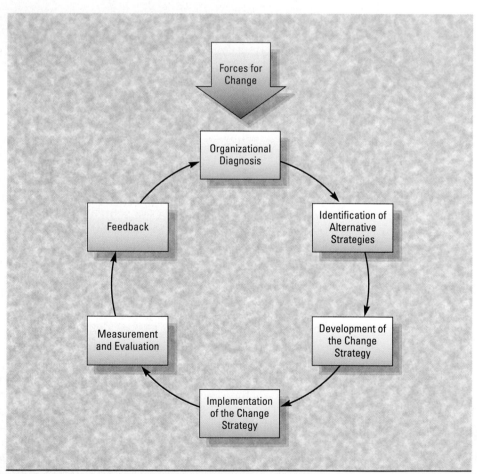

Source: Gene E. Burton, "Organizational Development—A Systematic Process," *Management World,* March 1976. Reprinted with permission from the Administrative Management Society, Willow Grove, PA. Copyright 1976 AMS.

The Strategies of Organizational Development

Exhibit 9.6 describes the tools and methods that managers who apply OD strategies are likely to use. These managers may choose one or more of these strategies. The choice depends on the circumstances. Limits on time, money, and skill at implementing a strategy are just a few restrictions the managers may have to take into account.

　　　The choice of a strategy is usually the result of conferences and discussions involving those who will be most directly affected. The participants' experiences, feelings, and perceptions help determine if their parts of the organization are ready for change and OD techniques. A high level of receptiveness to change is crucial to the success of OD.

Exhibit 9.6

Tools and methods for applying organizational development strategies.

DIAGNOSTIC STRATEGIES	
Consultants	This strategy consists of bringing in objective outsiders (consultants) to analyze and conduct audits of existing policies, procedures, and problems. Consultants can be individuals or groups and may act as change agents as well.
Surveys	Surveys consist of interviews or questionnaires used to assess the attitudes, complaints, problems, and unmet needs of employees. Surveys are usually conducted by outsiders and guarantee anonymity to participants.
Group discussions	Group discussions are periodic meetings conducted by managers to uncover problems and sources of their subordinates' discomfort and dissatisfaction.
CHANGE STRATEGIES	
Training programs	Training programs are ongoing or special efforts to improve or increase skill levels, change or instill attitudes, or increase the knowledge needed to perform present jobs more effectively and efficiently.
Meetings and seminars	As change strategies, meetings or seminars are gatherings held to explore mutual problems and seek mutually agreeable solutions. Such group sessions may be chaired by insiders or outsiders and may be used to prepare people for changes in advance of implementation.
Grid OD	Grid OD is a six-phase program based on the leadership grid. Its purpose is management and organizational development. The first two phases focus on management development. The last four phases are devoted to organizational development. The six phases are laboratory training, team development, intergroup development, organizational goal setting, goal attainment, and stabilization.

Evaluating the Effectiveness of OD

Since organizational development is an ongoing, long-term effort to introduce lasting change in an organization's technology, structure, and people, a successful OD program takes a significant investment of money and time. Both are needed to adequately diagnose the problem, select the strategy, and evaluate the effectiveness of the program.

One way to measure effectiveness is to compare the results of the program to the goals before it was implemented. Were the goals met? If not, why not? Perhaps they were too rigid and too hard to achieve. Perhaps the problems were inadequately defined, and the inadequate definition resulted in the choice of an inappropriate solution. Perhaps managers tried to institute changes before people were prepared for them. Regardless of the cause, the results of the OD analysis will provide feedback needed for later changes.

In the final analysis, OD, like any other management effort, is only as effective as the quality of its inputs and the skills of those making the analysis. Successful OD is based on solid research and clear goals and implemented by effective change agents who use appropriate methods.

GLOBAL APPLICATIONS
Adapting to a New Culture

American executives are facing the need to change as they start working for Japanese companies. This is particularly true in the auto industry, where Americans must adapt and mesh with the new culture. To help in the transition, each American must work closely with a Japanese executive who serves as a coordinator, interpreter, and friend.

The American executives have found their task to be challenging, confusing, and rewarding. At the Big Three American auto makers, junior executives traditionally advanced by showing decisiveness, self-assurance, and the ability to inspire awe among the workers. Japanese auto makers expect other skills. Among other things, managers must be able to promote a questioning attitude among subordinates. They are expected to build consensus rather than make independent decisions.

In return, the successful manager receives a lot of authority.

The American executives must adopt two key values. First, service, not tradition, counts. In choosing staff, managers may draw from outside candidates rather than promote from within, if that's where the talent lies. Second, managers must value peer review. They must run their new ideas through a gauntlet of co-workers rather than submit them directly to department chiefs. This process subjects each new idea to the "five whys." Each time an executive answers one question, a peer asks why. The executive must either give a more precise answer or admit that the idea needs more study.

Although not all American executives have become immersed in this changed culture, those that do have thrived. Why? In these companies, executives have tremendous responsibility—far more than in Detroit. ▲

For more about the changes in the auto industry, see Doron P. Levin, "Adjusting to Japan's Car Culture," *New York Times,* March 4, 1992, pp. C1, C3.

OD is an expression of managers' efforts to stay flexible. These managers recognize that events inside and outside their organization can happen quite suddenly and create pressure for change. OD provides the personnel and mechanisms to deal with change; control its evolution; and direct its impact on organizational structure, technology, and people.

Future Trends

According to experts (Want, 1990), managers of the future will have to take the following actions to manage change in the turbulent business climate:

- Ensure that the organizational culture promotes innovation

- Continuously monitor the external environment and be prepared to institute more change

- Develop flexible strategies for change—those that can apply to more than one situation

- Cultivate leadership qualities that advance initiative and flexibility

- Design an information system that provides, to many employees at all times, up-to-date and accurate data on the status of the organization and the environment

- Create organizational structures that open all employees to the possibility of change

C H A P T E R　S U M M A R Y

- Each organization has a system of shared beliefs, values, and norms that is unique to it. The system is called the organizational culture. This culture helps employees develop a sense of group identity and pride, valuable contributors to organizational effectiveness.

- The factors that influence culture are key organizational processes, employees and other tangible assets, formal organizational arrangements, the dominant coalition, the social system, technology, and the external environment. These factors interact with each other.

- The culture becomes apparent to the organization's members through statements of principle, stories, slogans, heroes, ceremonies, symbols, climate, and the physical environment.

■ Managers and employees create organizational culture through intentional culture-building activities, and unconsciously, by following recurrent behavior patterns. Culture also affects how managers and employees perceive the world and identify problems.

■ Organizational culture affects organizational performance. Three factors help determine the effectiveness of organizational culture: coherence, pervasiveness and depth, and adaptability to the external environment.

■ A company can enhance control and survival by adopting planned change, which involves anticipating changes in the external and internal environments and then developing a response that will maximize success. A change agent helps implement that change.

■ Organizations change over time, evolving through five phases: creativity, direction, delegation, coordination, and collaboration. Each phase eventually results in a crisis that must be resolved.

■ In a program of planned change, managers must follow nine steps: recognizing the need for change, developing goals, selecting a change agent, diagnosing the problem, selecting the intervention method, developing a plan and approach, implementing the plan, and following up and evaluating the change.

■ Managers can help create a climate that promotes change by cultivating mutual trust, organizational learning, and adaptability.

■ Managers must be aware of sources of resistance to change—habit, or fear of loss of security or power, for example—and develop techniques to overcome them. Techniques to overcome resistance include participation, open communication, advance warning, sensitivity, and security.

■ Change efforts can fail for a number of reasons, including faulty thinking or an improperly followed process, lack of resources or commitment, poor timing, or a resistant cultural climate.

■ To change people's behavior, managers can follow a process of unfreezing the undesired behavior, changing to the new behavior, and refreezing the desired behavior. Another technique is to strengthen the forces that lead a person to change and weaken or remove those that lead to resistance. In either case the goal is to render the driving forces strong enough to enable the change.

■ Companies that wish to achieve long-term policies of ongoing change institute programs of organizational development. There are many OD techniques; change agents choose one in consultation with organization members.

S K I L L - B U I L D I N G

Refer to your current or past work experience in answering the following questions about organizational culture.

1. What was the culture like in your organization? What values were shared by its members? What was the customary way of doing things? What norms, philosophies, and attitudes did new employees have to learn and commit themselves to?

2. Were there any written guidelines or principles as evidence of the culture?

3. What evidence of the culture could be interpreted from stories, slogans, heroes, ceremonies, symbols, climate, or the physical environment?

4. Did managers seem to have a planned approach to change? Or did they merely react to change? Explain your answer.

5. How did any changes and the management of change affect organizational culture?

6. What, if any, resistance to change occurred? Why did it arise? How did management respond?

R E V I E W   Q U E S T I O N S

1. Review this chapter's essential terms and look up the meanings of those you cannot define.

2. What are the seven factors that influence culture? Use specific examples to explain how they interact.

3. How is culture evidenced?

4. How does culture influence organizational effectiveness? What factors contribute to an effective culture?

5. What are the four kinds of change that can occur in an organization?

6. What are the differences between planned and unplanned change?

7. What are the steps of planned change?

8. What elements of a manager's philosophy promote change?

9. Describe three reasons that people resist change, and explain what managers can do to overcome resistance.

10. What are three reasons that change efforts fail?

11. Why do organizations adopt an organizational development program?

R E C O M M E N D E D   R E A D I N G

Arrington, Lance. "World Class Quality: Different Cultures—Common Language," *Vital Speeches* (September 1, 1991), pp. 69–73.

Choate, Scott. *Your Guide to Corporate Survival* (Clearwater, FL: CC Publications), 1991.

Collins, J. C., and J. I. Porras. "Organizational Vision and Visionary Organizations," *California Management Review* (Fall 1991), pp. 30–52.

Fisher, Shirley, and Gary L. Cooper. *On the Move: The Psychology of Change and Transition* (New York: Wiley), 1991.

Helmstetter, Shad. *You Can Excel in Times of Change* (New York: Simon & Schuster), 1991.

Kinkhead, R. W., and D. Winokur. "Navigating the Seas of Cultural Change," *Public Relations Journal* (November 1991).

Lyons, Daniel J. "Hard Times Hit Peter Norton Computing As Old Culture Dies," *PC Week* (February 19, 1990), p. 132.

Morgan, James C., and Jeffrey J. Morgan. *Cracking the Japanese Market: Strategies for Success in the Global Economy* (New York: Macmillan), 1991.

Osborne, R. L. "Core Value Statements: The Corporate Compass," *Business Horizons* (November–December 1991), pp. 27–34.

Turner, Barry. *Organizational Symbolism (Studies in Organizations)* (Hawthorne, NJ: Walter DeGruyter), 1991.

R E F E R E N C E S

Argyris, Chris, and Don Schon. *Organizational Learning: A Theory of Action Perspective* (Reading, MA: Addison-Wesley), 1978.

Barnes, Louis B. "Managing the Paradox of Organizational Trust," *Harvard Business Review* (March–April 1981), pp. 107–118.

Bender, Marilyn, and Selig Altschul. *The Chosen Instrument: Pan Am, Juan Trippe, the Rise and Fall of an American Entrepreneur* (New York: Simon & Schuster), 1982.

Brenner, Joel Glenn. "The World According to the Planet Mars," *Dallas Morning News,* April 19, 1992, pp. 1H, 2H, 7H.

Burton, Gene E. "Organizational Development—A Systematic Process," *Management World* (March 1976).

Business Week (February 8, 1993). "IBM After Akers," pp. 22–24.

Deal, Terrence E., and Allan A. Kennedy. *Corporate Cultures: The Rites and Rituals of Corporate Life* (Reading, MA: Addison-Wesley), 1982, p. 25.

Dubrin, Andrew J. *Fundamentals of Organizational Behavior* (New York: Pergamon), 1974, pp. 331–361.

Greiner, Larry E. "Evolution and Revolution as Organizations Grow," *Harvard Business Review* (July–August 1972), pp. 55–64.

Greiner, Larry E. "Patterns of Organizational Change," *Harvard Business Review* (May–June 1967), pp. 119–130. Much of this section derives from this source.

Holusha, John. "A New Soft Edge for 'Neutron Jack,'" *New York Times,* March 4, 1992, pp. C1, C3.

Kotter, John P. *Organizational Dynamics: Diagnosis and Intervention* (Reading, MA: Addison-Wesley), 1978. Much of this section derives from this source.

Kotter, John, and James Heskett. *Corporate Culture and Performance* (New York: Free Press), 1992, pp. 11, 12.

Kupfer, Andrew. "Apple's Plan to Survive and Grow," *Fortune* (May 4, 1992), pp. 68–72.

Lammers, Terry. "The New Improved Organization Chart," *Inc.* (October 1992), pp. 147–149.

Lewin, Kurt. "Frontiers in Group Dynamics: Concept, Method, and Reality in Social Science," *Human Relations* 1 (1947), pp. 5–41.

Nadler, David A. "The Fine Art of Managing Change," *New York Times,* November 29, 1987, p. F3.

Newsweek (February 8, 1993). "Available: One Impossible Job," pp. 44–51.

Peters, Thomas J., and Robert H. Waterman. *In Search of Excellence: Lessons from America's Best-Run Companies* (New York: Harper & Row), 1982, p. 173.

Richman, Tom. "The Master Entrepreneur," *Inc.* (January 1990), p. 50.

Robbins, Stephen P. *Management,* 3rd edition (Englewood Cliffs, NJ: Prentice-Hall), 1991, p. 72.

Sonnenburg, Paul, and William Schoneberger. *Allison: Power of Excellence, 1915–1990* (Malibu, CA: Coastline), 1990.

Want, Jerome H. "Managing Change in a Turbulent Business Climate," *Management Review* (November 1990), pp. 38–41. This section is based in part on this source.

GLOSSARY OF TERMS

change   Any alteration in the present work environment. The shift may be in the way things are perceived or in how things are organized, processed, created, or maintained.

change agent   A person who implements change.

force-field analysis   A technique to implement change by determining which forces drive change and which forces resist it.

management by reaction   A management method that does not anticipate change but merely reacts to it.

mutual trust   The ability to rely on someone based on his or her character, ability, and truthfulness.

organizational climate   The quality of the work environment as experienced by employees.

organizational culture   A system of shared beliefs, values, and norms that define what is important to the organization, how people should behave, how they should interact with each other, and what they should be striving for.

organizational development (OD)   A process of conducting a thorough analysis of an organization's problems and then implementing long-term solutions to solve them.

organizational learning   The ability to integrate new ideas into established systems to produce better ways of doing things.

planned change   A philosophy that involves trying to anticipate what changes will occur in both the external and internal environments and then developing a response that will maximize success.

subculture   Within an organization, a unit that forms because people share values, norms, and beliefs.

three-step approach   A technique of behavior modification consisting of three phases—unfreezing, changing, and refreezing—that is used to implement change.

C A S E   P R O B L E M
Change Can Be Painful

Most executives agree that change requires time and effort. Few, however, can accurately estimate the time and effort it will take to drive change through a large organization. To implement the change, executives must both exhibit and demand flexibility, nimbleness, and customer focus. Year after year, corporations centralize, decentralize, reorganize, and re-engineer—many times to no avail. Three major American corporations have unsuccessfully dealt with the change process in recent years: Sears, IBM, and Ford.

At Sears, CEO Edward A. Brennan called for a change in the Merchandise Group. His goal was to have both store and catalogue associates be more responsive to customer needs. After making the directive known, Brennan took a tour of operations in 10 cities and reported to shareholders: "The mood is much improved, and our people are committed to winning." Insiders at Sears didn't reflect that optimistic view. They wondered who Brennan had been talking to. Employees watched as the CEO spent time golfing and politicking. More and more of them were laid off and a pay freeze continued.

In 1992, CEO John Akers took massive measures to shore up IBM. He reduced the work force by 40,000 workers. He broke the company into 13 relatively independent operating divisions. Despite these efforts, the company posted a loss of nearly $5 billion (*Newsweek,* 1993). The stock slid to a 17-year low, below $46 per share. Akers stepped down, and IBM directors started 1993 by searching for a new chief executive officer. In commenting on the situation, one expert reported, "The company was less devoted to bringing on the future than to preserving its past success. The problem has never been technology, it's been lethargy and bureaucracy" (*Business Week,* 1993).

Ford needed to respond to fierce foreign competition and plummeting profits. It shut factories, adopted quality processes, developed progressive labor relations with unions, and attempted to forge long-term partnerships with suppliers. But when the fat profits returned, so did corporate complacency. The company's replacement cycle remained twice that of competitors. In addition, it angered its supplier partners by demanding an across-the-board price cut.

Q U E S T I O N S

1. Which two of the companies have ignored the importance of culture in implementing change? Cite examples to support your answer.

2. How would you describe Edward Brennan's approach to change? How would you have attempted to implement his objectives?

3. What lesson can be learned from the change process at Ford?

For more about implementing change, see Keith B. Hammond, "Why Big Companies Are So Hard to Change," *Business Week,* July 17, 1992, pp. 28–29.

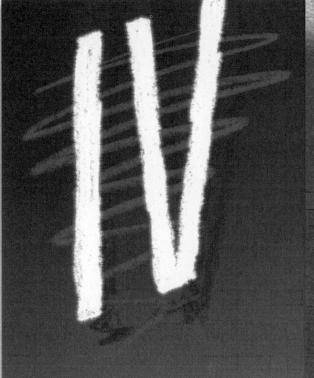

P · A · R · T

Staffing and Leading

IV

Staffing

LEARNING OBJECTIVES

After reading and discussing this chapter, you should be able to:

- Define this chapter's essential terms
- Explain the importance of the staffing function
- List and describe the steps in staffing
- Explain the significance of equal employment opportunity and affirmative action in the staffing process
- List and describe the steps in the selection process
- Identify the purposes of performance appraisal and explain why it should be objective
- Describe the social and cultural environments of staffing
- Describe the uses for promotions, transfers, demotions, and separations
- Describe the methods used in training and development
- Describe the components of an organization's compensation package

MANAGEMENT IN ACTION
Eaton Corporation

Eaton Corporation of Cleveland, Ohio, manufactures automotive parts and equipment. In 1992, *Fortune* magazine ranked it 128th in a list of the 500 largest U.S. corporations. In 1992 and 1993, *Fortune* placed Eaton in the "Most Admired" category in a list of corporations that produce automotive parts. Eaton's profits in 1991 were $74 million. The organization employs some forty thousand people in 130 plants around the world. Some workers are unionized, others are not.

Eaton's products are unglamorous and the corporation is virtually unknown outside of the automotive industry. Nevertheless, Eaton has some very innovative and highly motivated people at work, raising productivity and keeping the company lean and mean. Eaton's sales for 1992 were up 15%. Full-year profits for 1992 increased 120% over 1991 profits.

Eaton promotes the *kaizen* (continuous improvement) philosophy in both words and deeds. The corporation actively encourages every employee to take small steps to improve products and processes. Eaton managers are obsessive about controlling costs—an essential characteristic in the automotive industry, which cannot accept ever-increasing costs. Productivity has been a focus at Eaton for the past 20 years, and the focus has paid off. The corporation replaced eight unionized plants with 22 nonunionized factories in the South and Midwest. Eaton relies on machinery (some of it designed and built in-house) to do the most tedious work, releasing workers' talents for more creative uses.

Eaton recruits and encourages managers who are comfortable sharing information and responsibility with workers. Not all managers can tolerate such "encroachments" on their authority. At the Lincoln, Illinois, plant, two engineers who were being trained to work with teams of workers quit in protest.

Besides recruiting a particular kind of manger, Eaton fosters promotion

Teams focused on productivity *have helped Eaton Corporation increase sales and profits in the midst of an economic downturn.*

> The goal of information sharing is to get workers to understand what is happening and to enlist their support in improving the bottom line.

from within; 23 of the 57 salaried employees at the Lincoln plant rose through the ranks.

Information sharing is vital to the success of the teams. Data about yesterday's sales, the costs of labor, utilities, and materials, and more are reviewed each day. In the employee cafeteria, a television monitor reports the progress of individual teams, departments, and shifts. The goal of information sharing is to get workers to understand what is happening and to enlist their support in improving the bottom line. Judging from Eaton's productivity improvement, the information dissemination efforts are worthwhile. Productivity has increased 3% per year over the past 10 years. Furthermore, employees know that the more efficient the organization becomes, the more secure their jobs will be.

Teams of workers are rewarded with quarterly bonuses based on their plant's performance. In the first quarter of 1992, bonuses at the Lincoln plant averaged about $500 per worker. For perfect attendance, workers earn a cumulative bonus of $25 per year. There are noncash bonuses too—free lunches to celebrate a year without injuries, and "Eaton Bucks," credits earned for profit-boosting suggestions. Employees can use Eaton Bucks to purchase sporting goods and other items. In rewarding group performance rather than individual output, Eaton has left behind a system that led to inventories of low-quality parts. ▲

For more information about Eaton Corporation, see Thomas F. O'Boyle, "Working Together: A Manufacturer Grows Efficient by Soliciting Ideas from Employees," *Wall Street Journal,* June 5, 1992, p. A1; *Fortune,* April 20, 1992, "The Fortune 500: Special Report," pp. 224, 278; Kate Ballen, "America's Most Admired Corporations," *Fortune,* February 10, 1992, p. 72; *and Business Week,* June 30, 1992, "The Top 1,000 U.S. Companies Ranked by Industry," p. 165.

The Importance of Staffing

People are any organization's most valuable resource. Without dedicated, knowledgeable, and motivated employees, the best-laid plans will never bear fruit. Ben Tregoe, corporate strategy expert and chairman of Kepner-Tregoe, explained just how crucial the human factor is (Brown, 1991):

> One of the most serious reasons for America's lack of competitiveness is that top management does not understand that human resources and human issues are critical to the organization. More and more companies, as they move into global competitiveness, see that the one thing that can make a difference in the world market is people. Raw materials, technology and systems are available to everybody. The right people can be a unique commodity.

The primary purposes of **staffing** are to attract, develop, reward, and retain the human resources—the people—needed to accomplish an organization's goals and to assist all employees in gaining job satisfaction.

This chapter will explore the activities, methods, and principles of staffing in the United States. Chapter 20 will examine the staffing problems and methods of multinational companies.

The Responsibility for Staffing

In small organizations, every manager is responsible for the staffing function; even worker teams can participate. A large firm usually establishes a separate department dedicated to staffing. A subunit that focuses on staffing is usually called a personnel department, or a human resource department. Managers of such a department—**human resource managers,** or **personnel managers**—assist others by planning, organizing, staffing, coordinating, controlling, and sometimes executing specific personnel and human resource (P/HR) management functions.

Some human resource managers and practitioners are specialists who focus on a specific aspect of P/HR management—compensation, training, or recruiting, for example. Others are generalists who are responsible for several functions. This book will use the terms *human resource manager* and *human resource specialist* to refer to both groups.

The Staffing Process

Exhibit 10.1 summarizes the eight elements of the staffing process. The list that follows briefly describes each element.

- Human resource planning. This aspect of staffing involves assessing current employees, forecasting future needs, and making plans to add or remove workers. To adapt to changing strategies and changing needs, managers must continually update their plans.

- Recruiting. In this step, managers with positions to fill look for qualified people inside or outside the company.

- Selection. This step involves testing and interviewing candidates and hiring the best available.

1. Human Resource Planning

2. Recruiting

3. Selection

4. Orientation

5. Training and Development

6. Performance Appraisal

7. Compensation

8. Employment Decisions: Transfers, Promotions, Demotions, Layoffs, and Firings

- Orientation. In this phase of staffing, new employees learn about their surroundings, meet their co-workers, and learn about the rules, regulations, and benefits of the company.

- Training and development. To train and develop employees, employers establish programs to help workers learn their jobs and improve their skills.

- Performance appraisal. As part of the controlling function of management, managers must establish the criteria for evaluating work, schedule formal sessions to discuss evaluations with employees, and determine how to reward high achievers and motivate others to become high achievers. All these tasks are part of the performance-appraisal element of staffing.

- Compensation. This aspect of staffing relates to establishing pay and, in some cases, benefits.

- Employment decisions. Workers' careers involve transfers, promotions, demotions, layoffs, and firings. Making decisions about these career developments is part of the staffing process.

Not all the elements of the staffing process are components of every staffing problem. Recruiting, for example, is not necessary unless new employees are needed. Some elements are constants, however. Planning, training, and appraisal accompany the primary management functions. Therefore, every manager must be concerned about staffing.

The Staffing Environments

Staffing, like other managerial functions, is subject to outside influences. Events and pressures from many sources in an organization's external environment—customers, suppliers, and competitors, for example—influence staffing and dictate the human resource plans and strategies necessary to carry them out.

The Legal Environment

The laws and principles that govern a community inevitably affect the way companies do business. Consider just a few of the legal issues that pertain to even the smallest company: contracts, criminal law, negligence, and equity. A legal concept that has a great impact on organizations today is the idea that the law is a tool to correct and prevent wrongs to individuals and groups. Laws and legal principles act as controls on managers who discharge staffing responsibilities.

Executive orders and laws generated by federal, state, county, and city agencies regulate how companies, usually those with 15 or more employees, must conduct staffing. So complex are these regulations, and so great is the potential for harm due to noncompliance, that many large companies and institutions hire attorneys and specialists to deal with reporting and disclosure requirements.

Exhibit 10.2 highlights federal laws regarding three topics: equal employment opportunity, affirmative action, and sexual harassment. The paragraphs that follow will review each topic.

Equal Employment Opportunity Federal laws prohibit discrimination in employment decisions. **Discrimination** means using illegal criteria in staffing. Laws that prohibit discrimination are designed to guarantee **equal employment opportunity**. Antidiscrimination laws are enforced by the Equal Employment Opportunity Commission (EEOC).

According to the United States Senate (1972), it is unlawful for an employer to do either of the following:

1. To fail or refuse to hire or to discharge an individual solely on the basis of race, color, religion, sex, age, national origin, or handicap

2. To limit, segregate, or classify employees or applicants for employment in any way that would tend to deprive the individual of employment opportunities solely on the basis of race, color, religion, sex, age, national origin, or handicap

Federal law has created protected groups—women, the handicapped, and minorities. Other protected groups include:

- Hispanics

- Asian-Americans

- Blacks not of Hispanic origin

- American Indians

- Alaskan Natives

By law, managers must refrain from employment decisions that produce a disparate impact on these protected groups. A **disparate impact** is any result that harms one group more than another. Not hiring an applicant because she is a woman causes a disparate impact. Using an employment test that eliminates a significantly greater percentage of protected groups than unprotected groups also causes a disparate impact. The actions in both these cases are considered discriminatory under law. The organization and the managers involved in the discriminatory decisions would be subject to criminal penalties. To avoid breaking equal opportunity laws,

Exhibit 10.2

U.S. federal legislation related to staffing.

Federal Legislation	Description of Provisions
Equal Pay Act of 1963	Prohibits paying employees of one sex less than employees of the opposite sex for doing roughly equivalent work. Applies to private employers.
Title VI 1964 Civil Rights Act	In staffing decisions, prohibits discrimination based on race, color, religion, sex, or national origin. Applies to employers receiving federal financial assistance.
Title VII 1964 Civil Rights Act (amended 1972)	Prohibits discrimination based on race, color, religion, sex, or national origin. Applies to private employers of 15 or more employees; federal, state, and local governments; unions; and employment agencies.
Executive Orders 11246 and 11375 (1965)	In staffing decisions, prohibits discrimination based on race, color, religion, sex, or national origin. Establishes requirements for affirmative action plans. Applies to federal contractors and subcontractors.
Age Discrimination in Employment Act of 1967 (amended 1978)	Prohibits age discrimination in staffing decisions against people over 40 years of age. Applies to all employers of 20 or more employees.
Title I 1968 Civil Rights Act	Prohibits interference with a person's exercise of rights with respect to race, color, religion, sex, or national origin.
Rehabilitation Act of 1973	In staffing decisions, prohibits discrimination based on certain physical and mental handicaps. Applied to employers doing business with or for the federal government.
Vietnam Era Veterans Readjustment Act of 1974	In staffing decisions, prohibits discrimination against disabled veterans and Vietnam-era veterans.
Privacy Act of 1974	Establishes the right of employees to examine letters of reference concerning them unless the right is waived.
Revised Guidelines on Employee Selection (1976, 1978, and 1979)	Establishes a single set of guidelines that define discrimination on the basis of race, color, religion, sex, and national origin. The guidelines provide a framework for making legal employment decisions about hiring, promoting, and demoting and for the proper use of tests and other selection procedures.
Pregnancy Discrimination Act of 1978	Prohibits discrimination in employment based on pregnancy, childbirth, or related medical conditions.
Equal Employment Opportunity Guidelines of 1981— Sexual Harassment	Prohibits sexual harassment when such conduct is an explicit or implicit condition of employment, if the employee's response becomes a basis for employment or promotion decisions, or if it interferes with an employee's performance. The guidelines protect men and women.

Exhibit 10.2

(continued)

Federal Legislation	Description of Provisions
Equal Employment Opportunity Guidelines of 1981— National Origin	Identifies potential national-origin discrimination to include fluency-in-English job requirements and disqualification due to foreign training or education. Identifies national-origin harassment in the work environment to include ethnic slurs and physical conduct with the purpose of creating an intimidating or hostile environment or unreasonable interference with work.
Equal Employment Opportunity Guidelines of 1981— Religion	Determines that employers have an obligation to accommodate religious practices of employees unless they can demonstrate that doing so would result in undue hardship. Accommodation may be achieved through voluntary substitutes, flexible scheduling, lateral transfer, and change of job assignment.
Mandatory Retirement Act (amended 1987)	Determines that employees may not be forced to retire before age 70.
Americans with Disabilities Act of 1990	Prohibits discrimination on the basis of physical or mental handicap.

managers should avoid using any criteria not related to the job when making decisions to recruit, hire, promote, train, develop, reward, or fire an employee.

Seven states and about twenty municipal governments have added homosexuals to the list of protected groups. Doing so forbids, in applicable jurisdictions, employment discrimination on the basis of sexual orientation or sexual preference. In 1991 and 1992, MCA (a unit of Matsushita Electric Industrial Company and the parent of Universal Studios) adopted nondiscrimination policies regarding homosexuals. Fox, Inc. and the Disney Company have adopted such policies as well (Jefferson, 1992).

Affirmative Action   Some laws go beyond prohibiting discrimination. Laws that mandate **affirmative action** require employers to make an extra effort to employ protected groups. Affirmative action laws apply to employers that have, in the past, practiced discrimination or failed to develop a work force that is representative of the whole population of their community. (Under current laws, affirmative action is not required with regard to handicapped Americans.) The fact that an organization has an affirmative action plan does not necessarily mean that the organization practiced unfair employment practices in the past, however. Managers of many organizations choose to develop affirmative action plans even when the law does not require them to do so. Affirmative action plans must include goals and timetables for achieving greater representation of and equity for protected groups.

When Anita Hill took a stance against Supreme Court nominee Clarence Thomas, the issue of sexual harassment gained unprecedented attention. Since the hearings, many other women have spoken out, and American business has been forced to reconsider how men and women interact in the workplace.

Sexual Harassment   Title VII of the Civil Rights Act and guidelines established by the EEOC prohibit sexual harassment (Moskal, 1989). **Sexual harassment** includes unwelcome sexual advances, requests for sexual favors, and other verbal or physical conduct of a sexual nature when

1. Submission to such conduct is an explicit or implicit term or condition of employment

2. Submission to or rejection of such conduct is used as a basis for any employment decision

3. Such conduct has the purpose of unreasonably interfering with the individual's work performance or creating an intimidating, hostile, or offensive working environment

This issue exploded into the national spotlight in 1991, when hearings of the Senate Judiciary Committee were broadcast on television. The hearings concerned allegations made by Anita Hill, a University of Oklahoma law professor. Hill alleged sexual harassment by her ex-boss Clarence Thomas, who at the time of the hearings was a nominee for the Supreme Court. As a result of the hearings unprecedented attention was focused on the importance and consequences of sexual harassment. Managers in every industry should work to prevent harassment and establish procedures for dealing with it properly when it does occur. Sexual harassment can severely damage morale and undermine productivity and quality.

Violations of sexual harassment laws can be expensive. Settlements have been as large as $500,000. Louis W. Brydges, Jr., a management-labor attorney in Chicago, urges companies to create a policy statement telling everyone in the workplace that sexual harassment will not be tolerated and that those engaging in it will be disciplined (Kleiman, October 15, 1991).

The Social and Cultural Environment

The U.S. labor force is becoming more culturally diverse. According to the U.S. Bureau of Labor Statistics, in 1970 about 55 million workers were male and 33 million were female; about 9 million were African-American and fewer than 5 million were Hispanic. In 1991 there were 70 million males, 57 million females, 13.5 million African-Americans, and nearly 10 million Hispanics. In addition, the average age of American workers is declining. In 1970, the average age was 39. In 1991, it was just under 38. This is due, in part, to large numbers of immigrants (mainly Asians and Latin Americans).

In 1990 Towers Perrin and the Hudson Institute surveyed corporate America to determine the staffing problems that exist and the trends that will affect America's future work force. Here are a few of their findings (TPF&C Company, 1990):

- Hiring is a problem for employers. More than one-third of the corporations responding to the survey reported some difficulty in recruiting in all employee categories. Some reported the need to review 10 or more applicants per position to be filled. Turnover is increasing too. According to the survey, the average rate of employee turnover per year is 28%.

- Increasingly, applicants do not have the basic skills that employers need. About 60% of survey respondents reported that the major reason they rejected applicants was poor writing and verbal ability. Another 18% pointed to math deficiencies as the reason for rejection.

- The work force is growing increasingly heterogeneous. Diverse populations bring with them differing attitudes and values about work, family, and job satisfaction. Most employees want work environments that accept their cultural orientations and their commitments to personal goals.

Cultural Diversity   America's history is the story of different races, ethnic groups, and cultures. Coping with cultural diversity is nothing new for American managers; valuing cultural diversity in the work force is (Perry and Perry, 1991).

In the past, most managers tried to create a homogeneous work force—to treat everyone in the same way and make people fit the dominant corporate culture. These efforts did not always build a stable, committed group of employees. What was needed—and what is rapidly appearing in enlightened corporations—is respect for what workers from different backgrounds bring to the workplace. Across America, managers are participating in workshops designed to facilitate understanding among diverse groups, not just tolerance of one another's existence.

One innovator in the effort to build respect for diversity is Levi Strauss & Company of San Francisco. For several years the company has conducted workshops to help employees air grievances and dispel tension in the workplace. Through participating in these sessions, workers and managers gain new insights and appreciation for differing perspectives and cultural values. With the growing emphasis on teams and the increasing presence of foreign managers and their cultures, employees and managers must learn to tap the power that comes from differing points of view.

Glass Ceilings and Glass Walls   The terms *glass ceiling* and *glass wall* refer to invisible barriers of discrimination that block the careers of women and other protected groups (Kleiman, April 13, 1992). A glass ceiling is discrimination that keeps individuals from protected groups out of upper-level management jobs; a glass wall prevents them from pursuing fast-track career paths. Do these invisible barriers really exist? The data indicate that *something* is keeping protected groups out of the top jobs. In 1990, a federal study surveyed 94 major corporations. The study revealed that only 16.9% of managers at all levels were women and only 6% were minority members. Among top managers, only 6.6% were women and 2.6% were minorities. These numbers suggest one reason why women earn about 72 cents for every $1 earned by men (*Fortune,* April 20, 1992).

In 1992, Catalyst, a nonprofit research organization that focuses on women's issues in the workplace, conducted another survey about job discrimination. The survey revealed that human resource managers often steer women away from jobs in marketing and production. Stereotyped as support providers, women end up in staff positions. One reason for the perpetuation of the stereotype is that many men, especially those in the upper ranks of management, feel uncomfortable dealing with women. The Catalyst study suggested that women should "find out what type of experience companies require of their executives and then seek to get it." The report also suggested that "companies should create programs to encourage mentoring and career development and to discourage gender stereotyping" (Fuchsberg, 1992).

The cost of discrimination against women can be high in terms of lost morale, commitment, and productivity. Penalties can be high as well. In 1992 State Farm Insurance paid $157 million to settle a case filed by 814 women. The women claimed that because of their sex, State Farm had refused to give them lucrative sales jobs. In addition to the settlement, the women's claims led to changes in the recruiting and hiring of State Farm agents in California. An affirmative action plan, in place since 1988, requires the company to hire women for 50% of the sales agent jobs to be filled through 1998.

Many companies recognize that glass ceilings and glass walls exist and have worked hard to eliminate them. American Airlines requires corporate officers to submit detailed, cross-functional plans regarding the development of all high-potential women in middle management and above (Fuchsberg, 1992). Anheuser-Busch has a management-development program that moves women and minorities from jobs in inventory to jobs as coordinators and then to supervisory positions. Johnson & Johnson, the pharmaceutical giant, operates workshops to sensitize managers and supervisors to the problems of those striving for the top. The company has a significant number of women and minorities in high positions (Kleiman, April 13, 1992).

AIDS and Drug Testing   Acquired immune deficiency syndrome (AIDS) is a frightening condition that—until medical progress can prevent it—leads to death. HIV, the virus that causes AIDS, cannot be casually transmitted. But fear of AIDS is a reality in the workplace. Companies need policies telling employees and managers how to deal with the issue. Federal law prohibits discrimination against employees suffering from AIDS and any other contagious diseases (Stodghill, 1993). Will a company accommodate the employee who does not want to work with an employee who has HIV? What will management do when an employee's routine physical reveals that he or she is HIV positive?

Most of America's largest companies have had experience with employees who are suffering from some sort of drug addiction. Less than half of these companies have drug policies. Employees with drug or alcohol dependencies can and do cause losses to their companies, themselves, and others. Workers with drug problems compromise safety, quality, and productivity. One study estimated the loss from drug-related absenteeism and turnover in the United States to be nearly $50 billion a year (Hoerr, 1988).

According to the 1990 Americans with Disabilities Act, drug-addicted employees are protected from discrimination if they are currently enrolled in legitimate drug-interdiction programs or have completed such programs and are drug-free. Testing for drugs raises issues about employee privacy, because most drug tests involve blood and urine analysis. These tests can reveal conditions that an employer has no business knowing about. In addition, drug tests can produce false positive results. Many companies require drug testing for all applicants, and some require random testing of current employees involved in work that is potentially hazardous to themselves or others. Where a work force is unionized, it is wise to involve the union in any drug-testing efforts before they are instituted.

Genetic Screening   Medical tests of a person's genetic makeup can identify his or her predisposition to diseases like heart disease and certain types of cancer. Such tests can be used to deny employment, insurance, and advancement (Hoerr, 1988). Few bans on genetic screening currently exist. Those that do are state and local efforts; no federal laws address the issue. To prevent confusion and injustice, however, employers must develop policies about the use of genetic screening.

The Union Environment

According to the U.S. Bureau of Labor Statistics, unions represented 16.1% of American workers in 1992. That figure represented a significant decrease; in 1977, 22.6% of American workers had union representation. From 1977 to 1992, union representation in the private sector fell from 23.3% to 11.9%. What few gains unions have made came by adding government workers to their ranks (Milbank, 1992). Government employees now represent about 40% of organized union membership. With the decline of manufacturing jobs in America, unions have turned to recruiting white collar and service workers. Most union members belong to unions affiliated with the American Federation of Labor/Congress of Industrial Organizations (AFL/CIO). The AFL/CIO had 13.9 million members in 1991.

Companies that employ unionized workers must bargain collectively to create a contract, to enforce that contract, and to process complaints (called grievances) about how the contract is enforced. Unions typically bargain for their members' wages, hours, and working conditions. Whether the issue is employment, work methods, equipment, safety, or productivity improvement, a union can impede or support changes that managers want to make.

Collective Bargaining   In **collective bargaining**, negotiators from management and a union sit down together and try to agree on the terms of a contract that will apply to the union's members for a fixed period of time. Both parties prepare for these negotiations by analyzing past problems and agreements, polling their constituents, building a list of demands, and creating strategies. Both want what they perceive to be the best deal for themselves, given their respective needs and priorities. Negotiations usually begin before an existing contract expires, and negotiators try to reach a new agreement while the contract is still in effect.

The principal issues in labor negotiations today are job security, strike prevention, and support for quality and productivity improvement efforts that will help organizations survive. According to the U.S. Bureau of Labor Statistics, work stoppages (strikes) involving 1,000 or more employees have declined from 80 in 1983 to about 40 in 1991.

One reason for the decline is managers' increasing tendency to hire workers to replace those who strike. When managers hire replacement workers, union members have fewer jobs to go back to if and when the strike ends. This was the case in the prolonged Caterpillar strike of 1991–1992. When union members decided to return to work (before reaching agreement on a final contract), they found that the company had hired replacement workers who stayed on as permanent employees. Increasingly, results like this have turned workers away from unions.

Grievance Processing A labor agreement (contract) provides a process by which managers and workers can file grievances: complaints alleging that a contract violation has taken place. The process of filing a grievance usually begins at the lowest level. If no settlement can be reached at that level, the complaint is brought before those at successively higher levels. A grievance can progress to the point that it becomes a focus for top managers and union officials. When these parties cannot agree, a third party may be called in. Third parties are usually neutral professionals hired to recommend or enforce a settlement. A third party can be a mediator or an arbitrator. Mediators make recommendations. Arbitrators suggest settlements that are enforced. Arbitrators have the power to hold hearings, gather evidence, and render a decision to which both parties agree in advance to adhere.

Human Resource Planning

In planning to meet staffing needs, managers must know their organization's plans and what human resources are available. They study existing jobs by performing job analyses. They review their firm's past staffing needs, inventory current human resources, forecast personnel needs in light of strategic plans, and compare their human resource inventory to the forecast. Then, with line managers, they construct plans to expand the company's employee roster, maintain the status quo, or reduce the number of jobs. Exhibit 10.3 illustrates this process.

The Job Analysis

Before managers can determine personnel needs, they must perform a **job analysis** for each job. The first step in a job analysis is to prepare up-to-date descriptions that list the duties and skills required of each job holder. Then managers must compare all the analyses to ensure that some job holders are not duplicating the efforts of others. This comparison enhances effectiveness and efficiency in the organization.

Exhibit 10.3

The human resource planning process.

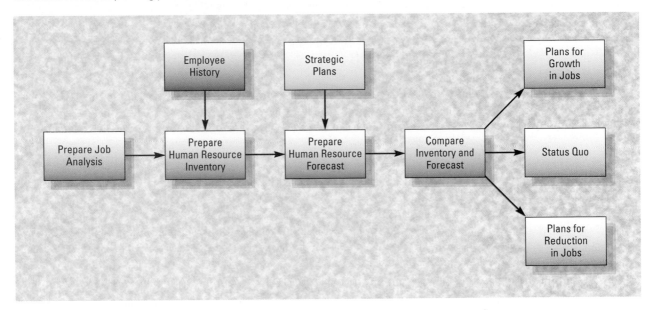

To prepare an in-depth study of jobs, some companies employ job analysts. To do their work, job analysts (1) observe the job holder executing his or her duties; (2) review questionnaires completed by the job holder and supervisor; (3) conduct interviews with both; or (4) form a committee to analyze, review, and summarize the results. Job analysts may study more than one job holder in a job category over several months.

The job analysis produces two coordinated documents: a *job description* and a *job specification.* Exhibit 10.4 presents an example of a job description. A job description cites the job title and the purpose of the job. It lists major work activities, the levels of authority above and below the job holder, the equipment and materials the job holder must use, and any physical demands or hazardous conditions the job may involve.

Exhibit 10.5 presents an example of a job specification. A job specification lists the human dimensions that a position requires. These include education, experience, skills, training, and knowledge. To avoid even the appearance of discrimination, those who create job specifications must take care to list only those factors directly linked to successful work performance.

Managers should review job descriptions and specifications regularly (usually each year) to ensure that they continue to reflect the positions they refer to. Jobs evolve with time as changes in duties, knowledge bases, and equipment take place; the documents should reflect that evolution. When new positions are added to the organization, job descriptions and specifications must be created.

Exhibit 10.4

An example of a job description.

I Job Identification

Position Title: Customer-Service Representative

Department: Policyholders' Service

Effective Date: March 1, 1995

II Function

To resolve policyholders' questions and make corresponding adjustments to policies if necessary after the policy is issued

III Scope

(a) Internal (within department)
Interacts with other members of the department in researching answers to problems

(b) External (within company)
Interacts with Policy Issue in regard to policy cancellations, Premium Accounting in regard to accounting procedures, and Accounting in regard to processing checks

(c) External (outside company)
Interacts with policyholders, to answer policy-related questions; client-company payroll departments, to resolve billing questions; and carriers, to modify policies

IV Responsibilities

The job holder will be responsible for:

(a) Resolving policyholder inquiries about policies and coverage

(b) Initiating changes in policies with carriers (at the request of the insured)

(c) Adjusting in-house records as a result of approved changes

(d) Corresponding with policyholders regarding changes requested

(e) Reporting to the department manager any problems he or she is unable to resolve

V Authority Relationships

(a) Reporting relationships: Reports to the manager of Policyholders' Service

(b) Supervisory relationship: None

VI Equipment, Materials, and Machines

Personal computer, calculator, and VDT

VII Physical Conditions or Hazards

95% of the duties are performed sitting at either a desk or VDT

VIII Other

Other duties as assigned

Exhibit 10.5

An example of a job specification.

I Job Identification

Position: File/Mail Clerk

Department: Policyholders' Service

Effective Date: March 1, 1995

II Education

Minimum: High school or equivalent

III Experience

Minimum: Six months of experience developing, monitoring, and maintaining a file system

IV Skills

Keyboarding skills: Must be able to set up own work and operate a computer and typewriter. No minimum WPM.

V Special Requirements

(a) Must be flexible to the demands of the organization for overtime and change in workload

(b) Must be able to comply with previously established procedures

(c) Must be tolerant of work requiring detailed accuracy (the work of monitoring file signouts and filing files, for example)

(d) Must be able to apply systems knowledge (to anticipate the new procedures that a system change will require, for example)

VI Behavioral Characteristics

(a) Must have high level of initiative as demonstrated by the ability to recognize a problem, resolve it, and report it to the supervisor

(b) Must have interpersonal skills as demonstrated by the ability to work as a team member and cooperate with other departments

The Human Resource Inventory

The human resource inventory provides information about an organization's present personnel. The inventory is a catalog of the skills, abilities, interests, training, experience, and qualifications of each member of its present work force. A human resource inventory tells managers the qualifications, length of service, responsibilities, experiences, and promotion potential of each person in the firm. This information is updated periodically and supplemented by the most recent appraisals given to job holders. What emerges is something similar to Exhibit 10.6, a plan for staffing changes in management ranks. Developing such a chart makes managers aware of strengths and weaknesses in the current personnel base and allows them to develop a managerial succession plan.

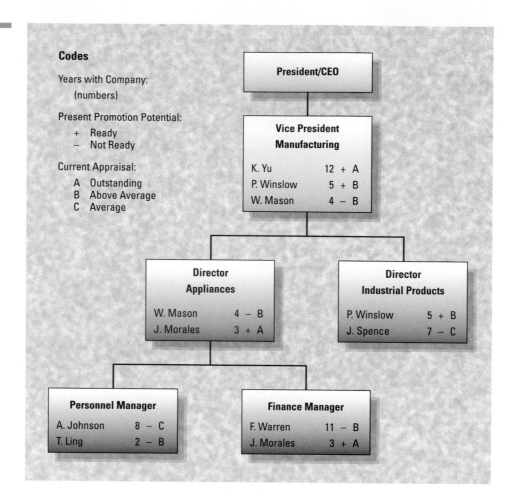

Codes

Years with Company:
(numbers)

Present Promotion Potential:
+ Ready
− Not Ready

Current Appraisal:
A Outstanding
B Above Average
C Average

President/CEO

Vice President Manufacturing

K. Yu	12	+	A
P. Winslow	5	+	B
W. Mason	4	−	B

Director Appliances

W. Mason	4	−	B
J. Morales	3	+	A

Director Industrial Products

P. Winslow	5	+	B
J. Spence	7	−	C

Personnel Manager

A. Johnson	8	−	C
T. Ling	2	−	B

Finance Manager

F. Warren	11	−	B
J. Morales	3	+	A

Human Resource Forecasting

When forecasting an organization's personnel requirements, managers need to consider the strategic plans of the company and its normal level of attrition. Strategic plans determine the company's direction and its need for people. A long-term plan to stabilize the company at its present employment level will mean the need to replace those who leave.

Consider how a fictional furniture-making company translates strategic plans into actual personnel requirements. Suppose managers decide to increase production by 30% to meet a forecast increase in long-term demand. They analyze present capabilities, reject the use of overtime, and decide to add a third shift within three months. Using up-to-date job descriptions and specifications for the jobs to be added, managers determine how many and what kinds of employees to hire: nine production workers. Then the managers look at anticipated turnover in the existing shifts and support personnel. They decide to, over the next three months, hire two new employees to replace retiring employees. Therefore, the managers must acquire 11 new hires over the next three months.

Inventory and Forecast Comparison

By comparing the inventory and the forecast, managers determine who in the organization is qualified to fill the projected openings and which personnel needs must be met externally. At the furniture company, managers decide that most of the needed personnel must come from outside, because many of the positions are entry-level jobs and members of the existing work force will be needed to replace retiring workers.

If the managers decide to try to fill some of the vacancies from within, the first question is whether present employees qualify. If so, the managers must advertise the jobs within the company and encourage employees to apply for them. If current employees do not qualify, the next question is whether, through training and development, they can achieve the qualifications. If so, and if the company can afford the money and time, managers should prepare a plan to provide the needed training and development.

Recruitment, Selection, and Orientation

With the forecast and inventory complete and job descriptions and specifications in hand, managers begin **recruiting**—the process of locating and soliciting a sufficient number of qualified candidates. Sources of applicants should include employed and unemployed prospects and temporary-help services. Managers may also want to investigate the option of leasing employees. This option involves working with a company that hires workers to lease to a client firm. The lease company hires, fires, complies with all government regulations, pays the leased employees, and is responsible for all human relations functions.

Strategies for Recruiting

At the furniture-making company, managers decide to look outside for the needed applicants. This decision presents several options. They can call private or state-operated employment services. They can run ads in newspapers and other publications, including trade journals and papers that appeal to racial and ethnic minorities. They can ask current employees to recommend qualified friends and relatives. (Many companies offer bonuses to employees who refer people who are eventually hired.) They can contact schools and offer a training program, and they can participate in job fairs. The managers can ask neighborhood and community groups to help them reach minorities and other protected groups and encourage them to apply for the jobs. If the company employs union labor, managers can contact trade unions in their search for skilled workers.

Internship and apprenticeship programs are a proven way to gain access to needed talent. Precision Metal Forming Industries of Williamsport, Pennsylvania, a small firm employing 50 people, joined forces with five other metalworking companies in its area to establish a school-to-work transition project. With six employers, seven high schools, and 12 students participating, the program (backed by private and government funding) gives students postsecondary credits and a certification of competence in entry-level metalworking skills. During the two-year program, students complete high school, earn minimum wage, and earn

F O C U S   O N   Q U A L I T Y

Apprenticeships in Germany

In Germany, high-school dropouts are channeled into apprenticeship programs where, within three to four years, they acquire the skills needed to fill entry-level positions. Each year they are paid about 20% of what they will earn in the first year after they complete their apprenticeships. The apprentices begin by becoming familiar with materials and tools. They progress to learning about manufacturing processes and becoming computer literate.

Apprenticeships in Germany are not limited to manufacturing jobs. The practice has spread to just about every vocation imaginable. Many believe that the proliferation of apprenticeship programs in Germany is one reason that German products have a reputation for quality and dependability.

A student in a vocational school spends one day a week in classes and four days learning on the job. "After the final examination, at least 90% of the trainees get a permanent job," says Sigrid Kuemmerlein of the Association of German Chambers of Industry and Commerce, which runs the system. "Through their training, apprentices have become integrated in a business, and the businesses themselves are interested in taking them on."

The program is experiencing difficulties, however. These days, German youth seem less interested in the traditional trades; instead, they prefer to enter white-collar occupations in computer science or service industries. There is a growing shortage of skilled workers and apprentices for the handicraft trades. In addition, young Germans are showing an increasing desire to attend college. In 1990, for the first time, there were more college students than apprentices. All together there are currently about 1.5 million filled apprenticeship positions, the lowest number in years. ▲

Adapted from Alice Siegert, "Young Apprentices Bolster Western Germany's Labor Market," *Chicago Tribune,* June 7, 1992, sec. 7, p. 6.

---

prejourneyman status in metalworking (Milbank, 1992). Many students who participate in internship and apprenticeship programs become full-time employees of the companies that sponsored them.

The Selection Process

Selection is the process of deciding which candidate out of the pool of applicants possesses the qualifications for the job to be filled. Selection begins where recruiting ends. Its goal is to eliminate unqualified candidates through use of the screening devices shown in Exhibit 10.7. The paragraphs that follow will discuss these devices.

The Application Form   Usually, a prospective employee must fill out an application form as part of the selection process. An application form summarizes the candidate's education, skills, and experiences relating to the job he or she is applying for. To avoid discrimination in the selection process, employers must not ask for information that is unrelated to the candidate's ability to perform the job successfully. Questions regarding home ownership, marital status, age, ethnic or racial background, and place of birth are usually irrelevant. When used properly, the completed application yields needed information. In addition, it indicates a person's ability to follow simple instructions and use basic language skills.

Exhibit 10.7

The screening devices of the selection process.

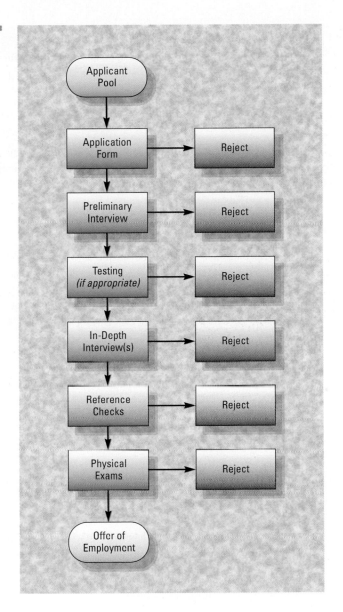

The Preliminary Interview In small firms, a job candidate's first interview at a firm may be conducted by the very manager for whom the person hired will work. In large companies, someone from the human resource staff may be the designated screening interviewer. In very large or sophisticated firms, a human relations specialist may conduct the preliminary interview. If a team has authority to hire, several team members may question each applicant. This is usually the case if the team is self-managing.

A preliminary interview may be structured—scripted with specific questions—or unstructured. An unstructured format allows an applicant relative freedom to express thoughts and feelings. An interviewer uses the preliminary meeting to verify details from the application form and to obtain information

The best general guideline to follow on employment application forms and in interviews is to ensure that information elicited relates to qualifications for effective performance on the job. The topics listed in bold in this exhibit are especially sensitive.

Age? Date of birth? In general, asking whether a candidate is under 18 or over 70 is permissible.

Arrests? Since an arrest is no indication of guilt and because, proportionally, minorities are arrested more than those in other segments of the population, questions about arrests are probably discriminatory. Such an inquiry is prohibited by the Illinois Department of Human Rights.

Convictions (other than traffic violations)? Military record? Questions about convictions are generally inadvisable, though they may be appropriate for screening candidates who have been convicted of certain offenses and are under consideration for certain kinds of jobs. Questions about less-than-honorable military discharges are likewise inappropriate unless the job involves security issues. In general, a candidate can be asked what branch of service he or she served in and what kind of work the candidate did. If information about convictions or military discharge is necessary, exercise care in how it is used; avoid possible discrimination.

Available for Saturday or Sunday work? Although knowing when employees are available to work is important, a question about availability on certain days may discourage applicants from certain religious groups. If business requirements necessitate such a question, indicate that the employer will make an effort to accommodate the religious needs of employees.

Age and number of children? Arrangements for child care? Although the intent of these questions may be to explore a source of absenteeism or tardiness, the effect can be to discriminate against women. Do not ask questions about children or their care.

Credit record? Own a car? Own a home? Unless the person hired must use personal credit, a personal car, or do business from a home he or she owns, avoid these questions. They could discriminate against minorities and women.

needed to continue the selection process. Interviewers must avoid topics that are not related to the applicant's abilities to perform successfully on the job. An ability necessary to perform a job is called a bona fide occupational qualification. For example, if a job involves work in a men's locker room, a question about the sex of the applicant is probably not discriminatory because it asks about a bona fide occupational qualification.

Employers and job candidates must be particularly sensitive to the potential for discrimination in interviews. Because both parties must avoid sensitive issues, Exhibit 10.8 presents some interviewing guidelines prepared by one state employment agency.

Exhibit 10.8

(continued)

Eyes? Hair color? Eye and hair color are not related to job performance and may serve to indicate an applicant's race or national origin.

Fidelity bond? Since a bond may have been denied for an arbitrary or discriminatory reason, use other screening considerations.

Friends or relatives? This question implies a preference for friends or relatives of employees and is potentially discriminatory because such people are likely to reflect the demography of the company's present work force.

Garnishment record? Federal courts have held that wage garnishments do not normally affect a worker's ability to perform effectively on the job.

Height? weight? Unless height or weight relates directly to job performance, do not ask about it on an application form or in an interview.

Maiden name? Prior married name? Widowed, divorced, separated? These questions are not related to job performance and may be an indication of religion or national origin. These inquiries may be appropriate, however, if the information gained is needed for a pre-employment investigation or security check.

Marital status? A federal court has held that refusal to employ a married woman when married men occupy similar jobs is unlawful sex discrimination. Do not ask about an applicant's marital status.

Sex? State and federal laws prohibit discrimination on the basis of sex except where sex is a bona fide occupational qualification necessary to the normal operation of business.

NOTE: *If certain information is needed for postemployment purposes, such as in the administration of affirmative action plans, the employer can obtain it after the applicant has been hired. Keep this data separate from data used in career advancement decisions.*

Source: Illinois Department of Employment Security.

Testing   According to Equal Employment Opportunity Commission guidelines, a **test** is any criterion or performance measure used as a basis for any employment decision. Such measures include interviews, application forms, psychological and performance exams, physical requirements for a job, and any other device that is scored and used as a basis for selecting an applicant (*Federal Register,* 1978). All tests used for screening should attempt to measure only performance capabilities that have been or can be proven to be essential to successful performance of the job (Kleiman, February 9, 1992).

Regardless of the tests used, employers must avoid producing a disparate impact—that is, creating a test that one demographic group is more likely to do better on than another. Employers must also ensure that each test has validity. A test with validity is a predictor of future performance on a specific job. A person receiving a high score on a valid test will be able to perform the related job successfully. Those who perform poorly on the test would perform poorly on the job. If test performance does not correlate to job performance, the test is probably invalid.

Assessment centers specialize in screening candidates for managerial positions. Tests administered at assessment centers attempt to analyze a person's ability to communicate, decide, plan, organize, lead, and solve problems. The testing techniques used include interviews, in-basket exercises (tests that present a person with limited time to decide how to handle a variety of problems), group exercises intended to uncover leadership potential and the ability to work with others, and a variety of hands-on tasks. The assessments usually last several days and take place away from the usual job site. Many large companies, especially Japanese employers, use assessment centers to determine who will make it into a company or up its corporate ladder. The results from assessment centers are usually more accurately predictive than paper-and-pencil exercises that assess managerial ability.

The In-Depth Interview   An in-depth interview is almost always conducted by the person or persons for or with whom the applicant will work if hired. The goal of an in-depth interview is to determine how well the applicant will fit into the organization's culture and the subsystem in which he or she would work. Eaton Corporation, for example, screens its applicants to be certain they will be willing to share authority. In-depth interviews may or may not be structured. They can be used to relay information specifically related to the job and its environment as well as to talk about benefits, hours, and working conditions. Applicants who have passed through the initial screenings and progress to in-depth interviews need the endorsement of the person for whom they will work. Without this person's commitment to the success of the new hire, the applicant's future at that firm is in doubt. As is the case with application forms and preliminary interviews, interviewers must take care to avoid topics that could lead to accusations of employment discrimination.

Reference Checks   A recent article (Kleiman, February 9, 1992) reported that most employers conduct fairly extensive background checks:

- 84% verify education and past-employment claims

- 60% contact persons listed as references

- 63% review school transcripts

Checking an applicant's past can present problems. First, employers must avoid background checks that could be discriminatory. Checks of credit history and arrest records, for example, are discriminatory. Second, checking references can be difficult because most former employers refuse to cooperate. They may avoid saying anything negative for fear of a defamation-of-character lawsuit by the ex-employee. According to one recent survey (Amend, 1990), 41% of companies surveyed prohibited current employees from giving references about ex-employees.

The Physical Exam   According to one article (Kleiman, February 9, 1992), 52% of employers surveyed asked applicants to take a pre-employment physical exam as part of the selection process; 19% asked for a medical history without a physical exam. Employers use physical exams and medical histories to prevent insurance claims for illnesses and injuries that occurred prior to employment. They also detect communicable diseases and certify that an applicant is physically capable of performing his or her job. If the job description cites physical demands, they must be valid. According to the Americans with Disabilities Act, employers must make reasonable accommodations for the physically impaired and not use physical barriers as an excuse for not hiring.

The Offer of Employment   At this point, the manager or team offers the job to the top-rated applicant. This step may involve a series of negotiations about salary or wage, work schedule, vacation time, types of benefits desired, and other special considerations. With the diversity of the work force of today, an employer may have to accommodate an employee's handicap, make time for him or her to get children off to school or be at home when they return, or to arrange for daycare. Federal law requires that within 24 hours from the time of hiring, the new employee must furnish proof of U.S. citizenship or the proper authorization needed to work in the U.S. as a legal alien.

Orientation

The previous steps in the selection process have done much to familiarize the newcomer with the company and the job. What the new hire needs now is a warm welcome so he or she can begin contributing as soon as possible. The newcomer needs to be introduced to his or her workstation, team, and co-workers. Managers and co-workers should answer the new employee's questions promptly and openly. Someone should explain work rules, company policies, benefits, and procedures and fill out the paperwork necessary to get the new person on the payroll. All employee assistance programs should be explained, and the new hire should be told how to take advantage of them.

All this can be done in stages and by several different people. Human resource specialists may handle the paperwork while team members or a supervisor take charge of introductions to the work area and co-workers. All equipment, tools, and supplies that the newcomer needs should be in place when he or she reports for work.

It is important that first impressions and early experiences be realistic and as positive as possible. **Orientation** is the beginning of a continuing socialization process that builds and cements employees' relationships, attitudes, and commitment to the company. Orientation should be thoroughly planned and skillfully executed.

Training and Development

Training teaches skills for use in the present and near future. Development focuses on the future. Both involve teaching the particular attitudes, knowledge, and skills a person needs. Both are designed to give people something new, and both have three prerequisites for success: (1) Those who design training or development programs must create needs assessments to determine what the content and objectives of the programs should be; (2) the people who execute the programs must know how to teach, how people learn, and what individuals need to be

Training unlocks the potential of a company's work force by helping employees develop their skills. At Aetna Insurance Company, employees can take courses via the Aetna Television Network.

taught; and (3) all participants—trainers, developers, and those receiving the training or development—must be willing participants.

American employers spend in excess of $210 billion each year to provide training and development for their employees (Kleiman, January 12, 1992). In most U.S. businesses, training and development are continual processes. The American Society for Training and Development named the Xerox Corporation as one of several businesses with the best training systems. Xerox spends about 4% of its payroll (between $250 million and $300 million per year) for training its 110,000 employees. Xerox has its own training center in Leesburg, Virginia, and the corporation employs 120 trainers who train 12,000 employees annually. An additional 21,000 employees receive at least 40 hours of training each year at a district headquarters (Kleiman, January 12, 1992).

The Purposes of Training

Training has five major aims: to increase knowledge and skills, to increase motivation to succeed, to improve chances for advancement, to improve morale and the sense of competence and pride in performance, and to increase quality and productivity. In the culturally diverse work force of today, employees often need to improve their ability to handle English, to gain an appreciation of the organization's diverse cultures, and to learn how to cope with the many changes that occur on the job, such as new technologies, methods, and duties.

The Challenges of Training

According to the Southport Institute for Policy Analysis, half of America's businesses that employ fewer than 50 people report that 40% of their work forces (some 10 million employees) have serious problems with reading, writing, and math. For this reason, many firms need to conduct remedial training so that workers can cope with job demands and prepare themselves for positions of greater responsibility (*Chicago Tribune,* June 5, 1992).

One answer to language and illiteracy problems is job re-design. The re-designed jobs avoid, as much as possible, the need to rely on English and math. "Some warehouses use computers with speech capability to tell forklift operators who cannot read where they should go in the warehouse. Some construction firms rely on portable computers with touch-activated display screens that allow workers to record their reports by touching appropriate pictures on the screens" (Bulkeley, 1992).

Another challenge is America's increasingly diverse work force, which is currently made up of about 18% minorities. By the year 2000, that figure will rise to 25%. By the year 2005, the population of California is expected to consist of 50% minorities speaking 80 different languages (Jamieson and O'Mara, 1991).

Immigrants, many highly educated in their home countries, bring motivation and skills to the workplace. But they also bring cultural values and norms that may make it difficult for them to find well-paying jobs. Aside from their language difficulties, their views about the value of time, the relative importance of work and family, and how people should interact at work may not mesh with those of the dominant culture or the current mix of cultures.

The Techniques of Training

A company can train employees in various places. A trainee can be sent to a job site, a corporate training center, a college classroom, or various workshops, seminars, and professional gatherings. When training is done by the employer in-house, it commonly takes the following forms:

- On-the-job training (OJT). In this approach, an employee learns while the job is being performed. Training proceeds through coaching or by the trainee observing proficient performers and then doing the work. Apprenticeships and internships are on-the-job training programs.

- Machine-based training. In this technique, trainees interact with a computer, simulator, or other type of machine. The environment is usually controlled and the interaction is one-on-one. The trainees proceed at their own pace or at a pace set by the training equipment.

- Vestibule training. This system simulates the work environment by providing actual equipment and tools in a laboratory setting. The noise and distractions of a real work area and the pressure of meeting production goals are absent, so the trainee can concentrate on learning.

- Job rotation. In a job-rotation program, trainees move from one job to another. The temporary assignments allow them to learn various skills and acquire an awareness of how each job relates to others. In the process, trainees become more valuable because they develop the flexibility to perform many tasks. Internships utilize this form of training. (Job rotation is also used as a development technique.)

Regardless of the techniques used, training must be realistic. It must teach what is necessary in ways that can be directly applied to the work setting once training ends. Progress must be monitored to determine how well trainees are mastering the material.

The Purposes of Development

Development is a way of preparing someone for the new and greater challenges he or she will encounter in another, more demanding job. Workers seek development opportunities to prepare for management positions; supervisors need development to prepare to move into middle management. All development is really self-development. Without a personal commitment, development cannot occur. People can be pressured into training just to keep their jobs, but development, when offered, can be rejected. Employees cannot depend on their employers for development opportunities. Small companies cannot afford it, and many large employers will not pay for development when it is not directly related to an employee's current job or career track.

The Techniques of Development

Development techniques include job rotation, sending people to professional workshops or seminars, sponsoring memberships in professional associations, paying for an employee's formal education courses, and granting a person a sabbatical (leave of absence) to pursue further education or engage in community service. An employee should regard a company-sponsored program as a reward and as a clear statement about his or her worth to the company. Such programs are conduits through which workers can gain prestige, confidence, and competence.

Development efforts should never end; indeed, they can be part of a daily routine. By reading professional journals and business publications regularly and by interacting with experts at professional meetings, employees can help keep themselves up-to-date. Another approach to development involves volunteering for difficult assignments. Meeting tough challenges encourages a person to expand his or her abilities.

Another form of development can be extremely significant: mentoring. Mentors are professionals who are one or two steps above a person in his or her profession. Mentors can come from a person's present environment or from another organization. Whatever their affiliation, mentors are willing to share experiences and give competent advice about handling advancement opportunities, company politics, and self-development.

Performance Appraisal

In most organizations some assessment of job performance takes place every day, at least informally. When results for a given period are summarized and shared with those being reviewed, **performance appraisal** becomes a formal, structured system designed (in line with legal limits) to measure the actual job performance of an employee by comparing it to designated standards. These standards are introduced and reinforced in the selection and training processes.

Evaluating performance is a necessary part of managing people. Appraisals should be aimed at improving not only the individual's work but also the training and support offered by the organization.

The Purposes of Performance Appraisal

Most organizations use appraisals to:

- Provide feedback about the success of previous training and disclose the need for additional training

- Develop individuals' plans for improving their performance and assist them in making such plans

- Determine whether rewards such as pay increases, promotions, transfers, or commendations are due or whether warning or termination is required

- Identify areas for additional growth and the methods that can be utilized to achieve it

- Develop and enhance the relationship between the person being evaluated and the supervisor doing the evaluation

- Give the employee a clear understanding of where he or she stands in relation to the supervisor's expectations and in relation to the achievement of specific goals

Company policy establishes the frequency and form of the appraisal. Whatever form evaluations take, managers should provide daily feedback to an employee about performance. The employee's team members should do the same. If feedback is continual, the formal annual or semiannual performance appraisal will contain no surprises.

The Components of Appraisal Systems

Performance appraisal systems include three major components:

- The criteria (factors and standards) against which the employee's performance is measured. Criteria could include quality of work, efforts at improvement, specific attitudes, and quantity of output.

- The rating that summarizes how well the employee is doing.

- The methods used to determine the ratings. Methods could involve specific forms, people, and procedures.

Different personalities, jobs, organizations, and subsystems call for different criteria, ratings, and methods. According to Dr. Susan Resnick-West, co-author of *Designing Performance Appraisal Systems,* the major predictor of the effectiveness of a performance system is whether it is tailored for individuals. Factors that system designers should consider include task competency, previous experience, educational levels, and individual preferences (Mohrman, Resnick-West, and Lawler, 1989).

Appraisal systems can be classified as subjective or objective. Subjective systems allow raters to operate from their own personal points of view. Raters may be allowed the freedom to create factors, define what each factor means, and determine the employee's proficiency in each category. Exhibit 10.9 shows how one rater uses a simple matrix of four categories—Time Management, Attitude, Knowledge of Job, and Communication—and the proficiency categories Excellent, Good, Fair, and Poor. But what do these words mean? How is the rater defining each? In comparison to another person or to an ideal? Definitions used by one rater using this form may vary from those of another. Worse, the evaluator's stereotypes of and prejudices against an employee may become factors in the evaluation. Subjective methods and forms are difficult to justify when faced with accusations of discrimination. An employer should make every effort to keep subjectivity out of ratings.

Objective performance appraisals attempt to remove rater biases. Criteria are clearly defined and shared with the employer well in advance of the actual rating. Exhibit 10.10 shows just how concrete standards can be. An objective approach causes little confusion about the factors used for evaluation.

Appraisal Methods

Three appraisal methods dominate current practice: management by objectives, behaviorally anchored rating scales, and computer monitoring. After a brief look at each type, this chapter will examine the legal constraints on all rating methods.

Exhibit 10.9

A subjective performance appraisal system.

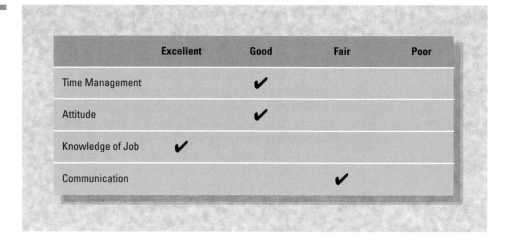

	Excellent	Good	Fair	Poor
Time Management		✔		
Attitude		✔		
Knowledge of Job	✔			
Communication			✔	

Exhibit 10.10

A portion of an objective performance appraisal system.

Performance Aspect	Rating				
	1	*2*	*3*	*4*	*5*
1. Self-Improvement Consider the desire to expand present capabilities in both depth and breadth. ☐ *No opportunity to observe.*	No interest in learning additional duties.	Limited interest in expanding job assignments; little interest in preparing for advancement.	Has demonstrated interest in additional assignments and shown some interest in and preparation for advancement.	Has shown extra effort to learn additional duties. Advancement preparation undertaken.	Very inquisitive concerning all phases of job-related assignments. Advancement preparation undertaken.
2. Attendance Consider the regularity with which the employee reports to work.	Excessively absent.	Frequently absent.	Occasionally absent.	Rarely absent.	Almost never absent.
3. Punctuality Consider number of occasions late. ☐ *Punctuality is not essential to this job.*	Excessively tardy.	Frequently tardy.	Occasionally tardy.	Rarely tardy.	Almost never tardy.
4. Work Planning Consider how the work load is planned and organized for maximum efficiency. ☐ *No opportunity to observe.*	Unsystematic, unable to organize work load.	Fair on routine but unable to organize variations effectively.	Efficient under normal conditions. Gives priority to important jobs.	Skillful in organizing and planning work. Meets emergencies promptly.	Exceptional efficiency. Keeps priority items in proper perspective.

Management by Objectives   Recall from Chapter 4 that a management by objectives (MBO) system requires a manager and subordinate to meet periodically to agree on specific performance goals for the subordinate over a fixed period. At the end of that period, an employee working under MBO is evaluated in regard to the number of goals met, how effectively and efficiently each one was achieved, and the growth that took place during the effort. Evaluators take into account the difficulties that the employee had to overcome to reach those goals.

Behaviorally Anchored Rating Scales   BARS, or behaviorally anchored rating scales, identify specific behaviors that correspond to different levels of performance. Each behavior corresponds to a numeric rating. Exhibit 10.10 illustrated a behaviorally anchored rating scale. The employee's overall rating is the sum of the points earned in each category.

Computer Monitoring   A computer monitoring system tracks an employee's performance as it is taking place. The performance of those who work with computers or computerized equipment can be evaluated in terms of the amount of time their machines are operating productively, the number of keystrokes per minute, or total output. Managers can compare the ratings of various employees in similar jobs and rank workers according to productivity. Managers can use performance averages to set or confirm existing standards. Retailers, banks, insurance companies, telephone companies, and transport firms use computer monitoring as one objective measure of employee performance.

The Legality of Appraisals

An analysis of U.S. Supreme Court rulings over the past 25 years reveals that performance appraisals are likely to be illegal if:

- The instruments used are invalid

- Standards are not job-related and objective (quantifiable and observable)

- The results of the process have a disparate impact on women, the handicapped, or minorities

- The scoring method is not standardized

- People who are performing similar jobs are evaluated differently, using different forms, factors, or processes

- Evaluative criteria are not developed according to EEOC guidelines

- Employees are not warned of declining or substandard performance

- The evaluation is not based on the employee's current duties

In addition, the ranks of performance appraisers should be filled by women, handicapped people, and minorities in a proportion that is representative of the community at large.

Raters must be trained to carry out performance appraisals consistently and in accordance with legal requirements. Lawrence H. Peters, professor of management at Texas Christian University, gave practical advice to raters and ratees: "It's hard to remember what the employee did 12, 11, or 10 months ago. It's important for managers to keep information as it occurs, and if you don't, stop and take time to collect your thoughts before the performance review. Employees should do the same" (Kleiman, February 2, 1992). In addition, raters need to reserve adequate facilities and time to review appraisals with subordinates.

The Implementation of Employment Decisions

As you recall, employment decisions include decisions about promotions, transfers, demotions, and separations (voluntary or involuntary). These changes are influenced by appraisals and by how an organization recruits, hires, orients, and trains. All employment decisions mean change—change that has a ripple effect throughout an organization's subsystems and its ability to interact with the external environment.

Promotions

Promotions are job changes that lead to higher pay and authority and which reward devoted, outstanding effort. They serve as incentives as well, offering the promise of greater personal growth and challenges to those who seek them. Employees usually earn a promotion by exhibiting superior performance and going beyond that which is expected.

Sometimes past performance is not the sole criterion for a promotion. Affirmative action requires that underrepresented groups such as women and minorities be better represented at all levels within an organization. Therefore, affirmative action goals may dictate that members of these groups be given special status in hiring and promoting decisions. In many union agreements, seniority is the most significant factor influencing promotion decisions.

Transfers

Opportunities for promotion are not as available now as they were only a few years ago. The leaner, flatter management structures of today and the trend toward teams mean there simply are not a large number of openings. According to Marilyn M. Kennedy, editor of the newsletter *Kennedy's Career Strategist*, **transfers**—lateral moves that require new skills—may be a company's only means of retaining talent (Rigdon, 1992).

> Companies that have restructured have taken steps to make sideways moves more palatable. RJR-Nabisco's Nabisco Foods Group (in New Jersey) recently added tiers to its pay scales so that workers who move sideways have a better chance of getting pay raises instead of cuts. Corning Inc., which has long wooed recruits by promising them they can "change careers without changing companies," recently began offering five percent raises to managers who make lateral moves. The policy comes on the heels of restructuring.

For years companies have used lateral moves in attempts to train and develop employees. Job rotation is one way of exposing people to different aspects of an operation and helping them see the big corporate picture. Transfers can help people advance by moving them from an area where few opportunities exist to an area that offers a less congested career track.

Demotions

A **demotion** is a reassignment to a lower rank in an organization's hierarchy. In the business climate of today, demotions are rarely used as punishment. (Ineffective performers are fired, not retained.) Demotions are used to retain employees who lose their positions through no fault of their own. Some people prefer taking a lower-status, lower-paying job to the alternative of being laid off. Others choose a demotion to decrease stress, allow themselves more freedom to pursue outside interests, or meet challenges such as having to care for children or an elderly parent.

Some companies have established what have become known as "mommy tracks"—temporary career interruptions for parents. Mommy tracks allow a parent to take care of children from pregnancy through the preschool years. By offering adjustments such as part-time work, a mix of telecommuting and in-house office hours, and flexible work schedules, companies help valued employees cope with new interests and demands on their time. But as Beck (1992) notes, some of these arrangements have drawbacks:

> Unfortunately, many employers still exact a steep price for non-standard work arrangements. Part-time work typically pays low wages and usually includes few if any benefits. Even women at middle-management levels or on fast professional tracks find that cutting back on work hours and trying other strategies to eke out more time for family cut chances for promotion.

Separations

A **separation**, the departure of an employee from an organization, may be voluntary or involuntary. Voluntary separations include resignations and retirements. Involuntary separations include layoffs and firings. Employers sometimes encourage voluntary separation by offering incentives to encourage employees to retire early. In May 1992 Digital Equipment Corporation offered 7,000 employees an early-retirement buy out; 3,000 accepted (Wilke, 1992). Involuntary separations seem to be on the rise in U.S. business. Layoffs due to declining business, personal performance, or company bankruptcies (as in the cases of Pan Am and Eastern Airlines) have cost millions of Americans their jobs.

Layoffs   Although downsizing can make companies more competitive, it can also undermine the loyalty of employees threatened with layoffs. According to Sanford M. Sherizen, a Massachusetts-based computer security consultant, downsizing leads to more responsibility for fewer people, which means less time to devote to the security of information systems. An insecure system practically invites a disgruntled employee to destroy data or leave behind a computer virus that will sabotage the system after the employee has left (Steinert-Threlkeld, 1992). An information security consultant, William H. Murray, says that the best way to protect a company against sabotage is to take steps to prevent employee disaffection—to treat those who must leave as well as possible before the layoff and compensate remaining employees fairly. According to Murray, most revenge comes from those who conclude that their contributions are unrecognized. People need to know they are appreciated day by day (Steinert-Threlkeld, 1992).

As alternatives to layoffs, many companies are implementing other strategies. Some have enacted hiring freezes, which allow normal attrition to reduce the work force. Other strategies include job sharing, restricting the use of overtime, retraining and re-deploying workers, reducing hours, and converting managers to paid consultants. Managers at Unarco, a manufacturer of shopping carts, pride themselves on the company's no-layoff policy. Unarco managers find useful employment for displaced workers by relying on retraining and normal attrition.

Unarco managers and managers everywhere have good reasons to avoid layoffs. Layoffs can be extremely expensive. Processing paperwork, closing facilities, and paying severance costs and higher unemployment-insurance premiums can cost thousands of dollars. The psychological costs are high as well. Those left behind after layoffs are fearful and insecure; those laid off are more likely than employed people to experience family problems, suffer divorce, or commit suicide.

Exit Interviews   Exit interviews are voluntary discussions between managers and employees who are being laid off or who are leaving voluntarily. A recent survey found that 96% of companies responding to the survey conducted exit interviews. The subjects discussed in the interviews included job satisfaction, working conditions, and compensation (Kleiman, October 13, 1991). Because the costs of laying off and replacing workers are high, a manager should use exit interviews to find out about factors that could cause employees to leave. Once the manager identifies a problem, he or she should fix it. Managers should realize, however, that exit interviews have a limitation. Because departing employees may not wish to leave a negative impression, they may not be totally open and honest. The fact that exit interviews do not reveal a cause for employee dissatisfaction does not necessarily mean that a cause does not exist.

Compensation

Compensation includes all forms of financial payments to employees: salaries and wages, benefits, bonuses, gain sharing, profit sharing, and awards of goods or services. The trend today is to offer increases in compensation in response to increases in performance that add value to the organization, its services, or its products. Increasing compensation is a way of retaining employees who have proved themselves valuable. This makes sense: As employees become more valuable, losing them becomes more costly.

The Purposes of Compensation

Compensation has three primary purposes: to attract, help develop, and retain talented performers. The level of compensation offered by a firm can either increase or decrease a company's attractiveness to job seekers. Compensation should encourage workers to continually improve their performance and to make themselves more valuable both to themselves and to their employers. Compensation must also anchor valued employees to the company, discouraging them from leaving to find other employment. People who consider their compensation fair and adequate feel that they are being treated with recognition and respect. They feel that the organization is giving them a fair return on their investment of time, energy, and commitment. Finally, compensation should give employees a sense of security, freeing them to unleash their full energies without the distraction that comes with the inability to meet financial needs.

The Factors That Influence Compensation

When designing a compensation package for employees, managers should be concerned about being equitable, meeting legal and strategic requirements, and linking compensation philosophy to various market factors. When certain types of workers are in short supply, managers may have to offer premium compensation to attract or hold them. Similarly, managers who decide to make their organization a leader in terms of the compensation it offers will probably be able to attract and keep the best employees.

The U.S. Fair Labor Standards Act, passed in 1938 and amended many times, relates to the payment of wages and overtime to workers under 18 years old. Other federal laws address the level of wages that must be paid to workers in companies doing business with the federal government. Some local and state laws affect compensation systems, and union contracts set wages and restrict compensation decisions in the organizations that are party to them.

Wages and Salaries

To determine the worth of each job and establish a compensation package for each that is fair in relation to all jobs, organizations use a process called **job evaluation**. Job evaluations are usually done by human resource compensation specialists. To complete the evaluation process, the specialist works with a manager with firsthand knowledge of the job and the employee or employees who hold the job.

I S S U E S   A N D   E T H I C S

BELL Spells Trouble

Pensions are often the only income that former employees can count on to see them through their retirement. Many people labor for many years to gain the security that pensions promise. Employers use their pension programs as incentives to attract competent employees and as "golden handcuffs" to keep people from leaving.

In the 1970s and 1980s a major manufacturer of packaging conducted a covert campaign to keep employees from getting their pensions. Under its pension program, employees became vested, or eligible for their pensions, upon the completion of 20 years of service. Managers devised a program called BELL to alert managers in advance of each worker's twentieth anniversary. The company would then lay off the worker, sometimes on the day before the anniversary, leaving the impression that the layoff was temporary. Since layoffs were fairly common, most employees saw no cause for alarm. But the company never called back workers who were just short of being vested. Therefore, the workers never qualified for their pensions.

Over a period of about 15 years, the company systematically removed all workers who had achieved more than 19 but fewer than 20 years of service—some 3,000 people. These people banded together and filed a class-action lawsuit claiming discrimination. In 1991 the company agreed to a settlement of $715 million to be divided among the parties to the suit.

BELL, it turns out, was an acronym for "limit liability for employee benefits" (spelled backwards). ▲

One common job evaluation method involves grouping jobs by type and then choosing factors common to each type. For example, two groups of jobs that job evaluation specialists often define are manufacturing jobs (wage jobs) and sales jobs (salary jobs). An evaluation might involve examining each type of job in light of the responsibility, education, skills, training, experience, and working conditions that are common to it. Then the evaluator assigns various levels within each factor and assigns point values to each level as measures of achievement.

To illustrate this process, suppose the job being analyzed is that of an industrial products sales professional. The evaluator chooses experience as an evaluation factor and defines experience as number of years in the selling profession. The levels for this factor might be one year or less of experience, one to three years of experience, three to five years of experience, and more than five years of experience. By assigning points to each level, the specialist shows the relative value the organization places on each. If the top level is worth 10 points and the previous one is worth 5 points, the organization is saying that more than five years of experience is twice as valuable as three to five years of experience.

Once all jobs have been evaluated, they can be grouped by total points into what are usually called job grades, or classifications. Evaluators then rank, by point total, jobs within each grade. For example, all jobs with point totals between 0 and 200 might be in the same grade. What emerges is a "job ladder" that shows jobs with the fewest total points at the bottom. At the top are the jobs with the most points. Evaluators assign a salary range to jobs in the same grade. Exhibit 10.11 shows the result of a typical job evaluation.

Exhibit 10.11

The result of a typical job evaluation.

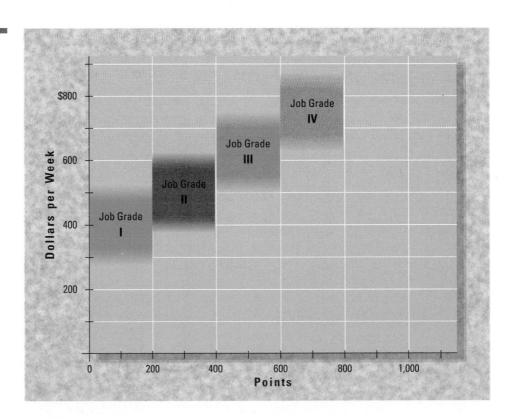

Job evaluation requires skill, up-to-date job descriptions and specifications, knowledge, and ample time. Many companies conduct pay surveys within their industries as a base for beginning the job evaluation process or as a substitute for it. Pay surveys show what competitors pay for comparable jobs. These rates of pay may be available through industry and trade associations as well as from the federal government. Not all jobs must be compared with the survey results; the evaluator compares only those that are representative of their grades or classes. Compensation for the other jobs is established in relation to the jobs that are compared.

In the final analysis, the minimum and maximum compensation assigned to a job are determined by an organization's ability to pay, market conditions for specific types of jobs, and the organization's strategies and philosophy about employee compensation.

Benefits

In 1990 American employers spent a record amount on employee **benefits**—the compensation employees receive from their employers that is not wages, salaries, or bonuses. On average, employers spent $12,402 per full-time employee to provide legally required benefits (Social Security, workers' compensation, and unemployment insurance) along with voluntary programs like paid holidays and vacations, profit sharing, health and life insurance, retirement programs, and bonuses. Nationwide in 1990, employers spent an average of 38.4% of their payroll costs (over $1 trillion) to provide employee benefits (Thompson, February 1992).

The industry with the highest benefit costs—an average $16,330 per employee—was the public utilities group. The group with the lowest was department stores—$5,287 (Thompson, February 1992). Legally required benefits accounted for 23% of the 1990 benefit costs. Medical benefits and other types of insurance programs accounted for 27%. Retirement compensation took 13%, and vacations and other benefits such as leaves and child care cost 37% (Main, 1991).

Perhaps no single issue in American society today is as important as health care and the cost of providing it. Concern about health care and medical costs was often the focus of the U.S. elections in 1992. As President Bill Clinton and the 103rd Congress took office in January 1993, the issue seldom left the spotlight. The task of resolving this crucial issue will almost certainly fall to imaginative and dedicated managers.

For U.S. companies, the cost of the medical-insurance benefit continues to rise steeply, seriously affecting the overall cost of doing business. In 1991 U.S. employers spent an average of $3,573 per worker to purchase health insurance. The 1991 figure represented a 13% increase from the previous year (Thompson, May 1992). The high cost of medical insurance has prevented some companies from offering any medical benefits whatsoever.

To accommodate a changing and diverse work force, many companies do manage to offer a number of innovative benefits. Many employees now have access to daycare for their children through company-sponsored programs or child-care allowances. Flexible scheduling allows employees to determine how they will fulfill their time commitments to their companies. They can choose to come early, leave late, or even work a four-day week—just as long as they work a specified amount of time and are present for specified hours. Job sharing allows

A benefits package should be designed to attract, develop, and retain talented and committed workers. Managers must plan benefits to fit their available financial resources and the current market conditions.

two people to split a single job, each working part-time. Telecommuting allows workers to work at home while communicating via telephone, computers, and fax machines. Parental leaves were growing in popularity even before they were mandated in 1993 by the first federal legislation signed by President Clinton. Parental leave offers new fathers and mothers time off (with or without pay) to care for newborns. For employers, these and other programs are alternatives to losing capable people who must cope with life changes.

An organization offers benefits, like other forms of compensation, so that it can attract, develop, and retain talented and committed workers. As with wages and salaries, managers plan benefits according to their organizations' financial resources and strategies and the market conditions the organization faces.

Executive Compensation

In addition to salaries and the benefits all other employees in their firm receive, executives—members of top management—may also receive benefits unique to their status. These benefits are called perquisites, commonly known as **perks** (Bennett, 1992). In 1991 the highest-paid chairman and CEO in the United States was Roberto C. Goizueta of Coca-Cola. Goizueta received $58.9 million, $56 million of which was in the form of a stock grant (Tully, 1992). Stock grants are the fastest-growing element in executive compensation.

Along with stock grants and stock options, top executives usually receive bonuses on the basis of company performance. They can receive generous expense accounts, travel and lodging allowances, new homes at no personal cost, and memberships in clubs and associations.

According to Graef Crystal, a compensation specialist, the average American CEO earns $2.8 million in direct compensation, about 160 times as much as their companies' average worker earns. Comparable Japanese CEOs earn between 10 and 20 times the average Japanese worker's pay (Healey and Osborn, 1992).

GLOBAL APPLICATIONS
Staffing the Japanese Way

Staffing practices of American and Japanese companies differ in important ways. Each is a product of its country's culture; the shrinking business world, however, means that each must learn the strengths of the other. Here are some of the major distinctions of the Japanese way:

- Large Japanese companies competing in international markets offer lifetime employment to their employees. Once a person joins the company, its managers will do whatever is necessary to keep that person usefully employed.

- The Japanese prefer to train employees to do a variety of tasks. Job descriptions, where they exist, are usually broad and do not list specific duties. They focus instead on skills. People are expected to do what they know how to do when and where it is necessary.

- Before taking action, Japanese managers seek consensus—unanimous agreement by a group on what needs to be done and how to proceed. Even at the lowest level of a company, teams of workers conduct business in the same way.

- Japan lacks meaningful antidiscrimination laws; non-Japanese people as well as women are openly discriminated against. In foreign operations, however, Japanese companies must abide by the host country's laws.

- In Japan, recruiting for entry-level management jobs takes place at schools and universities.

From then on, management jobs are usually filled from within. Japanese employers promote by tapping the pool of employees who intend to spend their careers with just one employer.

- Japanese companies tend to use the techniques of the assessment center to screen applicants. They rely heavily on in-depth interviews as well as hands-on exercises to determine applicants' attitudes, commitment, and talents.

- Job rotation as a means for training and development is more common in Japan than in the United States. Japanese employees move through jobs in one area and also cross functional lines. Japanese managers tend to stay in a job for a longer period of time than the typical American manager does.

- In Japan, employee appraisals are part of the mentoring process. Those who conduct the evaluations try hard not to embarrass an employee. Japanese appraisals tend to be less formal than American appraisals.

- Salaries and promotions for Japanese employees are typically linked to seniority and experience. Wages and salaries are usually lower than they are in the United States.

- Forced retirements are still common in Japanese companies. They usually occur before an employee is over 60 years old. ▲

According to Ira Kay, a management consultant with the Hay Group (*Business Week*, January 27, 1992):

> [American CEOs of companies with revenues between $500 million and $800 million] enjoy pay levels that are 13.6 times those of entry-level professionals. For Italy, Germany, Britain, and Japan, such multiples are comparable, ranging from 12.1 to 13.1.

In recent years, however, discussion of "excessive" executive compensation has appeared in popular periodicals and the business press.

Future Trends

Looking toward the future of staffing reveals four areas that are likely to become increasingly more important:

- Top managers' compensation. A number of recent articles on this subject indicate that American executives' pay and benefits are out of line when compared with compensation systems around the world. The IRS and Congress are currently considering ways to cap executives' pay.

- Privacy issues. Concerns over privacy will grow in significance and begin to cost employers additional time and money. Tests for honesty, AIDS, drug use, and genetic predispositions to disease are just four of the hot topics that relate to privacy.

- Work force diversity. The growing numbers of Asian-, Hispanic-, and African-Americans bring special strengths and needs to the workplace. Forecasts show that businesses will become increasingly dependent on these protected groups. Programs in the workplace that respond to cultural diversity are in growing demand.

- Meeting employees' needs. Employers will be under greater pressure to modify tasks and work procedures to accommodate employees. Managers and organizations will have to become more flexible.

C H A P T E R S U M M A R Y

- People are an organization's most important asset. Staffing is the process of attracting, developing, rewarding, and retaining competent people.

- Staffing is part of every manager's job. It requires expertise and a knowledge of applicable law. Managers must provide equal opportunity in all employment decisions, especially with respect to protected groups.

- Many companies must make their human resource decisions in the context of agreements made with labor organizations and through collective bargaining.

- Human resource planning begins with a job analysis. Performing a job analysis involves creating descriptions of all jobs in an organization and their necessary qualifications. The descriptions are compared to ensure efficiency within the organization.

- Human resource forecasting attempts to predict the future personnel needs of an organization. When the forecast is compared with the inventory of personnel, managers learn whether they need to recruit new employees.

■ Recruiting brings people into an organization or encourages existing employees to move up into other jobs. Selection involves a series of employment tests and interviews that attempt to find a worker who is qualified for the job and can fit into the organizational culture. Hiring decisions must be based on real job requirements, not discrimination.

■ Employers orient new employees to their new surroundings to welcome them and introduce them to the company, its procedures, and its people.

■ The goal of training and development is the improvement of employees' skills. Training focuses on short-term improvement; development focuses on long-term improvement. All development is self-development. It can occur only if the employee is willing.

■ Employers should evaluate the performance of workers on a daily basis. A formal performance appraisal should occur regularly. Formal appraisals provide a basis for decisions about raises, promotions, demotions, and firings. These decisions must be based on actual performance, not personal characteristics.

■ Compensation systems are created to obtain, develop, and retain talented workers. Compensation includes salary, wages, commission, and fringe benefits. Benefits can range from legally mandated items such as Social Security and unemployment compensation to optional benefits such as vacations, holidays, health insurance, and pension plans.

S KILL - B UILDING

Towers Perrin and associates from the Hudson Institute interviewed 645 human resource executives.* The researchers' findings are published in Workforce 2000—Competing in a Seller's Market: Is Corporate America Prepared? *The quiz that follows asks you to predict some of the findings. Answer each question and then check the answers, which follow. You're in for some real surprises!*

1. The percentage of companies surveyed that are already having some or great difficulty finding professional and technical employees is between:

   a. 18%–24%   b. 63%–70%   c. 46%–51%

2. The percentage of companies surveyed that are currently encountering shortages of managerial or supervisory employees is:

   a. 49%   b. 64%   c. 31%

---

* See Towers Perrin and Hudson Institute, *Workforce 2000—Competing in a Seller's Market: Is Corporate America Prepared?* (Valhalla, NY: Towers Perrin), 1990. The quiz is adapted from TPF&C Company, *TPF&C Letter* 255, August 1990, pp. 2–3. Used with permission of the publisher.

3. Link the industry group listed in the left column to the employee category in which it is now experiencing widespread shortfalls:

   Health care   a. Professional

   Manufacturing   b. Management/supervisory

   Consumer products   c. Skilled crafts

   Services   d. Secretarial/clerical

   Utilities   e. Technical

4. To find a single suitable entry-level job candidate, over one-quarter of the survey companies report screening:

   a. More than 20 candidates

   b. Fewer than 5 candidates

   c. Between 10 and 20 candidates

5. The average first-year turnover rate for new entry-level hires at the companies surveyed is:

   a. 17%   b. 34%   c. 28%

6. Employees over the age of 40 make up what percentage, on average, of the surveyed companies' work forces?

   a. 27%   b. 39%   c. 43%

7. One-quarter of the companies surveyed report that minorities now constitute what percentage of their work force?

   a. More than 35%   b. Less than 20%   c. More than 25%

8. The survey companies report that women currently constitute what percentage of their work force:

   a. 50%   b. 56%   c. 42%

9. Participants' single greatest concern about managing a racially, ethnically, and sexually diverse work force is:

   a. Communication difficulties

   b. Supervisors' inability to deal with a mixed employee group

   c. Promotability

10. The single most common strategic step that the companies surveyed have taken to adapt to shifting demographics is:

    a. Raising salaries

    b. Increasing use of technology or automation

    c. Enhancing benefits

Answers: 1 b.   2 a.   3 Health care, b; Manufacturing, a; Consumer products, e; Services, d; Utilities, c.   4 a.   5 c.   6 b.   7 c.   8 a.   9 b.   10 c.

R E V I E W   **Q** U E S T I O N S

1. Review this chapter's essential terms and look up the meanings of those you cannot define.

2. Why is staffing important to an organization?

3. Describe the major steps in the staffing process.

4. Why are the concepts of equal employment opportunity and affirmative action so important to the staffing process?

5. What are the major social and cultural issues facing managers today?

6. How do managers go about planning human resources?

7. What strategies can managers follow to recruit new employees?

8. What are the steps in the selection process?

9. Describe the aims of training and development and contrast these two activities.

10. What are the major purposes of the performance appraisal? What methods can a manager use to make appraisals objective?

11. For what purposes and under what conditions do managers promote, transfer, demote, or fire employees?

12. What are the major purposes of an organization's compensation program?

R E C O M M E N D E D   **R** E A D I N G

Boyett, Joseph H., and Henry P. Conn. *Workplace 2000* (New York: Penguin), 1991.

Chisman, F. P. et al. *Leadership for Literacy: The Agenda for the 1990s* (San Francisco: Jossey-Bass), 1990.

Crystal, Graef S. *In Search of Excess* (New York: Norton), 1992.

Magnet, Myron. "The Truth About the American Worker," *Fortune* (May 4, 1992), pp. 48–66.

Schwartz, Felice. *Breaking with Tradition: Women and Work, the New Facts of Life* (New York: Warner), 1992.

Thomas, Jr., R. R. "From Affirmative Action to Affirming Diversity," *Harvard Business Review* (March–April 1990), p. 116.

R E F E R E N C E S

Amend, Patricia. "Job References Hard to Come by These Days," *USA Today,* February 2, 1990, p. 4B.

Beck, Joan. "Matching the Workplace to the Work Force," *Chicago Tribune,* March 9, 1992, sec. 1, p. 15.

Bennett, Amanda. "Executive Pay: A Little Pain and a Lot to Gain," *Wall Street Journal,* April 22, 1992, p. R1.

Brown, Donna. "HR: Survival Tool for the 1990s," *Management Review* (March 1991), p. 10.

Bulkeley, William M. "Computer Use by Illiterates Grows at Work," *Wall Street Journal,* June 9, 1992, p. B1.

Business Week (January 27, 1992). "Just How Excessive Are the Pay Scales of U.S. CEOs?" p. 22.

Chicago Tribune (June 5, 1992). "Workers Lack Three R's, Hurting Small Firms, Study Says," sec. 3, p. 3.

Federal Register 43, #156 (August 1978). "Uniform Guidelines on Employee Selection Procedures," pp. 38,295–38,309.

Fortune (April 20, 1992). "Pay Gap Between the Sexes (Cont'd)," p. 20.

Fuchsberg, Gilbert. "Study Says Women Face Glass Walls as Well as Ceilings," *Wall Street Journal,* March 3, 1992, pp. B1, B8.

Healey, James R., and Michelle Osborn. "Bush Contingent Takes Heat over CEO Pay," *USA Today,* January 8, 1992, sec. B, p. 1.

Hoerr, John, et al. "Privacy," *Business Week* (March 28, 1988), pp. 61, 65.

Jamieson, David, and Julie O'Mara. *Managing Workforce 2000* (San Francisco: Jossey-Bass), 1991, p. 21.

Jefferson, David J. "MCA to Extend Health Insurance to Gay Couples," *Wall Street Journal,* May 18, 1992, p. B5.

Kleiman, Carol. "Dealing with Harassment," *Chicago Tribune,* October 15, 1991, sec. 3, p. 1.

Kleiman, Carol. "Employee Reviews Merit Close Attention," *Chicago Tribune,* February 2, 1992, sec. 8, p. 1.

Kleiman, Carol. "Employer-Based Training Is a Growing Job Source," *Chicago Tribune,* January 12, 1992, sec. 8, p. 1.

Kleiman, Carol. "From Genetics to Honesty, Firms Expand Employee Tests, Screening," *Chicago Tribune,* February 9, 1992, sec. 8, p. 1.

Kleiman, Carol. "Some Firms Breaking Glass Ceiling," *Chicago Tribune,* April 13, 1992, sec. 4, p. 7. Also see Fuchsberg, 1992.

Kleiman, Carol. "Worker Skepticism Aside, Firms Like Exit Interviews," *Chicago Tribune,* October 13, 1991, sec. 8, p. 1.

Main, Jeremy. "The Battle over Benefits," *Fortune* (December 16, 1991), p. 91.

Milbank, Dana. "On the Ropes: Unions' Woes Suggest How the Labor Force in the U.S. Is Shifting," *Wall Street Journal,* May 5, 1992, p. A1.

Mohrman, Jr., Allan; Susan Resnick-West; and E. E. Lawler III. *Designing Performance Appraisal Systems: Aligning Appraisals and Organizational Realities* (San Francisco: Jossey-Bass), 1989.

Moskal, Brian S. "Sexual Harassment '80s Style," *Industry Week* (July 2, 1989), p. 24.

Perry, John A., and Erna K. Perry. *Contemporary Society: An Introduction to Social Science* (New York: HarperCollins), 1991, p. 94.

Rigdon, Joan E. "Using Lateral Moves to Spur Employees," *Wall Street Journal,* May 26, 1992, pp. B1, B5.

Steinert-Threlkeld, Ton. "Computer Revenge a Growing Threat," *Chicago Tribune,* March 9, 1992, sec. 4, p. 3.

Stodghill, Ron. "Managing AIDS," *Business Week* (February 1, 1993), pp. 48–52.

Thompson, Roger. "Costs for Firms Set a Record," *Nation's Business* (February 1992), p. 43.

Thompson, Roger. "Employers' Costs for Employees Soar," *Nation's Business* (May 1992), p. 62.

TPF&C Company. *TPF&C Letter* 225 (August 1990). (The cited text is abstracted from Towers Perrin and Hudson Institute. *Workforce 2000—Competing in a Seller's Market: Is Corporate America Prepared?* [Valhalla, NY: Towers Perrin], 1990.)

Tully, Shawn. "What CEOs Really Make," *Fortune* (June 15, 1992), p. 94.

United States Senate, Subcommittee on Labor of the Committee on Labor and Public Welfare. Equal Employment Opportunity Act of 1972 (March 1972), p. 3.

Wilke, John R. "Digital's Offer to Employees Proves Popular," *Wall Street Journal,* June 1, 1992, p. B6.

G L O S S A R Y   O F   T E R M S

affirmative action   A plan to give members of specific groups priority in hiring or promotion. An affirmative action plan cites specific goals and the time period in which they will be achieved. For organizations that have discriminated against particular groups in the past, affirmative action is mandatory. Other organizations institute affirmative action plans by choice.

assessment center   A place where candidates are screened for managerial positions. Screening in an assessment center usually involves extensive testing and hands-on exercises.

benefit   Legally required or voluntary compensation provided to employees in addition to their salaries or wages.

collective bargaining   Negotiation between a union and an employer in regard to wages, benefits, hours, rules, and working conditions.

compensation   All forms of financial payment to employees. Compensation includes salaries, wages, and benefits.

demotion   A reduction in an employee's status, pay, and responsibility.

development   Efforts to acquire the knowledge, skills, and attitudes needed to move to a job with greater authority and responsibility.

discrimination   Using illegal criteria while making employment decisions. Discrimination results in an adverse impact on members of protected groups.

disparate impact   The result of using employment criteria that have a significantly greater negative effect on some groups than on others.

equal employment opportunity   Legislation designed to protect individuals and groups from discrimination.

human resource manager   A manager who fulfills one or more personnel, or human resource, functions.

job analysis   A study that determines the duties associated with a job and the human qualities needed to perform it. A job analysis results in the preparation or updating of a job description and job specification.

job evaluation   A study that determines the worth of a job in terms of its value to an organization. Job evaluations are used to determine compensation levels.

orientation   Introducing new employees to the organization by explaining their duties, helping them meet their co-workers, and acclimating them to their work environment.

performance appraisal   A formal, structured comparison between employee performance and established quantity and quality standards.

perk   A payment or benefit received in addition to a regular wage or salary. Executives usually receive perks.

personnel manager   *See* human resource manager.

promotion   A job change that results in increased status, compensation, and responsibility.

recruiting   Efforts to find qualified people and encourage them to apply for positions that need to be filled.

selection   Evaluating applicants and finding those best qualified to perform a job and most likely to fit into the culture of the organization.

separation   The voluntary or involuntary departure of employees from a company.

sexual harassment   Unwelcome verbal or physical conduct of a sexual nature that (1) implies, directly or indirectly, that sexual compliance is a condition of employment or advancement, or (2) interferes with an employee's work performance.

staffing   Efforts designed to (1) attract, develop, reward, and retain the people needed to accomplish an organization's goals and (2) promote job satisfaction.

test   Any criterion used as a basis for an employment decision.

training   Giving employees the knowledge, skills, and attitudes needed to perform their jobs.

transfer   Moving an employee to a job with similar levels of status, compensation, and responsibility.

C A S E   P R O B L E M
Employees Put Great Stock in Company Profits

Science Applications International Corporation (SAIC) is a high-tech research firm that recently earned $1.3 billion in one year. Over the last 20 years, the value of SAIC stock has grown by a 27% annual compound rate. Don't go to your broker with a buy order, however; outsiders find it nearly impossible to purchase SAIC stock. SAIC workers and directors own 46% of the stock, and 41% is reserved for the employee stock ownership and retirement plans. Nearly all the rest of the shares are in the hands of ex-employees.

Founder and nuclear physicist J. Robert Beyster credits employee ownership for his company's success. Beyster believes that because everyone's personal prosperity is linked to the prosperity of the company, employees are committed to helping the company do well. Beyster takes the use of stock as an incentive one step further: He insists on linking stock ownership to performance. As he explains it, performance is measured on "among other things, sales targets or how well a manager handles contracts. Only employees who are recommended by the managers can buy stock on SAIC's quarterly trading days."

The company was heavily involved in defense work but has managed to shift with the times. SAIC geologists, hydrologists, and other experts now work on problems involving health care, global warming, and hazardous-waste disposal.

Q U E S T I O N S

1. Do you agree that SAIC's excellent growth is due in large measure to the fact that employees own so much of its stock? Why?

2. Does the fact that most of the employees are technical experts with advanced degrees make a difference in the way a company is managed? If so, how?

3. Do you think it is important to share in the ownership of the company you work for? What are the risks connected with tying your pension to an investment in your company's stock?

For more information about SAIC, see Nancy J. Perry, "Talk About Pay for Performance!" *Fortune*, May 4, 1992, p. 78.

Communication: Interpersonal and Organizational

LEARNING OBJECTIVES

After reading and discussing this chapter, you should be able to:

- Define this chapter's essential terms
- List the primary purposes for communicating
- Diagram the communication process and label all its parts
- List and explain the barriers to interpersonal communication and suggest remedies to overcome them
- Describe the formal organizational communication channels: upward, downward, and horizontal
- Describe the informal communication channel known as the grapevine
- List and explain the barriers to organizational communication
- Explain the responsibilities of senders and receivers
- Describe the importance of listening in communication

MANAGEMENT IN ACTION
Magma Copper Company

When **Magma Copper Company** became a standalone operation after a divestiture in 1987, it was a troubled company. Negotiations in 1986 with the mine workers' union had committed the company to paying bonuses it could not afford. Workers had already given up 22% of their wages.

In 1989, during labor negotiations with the company's six different unions, managers agreed to restore half the wages but found themselves facing hostile workers who mistrusted them. At the same time, costs were out of control and interest on the company's $400-million debt was eating up its cash flow. Magma's CEO, J. Burgess Winter, knew labor relations had to improve. If a turnaround was to take place, employees and management had to work together.

Over the next three years, the corporation spent $3 million and 300,000 hours to bring the warring factions together. The beginning was less than a success. At a kickoff dinner party, managers and labor officials refused to talk or eat with one another. But within two days, the parties reached an agreement to establish work teams

***Magma is red hot** after facing cold facts about poor labor relations, high costs, and crushing debt. Communication was the answer.*

and share decisions with workers. The company provided information and financial data through day-long workshops and taught everyone what the facts meant. It took time for labor leaders and employees to be convinced of the need to cooperate. By the time labor negotiations began in 1991, however, the employees understood the difficulties facing the company and most were comfortable with the new working arrangements. The unions did not ask for large wage increases. Both sides agreed to a 15-year collective bargaining agreement that prohibits lockouts by management and strikes by labor for at least seven years.

Work teams run nearly everything at Magma these days. Five-worker tank-car crews are self-managing. The elimination of some supervisory positions has lowered management costs, and productivity (measured in pounds of ore produced per shift) has increased by 43% since 1988. Total pounds of copper produced has increased to the point of overtaxing the company's smelter capabilities. Bonuses are now linked to improvements in operations, not to rises in

copper prices. The new system is working well; both mine and smelter workers earned bonuses in 1991.

The company is also working hard to make a new mine successful. Magma assembled a team of about 150 miners to determine how to reduce the mine's costs from $6.50 per ton to the needed $4.00 per ton. The team threw out accepted union practices and came up with new designs for more efficient mining techniques and teams. Their efforts have brought costs to $4.60 per ton and are continuing.

The company's labor wars are over and employees are committed to their company's survival. By spring 1992, Magma Copper Company had brought its costs into line and had significantly reduced its debt and interest payments. The key to the turnaround was communication between management and labor. ▲

▶ Magma assembled a team of about 150 miners to determine how to reduce the mine's costs. The team threw out accepted union practices and came up with new designs for more efficient mining techniques and teams.

For more about Magma Copper Company, see Marj Charlier, "Magma Copper Heals Its Workplace and Bottom Line," *Wall Street Journal,* April 6, 1992, p. B4.

The Importance of Communication

Communication is the process through which people and organizations accomplish objectives. By communicating with others we share attitudes, values, emotions, ambitions, wants, and needs. Behind most successes is effective communication—that which is well planned and thoughtfully executed. But the process of communication is difficult. Failed plans are often the result of failed attempts at communicating.

Successful managers effectively communicate their vision for a work unit or the company as a whole. At Wal-Mart, Sam Walton's vision to make the customer number one led his company to its place as the most successful retailer in American history. Here are a few thoughts from Sam Walton (1992) about the importance of communication:

> Communicate everything you possibly can to your partners. The more they know, the more they'll understand. The more they understand, the more they'll care. Once they care, there is no stopping them. If you don't trust your associates to know what's going on, they'll know you don't really consider them partners. Information is power, and the gain you get from empowering your associates more than offsets the risk of informing your competitors.

Listen to everyone in your company. And figure out ways to get them talking. The folks on the front lines—the ones who actually talk to the customer—are the only ones who really know what's going on out there. You'd better find out what they know. This really is what total quality is all about. To push responsibility down in your organization, and to force good ideas to bubble up within it, you must listen to what your associates are trying to tell you.

Managers at Magma Copper Company realized just how important these concepts are. They shared information, empowered workers, and unleashed talents to solve problems that threatened the firm's survival. Once management and labor agreed on the facts of the company's condition and what was needed to improve it, they pulled together to accomplish a dramatic turnaround.

Increasingly, managers are seeing the value of keeping in touch with employees. A 1991 poll of 212 CEOs revealed that nearly 60% conduct employee surveys. When asked what their companies had done in recent years that most helped improve communication and productivity, 41% listed regular meetings with employees, 16% cited internal newsletters and bulletins, 11% listed efforts to involve teams and employees, 7% listed organizational delayering and middle-management training, and 6% cited efforts to improve communication among all layers of management. Richard F. Teerlink, CEO of Harley-Davidson, said: "It's a matter of top management getting out and talking with people, not at people." Alan G. Hassenfeld, CEO of Hasbro, added: "We have a program called 'write to the top' in which everyone is encouraged to write to me about anything that's on their minds, and it's read only by me" (Fisher, 1991, "CEOs").

People in organizations need each other. They must coordinate and pool their efforts to achieve their goals and avoid waste and confusion. They must focus on the needs of customers, those inside as well as outside the company. They must be able to articulate their needs so that they can work cooperatively. They must be free to express what they know and believe in order to capitalize on opportunities for meaningful change. Managers who really believe that their people are the organization's most valuable resource will make communicating with those people their most vital process.

The Communication Process

Communication is the transmission of **information**—data in a coherent, usable form—from one person or group to another. Rational communicators strive to achieve a common **understanding**—agreement about the meaning and intent of the message—among all parties to each communication. Although much of the information that managers rely upon is in numeric form, the greatest portion of managerial activity depends upon verbal communication and competent use of language. Able communicators respect the conventions of language—spelling, grammar, and punctuation. They know precisely what they wish to say and thoughtfully select the best way to say it. In addition, the communicator needs to be certain that the person who receives the information actually understands the message.

Communication is a process—a set of steps usually taken in a definite sequence. The initiator of communication is called a **sender**; the person or group that gets the communication is the **receiver**. The information that the sender

Exhibit 11.1

A model of the communication process.

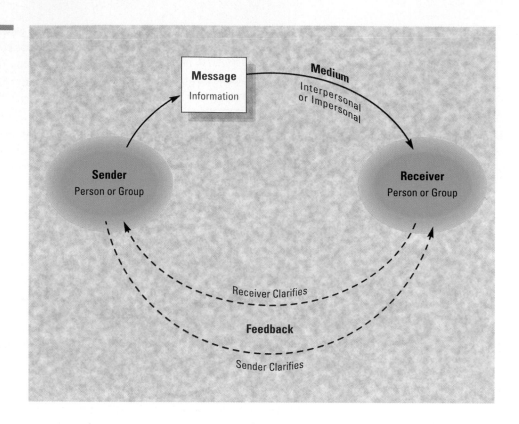

wants to transmit is the **message**. The means chosen by the sender to transmit the message is the **medium**, or channel. Finally, the process must provide mechanisms through which both sender and receiver can determine if the intended communication has taken place and mutual understanding achieved. That mechanism provides **feedback**—information the receiver provides to show how he or she perceived the sender's message. In providing feedback the receiver becomes a sender and the original sender becomes a receiver; the process of sending and receiving refining messages proceeds until both communicators believe that understanding has taken place. The more carefully crafted and unambiguous the message is, the less the feedback will be required to achieve understanding. Exhibit 11.1 models the communication process.

To illustrate the communication process, consider an example involving Harry Trent, a manufacturing director. Harry calls Anita Raton, the human resource manager for his company, and says, "I need a replacement employee." In response to the message, Anita says, "What kind of skills do you need? For which department?" The receiver is seeking clarification of the original message and becomes a sender in doing so. Harry now shifts to being a receiver and must clarify his original message before responding and becoming a sender again. Many conversations flow in this manner because the sender transmits an incomplete message—one that requires the receiver to ask for additional information so that understanding can take place. Harry failed to refine his message before he initiated the communication process.

Mediums of Communication

Communication mediums are verbal (spoken or written words) and nonverbal (images, facial expressions, gestures, and body language).

Verbal Communication

Spoken verbal messages can be delivered face-to-face or by electronic means, such as telephone, voice and video recordings, and sophisticated computers with voice and video capabilities. Written verbal mediums range from memos, letters, and reports to facsimiles (faxes), electronic mail (e-mail), and a wide array of printed pieces—manuals, newsletters, newspapers, magazines, and more.

The sender's choice of medium is influenced by several factors: the content of the message, the importance of feedback, the number of intended receivers, the receiver's and sender's preferences and characteristics, the sender's and receiver's locations and environments, and the technologies available. Communication requiring immediate, two-way feedback and a personal touch should be oral and in person. If the message is complicated and requires a considered response, communication should be written.

Conversation, perhaps the most common communication medium for managers, takes place on the shop floor, in the office, over the telephone, at lunch, on the way to meetings, and in group settings. Conversation should be used when the message is for one person and requires personal contact, or when give-and-take is vital. Henry Mintzberg (1973) studied five CEOs and found that they spent 78% of their time talking with others. These conversations were generally short—49% of their daily encounters lasted less than nine minutes; only 10% lasted longer than an hour.

John Kotter found virtually the same results. The 15 executive general managers he studied spent 76% of their time talking with others (Deutschman, 1992). As Suzanne Rinfret Moore, who directs three companies, reported (Deutschman, 1992):

> Someone can say to me in 30 seconds what it might take 15 minutes to write in a memo—and it generates the ability to think on your feet.... [Oral communication] fosters creativity for yourself and the people you work with. Access is critical. I want people who can come to my door. They're not time bandits.

Oral communication cannot always substitute for the written word, however. The process of preparing a written document allows careful consideration. The initiator can precisely determine and control the content, organization, complexity, tone, and style of the message. Receivers can digest such communications according to their own schedule and at their own pace. They can prepare considered responses. A written message can be enriched with graphics and other illustrations. In addition, writing tends to support confidentiality. Among the countless variations of written communications are letters, memos, outlines, reports, procedures manuals, press releases, contracts, advertisements, and forms. Exhibit 11.2 suggests conventional applications for common written communication tools.

Written forms of communication have disadvantages. They are impersonal, do not provide the immediacy of face-to-face contact, and do not elicit immediate feedback.

Letters	For correspondence with persons or groups outside an organization. Usually produced in a format—a form letter or block-style letter, for example.
Memos	For routine correspondence with superiors, subordinates, and peers. Memos should contain the date, the names of intended receivers and their titles, the subject of the correspondence (ideally only one subject per memo), the message, and the name and title of the sender. The ideal memo is no more than one page long.
Outlines	For indicating the structure of a lecture, report, or agenda and to order major and minor points. Outlines are useful in developing tables of contents and summaries.
Reports	For reporting the results of an investigation or routine and ongoing activities. Report formats range from fill-in-the-blank styles to manuscripts with or without statistical data. The format is often prescribed.

Some forms of written communication—such as notices on bulletin boards, handbooks, and newsletters—are by their nature impersonal. Do not rely on these tools when timely feedback or elaboration is needed or when the message is critical. Receivers read these communications casually. If communication is vital, use tools of this nature as supplements to immediate tools.

Nonverbal Communication

Nonverbal communication consists of messages transmitted without the use of words. Nonverbal transmitters include facial expressions, gestures, and body language (posture, placement of limbs, and proximity to others). Photographs, charts, and videos also convey information nonverbally. Visual transmitters are powerful and persuasive tools that enable senders to send messages that are nearly impossible to communicate verbally. Imagine trying to use words alone to convey the information contained in an architect's drawing. As an exercise, examine the diagram in Exhibit 11.3. Now, using only words, describe the diagram to a friend and ask him or her to draw what you describe. In a few frustrating moments, the value of visuals should be apparent.

Research and your own experiences indicate that a sender's body language and other nonverbal expressions help a receiver to understand the sender's feelings and intent. The upset boss communicates emotions through facial expressions, clenched fists, aggressive gestures, a louder-than-normal voice, closer-than-normal physical presence, and eye-to-eye contact that is direct and intense.

Suppose a manager remains seated behind the desk when a visitor arrives, refuses to look at the person, and grunts an acknowledgment of the visitor's presence. These behaviors transmit one or more of the following messages to the visitor: "This person is not pleased to see me," "I have done something to annoy this person," "This person does not respect me," or "Maybe this is not a good time

Exhibit 11.3

An exercise in nonverbal communication.

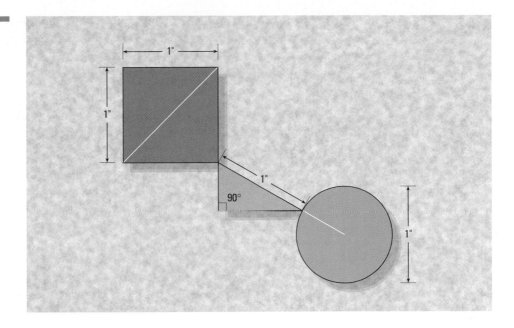

to visit with this person." The manager sends quite a different set of messages if he or she rises and extends a hand, seeks eye contact, smiles broadly, and says, "It's great to see you. Have a seat!"

Senders and receivers must be aware of the messages inherent in nonverbal communication. When nonverbal cues seem to contradict the sender's verbal messages, the receiver tends to believe the nonverbal message.

Interpersonal Communication

Interpersonal communication involves real-time face-to-face or voice-to-voice (telephone) conversation that allows instant feedback. Such communication recently acquired a new dimension. AT&T's VideoPhone, developed by Compression Labs and introduced in January 1992, utilizes an electronic technique called video compression to send moving pictures over telephone lines. The device can be used for individual conversations and videoconferencing. In addition, Compression Labs has perfected a device that will allow an Apple computer to become a video phone (Schneidawind, 1992).

A number of companies now use satellite-transmitted videoconferences for interpersonal communication. K Mart, for example, regularly runs videoconferences involving managers at its Michigan headquarters and those in its 2,300 stores nationwide. The headquarters managers make a presentation, and the store managers are invited to ask questions (Comins, 1992).

Interpersonal communications are appropriate for discussing matters that require give-and-take between participants. Applications include discussions about a performance appraisal; MBO sessions; conversations in which praise or criticism is given; and coaching, counseling, or training sessions. Meetings and conferences are useful forms of interpersonal communication when the issues affect others or require input from more than one or two parties. Brainstorming sessions, quality circles, committee meetings, and contract negotiations are but a few uses for interpersonal communication (Plunkett and Fournier, 1991).

Communication and Teams

Teams are taking an increasingly large role in organizations. Managers find that by putting workers together, they can get better work. Chapter 14 will explore team dynamics in detail; this chapter will focus on the management of team communication.

Team members generally engage in four kinds of communication. They exchange views, discuss work, deliberate on a problem or issue, and transmit information.

Whether a team is a permanent work group or temporarily gathered to address an issue, team members share a leader, a goal or goals, related activities (though each member may have a distinct role), and mutual dependency. Each individual possesses unique traits, of course, but the shared characteristics build group identity. In fact, group members often develop common perspectives about

***Team meetings** don't need a formal setting to be effective. An impromptu gathering to quickly discuss ideas and transmit information is more efficient than tracking down team members individually.*

management and the organization. These shared viewpoints arise first from the fact that group members affect each other and also from the fact that communications within the group transmit and reinforce similar attitudes. One key to managing intergroup communication, then, is to ensure that the viewpoints being shared are positive and match the organization's culture and goals.

Much team communication revolves around getting the job done—copywriters talk to product managers about a product's features and target market, and designers discuss page layouts with copywriters. A manager's main concerns with this kind of communication are to ensure that people send and receive accurate information, that all team members get the information they need when they need it, and that team members show sensitivity to one another's ideas and concerns.

The third kind of team communication takes place when a group meets to explore an issue, determine how to implement a procedure, solve a technical problem, or make a pricing decision. Group decision making offers many benefits. Hearing multiple perspectives can help a person generate more ideas than he or she could generate alone; the interaction of people can create a powerful synergy. In addition, participation increases commitment to the decision (see Chapter 6). But group deliberations must be carefully managed to ensure that they are effective. Managers must set a clear agenda for the meeting and keep the discussion to the point. They need to ensure that all group members participate by channeling discussion to avoid domination by a few. They must keep an eye on the clock so the meeting does not waste time.

The fourth type of intrateam communication involves the transmission of information. Whether a manager is informing team members about a new organizational policy or a team member is passing on the findings of a telephone conversation with a consultant, a team meeting is ideal for this kind of communication. Telling five people at once is far more efficient than seeking out and telling each one individually. Also, when information is transmitted to several people at a time, the chance of each team member receiving the same information increases. Finally, having the team assembled to hear this kind of message provides the opportunity for team members to discuss its implications (Plunkett and Fournier, 1991).

Barriers to Interpersonal Communication

Leonard R. Sayles and George Strauss (1966) identified common barriers to interpersonal, or face-to-face, communication; the paragraphs that follow summarize the barriers they defined. These barriers can be overcome in large measure by following the guidelines for improving communication that appear toward the end of this chapter.

Diction and Semantics   Diction—the choice and use of words in speech and writing—significantly affects communication. **Semantics**, the study of the meaning of words, confirms that words may possess different meanings for different people. In everyday usage, abstract words such as *liberal, conservative,* and *motivate* create different images for senders and receivers. Business terms can cause the same problems. Terms such as *discipline* and *grievance* usually convey both negative and positive connotations and may have a strong emotional impact. The effective communicator is sensitive to such effects.

Jargon—the specialized or technical language that develops in trades, professions, and other groups—poses its own set of hazards. Each corporate culture, subculture, unit, and division has its own unique terminology and slang expressions. Computer experts talk about bits, bytes, and boilerplate. Financial managers use terms like *leverage, equity,* and *depreciation.* When members of these subcultures attempt to communicate with those outside their group by using these expressions, confusion can result.

The lesson for communicators is clear: Strive for language that means the same thing to receiver and sender. The sender who has any doubt about the possible interpretation of unusual, specialized, or vague words should take extra care to ask receivers if they understand the terms. Communication with newcomers to American culture and language deserves special attention. Local English is treacherous to speakers who tend to take things literally and may be unaware of slang and jargon. The meaning of *chewing the fat* differs significantly in Cleveland and Nome.

Expectations of Familiarity   How many times have you been in conversation and tuned out the speaker because you absolutely knew what he or she was going to say? People do this because they are familiar with a speaker's thoughts on particular topics. The speaker begins with a statement and tone that sounds similar to openings used in the past. At that moment, listening stops. When a parent begins by saying "When I was your age…," the child tunes out. When the boss begins with "When I did your job, I…," the subordinate tunes out. Failure to listen because of the listener's expectation of familiarity is a factor that inhibits communication.

When addressing people on familiar topics, senders should engage their receivers by asking questions about their understanding and current knowledge of the topic. If receivers already know what a sender wants to communicate, no further effort is needed. If what is about to be sent is new, senders should state that fact and proceed to convey the new data.

The Source's Lack of Credibility   If a sender has credibility in the receiver's mind, the message will be received more readily than if the sender lacks credibility. When a person proven to have knowledge and a successful track record speaks about his or her specialty, people tend to listen. The finance manager is presumed to have more expertise in budgetary matters than the marketing manager. The experienced plant manager's ideas about how to handle a maintenance problem should prevail over those of his or her new apprentice. But new and inexperienced employees often bring an unbiased and fresh approach to problems. They may spot more effective or efficient ways to get things done. Their ideas deserve a hearing. Empowering employees means giving them the freedom and authority to offer suggestions and devise new solutions.

Preconceived Notions   If the new and different viewpoint the receivers hear contradicts what they "know" to be true, the receivers do not accept them. In reacting this way, the receivers close their minds and inhibit growth and change. They shut others out even though the others could be the means of the receivers' own growth and development.

Stereotypes can inhibit interaction and communication. Preconceptions about a person's race, nationality, gender, sexual orientation, or physical ability must be set aside for an honest, open exchange of ideas.

Differing Perceptions   Most organizations include people from different social, economic, and cultural backgrounds. These people may hold different values, beliefs, expectations, and goals. Many do not even share a common language. These differences contribute to differing **perceptions**—ways of observing and the bases for making judgments. Predetermined sets of conventional and over-simplified beliefs about groups of people—**stereotypes**—cause positive or negative reactions to those groups. "He's Hispanic, so he must be…," "Women just don't…," and "Germans always…" are expressions of stereotypes. Stereotypes can inhibit interaction and communication. See this chapter's Skill-Building exercises to gain further insight into stereotyping.

Conflicting Nonverbal Communication   A person who frowns while saying "I feel great" is sending conflicting messages. The manager who squirms in her seat and keeps checking her watch while telling us to continue a conversation is really telling us to stop.

A person's physical appearance and behavior send messages. Suppose a manager urges employees to strive for thoroughness. The urgings are likely to go unheeded if the manager always looks sloppy. Whatever a manager says about the need for continual improvement may be mitigated if he or she is never on time for meetings. Tardiness says that other things are more important, that the meeting is unnecessary, or that other peoples' time has no value.

Emotions   Tempers interfere with reason and understanding; therefore, they inhibit communication. Sender and receiver become opponent and adversary. When the head coach of the Chicago Bears lost his temper on the sidelines during a football game in October 1992, sports commentators and some team members claimed that it turned the momentum in favor of the opposing team. The Bears had a 14-point lead at the time but scored no more points and lost the game. Attempts at achieving a meeting of the minds dissolved into name calling and offensive remarks and behaviors. Messages communicated in anger can be damaging to people and their relationships for some time to come. Once offensive words are spoken, they cannot be unsaid. Apologies will not erase the hurt that receivers felt.

The best way to overcome the barriers to communication that emotions can pose is to develop a sense of timing. A sense of timing helps a sender know the best time to initiate a communication. Sam shows sensitivity to timing when he says, "I wouldn't see the boss today. He's just heard that his new budget was rejected." Similarly, the end of a tiring workday is not the best time to attempt to communicate complex messages. People are usually not in the proper condition to make communication successful.

Noise   Anything in the environment that interferes with the sending and receiving of messages is **noise**. If you have ever tried to speak over the roar of machinery or over a telephone with a bad connection, you know how noise interferes with communication. When people have to shout to be heard or are overburdened with irrelevant messages, they are experiencing noise.

Organizational Communication

Now that you understand how people communicate on an interpersonal level, you are ready to explore organizational communication. This section will begin by discussing the **formal communication channels**, the channels that result from a company's organizational structure. These designated pipelines for messages run in three directions: upward, downward, and horizontally. Managers are charged with the responsibility of creating, using, and keeping these channels open and available to organization members. The channels act as connections between members and outsiders and as paths through which official communications flow.

One look at an company's formal organization chart will reveal who is connected to whom and, therefore, in which directions communications will flow. Exhibit 11.4 shows a formal organization chart and the communication links between line and staff managers. Remember that communication is a two-way effort, so these channels carry messages from, as well as to, the persons they link.

In the not-too-distant past, formal communication flowed down from the top and rarely in any other direction. A strict chain of command existed at each level and in every work unit or subsystem. Feedback efforts were difficult and time-consuming. A great dependence on paper and written communication was the norm. Orders were given, procedures were written, and those who received them obeyed them.

Today, organizations emphasize electronic means of communicating, empowerment of employees, flexibility, and integrated teams. Therefore, compared to the past, more communication flows from the bottom up and from side to side.

Because layers of middle management have been removed, communications today are faster, more direct, and subject to less filtering than in the past. Computer networks, fax machines, satellite communications, and teleconferencing link those

Exhibit 11.4

The organization's formal channels for communication.

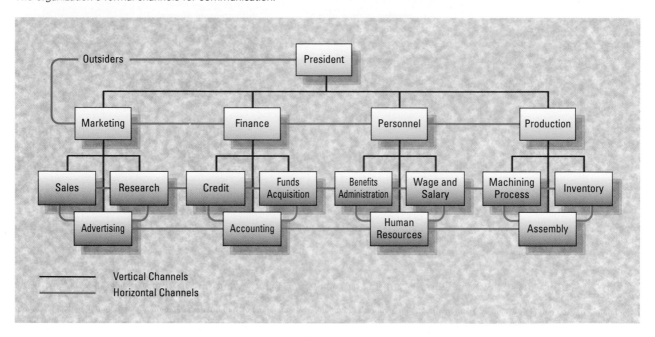

who must work together—even if they are in another part of town or in another country. With a laptop computer, a modem, a telephone, and a fax machine, an employee is never out of touch. Today, managers and workers occupy offices that are, in effect, without walls.

Formal Downward Channels

Downward communication conveys the kinds of information shown in Exhibit 11.5. Along with the messages themselves, managers should communicate the reasoning behind the messages—why things are being done and the advantages and disadvantages that may result to all concerned. Sharing reasons has the effect of bringing others into the decision-making process. As Chapter 6 reported, the results can be extremely beneficial.

Downward communication takes place daily, in on-the-job conversations and interactions between managers or team leaders and their subordinates. Downward communication can be one-on-one or take place in large meetings. Magma Copper's efforts at communication began with top management explaining the company's position to employees. Typical devices used to carry downward communication are company procedures manuals, newsletters, public relations announcements, annual statements, and various types of memos, reports, letters, and directives.

The co-founders of Zingerman's Deli in Ann Arbor, Michigan, began their company newsletter when the deli got too large for them to talk to all 130 employees.

Exhibit 11.5

Subjects for downward, horizontal, and upward communication.

DOWNWARD COMMUNICATION	
CEO's vision	Job designs
Changes in rules or procedures	Performance appraisals
Company mission	Policies
Delegation of authority	Solutions
Development	Staff managers' advice
Feedback	Strategic goals
Incentives	Training

HORIZONTAL COMMUNICATION	
Coordination efforts	Information about customers
Efforts to seek assistance	Information about suppliers
Feedback	

UPWARD COMMUNICATION	
Complaints	Requests for assistance
Feedback	Status reports
Recommended solutions	

The co-founders justify the cost of the newsletter, $2,000 a year, because it gives them a way to communicate with their workers. As Spragins reported (1992), the co-founders give three reasons for the newsletter's positive reception:

- Nothing gets published that is offensive or a put-down.

- The editor receives extra pay for producing the newsletter. Therefore, the editor has an incentive for producing a quality communication that will appeal to the workers.

- Some 30% of the newsletter's content is created by the front-line employees (the remainder comes from the managers and co-founders).

Formal Horizontal Channels

As Exhibit 11.5 showed, horizontal channels connect people of similar rank and status with customers and suppliers inside and outside an organization. Through horizontal channels, workers provide feedback, keep people informed, coordinate activities, seek assistance, and stay close to the customers. Staying close to

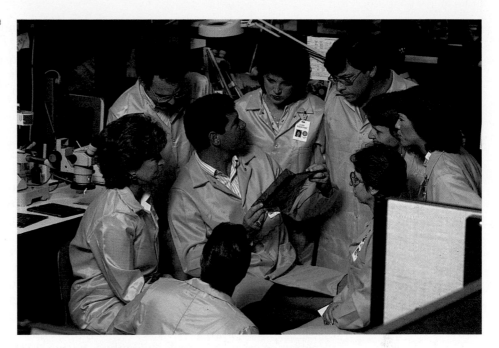

Horizontal communication *is at the core of the team concept, an approach to management that encourages direct interaction, bypassing layers of hierarchy. These Westinghouse employees solve problems by working in "quality circles."*

customers can mean literally staying close. One source described how United States Surgical communicates with its customers:

> In any ten-day period, sales representatives of United States Surgical visit every one of the 5,000 American hospitals where surgery is performed. They gown up and march right into operating rooms to coach surgeons in the use of the complex instruments their company makes. They listen to what the doctors like and don't like, need and don't need.

Such tactics have allowed managers to sense customers' needs and develop products to meet them. The approach works: United States Surgical claims 85% of its market (*Fortune*, May 18, 1992).

Toll-free long-distance telephone lines for customers are horizontal channels that connect consumers with those in the company, no matter what level, who can best answer their questions or meet their needs. WordPerfect Corporation is renowned in the PC world for the rapid and exhaustive telephone support it supplies for consumers of many of its software products.

Horizontal communication channels are used to set goals; define roles; create, examine, and improve methods; improve working relationships; define, investigate, and solve problems; and gather, process, and distribute information.

Horizontal communication is becoming increasingly important as managers institute more and more work teams. One observer pointed out the advantages of horizontal communication and the team approach: "Information moves straight to where it's needed, unfiltered by a hierarchy. If you have a problem with people upstream from you, you deal with them directly, rather than asking your boss to talk to theirs." Workers at Kodak's black-and-white film operations, called zebras, have worked in teams for more than two years. The teams work closely with the customers, communicating constantly about schedules, new products, and other customer needs.

Professor Shoshana Zuboff of Harvard University calls for all companies to "informate" employees by placing the corporation at their fingertips—giving them real-time access to all the information and experts in the system (Peters, 1991).

Formal Upward Channels

Upward communication provides the feedback required by downward communication. It allows workers to request assistance in solving some problems, and it provides a means for workers to recommend solutions to others. Workers also use upward communication to provide status reports and inform higher authorities about employee complaints. The tools of upward communication are employee surveys; newsletters; regular meetings between managers and their subordinates; suggestion systems; team meetings; and an open-door policy, which provides employee access to managers.

When asked what their companies had done to improve communication and productivity, CEOs responding to a survey cited several actions that related to upward communication. These included meeting regularly with employees, delayering the organization, broadening participation in decision making, and instituting grievance panels and hotlines (Fisher, 1991, "CEOs").

An attitude survey of 750,000 middle managers conducted by Hay Research showed that improvements in upward communication are still needed, however.

Status reports *are typical of the information that flows upward in an organization. According to one survey, however, upper management doesn't listen closely enough to the problems and complaints of lower levels.*

Though more than half of the managers rated their companies favorably in terms of providing information to employees, fewer than half rated top management favorably in terms of listening to employees' problems and complaints (Fisher, 1991, "Morale").

Managers must regularly leave their offices and touch base with people in the field. This management technique is known as management by wandering around. As one writer commented, "Even anonymous polls may not elicit truthful responses, and there is nothing quite like being there face to face" (Fisher, 1991, "Morale"). Management by wandering around has been one of Wal-Mart's secrets to success for many years.

Karl Krapek, head of United Technologies' Carrier Corporation, has had meals with more than 9,000 employees over the past few years. He's found that he gets substantive messages. Says Krapek, "The main thing is not to come with prepared notes. You want to get a dialogue going. You want people to speak up. People don't crab about their parking space or their merit raise. They usually want to know why we do certain things that don't help the customer" (Fisher, 1991, "Morale").

Some managers and their organizations have learned that it pays to listen to employees. According to the National Association of Suggestion Systems (NASS), employee suggestions saved more than 1,000 American businesses $2.3 billion in 1990. In 1991, the NASS Suggester of the Year award ($37,500) went to an American Airlines mechanic for his suggestion for a tamper-proof airport security door (West, 1991).

FOCUS ON QUALITY
The Power of Information

Combining effective communication and polling techniques, J. D. Power III developed the customer satisfaction index (CSI). He introduced the CSI in 1981, and it has been used ever since to rate cars. Power's firm, J. D. Power and Associates, now conducts 12 studies of auto makers and their dealers. It has launched a Canadian CSI and, with Japan's Research & Development Inc., a Japanese CSI. The company is also working to set up CSIs in Europe and Australia. Along with industry-wide studies and private research for individual clients, Power provides training to individual auto makers and dealers who want to learn how to satisfy customers.

To compile its ratings, Power and Associates mails surveys to registered car owners. The six- to eight-page questionnaires are sent to about 70,000 car owners. In exchange for 30 to 40 minutes of their time, respondents get a dollar bill.

The incentive must work—the response rate averages 38% and sometimes hits 50%, a high rate for such surveys. Only about 150 completed questionnaires on each model are sufficient to yield results with statistical validity.

The high response rate and the quality of Power's analyses put the company in a unique position to transmit valuable information from consumers to producers. Keeping the information away from his competitors has not been easy. In 1992, Power sued a company that hired two of his former employees, and those employees, for stealing company secrets. ▲

For more about J. D. Power, see Alex Taylor, "More Power to J. D. Power," *Fortune,* May 18, 1992, pp. 103–106.

Formal Communication Networks

Formal communication networks are electronic links between people and their equipment and between people and databases that store information. Organizations have linked their desktop computers for years. Since the 1970s, supermarkets and other large retailers have maintained computer links between their stores, headquarters, distribution centers, and suppliers. Xerox Corporation's research operations in Palo Alto, California, have videoconferencing links between employee lounges and various departments and buildings. The links allow researchers to confer easily (Ryan, 1992).

At Boeing, employees engage in brainstorming sessions by computer. Using special software called groupware, which tracks all brainstormers' contributions, Boeing has slashed the team size for most projects by 90%. One team designed a control system for machine tools in 35 days—a task that would have taken a year in the old days (Kirkpatrick, 1992).

According to one observer, electronic links help forge a sense of belonging. "Researchers find that electronic-mail users are more likely to feel committed to their jobs than do the unplugged. No similar data yet exist for groupware, but anecdotal evidence so far suggests it creates an even more powerful sense of belonging" (Kirkpatrick, 1992). Carl Di Pietro, a human resource executive at Marriott, has used groupware to run meetings. In describing the experience, he reported: "In my 30 years, it's the most revolutionary thing I've seen for improving the quality and productivity of meetings. It gets you closer to the truth." He adds that it enables a group to come to a consensus and the members to become more committed to decisions of the group. In addition, Di Pietro reported that groupware can overcome the difficulties that cultural diversity sometimes presents. "You don't know if that idea you're reading comes from a woman or a man, part of the minority or majority, or a senior or junior person. People begin to say, 'Hey, we've got a lot in common with each other'" (Kirkpatrick, 1992).

Informal Communication Channels

The formal communication channels designed by management are not the only means of communication in an organization. **Informal communication channels** carry casual, social, and personal messages on a regular basis in or around the workplace. These channels are often called, collectively, the **grapevine**. Informal communication channels disseminate rumors, gossip, accurate as well as inaccurate information, and, on occasion, official messages. Anyone inside or outside an organization can originate a grapevine message. Grapevine messages are transmitted in many ways—face-to-face and by telephone, e-mail, or fax.

Messages transmitted through informal channels usually result from incomplete information from official sources, environmental influences in the organization or outside it, and the basic human needs to socialize and stay informed. When changes occur, people like to speculate about what they will mean. When people feel insecure or fearful because of cutbacks and layoffs, rumors fly about what will happen next. When Jill is absent from her job, friends and co-workers want to know why. People who are the first to know something special usually want to share their new knowledge with others. Exhibit 11.6 shows how messages might travel through the grapevine.

Exhibit 11.6

The grapevine in action.

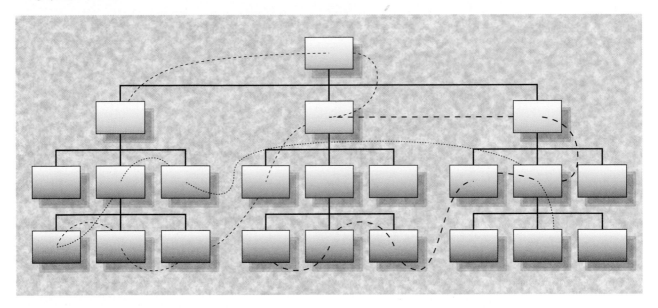

The grapevine has a number of characteristics:

- It can penetrate the tightest security.

- It is fast (with or without electronic links).

- It tends to carry messages from anonymous sources.

- Its messages are difficult to stop or counter once they get started.

- It is accessible to every person in an organization.

- It can be supportive of or an obstacle to management's efforts.

In most organizations, relatively few individuals disseminate most of the grapevine messages. These people create networks through which the messages are carried. Managers need to be attuned to the grapevine—that is, they should be aware of the messages it carries and the people who control it. They should not, however, use it as a formal communication channel. Inaccurate messages must be countered with the truth as soon as possible.

Exhibit 11.7 illustrates four common grapevine configurations. The most common is the cluster chain. Through it, an initiator—A, in this case—sends a message to a cluster, or group, that consists of B, E, and L. Through their own connections these three send the message to others. Each party involved usually distorts the message. Not all recipients carry the message to others. If a recipient has no interest in a grapevine communication or disagrees with it, he or she probably does not repeat it.

Exhibit 11.7

Four common grapevine configurations.

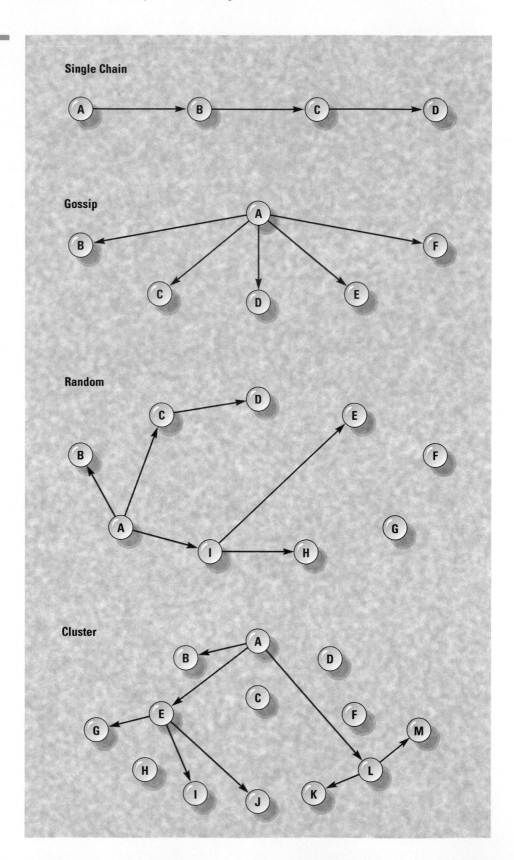

Barriers to Organizational Communication

Communication in organizations can be blocked by interpersonal barriers and by barriers that are part of the organizational environment. The way workstations are positioned in an office or factory can enhance or hinder communication, for example. People who cannot see each other or who are not physically close to one another may find it difficult to stay in touch, although telephones, e-mail, and fax machines can diminish the difficulty. Some managers have found that people seek each other out more often in a building equipped with escalators than in one with stairways or elevators. Escalators, they believe, offer relative privacy and allow senders and receivers to pay more attention to each other.

The paragraphs that follow will review several barriers to organizational communication.

Overload In the context of communication, the term *overload* means too much information. Everyone receives dozens of pieces of junk mail at home each week. The same thing occurs in plants and offices every day. People receive information they do not need. This overload is a type of noise, and employees must waste time trying to sort through it. One job for a company's management information system specialist is to make certain that people receive only what they need and that they receive it in the form that is most useful to them.

Filtering by Levels The management levels in a company can become barriers to communication. According to Keith Davis (1989), the more levels that information has to pass through, the more it can be embellished or filtered. The message the last receiver receives may bear little resemblance to the original communication. The current trend toward flattened organizational structures should help to prevent such distortion.

Timing Communications that must pass through several hands can be delayed in the process. Anything in an organization that prevents the free and quick flow of needed information impedes communication. The spread of high-speed communication technologies (such as e-mail) and the growing use of teams (whose members are trained to recognize the need to share information) are expected to reduce barriers to prompt communication.

Lack of Trust and Openness Companies that are secretive about sharing vital information with employees lack openness; such behavior says that they do not trust their employees. A lack of openness in organizational communications derives from a lack of trust or from the fear that wrongdoing will be exposed. Workers and managers at Bell Atlantic play games to develop good working relationships and mutual trust. Each year, in a 2½-day seminar, everyone from the chairman of the board to the customer-service representatives undergoes the same training program. The session consists of games such as blindfolded dart throwing. Blindfolded throwers have little chance of hitting the target unless others coach them. "It's just a silly dart game," says CEO Raymond Smith, "but people never forget it" (Huber, 1992).

Inappropriate Span of Control If a manager supervises more people than time and energy permit, communication suffers. The manager who has too few

I S S U E S   A N D   E T H I C S
Do We Need to Leash Electronic Watchdogs?

n today's electronic environment, people often socialize by using the company's e-mail. Gossip, recipes, social invitations, and rumors all appear in electronic mailboxes. Employers have ways of accessing private e-mail once it is in the computer system. Some employees have been fired on the basis of information that was contained in their electronic mailboxes.

By looking at the contents of e-mail, for example, employers have discovered that employees were communicating confidential information to un-authorized persons or using company time to run a personal business.

Since 1986 a federal law has restricted third-person access to e-mail messages, but the law does not deal directly with an employer's right to scan the contents of e-mail.

For many years, employers have used electronic monitoring to keep track of how employees are using their computers. Many employees are evaluated, in part, on the findings of systems that keep track of computer keystrokes, number of orders processed, and the amount of time employees are actively using their computers. The issue with electronic eaves-dropping and monitoring is one of privacy.

What do you think about an employer using a computer system to monitor your performance? Should supervisors be allowed to read the personal messages sent between employees at work? Do you see broader social or ethical conflicts in this issue? ▲

people to oversee may become overbearing and attempt to communicate too much. The more that leaders empower their people by delegating authority and providing quick access to needed information, the less they need to worry about keeping communication effective. Well-trained self-managing work teams know that when they need help, all they have to do is seek it. Until then, the manager should observe, track, and facilitate as needed.

Change   Changes anywhere in a company can hurt or hinder communication. When a new manager takes over, he or she invariably introduces changes in goals, methods, and communication style. What matters is how well people are prepared to cope with the changes. Larry Senn, head of Senn-Delaney Leadership Consulting Group in California, had this advice: "Take the time to describe your expectations to people. In a small organization, one person who's not open to change and not a team player can really gum up the works" (Huber, 1992).

Rank or Status in the Company   Unfortunately, in too many organizations the higher a manager is in the hierarchy, the less available he or she seems to be to others. Rank or status can make others timid and hesitant to communicate, or willing to communicate good news only. Some people in high positions begin to imagine that they are something special, an attitude that leads them to avoid listening to what subordinates have to offer.

In *Riding the Runaway Horse,* Charles C. Kenney (1992) examined the fall of Wang Laboratories. He attributed the company's decline to, among other things, an unwillingness to respect diverse opinions and stay close to customers. An

Wang, the founder, created two classes of stock to avoid stockholder influences on his decisions. He delayed moving into the personal computer field until that field fell to others. He announced the development of new products when the products were nothing but ideas on paper. And, on his deathbed in 1989, he fired his son and president, Fred Wang, so that Fred would be blamed for the company's failures. In the words of a former president at Wang, John Cunningham, An Wang had become "a humble egomaniac."

Managers' Interpretations Managers, like everyone else, are people with biases, stereotypes, values, needs, morals, and ethics. How they perceive their world determines how they will react to it. Managers will communicate where, when, what, and to whom they believe they must. As an example, consider the manager who is facing a crisis and asks for emergency funding for additional overtime. He needs the approval quickly. But the finance manager who receives the request is in no hurry. She wants to defer the request until next year's budget kicks in, in about two months. When pressured for a decision, she responds: "You'll get the money you requested when I decide to give it." Both managers have different needs and agendas. Both have differing perspectives, priorities—and levels of courtesy.

Electronic Noise Modern electronics have added yet more noise to the work environment. Breakdowns, overloads, static on the line, and ill-trained operators are barriers to organizational communication. Voice-mail systems can be barriers to communicating, especially for people unaccustomed to them. Managers should remain aware of potential difficulties and take steps to smooth or eliminate them where possible.

Improvement of Communication

Being adept at communicating involves individual skills as well as organizational frameworks and aids. Both the sender and the receiver have distinct responsibilities in the communication process. Meeting those responsibilities can help both parties avoid or overcome barriers to communication.

Responsibilities of Senders

Those who send messages must shape them and be aware of how they are received. The paragraphs that follow discuss the sender's responsibilities.

Be Certain of Intent The sender's first task is to be clear about the intent of the message. Exhibit 11.8 lists some typical goals of communication. As the exhibit shows, the goals often vary according to the receiver. One goal common to all messages is that the receiver understand them.

Know the Receiver and Construct the Message Accordingly The sender should acquire as much information as possible about the individual or group that is to receive the message. Senders need to know the receiver's job, experience, personality, perceptions, and needs. If the sender and receiver use different native languages, are from different cultures, or have had significantly

Exhibit 11.8

Typical communication goals.

When Communicating with Superiors

- To provide responses to requests
- To keep them informed of progress
- To solicit help in solving problems
- To sell ideas and suggestions for improvement
- To seek clarification of instructions

When Communicating with Peers

- To share ideas for improvement
- To coordinate activities
- To provide assistance
- To get to know them as individuals

When Communicating with Subordinates

- To issue instructions
- To persuade and sell
- To appraise performance
- To compliment, reward, and discipline
- To clarify intentions and instructions
- To get to know them as individuals

different experiences, the sender must be aware of the barriers these differences could pose. For instance, pictures and charts may be the best way to communicate when senders and receivers do not speak the same native languages.

Senders must choose words with receivers' vocabularies in mind, not their own. While composing a message, senders should try to imagine themselves as the receiver and ask themselves if they would understand it. One basic goal of all communication is to help the receiver view the content of the message as the sender does. The sender should emphasize aspects of the message that relate to the receiver. If the message announces a change, the sender should point out the advantages that will result for the receiver. If the purpose is to ask for assistance, the sender should cite what the receiver will gain by providing it.

Select the Proper Medium   The choice of a medium to carry the message depends in part on the content of the message. Confidentialities and praise always call for a personal touch. If the receiver is in a remote location or if the matter is complex and lengthy, putting it in writing might be the best choice. If the receiver prefers a given medium, the sender should try to use that method. A sightless person may prefer a voice message or one encoded in Braille. A person who has a hearing difficulty may prefer a visual presentation. Finally, the sender must consider

Choosing the medium is an important part of effective communication. Often, complex ideas are best expressed using nonverbal means such as charts and graphs.

the physical and emotional environment to be faced when attempting to communicate. What kind of noise will there be?

Time the Transmission　The timing of the communication affects its success. The sender's needs along with the receiver's must be considered in determining the best time. A supervisor may want to talk with a subordinate at 4:00 p.m., but if the worker leaves at 3:30 p.m., 4:00 is an inappropriate time. Business communications should be delivered to people who are in a receptive mood and under the proper circumstances. Important discussions about a new budget would be inappropriate at a company picnic or when people are on their breaks. People who are clearly overwhelmed with work when a message sender contacts them cannot give their full attention to the message.

Seek and Give Feedback　Senders have the primary responsibility to make certain that their messages have been received and understood. The only way to make certain is to get feedback. The sender cannot settle for the response, "I understand." If receivers have no questions, the sender should have some. One technique to assess understanding is to ask the receiver to restate the message using his or her own words. Another approach is to ask questions to check on the receiver's grasp of specifics.

　　As the receiver engages in feedback, he or she may ask questions that require responses from the sender. At this time the sender must understand how the receiver has interpreted the message and then take the actions needed to clear up any misunderstandings.

GLOBAL APPLICATIONS
The Growing Importance of Meetings

Planning meetings is a huge industry worldwide. In the United States during 1991, the meeting-planning industry took in more than $56 billion, and more than 82 million delegates attended 260,000 meetings. Professional meeting planners take care of all the negotiations necessary to reserve facilities and make all other arrangements. There are even companies around the world that specialize in nothing but planning meetings for corporate clients. Meetings are held for training and development, to keep organization members informed of results and pending changes, to coordinate activities, to build teams, and to plan for the future. They utilize the latest in communication technology, such as interactive video through satellite links.

With so many businesses diversifying, creating autonomous divisions, and engaging in global operations, meetings have become an important part of networking. The communications manager of an international consulting firm reported: "Because we are a global company [with 35 offices worldwide], it's important for our officers to get together to build relationships and network with each other. We feel there's always a need for more training and development of our people." As long as managers concur, the meeting-planning industry will prosper. ▲

For more about meetings, see Carol Kleiman, "Demand Still Strong for Meeting Planners," *Chicago Tribune,* August 23, 1992, sec. 8, p. 1.

Responsibilities of Receivers

Just as senders have specific obligations, so do receivers. The paragraphs that follow discuss these responsibilities.

Listen Actively   A receiver must listen attentively to the message being sent. Listening attentively requires that receivers block out distractions that can interfere with communication. Because people speak more slowly than listeners can process words, listeners' minds are often tempted to wander. Receivers must not attempt to pass judgment on the sender or the message until the message has been completely transmitted. Being critical distracts from listening. According to John J. Gabarro (1991), a professor of human resource management at the Harvard Business School, "The greatest barrier to effective communication is the tendency to evaluate what another person is saying and therefore to misunderstand or to not really 'hear.'"

Active listeners take notes and list any areas where a sender's meanings are unclear. Good listeners ask questions to clarify messages. They observe gestures, tone of voice, facial expressions, and body language and note contradictions between them. If necessary, they seek explanations for the contradictions.

Be Sensitive to the Sender   Senders communicate because they believe they must. They pick a certain medium, time, and receiver because they see these elements of communication as appropriate. Receivers should approach every communication with the assumption that the message is important to the sender.

Active listening means giving full attention to the sender of the message, suspending judgment until the message is complete, and asking for clarification of anything left unclear.

They should try to discover why that is so and what value the message has for them as receivers. Being sensitive means not interrupting or distracting the speaker. If a sender has difficulties in making the message clear, the receiver must try to help or act to postpone communication until the sender is better prepared.

Indicate an Appropriate Medium   Receivers can often facilitate communication by stating a preference for a certain medium. Many managers want to receive important messages in writing so that they can study and store them. E-mail, faxes, letters, memos, and reports can meet these requirements. Sometimes the request is for a face-to-face meeting so that two or more people can interact. Expressing a preference speeds up a communication effort and removes possible guesswork by the sender. Both parties, therefore, should be more comfortable. Of course, company rules and procedures or a union contract often specify various mediums as appropriate for handling routine communications.

Initiate Feedback   Receivers bear the primary responsibility for providing feedback. Until the receiver states his or her interpretation of the message, the sender will never know if it was understood. Similarly, the receiver cannot be certain that he or she has understood the sender's intentions until the receiver summarizes the message and receives confirmation that the summary was correct. When a receiver cannot restate a message, it is a sure sign that it was not understood.

The Ten Commandments of Good Communication

The American Management Association has prepared guidelines for effective communicating. Exhibit 11.9 presents these guidelines.

1. Clarify your ideas before communicating. The more systematically the problem or idea to be communicated is analyzed, the clearer it becomes. This is the first step toward effective communication.

2. Examine the true purpose of each communication. Before you communicate, ask yourself what you really want to accomplish with your message—obtain information, initiate action, change another person's attitude? Identify your most important goal and then adapt your language, tone, and total approach to serve that specific objective.

3. Consider the total physical and human setting whenever you communicate. Meaning and intent are conveyed by more than words alone.

4. Consult with others, when appropriate. Frequently, it is desirable or necessary to seek the participation of others in planning a communication or developing the facts on which to base it.

5. Be mindful, while you communicate, of the overtones as well as the basic content of your message. Your tone of voice, expression, and apparent receptiveness to the responses of others have tremendous impact on those you wish to reach.

6. Take the opportunity, when it arises, to convey something of help or value to the receiver. Consideration of the other person's interests and needs will frequently highlight opportunities to convey something of immediate benefit or long-range value to the receiver.

7. Follow up your communication. Unless you follow up, your best efforts at communication may be wasted and you may never know whether you have succeeded in expressing your meaning and intent.

8. Communicate for yesterday and tomorrow as well as today. Although a message may be aimed primarily at meeting the demands of an immediate situation, it must be planned with the past in mind if it is to maintain consistency in the receiver's view. More important, it must be consistent with long-range interests and goals.

9. Be sure your actions support your communications. In the final analysis, the most persuasive kind of communication is not what you say but what you do. When a person's actions or attitudes contradict his or her words, we tend to discount what that person has said.

10. Seek not only to be understood but to understand—be a good listener. When we start talking, we often cease to listen in that larger sense of being attuned to the other person's unspoken reactions and attitudes.

Future Trends

Several trends are in evidence in the area of communications:

- Globalization. As the number of joint ventures and global enterprises increases, so will the difficulties partners face when communicating with one another. In many multinational corporations, the official spoken language depends upon a manager's location. In the Swiss offices of a British multinational company, managers communicate in German even though they are of several different nationalities. A Japanese company with plants in the United States has a few Japanese nationals in top management but depends upon an American work force. English is the official language in these U.S. operations except when the top officials wish to exclude their American subordinates. Too often, business partners must speak to one another with translators who often find it difficult to translate terms precisely (if at all). Or, they may translate them too literally, a practice that leads to misunderstandings. Clearly, language training will become increasingly important in multinational companies.

- Technology. The introduction of new electronic technologies will continue at a rapid pace. Although these tools—e-mail, faxes, and voice mail—have become indispensable, they do present a danger. Workers may become so reliant on them that they forget the importance of nonverbal communication and the need to engage in the personal, social, and face-to-face interactions that are necessary to bring people closer, develop trust, and foster team spirit and cooperation. To prevent complete reliance on electronic communication, businesses will continue to increase the number of meetings and videoconferences they use each year.

- Cultural diversity. Given the changing demographics of the United States and the increasing international presence in U.S. companies, the number of programs to teach the value of cultural diversity will continue to grow. These programs will also seek to foster corporate culture.

C H A P T E R   S U M M A R Y

- Communication is the transmission of information and understanding from one person or group to another.

- Communicating is a complex process with five specific elements: the sender, the message, the medium, the receiver, and feedback. Feedback is information about the receiver's perception of the sender's message.

- Communication may be verbal—spoken or written—or nonverbal—using actions and images. The appropriate medium depends upon such factors as the technology available, the number of people receiving the message, and the relative need for feedback.

■ Several barriers can interfere with interpersonal communication; they must be recognized, prevented, or overcome.

■ Formal organizational communication may be vertical (upward or downward) or horizontal. It, too, has barriers that must be recognized, prevented, or overcome.

■ Communication networks help people at all levels of an organization gain access to information.

■ Informal channels of communication are known collectively as the grapevine. They carry both fact and fiction. Managers need to monitor the grapevine closely and quickly correct inaccurate messages.

■ Each party to a communication has specific responsibilities. Those of the sender involve clarifying the message and understanding the receiver, who should listen attentively and provide feedback.

■ All of us need to develop our communication skills in order to engage in the communication process more effectively.

S K I L L - B U I L D I N G

All people possess some biases, stereotypes, and general perceptions that affect communication efforts. Left unchecked, these mindsets can degrade the ability to include people and show them proper respect. In general, a person's race, ethnic background, sex or sexual orientation, color, or handicap should not be a part of a communication unless it is vital to the content of a message. The following exercises ask you to spot a bias and then take action to eliminate it.

In the list that follows, see if you can detect the kind of bias the words illustrate and then find alternative words or phrases that eliminate the bias. The first term has been done as an example.

Biased	**Nonbiased Alternative**
1. Businessman	*Owner, manager, or executive*
2. Bill's Mexican friend	_____

Biased	Nonbiased Alternative
3. Crippled people	_____
4. Ladylike	_____
5. Housewife	_____
6. The girls in the typing pool	_____
7. Colored people	_____
8. Mary's husband	_____
9. Al's female assistant	_____
10. Manpower	_____

R E V I E W   Q U E S T I O N S

1. Review this chapter's essential terms and look up the meanings of those you cannot define.

2. What are the primary purposes of communication? How can you measure the effectiveness of a communication effort?

3. What are the essential elements in the communication process?

4. What are the major barriers to interpersonal communication? What can be done to overcome each?

5. What are the three formal channels used in organizational communication? What kind of messages does each carry?

6. What is the informal communication channel found in business, and what kind of information does it usually convey?

7. What are the major barriers to organizational communication? What can be done to overcome each?

8. What are the major responsibilities of senders and receivers?

9. Why is listening so important in the effort to communicate?

R E C O M M E N D E D   R E A D I N G

Adler, Ronald B. *Communicating at Work: Principles & Practices for Business and the Professions,* 3rd edition (New York: Random House), 1990.

Beechhold, Henry R. "Classic Writing Tips, Always Worth Remembering: Here Are Nine Ways to Improve Your Business Communications," *Home Office Computing* (July 1990), pp. 22–23.

Bonner, William H. *Communicating in Business: Keys to Success,* 6th edition (Houston: Dame Publications), 1990.

Bylinsky, Gene. "A U.S. Comeback in Electronics," *Fortune* (April 20, 1992), pp. 77–78, 82, 84–85.

Cohn, Elizabeth, and Susan Kleimann. *Writing to Please the Boss* (Rockville, MD: Scandinavian PC Systems), 1990.

Dulek, Ronald, and John S. Felden. *Principles of Business Communication* (New York: Macmillan), 1990.

Huber, Janean. "The Big Picture: Learning from Big Business," *Entrepreneur* (June 1992), pp. 184, 186–187.

Massimilian, Richard D. "The New Language Barrier: Closer to Home Than You Think," *Business Horizons* (July–August 1990), pp. 52–58.

Tannen, Deborah. *You Just Don't Understand* (New York: Ballantine), 1990.

Welles, Edward O. "Quick Study," *Inc.* (April 1992), pp. 67–68, 70, 72, 74, 76.

R E F E R E N C E S

Comins, Jr., Frederic M. "Renewal at K-mart," a letter to the editor of *Harvard Business Review* (September–October 1992), p. 176.

Davis, Keith. *Human Behavior at Work: Organizational Behavior* (New York: McGraw-Hill), 1989.

Deutschman, Alan. "The CEO's Secret of Managing Time," *Fortune* (June 1, 1992), pp. 136, 140, 144, 146.

Fisher, Anne B. "CEOs Think That Morale Is Dandy," *Fortune* (November 18, 1991), pp. 83–84.

Fisher, Anne B. "Morale Crisis," *Fortune* (November 18, 1991), pp. 70, 76.

Fortune (May 18, 1992). "Getting Hot Ideas from Customers," p. 86.

Gabarro, John J. "Retrospective Commentary," *Harvard Business Review* (November–December 1991), p. 108.

Huber, Janean. "The Big Picture: Learning from Big Business," *Entrepreneur* (June 1992), pp. 186–187.

Kirkpatrick, David. "Here Comes the Payoff from PCs," *Fortune* (March 23, 1992), pp. 93, 96, 100.

Kenney, Charles C. *Riding the Runaway Horse* (New York: Little, Brown), 1992.

Mintzberg, Henry. *The Nature of Managerial Work* (New York: Harper & Row), 1973.

Peters, Tom. "Steps to Turn Workers into Business People," *Chicago Tribune,* November 25, 1991, sec. 4, p. 4.

Plunkett, Lorne C., and Robert Fournier. *Participative Management* (New York: Wiley), 1991, pp. 123–124, 126–127.

Ryan, Nancy. "Interaction on the Way for Offices," *Chicago Tribune,* June 9, 1992, sec. 3, p. 1.

Sayles, Leonard R., and George Strauss. *Human Behavior in Organizations* (Englewood Cliffs, NJ: Prentice-Hall), 1966, pp. 93–94, 238–246.

Schneidawind, John. "Firm Connects on VideoPhone," *USA Today,* January 8, 1992, p. 3B.

Spragins, Ellen E. "An Employee Newsletter with Zing," *Inc.* (April 1992), p. 121.

Walton, Sam, with John Huey. *Sam Walton: Made in America* (New York: Doubleday), 1992, pp. 247–248.

West, Phil. "Here's a Suggestion for Managers: Listen to the Employees," *Chicago Sun-Times,* September 12, 1991, p. 61.

G L O S S A R Y   O F   T E R M S

communication   The transmission of information and understanding from one person or group to another.

diction   The choice and use of words in speech and writing.

feedback   Information about the receiver's perception of the sender's message.

formal communication channels Management-designated pipelines used for official communication efforts. Formal communication channels run up, down, and across the organizational structure.

formal communication network An electronic link between people and their equipment and between people and databases.

grapevine *See* informal communicaton channels.

informal communication channels The informal networks that exist outside the formal channels. People use informal channels to transmit casual, personal, and social messages at work.

information Processed data that is useful to the receiver.

interpersonal communication Face-to-face or voice-to-voice (telephone) conversations that take place in real time and allow instant feedback.

jargon The specialized technical language of a trade, profession, subculture, or other group.

medium The means by which a sender transmits a message.

message The information that the sender wants to transmit.

noise Anything in the environment of a communication that interferes with the sending and receiving of messages.

nonverbal communication Images, actions, and behaviors that transmit messages.

perceptions Ways in which people observe and bases for their judgments about the stimuli they experience.

receiver The person or group for whom a communication effort is intended.

semantics The study of the meanings of words.

sender The person or group that initiates the communication process.

stereotype Predetermined belief about a group of people.

understanding The situation that exists when all senders and receivers agree about the meaning and intent of a message.

C A S E   P R O B L E M
The Gap

he Gap is a highly successful chain of 1,200 retail clothing stores that offer shoppers a clean, well-lighted place to buy colorful, comfortable clothes. Founder and chairman Donald G. Fisher started The Gap in 1969 as a store where customers could buy jeans that fit. He added clothes under his store brand and displayed them on pipe racks, but found that he could sell them at discount prices only. In 1983 Fisher sought help from Mickey Drexler, then ex-president of Ann Taylor Stores.

Drexler began by restructuring The Gap. Deciding that the merchandise didn't sell because it was of poor quality, Drexler promoted a new approach: He instructed designers to create clothes that they would want to wear. Rather than relying on quantitative models, he made product decisions based on intuition—and then pulled goods that didn't sell. He threw out the pipe racks and junky clothes and emphasized jeans and sweats. He placed the goods along wide aisles and within easy reach of customers. He then boosted quality with the already established network of suppliers. Today 200 quality control inspectors check goods in factories in 40 countries. By controlling design, materials, and manufacturing, The Gap manages to create high-quality goods at low cost. It uses an automated distribution center to funnel clothes to its retail outlets.

Drexler stays in close touch with his company's stores and New York designers. He tries to balance the designers' ideas about what will sell with his own and those of store managers. Every eight weeks a new line enters the stores. The leftovers end up in a markdown section. The stores now carry only the company's brand of clothes, including shoes and baby clothes, and The Gap is planning new products for adults, such as lines of neckties and sportcoats. In 1986, frustrated about the poor selections in kids' fashions, Drexler launched GapKids, a spinoff chain consisting of 215 stores. The Gap has also established stores in England and Canada.

Today the company is so big and growing so fast that bureaucracy could become a problem. But Drexler is no stranger to bureaucracies. He fought them at Bloomingdale's and Saks Fifth Avenue, and he is likely to do so again, at The Gap.

Q U E S T I O N S

1. One of the secrets to The Gap's success is president Mickey Drexler's intuition about which fashions will sell. Do you see a potential problem with this? If so, what is it?

2. In what ways has being tied so closely with suppliers been important to The Gap?

3. What do you think of the company's strategy of introducing new lines every eight weeks? What are some advantages and disadvantages?

4. What led to the establishment of GapKids?

For more about The Gap, see Russell Mitchell, "The Gap," *Business Week,* March 9, 1992, pp. 58–64.

Human Motivation

LEARNING OBJECTIVES

After reading and discussing this chapter, you should be able to:

- Define this chapter's essential terms

- Discuss the factors that stimulate and influence motivation

- Differentiate between content and process theories of motivation

- List the five levels of needs according to Maslow and give an example of each

- Discuss the impact of hygiene and motivation factors in the work environment

- Explain the characteristics of a person with high achievement needs

- Identify the needs associated with ERG theory

- Discuss the relationship between expectations and motivation

- Explain the relationship between reinforcement and motivation

- Explain how equity influences motivation

- Explain how goals influence motivation

- Discuss the importance of a manager's philosophy of management in creating a positive work environment

- Describe how managers can structure the environment to provide motivation

M A N A G E M E N T   I N   A C T I O N
Omni Hotels Thrive on Empowerment

Five years ago, senior managers at Omni Hotels were unhappy with two situations: (1) low customer satisfaction as revealed in customer comment cards and (2) high employee turnover. These obstacles to improving performance became twin challenges. Omni's solution was an unconventional one: to establish an empowerment program to give frontline employees the tools and the authority to solve customer problems themselves.

To develop this motivated environment, Omni created three programs. The first element, Omni Service Tradition (OST), gave first-line employees, department by department, an opportunity to address the problems that customers cited in their comment cards. The OST meetings also provided a forum for improving the communication process required in finding cross-departmental solutions.

On the front lines, Omni employees are encouraged to think on their feet to solve guest problems and to provide better service.

The second program was designed to create a pervasive corporate culture that would permeate all levels of the organization. With this in mind, the company created Omni Service Champions (OSC), "a comprehensive approach to recognizing and rewarding hourly employees who demonstrate exemplary commitment to serving customers and fellow employees." The OSC program singles out those employees who are "naturals"—able to help others in a smooth and easy way—in delivering service. The program includes medals for employees who are commended, over half a million dollars in cash prizes, and trips. It is, in essence, an incentive program for frontline employees.

The third element, and the one most responsible for success, is the program called Power of One, which fosters independent thinking on the part of frontline employees. The program outlines 19 guidelines for autonomous employee behavior that boosts service. One guideline, for example, is "Make decisions that benefit the guests: Bend the rules sometimes." Every employee, from top to bottom, received orientation in the Power of One principles. They viewed videos, participated in workbook sessions, and received a pocket card that listed the 19 behavior models.

To date, Power of One has succeeded in improving guest satisfaction by 25%. And the employee turnover rate has dropped from 65% to 42%. In light of industry statistics, the improvement is nothing short of staggering. ▲

❝ Make decisions that benefit the guests: Bend the rules sometimes. ❞

— From the **Power of One** guidelines, Omni Hotels

For more about Omni Hotels, see Joy Lesser, "From the Bottom Up: A Toast to Empowerment," *Management Review,* May 1992, pp. 2–4.

The Challenge of Motivation

What do Southwest Airlines, Chili's restaurants, Chaparral Steel, and Omni Hotels have in common? One answer is success. Although these organizations offer different products in different marketplaces, they all have become successful. But if you entered each workplace, you would notice another important similarity. In each organization, the morale is excellent. **Morale** is the attitude, or feelings, the workers have about the organization and their total work life (Straub and Attner, 1991). The CEOs of each company and their management teams have created a positive work environment. In their own unique way, each organization has taken steps to enhance the **quality of work life** (**QWL**) (Case, 1992). QWL efforts focus on

Exhibit 12.1

Factors that enhance the quality of work life.

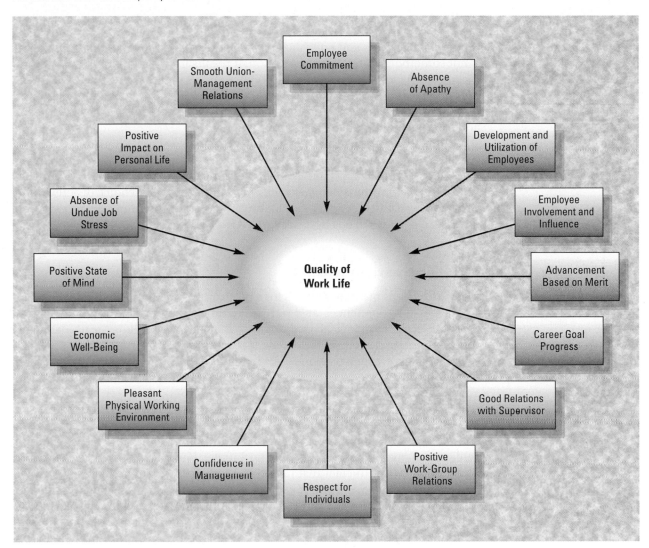

enhancing workers' dignity, improving their physical and emotional well-being, and enhancing the satisfaction individuals achieve in the workplace. By developing a positive work environment, management teams can capture the commitment of their employees. The result is employees who are truly motivated—they want to do their jobs well. Such commitment, combined with the skill to do the job, creates an energetic, highly competent labor force to work in partnership with management. Exhibit 12.1 shows the factors that enhance the quality of work life.

The managers at Southwest Airlines, Chili's, Chaparral Steel, and Omni Hotels have met one of the great management challenges: They have discovered how to motivate employees. These managers recognized that motivation is not magic, but a set of processes that influence behavioral choices (Steers and Porter, 1987).

The Basics of Motivation

Modern researchers and enlightened managers have discovered that motivation is not something that is done to a person. It results from a combination of factors, including an individual's needs, the ability to make choices, and an environment that provides the opportunity to satisfy those needs and to make those choices. **Motivation** is the result of the interaction between a person's internalized needs and external influences that determine behavior.

People make conscious decisions for their own welfare. Why do you do what you do? Why do you choose to go to school and someone else does not? Why do you choose to study hard and someone else does not? The study of motivation concerns what prompts people to act, what influences their choice of action, and why they persist in acting in a certain way. The starting point in such a study is to examine a person's needs by using a motivation model.

The Motivation Model

A person's needs provide the basis for a motivation model. **Needs** are deficiencies that a person experiences at a particular time. They can be physiological or psychological. Physiological needs relate to the body and include the needs for air, water, and food. Psychological needs include the needs for affiliation and self-esteem. Needs create a tension (stimulus) that results in wants. The person then develops a behavior or set of behaviors to satisfy the wants. The behavior results in action toward goal achievement (Davis and Newstrom, 1992).

Exhibit 12.2 offers a rudimentary example of the motivation model. A person feels hunger (a need). Recognition of the need triggers a want (food). The person chooses to cook a hamburger (behavior) and then he eats it (he takes action to achieve the goal). Satisfied, he feels no hunger (feedback). When the model is modified to reflect the fact that behavior is subject to many influences, it grows more complex. Why did the person in the example choose a hamburger, not cereal? Why did he prepare the hamburger himself instead of buying it? Has the person previously practiced the behavior? If so, did it satisfy the need? The integrated motivation model—by addressing more complex influences on motivational choices—provides these explanations.

The Integrated Motivation Model

Unsatisfied needs stimulate wants and behaviors. In choosing a behavior to satisfy a need, a person must evaluate several factors:

1. Past experiences. All the person's past experiences with the situation at hand enter into the motivation model. These include the satisfaction derived from acting in a certain way, any frustration felt, the amount of effort required, and the relationship of performance to rewards.

Exhibit 12.2

The basic motivation model.

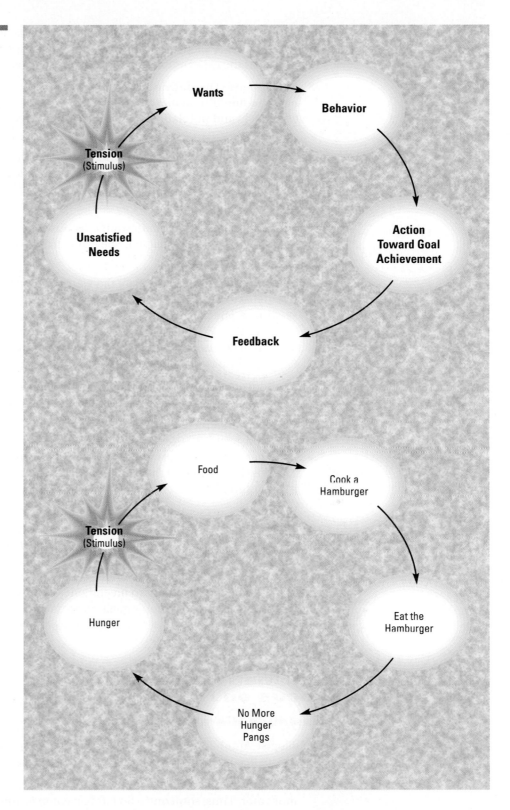

2. Environmental influences. The choices of behaviors are affected by the environment, which in a business setting comprises the organization's values as well as the expectations and actions of management.

3. Perceptions. The individual is influenced by perceptions of the expected effort required to achieve performance, and the value of the reward both absolutely and in relation to what peers have received for the same effort.

In addition to these three variables, two other factors are at work: skills and incentives. Skills are a person's performance capabilities; they result from training. Incentives are factors created by managers to encourage workers to perform a task.

Look at the motivation process again, this time from a business perspective:

1. Unsatisfied needs stimulate wants. In this situation, a first-level manager feels the need to be respected. She wants to be recognized by her boss as an outstanding employee.

2. Behavior is identified to satisfy the want. The first-level manager identifies two behaviors that can satisfy the want: volunteering to write a report or seeking a special project. To consider which behavior to choose, she consciously evaluates the rewards or punishments associated with the performance (incentives); her abilities to accomplish the activities identified (skills); and past experiences, environmental influences, and perceptions.

3. The individual takes action. Based on her analysis, the first-level manager selects what she considers the best option (behavior) and then takes action.

4. The individual receives feedback. The response the manager gets from her boss constitutes the feedback in this case. If the response is positive, the manager has done more than help the first-level manager meet her need. The boss has increased the likelihood that the manager will behave similarly in the future.

Exhibit 12.3 presents the integrated motivation model, which shows how experience, environment, and perceptions influence decision making.

The integrated motivation model is useful in exploring theories of motivation in two categories: content and process. Content theories emphasize the needs that motivate people. If managers understand workers' needs, they can include factors in the work environment to meet them, thereby helping direct employees' energies toward the organization's goals. Process theories explain how employees choose behaviors to meet their needs and how they determine whether their choices are successful (Daft, 1991).

Content Theories: Motivation Theories That Focus on Needs

Maslow's Hierarchy of Needs

Psychologist Abraham H. Maslow (1943) based his study of motivation on a hierarchy of needs. His theory is based on four premises:

1. Only an unsatisfied need can influence behavior; a satisfied need is not a motivator. Thus, someone who has just eaten is unlikely to want food until the hunger need arises again.

Exhibit 12.3

The integrated motivation model.

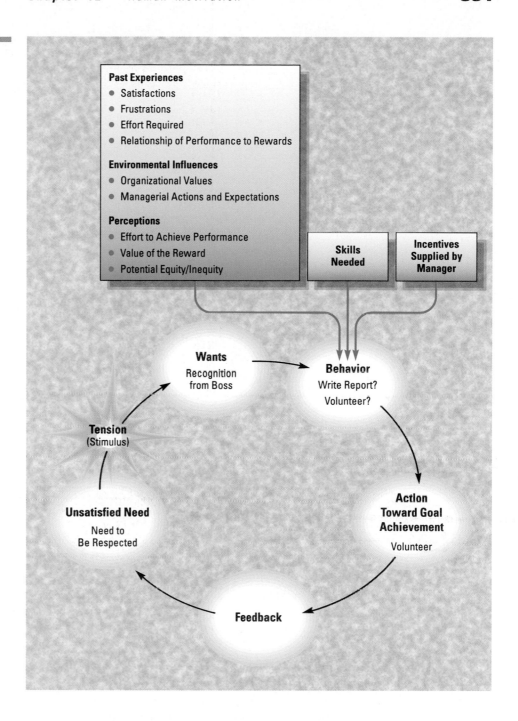

2. A person's needs are arranged in a priority order of importance. The hierarchy goes from the most basic needs (such as water or shelter) to the most complex (esteem and self-actualization).

3. A person will at least minimally satisfy each level of need before feeling the need at the next level. Someone must feel companionship before desiring recognition.

Exhibit 12.4

Abraham Maslow's hierarchy of human needs.

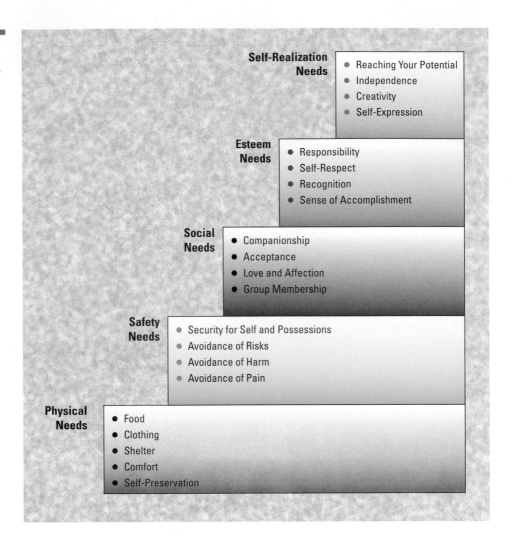

4. If need satisfaction is not maintained at any level, the unsatisfied need will become a priority once again. For example, for a person who is presently feeling social needs, safety will become a priority once again if he or she is fired.

The Five Levels of Needs   Exhibit 12.4 displays Maslow's hierarchy of needs. The exhibit lists the needs in order of priority, from bottom to top. The first category is composed of physiological (physical) needs. These are the primary, or basic-level, needs: the needs for water, air, food, shelter, and comfort. In the working environment, managers try to satisfy these needs by providing salaries and wages that allow employees to buy the basic necessities. While the employee is at work the manager meets these needs by providing water fountains, clean air, no objectionable odors or noises, comfortable temperatures, and lunch breaks.

When physiological needs are met to the individual's satisfaction, the next priority becomes safety—the need to avoid bodily harm and uncertainty about one's well-being. Safety is closely allied to security, the freedom from risk or danger. Behaviors that reflect safety needs include joining unions, seeking jobs with tenure, and choosing jobs on the basis of health insurance and retirement programs. All of us desire a work environment in which we can be free from threats to our physical and emotional sense of security (Maslow, 1943). Managers attempt to satisfy safety needs by providing salary, benefits, safe work conditions, and job security.

Social needs become dominant when safety needs have been minimally gratified. People desire friendship, companionship, and a place in a group. Love needs include the needs for giving and receiving love (Maslow, 1943). At work employees meet social needs by interacting frequently with fellow workers and through acceptance by others. The typical conversation at the water cooler reflects employees' needs to interact socially as well as in their official business roles. The groups that employees form at lunchtime are also a result of their need to be social. Managers can meet these needs by supporting employee get-togethers—birthday parties, lunches, and sports teams.

The next level in the hierarchy, esteem needs, includes the desire for self-respect and for the recognition of one's abilities by others. Satisfaction of these needs gives pride, self-confidence, and a genuine sense of importance. Lack of satisfaction of these needs can result in feelings of inferiority, weakness, and helplessness. Work-related activities and outcomes that help meet individual esteem needs include successfully completing projects, being recognized by peers and superiors as someone who makes valuable contributions, and acquiring organizational titles. Sam Walton of Wal-Mart recognized the importance of this need in creating Sam's Rules for Building a Business. In Walton's words: "Rule 5: Appreciate everything your associates do for the business…nothing else can substitute for a few well-chosen, well-timed, sincere words of praise" (Trimble, 1992). At Omni Hotels, the Omni Service Champions program helps employees meet esteem needs.

Maslow's highest need level, self-realization, relates to the desire for fulfillment. Self-realization (also called self-actualization) represents the need to maximize the use of one's skills, abilities, and potential. If an employee wants a college degree, a manager can help meet the employee's need by providing a flexible work schedule, tuition reimbursement, and opportunities to apply classroom theory on the job.

Implications for Managers   Maslow's needs theory applies to all environments, not specifically to the workplace. Nevertheless, it presents a workable motivation framework for managers. By analyzing employees' comments, attitudes, quality and quantity of work, and personal circumstances, the manager can identify the particular need level that individual workers are attempting to satisfy. Then the manager can attempt to build into the work environment opportunities that will allow individuals to satisfy their needs. Exhibit 12.5 lists five common circumstances and the needs that are likely to accompany them. The exhibit also lists ways the manager can facilitate need satisfaction.

Because people are unique in their perceptions and personalities, applying the needs theory poses some difficulties. Just as one motive may lead to different behaviors, similar behavior in individuals can spring from different motives. The act of working hard on a new project, for instance, can arise from many needs.

Exhibit 12.5

Five common worker needs and appropriate managerial responses.

Workers' Circumstances	Levels of Need Demanding Satisfaction	Need-Satisfying Actions
Employee has two children entering college next year	Physiological/Safety	Increase pay or train and promote employee to higher-paying job if justified; confirm job security.
Worker feels concern about a competitor's purchase of the firm	Safety	If possible, reassure worker that jobs will not be eliminated; otherwise, frankly admit that certain jobs will be abolished. Encourage and assist those affected to seek employment elsewhere.
Worker feels uncomfortable as a new addition in a closely knit work group	Social	Invite subordinates to a social evening at your home, creating an opportunity for the newcomer to meet peers in an informal setting. Encourage the new worker to participate in company recreational activities. Sponsor the new worker for membership in professional organizations.
Employee feels unappreciated	Ego/self-esteem	Examine the employee's job performance and find reasons for praise. Accept the employee's suggestions where applicable. Build closer rapport.
Worker wants to get ahead in the organization and has a general idea of an ultimate employment goal in the company	Self-realization/ self-actualization	Provide specific guidance in pinpointing ultimate goal; help chart career path. Facilitate educational improvement. Provide opportunities for job experience and company recognition.

Some people apply themselves in order to grow and develop; others do so to be liked. Still others wish to earn more money to enhance their sense of security. And yet others want the recognition that success will bring. For this reason, managers must use care when assessing motives simply by observing behavior.

An unmet need can frustrate an employee. It will continue to influence his or her behavior until it is satisfied, either on the job or off. The means of satisfaction might mesh with the organization's goals and processes. On the other hand, it could compete or even conflict with them. The esteem need, for example, can be satisfied by involvement with work-related groups or groups outside the work environment.

The level of need satisfaction constantly fluctuates. Once a need is satisfied, it ceases to influence behavior only for a time. Needs do not remain fully satisfied over the long term.

Herzberg's Two-Factor Theory

Psychologist Frederick Herzberg (1975) and his associates developed a needs theory called the two-factor, or hygiene-motivator, theory. Herzberg's theory defines one set of factors that lead to job dissatisfaction; these factors are called hygiene factors. The theory also defines a set of factors that produce job satisfaction and motivation; these factors are called motivators.

Hygiene Factors   According to Herzberg, a manager's poor handling of **hygiene factors** (often referred to as maintenance factors) is the primary cause of unhappiness on the job. Hygiene factors are extrinsic to the job—that is, they do not relate directly to a person's actual work activity. Hygiene factors are part of a job's environment; they are part of the context of the job, not its content. When the hygiene factors that an employer provides are of low quality, employees feel job dissatisfaction. When the factors are of sufficient quality, they do not necessarily act as motivators. High-quality hygiene factors are not necessarily stimuli for growth or greater effort. They lead only to employees' lack of job dissatisfaction (Herzberg, 1975). Hygiene factors include:

- Salary. To prevent job dissatisfaction, a manager should provide adequate wages, salaries, and fringe benefits.

- Job security. Company grievance procedures and seniority privileges contribute to high-quality hygiene.

- Working conditions. Managers ensure adequate heat, light, ventilation, and hours of work to prevent dissatisfaction.

- Status. Managers who are mindful of the importance of hygiene factors provide privileges, job titles, and other symbols of rank and position.

- Company policies. To prevent job dissatisfaction, managers should provide policies as guidelines for behavior and administer the policies fairly.

- Quality of technical supervision. When employees are not able to receive answers to job-related questions, they become frustrated. Providing high-quality technical supervision for employees prevents frustration.

- Quality of interpersonal relations among peers, supervisors, and subordinates. In an organization with high-quality hygiene factors, the workplace provides social opportunities as well as the chance to enjoy comfortable work-related relationships.

Motivation Factors   According to Herzberg, **motivation factors** are the primary cause of job satisfaction. They are intrinsic to a job and relate directly to the real nature of the work people perform. In other words, motivation factors relate to job content. When an employer fails to provide motivation factors, employees experience no job satisfaction. With motivation factors, employees enjoy job satisfaction and provide high performance. Different people require different kinds and degrees of motivation factors—what stimulates one worker may not affect another. Motivation factors also act as stimuli for psychological and personal growth. These factors include:

- Achievement. The opportunity to accomplish something or contribute something of value can serve as a source of job satisfaction.

- Recognition. Wise managers let employees know that their efforts have been worthwhile and that management notes and appreciates them.

- Responsibility. The potential for acquiring new duties and responsibilities, either through job expansion or delegation, can be a powerful motivator for some workers.

- Advancement. The opportunity to improve one's position as a result of job performance gives employees a clear reason for high performance.

- The work itself. When a task offers the opportunity for self-expression, personal satisfaction, and meaningful challenge, employees are likely to undertake the task with enthusiasm.

- Possibility of growth. The opportunity to increase knowledge and personal development is likely to lead to job satisfaction.

Exhibit 12.6 illustrates the hygiene and motivation factors. The hygiene factors relate to responses that range from no dissatisfaction to high dissatisfaction. The motivators, if present in the work environment, can provide low to high satisfaction. If not present, no satisfaction can result.

Implications for Managers   Herzberg's theory relates specifically to the work environment. Managers can use their knowledge of hygiene factors and

Exhibit 12.6

The results of hygiene factors and motivation factors.

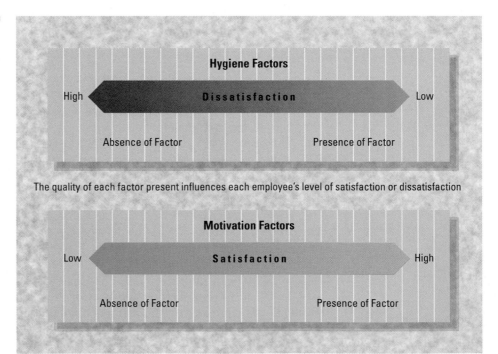

motivation factors to build an environment that supports high achievement and boosts morale.

Note that nearly all supervisors have the power to heighten the motivation factors in the workplaces they manage. They can do this by granting more responsibility to employees, praising their accomplishments, and making them feel that they are succeeding. Top managers at Du Pont, Tandem Computer, Southwest Airlines, and countless other companies have come to the same conclusion: Motivated employees believe they have control over their jobs and that they can make a contribution (Wilson, 1992). This belief provides the basis for team management, empowerment, and intrepreneurship—all to be explored later in this chapter.

McClelland and the Need for Achievement

David McClelland (1971) developed a needs theory that holds that certain types of needs are learned during a lifetime of interaction with the environment. McClelland's three needs relate to:

- Achievement, or the desire to excel or achieve in relation to a set of standards

- Power, or the desire to control others or have influence over them

- Affiliation, the desire for friendship, cooperation, and close interpersonal relationships

Achievement relates to individual performance. Power and affiliation, on the other hand, involve interpersonal relationships.

Studies of achievement motivation have produced two important ideas: (1) A strong achievement need relates to how well individuals are motivated to perform their work, and (2) the achievement need can be strengthened by training.

McClelland's needs theory recognizes that people may have different mixtures or combinations of the needs; an individual could be described as a high achiever, a power-motivated person, or an affiliator.

The High Achiever   McClelland and an associate, David Burnham (1976), defined the characteristics of the high achiever. They believed the high achiever:

- Performs a task because of a compelling need for personal achievement, not necessarily for the rewards associated with accomplishing the task. The desire to excel applies to both means and end; the high achiever wants to do the job more efficiently than it has been done before as well as do a good job.

- Prefers to take personal responsibility for solving problems rather than leave the outcome to others. Achievers may be viewed as loners. At times they may appear to have difficulty delegating authority.

- Prefers to set moderate goals that, with stretching, are achievable. For the achiever, easy goals with a high probability of success provide no challenge and thus no satisfaction. Difficult goals with a low probability of success would require an achiever to gamble on success.

Because the achiever likes to be in control, an outcome that depends on chance is unacceptable.

- Prefers immediate and concrete feedback about performance, which assists in measuring progress toward the goal. The feedback needs to be in terms of goal performance (rather than personality variables) so the achiever can determine what needs to be done to improve performance.

The Power-Motivated Person   The person with a strong desire for power needs to acquire, exercise, and maintain influence over others. Such persons compete with others if success will allow them to be dominant. The power-motivated person does not avoid confrontations.

The Affiliator   The person with a high need for affiliation wants to be liked by other people, attempts to establish friendships, and seeks to avoid conflict. The affiliator prefers conciliation.

Implications for Managers   Based on McClelland's theory, managers should work to identify and develop high achievers. Managers can help high achievers set goals and fulfill their desire for responsibility by allowing them to participate, delegating authority to them, and using management by objectives (see Chapter 4). To work effectively with high achievers, managers should provide immediate, concrete feedback.

Managers should recognize that the use of power is a necessary part of corporate life and that those who are motivated by power can serve a necessary and useful part in an organization. Managers must be aware, however, of the negative aspect of power as a motivator: Many who seek power seek it solely for personal benefit. The power-motivated person may not, therefore, have the organization's best interests at heart. In working with employees who are affiliators, managers must be aware that the employees' desire to avoid conflict may prevent them from handling organizational conflict effectively.

Exhibit 12.7 shows how the three needs theories relate. Each theory provides the manager with a different viewpoint from which to understand the cause of behavior. Herzberg's hygiene factors relate to Maslow's lower-level needs; Herzberg's motivation factors relate to the higher-level needs, as do McClelland's needs for power and achievement.

Alderfer's ERG Theory

Clayton Alderfer (1972) proposed a needs theory that compressed Maslow's five need levels into three. The three need levels of Alderfer's theory are:

- Existence. Existence needs relate to a person's physical well-being. (In terms of Maslow's model, existence needs include physiological and safety needs.)

- Relatedness. This level includes needs for satisfactory relationships with others. (Relatedness needs correspond, in terms of Maslow's model, to social needs.)

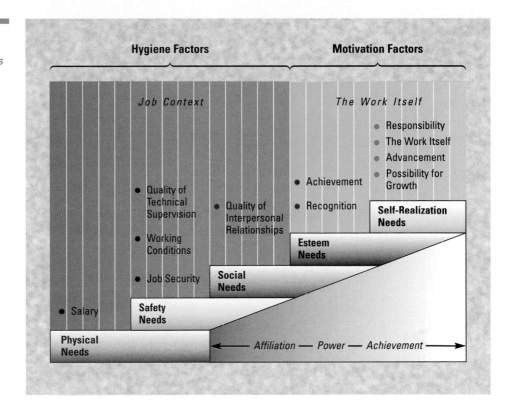

- Growth. Growth needs call for the realization of potential and the achievement of competence. (In terms of Maslow's model, growth needs include esteem and self-realization needs.)

The name of Alderfer's theory is the **ERG theory**. The name derives from the first three letters of each of the needs Alderfer defined.

Maslow and Alderfer agreed that an unsatisfied need is a motivator and that, as lower-level needs are satisfied, they become less important. But Alderfer believed that higher-level needs become more important as they are satisfied. If a person is frustrated at attaining more of a need, the individual might return to a lower-level need. For example, the employee frustrated in an attempt to achieve more growth could re-direct energies to, say, becoming part of a group. When high-tech, computer-related businesses in the Silicon Valley began to retrench after a period of expansion, managers who had been focusing on furthering their growth needs began to seek new organizations to meet their existence needs.

Exhibit 12.8 illustrates the relationship between the theories of Maslow and Alderfer.

Implications for Managers   According to Alderfer, managers should realize that a person can voluntarily move down the needs hierarchy if attempts to achieve needs are frustrated. To maintain high levels of performance, managers should provide opportunities for employees to capitalize on the increased importance of higher-level needs.

Exhibit 12.8

A comparison of the theories of Maslow and Alderfer.

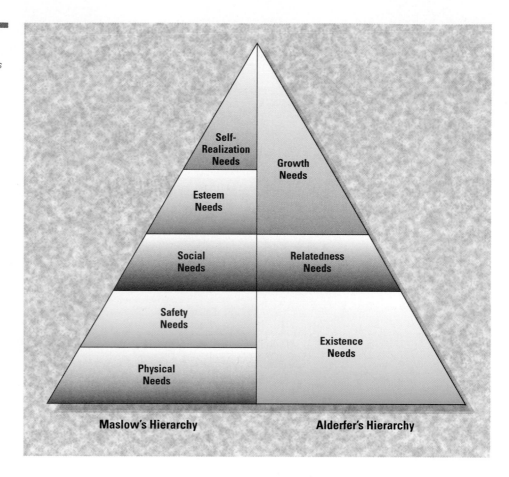

Process Theories: Motivation Theories That Focus on Behaviors

Now that you have examined four motivation theories relating to the individual's needs, you can explore four theories about why people choose a particular behavior to satisfy their needs. This section will discuss four behavior-oriented theories: expectancy theory, reinforcement theory, equity theory, and goal-setting theory. Each derives from the factors summarized in Exhibit 12.3: past experiences, environmental influences, and perceptions.

Expectancy Theory

Developed by Victor Vroom (1964), **expectancy theory** states that, before choosing a behavior, an individual will evaluate various possibilities on the basis of anticipated work and reward. Motivation—the spur to act—is a function of how badly we want something and how likely we think we are to get it. Its intensity functions in direct proportion to perceived or expected rewards. Expectancy theory includes three variables:

- Effort-performance link. Will the effort achieve performance? How much effort will performance require? How probable is success?

I S S U E S   A N D   E T H I C S
The Problem with Valuable Employees

The **secret** to a manager's success is a highly productive, well-performing department. A manager who has created an environment where people are motivated and productive often develops star employees. Then he or she finds that the stellar talent attracts the attention of those in other departments. The manager receives queries, off the record: Would the employee be interested in a move to a new job in another functional unit? The new position may well represent a growth opportunity for the employee. If the move represents a significant loss for the employee's current manager, however, the current manager may choose not to tell the star employee about the opportunity.

Is it ethical not to tell an employee about a growth opportunity in another department? Why? If you were a manager who had a number of talented employees, would your answer be different? Why? What can a manager do to make the loss of star talent less of a problem? ▲

- Performance-reward link. What is the possibility that a certain performance will produce the desired reward or outcome?

- Attractiveness. How attractive is the reward? This factor relates to the strength or importance of the reward to the individual and deals with his or her unsatisfied needs.

To see how expectancy theory can be applied, consider an example. Suppose that, late one Friday afternoon, John Friedman's boss asks him to develop a presentation of six-month budget results. The presentation is due the following Monday. John realizes he can complete the four-hour project in one of two ways: He can stay at the office and do the work, or he can take the work home over the weekend.

John evaluates the first option, staying at work for the needed four hours. He realizes that staying will result in a completed presentation by Monday (effort-performance link). He knows from past experience that a completed project will result in recognition from his boss (performance-reward link). John has a high regard for this recognition, because it will eventually lead to a promotion. Working late on Friday will, however, interfere with existing plans and may cause domestic problems. (The domestic problems affect the attractiveness of the reward.)

As John evaluates the second option, taking work home, he realizes that the effort-performance link and the performance-reward link will be the same as in option 1. But, by taking the work home, John can avoid the negative consequences of interfering with social plans. (This makes the reward seem more attractive.) John chooses the second option.

In his decision making, John asked himself a series of questions. "Can I accomplish the task?" Yes, it will take four hours, but I can do it. "What's in it for me?" When I do the task it can bring both positive and negative results (option 1) or just positive results (option 2). "Is it worth it?" The positive is, but the negative isn't. Study Exhibit 12.9 and determine the stage of the expectancy theory to which each question pertains.

Exhibit 12.9

A model of expectancy theory.

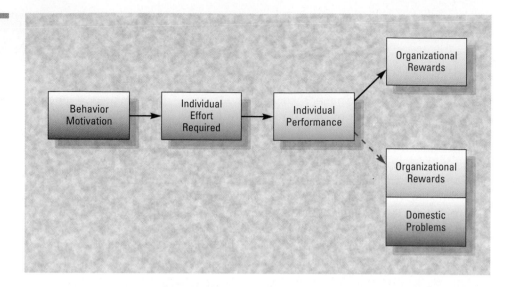

Implications for Managers   According to expectancy theory, behavior is heavily influenced by perceptions of the outcomes of behavior. The individual who expects an outcome, possesses the competence to achieve it, and wants it badly enough, will exhibit the behavior required by the organization. The person who expects that a specific behavior will produce an outcome perceived as undesirable will be less inclined to exhibit that behavior. A manager who knows each subordinate's expectations and desires can tailor outcomes associated with specific behaviors to produce motivation (Vroom, 1964; Porter and Lawler, 1968). To motivate behavior, managers must:

- Understand that employees measure the value associated with the assignment. As a manager, you get from your people what you reward, not what you ask for.

- Find out what outcomes are perceived as desirable by employees and provide them. Outcomes may be intrinsic (experienced directly by the individual) or extrinsic (provided by the company). A feeling of self-worth after doing a good job is intrinsic; the promotion that the job produces is extrinsic. For an outcome to be satisfying to an employee, the employee must recognize it as an outcome that relates to his or her needs and one that is consistent with his or her expectations of what is due (Schuler, 1987).

- Make the job intrinsically rewarding. If this is a valued outcome, it is critical for managers to provide experiences that enhance an employee's feeling of self-worth.

- Effectively and clearly communicate desired behaviors and their outcomes. Employees need to know what is acceptable and what is unacceptable to the organization.

- Link rewards to performance. Once the acceptable performance level is attained, rewards should quickly follow.

Exhibit 12.10

How the reinforcement process affects behavior.

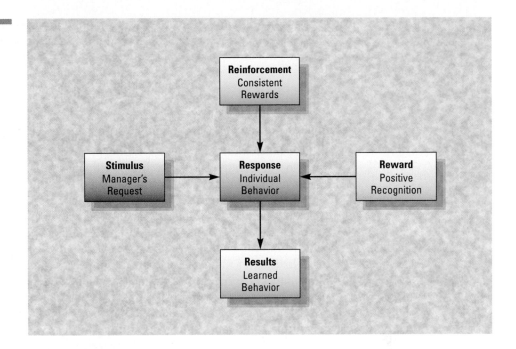

- Be aware that people and their goals, needs, desires, and levels of performance differ. The manager must set a level of performance for each employee that is attainable by that person.

- Strengthen each individual's perceptions of his or her ability to execute desired behaviors and achieve outcomes by providing guidance and direction.

Reinforcement Theory

Another theory that examines the reasons for behavior has foundations in the work of B. F. Skinner (1969) in regard to operant conditioning. **Reinforcement theory** holds that a person's behavior in a situation is influenced by the rewards or penalties experienced in similar situations in the past. John, the employee who was faced with the task of preparing a budget presentation, received praise from his boss for expending extra effort in the past. This positive reinforcement influenced John's behavior when the boss had another last-minute request.

Reinforcement theory introduces a major point that managers should understand: Much of motivated behavior is learned behavior (Tarpy, 1974). The employee learns over time what type of performance is acceptable and what is unacceptable. This learning influences future behavior. Exhibit 12.10 shows how reinforcement affects behavior.

Types of Reinforcement Managers can choose from four main types of reinforcement: positive reinforcement, avoidance, extinction, and punishment. Of these four approaches, positive reinforcement most often leads to long-range growth in individuals by producing lasting and positive behavioral changes.

To increase the probability that an individual will repeat a desired behavior, a manager provides positive reinforcement after desired behavior occurs. Positive reinforcers can be praise, pay, or promotions—elements normally regarded as favorable by employees. The Omni Service Champions program offers the positive reinforcers of medals and prizes.

Avoidance attempts to increase the probability that a positive behavior will be repeated by showing the consequences of behavior the manager does not desire. The employee is allowed to avoid those consequences by displaying the desired behavior. For example, a manager has a policy of penalizing all employees who do not turn in reports on time. As long as the threat of punishment is there, employees will be motivated to turn in reports on time.

Extinction consists of ignoring the behavior of subordinates in order to weaken the behavior. Managers can use this approach when behavior is temporary, atypical, and not serious in terms of its negative consequences. The supervisor's hope is that the behavior will soon go away or disappear if ignored.

Extinction might be appropriate in a situation of changed circumstances. Say a manager and an employee have developed the habit of talking during working hours about off-the-job topics. After the manager is promoted to another job in another area, the employee continues to drop by, a practice that makes the manager uncomfortable. If the manager continues to work while the employee is there, the employee will eventually get the message and the behavior will be extinguished.

Punishment is an attempt to decrease the recurrence of a behavior by applying negative consequences. Loss of privileges, docked pay, and suspensions are forms of punishment. The trouble with punishment as a response to behavior is that the person will learn what not to do, but will not necessarily learn the desired behavior.

Reinforcement is affected by time. The closer the reinforcement is to the behavior, the greater the impact it will have on future behavior.

Implications for Managers   Reinforcement theory has several implications for managers. First, managers should bear in mind that motivated behavior is influenced by learning what is acceptable and unacceptable to the organization (Hamner, 1974).

In addition, in working with employees to develop motivated behavior, managers should:

- Tell individuals what they can do to get positive reinforcement. The establishment of a work standard lets all individuals know what behavior is acceptable.

- Tell individuals what they are doing wrong. The person who does not know why rewards are not forthcoming may be confused. Information allows a person to improve motivated behavior.

- Base rewards on performance. Managers should not reward all individuals in the same way. If the manager gives the same rewards to all employees for all performances, he or she loses motivational opportunities.

- Administer the reinforcement as close in time to the related behavior as possible. To achieve maximum impact, the appropriate reinforcement should immediately follow performance.

- Recognize that failure to reward can also modify behavior. If a manager does not praise a subordinate for meritorious behavior, the subordinate can become confused about the behavior the manager wants.

Equity Theory

Another view of motivation, **equity theory**, states that peoples' behavior relates to their perception of the fairness of treatment they receive. Most professional athletes use equity arguments to support their salary demands. They point to publicized salaries received by peers as justification for their negotiating stands. But equity theory also involves the fairness that an individual perceives in the relationship between effort expended and reward.

People determine equity by calculating a simple ratio: the effort they are expected to invest on the job (their input) in relation to what they expect to receive after investing that effort (their outcome or reward). As Exhibit 12.11 shows, this input-outcome ratio should provide a means of comparison with the ratios of other individuals or groups. Equity exists when the ratios are equivalent. Inequity exists when, in the employee's mind, inputs exceed the relative or perceived values of outcomes (Adams, 1963).

Consider an example: Ellen McCann has been working as a salesperson for 10 months. In this time, she has gone to sales school three times (achieving superior ratings in all categories), consistently achieved 125% of sales quota, and won two local sales contests. In recognition of this achievement, Ellen's boss gave her a $150-per-month raise. Ellen's motivation has dropped noticeably in the past month, however. Why? She learned that a salesperson with no prior experience had been hired at $1,550 per month—$50 more than Ellen is making! As Ellen said, "It's not fair! If they can do that, I'm going to start to look around for an employer who will appreciate me."

This example leads to two points about equity theory. First, when an individual perceives himself or herself as the victim of inequity, one of three

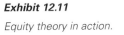

Exhibit 12.11

Equity theory in action.

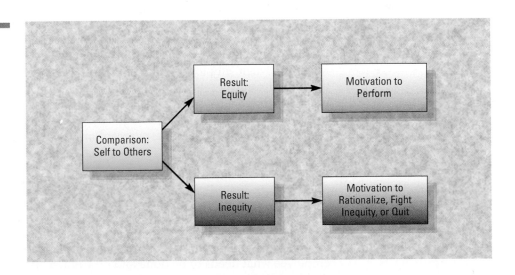

responses occurs. The person can decide to escape the situation ("I quit"), put the input-outcome ratios in balance ("I'll do less" or "I want a raise"), or attempt to change perceptions ("It's really fair because…").

The second important point about equity theory concerns the referent the person selects for comparison. There are two categories: other and system. In the example of professional athletes, the "other" category includes those persons in the same job, same company, or same profession or those with similar backgrounds or in the same circle of friends. The system is the referent when the individual recognizes the presence of organization-wide policies and procedures: "If those people are allowed overtime, I should have overtime when I need it to complete my work" (Goodman and Fredman, 1971).

Implications for Managers   Equity theory emphasizes that employees are motivated by absolute rewards and the relative rewards available in the system. More important, employees make conscious comparisons of equity that influence their motivation levels. Therefore, managers must make conscious efforts to establish and retain equity in the work environment. In addition, managers need to recognize that perceptions of equity are not a one-time occurrence. Present perceptions are affected by past perceptions. By bearing this in mind, a manager may be able to identify the incident that served as the straw that broke the camel's back.

Goal-Setting Theory

The fourth behavior-oriented theory, **goal-setting**, states that people's behavior is influenced by the goals that are established for them. In essence, goals tell an employee what needs to be done and how much effort will need to be expended (Robbins, 1991).

Goal-setting theory is similar to expectancy theory in that it focuses on the conscious choices a person makes. According to the theory, (1) managers should set goals for employees and (2) employees and managers should develop goals together.

Implications for Managers   According to goal-setting theory, managers should:

- Work with employees in setting goals to provide targets for motivation.

- Make goals specific rather than general. The goal of "Do your best" is not as effective as "Complete the project by June 15 with no budget overruns."

- Provide feedback on performance. Feedback acts as a guide to behavior. It helps identify shortcomings in performance and provides the means for corrective action.

Building a Philosophy of Management

The theories of Maslow, Herzberg, McClelland, and Alderfer offer valuable insight into the needs that trigger motivated behavior. The theories of expectancy, reinforcement, equity, and goal setting reveal the why of motivation—why employees display different types of motivated behavior. Each theory makes an important contribution to understanding the motivation of an employee, and each provides input for the motivation model.

Familiarity with theories of motivation allows a manager an educated viewpoint from which to consider how to develop motivated workers, capture commitment, and develop a positive work environment.

One significant factor that sets the foundation for creating a positive work environment is a manager's **philosophy of management**, or attitude about work and the people who do work. A manager's philosophy of management incorporates and reflects personal beliefs about human nature in the work setting—about worker attitudes and characteristics, employee maturity, and the influence of management expectations on employee behavior. A manager's philosophy influences the motivation approaches he or she will select. Managers who think subordinates are ambitious and eager, wish to do work well, want to be independent, and enjoy work will take far different actions than managers who think subordinates are lazy and work only to attain security.

To develop a philosophy of management, there are three concepts describing human nature that should be incorporated: Theory X and Theory Y, Argyris's maturity theory, and the development of expectations.

Theory X and Theory Y

Douglas McGregor (1960), a professor of industrial management, said that an individual's management philosophy reflects one of two sets of assumptions about workers. He called the two sets Theory X and Theory Y. Theory X is a philosophy of management with a negative perception of subordinates' potential for work and attitudes toward work. It assumes that subordinates dislike work, are poorly motivated, and require close supervision. A manager with these beliefs tends to control the group, use negative motivation, and refuse to delegate decision making. Exhibit 12.12 lists the components of Theory X.

Exhibit 12.12

Assumptions about workers according to Theory X and Theory Y.

Theory X	Theory Y
People basically dislike work and avoid it whenever possible.	Most people find work as natural as play or rest and develop an attitude toward work based on their experience with it.
Because most people dislike work, they have to be closely supervised and threatened with punishment to reach objectives.	People do not need to be threatened with punishment; they will work voluntarily toward organizational objectives to which they are committed.
Most people prefer to be told what to do, have little ambition, want to avoid responsibility, and want security above all else.	The average person working in an environment with good human relations will accept and seek responsibility.
Most people have little creativity. They are not capable of solving problems. Rather, they must be directed.	Most people possess a high degree of imagination, ingenuity, and creativity with which to solve organizational problems.
Most people have limited intellectual potential. Contributions above basic job performance should not be expected.	Although people have intellectual potential, modern industrial life utilizes only part of it.

Theory Y, on the other hand, is a philosophy of management with a positive perception of subordinates' potential for and attitudes toward work. It assumes, as Exhibit 12.12 shows, that subordinates can be self-directing, will seek responsibility, and find work as natural as play or rest. The outcome of this belief is a manager who encourages people to seek responsibility, involves people in decision making, and works with people to achieve their goals.

The important point about Theory X and Theory Y is that a management philosophy influences the type of work climate the manager endeavors to create and, ultimately, how the manager treats people.

Argyris's Maturity Theory

A manager's philosophy incorporates his or her attitude toward employee maturity. The work of Chris Argyris (1957) summarized these attitudes. Argyris related the

FOCUS ON QUALITY
Clothes Make the Team

At quality-obsessed factories, how do managers dress for success? Not in Armani suits or Ann Taylor dresses. To break down barriers between white- and blue-collar workers, many managers have shed their traditional forms of apparel.

The goal of this growing trend is to help establish the atmosphere of openness and democracy that is essential to quality programs. At the Bridgestone/Firestone plant in Warren County, Tennessee, everyone—workers and managers, men and women—wears identical shirts. The shirt, with blue and white stripes, has a name tag on the right side and the company logo on the left. The uniform symbolizes the view that, although people have different roles, everyone is equal. This seemingly minor change has produced two results: Employees have become more committed to the

Team uniforms *are a powerful way to build camaraderie. These Bridgestone/Firestone workers wear the company colors.*

organization, and they have embraced the concept of quality teams.

Another example of such democratic dressing emerged at Duke Power in North Carolina. As the result of a recommendation by a committee of employees, all hard hats are now white. The all-white approach replaces a scheme that used about 15 colors—welders wore green, meter readers yellow, and janitors blue, for example. The change has helped to eliminate an imposed status structure and led to implementation of cross-functional quality teams.

With quality as the goal, many companies are making changes. Some may relate to complex technology; others, such as the way people dress, are symbolic. Because symbolic actions affect the way people feel, they can have an important effect on the motivation of a work force. ▲

For more about the relationship between democratic dressing and quality, see Maurice Drake, "Dressing Down Helps Break Work Barriers," *USA Today*, June 19, 1992, p. 2B.

---

development of individual maturity to the structure of organizations. Argyris believed that people develop along a continuum from immaturity to maturity. People who have reached maturity:

- Tend to be active rather than passive

- Are independent rather than dependent

- Are self-aware rather than unaware

- Are self-controlled rather than controlled by others

Argyris's concern was that a mature personality conflicts with typical organizations in four ways:

- The formal chain of command limits self-determination, making individuals passive and manager dependent.

- The span of control decreases a person's self-determination.

- Unity of direction places objectives under the control of one manager. It limits the employee's ability to define objectives.

- Specialization of labor limits initiative and self-determination.

Managers who create work environments that are obstacles to mature employees set up themselves and their organizations for failure. Mature people confronted with rigid, limiting circumstances become passive and dependent. They cannot grow, and they can rarely see long-term implications. Recognition of these realities in recent years has fueled the growth of the movement to employee empowerment, which this chapter will discuss later.

The Development of Expectations

In developing a philosophy of management, a manager must consider the importance of expectations. A manager must communicate his or her expectations directly to employees. John L. Single (1980) reports that:

- Subordinates do what they believe they are expected to do.

- Ineffective managers fail to develop high expectations for performance.

- Managers perceived as excellent create high expectations that their employees can fulfill.

The last point, that employees fulfill their manager's expectations, is often referred to as the self-fulfilling prophecy. It is a key management concept. Sam Walton believed in it so much that it became "Rule 3 of Sam's Rules for Building a Business: Motivate your partners. Money and ownership aren't enough....Set high goals, encourage competition, and then keep score" (Trimble, 1992).

Incorporating expectations into management requires two phases. The first consists of developing and communicating expectations of performance, group citizenship, individual initiative, and job creativity. The second involves consistency. The manager must be consistent in his or her expectations and in communicating them. Consistency will produce reinforcement and, in the end, promote stability and reduce anxiety. Employees will know what the boss expects.

Managing for Motivation

With a well-rounded, people-centered philosophy in place, a manager is ready to motivate by creating a positive, supportive work environment. This section will discuss how to manage for motivation: how to treat people as individuals, provide support, recognize cultural diversity, empower employees, provide an effective reward system, re-design jobs, promote intrapreneurship, and create flexibility in work.

Treating People as Individuals

All of us are different. We think differently. We have different needs and wants, and we cherish different values, expectations, and goals. Each wants to be treated as a special person because each of us is a special person. What is more, we change. Today, a person's links to others may be paramount; a year from now, recognition for accomplishment may be the driving passion.

The work force is becoming increasingly diverse. Some observers (Howe and Strauss, 1992) have focused on Baby Boomers, Twentysomethings, and Thirteeners. You do not have to give more than a cursory glance, however, to be aware of the many groups in the labor force: ethnic and racial groups, senior citizens, women, and working mothers, to name just a few (Mills and Cannon, 1992).

Successful managers recognize people as individuals and work with their particular differences. Such recognition goes further: The successful manager knows that, because each of us is an individual, each of us is motivated differently. The more managers know about motivation, the more successful they will be in working with people.

Providing Support

To develop motivated employees, a manager must provide a climate in which each employee's needs can be met. A starting point is to facilitate attainment of the employee's goals. The manager does this by removing barriers, developing mutual goal-setting opportunities, initiating training and education programs, encouraging risk taking, and providing stability.

Two other actions can provide support and enhance the environment. First, openly appreciate the contributions of the employee. According to Jill Barad, the president of Mattel USA (Oliver, 1992):

> Taking time to tell people how good they are is one of the best ways management can reward people for their efforts. We in management tend to focus on what's *not* being done, how people are not performing instead of recognizing that our people *are* performing. We must constantly remind people of their strengths so they can make the most of those behaviors.

Second, show sensitivity to employees' needs for equity. Each employee must feel that he or she is receiving a fair exchange for his or her input into the company and in comparison to other employees. This point is supported by Norman Brinker, CEO of Chili's and Macaroni Grill restaurants (Hall, 1992): "Compensation has to be equitable. From the top to the bottom of the organization, the program must recognize the value of inputs into the company. Everyone is aware of everyone else."

Recognizing Cultural Diversity

Part of working with people as individuals is the ability to recognize and incorporate the value of cultural diversity within the workplace. The ethnic composition of the work force is changing, and with it workers' needs, goals, and values. Minorities— African-Americans, Hispanics, and Asians—are collectively becoming the majority in the workplace (Schlossberg, 1991).

Managers today *face the challenge of an increasingly diverse mix of cultures comprising the work force. Understanding, appreciating, and actually utilizing their inherent differences is a key to motivation.*

Managers need to respond by understanding, appreciating, and actually utilizing differences. As the cultural elements in the work force continue to change, traditional programs for training, mentoring, and compensation may have to be modified (Ettorre, 1992).

Umanoff and Parsons, a New York City bakery, has recognized and incorporated cultural diversity within the workplace (Nelton, 1992). Its senior management team, composed of three men and three women, includes people from five diverse cultures: Jamaican, American, Haitian, Hispanic, and Russian. Half the work force of the bakery is foreign-born; the workers come from Haiti, Trinidad, Grenada, the Dominican Republic, and Russia. The diversity brings contrasting viewpoints, experiences, and needs to the work environment. With these in mind the company has devised innovative training programs, mentor programs, and cross-cultural teams.

Empowering Employees

"You want motivated workers?" asks Peter C. Fleming (1992), vice president of Prudential Insurance Company. "Just empower them and you will see what motivation and ownership means." As presented by management consultant Tom

Peters (1990), **empowerment** occurs when individuals in an organization are "given autonomy, authority, [and are] trusted and encouraged to break the rules in order to get on with the job."

Empowerment is designed to unshackle the worker and make the job—not just part of the job—the worker's. As we have seen, employees of Omni Hotels are now partners in the work setting; so are workers at Prudential. They make decisions that formerly were made by the manager. Empowerment results in greater responsibility and innovation and a willingness to take risks. Ownership and trust, along with autonomy and authority, become a motivational package.

Another company that is reaping the benefits of empowerment is Reflexite Corporation of New Britain, Connecticut. *Inc.* magazine recently named Reflexite's 240 employees its Entrepreneurs of the Year. CEO Cecil Ursprung says of the employees, "They wanted more than money—they wanted to be committed to something, and they wanted power over the decisions affecting their work lives. Give them that and they would repay the company a thousand times over" (Case, 1992). Empowerment, in the form of work teams responsible for production and quality, has given the employees just such control. The teams plan the production operation, work with suppliers, respond to customer questions, and are accountable for bottom-line decisions. The quality team, composed of members from all production operations, has established individual responsibility for quality assurance as an organizational value. At Reflexite the results can be seen in increased productivity, attainment of quality goals, and a committed work force.

Providing an Effective Reward System

To motivate behavior, an organization must provide an effective reward system. Given the belief that all people are individuals with different needs, values, expectations, and goals, the reward system must accommodate many variables.

According to David D. Van Fleet (1991), an effective reward system has the following characteristics:

- Rewards must satisfy the basic needs of all employees. Pay, for example, must be adequate, benefits reasonable, and vacations and holidays appropriate.

- Rewards must be comparable to those offered by competitive organizations in the same area. For example, the pay offered for the same job should be similar to that offered by a competing company. In addition, benefits packages and other programs should be similar from company to company.

- Rewards must be equally available to people in the same positions and be distributed fairly and equitably. People performing the same job need to have the same options for rewards and also be involved in the decision governing which rewards they receive. When employees are asked to complete a special task or project, the employees should have the opportunity to determine the reward they value—a day off or extra pay.

- The reward system must be multifaceted. Because all people are different, managers must provide a range of rewards that focus on different aspects—pay, time off, recognition, or promotion. In addition, managers should provide several different ways to earn these rewards.

This last point is worth noting. With the widely developing trend toward empowerment in American industry, many are beginning to view traditional pay systems as inadequate. In a traditional system, people are paid according to the positions they hold, not the contributions they make. As organizations adopt approaches built upon teams, customer satisfaction, and empowerment, workers need to be paid differently. Companies like Monsanto and Procter & Gamble have already responded. Monsanto has more than 40 pay plans—designed by employee design teams—and P&G has a pay system that provides rewards based on skill levels (Verespej, 1992).

Re-Designing Jobs

Jobs are important motivational tools because what they contain may provide a means to meet an employee's needs. Managers need to know what elements of a job provide motivation and then apply the concepts of **job re-design**, the application of motivational theories to the structure of work, to increase output and satisfaction.

Principles of Job Re-Design   Recent trends in management have attempted to increase output and satisfaction in several ways. Jobs and organizations have been re-examined with the aim of putting challenge and other psychological rewards back into work. To this end, managers have assigned many repetitive tasks to robots and other kinds of computer-assisted machinery. Training and development programs have been devised that enable people to perform more demanding tasks and jobs.

Job re-design requires a knowledge of and concern for the human qualities that people bring with them to the organization—such things as their needs and expectations, perceptions and values, and level of skills and abilities. Job re-design also requires knowledge of the qualities of jobs—the physical and mental demands made on those performing the job and the environment in which the job is performed. Job re-design usually tailors a job to fit the person who must perform it. The beginner who holds a re-designed job gets pieces of the work in measured increments until he or she masters the tasks required to complete the whole job. Workers who have more experience and who are becoming bored with their jobs may be given more challenging tasks and more flexibility or autonomy in dealing with them.

The two approaches to job re-design relate to job scope and job depth. **Job scope** refers to the variety of tasks incorporated into a job. **Job depth** refers to the degree of discretion the person possesses to alter a job. Job re-design alternatives include job enlargement, job rotation, and job enrichment.

Job Enlargement   To increase the number of tasks a job includes, not the quality or the challenge, is to implement **job enlargement**. Often called horizontal loading, job enlargement may attempt to demand more of the same from an employee or to add other tasks containing an equal or less amount of meaning or challenge. Underworked employees benefit from job enlargement. These people need to be kept constantly busy and occupied with routine tasks that they understand and have mastered. Their sense of competence improves as their

Re-designing jobs to better fit the needs and expectations of workers is one way to bring fresh enthusiasm to the task. Assigning more challenging work with more autonomy prevents burnout of valuable, experienced personnel.

volume of output increases. But some people simply seek more challenge; job enlargement is not an appropriate strategy for them.

Job Rotation   Temporarily assigning people to different jobs, or tasks to different people, is **job rotation**. The idea is to add variety and to emphasize the interdependence of a group of jobs. Managers involved in job rotation gain knowledge about the operations of specific departments. Assembly-line workers may be assigned one set of tasks one month and another set the following month. Office workers may swap jobs for a time to learn additional dimensions of the office's responsibilities, to gain additional insights, and to enable them to substitute for one another in times of need.

At the Tony Lama Company—a boot manufacturer in El Paso, Texas—customer-service department employees work in the store for one week. Similarly, salespeople work a week in the shipping department. The experiences broaden employees' perspectives. Job rotation can be used to cross-train or to facilitate permanent job transfers or promotions. Workers who can benefit from job rotation are those who are interested in or ready for promotion and those who need variety.

Job Enrichment   Frederick Herzberg (1975) pointed out that jobs can allow workers to satisfy some of their psychological needs. **Job enrichment** is the result of designing jobs that can enhance psychological satisfaction. (Herzberg referred to job enrichment as vertical job loading.) Job enrichment should include the following elements:

- Variety of tasks. An enriched job introduces an employee to new and more difficult tasks he or she has not previously handled.

- Task importance. An employee with an enriched job handles a complete natural unit of work and also handles specific or specialized tasks that enable him or her to become an expert.

- Task responsibility. An employee with an enriched job is accountable for his or her work and can exercise authority in the course of job activities.

- Feedback. Workers in enriched jobs receive periodic and specialized reports that are delivered directly to them.

Experiments with job enrichment vary widely in approach, scope, and content. Most efforts at job enrichment increase the workers' control over work. In some companies, job enrichment means that supervisors and workers meet regularly to discuss mutual problems and that managers solicit employee suggestions for improvement. Volvo pioneered the concept of having a team of

---

GLOBAL APPLICATIONS
Motivation the Japanese Way

apanese companies have a secret for success. They have broken down the "us versus them" barrier that so often harms the American working environment by pitting management against labor. When an employee of Toyota thinks "us versus them," *them* is more likely to be Nissan or General Motors than Toyota managers. Japanese managers achieve this attitude by creating a feeling that employees and managers share a common fate. A well-run Japanese corporation is of, by, and for its people.

The Japanese do not forget that a business organization is made up of people and can function no better than they do. Japanese managers believe that the company's employees, not its machines, are its most important assets. Therefore, employees are to be valued, nurtured, and, except in extreme situations, retained. As a result, Japanese companies train their employees, guarantee them job security, and offer career paths that remain as long as the company is successful.

Although Japanese companies have management hierarchies, the organizations are run by the employees. Many top corporations are run by consensus. Work is organized for teams that include those from the executive suite as well as workers on the factory floor. Important ideas and decisions come up from below at least as frequently as they come down from the top. Ordinary workers are encouraged to make on-the-spot decisions rather than leave their brains at the door.

Japanese companies have been successful in incorporating the elements identified as supporting motivation. They have been rewarded by a committed, motivated work force. ▲

For more about creating a motivated work environment, see Alan S. Blinder, "How Japan Puts the Human in Human Capital," *Business Week,* June 11, 1992, p. 20; and Frank Gibney, *Japan: The Fragile Superpower* (Rutland, VT: Charles E. Tuttle), 1987, pp. 161–208.

employees work on the entire auto-assembly operations to produce a single car. The result was increased employee commitment, increased productivity, and decreased quality defects. Many manufacturers have allowed skilled machine operators to set up their machines, maintain them, plan their own work flow and pace, and inspect their own output.

For job enrichment to be successful, participation must be voluntary and management must be competent in its day-to-day operations as well as in its efforts at job enrichment. However, managers and workers can be expected to resist some efforts at job enrichment (see Chapter 9 for an analysis of resistance to change). And, once introduced, changes do not yield improvements overnight—mistakes can be made in the implementation of job enrichment programs and setbacks can occur. Nevertheless, companies that undertake job enrichment usually heighten morale and improve productivity.

Promoting Intrapreneurship

As an organization grows, it has a tendency to establish rules, policies, and procedures. The formal control systems that become established along with bureaucratic procedures cause it to lose innovative energy. The corporate environment can stifle the creative energy of entrepreneurial employees. To meet their need for creativity, these employees often leave and create their own organizations.

Recognizing this problem—and the losses their organizations suffer as a result—the top managers of many large corporations are trying to foster environments that promote corporate entrepreneurship, or intrapreneurship (Winters and Murfin, 1988). **Intrapreneurship** occurs when entrepreneurship exists within the boundaries of a formal organization. It is, in essence, a process whereby an individual pursues a new idea and has the authority to develop and promote it within the organization. According to Kuratko and Hodgetts (1989), a manager can foster intrapreneurship by following these guidelines:

- Encourage action.
- Use informal meetings whenever possible.
- Tolerate—do not punish—failure and use it as a learning experience.
- Be persistent.
- Reward innovation for innovation's sake.
- Plan the physical layout to encourage informal communication.
- Reward and/or promote innovative personnel.
- Encourage people to go around red tape.
- Eliminate rigid procedures.
- Organize people into small teams to pursue future-oriented projects.

Managers who really want a climate of intrapreneurship cannot be timid. True intrapreneurs are not comfortable with structure—they will figure a way around orders that block their dreams. They will do any job that will make the project successful, always being true to their goals (Pinchot, 1985).

Workers are people, and people have lives outside the organization. Managers who want to attract, keep, and motivate these workers will provide job enhancements like flextime, job sharing, and allowing them to share lunch with their children.

Creating Flexibility

Another way managers can motivate workers is to provide them with flexibility in work through flextime, a compressed workweek, or job sharing.

Flextime   Flextime allows employees to decide, within a certain range, when to begin and end each workday. It allows them to take care of personal business before or after work, vary their daily schedules, and enjoy more control over their lives. Companies that have adopted this approach report decreases in absenteeism, lower turnover, less tardiness, and higher morale (Bahls, 1992).

Compressed Workweek   A **compressed workweek** allows employees to fulfill their work obligation in less than the traditional five-day workweek. The most often-used schedule consists of four 10-hour days.

The approach—like flextime—provides more time for personal business and recreation. Employees who adopt it report heightened job satisfaction. Nevertheless, not all managers are supportive of the idea. Some managers think that compressed workweeks make scheduling much more difficult. They fear that providing employee coverage at all times may be impossible if people are in and out. Other managers fear loss of control (*Dallas Morning News,* February 16, 1991).

Job Sharing   Job sharing, or twining, permits two part-time workers to divide one full-time job. Such an occupational buddy system is ideal for parents who are raising school-age children or those who prefer part-time employment. The benefit from an employer's standpoint is that the employer gets the advantage of ideas from two sources but has to pay for only one salary and only one set of benefits.

Future Trends

In the future, four factors will challenge the motivational energies of management:

- The work force will continue to reflect greater and greater cultural diversity. This broad diversity will require managers to change reward systems and work even harder to provide a work climate that meets the needs of workers with an even more varied set of values, attitudes, and beliefs.

- The gender mix of the work force will continue to change. Women will constitute a greater percentage of the work force. This will require management to change to meet the needs generated by family concerns. There may be increased use of flextime and job sharing.

- The movement toward worker empowerment will continue, requiring managers to rethink and retrain.

- The number of opportunities for promotions will decrease. Downsizing will leave fewer managerial positions; therefore, managers will have to keep employees motivated without offering promotions.

C H A P T E R S U M M A R Y

- By developing a positive work environment, managers can capture the commitment of employees and have truly motivated workers.

- Motivation is not something done to a person; it is an impulse to action that grows out of a person. The factors that contribute to motivation include the individual's needs, his or her ability to make choices, and whether the environment developed by management provides the employees the opportunity to satisfy those needs and make those choices.

- The theories of motivation fall into two categories: process theories and content theories.

- Maslow's theory establishes five categories of needs that motivate human behavior: physiological (physical); safety, or security; love, or social; esteem; and self-realization, or self-actualization.

- Herzberg's hygiene factors (salary, job security, working conditions, and so on) are the primary elements involved in job dissatisfaction. When present in sufficient quality, they have no effect; when absent, they can lead to job dissatisfaction. Motivation factors (which include recognition and responsibility) are the primary elements involved in job satisfaction. When present, they can stimulate personal and psychological growth.

- The three needs defined by McClelland (achievement, power, and affiliation) relate to task accomplishment. They can be strengthened through training.

- The ERG theory of Alderfer identifies three levels of needs: existence, relatedness, and growth.

- Vroom's expectancy theory states that a person's behavior is influenced by the value of the rewards, the relationship of rewards to performance, and the efforts required for performance.

- According to reinforcement theory, employees learn motivation. The consequences of behavior influence choices in subsequent situations.

- Equity theory states that employees compare the reward they earn to the amount of effort they expend and to the rewards of other employees. These comparisons influence their levels of motivation.

- Goal-setting theory states that a person's behavior is influenced by the goals that are set. The goals tell an employee what needs to be done and how much effort will need to be expended.

- A philosophy of management can set the foundation for a positive environment. The philosophy should include Theory Y, Argyris's views on maturity, and the development of expectations.

- To develop motivated employees, a manager must treat people as individuals, provide a supportive climate, recognize cultural diversity, empower workers, establish an effective reward system, re-design jobs, promote intrapreneurship, and create a flexible working environment.

S K I L L - B U I L D I N G

The following statements are designed to allow you to evaluate the motivational climate of a company you now work for or have worked for in the past. On a scale of 1 (disagree) to 10 (agree), rate the company. Then total the points and read the interpretation that follows to see how your company stands.

1. The wages I receive are satisfactory.

2. The working conditions are satisfactory.

3. The supervision I receive is satisfactory.

4. The work I do provides me with satisfaction.

5. The rewards I receive are satisfactory for the amount of effort I put into the job.

6. The rewards I receive are fair compared to what others receive for the same work.

7. The goals set for completing my job are challenging.

8. The work I do provides recognition.

9. My supervisor is consistent with each employee in providing rewards for equal work.

10. The work I do provides a chance for advancement.

11. The work I do provides opportunity for additional responsibility.

Interpretations of scores:

0–55	You and your company are in trouble.
56–75	You and your company have a chance.
76–90	You and your company are working together.
91–110	Don't leave.

R E V I E W   Q U E S T I O N S

1. Review this chapter's essential terms and look up the meanings of those you cannot define.

2. What stimulates motivation? What three factors influence the behavior an individual will choose to satisfy a stimulus?

3. On what do content theories of motivation focus? What theories are included in this category? On what do process theories of motivation focus? What theories belong in this category?

4. List and explain the five categories of human needs identified by Abraham Maslow. Why are the needs arranged in a hierarchy?

5. Define Frederick Herzberg's hygiene and motivation factors and give three examples of each. What is the importance of each set of factors to a manager?

6. Why is a high achiever likely to focus on goal setting, feedback, individual responsibility, and rewards?

7. What three needs does Clayton Alderfer's ERG theory identify?

8. Apply expectancy theory to your classroom experience. Explain your motivation for grades in relationship to the value of the reward (grade), the relationship of the reward to performance (tests, papers), and the amount of effort required to receive the grade (time spent in class and studying).

9. Cite an experience in which your behavior (motivation) was influenced by past consequences.

10. Describe the two factors a person uses to determine equity in a work situation.

11. What influence on behavior and motivation is the result of employee goal setting?

12. What is the importance of a manager's philosophy in creating a positive work environment?

13. How can a manager influence motivation through empowerment, intrapreneurship, and recognition of cultural diversity?

R E C O M M E N D E D   **R** E A D I N G

Bray, Douglas. *Working with Organizations and Their People* (New York: Guilford), 1991.

Day, Charles R. "After Empowered...What Do the Empowered Owe Their Managements?" *Industry Week* (June 3, 1992), p. 5.

Lawrence, Paul R. *The Changing of Organizational Behavior Patterns* (New Brunswick, NJ: Transaction Publishers), 1991.

Leinberger, Paul, and Bruce Tucker. *The New Individualists: The Generation After the Organization Man* (New York: HarperCollins), 1991.

Levitt, Theodore. *Thinking About Management* (Scottsdale, AZ: Freedom Press), 1991.

McKenna, Joseph F. "What Can Restore Fading Loyalty," *Industry Week* (February 4, 1992), pp. 50–52.

Moskal, Brian S. "Is Industry Ready for Adult Relationships? Among Top Executives, Optimism Abounds About Employee Involvement and Participative Management," *Industry Week* (January 21, 1992), pp. 18–23.

Shatzer, L., and L. Schwartz. "Managing Intrapreneurship at AT&T," *Management Decisions* (November 1991), pp. 15–18.

Szathmary, Richard. "Incentives in Times Like These," *Sales & Marketing Management* (April 1992), pp. 98–103.

Vecchio, Robert P. *Organizational Behavior,* 2nd edition (Homewood, IL: Dryden Press), 1991.

R E F E R E N C E S

Adams, J. Stacy. "Toward an Understanding of Equity," *Journal of Abnormal and Social Psychology* (November 1963), pp. 422–436.

Alderfer, Clayton. *Existence, Relatedness, and Growth: Human Needs in Organizational Settings* (New York: Free Press), 1972.

Argyris, Chris. *Personality and Organization* (New York: Harper & Brothers), 1957.

Bahls, Jane Easter. "Getting Full-Time Work from Part-Time Employees," *Management Review* (February 1992), pp. 50–52.

Case, John. "Collective Effort," *Inc.* (January 1992), pp. 32–35, 38, 42–43.

Daft, Richard L. *Management,* 2nd edition (Homewood, IL: Dryden Press), 1991, pp. 404–410.

Dallas Morning News (February 16, 1991). "Four Day Week—The Jury Is Still Out," p. D1.

Davis, Keith, and John W. Newstrom. *Human Behavior at Work: Organizational Behavior,* 9th edition (New York: McGraw-Hill), 1992, p. 105.

Ettorre, Barbara. "Breaking the Glass... Or Just Window Dressing," *Management Review* (March 1992), p. 17.

Fleming, Peter C. "Empowerment Strengthens the Rock," *Management Review* (March 1992), pp. 34–37.

Goodman, Paul S., and Abraham Fredman. "An Examination of Adam's Theory of Inequity," *Administrative Science Quarterly* (December 1971), pp. 271–288.

Hall, Cheryl. "The Brinker Touch," *Dallas Morning News,* March 3, 1992, p. 23H.

Hamner, W. C. "Reinforcement Theory and Contingency Management in Organizational Settings," *Organizational Behavior and Management: A Contingency Approach,* H. L. Tosi and W. C. Hamner, editors (New York: Wiley), 1974, pp. 86–112.

Herzberg, Frederick. "One More Time: How Do You Motivate Employees?" *Business Classics: Fifteen Key Concepts for Management Success* (Cambridge, MA: Harvard Business Review), 1975, pp. 16–17.

Howe, Neil, and William Strauss. "The New Generation Gap," *The Atlantic* (December 1992), pp. 67–89.

Kuratko, Donald F., and Richard M. Hodgetts. *Entrepreneurship: A Contemporary Approach* (Chicago: Dryden Press), 1989.

Maslow, Abraham H. "A Theory of Human Motivation," *Psychological Review* 50 (1943), pp. 370–396.

McClelland, David C. *The Achieving Society* (New York: Van Nostrand Reinhold), 1971.

McClelland, David C., and David Burnham. "Power Is the Great Motivator," *Harvard Business Review* (March–April 1976), pp. 100–110.

McGregor, Douglas. *The Human Side of Enterprise* (New York: McGraw-Hill), 1960, pp. 23–27.

Mills, D. Quinn, and Mark D. Cannon. "Managing the New Work Force," *Management Review* (June 1992), p. 38.

Nelton, Sharon. "Winning with Diversity," *Nation's Business* (September 1992), pp. 18–21.

Oliver, Joyce Ann. "Mattel Chief Followed Her Vision," *Marketing News* (March 16, 1992), p. 15.

Peters, Tom. "Time-Obsessed Competition," *Management Review* (September 1990), p. 18.

Pinchot, Gifford. *Entrepreneuring* (New York: Harper & Row), 1985.

Porter, L. W., and E. E. Lawler. *Managerial Attitudes and Performance* (Homewood, IL: Richard D. Irwin), 1968.

Robbins, Stephen P. *Organizational Behavior: Concepts, Controversies, and Applications,* 5th edition (Englewood Cliffs, NJ: Prentice-Hall), 1991, p. 209.

Schlossberg, Howard. "Internal Marketing Helps Companies Understand Culturally Diverse Markets," *Marketing News* (January 21, 1991), pp. 7, 9.

Schuler, Randall S. *Personnel and Human Resource Management,* 3rd edition (St. Paul, MN: West), 1987, pp. 41–43.

Single, John L. "The Power of Expectations: Productivity and the Self-Fulfilling Prophecy," *Management World* (November 1980), pp. 19, 37–38.

Skinner, B. F. *Contingencies of Reinforcement* (New York: Appleton-Century-Crofts), 1969.

Steers, Richard M., and Lyman W. Porter, editors. *Motivation and Work Behavior,* 4th edition (New York: McGraw-Hill), 1987, pp. 3–4.

Straub, Joseph, and Raymond Attner. *Introduction to Business,* 4th edition (Boston: PWS-Kent), 1991, p. 182.

Tarpy, R. M. *Basic Principles of Learning* (Glenview, IL: Scott, Foresman), 1974, pp. 71–79.

Trimble, Vance H. *Sam Walton: The Inside Story of America's Richest Man* (New York: Signet), 1992, p. 109.

Van Fleet, David D. *Contemporary Management,* 2nd edition (Boston: Houghton Mifflin), 1991, p. 371.

Verespej, Michael A. "Pay-for-Skills: Its Time Has Come," *Industry Week* (June 15, 1992), pp. 22–30.

Vroom, Victor H. *Work and Motivation* (New York: Wiley), 1964.

Wilson, Larry. "Creating the Best Work Culture: How Managers Can Avoid the Trap of Ignoring the 'People' Skills in Dealing with Their Employees," *Nation's Business* (April 1992), p. 38.

Winters, Terry E., and Donald L. Murfin. "Venture Capital Investing for Corporate Development Objectives," *Journal of Business Venturing,* Summer 1988, p. 207.

G L O S S A R Y   O F   T E R M S

compressed workweek   A schedule that allows employees to fulfill weekly time obligations in less than the traditional five-day workweek.

empowerment   A method to increase motivation. Empowerment occurs when an individual receives autonomy, authority, and trust and is encouraged to break rules in order to get the job done.

equity theory   A motivation theory that states that comparisons of relative input-outcome ratios influence behavior choices. A worker mentally calculates the ratio of input (efforts) to outcome (rewards) and then compares it to others' ratios to see if equity exists.

ERG theory   A motivation theory that establishes three categories of human needs: existence needs, relatedness needs, and growth needs.

expectancy theory   A motivation theory that states that three factors influence behavior: the value of rewards, the relationship of rewards to necessary performance, and the effort required for performance.

flextime   An employment alternative that allows employees to decide, within a certain range, when to begin and end each workday.

goal-setting theory   A motivation theory that states that behavior is influenced by goals. Goals, whether set by a manager or by a worker and manager together, tell the employee what needs to be done and how much effort he or she must expend.

hygiene factors   The causes most closely identified with unhappiness on the job. These extrinsic factors, provided by management, can result in no job dissatisfaction when they are of high quality. They are not necessarily motivators for growth or greater effort, however.

intrapreneurship   Entrepreneurship within an organization. A company that values intrapreneurship allows employees flexibility and authority in pursuing and developing new ideas.

job depth   An element of job re-design that refers to the degree of discretion an employee has to alter a job.

job enlargement   Increasing the variety or the number of tasks a job includes, not the quality or the challenge of those tasks.

job enrichment   Designing a job to provide more responsibility, control, feedback, and authority for decision making.

job re-design   The application of motivational theories to the structure of work, to increase output and satisfaction.

job rotation   Temporarily assigning people to different jobs, or tasks to different people, on a rotating basis.

job scope   An element of job re-design that refers to the variety of tasks incorporated into a job.

job sharing   A technique to provide flexibility in work by permitting two part-time workers to divide one full-time job.

morale   The attitude, or feelings, workers have about the organization and their total work life.

motivation   The result of the interaction of a person's internal needs and external influences. Motivation involves perceptions of equity, expectancy, previous conditioning, and goal setting. Motivation determines behavior.

motivation factors   The conditions that can lead to an individual's job satisfaction. They are intrinsic to the job and offer satisfactions for psychological needs.

needs   Physical or psychological conditions that act as stimuli for human behavior.

philosophy of management   A manager's attitude about work and the people who perform it. A manager's philosophy influences the motivation approaches he or she selects.

quality of work life (QWL)   A term used to describe managers' efforts to enhance the dignity of workers by improving their physical and emotional well-being and enhancing the satisfactions that work can provide.

reinforcement theory   A motivation theory that states that a supervisor's reactions and past rewards and penalties affect behavior.

C A S E P R O B L E M
Building Commitment and Motivation

How does being obsessed with quality lead to motivated workers? According to John Wallace, CEO of Wallace Company, a winner of the Malcolm Baldridge National Quality Award, "It forces you to take a critical look at your entire operation—employees, systems, finances, suppliers, customer relations."

When Wallace Company committed to pursue quality in every facet of its operations, the company focused on the employees as the most critical ingredient. "If employees are not motivated and committed, they cannot and will not pursue quality, they will be dissatisfied."

Responding to the challenge, Wallace provided new tools to employees who asked for them; put a fresh coat of paint on the offices, warehouse, and manufacturing facilities; and improved a company car plan that applied to outside salespeople. The company even updated its entire fleet of trucks—more than fifty 18-wheelers—at a time when it seemed desperately unable to afford the expense.

The company began to address the administrative concerns of the employees by evaluating policies on vacation, sick leave, and personal leave. These policies were changed to be more competitive with those of other firms. The compensation system was re-designed to reflect the contributions made by the employees. Grievances over unfair policy administration were reduced to zero.

Wallace introduced a comprehensive training program for all levels of employees. "The training programs have been really important to a lot of us," noted a shipping supervisor. "Unlike some groups of employees in the company, many of the staff in our area didn't go to college or even finish high school."

Managers took two additional actions in the process of reshaping the organization. First, they recognized that the company needed a new mission statement to direct the energies of the employees and management. Several employees were asked to help develop an initial draft. The draft was distributed to all employees, who were asked to suggest changes or add their own values and views. Three drafts and six months later, the process produced the mission statement in use today. Though the statement took a long time to create, it elicits total commitment from the work force.

The second action was to create teams. Teams were established to focus on quality, production, customer service, and order processing. Each team developed its own set of goals, evaluated its work, and made modification when needed. The team structure put employees in charge of their own destiny. The teams allowed employees to discover what they were capable of producing and the value of their products to themselves and the company.

The actions taken by Wallace Company resulted in a motivated work force. As people realized they had made a difference, a sense of unity emerged. On a daily basis, employees at all levels began to challenge old concepts and try new ideas.

Q U E S T I O N S

1. Which motivation theories did Wallace Company apply in developing its overall motivation strategy?

2. What specific elements of each theory did the company address with its actions? Provide examples to support your answers.

3. Did the company focus on content theories, process theories, or both? Explain your answer.

For more about building commitment and motivation, see David Altany, "Cinderella with a Drawl," *Industry Week,* January 6, 1992, pp. 49–51.

13

Leadership

L E A R N I N G   O B J E C T I V E S

After reading and discussing this chapter, you should be able to:

- Define this chapter's essential terms
- Distinguish between managers and leaders
- Discuss a leader's use of task-centered and people-centered approaches
- Discuss the three kinds of power that leaders can possess
- Describe the three interacting factors that create a manager's leadership style
- Differentiate between positive and negative motivation
- Discuss the three styles of leadership and their appropriate use
- Explain how to use the managerial grid
- Compare and contrast the contingency, path-goal, and life-cycle theories of leadership

MANAGEMENT IN ACTION

"Male" and "Female" Approaches to Leadership

A recent study by the National Association of Women Business Owners showed that 5.4 million U.S. businesses are owned by women. The same source revealed that women-owned businesses employ some 11.7 million Americans. Women have been starting businesses at a higher rate than men, and the study predicted that during 1992 women-owned businesses would create more jobs and employ more people than would the 500 largest corporations in America.

Women own businesses in every sector of the U.S. economy; the greatest percentage is in retail (40%). Of women-owned business, 9% generate over $1 million per year in sales. Most women owners are active in the management of their businesses. According to *Inc.* magazine, of America's 500 fastest-growing private companies, 8% have women as CEOs and nearly one-third have husband-and-wife teams in charge.

Leadership styles *can include traits considered "masculine" or "feminine," combined in the best way to get the job done.*

A survey of 456 executives (355 women and 101 men) revealed some interesting differences between the ways in which both sexes approach their leadership roles. Women respondents favored being interactive—encouraging others to participate and making subordinates feel good about themselves, their contributions, and their organizations. Interactive leaders attempt to create a group identity in a variety of ways. One way is to encourage others to have a say in almost every aspect of work, from setting performance goals to determining strategy. To facilitate inclusion, interactive leaders create mechanisms to get people to participate, using a conversational style that encourages involvement.

The majority of the male respondents described their styles of leadership as a set of "transactions with subordinates—exchanging rewards for services rendered or punishment for inadequate performance."

429

Gender-neutral traits were adaptiveness, tactfulness, sincerity, efficiency, and reliability.

University of Chicago sociology professor Pauline B. Bart has studied how women lead. Bart believes that women with female models are more inclusive, cooperative, nurturing, and less power-obsessed than women who have adopted men as their role models. Author, professor, and senior program associate for the Center for Creative Leadership, Carole Leland observed that:

> Many women, in the face of discrimination, have learned to do the things men have learned to do—and they've survived by exercising control....But leadership traits such as being 'inclusive and non-hierarchical' are more likely to be found among women.

▶ The "best" style depends on organizational context. Both men and women can learn much from each other.

Men reported that they were more likely than women to use power that comes from their "organizational position and formal authority."

The men and women surveyed claimed to have an equal mix of traits considered to be feminine, masculine, and gender neutral. Feminine traits included understanding, compassion, sensitivity, and dependency. Masculine traits included dominance, toughness, assertiveness, and competitiveness.

Some men lead with what are considered feminine traits; some women lead with so-called masculine traits. And both men and women vary their approaches as circumstances dictate. A detrimental trait under one set of circumstances becomes a beneficial trait under another.

The "best" style depends on organizational context. Both men and women can learn much from each other. ▲

For more about male and female leadership styles, see "Women Entrepreneurs: A Pretty Big Game," *Nation's Business,* August 1992, p. 53; Carol Kleiman, "Women-Owned Firms on Upswing Despite Recession," *Chicago Tribune,* July 13, 1992, sec. 4, p. 3; Martha E. Mangelsdorf, "Behind the Scenes," *Inc.,* October 1992, p. 78; Judy B. Rosener, "Ways Women Lead," *Harvard Business Review,* November–December 1990, pp. 119–125; Carol Kleiman, "Male, Female Leadership a Study in Contrasts," *Chicago Tribune,* sec. 4, p. 3.

Leadership Defined

Leadership is part of the seamless fabric of management functions. The concepts of leadership, communication, and motivation are inextricably interrelated, and they are closely linked to the manager's directing and controlling tasks. **Leadership**, in its management application, is the process of influencing individuals and groups to set and achieve goals. **Influence** is the power to sway other people to one's will. Leaders guide, direct, show, and inspire—all these activities are components of management. This chapter will examine the nature of leadership, the theories and principles of leadership, and its importance to managers and organizations.

Leadership involves three sets of variables: the leader, those being led, and the circumstances in which leadership is exercised. All three variables change constantly. When head coach Jackson of the Chicago Bulls prepares his team to take on an opponent, he is exercising leadership. Each opponent, game, and play present the coach, his staff, and their players with new challenges and demands. When David Nagel, head of Apple Computer's advanced technology group, works with his teams to create new software and digital devices, he is leading. His teams' efforts are influenced by the quality of his leadership, the abilities and motivations of team members, and the internal and external limits and challenges they encounter in each situation.

What qualities must a leader have? As Kleiman (1992) reported, Jeffrey Christian, president and chief executive officer of a Cleveland-based executive search firm, looks for managers

> who are high impact players, change agents, drivers and winners—people who are extremely flexible, bright, tactical and strategic, who can handle a lot of information, make decisions quickly, motivate others, chase a moving target and shake things up. Previously, corporate recruiting emphasized credentials [schooling] and experience, which are still important, but . . . you can't teach good leadership or how to be excited about life.

Robert K. Greenleaf, former director of management research at AT&T and founding director of the Center for Applied Ethics, said: "The leader exists to serve those whom he nominally leads, those who supposedly follow him. He (or she) takes *their* fulfillment as his (or her) principal aim" (Kiechell, 1992). The servant-leader takes people and their work seriously, listens to and takes the lead from the troops, heals, is self-effacing, and sees himself or herself as a steward (Kiechell, 1992).

Leadership Traits

Early theories about leadership suggested that excellent leaders possessed certain traits, or personal characteristics, that lay at the root of their ability to lead. Following World War II, the U.S. Army surveyed soldiers in an attempt to compile a list of traits shared by commanders who soldiers perceived as leaders. The resulting list, which included 14 traits, was clearly inadequate to describe leadership. No two commanders displayed all the traits, and many famous commanders lacked several.

More recently, Gary A. Yukl (1981) constructed a list of traits and skills commonly associated with effective leaders. Exhibit 13.1 presents these traits. Yukl's list suggests that a leader is strongly motivated to excel and succeed.

No list of leadership traits and skills can be definitive, however, because no two leaders are exactly alike. Different leaders working with different people in different situations need different traits. If people in charge possess what is needed when it is needed, they should be able to exercise effective leadership.

William H. Peace is a former executive with Westinghouse and United Technologies. Now he is director and executive consultant with Doctus Management Consultancy of Chester, England. In the course of his career, Peace has learned that certain traits serve him well in management jobs. In an article for

Traits	Skills
Adaptable	Cleverness (intelligence)
Alert to social environment	Conceptual ability
Ambitious and achievement-oriented	Creativity
Assertive	Diplomacy and tact
Cooperative	Fluency in speaking
Decisive	Knowledge about the group task
Dependable	Organizational (administrative) ability
Dominant (desires to influence others)	Persuasiveness
Energetic (high activity level)	Social ability
Persistent	
Self-confident	
Tolerant of stress	
Willing to assume responsibility	

Source: Gary A. Yukl, *Leadership in Organizations*, p. 70. Adapted by permission of Prentice-Hall, Inc., Englewood Cliffs, NJ. Copyright 1981.

Harvard Business Review, Peace (1991) noted the importance of intelligence, energy, confidence, and responsibility. He differed from some observers in his emphasis on candor, sensitivity, and a "certain willingness to suffer the painful consequences of unpopular decisions." Peace called using these traits in management "soft management." As the Management in Action feature that opened this chapter noted, personal traits are often perceived as masculine, feminine, or gender neutral. All constructive traits are valuable and have their place in the exercise of leadership.

Leadership Skills

A person's skills are the competencies and capabilities he or she possesses. Look again at Exhibit 13.1 and notice that many of the skills Yukl identified are primarily useful in dealing with others. These skills include diplomacy, fluency in speech (communication skills), persuasiveness, and social ability. Some of the traits listed imply the existence of skills. For example, being decisive means that one has skill in making decisions by both rational and intuitive means.

Chris Carey, president of Datatec Industries, which makes in-store computer systems, believes that subordinates should evaluate their bosses in what he calls reverse performance reviews. He has his 318 employees score their managers' skills in areas such as coaching, listening, praising, and responsiveness. Employees rate upper managers in terms of support of employees, articulation of goals, attention to employee ideas, and fairness. The surveys are anonymous and the results are shared. Formal, top-down appraisals follow within a month. "Scheduling the reviews back-to-back underscores the fact that everyone can perform better and everyone has a chance to say how that will happen" (*Inc.*, October 1992).

Leadership Behaviors

Gary Yukl (1981) and his colleagues determined 19 categories of "meaningful and measurable" leadership behavior. Exhibit 13.2 presents the Yukl group's categories along with definitions and examples. As you examine these behaviors—the things leaders do in the everyday exercise of leadership—relate them to the traits and skills discussed earlier. Then link the concepts to what you know about human behavior and motivation as described in Chapter 12.

Exhibit 13.2

The Yukl group's 19 categories of leadership behavior.

1. **Performance emphasis:** The extent to which a leader emphasizes the importance of subordinate performance, tries to improve productivity and efficiency, tries to keep subordinates working up to their capacity, and checks on their performance.

    Example: My supervisor urged us to be careful not to let orders go out with defective components.

2. **Consideration:** The extent to which a leader is friendly, supportive, and considerate toward subordinates and strives to be fair and objective.

    Example: When a subordinate was upset about something, the supervisor was sympathetic and tried to console him.

3. **Inspiration:** The extent to which a leader stimulates subordinates' enthusiasm for the work of the group and says things to build subordinates' confidence in their ability to perform assignments successfully and attain group objectives.

    Example: My boss told us we were the best design group he had ever worked with, and he was sure that our new product was going to break every sales record in the company.

4. **Praise-recognition:** The extent to which a leader provides praise and recognition to subordinates with effective performance, shows appreciation for their special efforts and contributions, and makes sure they get credit for their helpful ideas and suggestions.

    Example: In a meeting, the supervisor told us she was satisfied with our work and that she appreciated the extra effort we had made this month.

5. **Structuring reward contingencies:** The extent to which a leader rewards effective subordinate performance with tangible benefits. Such benefits include pay increases, promotions, preferred assignments, a better work schedule, and time off.

    Example: My supervisor established a new policy that any subordinate who brought in a new client would earn 10% of the contracted fee.

Exhibit 13.2 (continued)

6. **Decision participation:** The extent to which a leader consults with subordinates and otherwise allows them to influence decisions.

    Example: My supervisor asked me to attend a meeting with him and his boss to develop a new production schedule. He was very receptive to my ideas on the subject.

7. **Autonomy-delegation:** The extent to which a leader delegates authority to subordinates and allows them to determine how to do their work.

    Example: My boss gave me a new project and encouraged me to handle it as I think best.

8. **Role clarification:** The extent to which a leader informs subordinates about their duties and responsibilities, specifies the rules and policies that must be observed, and lets subordinates know what is expected of them.

    Example: My boss called me in to inform me about a rush project that must be given top priority, and she gave me some specific assignments related to this project.

9. **Goal setting:** The extent to which a leader emphasizes the importance of setting specific performance goals for each important aspect of a subordinate's job, measures progress toward the goals, and provides concrete feedback.

    Example: The supervisor held a meeting to discuss the sales quota for next month.

10. **Training-coaching:** The extent to which a leader determines training needs for subordinates and provides any necessary training and coaching.

    Example: My boss asked me to attend an outside course at the company's expense and said I could leave the office early on the days classes were to be held.

11. **Information dissemination:** The extent to which a leader keeps subordinates informed about developments that affect their work, including events in other work units or outside the organization; decisions made by higher management; and progress in meetings with superiors or outsiders.

    Example: The supervisor briefed us about some high-level changes in policy.

12. **Problem solving:** The extent to which a leader takes the initiative in proposing solutions to serious work-related problems and acts decisively to deal with such problems when a prompt solution is needed.

    Example: The unit was short-handed due to illness, and we had an important deadline to meet. My supervisor arranged to borrow two people from other units, so we could finish the job today.

13. **Planning:** The extent to which a leader decides how to organize and schedule work efficiently, plans how to attain work-unit objectives, and makes contingency plans for potential problems.

    Example: My supervisor suggested a shortcut that allows us to prepare our financial statements in three days instead of the four days it used to take.

14. **Coordinating:** The extent to which a leader coordinates the work of subordinates, emphasizes the importance of coordination, and encourages subordinates to coordinate their activities.

    Example: My supervisor encouraged subordinates who were ahead in their work to help those who were behind. By helping each other, all the different parts of the project will be ready at the same time.

15. **Work facilitation:** The extent to which a leader obtains for subordinates any necessary supplies, equipment, support services, or other resources; eliminates problems in the work environment; and removes other obstacles that interfere with the work.

    Example: I asked my boss to order some supplies, and he arranged to get them right away.

Exhibit 13.2 *(continued)*

16. **Representation:** The extent to which a leader establishes contacts with other groups and important people in the organization, persuades them to appreciate and support the leader's work unit, and influences superiors and outsiders to promote and defend the interests of the work unit.

> *Example:* My supervisor met with the data processing manager to ask for revisions to the computer programs. The revised programs will meet our needs more effectively.

17. **Interaction facilitation:** The extent to which a leader tries to get subordinates to be friendly with each other, cooperate, share information and ideas, and help each other.

> *Example:* The sales manager took the group out to lunch to give everybody a chance to get to know the new sales representative.

18. **Conflict management:** The extent to which a leader restrains subordinates from fighting and arguing, encourages them to resolve conflicts in a constructive manner, and helps settle disagreements between subordinates.

> *Example:* Two members of the department who were working together on a project had a dispute about it. The manager met with them to help resolve the matter.

19. **Criticism-discipline:** The extent to which a leader criticizes or disciplines a subordinate who shows consistently poor performance, violates a rule, or disobeys an order. Disciplinary actions include official warnings, reprimands, suspensions, and dismissals.

> *Example:* The supervisor, concerned that a subordinate repeatedly made the same kinds of errors, made sure that the subordinate was aware of expectations concerning quality.

Source: Gary A. Yukl, *Leadership in Organizations*, pp. 121–125. Adapted by permission of Prentice-Hall, Inc., Englewood Cliffs, NJ. Copyright 1981.

The first behavior Yukl listed, performance emphasis, remains a popular focus for managers and business writers. The movement in business today is to pay people for what they learn and to reward them for their individual and group performance. At Lyondell Petrochemical, owned half by its employees and half by Atlantic Richfield (Arco), "Managers and workers tackle new undertakings in teams, which get bonuses if their ideas fly" (Nulty, 1992). By putting their emphasis and money where their words are, company managers emphasize performance and productivity.

Management Versus Leadership

Management and *leadership* are not synonyms. Managers plan, organize, staff, direct, and control. They may or may not be effective in influencing their subordinates or team members to set and achieve goals. Ideally, leadership and management skills combine to allow a manager to function as a leader, as Exhibit 13.3 suggests. The manager who gives orders and explicit instructions to experienced people, for instance, is not leading but actually impeding productivity. Planning effectively helps one to become a manager; enabling others to plan effectively is leading. Leaders empower—they give people the things they need to

Exhibit 13.3

*The relationship between
management and leadership.*

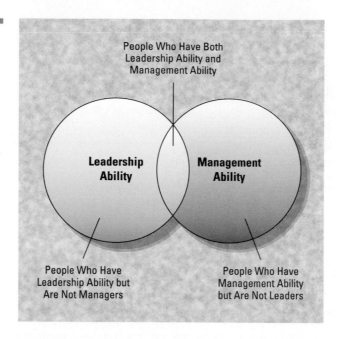

People Who Have Both
Leadership Ability and
Management Ability

Leadership
Ability

Management
Ability

People Who Have
Leadership Ability but
Are Not Managers

People Who Have
Management Ability
but Are Not Leaders

grow, to change, and to cope with change. Leaders create and share visions, generating strategies to bring the visions to reality.

According to Datatec's Chris Carey, empowering people requires a corporate culture that makes empowerment a core value. His company worked hard to create a culture that has as "its core values: honesty, openness, empowerment, and acceptance of failure" (*Inc.,* October 1992).

John P. Kotter and James L. Heskett (1992), in *Corporate Culture and Performance,* listed organizations that had made major cultural changes. The leaders of these organizations first had to realize that change was needed. Then they had to communicate to employees the facts that pointed to a crisis or potential crisis so the employees would perceive the need to change. Finally, as Kotter and Keskett described, these leaders

> developed or clarified their visions of what changes were needed.... After perceiving some minimum readiness on the part of their managers, the leaders then began communicating their visions of what changes were necessary. These visions always carried some general message about key constituencies, especially customers.... [Also] included was information about more specific strategies and practices that were seen as needed to deal with the current business climate or competitive situation.

As the leaders' visions and strategies were conveyed, they won allies and became role models for other managers. "Their ability to change and play a useful leadership role signaled that others could also" (Kotter and Heskett, 1992). Such leaders are often called transformational leaders, because they are able to create fundamental changes in their organizations' values, missions, and cultures. Exhibit 13.4, which is based on John P. Kotter's work, further differentiates between

Exhibit 13.4

The differences between management and leadership.

Management	Leadership
Planning and budgeting. Establishing detailed steps and timetables for achieving needed results and then allocating the resources necessary to make them happen.	**Establishing direction.** Developing a vision of the future, often the distant future, and strategies for producing the changes needed to achieve that vision.
Organizing and staffing. Establishing a structure for accomplishing plan requirements, staffing that structure with individuals, delegating responsibility and authority for carrying out the plan, providing policies and procedures to help guide people, and creating methods or systems to monitor implementation.	**Aligning people.** Communicating the direction by words and deeds to all those whose cooperation may be needed to influence the creation of teams and coalitions that understand the vision and strategies and accept their validity.
Controlling and problem solving. Close monitoring of results in terms of the plan, identifying deviations, and then planning and organizing to solve these problems.	**Motivating and inspiring.** Energizing people to overcome major political, bureaucratic, and resource barriers by satisfying basic, but often unfulfilled, human needs.
Produces a degree of predictability and order and consistently achieves the key results expected by various stakeholders (for customers, being on time; for stockholders, being on budget).	*Produces change, often to a dramatic degree, that has the potential of being extremely useful (for example, developing new products that customers want or new approaches to labor relations that help make a firm more competitive).*

Source: John P. Kotter, *A Force for Change: How Leadership Differs from Management* (New York, Free Press), 1990, p. 6.

management and leadership. Notice how Kotter's list of leadership behaviors emphasizes people skills and motivational connections.

Bruce R. Ellig, vice president of personnel of Pfizer, discussed leadership in regard to change in the context of a chief personnel officer's role: "To get the CPO job, the key requirement is the ability to identify and lead needed organizational change that will serve both of personnel's customers: management and the employees" (Ellig, 1991).

Sam Walton (1992), founder of Wal-Mart, wrote about the importance of change to his company, noting that strong corporate culture can create a resistance to change:

> When folks buy into a way of doing things, and really believe it's the best way, they develop a tendency to think that's exactly the way things should always be done. So I've made it my own personal mission to ensure that constant change is a vital part of the Wal-Mart culture itself. I've forced change—sometimes for change's sake alone—at every turn in our company's development. In fact, I think one of the greatest strengths of Wal-Mart's ingrained culture is its ability to drop everything and turn on a dime.

These words also indicate why Sam Walton is such a good example of a leader-manager.

Power and Leadership

Power gives people the ability to exert influence over others, to get them to follow; it makes leadership possible. Leaders possess power, as do all managers whether or not they are leaders. Possessing power can increase the effectiveness of managers by enabling them to inspire people—to get them to perform willingly, without relying solely on formal managerial authority. Formal authority grants a manager legitimate power, but expert and referent power exist as well.

Legitimate Power

Managers' formal authority derives from their positions in their organizations' hierarchies and is usually specified in each position's job description. Authority gives managers power or influence over others because it enables them to use organizational resources, appraise the work of others, and punish or reward performance. People work to please those who hold authority over them. Therefore, the power gained from authority is called **legitimate power**.

A worker engaged in training a newcomer normally has the authority to exercise influence over the trainee through appraisals and rewards for mastering the material being taught. When Ukari, a member of a self-managing worker team, asks for help from the team leader (another team member) and then acts on that advice, she is being influenced by a peer who has authority. When legitimate power is coupled with one or more of the additional kinds of power, the person holding that power is capable of being a leader.

Expert Power

Influence over others that comes from one's abilities, skills, knowledge, and experience is called **expert power**. The old-timer holds expert power over newcomers and apprentices. The boss who held your job before you has it too. When your doctor tells you to go home, spend the next three days in bed, and take specific medication, you do it. Most professionals who are paid for their opinions and advice exercise expert power over their clients.

Referent Power

Power that comes to people because of the kind of persons they appear to be is known as **referent power**. Referent power is sometimes called charismatic power, and it derives from personal magnetism or charm. Your personality, sense of humor, openness, honesty, and other endearing traits draw others to you and can create bonds of trust and friendship. When Jack praises his boss for her tact, honesty, and courtesy in handling a problem, he is talking about the way in which she uses her referent power. Many leadership traits and skills generate referent power for those who possess them.

Leadership Styles

From the discussion of leadership and its power bases, turn now to the dynamic interaction between a leader and other people. The perceived approaches and behaviors a manager uses to influence others constitute the manager's **leadership style** (Davis and Newstrom, 1989). Managers' leadership styles result from their philosophies about motivation, their choices of decision-making styles, and their areas of emphasis in the work environment—whether they focus on tasks or people.

Positive Versus Negative Motivation

Leaders influence others to achieve goals through their approach to motivation. Depending on the style of the manager, the motivation can take the form of rewards or penalties (Davis and Newstrom, 1989). Exhibit 13.5 presents a continuum containing positive and negative motivations. Leaders with positive styles use positive motivators. They motivate by using praise, recognition, or monetary rewards or by increasing security or granting additional responsibilities.

A negative leadership style incorporates coercion known as **sanctions**—fines, suspensions, termination, and the like. The manager who says "Do it my way or else," employs negative motivation. Implied in the statement is the manager's willingness to exercise disciplinary powers; the subordinate's failure to comply would be an act of insubordination.

Exhibit 13.5

A motivation continuum.

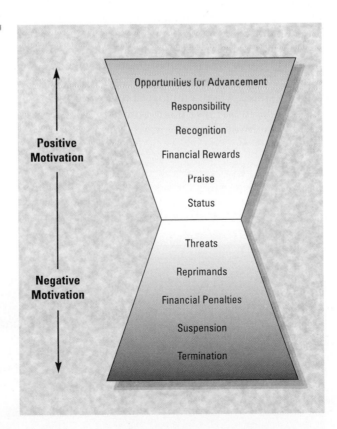

Positive leadership styles encourage development of employees and higher levels of job satisfaction (Keller and Szilagyi, 1978). Negative leadership styles are based on the manager's ability to withhold items of value from employees. The result of negative leadership may be an environment of fear, where managers are viewed with distrust and seen as dictators rather than leaders or team players.

Decision-Making Styles

Another element in a manager's leadership style is the degree to which he or she shares decision-making authority with subordinates. Managers' styles range from not sharing at all to completely delegating decision-making authority. Exhibit 13.6 shows the degrees of sharing as a continuum, with the range of styles categorized in three groups: autocratic style, participative style, and free-rein style. Which style a manager chooses should relate to the situation encountered.

The Autocratic Style   A manager who uses the **autocratic style** does not share decision-making authority with subordinates. The manager makes the decision and then announces it. Autocratic managers may ask for subordinates' ideas and feedback about the decision, but the input does not usually change the decision unless it indicates that something vital has been overlooked. The hallmark of this style is that the entire process is executed by the manager, who retains all the authority. Consequently, the autocratic style is sometimes called the "I" approach.

Under certain conditions, the autocratic style is appropriate. When a manager is training a subordinate, for instance, the content, objectives, pacing, and execution of decisions properly remain in the hands of the trainer. (The manager should elicit feedback from the trainee, however.) During a crisis—a hazardous-materials spill or bomb threat, say—leaders are expected to take charge, issue orders, and make decisions. When a subordinate directly challenges a manager's authority, an autocratic response may be needed to preclude acts of insubordination. In circumstances where employees have not been empowered to make decisions, supervisors must make them. Some subordinates do not want to share authority or become involved in any way beyond the performance of their routine duties.

Exhibit 13.6

Leadership styles and the distribution of decision-making authority.

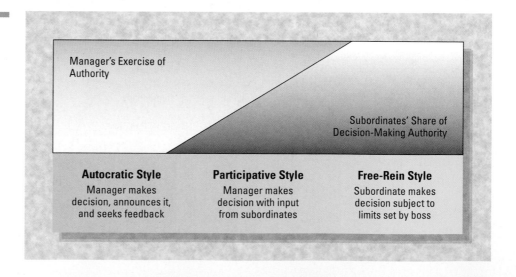

Manager's Exercise of Authority

Subordinates' Share of Decision-Making Authority

Autocratic Style	**Participative Style**	**Free-Rein Style**
Manager makes decision, announces it, and seeks feedback	Manager makes decision with input from subordinates	Subordinate makes decision subject to limits set by boss

Managers should respect these preferences but also make incentives and growth opportunities available.

To use the autocratic style effectively, managers must know what needs to be done and they must possess expert power. The autocratic style is effective when managers face issues that they are best equipped to solve, create solutions whose implementation does not depend on others, and desire to communicate through orders and instructions. If these conditions do not exist, one of the other two leadership styles is probably more appropriate.

The Participative Style Managers who use the **participative style** share decision-making authority with subordinates. The degree of sharing can range from the manager's presenting a tentative decision that is subject to change, to letting the group or subordinate participate in making the decision. Sometimes called the "we" approach, participative management involves others and lets them bring their unique viewpoints, talents, and experiences to bear on an issue. This style is strongly emphasized today because of the trends toward downsizing, employee empowerment, and worker teams.

A consultative and democratic approach works best for resolving issues that affect more than just the manager or decision maker. People affected by decisions support them more enthusiastically when they participate in the decision making than when decisions are imposed on them. Also, if others in a manager's unit know more than the manager does about an issue, common sense urges their inclusion in decisions concerning it.

Before subordinates can be brought into the process, mutual trust and respect must exist between them and their managers. The subordinates must be willing to participate and trained to do so. People need training in rational decision making. They must also possess the related skills and knowledge needed to cope with the problems they are expected to solve. It takes time to give people the confidence

Participation in management decisions is the hallmark of the more democratic style favored today, reflecting the trend toward downsizing, employee empowerment, and worker teams.

and competence needed to make decisions. Managers must have the time, means, and patience to prepare subordinates to participate. But when employees participate, they devise solutions that they feel they own. This sense of ownership increases their commitment to making the solutions work.

Inc. magazine (October 1992) reported that at Datatec the participation of employees is encouraged even in the matter of their bosses' appraisals. Datatec managers believe that

> giving employees the chance to appraise their bosses forces a company to live up to its commitment to participative management. [Managers are asked] to conduct one-on-one reverse appraisals with subordinates. Employees who find appraising their bosses simply too discomforting may choose to talk to another manager. [President] Carey wants to make sure that problems don't get buried just because they're prickly ones.

Limits on subordinates' participation must be clearly spelled out beforehand; there should be no misunderstandings about who holds authority to do what. Mistakes will be made and some waste will occur, but the power of the participative style to motivate and energize people is great. In many organizations, such as Datatec, managers must use this style; corporate culture and policies demand it.

FOCUS ON QUALITY
Participation Leads to Success

Jack Stack, CEO of Springfield Remanufacturing Company and author of *The Great Game of Business,* believes that "the best, most efficient, most profitable way to operate a business is to give everybody in the company a voice in saying how the company is run and a stake in the financial outcome, good or bad." He and his 650 employees remanufacture engines and engine components, but Stack believes that his real business is education:

> We teach people about business. We give them the knowledge that allows them to go out and play the Game…. We try to take ignorance out of the workplace and force people to get involved, not with threats and intimidation but with education…. To do that you have to knock down the barriers that separate people, that keep people from coming together as a team.

In other words, Stack leads by enabling others to do so.

Employees learn from each other through classes and tutoring. Their managers provide them with all the facts relating to how their business is run and how it is doing. Along with their willingness to learn and help their company win what Stack calls "the great game of business" comes job security and a share in the profits. At Springfield Remanufacturing, people share authority and learn to do more than one job. All the employees think and act like owners because they are. Stack has learned what happens when all employees embrace the same goals; work together as a team to achieve them; have the information, understanding, and knowledge they need to make a decision; and possess the will to act quickly: Quality and success will follow. Stack has been successful in achieving success for his company. From 1983 to 1986, the company went from a loss to a profit before taxes of $2.7 million. By 1991, annual sales hit about $70 million and the work force grew from 119 to 650. ▲

For more about participative leadership, see Jack Stack, *The Great Game of Business,* Bo Burlingham, editor (New York: Doubleday/Currency), 1992; and Jack Stack, "The Great Game of Business," *Inc.,* June 1992, pp. 53–62.

The free-rein style of leadership allows individuals to operate independently, consulting a manager only when necessary.

The Free-Rein Style   Often called the "they" approach, or spectator style, the free-rein style empowers individuals or groups to function on their own, without direct involvement from the managers to whom they report. The style relies heavily on delegation of authority and works best when the parties have expert power, when participants have and know how to use the tools and techniques needed for their tasks. Under this style, managers set limits and remain available for consultation. The managers also hold participants accountable for their actions by reviewing and evaluating performance.

Free-rein leadership works particularly well with managers and experienced professionals in engineering, design, research, and sales. Such people generally resist other kinds of supervision.

In most organizations, managers must be able to use the decision-making style that circumstances dictate. Lee is new, so he needs to use an autocratic approach until he develops the confidence and knowledge to perform independently or until he joins a team. Kim, experienced in her job and better at it than anyone else, will probably do well under a participative or free-rein approach. Because people and circumstances constantly change and because subordinates must be prepared for change, the effective manager switches from one leadership style to another as appropriate.

Task Orientation Versus Employee Orientation

Yet another element of leadership style is the manager's philosophy about the most effective way to get work done. Leaders can adopt a focus on task (a work, or task, orientation) or a focus on employees (a relationship, or people-centered, approach). Depending on the manager's perspective and situation, these two approaches can be used separately or in combination.

A task focus emphasizes technology, methods, plans, programs, deadlines, goals, and getting the work out. Typically, the manager who focuses on a task uses the autocratic style of leadership and issues guidelines and instructions to subordinates. A task focus works well in the short run, especially with tight schedules or under crisis conditions. Used over the long term, however, a task focus can create personnel problems. It may cause the best performers, who desire flexibility and freedom to be creative, to leave the group, and it may increase absenteeism and decrease job satisfaction (Likert, 1976).

The manager who focuses on employees emphasizes workers' needs. He or she treats employees as valuable assets and respects their views. Building teamwork, positive relationships, and mutual trust are important activities of the people-centered leader. By focusing on employees a manager can increase job satisfaction and decrease absenteeism (Likert, 1976).

The University of Michigan Studies   In the 1970s researchers at the University of Michigan compared the behaviors of effective and ineffective supervisors. The researchers' findings indicated that supervisors who focused on their subordinates' needs ("employee-centered leaders") were the most effective, building high-performance teams that reached their goals. The less-effective supervisors ("job-centered leaders") tended to focus on tasks and were more concerned with efficiency and meeting schedules (Likert, 1979).

The Ohio State University Studies   Researchers at Ohio State University surveyed hundreds of leaders in the 1970s. The researchers studied their behavior in terms of two factors: consideration and initiating structure. *Consideration* was defined as concern for subordinates' ideas and feelings (what the University of Michigan studies referred to as an employee focus). Leaders who rated high in consideration communicated openly, developed teams, and focused on subordinates' needs. *Initiating structure* was defined as concern for goal achievement and task orientation (what the Michigan studies called job focus). Leaders who rated high in initiating structure were concerned with deadlines, planning work, and meeting schedules (Schriesheim and Bird, 1979).

The researchers found that leaders had one of four combinations of the two behaviors: high consideration and low initiating structure, low consideration and high initiating structure, low consideration and low initiating structure, and high consideration and high initiating structure. The researchers concluded that the last combination resulted in the greatest job satisfaction and performance by subordinates (Schriesheim and Bird, 1979).

Since the Ohio State studies, additional research suggests that the approach a manager takes should vary, depending upon the people involved and the situation. In a crisis, managers should focus on task. When training people to become a self-managing work team, managers should focus on people—their needs to cooperate, get to know one another, and develop relationships. Managers, these studies suggest, must be flexible and provide the kind of leadership their people and situations require.

Exhibit 13.7

The managerial grid.

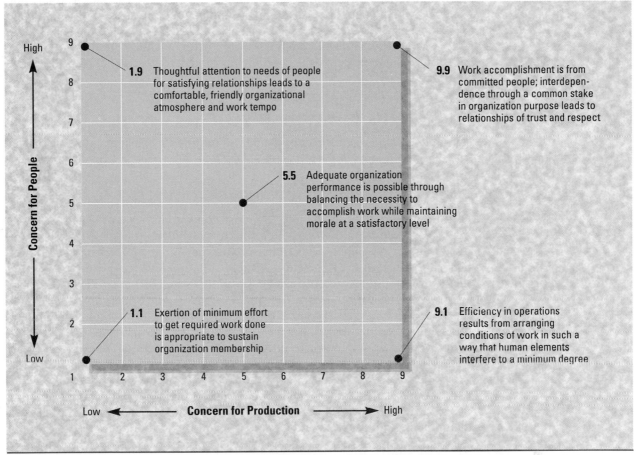

Source: Adapted from Robert R. Blake and Anne Adams McCanse, *Leadership Dilemmas—Grid Solutions* (Houston: Gulf). Reprinted by permission of the owners. Copyright 1991 by Scientific Methods, Inc.

The Managerial Grid Robert R. Blake and Jane S. Mouton of the University of Texas created a two-dimensional model for visualizing the continuum from task focus to employee focus (Blake et al., 1964). They called the model the **managerial grid.** As Exhibit 13.7 shows, the model presents two axes, one that rates concern for people and another that rates concern for production. (These axes clearly correspond to employee- and job-centeredness in the University of Michigan studies, and consideration and initiating structure in the Ohio State studies.) The ratings are stated in terms of a 9-point scale, with 1 representing low concern and 9 representing high concern. The grid effectively summarizes positions that managers and leaders can take under a variety of circumstances.

If you are a manager, see if you can place your focus on the grid in relation to a specific subordinate. If you are not a manager, try placing your boss's focus. Then ask yourself if the focus is appropriate. Such an analysis typifies one use of the grid—it is an effective tool for management training and development.

In choosing a leadership style, a manager must adapt to the situation while evaluating motivational strategy, decision-making style, and the merits of a task or employee focus. The style a manager chooses is influenced by the leader's philosophy, background, and perceptions; the personalities, backgrounds, and needs of subordinates or team members; and external pressures, influences, and constraints.

The next section will examine three theories of leadership that incorporate these situational elements: the contingency model, the path-goal theory, and the life-cycle theory.

Theories of Situational Leadership

Three general theories of leadership address adaptation of leadership to situations. All have strong roots in the motivational theories discussed in Chapter 12.

Fiedler's Contingency Model

Fred E. Fiedler (1974) holds that the most appropriate style of leadership for a manager depends on the manager's situation. Fiedler's model of management, the **contingency model**, suggests that a manager should choose task or employee focus according to the interaction of three situational variables: leader-member relations, task structure, and leader position power. Because Fiedler's model emphasizes the importance of the situation, Fiedler's work is sometimes called the theory of situational leadership. Exhibit 13.8 shows Fiedler's contingency model.

The solid line plotted at the top of Exhibit 13.8 reveals the recommended focus for specific situations. To understand the recommendations and how they were reached, you must understand the variables the model uses.

The scale of leader-member relations refers to the degree to which the leader is or feels accepted by the group. Measured by the observed degree of mutual respect, trust, and confidence, this acceptance is rated as good or poor. In a good relationship, the leader should be able to inspire and influence subordinates. If the relationship is poor, the manager may have to resort to negotiating or to promising favors to get performance.

The task structure ratings relate to the nature of subordinates' jobs or tasks. A structured task is or can be broken into procedures. It is narrowly defined and may be machine-paced, and it tends to be full of routines that are repeated regularly. Data entry clerks, file clerks, and supermarket checkers hold structured jobs. An unstructured job includes complexities, variety, and latitude for creative expression. Researchers, managers, design engineers, and most professionals hold unstructured jobs.

The ratings for leader position power describe the organizational power base from which the leader operates. To what degree can the leader reward and punish? With whom is the leader allied? The leader's connections, legitimate power, expert power, and referent power determine weakness or strength—the ability to exercise a little influence or a great deal of influence inside the organization.

Note position I in Exhibit 13.8. In a situation displaying good leader-member relations, structured tasks, and strong leader position power, the contingency model tells the leader to adopt a task orientation. At position VII, a nearly equal blend of employee- and task-orientation is best. Employee-oriented leaders

Exhibit 13.8

Fiedler's contingency model, depicting the interaction of leadership orientations with situational variables.

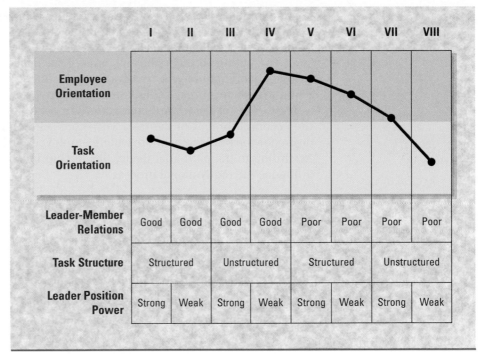

perform best under conditions associated with positions IV, V, and VI. When a manager is promoted or given a temporary assignment—as project leader or product design team leader, for example—he or she will find a new combination of people and circumstances. Each combination calls for a fresh assessment of Fiedler's three variables.

House and Mitchell's Path-Goal Theory

Robert J. House and Terrence R. Mitchell (1974) developed the **path-goal theory** of leadership. Their theory relates to the behaviors a leader can use to stimulate subordinates' motivation to achieve both personal and organizational goals and rewards (House, 1971). The path-goal theory suggests that a leadership style is effective or ineffective on the basis of how successfully leaders influence and support their subordinates' perceptions of:

● Goals that need to be achieved

● Rewards for successful performance

● Behaviors that lead to successful performance

According to the path-goal theory, leaders can influence subordinates' motivation by (1) teaching employees the competencies they will need to perform successfully and gain rewards, (2) tailoring rewards to meet employees' needs, and (3) acting to support subordinates' efforts. Teaching (coaching, development, and training) builds confidence and competencies. Adapting rewards to the specific needs of individual employees makes them more appealing. Supportive behaviors assist subordinates as necessary, enabling them to achieve both personal and organizational goals.

The path-goal theory has its basis in the expectancy theory of motivation. In that theory, employees' motivations are influenced by their perceptions of what a task requires, their confidence in their abilities to perform, the attractiveness of the reward being offered, and the relationship of the reward to the accomplishment of the task. The more self-confidence and the greater the desire for the reward, the more willing employees will be to perform as required. According to the path-goal theory, leadership behaviors and situational factors influence the motivational process.

Leadership Behaviors   House and Mitchell (1974) based their theory on the following two assumptions:

1. A leader's behavior is acceptable and satisfying to subordinates to the extent that they view it as either an immediate source of satisfaction or as an instrument to some future satisfaction.

2. A leader's behavior will increase subordinates' efforts if it links satisfaction of their needs to effective performance and supports their efforts to achieve goals.

These two assumptions tell managers to increase the number of ways in which performance can be deemed successful, to clear away barriers to successful outcomes, and to help subordinates see these outcomes as desirable (House and Mitchell, 1974). To enable leaders to do these things, the theory provides four kinds of leadership behavior:

- Instrumental behavior (task-oriented). This behavior, sometimes called directive behavior, involves the planning, directing, monitoring, and task-assignment aspects of leadership. It can be prescriptive. A manager who uses instrumental behavior establishes precise procedures, goals, and timetables and utilizes the autocratic style of leadership. This behavior can be used to increase an employee's work effort or to clarify outcomes.

- Supportive behavior (employee-oriented). This behavior creates a climate of mutual trust and respect between leaders and followers. It involves the coaching, counseling, and mentoring aspects of leadership. Supportive behavior requires open communication and a leader's honest concern for subordinates' needs. This type of behavior builds teams.

- Participative behavior (employee-oriented). In this behavior, a leader solicits and uses subordinates' ideas and contributions and involves subordinates in decision making. During the planning and execution phases of an operation, the manager tries to obtain input from everyone concerned. Supportive behavior promotes participative behavior. The reverse is true as well. Participative behavior builds team spirit, values individuals and their contributions, and encourages development through exposure to others' points of view and experience.

D. Wayne Calloway, CEO of PepsiCo, places great emphasis on empowerment. His enlightened management tactics have created a more powerful work force.

- Achievement-oriented behavior (employee-oriented). A leader who shows this type of behavior helps subordinates grow and increases their competencies through training and development. The leader's primary aim is to improve subordinates' abilities and performance, thus making the employees more valuable to themselves and their organization. Instrumental behavior, supportive behavior, and participative behavior increase a leader's ability to engage in achievement-oriented behavior, which paves the way for subordinates' advancement.

CEO D. Wayne Calloway heads up the 300,000 employees of PepsiCo's worldwide operations. His regular routines include all four types of behavior that House and Mitchell described. He uses instrumental behavior in his hands-on approach to hiring, strategic planning, and executive appraisals. He interviews all job candidates for positions at the vice-presidential level or above, and some 75 executives each year. Twice a year Calloway is personally involved in evaluating some 600 managers (Konrad and Rothman, 1992).

Calloway uses supportive behavior in a company-wide drive to build on past decentralization with renewed efforts at empowerment. His participative behavior includes encouraging employees—everyone from route salespeople to restaurant workers—to recommend ways to improve the business. In 1991, for example, Calloway introduced the Great PepsiCo Brainstorm, in which employees won prizes for contributing ideas. His achievement-oriented behavior includes encouraging people to take risks and rewarding them for their initiative, whether it leads to success or failure (Konrad and Rothman, 1992).

Situational Factors   Two situational factors are important components in the path-goal theory: the personal characteristics of subordinates and the work environment. These two factors influence the behavior a leader should choose.

The personal characteristics of subordinates include their abilities, self-confidence, personal needs and motivations, and perceptions of their leaders. When subordinates exhibit low levels of performance, leaders must be ready to provide coaching, training, and direction. The leader must ensure that the rewards offered for outstanding performance are rewards that appeal to employees.

Factors in the work environment include the organization's culture and subcultures, the philosophy of management, how power is exercised, policies and rules, and the extent to which tasks are structured. These factors are environmental pressures beyond the abilities of employees to control, but they affect employees' abilities to accomplish tasks and achieve goals.

Leaders must know what their people want from work, what their motivations are, and what stands between them and successful performance. Leaders must provide to each person the appropriate leadership, depending upon the employees and the environmental conditions. Where skills are weak, instrumental behavior is called for; when subordinates lack motivation, achievement-oriented behavior may be appropriate.

Managers at Collins & Aikman, a carpet manufacturer, decided to give their employees what they needed: new technology. Instead of opting for cheap labor overseas as a means to stay competitive, the company chose to invest in its U.S. work force and operations and install state-of-the-art equipment. In their Georgia plant, the primary tufting and shearing machines were to be linked to computers. But the prospect of working with computers terrified many of the firm's 560 employees. Almost one-third of the workers had not finished high school; some could not read or write (Cooper, 1992).

A needs assessment revealed that only 8% of the workers possessed the skills needed to adjust to the new high-tech environment. Collins & Aikman provided basic literacy training at a cost of about $1,200 per worker, and the employer implemented other in-house training programs as well. Productivity and employee self-confidence rose, and so did a flood of workers' suggestions about how to improve just about every phase of the operation. Production rejects fell by 50%, and workers needed less assistance from supervisors (Cooper, 1992).

Hersey and Blanchard's Life-Cycle Theory

Paul Hersey and Kenneth H. Blanchard (1982) developed the **life-cycle theory** of leadership. As Exhibit 13.9 shows, the life-cycle theory relates leadership behavior to subordinates' maturity levels. Immature employees (new and inexperienced) require leadership with a high task–low relationship focus (the lower-right quadrant in the exhibit). As people learn and mature in their jobs, they become increasingly able to direct themselves and participate in decision making. Employees develop relationships with their co-workers, team members, and superiors that lead to mutual respect and trust. New skills and knowledge make employees more valuable to themselves and their organizations. As they progress in their organizational lives, employees require from their leaders first a high task–high relationship focus, followed by a high relationship–low task approach, and finally a low task–low relationship focus.

Exhibit 13.9

Adaptation of Hersey and Blanchard's life-cycle theory of leadership.

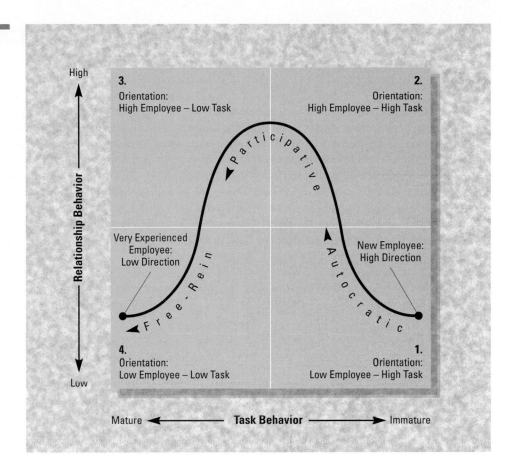

For employees described in quadrant 1 of Exhibit 13.9, an autocratic leadership style would be appropriate. For employees described in quadrants 2 and 3, the manager should move to a participative style. For those described in quadrant 4, the free-rein style is appropriate. Stated in terms of path-goal theory behaviors, quadrant 1 calls for instrumental behavior. Quadrants 2 and 3 call for supportive, participative, and achievement-oriented behaviors. By the time employees attain the characteristics described in quadrant 4, they should be operating in a relatively autonomous way, turning to the manager or higher authority on an as-needed basis.

Hersey and Blanchard built on and combined ideas from the managerial grid and path-goal theory. Their theory does not allow for changes in situations, however, and it assumes that leaders are capable and mature.

Challenges Facing Leaders

Leaders provide vision. They also supply incentives that enlist the support of others in making the vision a reality. Leaders keep people focused on what is important and what must be done. They set examples and foster values that become part of their organizations' cultures. Leaders are change agents, sensing the need for change and creating strategies that will help to initiate it.

Was the System to Blame?

The California Department of Consumer Affairs charged a national retailer's automobile-repair operation with defrauding consumers with overcharges and unneeded repairs. The chairman of the retail outfit claimed that his company's incentive policy contributed to the problem. The policy rewarded service advisors who met sales quotas on specific auto parts and paid the advisors on a commission-only basis for repairs customers authorized. This policy, the chairman said, was to blame for "creating an environment where mistakes did occur." He took final responsibility for the policies by stating, "The buck stops with me."

The chairman changed the company's compensation policies to remove the incentives that led to the abuses, and he publicly announced the changes through a press conference and television commercials. The retailer's auto centers now emphasize quality rather than quantity.

Do you think that the commission system encouraged sales advisors to overcharge customers and sell them repairs they did not need? Do the service advisors bear any responsibility for their actions? If so, what? Besides changing the compensation system, is there anything else you would advise the chairman to do? ▲

One leader who takes his role as change agent seriously is CEO Harold McInnes, who heads AMP, a business that supplies electrical connectors. From its headquarters in Pennsylvania, AMP does business through 30 wholly owned foreign subsidiaries around the globe. McInnes's vision is to build on his company's position by devoting 9% of sales dollars to R&D each year. He believes this investment will allow the company to move from being a supplier of connectors to being a provider of larger, more complete subsystems. McInnes calls the process "moving up the food chain." One strategy for achieving McInnes's vision is to couple AMP's sales engineers with product-design teams at customers' locations. "That way, when the whizzes at DEC or Apple Computer sit down to formulate next-generation products, AMP people are right there determining which AMP subsystems can be designed into them." Harold McInnes plans to ensure that his company will thrive in the future (Erdman, 1992).

Leadership Throughout an Organization

It is not enough to have a leader at the top of an organization. Leadership must be exerted at all levels, or change will be resisted and blocked. Leaders must occupy top, middle, and supervisory ranks. Workers in self-directed teams need leaders too. Staff development and training efforts (see Chapter 10) should encourage and empower people to become leaders at every level.

If one story illustrates the value of leadership at all levels of a company, it is the dramatic turnaround of Harley-Davidson, the motorcycle maker. Harley-Davidson tried various approaches to improving the quality and dependability of its motorcycles. Results were insignificant until managers discovered the power within their own work force.

In the 1980s Harley managers decided to replace the obsolete manufacturing system in its Pennsylvania plant and introduce a just-in-time inventory system. To implement the new system, Harley took a step that was unusual for that time: Managers involved employees in deciding how to handle the changeover. Instead of having managers and engineers make all the decisions and announce them to workers, Harley managers spent several months discussing the desired changes with everyone. After all parties helped decide on the changes, everyone cooperated to make them work (Boyett and Conn, 1991).

Employee involvement worked so well that management decided to enlist employees in solving quality problems. Employees learned how to use statistical tools for monitoring and controlling the quality of their own work; managers and supervisors were trained as team leaders. Both quality and morale improved. Employee involvement, just-in-time inventory, and statistical operator control became part of what Harley came to call its productivity triad (Boyett and Conn, 1991). Employees were empowered to monitor their own work, resolve problems, and implement their own solutions. Managers worked with teams, sharing authority and supporting team efforts in every way possible.

Leadership and Rapid Response

Constantly changing demands challenge a leader's effectiveness. As culturally diverse organizations evolve, the leader's constituencies grow increasingly complex. Different circumstances and demands call for different kinds of direction, change, and strategies. In a business world based on high technology, speed is essential: In Sam Walton's words, a company must be able to "turn on a dime."

CEO Arthur Shoring of Topps, the maker of trading cards sold with bubble gum, illustrates the ability to turn on a dime. Topps has an extraordinary capacity to capitalize quickly on fads. During the Persian Gulf War, Shoring watched a TV broadcast about children who feared that Iraqi missiles might hit the United States. In response, Shoring launched a line of Desert Storm trading cards that pictured and described American weaponry. The process, from idea to store shelf, took six weeks. The line was, of course, a smash hit for Topps (Teitelbaum, 1992).

Leadership and Tough Decisions

Anyone can lead when decisions are easy and please constituencies. But leaders must often make unpopular, difficult decisions that adversely affect people inside and outside an organization. Leaders need the courage to see their decisions through and to face consequences. Leaders must have the ability to do—within legal, moral, and ethical boundaries—what is best for their organizations.

In a crisis, a company may turn to an outsider for guidance. Niagara Mohawk Power of Syracuse, New York, turned to an insider, Bill Donlon. Maintenance problems had caused the shutdown of a nuclear power station, forcing the company to buy electricity from rival producers. Cost overruns from the construction of a second nuclear plant were also hurting the bottom line. Donlon turned the company around by bringing in 20 new senior officers, reassigning key staff, terminating poor performers, reassessing the functions of all 11,000 employees, and enlisting everyone's help in establishing changes and productivity savings. "The whole system just wasn't working any longer," said Donlon. "It was apparent to me that we had to change" (Losee, 1992).

Donlon converted his vertical organization into four separate units—nuclear, gas customer service, electric customer service, and electric supply and delivery. Each unit was responsible for its own profit and for developing its business. To keep productivity high, Donlon deployed a new incentive plan that gives manager and officer bonuses from 15% to 35% of salary if they meet performance goals (Losee, 1992). He negotiated with his most important constituencies—customers and regulators—and in two years recaptured their trust. Profits rose over five years, and customer complaints dropped by 27%. A deep and lasting change was made by an inside change agent and leader-manager.

Just as Donlon asked hard questions and made tough decisions, so did Richard Stegemeier, CEO of Unocal. His goal was to set his company on the right course and bring it back from deep indebtedness. The answers to the questions Stegemeier asked led him to take drastic measures; he closed gas stations, shut down refineries, and consolidated domestic operations. The result: Unocal is on the road to recovery (Murray, 1990).

How Managers Can Become Better Leaders

Becoming a better leader begins with efforts to know oneself. Each manager has diverse values, needs, goals, ethics, strengths, and weaknesses; these determine how he or she will use the arts of management and leadership. An individual's philosophy about work and about the people who perform it will influence approaches to leadership. Managers who respect individuals will value diversity

The fine art of leadership is not the same as management ability. Both sets of skills are needed to keep organizations directed and productive.

and treat each person with dignity. Managers who value security above all else may be too cautious, unwilling to make tough decisions and take their consequences. Conversely, managers who value growth and challenge will seek new approaches, take on tough assignments, and willingly endure personal sacrifice to improve themselves, their subordinates, and their organizations. Such managers will encourage others to do the same.

Because leadership is situational, leaders must be adaptable. They must build teams and work with them. Leaders must willingly and ably exercise different leadership styles and utilize the behaviors discussed in this chapter. Only by doing so will their businesses be able to turn on a dime—a capability that the business environment of today requires. Managers must provide a vision and "sell" it to their constituents. They need to sense the need for change, prepare themselves and their team members for change, and articulate what is needed for change. Then they must act as change agents. They can do all these things only by staying current in their fields, remaining open to what is new and different, and committing themselves to constant efforts at self-improvement through the adoption of the *kaizen* philosophy.

GLOBAL APPLICATIONS
American and Japanese Leadership Styles

Several differences distinguish American and Japanese managers' approaches to leading. *Business Week* (May 7, 1990) reported on the differences in empowerment and participation.

The most profitable Japanese-owned companies in the U.S. are those that delegate a high degree of authority to their American managers. That is a key finding of a study by the University of Michigan School of Business Administration and Egon Zehnder International, an executive search firm, based on a survey of 133 top American executives employed by 32 Japanese companies.

The study also found that many American managers in Japanese companies complained that they were given little access to strategic information and felt "locked out" of decision making and product planning. Performance reviews were irregular or nonexistent. Consequently, the more aggressive and ambitious American managers tended to quit because they believed opportunities for promotion above certain levels were restricted (*Business Week,* May 7, 1990). In Japan, these same companies do involve employees at every level in collaborative decision making and open communication.

With regard to Japanese practices in management development, many Japanese companies send their employees to American business schools to earn a Master of Business Administration (MBA) degree at company expense. But the returning graduates find little use or respect for their MBAs among their Japanese colleagues. Ono (1992) cited the reason:

[Japanese companies] send students abroad under the life-time employment system to ensure that there will be more English speakers who are familiar with Western business practices. Some managers regard business schools as a kind of high-level English language school, returning students say, or consider the two years [to earn the degree] as more or less a paid vacation. Nearly a third of 68 Toyota-sponsored business school graduates have left the company after returning.

In Japan, both Japanese and foreign companies have been more than willing to hire these disheartened employees whose educations have been paid for by their rivals. ▲

Leaders must be willing to suppress what may seem best for themselves and implement what is best for others—subordinates, customers, and their organizations. As a servant who tailors leadership style and behavior to fit others' needs, the true leader excels by doing what is best for others. Being a manager is tough, but being a leader-manager is tougher still.

Future Trends

In the 1990s, several business trends relate to leadership in organizations. These trends include the following:

- The traditional manager who relied on legitimate power and instrumental behavior is all but gone in America's medium- to large-sized companies. Managers who cannot adjust to team management, empower subordinates, and act as facilitators for their people will not last long in organizations.

- Downsizing and decentralization mean fewer opportunities for advancement and more competition than ever before for the positions that remain. The manager who can make the transition to leader-manager will have the best chance for advancement. Others with leadership ability will find additional opportunities as team leaders.

- More organizations are splitting themselves into self-managing divisions and units. The leadership these organizations need is from people who see the whole, not just one part. Cross-training through job rotation and understudy positions must occur to provide these companies with the well-rounded executives they need.

- Several large corporations have split the power of the CEO among two or more leaders. Microsoft has created a three-person presidency. Xerox (as the case problem at the end of this chapter will discuss) has created a six-person corporate position that replaces the president's role. If these experiments prove successful, more organizations are likely to follow suit and employ the technique of power splitting at lower levels.

- More and more managers will find themselves managing process teams that work on a horizontal level rather than vertically. Teams will control and drive all functions on one level, reporting results to a senior person and asking him or her for assistance as needed. Managers will have to depend on their subordinates' expert power to a greater extent than at present.

- Workplaces will show less and less evidence of members' status. Work environments will become more open, physically and intellectually. Barriers that separate people in any way and inhibit open communication will be eliminated. Managers who have a low need for status symbols will thrive in these environments.

- More and more employees will "own" their jobs, and those jobs will be less specific and include more tasks. Typical employees will need continual training to keep up with changes in the tools and technology they must use to monitor and lead individual and team efforts.

C H A P T E R   **S** U M M A R Y

- Leadership is the process of influencing individuals and groups to set and achieve goals. The terms *leadership* and *management* are not synonyms.

- The demands placed on leaders include the need to satisfy multiple constituencies, sense the need for and then successfully implement change, tailor their uses of power and their leadership behaviors to the needs of subordinates and circumstances, and inspire people to give their best.

- Leaders need vision. They must be able to articulate it and keep their people focused on and committed to it.

- Leaders can draw on three types of power: legitimate, referent, and expert.

- Leadership emphasizes positive motivational approaches. Negative approaches create an environment of fear.

- Sharing authority and empowering employees involves delegating authority, training employees in decision-making skills, and using the participative or free-rein leadership style.

- A leader needs to vary his or her focus—on employees or on tasks—depending on personal philosophy, background, and perceptions; the kind of subordinates and their needs and backgrounds; and the external pressures, influences, and constraints.

- Whether a manager should focus on employees or tasks depends on leader-member relations, how structured the task is, and how much power the leader has.

- Leaders must know how and when to engage in instrumental behavior, supportive behavior, participative behavior, and achievement-oriented behavior.

- Leaders and subordinates affect the leadership situation through their values, morals, ethics, needs, strengths, weaknesses, knowledge, skills, traits, behaviors, experiences, and levels of motivation.

- Environmental variables that affect a leader's approach include the type of work being performed, its structure, and the policies, cultures, rules, resources, and relationships in the organization.

- An effective leader varies his or her leadership style according to employees' levels of maturity. Inexperienced employees call for a task focus. With more experienced employees, the manager should maintain an employee focus.

- Leaders must be flexible and adaptable—equipped to give subordinates what they need when they need it so that they can reach both personal and organizational goals.

SKILL-BUILDING

The following questions are designed to allow you to apply the material in this chapter to a job you now hold or one you may have held in the past. By answering each question candidly, you will gain insight into the impacts that leaders can have on subordinates.

1. Is your manager a leader? In what ways is he or she a good or poor example to you?

2. Who are your manager's constituencies? Does he or she meet their needs?

3. Do you know of a tough decision your manager has had to face? What was it? How did your manager deal with its consequences?

4. What examples can you cite from your work experiences to support the statement that managers need to have vision? What visions have been communicated to you at work by managers?

5. Is your manager able to adapt approaches to meet your needs and the needs of your fellow employees?

6. Does your manager involve you in decisions and problems? Do you want to be involved?

REVIEW QUESTIONS

1. Review this chapter's essential terms and look up the meanings of those you cannot define.

2. Is a manager a leader? Explain.

3. Under what conditions should a leader adopt a task focus? An employee focus?

4. What kinds of power can leaders possess? Upon what is each based?

5. What three factors interact to create a manager's leadership style?

6. What is positive motivation? What is negative motivation? Cite examples of each.

7. Under what conditions should a leader use (1) autocratic leadership, (2) participative leadership, or (3) free-rein leadership?

8. What three factors interact with a manager's orientation according to the contingency theory?

9. What are the four types of leadership behaviors according to the path-goal theory of leadership?

10. What does the life-cycle theory consider that the managerial grid does not?

R E C O M M E N D E D   R E A D I N G

Bennis, Warren. "How to Be the Leader They'll Follow," *Working Woman* (March 1990), p. 42.

Crosby, Philip B. *Leading* (New York: McGraw-Hill), 1990.

Crosby, Philip B. *Running Things* (New York: McGraw-Hill), 1986.

Gitlow, Abraham L. *Being the Boss* (Homewood, IL: Richard D. Irwin), 1992.

Jamieson, David, and Julie O'Mara. *Managing Workforce 2000* (San Francisco: Jossey-Bass), 1991.

Kotter, John P. *A Force for Change: How Leadership Differs from Management* (New York: Free Press), 1990.

Kotter, John P. *The Leadership Factor* (New York: Free Press), 1988.

Petersen, Donald E., and John Hillkirk. *A Better Idea: Redefining the Way Americans Work* (Boston: Houghton Mifflin), 1991.

Plunkett, Lorne C., and Robert Fournier. *Participative Management: Implementing Empowerment* (New York: Wiley), 1991.

Yukl, Gary A. *Leadership in Organizations* (Englewood Cliffs, NJ: Prentice-Hall), 1981.

R E F E R E N C E S

Blake, Robert R.; Jane S. Mouton; Louis B. Barnes; and Larry E. Greiner. "Breakthrough in Organization Development," *Harvard Business Review* (November–December 1964).

Boyett, Joseph H., and Henry P. Conn. *Workplace 2000* (New York: Plume), 1991, pp. 330, 331.

Business Week (May 7, 1990). "Japanese Employers Are 'Locking Out' Their U.S. Managers," p. 24.

Cooper, Helen. "Carpet Firm Sets Up an In-House School to Stay Competitive," *Wall Street Journal,* October 5, 1992, pp. A1, A5.

Davis, Keith, and John Newstrom. *Human Behavior at Work: Organizational Behavior,* 8th edition (New York: McGraw-Hill), 1989, pp. 213, 215.

Ellig, Bruce R. "Do You Have the Right Stuff?" *HR Magazine* (October 1991), p. 40.

Erdman, Andrew. "Staying Ahead of 800 Competitors," *Fortune* (June 1, 1992), p. 111.

Fiedler, Fred E. "The Contingency Model—New Directions for Leadership Utilization," *Journal of Contemporary Business* 3, no. 4 (Autumn 1974), pp. 65–80.

Hersey, Paul, and Kenneth H. Blanchard. *Management of Organizational Behavior,* 4th edition (Englewood Cliffs, NJ: Prentice-Hall), 1982.

House, Robert J. "A Path-Goal Theory of Leader Effectiveness," *Administrative Science Quarterly* 16 (1971), pp. 321–338.

House, Robert J., and Terrence R. Mitchell. "Path-Goal Theory of Leadership," *Journal of Contemporary Business* 3, no. 4 (Autumn 1974), pp. 81–97.

Inc. (October 1992). "Managing People," p. 33.

Keller, Robert, and Andrew Szilagyi. "A Longitudinal Study of Leader Reward Behavior, Subordinate Expectations, and Satisfaction," *Personnel Psychology* (Spring 1978), pp. 119–129.

Kiechell III, Walter. "The Leader As Servant," *Fortune* (May 4, 1992), pp. 121, 122.

Kleiman, Carol. "1990s Will See Opportunity for New Breed of Manager," *Chicago Tribune,* March 22, 1992, sec. 8, p. 1.

Konrad, Walecia, and Andrea Rothman. "Can Wayne Calloway Handle the Pepsi Challenge?" *Business Week* (January 27, 1992), pp. 90, 91, 92.

Kotter, John P., and James L. Heskett. *Corporate Culture and Performance* (New York: Free Press), 1992, pp. 94–96.

Likert, Rensis. "From Production- and Employee-Centeredness to Systems 1–4," *Journal of Management* 5 (1979), pp. 147–156.

Likert, Rensis. *The Human Organization* (New York: McGraw-Hill), 1976.

Losee, Stephanie. "Revolution from Within," *Fortune* (June 1, 1992), p. 112.

Murray, Kathleen. "Unocal's New Man: Stegemeier Pares Debt, Refines Look of Company," *Orange County Register,* January 28, 1990, p. K2.

Nulty, Peter. "How to Live by Your Wits," *Fortune* (April 20, 1992), p. 119.

Ono, Yumido. "Japanese Firms Don't Let Masters Rule," *Wall Street Journal,* May 4, 1992, B1.

Peace, William H. "The Hard Work of Being a Soft Manager," *Harvard Business Review* (November–December 1991), pp. 40–47.

Schriesheim, C. A., and B. J. Bird. "Contributions of the Ohio State Studies to the Field of Leadership," *Journal of Management* 5 (1979), pp. 135–145.

Shartle, C. L. "Early Years of the Ohio State University Leadership Studies," *Journal of Management* 5 (1979), pp. 126–134.

Teitelbaum, Richard S. "Timeliness Is Everything," *Fortune* (April 20, 1992), p. 120.

Walton, Sam, with John Huey. *Sam Walton: Made in America* (New York: Doubleday), 1992, p. 169.

Yukl, Gary A. *Leadership in Organizations* (Englewood Cliffs, NJ: Prentice-Hall), 1981, p. 70, 121–125.

G L O S S A R Y   O F   T E R M S

autocratic style   A leadership approach in which a manager does not share decision-making authority with subordinates.

contingency model   A leadership theory that states that a manager should focus on either tasks or employees, depending upon the interaction of three variables—leader-member relations, task structure, and leader position power.

expert power   Influence due to abilities, skills, knowledge, or experience.

free-rein style   A leadership approach in which a manager shares decision-making authority with subordinates, empowering them to function without direct involvement from managers to whom they report.

influence   The ability to sway people to one's will.

leadership The process of influencing individuals and groups to set and achieve goals.

leadership style The perceived approaches and behaviors a manager uses to influences others.

legitimate power Authority possessed by managers and derived from the positions they occupy in the formal organization.

life-cycle theory A view of management that asserts that a leader's behavior toward a subordinate should relate to the subordinate's maturity level. The focus on tasks and relationships should vary as the subordinate matures.

managerial grid Blake and Mouton's two-dimensional model for visualizing the extent to which a manager focuses on tasks or employees.

participative style A leadership approach in which a manager shares decision-making authority with subordinates.

path-goal theory A view of management that asserts that subordinates' behaviors and motivations are influenced by the behaviors managers exhibit toward them. This theory suggests that leadership style should depend on the leader's influence and subordinate's perceptions, goals, rewards, and goal paths.

referent power Influence that comes to people because of the kinds of persons they seem to be—their traits, personalities, and attractiveness to others.

sanction A penalty—such as a fine, suspension, or termination—used to influence people's behavior.

C A S E   P R O B L E M

Teams at the Top

Many companies are concluding that the job of chairperson and president is too complex for one person to handle, especially in multistate and multinational environments. In 1992 Xerox, Microsoft, and retail leader Nordstrom Inc. moved to power sharing in their executive suites. According to University of Southern California business professor James O'Toole, "Corporate America is moving away from single, all-powerful chief executives. One person can't have all the wisdom." Deborah Ancona, associate professor of organizational studies at MIT's Sloan School of Management, adds: "The complexity of the task is becoming overwhelming for one person. There is too much for the CEO to do himself.... [Work] that used to be done sequentially now must be done in parallel."

At the Paris headquarters of Accor S.A., a French hotel and restaurant group, two people share the chairman's job—M. Dubrule and M. Pelisson. The two believe that their arrangement works because it is based on mutual trust. As Pelisson put it, "It took three years to become very confident in the other person. The key is the building of confidence." The two chairmen believe that they must extend the same degree of trust to their managers that they extend to each other. Their company is highly decentralized. "Managers in the group are required to consult with the chairmen on major strategic decisions, such as whether to focus their product expansion on Europe or on Asia. But once the long-term goals are set, managers may chart their own course."

At Seattle-based Nordstrom Inc., three Nordstroms share the chair, and four managers (three men and one woman) share the president's position. In the case of the chairpersons, the decisions are made by committee but are generally limited to controlling strategic direction. Day-to-day management is left to the four presidents. "Like the co-chairmen, the presidents have ample debate, they say, and resolve most disagreements by focusing on what would be best for the customer.... '[We] leave our egos at the doorstep.'" The co-presidents each concentrate on their specialty areas and act with great autonomy.

Xerox, the copier and printer giant, has a new corporate position that six top executives share. In place of a president, the company has a group headed by Paul Allaire, chairman and CEO; three operations executives; one head of corporate research and technology; and one head of corporate strategic services. Before the change, "a lot of operating decisions came to the corporate office. In many cases,

the people making decisions at corporate headquarters didn't have all the information that someone working today might have." The results were sluggish product development and lost opportunities.

David Nadler, president of Delta Consulting Group in New York, helped design the Xerox structure. He says competition for the top job—either covert or overt—is the main threat to team leadership in the executive suite.

The power-sharing technique has not yet stood the test of time. Those who are experimenting with it face many questions. How should the executives coordinate their efforts? What happens when a decision demands the expertise of two or more executives and overlaps the authority of each? Will two or more executives be able to act as swiftly in a crisis as one?

Q U E S T I O N S

1. What potential problems do you think co-presidents and co-chairpersons will face when sharing power?

2. Can power-sharing arrangements work in companies where lower levels do not have a high degree of operating autonomy? Why or why not?

3. Do you think that power-sharing arrangements are appropriate for small, local businesses? Why or why not?

For more about leadership variants, see: Dori Jones Yang, "Nordstrom's Gang of Four," *Business Week,* June 15, 1992, pp. 122–123; Amanda Bennett, "Firms Run by Executive Teams Can Reap Rewards, Incur Risks," *Wall Street Journal,* February 5, 1992, pp. B1, B2; Brian Coleman, "Accor Finds Success with Two Chairmen," *Wall Street Journal,* April 2, 1992, p. B6; and Suein L. Hwang, "Xerox Forms New Structure for Businesses," *Wall Street Journal,* February 5, 1992, p. B6.

14

Team Management and Conflict

L E A R N I N G   O B J E C T I V E S

After reading and discussing this chapter, you should be able to:

- Define this chapter's essential terms
- Identify the types of teams that organizations use
- Discuss potential uses of teams
- Use decision-making authority as a characteristic by which to distinguish team type
- Identify and discuss steps in establishing teams
- Identify and discuss the roles of team members
- Describe the four stages of team development
- Discuss team cohesiveness and team norms and their relationship to team performance
- Evaluate the benefits and costs of teams
- Discuss positive and negative aspects of conflict in an organization
- Identify the sources of conflict in an organization
- Describe a manager's role in conflict management and potential strategies to manage conflict

avoidance
cohesiveness
collaboration
committee
compromise
conflict
confrontation

cross-functional team
dysfunctional conflict
executive team
formal team
forming stage
free rider
horizontal team

norming stage
performing stage
product-development team
project team
quality assurance team
quality circle (QC)
self-directed work team

smoothing
storming stage
superordinate objective
task force
team
team norm
vertical team
work team

M A N A G E M E N T   I N   A C T I O N
Teams at Picker International

When you walk into the Picker International Computed Tomography (CT) Division plant in Eastlake, Ohio, you see two framed signs in the lobby. One is a list of work expectations—a list developed participatively by all Eastlake employees. The second is the CT Division's mission statement, which defines the rights and obligations of each employee. These documents set the tone for a self-styled, no-blame environment. They contribute to a world-class manufacturing operation that can be characterized as an empowered team workplace.

The parts of a body work as a system, like a well tuned team at Picker International, producers of tomographic images like these.

Frank Vorwald, manufacturing and quality manager at Picker (a manufacturer of computer-enhanced tomography systems), believes his role is to be head coach and let his teams play. To Vorwald's way of thinking, "Managers in the U.S. have had a tendency to feel we know more than the people on the floor. In actuality, it's the reverse. People on the floor know what it takes to get the job done."

With this guiding premise, the number of management levels has been reduced from nine to three. All staff members are salaried, and the environment focuses on team building and continual improvement. Employees are expected to change, react, and take chances—knowing that it is okay to make a mistake.

The approach has led to two distinctly different results. First, the production capability of the plant has doubled in the past five years. The increase is due to the efforts of the teams, not to an increase in staff. Second, employees solve problems. When pivot bearings do not fit, someone on the quality team or the production team jumps in and provides a solution, working with the supplier and the Picker employee identified as the champion/liaison. Regardless of which employees are involved, independence, self-direction, and empowerment are constant.

What does the future hold for the teams? For Vorwald and the other managers at Picker, the vision is for the employees to "own" more and more of the manufacturing process, until the managers do not even have to coach. ▲

For more about the team concept at Picker, see Joseph F. McKenna, "Coach Lets His Team Play the Game," *Industry Week,* May 4, 1992, pp. 17–18.

The Nature of Teams

A not-so-quiet revolution is taking place in American business. At companies such as Apple Computer, General Foods, Cypress Semiconductor, Levi Strauss, Xerox, and General Electric, teams are emerging as an organizational force (Stewart, 1992). Companies are realizing that the team approach can ignite superior performance. Teams in all their various forms—self-directed work teams, task forces, and project teams are but a few—are changing organizational structures, the way work is approached, the role of managers, and the involvement of workers (Cox, 1992).

This chapter will examine types of teams, how teams are created and managed, and their benefits and costs. You will see how to keep teams functioning effectively by managing conflict.

Teams Defined

In an organization, a **team** is a group of two or more people who interact regularly and coordinate their work to accomplish a common objective (Larson and LaFasto, 1989). Three points characterize a team:

- First, at least two people must be involved. The ultimate size of the group can vary depending on the nature of the assignment.

- Second, the members must interact regularly and coordinate their work. People who are in the same department but do not interact regularly are not a team. Nor are people who have lunch together every day but never actually coordinate their work.

- Third, members of a team must share an objective. Regardless of the objective—ensuring service quality, designing a new product, or reducing costs, for example—each member works toward a common end.

Characteristics of Effective Teams

Teams can and do function throughout organizations, as you will see shortly. Their effectiveness relates directly to how well managers engineer team structure and how team members behave. As Schein (1969) reported, the characteristics of effective teams include the following:

- Team members are committed to and involved in clear, shared goals.

- All team members feel free to express themselves and participate in discussions and decisions. Each member is valued and heard.

- Members trust each other. In discussions they openly disagree without fear of negative consequences.

- When needs for leadership arise, anyone feels free to volunteer. Team leadership varies with the situation.

- Decisions are made by consensus. All team members support final decisions.

Teamwork involves people who interact regularly and coordinate their work toward a common goal.

- As problems occur, the team focuses on causes, not symptoms. Likewise, when members develop solutions, they direct them at the causes of the problem.

- Team members are flexible in terms of work processes and problem solving. They search for new ways of acting.

- Team members change and grow. Growth is encouraged and supported by all.

Types of Teams

Many different types of teams are emerging in business organizations. These are **formal teams** created by management as a functioning part of the organizational structure. They are not informal nor are they created by social interaction. (For a discussion of informal groups, see Chapter 7.) In terms of origin, not function, two types of teams can be identified: vertical teams and horizontal teams.

Vertical Teams   A **vertical team**—sometimes called a command team or functional team—comprises a manager and subordinates in the formal chain of command. A vertical team may include as many as three or four levels of management. The Adstar Division of IBM is a vertical team that is restricted to a single functional department. Other examples of vertical teams are the human resource department at Citicorp, the accounting department at Archer Daniels Midland, and the quality control department at Picker International. Each conforms

Exhibit 14.1

Vertical and horizontal teams.

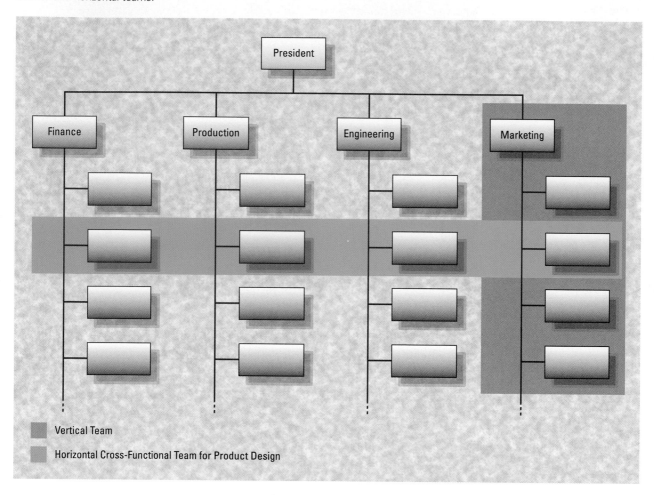

to the elements of the definition of *team:* Two or more people interact and coordinate their work for the purpose of achieving a common objective. The marketing department cited in Exhibit 14.1 is a vertical team, as are the finance, production, and engineering departments.

Horizontal Teams A **horizontal team** is made up of members drawn from different departments in an organization (Owens, 1989). In most cases, such a team is created to address a specific task or objective. The team may disband after the objective is achieved. Three common kinds of horizontal teams are task forces, cross-functional teams, and committees.

A **task force** is designed to accomplish a limited number of objectives or tasks, and it is composed of employees from different departments. A task force exists only until it meets the objectives. Master Industries, an injection-molding company in Ohio, formed a task force to implement a smoke-free policy in the workplace within 18 months. When this objective was attained, the task force disbanded (McKee, July 1992).

A **cross-functional team** harnesses the knowledge of people from various functional areas to solve operational problems. Like task forces, cross-functional teams focus on objectives, but they have an undefined life span. At Precision Industries, a distributor of industrial parts, a team of people from the collections, data entry, and customer-service departments meets on a regular basis with the firm's hardware developers. Their ongoing goal is to improve computer invoicing (Verespej, 1992). Exhibit 14.1 included a cross-functional product-design team.

A **committee** may be ad hoc (set up to do a job and then disbanded) or standing (permanent). The work of a standing committee—handling grievances, for instance—is ongoing. Commitee representatives may be chosen by functional area to reflect department views. Individuals are not necessarily chosen for specific technical ability, as members of a task force are. Thus, to ensure participation from all areas, a budget committee may have a representative from each of the major functional areas (Dumaine, 1992).

Philosophical Issues of Team Management

Given the current trend toward the team approach in American business, many managers are asking, "What can teams do?" and "How do they function within an organization?"

How to Use Teams

The purpose of a team is to accomplish one or more objectives. A team provides a vehicle for combining skills, securing commitment and involvement, and sharing expertise and opinions in the pursuit of a specific objective. The objective could be to improve quality, design a product, solve a problem, or carry out departmental work. Although managers may choose from unlimited team options, as Exhibit 14.2 suggests, four categories of teams are common: product-development, project, quality, and work teams.

Product-Development Teams Whether they are a task force or are cross-functional, **product-development teams** are organized to create new products. At Berrios Manufacturing Company, CEO Willis Berrios has created teams that combine people from different areas of expertise with the objective of smoothly bringing a new product to market. The teams include representatives from quality control, engineering, production, systems design, marketing, and manufacturing divisions (McKee, May 1992). Ingersoll-Rand's New Jersey–based Stryker Group used a product-development team to create a new power tool that went from design to production in just one year. The typical time to production before the implementation of teams was four years (Sheils, 1992).

Project Teams Instead of focusing on development of a single product, managers often assemble **project teams** (sometimes called problem-solving teams) to complete a specific task in an organization. Project teams flourish at Xerox, Apple Computer, Digital Equipment, Texas Instruments, General Dynamics, and

Exhibit 14.2

Potential uses for teams.

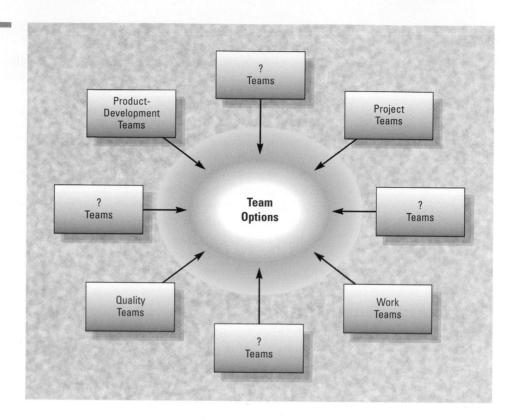

McDonnell Douglas (Benson, 1992). Teams of engineers move in to work out operating problems and harness their creativity to build strategic delivery systems.

Sometimes, to address an important project, teams operate outside the scope of the organizational structure. Although part of the formal organization, such teams maintain their own reporting structures. In these cases, members perceive their team as an independent and separate entity with plenty of "corporate breathing room" (Daft, 1991). At Apple Computer, the 150 software engineers working on the Taligent venture operate outside the normal structure on a high-risk, high-return project to develop a new operating system. At Digital Equipment Corporation, an acquisitions team, which evaluates other businesses as acquisition candidates, reports directly to the CEO (Kupfer, 1992).

Quality Teams In recent years, quality and quality assurance have become driving forces in American industry. Many firms have established quality teams, or teams that monitor and ensure quality. An early quality assurance tool was the quality circle. A **quality circle** (**QC**) is a group of volunteers from the same or related work areas who meet regularly to identify the quality issues facing the company or department and to offer suggestions for improvement. Other firms have developed **quality assurance teams**, whose mission is to guarantee the quality of services and products by visiting customers and working with vendors.

Work Teams When a company creates a small multi-skilled team that does all the tasks previously performed by individual members of a functional department

FOCUS ON QUALITY
Quality Teams Reform the Workplace

Ann Combs's co-workers used to hate to come to work in the morning. "There was no morale, absolutely none," says the Navy travel manager. Vernedia Arlington, an X-ray worker at Sentara Norfolk General Hospital in Virginia, felt the same way. She was about to quit, burned out after 15 years.

Then each woman joined small teams obsessed with improving quality. Action-minded dynamos were given free rein to radically reform their workplaces, improve quality, and make work productive and fun again. "Joining that team is the best thing that ever happened to me in my life," says Combs. "It has built up a camaraderie like you wouldn't believe."

Camaraderie. Commitment. Communication. Trust. They are the lifeblood of the quality movement. They are also vital to the five winners of the Quality Cup, an award created by Rochester Institute of Technology and *USA Today*. The Quality Cup honors teams of 5 to 20 people in five categories: manufacturing companies, service companies, government agencies, nonprofit institutions, and small businesses.

The first winners were Sentara Hospital, the Naval Aviation Depot Operations Center, Federal Express, U.S. Steel, and L-S Electro-Galvanizing. Each of the winners builds on a simple philosophy: People are smart; give them a chance to contribute and then get out of their way. Building upon the work of quality consultants such as W. Edwards Deming and Joseph M. Juran, management at the five cup winners empowered teams of hourly workers to attack problems and propose solutions. Then, and most important, the team members convinced management to listen to them and act on their suggestions.

Each team made stunning improvements in the workplace, rejuvenated morale, slashed bureaucracy, and eliminated waste.

- The 12-person Federal Express team revamped a sorting process and saved the overnight-delivery company nearly $1 million in 18 months. Prior to the team's innovative problem solving, up to 4,300 packages a month were missing flights.

- An hourly team at U.S. Steel slashed shipments of flawed steel by 78% and prevented U.S. auto makers from dumping the plant as a supplier.

- At Sentara Hospital, the doctors were waiting three days to get an X-ray image. When the quality team finished its analysis, the turnaround time was 20 minutes.

- Work teams of hourly employees at L-S Electro-Galvanizing literally run their company. They have taken on the responsibility for planning, operations, and quality assurance. The company's productivity increased 20%, and quality assurance programs saved the company $700,000 in one year.

- The team at the Naval Aviation Depot Operations Center streamlined purchasing and maintenance systems, saving the Navy $2 million a year. ▲

For more about quality awards, see John Hillkirk, "New Award Cites Teams with Dreams," *USA Today*, April 10, 1992, pp. 1D–2D.

---

or departments, the group is known as a **work team**. Work-team members assume responsibility for the function, sharing skills and complementing each other. The Defense Systems and Electronics Group of Texas Instruments, a Malcolm Baldridge National Quality Award winner, has 1,900 teams in operation. Under the team concept, members build entire product assemblies, and all members learn the requirements of each job (Wrolstad, 1992).

Exhibit 14.3

The continuum of autonomy.

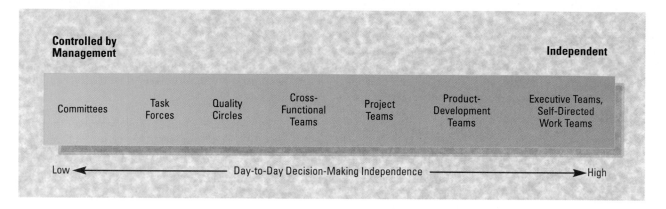

Controlled by Management						Independent
Committees	Task Forces	Quality Circles	Cross-Functional Teams	Project Teams	Product-Development Teams	Executive Teams, Self-Directed Work Teams

Low ◄─────────── Day-to-Day Decision-Making Independence ───────────► High

How Much Independence to Give Teams

How much authority and operating freedom should teams have? The continuum in Exhibit 14.3 shows the independence that various types of teams have in day-to-day operations.

Teams Closely Controlled by Management   Teams holding the least authority for decision making are committees, task forces, and quality circles. Although some task forces make decisions in regard to a narrowly defined charge, most task forces and operating committees are not decision-making bodies; they make recommendations to management. Quality circles have the ability to define quality, but they have little authority otherwise. Like the other closely controlled teams, the quality circle makes recommendations to management, which are usually conveyed by the circle facilitator, who is either a manager or a trained worker-facilitator (Reynolds, 1992).

Teams That Have Moderate Independence   Cross-functional, project, and product-development teams have more decision-making authority than closely controlled teams. Although empowered to make many decisions about the work at hand, the leaders of moderately independent teams are appointed by management. Therefore, the leaders of moderately independent teams tend to make decisions that support management. In addition, management controls budgetary decisions as well as team membership (Greenwald, 1992).

Independent Work Teams   Self-directed, or self-managed, work teams and executive teams are independent. Each controls day-to-day decision making.

A **self-directed work team** assumes complete responsibility for its work. The team manages itself, sets goals, takes responsibility for the quality of output, creates its own schedules, reviews its own performance as a group, prepares its own budgets, and coordinates its work with that done by the company's other departments or divisions. These teams plan, control, and improve operations, independent of formal management supervision (Byham, 1992).

Self-directed work teams are used anywhere in an organization where work units exist—in production, customer service, engineering, or design, for example. Companies using them report that team membership gives workers control over their jobs and a bigger stake in the company. These companies maintain that in self-directed work teams, creativity blossoms (Case, 1992). Managers at Texas Instruments are so pleased with self-directed teams that they plan to put 50% of their 15,000 nonteam employees in unsupervised teams by 1995 (Maney, 1992). "Self-directed work teams are," says Cecil Ursprung, CEO of Reflexite, "along with empowerment, the foundation for productivity, quality, and competitiveness in the marketplace (Magnet, 1992).

In the executive suites at Xerox, Nordstrom, and R. H. Macy, managers have decided that the jobs of chairman and president are too complex for one person to handle. As a result, these responsibilities are now in the hands of **executive teams**. The case problem in Chapter 13 discussed the executive teams at Xerox and Nordstrom. At Macy's, the chairman's position is shared by Myron Ullman, "a numbers man," and Mark Handler, a "style picker." With this team approach, both critical sides of the business receive optimum focus (Neuborne, 1992).

The Establishment of Team Organization

Team management represents a fundamental change from conventional ways of doing business, thinking, and managing. Consequently, the decision to adopt team management requires a philosophical commitment by top executives and careful, systematic implementation. The task of setting up work teams among employees must begin at the top (Brown, 1992).

The Process of Team Building

Successful team building requires a fresh assessment of the organization's basics. Exhibit 14.4 lists the steps involved (McKee, July 1992). The paragraphs that follow will describe each step in turn.

Assess Feasibility   Will the team approach work? For the organization new to teams, a feasibility study should be the starting point. The study should be a thorough, penetrating review of mission, resources (especially personnel), and current and projected circumstances. The study should provide reasonable estimates of how long it might take to institute teams and what kind of commitment is required.

Identify Priorities   An assessment of concerns by order of urgency should reveal the points where teams may be effective. The concerns could include, for example, customer needs, production process and capacity, and delivery systems.

Define Mission and Objectives   Before an organization begins to build teams, managers should take care that their mission and objectives are solid, well articulated, and accepted throughout the organization.

Exhibit 14.4

Steps in the process of team building.

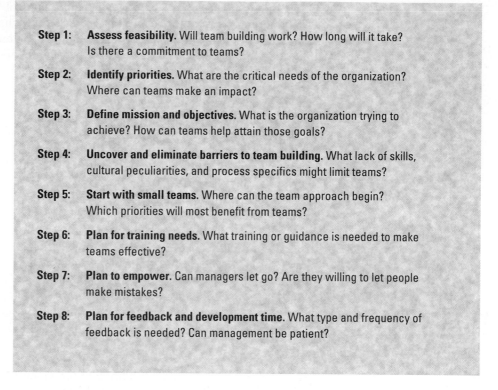

Step 1:	**Assess feasibility.** Will team building work? How long will it take? Is there a commitment to teams?
Step 2:	**Identify priorities.** What are the critical needs of the organization? Where can teams make an impact?
Step 3:	**Define mission and objectives.** What is the organization trying to achieve? How can teams help attain those goals?
Step 4:	**Uncover and eliminate barriers to team building.** What lack of skills, cultural peculiarities, and process specifics might limit teams?
Step 5:	**Start with small teams.** Where can the team approach begin? Which priorities will most benefit from teams?
Step 6:	**Plan for training needs.** What training or guidance is needed to make teams effective?
Step 7:	**Plan to empower.** Can managers let go? Are they willing to let people make mistakes?
Step 8:	**Plan for feedback and development time.** What type and frequency of feedback is needed? Can management be patient?

Uncover and Eliminate Barriers to Team Building   Three kinds of barriers impede teams: subject-matter barriers, process barriers, and cultural barriers.

- Subject-matter barriers arise when employees and managers are not sufficiently knowledgeable or technically proficient. Without adequate expertise, teams fail.

- Process barriers stem from unwieldy procedural approaches that limit teams' ability to do their work. Cumbersome approval processes and communication channels that follow the chain of command are incompatible with effective team operation.

- Cultural barriers are ways of thinking that run counter to the team approach. Especially in long-established firms, powerful departments may be unwilling to relinquish authority or to change cherished habits.

Such barriers must be identified and overcome; any one can stop teams cold.

Start with Small Teams   Begin team projects and planning in a pocket of the company—one of the clear priority areas. A sound idea is to begin by creating a design team that represents a cross-section of the company. The purpose of the team is not to design a product, but to create other teams.

Plan for Training Needs   At the outset, top or middle managers should offer their unreserved help and guidance to the teams as those groups refine their

Project teams focus their combined talents on specific problem-solving tasks. This approach works well at Lotus Development Corporation.

objectives and boundaries. Team members will probably need training in planning and the effective use of meetings. Members of cross-functional teams will need skills training.

Plan to Empower Executives and other managers must empower workers when creating teams. Senior people need to step back and let the team members make decisions and, if necessary, make mistakes and fail. Empowering involves giving team members the opportunities to fail as well as to succeed.

Plan for Feedback and Development Time Teams require feedback. Eventually, teams develop their own feedback mechanisms. Initially, however, it is vital that the team builders provide one. Simultaneously, in the team environment individuals must have ample opportunity to grow and develop. Managers must be patient.

Launching teams often raises unfamiliar issues and procedures. Companies that are beginning a team program can smooth the process by using consultants who specialize in team building. Skilled and experienced consultants can design a process, assist the organization in implementation, train workers and managers how to think in new ways about their new roles, and identify potential barriers.

Team-Building Considerations

Once top managers have decided to create teams and have prepared a comprehensive blueprint of the team-building process, they must make decisions about the details of specific teams. They must make decisions about team size and member roles, for example.

Team Size   Begin a team program by defining small teams—that is, teams that have fewer than 12 members. Small teams tend to reach consensus more readily than large teams. In addition, small teams allow more opportunity for interaction and self-expression and they tend not to break into subgroups. Small size allows members to use their diverse skills, to cross-train, and to solve problems aggressively. Actually, small teams retain their many advantages long after the start-up phase. Members of large teams often find interaction, communication, and the maintenance of unit cohesion difficult. In large teams, subgroups that have their own agendas can form, and conflict occurs more readily than in small teams (Shaw, 1985).

Member Roles   Effective teams display balance. Members possess diverse technical abilities and complementary interpersonal skills. Some members play task-oriented roles and others meet team needs for encouragement and harmony (Prince, 1989). Parker (1990) reported that the typical team includes the following task specialists:

- The contributor, a data-driven person who supplies needed information and pushes for high team performance standards

- The challenger, a team player who constantly questions the goals, methods, and even the ethics of the team

- The initiator, the person who proposes new solutions, new methods, and new systems for team problems

Roles for social specialists include:

- The collaborator, the "big picture" person who urges the team to stay with its vision and to achieve it

- The communicator, the person who listens well, facilitates well, and humanizes the work of the team

- The cheerleader, the person on the team who encourages and praises individual and team efforts

- The compromiser, the team member who will shift opinions to maintain harmony

Team members often play two or more of these roles and contribute dynamically to the essential balance. For sustained effectiveness, each team's task and interpersonal environments must sustain and invigorate members.

Management of Team Processes

Installing teams begins a remarkably complex and dynamic progression of interactive events. As businesses worldwide have experimented with teams, observers have hastened to gather and collate relevant data. As a result, much has been discovered and documented about how teams work, how they evolve and change, how they develop unique personalities, and how they should be managed for maximum advantage.

The Stages of Team Development

A soon as they are created, teams begin to develop in distinct stages (Tuckman, 1965; Gersick, 1989). Exhibit 14.5 shows the four stages of team development.

Forming During the **forming stage**, individual members become acquainted. Members test behaviors to determine which are acceptable and unacceptable to individuals and the group. This stage is marked by a high degree of uncertainty as individuals accept the power and authority of both formal and informal leaders. An important task for the designated team leader in this stage is to provide sufficient time and a suitable atmosphere in which team members can get to know one another and observe the emerging dynamic.

Exhibit 14.5

Stages of team development.

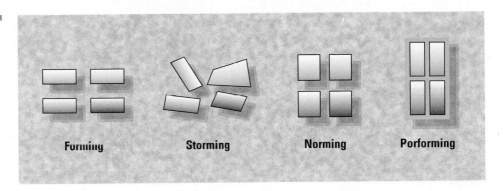

Forming   Storming   Norming   Performing

Storming In the **storming stage**, commonly marked by disagreement and conflict, personalities emerge and team members assert their opinions. Disagreements may arise over priorities, immediate goals, or methods. Coalitions or subgroups may emerge in the not-yet-unified team. The team leader's role now is to openly encourage the necessary interaction. Under competent leadership, the group can work through its disagreements and enter the next stage.

Norming As the tidy pattern in Exhibit 14.5 suggests, the team comes together in the **norming stage**. With disagreements and conflict resolved, the team achieves unity, consensus about who holds the power, and an understanding of the roles members will play. The focused team displays oneness, a sense of cohesion. The team leader builds on this newfound unity and helps to clarify the team's values and norms.

Performing In the **performing stage**, the team begins to function and moves toward accomplishing its objectives. Having accepted the oneness achieved during the norming stage, team members interact well with each other. They deal with problems, coordinate work, and confront each other if necessary. Now the team leader's role is to provide and maintain the balance between various members' requirements.

Small, highly cohesive teams are more effective than large, unfocused groups.
Team leaders should promote a clear direction and frequent interaction among members.

Team Cohesiveness

An important dimension of team dynamics is **cohesiveness**—the extent to which members are attracted to the team and motivated to remain together. In a highly cohesive team, members are committed to team activities, pull together to accomplish objectives, are happy with the success of the team, and are committed to staying in the team. On the other hand, members of uncohesive teams are not team-focused, are less concerned about team objectives, and are readier to leave the team.

Factors Determining Team Cohesiveness   Teams with few members, frequent interaction, clear objectives, and identifiable successes tend to be cohesive. Predictable results follow when these conditions are reversed. Teams are less cohesive when groups are large, when team size or members' locations prevent frequent interaction, when objectives are ambiguous, and when team efforts do not achieve identifiable success (Shaw, 1985). Exhibit 14.6 illustrates the factors that determine cohesiveness.

Exhibit 14.6

Determinants and results of
team cohesiveness.

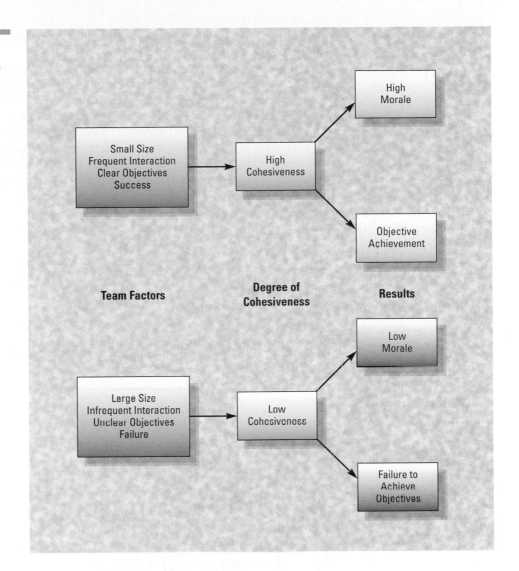

Results of Team Cohesiveness   Exhibit 14.6 also shows the outcome of team cohesiveness. High cohesiveness contributes to effectiveness and high morale. If cohesiveness is low, the team is less likely to achieve its objectives, and morale will be low (Cartright and Zandler, 1968).

Cohesiveness and success result from each other. High cohesiveness contributes to high achievement, which makes the team more cohesive. Knowing this, team leaders should foster cohesiveness by promoting clear direction, frequent interaction (in regard to work and nonwork topics), and small groups.

Team Norms

A **team norm** is a standard of behavior that all team members accept. Norms are the ground rules, or guidelines, that tell team members what they can or cannot do under certain circumstances; they provide boundaries of acceptable behavior. Individuals conform to these norms.

Team norms are set by the team itself. Through an informal process the key values, role expectations, and performance expectations emerge as norms. At Picker International, as the Management in Action feature that opened this chapter reported, team members developed a set of values and expectations. This list codified the team norms and was vital to the success of the team.

A key norm for teams is one that defines the acceptable level of performance—high, low, or moderate. Together with team cohesiveness, this norm is a critical determinant of team productivity. As Exhibit 14.7 shows, productivity is highest when the team is highly cohesive and has a high performance norm (quadrant A). Moderate productivity occurs when cohesiveness is low, because team members are less committed to performance norms (quadrant B). Low-to-moderate productivity occurs when cohesiveness is low and the performance norm is low (quadrant C). The lowest productivity occurs when the team members are highly cohesive in their commitment not to perform (quadrant D).

Team Personality

A team's personality is closely related to its norms (Greenwald, 1922). A personality for a team results from team members' cohesiveness and norms, the pressures

Exhibit 14.7

The effects of cohesiveness and performance norms on productivity.

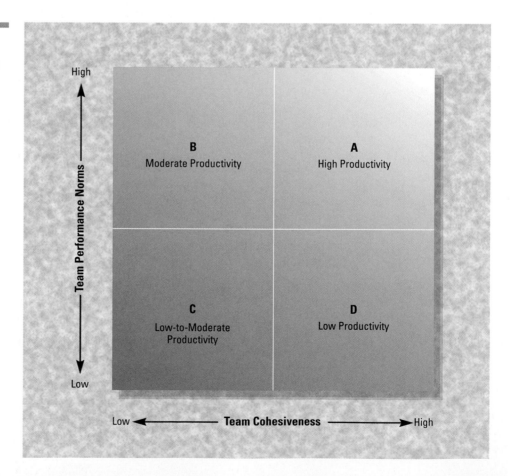

they face, their experiences, and their successes and failures. The team can be enthusiastic, energetic, or cooperative—or just the reverse. A team leader must monitor the personality of the team, identify its weaknesses and strengths, and then supply the leadership to remedy weaknesses and build on strengths.

Measurements of Team Effectiveness

The decision to create teams, like every management decision, generates benefits and costs. Team effectiveness is measured by weighing these benefits and costs.

The Benefits of Teams

If sound processes and techniques underlie team building and management, an organization can harness the benefits of teams. These benefits include synergy, increased skills and knowledge, flexibility, and commitment.

Synergy A team of employees working together develops synergy. The team produces more and generates more creativity and energy as a group than the individual members could produce working alone. Working in a team environment provides the camaraderie and sharing often absent from traditional work structures. At Conrail, Steelcase, and Goodyear, teams have facilitated prodigious increases in output—productivity increases as high as 70% (Greenwald, 1992).

Increased Skills and Knowledge In a team, the skills and knowledge of team members increase. This increase is due, in part, to cross-training. When individuals are exposed to more than one job, they acquire skills and knowledge from other workers. The result is people of increasing worth to themselves and to the company.

Flexibility As team workers become more adaptable in their attitudes and their capacity to perform, the organization gains flexibility and productivity. The broader knowledge base of team members allows them to adjust to changes in work demands and work flow and to respond constructively to emergencies. Moreover, the enhanced skill of individual team members permits improved response to organizational demands.

Commitment In an era highlighted by employee demotivation and lack of commitment, teams provide the opportunity for workers to "own" their work. As more companies move toward self-directed work teams and empowerment, the satisfaction and commitment level of employees increases. At Goodyear, CEO Stanley Gault proudly boasted, "The teams at Goodyear are now telling the boss how to run things—and I must say, I'm not doing a half-bad job because of it" (Greenwald, 1992).

The Costs of Teams

The major costs associated with implementing the team concept include power-realignment costs, training expenses, lost productivity, free-riding costs, and loss of productive workers.

Power-Realignment Expenses Implementing a team-centered approach results in the loss of power by lower- and middle-level managers. The power in the organization shifts from central management to the team and team worker. If adjustment is difficult and resistance occurs, the cost in time and money can be high.

Training Costs Employees may need retraining to be able to function in teams. The financial ramifications of retraining fall into two areas: costs for technical cross-training and for training in group dynamics. Of the two, the technical component is usually the easier to accomplish. Training in group dynamics is often hampered by the fact that many employees do not realize they need it. The processes of group decision making do not come naturally. Recall from Chapter 6 some of the potential pitfalls associated with group decision making: groupthink, excessive compromise, lost time, and lack of individual accountability. Team members need to be trained to avoid all these problems.

Lost Productivity Developing teams takes time, and time spent in team development is lost to production. The time spent selecting and retraining team members also lowers output of the product or service. In addition, team members need time to adjust to their new environment and roles. They will not reach peak performance overnight.

Free-Riding Costs Free riders are team members who receive the benefits of team membership but do not contribute their proportionate share. Free riding occurs because not all people are equally committed to team goals or exert the same amount of effort (Albanese and Van Fleet, 1985).

Loss of Productive Workers When companies move to a team system, there are workers who will not fit in. They do not want to think about their jobs, and they do not want increased responsibility. These workers may be forced out or resign voluntarily. Either way, the organization may lose skilled employees (Verespej, 1992).

Team and Individual Conflict

Whether a manager is working with teams or individuals, conflict inevitably occurs. Whenever people work together, the potential for conflict exists. **Conflict** is disagreement between two or more organizational members or teams (Stoner, 1986). Conflict occurs because people do not always agree—on goals, issues, perceptions, and the like—and because people inevitably compete.

Views of Conflict

What does a manager do when conflict occurs? The answer depends on the manager's views and beliefs about conflict (Thomas, 1976). Exhibit 14.8 shows three basic philosophical approaches to conflict.

The Traditional View The manager who views conflict as unnecessary and harmful to an organization fears conflict and eliminates all evidence of it. Such a

I S S U E S　　A N D　　E T H I C S
"Be a Team Player or Leave"

Companies have—at least on the surface—embraced teams, team concepts, and empowerment. With this transformation comes the need to change fundamentally the way managers and employees interact. Managers are no longer just managers; they have become facilitators. Employees experience a revolutionary change. They are transformed from being directed workers (workers who are told what to do) into being full-fledged decision-making partners.

In the typical style of American business, the wheels of change spin madly, taking the quick learners and adapters handily in tow and leaving behind those who are reluctant to change or slow to learn. Workers and managers who do not have transferable skills are quickly discarded. The modern business environment allows little time or chance for adaptation—especially for managers.

What ethical issues arise when people are told, "Be a team player or leave"? What obligations, if any, do companies owe to long-time employees who are unable to adapt to changed circumstances? Should state unemployment-insurance programs pay benefits to people who are laid off because they are unable or unwilling to perform as team members? Why or why not? ▲

manager holds the traditional view of conflict. If conflict does occur, the manager perceives it as a personal failure.

The Behavioral View　　The behaviorist recognizes that conflict frequently occurs because of human nature, the need to allocate resources, and organizational life. A manager who holds the behavioral view expects conflict. He or she believes that, on occasion, conflict can produce positive results. In general, however, a manager with a behavioral view believes that conflict is usually harmful. With this philosophical foundation, the manager's reaction to conflict is to resolve or eliminate it as soon as it occurs.

The Interactionist View　　A more current philosophy, the interactionist view, holds that conflict is not only inevitable but also necessary for organizational health. Furthermore, this view maintains that conflict can be good or bad, depending on how it is managed. A manager with an interactionist view attempts to harness conflict to maximize its positive potential for organizational growth and to minimize its negative effects.

The Positive and Negative Aspects of Conflict

A manager with an interactionist philosophy is able to identify the positive and negative aspects of conflict. The manager sees **dysfunctional conflict** as that which limits the organization's ability to achieve its objectives. Functional conflict, however, can support the objectives of the organization, especially when performance is low. People can be motivated to improve performance by competition—a kind of conflict—if they think their way is better than someone else's (Stoner, 1986).

Beliefs	Reactions
TRADITIONAL VIEW	
• Conflict is unnecessary	• Immediately stop conflict
• Conflict is to be feared	• Remove all evidence of conflict, including people
• Conflict is harmful	
• Conflict is a personal failure	
BEHAVIORAL VIEW	
• Conflict occurs frequently in organizations	• Immediately move to resolve or eliminate conflict
• Conflict is to be expected	
• Conflict can be positive but, more likely, it is harmful	
INTERACTIONIST VIEW	
• Conflict is inevitable in organizations	• Manage conflict to maximize the positive
• Conflict is necessary for organizational health	• Manage conflict to minimize the negative
• Conflict is neither inherently good nor bad	

Sources of Conflict

Competition is but one of many sources of conflict. Others include differences in objectives, values, and perceptions; disagreements about role requirements, work activities, and individual approaches; and communication breakdowns.

Competition   Competition can take the form of two individuals trying to outperform each other. Competition can also erupt over a struggle for limited resources. The manager of each work unit depends on an allocation of money, personnel, equipment, materials, and physical facilities to accomplish his or her objectives. Some managers inevitably receive fewer resources than others. This can lead not only to a lack of cooperation but to open conflict as well.

Conflict can also arise from competition for rewards associated with performance. Managed correctly, such conflict generates positive results.

Differences in Objectives   Individual employees' objectives may differ from those of the organization. An individual may aim to advance within an organization over a three-year period, whereas the organization may have a tradition of seasoning an employee over a longer period. There may be conflict in this situation.

Departments within an organization may develop conflicting objectives. For example, suppose the production division focuses its energies on manufacturing a product at the lowest possible cost. If the sales department wishes to promote high quality, conflict may arise.

Differences in Values and Perceptions   The value systems and perceptions of each individual differ from those of others. These differences can lead to conflict. For instance, an employee may place a high value on time with family. A manager may request frequent overtime or late hours, not understanding the employee's need for family time. An obvious value-system conflict arises.

Groups as well as individuals can have conflicting values and perceptions. Upper-level managers may perceive reports and procedures as valuable control devices designed to provide information. Line workers may view such paperwork as needless drudgery.

Disagreements About Role Requirements   When employees begin working in teams, their roles must change. Supposes, for example, that an employee who has received numerous rewards for individual performance must now play the unaccustomed role of team player. Conflict is likely to arise between the team and the individual.

Line and staff employees may find their new roles uncomfortable at first. In the team interaction of line and staff personnel, the line manager may expect the staff person to give advice, be supportive of the organization, and be action-oriented. The staff person may see himself or herself as one who provides answers, not advice. The staff person may be analytical (and sometimes critical) of the organization, and he or she may be reflective in reviewing potential alternatives. In such a case, conflict between the line and staff employees is almost certain.

Disagreements About Work Activities   Conflict between individuals and groups can arise over the quantity of work assigned or the relationship among the work units. In the first situation, the cause of conflict can be resentment because one group or individual believes the work load is inequitable.

Conflict over the relationships of work groups can take two forms. One group or individual may depend on another to complete work before starting its own. If the work is late or of poor quality, conflict can result. The other conflict situation arises when two work groups or individuals are purposely placed in competition with each other.

Disagreements About Individual Approaches   People exhibit diverse styles and approaches in dealing with others and with situations. One person may be reflective, speaking little until ready and then speaking wisely. Another person may be combative, often taking an argumentative approach, giving immediate responses with little thought, and pressuring for agreement.

Breakdowns in Communication   Communication is seldom perfect, and imperfect communication may result in misperception and misunderstanding. Sometimes a communication breakdown is inadvertent. Because the receiver is not listening actively, the receiver may simply misunderstand the sender. The result can be a disagreement about goals, roles, or intentions. Sometimes information is withheld intentionally, for personal gain or to embarrass a colleague.

Strategies for Managing Conflict

A manager must recognize potential sources of conflict and be prepared to manage it. A viable strategy for conflict management begins with an analysis of the conflict situation and then moves to the development of strategy options.

Analysis of the Conflict Situation

By answering three key questions, managers can analyze a conflict situation.

- Who is in conflict? The conflict may be between individuals, between individuals and teams, or between departments.

- What is the source of conflict? The conflict may arise from competition, personal differences, or organizational roles. Answering this question requires trying to view each situation through the eyes of the parties involved.

- What is the level of conflict? The situation may be at a stage where the manager must deal with it immediately. Or the conflict may be at a moderate level of intensity. If the goals of the work group are threatened or sabotage is occurring, the manager must take action immediately. If individuals or groups are simply in disagreement, a less immediate response is required.

Development of a Strategy

When the situation requires action, what options are available? A manager can consider seven possibilities. The paragraphs that follow will describe them.

Avoidance   Sometimes **avoidance** is the best solution. This calls for a manager to withdraw or ignore the conflict, letting the participants resolve it themselves. Avoidance is best when the conflict is trivial. The manager should not use it simply because he or she does not want to deal with the problem. Letting the parties disagree may be the best course if disagreement results in no consequences.

Smoothing   When using the option called **smoothing**, a manager diplomatically acknowledges conflict but downplays its importance. If there are no real issues to resolve, the approach may succeed in calming the parties. If there are real issues, however, this option will not work.

Compromise   With **compromise**, each party is required to give up something in order to get something. Each party moves to find a middle ground. Compromise

Conflict is a natural part of human interaction. Managers need to acquire and develop the skills necessary to resolve it or use it constructively.

can be effective when the parties in conflict are about equal in power, when major values are not involved, when a temporary solution to a complex issue is desirable, or if time pressures force a quick resolution.

Collaboration   In attempting **collaboration**, a manager promotes mutual problem solving by both parties. Each party seeks to satisfy his or her interests by openly discussing the issues, understanding differences, and developing a full range of alternatives. From this, the outcome sought is consensus—mutual agreement—about the best alternative.

Confrontation   If **confrontation** is used, the conflicting parties are forced to verbalize their positions and disagreements. Although this approach can produce stress, it can also be effective. The goal is to identify a reason to favor one solution or another and thus resolve the conflict. Many times, however, confrontation ends in hurt feelings and no resolution.

Appeals to Superordinate Objectives   Sometimes a manager can identify superordinate objectives that will allow the disputing parties to rise above their conflict. A **superordinate objective** is a goal that overshadows each party's individual interest. As an example, suppose individual work groups are vying for budget allocations in the face of an organizational downturn. If the two parties agree that reductions are in the best interest of the organization, each will move beyond the conflict.

GLOBAL APPLICATIONS
Teamwork Is the Edge

Japan's awe-inspiring business success has been attributed to corporate paternalism, lifetime employment, and robotic efficiency. A closer look reveals that the real key is the use of teams and teamwork from beginning to end of the product cycle.

Japanese companies are effective and efficient because they use interdepartmental teams to design products that meet needs from all perspectives. On the team are representatives from marketing, design, engineering, manufacturing, purchasing, and quality. The team approach keeps everyone involved at all times. It facilitates communication and ensures a design that everyone can live with.

The team structure in Japanese product design and manufacturing makes cooperation and collaboration a natural outcome. All the players are focused on the ultimate goal.

Toyota conceived and refined the team concept, and presently has thousands of teams in its operations. Toyota has thus been able to bring its products to the market in less time, with fewer design and system modifications, and with fewer customer complaints than companies operating without a team structure. Honda and Nissan have followed with parallel results.

In contrast, American companies often design products by sequentially transferring a developing item between departments—from marketing to design, to engineering, to manufacturing, and so on. This practice promotes poor intergroup communication and allows various departments to formulate goals that ultimately conflict.

With the team process as part of their operating culture, Japanese companies have established a competitive edge. ▲

For more about Japanese teamwork, see Garry Katzenstein, "Japanese Management Style," *Working Woman,* February 1992, pp. 50, 98.

Decisions by a Third Party   At times, the manager may turn to a third party and ask him or her to decide a conflict. The third party can be another supervisor, an upper-level manager, or someone from the human resource department. If the conflict is between two subordinates, the manager may be the third party.

Conflict Stimulation

At times a manager may wish to increase the level of conflict and competition in a work situation. The circumstances in which a manager might wish to stimulate conflict are these:

- When team members exhibit and accept minimal performance

- When people appear to be afraid to do anything other than the norm

- When team members passively accept events or behavior that should motivate action

Robbins (1986) reported that managers can choose from among five strategies to stimulate conflict:

- Bring in an outsider. A person from outside the organization or team—someone who does not have the same background, attitudes, or values—

may serve to establish the desired characteristics. A manager may have to bring in more than one outsider to make a difference.

- Change the rules. In some instances, a manager may choose to involve people who are not ordinarily included or exclude those who are usually involved. This alteration can stimulate the work environment. For example, a manager who is attempting to open up the environment may ask an informal leader to attend "management-only" meetings as a full participant. The result may be that both workers and managers gain new knowledge and change their actions.

- Change the organization. Another approach is to realign work groups and departments. A change in reporting relationships and the composition of work teams can allow individuals to have new experiences with people and perceptions.

- Change managers. Inserting a manager into a work group that can benefit from his or her style of leadership can be an appropriate response. The practice of rotating managers of work teams on a regular schedule can also stimulate groups.

- Encourage competition. A manager can encourage competition between groups or individuals by offering bonuses, travel, time off, or certificates of merit to employees who perform best.

Schein (1970) reported that the manager who chooses to encourage competition may reap one or more of the following benefits:

- An increase in cohesion within the competing group
- An increased focus on task accomplishment
- An increase in organization and efficiency

If the situation is not managed correctly, however, the competition can produce negative consequences:

- Communication between competitors may decrease or cease to exist.
- The competitor may be perceived as an enemy.
- Open hostility may develop between competitors.
- One competitor can sabotage the efforts of another.

Regardless of the strategy a manager selects when working with conflict, careful analysis and follow-up are required.

Future Trends

In the future, CEOs trying to gain a competitive edge will witness the following strategic shifts:

- Cross-functional teams will become more prominent, helping meet the need for greater flexibility and increased response time.

- The spreading use of teams will transform organizations into learning environments. The creativity and innovation that teams unleash will result in new skills, methods, and processes.

- Management levels will be replaced with a new team-centered orientation. Self-directed work teams will alter the role of management.

- Teams will empower employees and reorient managers. Managers will be transformed from controllers into facilitators. In the process, a generation of managers will retrain or perish.

- Teams will require unions to change. As traditional job structures evolve, so will the needs and expectations of workers. Union strategies will have to change to reflect the new needs and expectations.

CHAPTER SUMMARY

- Teams are rapidly emerging as an organizational force. A team is a group of two or more people who interact regularly and coordinate their work to accomplish a common objective.

- The two basic types of formal teams are vertical and horizontal.

- Teams can be used for product development, projects, quality assurance, and as work teams to replace operating departments.

- Teams possess different degrees of authority to function independently on a day-to-day basis. The ones with the most independence are self-directed, or self-managed, work teams and executive teams.

- A company that is establishing a team organization should follow a systematic process.

- Once top managers have made the decision to create teams, they need to consider the size of the teams and the roles the members will play, before choosing the team members themselves.

- The typical team goes through four phases of development: forming, storming, norming, and performing. An individual team develops its own degree of cohesiveness, its own norms, and its own personality.

- Evaluating a team requires examining its benefits versus its costs.

- Whether a manager is working with teams or individuals, conflict will inevitably occur. That conflict can be positive (functional) or negative (dysfunctional).

- Sources of conflict include competition; differences in objectives, values, and perceptions; disagreements about role requirements, work activities, and individual approaches; and breakdowns in communication.

- The first step in managing conflict is to analyze the situation to determine who is in conflict, the source of conflict, and the level of conflict.

- Options to resolve conflict include avoidance, smoothing, compromise, collaboration, confrontation, establishment of superordinate objectives, and involvement of a third party.

- At times, a manager may wish to stimulate conflict. The options are to bring in outsiders, change the rules, change the organization, change managers, and encourage competition.

S K I L L - B U I L D I N G

This exercise is designed to help you discover and evaluate the strategies you use to manage conflict. Place a mark in the appropriate column to indicate how often you do the following when you are in conflict with someone.

When I am in conflict with someone:

	Usually	Sometimes	Seldom
1. I explore our differences, not backing down but not imposing my view.	☐	☐	☐
2. I disagree openly and then invite more discussion about our differences.	☐	☐	☐
3. I look for a mutually satisfactory solution.	☐	☐	☐
4. Rather than let the other person make a decision with my input, I make sure I am heard and also that I hear the other out.	☐	☐	☐
5. I agree to a middle ground rather than look for a completely satisfying solution.	☐	☐	☐
6. I admit I am half wrong rather than explore our differences.	☐	☐	☐
7. I have a reputation for meeting a person halfway.	☐	☐	☐
8. I expect to get out about half of what I really want to say.	☐	☐	☐
9. I try to win over the other person.	☐	☐	☐
10. I work to come out victorious, no matter what.	☐	☐	☐
11. I never back away from a good argument.	☐	☐	☐
12. I would rather win than compromise.	☐	☐	☐

Scoring key and interpretation: Give yourself 5 points for each "Usually," 3 points for every "Sometimes," and 1 point for all answers of "Seldom." Then total the points for each set of statements, grouped as follows:

> Set A: Items 9–12
>
> Set B: Items 5–8
>
> Set C: Items 1–4

Treat each set separately. A score of 17 or above for any set is considered high. Scores of 12 to 16 are moderately high, scores of 8 to 11 are moderately low, and scores of 7 or less are considered low.

Sets A, B, and C represent different conflict-resolution strategies:

> A = Confrontation: I dominate.
>
> B = Compromise. We both give up something to get something.
>
> C = Collaboration. We both win.

Source: Adapted from *Managerial Skills for a New Era,* by Thomas J. Von Der Embse. Reprinted with permission of Macmillan Publishing Co.

R E V I E W   Q U E S T I O N S

1. Review this chapter's essential terms and look up the meanings of those you cannot define.

2. What are vertical teams? What are the three types of horizontal teams?

3. What is the purpose of a project team? How does it differ from a work team?

4. In terms of authority for day-to-day decisions, what is the difference between a self-directed work team and a product-development team?

5. What are the eight steps involved in the process of establishing teams?

6. What two major kinds of roles do team members play within a team? What is the importance of each role?

7. What are the four stages of team development? What occurs at each stage?

8. What is team cohesiveness? What factors contribute to high team cohesiveness?

9. What are the benefits associated with teams?

10. What are the positive and negative effects of conflict in an organization?

11. What are four potential sources of conflict in an organization? Explain each.

12. What strategies are available for conflict management? Explain each.

R E C O M M E N D E D 　 **R** E A D I N G

Brown, Tom. "Why Teams Go Bust," *Industry Week* (March 2, 1992), pp. 92–93.

Frohman, Mark. "The Aimless Empowered," *Industry Week* (April 20, 1992), pp. 64–67.

Garland, Ron. *Working and Managing in a New Age* (San Francisco: Jossey-Bass), 1991.

Hermann, Matthew. "Making Work into Teamwork," *Utne Reader* (March–April 1992), pp. 82–84.

Hirschhorn, Larry. *Managing in the New Team Environment* (Menlo Park, CA: Addison-Wesley), 1991.

Pascale, Richard T. *Managing on the Edge: How the Smartest Companies Use Conflict to Stay Ahead* (Kenmore, WA: S&S Enterprise), 1991.

Reingold, Howard. "The Virtual Workgroup," *Publishing* (April 1992), pp. 44–45.

Thompson, John. "Teams That Score Big on Productivity," *Business Week* (July 10, 1992), p. 104.

Tjesvold, Dean. *The Conflict Positive Organization: Stimulate Diversity and Create Unity* (Menlo Park, CA: Addison-Wesley), 1991.

Wellins, Richard S. *Empowered Teams. Creating Self-Directed Work Groups That Improve Quality, Productivity and Participation* (San Francisco: Jossey-Bass), 1991.

R E F E R E N C E S

Albanese, Robert, and David D. Van Fleet. "Rational Behavior in Groups: The Free-Riding Tendency," *Academy of Management Review* 10 (1985), pp. 244–255.

Benson, Tracy. "The New Leadership," *Industry Week* (June 1, 1992), pp. 12–16.

Brown, Tom. "Want to Be a Real Team?" *Industry Week* (July 20, 1992), p. 17.

Byham, William C. "Self-Directed Work Team Magic," *Board-Room Reports* (June 15, 1992), pp. 1–8.

Cartright, Dorwin, and Alvin Zandler. *Group Dynamics: Research and Theory*, 3rd edition (New York: Harper & Row), 1968.

Case, John. "Collective Effort," *Inc.* (January 1992), p. 35.

Cox, Allan. "The Homework Behind Teamwork," *Industry Week* (January 7, 1992), p. 21.

Daft, Richard L. *Management,* 2nd edition (Homewood, IL: Dryden Press), 1991, pp. 464–465.

Dumaine, Briane. "Unleash Workers and Cut Costs," *Fortune* (May 18, 1992), p. 88.

Gersick, Connie J. G. "Marking Time: Predictable Transitions in Task Groups," *Academy of Management Journal* (June 1989), pp. 274–309.

Greenwald, John. "Is Mr. Nice Guy Back?" *Time* (January 27, 1992), pp. 42–44.

Kupfer, Andrew. "Apple's Plan to Survive and Grow," *Fortune* (May 4, 1992), p. 72.

Larson, Carl E., and Frank M. J. LaFasto. *TeamWork* (Newbury Park, CA: Sage), 1989.

Magnet, Myron. "The Truth About the American Worker," *Fortune* (May 4, 1992), pp. 49–52.

Maney, Kevin. "Texas Instruments 10-Year Quality Quest," *USA Today,* October 15, 1992, p. 6B.

McKee, Bradford. "A Team Is As Strong As Its Weakest Link," *Nation's Business* (May 1992), p. 12.

McKee, Bradford. "Turn Your Workers into a Team," *Nation's Business* (July 1992), pp. 36–38.

Neuborne, Ellen. "Retailer Takes Team Approach," *USA Today,* April 29, 1992, p. 5B.

Owens, Thomas. "Business Teams," *Small Business Report* (January 1989), pp. 50–58.

Parker, Glenn. *Team Players and Teamwork* (San Francisco: Jossey-Bass), 1990.

Prince, George. "Recognizing Genuine Teamwork," *Supervisory Management* (April 1989), pp. 25–36.

Reynolds, Larry. "Quality Circles," *Management Review* (January 1992), 53–54.

Robbins, Stephen. *Managing Organizational Conflict,* 3rd edition (Englewood Cliffs, NJ: Prentice-Hall), 1986, p. 321.

Schein, Edgar. *Organizational Psychology,* 2nd edition (Englewood Cliffs, NJ: Prentice-Hall), 1970, pp. 32–34.

Schein, Edgar. *Process Consultation* (Reading, MA: Addison-Wesley), 1969, pp. 42–43.

Shaw, M. E. *Group Dynamics—The Psychology of Small Group Behavior,* 4th edition (New York: McGraw-Hill), 1985.

Sheils, Merry. "The Next Paradigm," *Chief Executive* (June 1992), p. 63.

Stewart, Thomas A. "The Search for the Organization of Tomorrow," *Fortune* (May 8, 1992), p. 93.

Stoner, James A. F. *Management,* 3rd edition (Englewood Cliffs, NJ: Prentice-Hall), 1986, pp. 85, 354–357.

Thomas, Kenneth W. "Conflict and Conflict Management," *Handbook of Industrial and Organizational Psychology,* Marvin Donnette, editor (Chicago: Rand McNally), 1976, pp. 889–935.

Tuckman, B. W. "Developmental Sequence in Small Groups," *Psychological Bulletin* 63 (1965), pp. 384–389.

Uris, Auren. *Techniques of Leadership* (New York: McGraw-Hill), 1964, p. 58.

Verespej, Michael A. "When Workers Get New Roles," *Industry Week* (February 3, 1992), p. 11.

Wrolstad, Mark. "For TI Defense Unit, It's Quality Time," *Dallas Morning News,* October 15, 1992, pp. 1D–2D.

G L O S S A R Y   O F   T E R M S

avoidance   A conflict strategy in which a manager ignores a conflict situation.

cohesiveness   The extent to which members are attracted to the team and motivated to remain together.

collaboration   A conflict strategy in which a manager focuses on mutual problem solving by both parties. Parties seek to satisfy their interests by openly discussing issues, understanding differences, and developing a full range of alternatives.

committee   A horizontal team designed to focus on one objective. Committee members represent functional areas. An ad hoc committee does one job and is then disbanded; a standing committee is permanent.

compromise   A conflict-resolution strategy in which each party gives up something.

conflict   A disagreement between two or more organization members or teams.

confrontation   A conflict strategy that forces parties to verbalize their positions and area of disagreement.

cross-functional team   A team designed to bring together the knowledge of various functional areas to work on solutions to operational problems. A cross-functional team has an undefined life span that is not tied to accomplishment of a specific objective.

dysfunctional conflict   Conflict that limits the organization's ability to achieve its objectives.

executive team   A team consisting of two or more people who do the job traditionally held by one upper-level manager.

formal team   A team created by upper-level managers to function as part of the organizational structure.

forming stage   The phase of team development in which team members are becoming acquainted.

free rider   A person who receives the benefits of team membership but does not do a proportionate share of work.

horizontal team   A team composed of members drawn from different departments.

norming stage   The phase of team development in which disagreement and conflict have been resolved and team members enjoy unity and focus.

performing stage   The phase of team development in which team members progress toward team objectives, handle problems, coordinate work, and confront each other if necessary.

product-development team   A team organized to create new products.

project team   A team organized to complete a specific task in the organization.

quality assurance team   A team created to guarantee the quality of services and products, visit customers, and work with vendors.

quality circle (QC)   A team of workers who meet voluntarily and regularly to identify quality issues and offer solutions.

self-directed work team   A self-managing team that is fully responsible for its own work. It sets goals, creates its own schedules and budgets, and coordinates work with other departments.

smoothing   A conflict strategy in which the manager diplomatically acknowledges that conflict exists but downplays its importance.

storming stage   The phase of team development characterized by disagreement and conflict as individual roles and personalities emerge.

superordinate objective   An objective that overshadows individual interests. A manager can appeal to superordinate objectives as a strategy for resolving conflict.

task force   A horizontal team composed of employees from different departments. A task force is designed to accomplish a limited number of objectives, and it exists only until objectives are met.

team   A group of two or more people who interact regularly and coordinate their work to accomplish a common objective.

team norm   A standard of behavior accepted by all team members.

vertical team   A team composed of a manager and subordinates.

work team   A team composed of multi-skilled workers. A work team does all the tasks previously done by individual members in a functional department or departments.

C A S E   P R O B L E M
Reviving the Camaro

Chevrolet had a problem. Its Camaro "muscle car"—a traditional lure for young buyers and a big part of Chevy's performance image—had become a clunky rattletrap. *Consumer Reports* magazine condemned it. Even sympathetic magazines for auto enthusiasts could not ignore loose gearshift levers, leaky windows, and chattering dashboards. Upper-level managers at GM had made the same observations. Sales were off. Quality ratings were way down. GM test results reported water leaks, squeaks and rattles, poor driveability, and electrical problems.

At GM, which is known for bureaucracy, the unheard of happened. A tiny eight-person team of engineers was hustled into being. Its task was reviving the Camaro. Richard De Vogelaere, the engineering manager who took on the mission, was told to spend no more than $5 million, fix the aging model before replacement models went into production, and stay in touch with the team working on the new models. The fact that his team members would have preferred to work on a new model rather than the old one did not make his task any easier.

Despite these obstacles, the team succeeded in repairing years of neglect. As a unit, it researched the file of customer complaints. It came up with solutions: new gaskets for fewer leaks, glued-together parts to eliminate squeaks, different assembly-line procedures to improve the fit of panels, and changes in wiring to cure stalling. The results speak for themselves. Operating with almost no administrative supervision, the team was able to improve quality and cut defects so substantially that warranty claims have fallen 50%. The bureaucrats were amazed.

Q U E S T I O N S

1. Was the Camaro team a vertical or horizontal team? Why?

2. What was the purpose of the team?

3. Would you consider the Camaro team a self-directed team? Why?

4. What does this example tell you about the power of teams?

P·A·R·T

Controlling

15

Controlling: Purpose and Process

LEARNING OBJECTIVES

After reading and discussing this chapter, you should be able to:

- Define this chapter's essential terms
- Discuss the relationship between controlling and the other four functions of management
- Explain the four steps in the control process
- Discuss the purposes of feedforward, concurrent, and feedback controls
- Describe the importance of a control system
- Discuss the characteristics of effective controls
- Explain the steps managers can take to make controls more effective

concurrent control

control process
control system

controlling
critical control point

feedback control
feedforward control
standard

M A N A G E M E N T   I N   A C T I O N
Combatting Crime at Convenience Stores

Between 1987 and 1992, the number of robberies at convenience stores in America grew from about 28,000 per year to nearly 40,000. A two-year study by the National Association of Convenience Stores (NACS) predicted that about one out of five convenience stores in the United States would be robbed in 1992. Besides the loss of money, armed robbery takes "a devastating psychological toll on employees" and has resulted in injuries and deaths. The study points out that some two-thirds of convenience store robberies happen in only 7% of the stores, and, once robbed, a store is likely to be robbed again.

The NACS has developed guidelines that stores can use to help control the risk of robbery:

- Cash in registers should be kept at a minimum by constantly placing large bills in a tamperproof safe. (Spectrum Stores, Inc. of Georgia keeps much less than $100 in any of its 42 stores' registers at any time.)

- Cash registers should be visible to passersby.

- Lighting should be bright in and around the store.

Convenient to criminals, neighborhood stores like this have become robbery targets, sparking the need for special controls.

- Clerks should be behind elevated checkout counters to improve their visibility.

- To reduce the chance of potential thieves using public phones inside the store, pay phones should be outside, at the side of the store.

- Parking lots should be watched carefully; people who back into parking places may be planning a quick getaway.

Experts on robbery prevention do not recommend the following steps:

- Bulletproof glass to protect employees (It can lead to a hostage situation.)

- Adding extra employees (Robbers who were interviewed in prison indicated that if they had a gun, they would not hesitate to rob a store with two or more people in it.)

- Fighting back (Those who resist are 49 times more likely to be killed than those who cooperate with a robber.)

Crown Central Petroleum has 82 stores in the South that are connected by a two-way television

> Once robbed, a store is likely to be robbed again.

monitoring system to a central security office. An agent in the office monitors store activity, calls out warnings over in-store loudspeakers, and calls police. The system costs about $380 per month per store. ▲

For more about preventing robbery, see Eugene Carlson, "Stop & Rob: Convenience Stores Combat Crime Rates," *Wall Street Journal,* October 6, 1992, p. B2.

The Nature of Control

Of all the management functions, this book discusses controlling last because it applies to each of the others. Without some way to monitor the execution of plans, managers would not know whether their work was effective or efficient. People and processes must be monitored to prevent, detect, and correct unacceptable differences between managers' expectations and actual results. The NACS guidelines mentioned in this chapter's Management in Action feature are control mechanisms to prevent and detect crime.

In its most basic form, **controlling** is the management function in which managers set and communicate performance standards for people, processes, and devices. A **standard** is any guideline or benchmark established as the basis for the measurement of capacity, quantity, content, value, cost, quality, or performance. Whether quantitative or qualitative, standards must be precise, explicit, and formal statements of the expected result. Once those who must abide by standards understand and can apply them, standards serve as mechanisms to prevent and detect unacceptable deviations from plans. Standards may be applied to people and processes before, during, and after work is performed.

This chapter will examine the need for controls, the control process, general types and characteristics of controls, and methods for making controls effective and efficient. Chapter 16 will examine specific kinds of controls that nearly every business organization uses.

Controlling and the Other Management Functions

As Bittel (1989) noted: "Controlling is the function that brings the management cycle full circle. It is the steering mechanism that links all the preceding functions of organizing, staffing, and directing to the goals of planning." The planning process determines the objectives that eventually become the foundation for controls. As the first function, planning is at the heart of all the others. The strategic objectives and plans made at the top level in an organization are derived from the organization's purpose and mission. From these plans flow the goals to be achieved by successively lower levels of management. As these plans and goals are developed, managers must establish controls to monitor progress toward them. The feedback from these controls should tell managers how each level of the organization— indeed, each individual—is progressing toward the relevant goals. The feedback may indicate that progress is proceeding as planned. If progress falls short of the plan, however, the feedback should indicate that managers need to change the plan (Odiorne, 1980).

When Cadillac, a division of General Motors, introduced the all-new 1992 Seville and El Dorado models, demand quickly exceeded initial estimates. Managers changed the production schedule so dealers had the supply to meet the demand. Shifts in production were possible because a control mechanism allowed for feedback from dealers about customer demand.

Budgets are both plans and controls. Budgets forecast the sources and amounts of funds that will flow into an organization over a period of time and allocate funds to various activities. Equally important, budgets help guarantee that funds are received and spent as planned. A brief look at an example illustrates how important controlling is and how it affects and is affected by the other four management functions.

Planning and Controlling   Based on market research, Procter & Gamble develops a plan to create and market a new soap. The plan calls for a 15% profit and a 10% share of the soap market. Along with these plans and goals, managers design and establish controls to provide feedback about profits, costs, sales, and market penetration. The company budgets for the added processes, facilities, supplies, training, and personnel required to produce the product and bring it to market. It must also monitor the sales of its other brands of soap to determine if the new brand is capturing sales from existing products rather than from competitors.

Organizing and Controlling   To accomplish its plans, Procter & Gamble modifies its organizational structure by adding a product team to launch the new soap. Senior managers delegate authority to the product-team manager, arrange to manufacture the soap in existing production facilities, and define and delegate authority to those who will assist the new team. They create controls to monitor production and determine whether the allocation of resources and authority has been appropriate to the job.

Staffing and Controlling   To accomplish its plans, Procter & Gamble must acquire workers at all levels and place them in the new positions. (Recruitment can occur inside and outside the organization.) Managers must establish a chain of command and a compensation plan for the new team. In addition, the new team members must be trained. As part of the staffing process, managers create controls to evaluate the effectiveness of the recruiting, hiring, compensation, and training of the new product team and those who assist the team in manufacturing and support positions.

Directing and Controlling   Employees in many different units—production, product team, sales, customer service, and advertising, for example—must work together to accomplish the goals established by the plan and within the means specified by the budget. Managers establish controls to ensure smooth work flow and progress toward goals. In addition, managers establish controls to enforce standards. For example, managers must evaluate workers and be evaluated themselves. Each employee must receive feedback in regard to his or her performance. Managers must reward success and take corrective action when appropriate. Managers must also establish methods of monitoring rewards and corrective actions.

In addition to its relationship to the other four functions, controlling meets a very practical need. Organizations have limited resources. The successful acquisition and use of these resources determine a firm's survival. No person or organization should expend resources to achieve a goal without arranging to monitor their use.

Controls in an Organization

At every level in an organization, managers need controls to prevent problems, to monitor activities, and to provide feedback about processes and people. Exhibit 15.1 displays the four primary types of controls, which monitor personnel, financial, informational, and operational activity.

Personnel Controls   Managers use various tools to control human resources. Human resource inventories, job descriptions, job specifications, and performance appraisals are but a few. Statistics can also be control measures. Statistics about absenteeism, lateness, safety, and costs provide managers with valuable information about personnel.

Financial Controls   Financial controls focus on income, expenditures, cash flow, asset mix, and the acquisition and investment of funds. As Chapter 16 will discuss, financial controls are among an organization's most useful tools. They help ensure access to sufficient funding, without which no organization can achieve its goals.

Exhibit 15.1

The four primary types of controls that monitor organizational activities and resources.

Control	Monitors
Personnel	Human resources, job content, performance, safety, and personnel cost
Financial	Income, expenditures, cash flow, asset mix, acquisition of funds, and investment of funds
Informational	Collection, processing, storage, security, and dissemination of data
Operational	Production, marketing, finance, and staff processes; inventory control; effectiveness of planning; abilities and methods used to meet customer needs

Informational Controls These controls help managers and others get the information they need to make timely and intelligent decisions. Many organizations operate management information systems that rely heavily on electronics to collect, process, disseminate, and store information. Information must be gathered from a variety of sources, inside and outside an organization. Every individual and group must determine what information is needed. Then the individual or group must ensure that the information is received, at the right time and place, in suitable quantity, quality, and format. Chapter 19 will focus on informational controls in the context of information management systems.

Operational Controls The fourth type of control, the operational controls, monitors anything that is not being monitored by a personnel, financial, or informational control. In general, this means that operational controls monitor the use of physical resources by every individual and group within an organization. (Chapter 18 will discuss operational controls further.) By using operational controls, managers ensure that:

- Policies are adequate

- Procedures (for such activities as purchasing, payroll, maintenance, and selling) are in place, communicated properly, and effective

- Inventories are adequate and secure

- Plans are effective

- Products and services meet internal and external customers' needs and expectations

The Control Process

You are now ready to examine the fours steps of the **control process**. As Exhibit 15.2 shows, the steps are (1) establishing performance standards, (2) measuring performance, (3) comparing measured performance to established standards, and (4) taking corrective action.

Establishing Performance Standards

As you know, a standard is a quantitative or qualitative measuring device designed to monitor people, money, capital goods, or processes. The exact nature of a standard depends on

- Who designs, works with, and receives the output from controls

- What is being monitored

- What is to be achieved through monitoring

- Where monitoring efforts will take place (location and functional area)

- When controls will be used (before, during, or after operations)

- What resources are available to expend on the controls

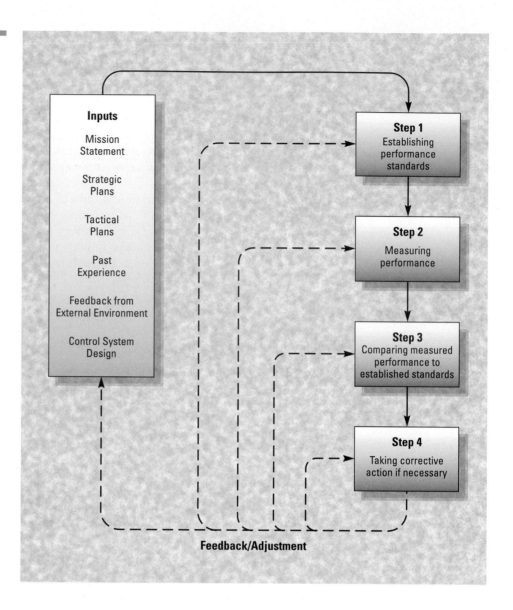

Exhibit 15.2

Steps in the control process.

Standards and controls usually deal with time, costs, quality, productivity, or behaviors. Once set, standards must be continually re-evaluated to ensure that they are still necessary and valid.

Time   The goal of standards that deal with time is usually to ensure sufficient time to achieve tasks. Standards for handling inventory ensure that goods are reordered before stock runs out. Standards for customer service demand that products be delivered at a time convenient for customers. Standards about feedback ensure that information reaches decision makers in time for them to make meaningful improvements to operations.

Time standards determine priorities, schedules, and sequences of events. Remember that to an organization, time is money. By controlling time, an organization can help control its finances.

F O C U S   O N   Q U A L I T Y
Total Quality Means Total Commitment

Total quality management (TQM) is a company-wide effort to make certain that quality is an integral part of an organization's culture and operation. Companies such as Motorola, Hewlett-Packard, Ford, and Xerox have made the commitment to TQM. In general, TQM embraces four essential elements:

- Intense efforts to satisfy customers.

- Accurate standards for and measurement of every critical operation. These standards help identify problems and eliminate their causes.

- Work relationships based on trust and teamwork. Central to TQM is empowerment—managers giving employees autonomy and support and motivating them to give their best. TQM must be part of suppliers' culture and activities as well.

- Continual improvement of processes, products, and services. TQM involves the *kaizen* philosophy and an ongoing quest for innovation.

As large firms adopt TQM, their suppliers find that they must also. "The quality movement is reaching critical mass, and those businesses that have not committed themselves to TQM will find it more and more difficult to meet their customers' demands, whether those customers are consumers or other firms." ▲

For more about TQM, see Michael Barrier, "Small Firms Put Quality First," *Nation's Business,* May 1992, pp. 22–23.

Costs   Money is a finite resource; few organizations ever seem to have enough of it. Budgets are created on the basis of what is needed and what is available. Many projects and product ideas are canceled for lack of funding or because they will cost more than the anticipated benefits are worth. Managers must use only the budgeted amount for each budgeted activity—or less, if possible. Like time, costs must be managed to get the most from each dollar.

In discussing costs, Sam Walton (1992) of Wal-Mart said:

> Control your expenses better than your competition. This is where you can always find the competitive advantage. For 25 years running—long before Wal-Mart was known as the nation's largest retailer—we ranked number one in our industry for the lowest ratio of expenses to sales. You can make a lot of different mistakes and still recover if you run an efficient operation. Or you can be brilliant and still go out of business if you're too inefficient.

Quality   Quality can be defined as how well the features and characteristics of a product or service satisfy customers' needs. Quality should be designed into processes, products, and services from their inception. The commitment to quality must be part of an organization's culture, and it must start with top managers. The top managers should involve everyone (including suppliers) in the quest for quality and use feedback from customers as one aspect of the quality control system. Thomas J. Barry (1991) of the American Society for Quality Control wrote:

> Measurement is the springboard to involvement, allowing the organization to initiate corrective action, set priorities, and evaluate progress. Standards and

measures should reflect customer requirements and expectations. Each employee must be a partner in achieving quality goals. Teamwork involves managers, supervisors, and employees in improving service delivery, solving systemic problems, and correcting errors in all parts of work processes.

To control quality, companies create quality assurance (QA) systems, "a validation process to ensure measurement accuracy and standardization. The QA system focuses on constant incremental quality improvement measurements and results" (Barry, 1991). Many organizations rely heavily on quantitative, statistical measures to ensure quality. Chapter 17 will explore the relationship between quality and productivity.

Productivity   Productivity is the amount of output achieved from a given set of inputs. Improvements in productivity should lead to improvements in both quality and profits, as Chapter 17 will discuss. Productivity can be measured quantitatively and qualitatively. Examples of quantitative measures of productivity include the number of customers served per hour and the total units produced per machine-hour of operation. Qualitative measures incorporate such factors as customer feedback—feedback about how well they were treated by a customer-service representative, for example. As Seidman and Skancke (1990) observed, "No job category is beyond measurement or evaluation. But remember, no single statistic that relates to worker effort should be regarded as an absolute measure of productivity."

Managers at General Foods decided to use a comprehensive approach to measuring productivity when they decided to become the nation's lowest-cost food producer. The company developed a sophisticated control system, the Plantwide Productivity Measurement Program, or PPMP. Using standard cost-accounting data, managers devised individual productivity indexes for each aspect of General Foods' many product lines. The component measures yielded an aggregate productivity index for each product or plant. By using PPMP, General Foods managers were able to identify production inefficiencies and meet cost-reduction targets (Seidman and Skancke, 1990).

Behaviors   Managers must take great care to ensure that standards do not encourage behaviors that compromise the organization's mission and goals. Salespersons evaluated solely by the sales revenue they generate may be tempted to treat all sales as equal rather than emphasize sales that yield the highest profits. Similarly, the division manager evaluated primarily against the short-term standard of quarterly profits may be tempted to ignore the long-term investment needed to ensure the organization's future survival. Control standards and measurements must seek to create compatibility between individual and organizational goals (Bittel and Ramsey, 1985).

Top managers at ConAgra, a giant producer of food products, discovered that standards emphasizing decentralization had led to behaviors that were undermining efficiency and profitability. As Lubove (1992) reported, ConAgra was operating as "a decentralized patchwork of business fiefdoms," unable to maximize its own potential. Each unit ordered packaging from different suppliers, for example, and made long-distance telephone calls over different networks. Each bought raw materials from outside suppliers that they could have bought from

ISSUES AND ETHICS
Cheaters Undermine Testing

With funding from Exxon Corporation, Professor Donald McCabe of the Rutgers University Graduate School of Management polled 16,000 graduate students at 31 universities. His goal was to investigate cheating patterns. Some 6,100 students (their anonymity guaranteed) responded to the survey. A sample of the results follows.

- Of business majors, 76% admitted to cheating on at least one test; 19% admitted to cheating on four or more tests.

- Of engineering students, 71% admitted to cheating at least once.

- Of medical students, 68% admitted to cheating at least once.

- Of government, or public service, students, 66% admitted to cheating at least once.

- Of law students, 63% admitted to cheating at least once.

What are the consequences of cheating for students who do not cheat? What do these survey results reveal about the effectiveness of present policies about cheating? What action do you think is appropriate to address the issue of cheating? Who should undertake such action? ▲

For more about this topic, see "Business Students Cheat Most," *Fortune,* July 1, 1991, pp. 14, 18.

---

one another. New CEO Philip Fletcher set out to achieve closer cooperation among the subsidiaries, especially in purchasing and distribution. "I want us to buy as a $20-billion-plus company but maintain [an] independent operating company culture" (Lubove, 1992).

Measuring Performance

After standards are established, managers must measure actual performance to determine variation from standard. The mechanisms for this purpose can be extremely sensitive, particularly in high-tech environments. Building modern airliners, for example, requires extraordinarily refined measurement and control systems. Along with visual inspections, technicians induce electric current in the metal surfaces to create magnetic fields. Any distortion in the fields indicates a problem (*Business Week,* November 18, 1991).

Computers are becoming increasingly important as tools for measuring performance. They can monitor people and operations as they occur, and they can store data to be used later. Many retail stores use computerized scanning equipment that simultaneously accesses prices and tallies sales and then tracks inventory by department, vendor, and branch store. The computerized scanning systems can also track the sales personnel, recording transactions and salesclerk activity. The displays and reports these systems produce often show current standards and actual performance measurements. Computerized systems of all kinds give managers the up-to-the-minute information they need to make sound decisions.

Comparing Measured Performance to Established Standards

The next step in the control process is to compare actual performance to the standards set for that performance. If deviations from the standards exist, the evaluator must decide if they are significant—if they require corrective action. If so, the evaluator must determine what is causing the variance.

To understand variance in regard to manufacturing, consider an operation that mills a billet of titanium into a complex shape to be used as an engine part. The established tolerance, or standard of variance, for the part is plus or minus 1/1000 inch from the specified dimensions. Periodically throughout the milling process, the machinist measures the part to be sure that it remains within tolerance. Any part milled beyond the tolerance must be rejected. A search for the cause of the unacceptable variance begins.

The source of a deviation may lie beyond the employee who first discovers it. Suppliers may have shipped faulty materials. Previous operators may have been poorly trained, dishonest about results, or misinformed about applicable standards. If equipment is in poor condition, it may be incapable of producing output that meets the standards—no matter how hard the operator tries. Determining the cause of substandard performance involves going beyond an examination of task performance, however. It involves examining the standards being applied and the accuracy of the measurement and comparison processes. As Bittel and Ramsey (1985) explained, the control may be too loose or too tight:

> If control is too loose, a deviation between actual and planned performance may result in poor coordination among organizational subunits and the failure to respond in time to unforeseen problems or opportunities. Loose control may also reduce some of the incentives for managers to meet their plans. On the other hand, tighter control generally calls for additional data collection, information processing, and management reporting. The cost and inconvenience of the 'red tape' associated with tight control is likely to be resented by the persons being controlled. Tight control may restrict the ability of lower-level managers to exercise imagination and initiative in response to changed conditions.

In the productivity- and quality-centered environment of today, workers and managers are often empowered to evaluate their own work for quality, productivity, and cost improvements. Individuals and groups throughout organizations are being given the responsibility to control their own behaviors and operations. By putting the authority to make decisions in the hands of those who are best equipped to make them, employees can respond almost instantly to substandard performance.

Taking Corrective Action

When an employee determines the cause, or causes, of a significant deviation from a standard, he or she must take corrective action to avoid repetition of the problem or defect. Policies and procedures may prescibe the actions. Such guidelines help shorten the time needed to react to deviations. Policies and procedures cannot be employed in all instances, however.

Managers of the Chi-Chi's restaurant chain observe a strict schedule of controls, double-checking every aspect of their operations. Quality control and the scheduling of operations is more difficult in a service operation than in manufacturing, yet just as important.

In some cases, pressures and controls imposed from outside an organization dictate the nature of corrective action. Equifax, a company that provides consumer credit reports, recently had to take action as a result of legal challenges. *Business Week* (July 13, 1992) reported the extent to which Equifax executives decided to change company practices:

> Equifax successfully avoided being sued when it agreed on June 30 [1992] to revamp its methods. After talks with attorneys general of 18 states, Equifax announced it would go beyond federal law to ensure the accuracy of its credit reports and correct errors promptly. Equifax said it would continue with many of the steps it had already taken, including installing new software, providing a toll-free number for consumer questions, looking into disputes within 30 days, and providing free copies of reports to consumers denied requests for credit. The state attorneys extracted a similar agreement last year from TRW, another leading credit report company.

Some corrective actions are automatic. Just as a thermostat can activate a heating or cooling system automatically, assembly operations with computer-guided equipment can sense deviations and take corrective actions without the need for human involvement. Managers must not overlook automatic controls when searching for the causes of substandard performance. Even automatic controls can malfunction on occasion.

Some corrective actions call for exceptions to prescribed modes of behavior. To retain the goodwill of a valued customer, for example, a manager may authorize an exception to the firm's refund policy. Some hotel and restaurant chains empower customer-service employees to "do whatever it takes" to guarantee customer satisfaction. If managers direct employees to do whatever it takes, the managers must allow the employees to use their discretion and judgment. The employees will face problems for which no guidelines exist—problems that will demand unique and creative solutions. Procedures, rules, and policies should not be substitutes for good judgment and employee initiative.

Types of Controls and Control Systems

This section will begin by discussing three types of controls: feedforward controls, concurrent controls, and feedback controls. Each focuses on a different point of a process—before the process begins, during the process, or after it ceases. Most experts agree that controls "are most economic and effective when applied selectively at the crucial points most likely to determine the success or failure of an operation or activity" (Bittel, 1989). A restaurant must focus on controlling the quality of its ingredients, their preparation, and their presentation. All these control points are critical to the restaurant's safe and effective operation. Poor ingredients will yield a bad meal, as will poorly cooked food. Poor customer service will alienate diners. Exhibit 15.3 shows how the three types of controls apply to restaurant operations.

Feedforward Controls

Controls that focus on operations before they begin are called **feedforward controls**. (These controls are sometimes called preliminary, screening, or prevention controls.) Feedforward controls are intended to prevent defects and deviations from standards. Locks on doors and bars on windows, safety equipment and guidelines, employee-selection procedures, employee-training programs, and budgets are all feedforward controls. When a manufacturer works closely with its suppliers to ensure that the suppliers deliver goods and services that meet standards, the manufacturer is implementing a feedforward control. A maintenance procedure that keeps equipment in top-notch shape is also a feedforward control. If the owner of a convenience store implements the recommendations about security that were cited at the beginning of this chapter, he or she would be implementing feedforward controls as well.

Concurrent Controls

Controls that apply to processes as they are happening are called **concurrent controls**, or steering controls. Consider word processing software, which allows a writer to change a document on a video display terminal before storing or printing it. The software provides concurrent control. A word processor's spelling checker also provides concurrent control.

Some concurrent controls are designed to provide readouts or audible warnings. Most photocopiers and computer printers, for example, have display panels that alert their users to malfunctions during operation. Many of the devices

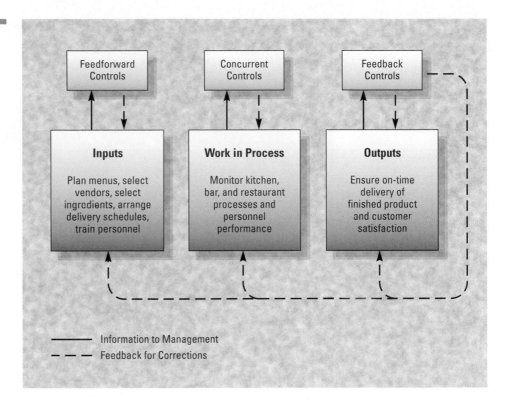

on the dashboard of an automobile are concurrent controls. The odometer keeps track of miles traveled; the speedometer tracks the speed of the vehicle. Various warning lights alert the driver to impending or actual problems, such as low levels of fuel or oil and problems with the brakes or computerized systems. The steering wheel is a concurrent control that allows a driver to make adjustments in the course of the vehicle. If you try to exit a newly built automobile without turning off the headlights, you will be concurrently controlled by a warning device, perhaps even a gently scolding electronic voice.

The most important concurrent control in any undertaking is often the skilled and experienced operator whose eyes, ears, and "feel" for the operation give timely warnings that things are not as they should be. Recognizing the importance of experienced employees as control mechanisms, many companies are enhancing workers' power to affect operations. The Cargill Company is America's largest privately held corporation, with operations in farming, transportation, merchandising, and agricultural processing. At Cargill's beef-packing plant in Alberta, Canada, 1,700 steers and heifers are butchered each day. On the swift-moving processing line, any employee who believes something is amiss has the power to halt the operation (Henkoff, 1992).

Feedback Controls

Controls that focus on the results of operations are called **feedback controls**. They are "after the fact," or postperformance, controls. They are called feedback controls because the information they provide is fed back into the process or to the

Collecting control data with VoCollect, this inspector calls out defects and the computer on his belt records them. This information can be used to pinpoint and eliminate problems in manufacturing.

controller, who must then make any necessary adjustments. "On a larger scale, however, measurements and comparisons made after an operation has been concluded (postperformance) serve to guide future planning, goals, inputs, and process designs" (Bittel, 1989). At the end of the year, for example, a manager should carefully review the budget control report. Which accounts were overdrawn? Which accounts retained a surplus? Were priorities established through the budget proper and in line with organizational demands? Why or why not? Lessons learned from historical information can be used to perform every task more effectively and efficiently. Everyone can learn from past performance.

A lack of feedback controls can lead to disaster, as it did in the case of United Way of America. In February 1992, allegations of mismanagement forced the longtime president of United Way, William Aramony, to resign. His resignation shook confidence in charity fundraising nationwide (Garland, 1992). Stanley C. Gault, chairman of Goodyear Tire & Rubber Company, expressed the feelings of many in corporate America when he said, "Where was the board [of directors? Where were] the outside auditors? [The indiscretions] should have been detected far earlier" (Garland, 1992). Pending an investigation of the problems, many local chapters of the nationwide charity withheld their contributions to headquarters. And many of them are examining their own accounting and fundraising methods to avoid any hint of scandal.

Recall the recommendations for store security presented at the beginnng of this chapter. The association that published the recommendations prepared the guidelines by using feedback from convicted store robbers.

Control Systems

Feedforward, concurrent, and feedback controls should be viewed as part of an overall **control system**. Able managers integrate suitable control combinations to enforce standards, make sure elements function smoothly with one another, and ensure that resources are used effectively and efficiently. Today companies are emphasizing feedforward and concurrent controls. They are avoiding dependence on feedback controls, which often provide information when it is too late to avoid losses.

Recall the example of Procter & Gamble, which was cited earlier in this chapter. When the company developed a new soap product, managers implemented controls as part of the planning process, to prevent problems from occurring and provide ongoing performance information. The feedforward controls included screening new hires, providing training for new personnel, creating budgets for new operations, and conducting market research.

As the project began, Procter & Gamble relied on concurrent and feedback controls. Managers evaluated the impact of the new soap on other brands. They assessed people's performance, compared actual to projected sales, and matched actual to projected profits. The resulting information was sufficiently detailed and complete to allow the executives to adjust ongoing operations. The information will also help them enhance the success of future product launches.

The Characteristics of Effective Controls

Controls at every level focus on inputs, processes, and outputs. But what characteristics make controls effective? Effective controls are focused on critical points and integrated into the corporate culture. They are timely and accepted by those who use them or abide by them. In addition, effective controls are economically feasible, accurate, and comprehensible. The paragraphs that follow will examine these characteristics.

Focus on Critical Points

Critical control points are all the operations that directly affect the survival of an organization and the success of its most essential activities. Critical control points exist in many areas of business activity—production, sales, customer service, and finance, for example. Controls should focus on those points at which failures cannot be tolerated and where time and money costs are greatest.

The objective is to apply controls to the essential aspects of a business, not the peripheral ones. Having a salesperson report on all the activities undertaken during a long sales trip would be one way to control. The resulting report would probably obscure the important issues, however, and the task of writing it would burden the salesperson. A simple report of actual sales calls and sales revenues would be far more relevant and effective.

Integration

Controls exhibit integration when the corporate culture supports and enforces them and when they work in harmony, not at cross-purposes. When controls and the need for them are consonant with the organization's values, the controls will be effective. Coordinated controls do not impede work; they function harmoniously to give people what they need to make informed judgments.

Many companies are focusing on the critical control point of worker health by banning smoking in the workplace. But many smokers (some 28% of working adults) are highly valued employees whose feelings must be addressed if managers plan to institute a no-smoking policy. The implementation of a smoking ban is a case where integrated controls—controls that reflect an organization's regard for health as well as a respect for personal rights—can make a great difference in workers' morale. Experts in implementing smoking bans report that employees need ample notice of the ban—a notice of two or three months is appropriate. Management can ask a voluntary committee of smokers and nonsmokers to recommend smoking and nonsmoking areas. Joseph Weintraub, president of a Massachusetts-based consultancy, says employees should be asked: "How can we make this work for everybody?" (Mangan, 1992). A participatory approach to the controlling effort protects employee morale and usually increases mutual support for controls.

When managers and employees trust each other, and workers at all levels believe that the controls are necessary, employees can be relied upon to implement the controls. When everyone accepts the organization's mission and culture, the corporate climate nourishes self-discipline and commitment. Work teams are self-policing and share values that are consistent with those of the organization. As workers enter these supportive environments, managers and co-workers take care to ensure that the newcomers "buy into" the culture (Walton, 1985).

Acceptability

People must agree that controls are necessary, that the particular kinds of controls in use are appropriate, and that the controls will not have negative impacts on individuals or their efforts to achieve personal goals. Controls that appear to be arbitrary, subjective, or an invasion of privacy will not elicit the support of those they affect. Likewise, controls that are redundant (except when necessary for health and safety) or too restrictive will go unsupported. In fact, such controls will stimulate covert and overt opposition. Too many controls, confusing controls, and too few controls create stress and resistance. Frustration, fear, and loss of motivation and initiative can result.

Timeliness

Controls must ensure that information reaches those who need it *when they need it;* only then can a meaningful response follow. One reason for setting deadlines is to ensure that information flows promptly. If deadlines are treated casually or unrealistically (if the manager always wants things yesterday), people will soon come to ignore them. In such a case, deadlines are totally ineffective as controls.

Ensuring timely flow is one goal of management information systems. K Mart employs modern technology to link its stores to headquarters and vendors. Among the sophisticated equipment the organization uses are point-of-sale devices that, via satellite, transmit merchandise information to buyers and vendors. The devices can also provide instant credit authorization to speed customer checkout. These tools saved enough money to pay for the satellite system in less than two years (Comins, 1992).

Economic Feasibility

The costs of a control system must be weighed against its benefits. If the resources expended on the controls do not return an equal or greater value, the controls are better left unimplemented. Suppose a costly security system includes highly trained personnel, sophisticated electronic surveillance equipment, and fingerprint scanning. Such a system is suitable for valuable capital equipment and facilities, but not the office supply cabinet.

Sometimes controls must be costly and redundant. Jet aircraft, nuclear power plants, hospital operating and intensive care facilities, and the space shuttle need redundant systems, or backup systems, to allow them to overcome a potentially life-threatening failure of the primary system. NASA will not launch the space shuttle if one of the three main computers on board is malfunctioning. Redundant and expensive controls are often required to prevent problems which, if they occur, would mean irrecoverable loss or irreparable damage far more costly than the controls.

Accuracy

Information is useful if it is accurate. Accuracy relates particularly to concurrent controls used to diagnose deviations from standards. Controls that offer inaccurate assessments feed decision makers the wrong input, which causes them to give inappropriate responses. When a project manager reports that production is two weeks behind schedule because of poor team attendance, her boss begins an investigation. It turns out that, though several people have been absent, they were not key to production. The delay was actually caused by the failure to properly plan the flow of work and set meaningful deadlines.

Comprehensibility

The more complex a control becomes, the more likely it is to create confusion. The simpler the control, the easier it will be to communicate and apply. Anyone who has struggled with assembly instructions for a hobby kit knows firsthand how rare well-written instructions are. Controls in the form of instructions are often complex because more than one person created, implemented, or interpreted them. Complexity can also result when control users lose sight of the purposes of the control.

Too many controls can lead to confusion. (The notion that if one control is good, two must be better, is common but incorrect.) Refinements in reporting procedures often lead to the proliferation of controls. The result can be a profusion of data that sidetracks control efforts.

Computers are reducing complexity and confusion in many environments. Bar codes attached to inventory items or materials moving along an assembly line simplify the process of tracking. Some computer software allows voice commands— even commands in a foreign language—to activate or access processes. Machines that use symbols rather than words further overcome language barriers. "Smart" software and a few keystrokes or flicks of a light pen can get things on track. All these innovations enhance communication by keeping it simple.

Control Monitoring

Controls are effective as long as they do what they are intended to do, do not generate opposition, and do not result in costs greater than the benefits they provide. Changing circumstances require organizations to monitor controls to ensure that they remain effective.

Monitoring Organizational Impacts

Managers need to know the impacts of controls. Controls can generate support or antagonism. Involving employees in the design of controls can help ensure support. Controls that employees believe are equitable seldom encounter resistance. When monitoring the impact of controls, managers can use the following techniques:

- Before-and-after comparisons. This approach assesses the organization's environment before and after implementation of the control, and notes differences that have occurred. If defects were 10 per 100 before the control and then dropped to 1 per 1,000 after the control was implemented, the organization should obviously retain the control and keep working on reducing the defects.

  Before-and-after comparison left no doubt that changes Jontee Accessories made in collection procedures were effective. The company, a manufacturer of hats and hair accessories, instituted the changes after experiencing difficulties in collecting on invoices. Instead of waiting for weeks to contact overdue customers, it now telephones each customer whose account is overdue by 10 days. Jontee now sets up special payment arrangements and allows financially troubled customers to return merchandise. The results? "We had an upsurge in payments, but more important, we were able to detect problems early on," says owner Francesca Kuglen. Mutual Life Insurance Company, the U.S. Chamber of Commerce, and *Nation's Business* designated the firm as California's 1992 Blue Chip Enterprise (*Nation's Business,* August 1992).

- Surveys of employees affected by the controls. A manager who wants to determine the impact of a control should collect relevant data at several points in time. Multiple surveys will not only reveal perceptions, but also show when the perceptions were formed. Positive feedback indicates that controls are accepted and integrated. Negative feedback can be further analyzed to determine the causes of resistance. Factors other than controls may affect perceptions. The manager must take care to consider all the changes that have taken place between measurements.

- Controlled experiments. To form a sound assessment of the effect of a change, scientific practice requires a survey of the changed group as well as of a group that works without the change. The unchanged group is called the control group. Both groups are studied to determine significant differences in their results, norms, values, perceptions, and behaviors. The technique of the controlled experiment isolates those effects that can be specifically linked to the change.

Updating Controls

Controls are designed to deal with specific people, processes, and circumstances. When any of these variables changes, managers need to re-evaluate the controls. Exhibit 15.4 presents a list of changes that usually call for a re-examination of an organization's controls.

　　　People tend to get comfortable with the way things are. Once controls are introduced, implemented, and yield results, people become complacent; the

Exhibit 15.4

Typical changes that require re-examination of controls.

- **Changes to mission.** What is the present purpose of the organization? Was the recent change planned? If not, how much of the change was driven by controls and the control system? Are the changes good? How will current plans affect the mission? Should the mission be changed again? If so, how? How will changes to the mission affect controls and the control system?

- **Structural changes.** Have the changes altered the organization's ability to meet its goals? What roles did controls and the control system play in making these changes come about? Have efforts at controlling affected the organization's span of control, chain of command, degree of decentralization, and job definitions? If so, have the effects been positive or negative? Are the controls worth any difficulties they have created? Have structural changes made changes to controls or the control system necessary?

- **Changes in decision making.** Did the control system alter the information flow required for decision making? Is there more decentralized decision making now than in the recent past? Is the quality of decisions being made today equal to that of the past? Is the management information system adequate? What roles have controls played in any of these issues? Do changes in decision making require changes in controls, the control process, or the control system?

- **Changes in human relations.** Do people enjoy working in the organization? Is there an unacceptable level of waste? Are high costs or frequent disciplinary actions, tardiness, or absenteeism related to personnel actions? Have quality and productivity been affected? Have there been changes to group norms and cultures? Has the interaction between managers and their subordinates improved or worsened? Are controls or control systems contributing factors to improvements or declines? Are changes needed in either the controls or the control system?

- **Technological changes.** What is the effect of recent technological change on controls and the control system? Are any changes in technology being planned? What will be their impacts on controls and the control process? Are the controls, control process, and control system using the latest beneficial technology? Should they be? Are the costs of using the latest technology worth its adoption?

GLOBAL APPLICATIONS
German Firms Relocate to Lower Costs

ontrolling costs lies at the heart of control efforts in many companies. The very survival of every organization demands that managers control costs.

German manufacturers are world famous for quality and precision engineering. But they are also notorious for having the world's highest average hourly labor costs. To reduce their costs, many German manufacturers are moving their manufacturing facilities to other countries. The newest of these will be BMW's production facilities in South Carolina. Daimler-Benz is examining the options of producing cars in Mexico and Russia. Of the $32 billion Volkswagen will spend on facilities by 1996, 50% will be spent outside Germany. Volkswagen executives plan to build low-cost production facilities in Portugal, Spain, Mexico, China, and Czechoslovakia. Siemens is moving some of its domestic production to Turkey and Eastern European nations.

The list keeps growing. German industry groups estimate that jobs are being exported at a rate of more than 100,000 a year, and that doesn't take into account foreign companies that may be bypassing Germany in favor of lower-cost European locations. German executives maintain that costs are often the driving motive for pulling out of Germany. In 1990 German companies invested a net of 29.8 billion marks abroad . . . while net foreign investments in Germany totaled 2.9 billion marks. The gap continued to widen in 1991. ▲

For more on this topic, see Terence Roth, "German Firms Bemoan Production Costs," *Wall Street Journal,* January 29, 1992, p. A10.

controls become a part of daily routine. But a continual repetition of the past means lost opportunities and delays in implementing needed changes. By simply relying on controls and systems that are in place, managers fail to make full use of the preventive nature of the controlling process. The instant that changes occur or are planned, managers should begin to determine if present controls will be adequate and applicable in the new situation. Invariably, changes are needed to the controlling effort as well. Controls themselves need to be controlled!

Future Trends

In regard to controls, a number of trends will continue:

- With growing decentralization and empowerment, the need for workers (individually and in teams) to plan, organize, direct, staff, and control their areas of influence will increase.

- Rapid advancements in technology will hasten feedback from all kinds of controls. Real-time, instant feedback will be possible in nearly every key operation.

- Controlling for quality will be the primary focus. Quality improvements must then be studied to assess their impacts on productivity.

- Changes will come more quickly to all organizations, creating the need to re-evaluate plans and controls more frequently.

High labor costs drive down profits and drive up prices. Many companies have had to move their manufacturing facilities into other countries in order to stay competitive.

- The expanded use of bar codes, which can be read by lasers, will speed the flow of information to managers and workers. Standard bar codes on most consumer products can hold 20 to 30 characters per inch. New codes under development can hold hundreds of characters per inch. The capacity of these new codes suggests many additional control applications.

C H A P T E R   S U M M A R Y

- Controlling affects and is affected by planning, organizing, staffing, and directing.

- The prudent management of resources is critical to the survival of an organization. Resources should not be acquired or used until effective means for monitoring acquisition and use are in place.

- Controls must be appropriate for the people, processes, and circumstances they will affect and which will affect them.

- Controls should be as simple as possible.

- Standards should deal with issues of quantity and quality.

- Controlling requires an organization to establish standards, measure performance, apply the standards to measured performances, and take corrective action when necessary.

- Key areas of focus for standards are time, cost, quality, productivity, and behavior.

- Feedforward controls focus on processes before they begin. Concurrent controls focus on processes as the processes occur, and feedback controls provide information about processes after they cease. Effective control systems employ all three types.

- Controls should focus on critical points. They should be integrated, acceptable, timely, economically feasible, accurate, and comprehensible.

- Keeping control devices current in terms of objectives and expectations is critical in making controls effective.

- Managers must monitor the organizational impact of controls to ensure that they remain effective.

S K I L L - B U I L D I N G

In answering the questions that follow, think about the job you have now or one that you have held in the past. Identify and list four control devices that you had to work with, and then answer the following questions:

1. What resources do you think each device was designed to control?

2. Were the standards established for each control quantitative or qualitative? Why?

3. Have any of the four controls presented a problem for you? If so, what was it?

4. What characteristics of effective controls do each of your controls have? Which characteristics do they lack?

R E V I E W   Q U E S T I O N S

1. Review this chapter's essential terms and look up the meanings of those you cannot define.

2. In what ways are planning, organizing, staffing, and directing linked to controlling?

3. What are the four steps in the control process, and what happens in each?

4. What purposes do feedforward, feedback, and concurrent controls serve for managers?

5. Why must controls be designed and implemented as a system?

6. What examples can you give for each of the seven characteristics of effective controls?

7. What actions can managers take to make controls more effective?

R E C O M M E N D E D   **R** E A D I N G

Aldag, Ramon, and Timothy M. Sterns. *Management* (Cincinnati: South-Western), 1991.

Barry, Thomas J. *Management Excellence Through Quality* (Milwaukee: ASQC Press), 1991.

Bittel, Lester R. *The McGraw-Hill 36-Hour Management Course* (New York: McGraw-Hill), 1989.

Drucker, Peter F. "The New Productivity Challenge," *Harvard Business Review* (November–December 1991), pp. 69–79.

Hinterhuber, Hans H., and Wolfgang Popp. "Are You a Strategist or Just a Manager?" *Harvard Business Review* (January–February 1992), pp. 105–113.

Hirschhorn, Larry, and Thomas Gilmore. "The New Boundaries of the 'Boundaryless' Company," *Harvard Business Review* (May–June 1992), pp. 104–115.

McIntyre, Thomas. *Behavior Management Handbook: Setting Up Effective Management Systems* (Needham Heights, MA: Allyn and Bacon), 1989.

Seidman, L. William, and Steven L. Skancke. *Productivity: The Proven Path to Excellence in U.S. Companies* (New York: Touchstone), 1990.

Warnick, Kevin. *Control Systems: An Introduction* (Englewood Cliffs, NJ: Prentice-Hall), 1989.

R E F E R E N C E S

Barry, Thomas J. *Management Excellence Through Quality* (Milwaukee: ASQC Press), 1991, pp. 5, 6.

Bittel, Lester R. *The McGraw-Hill 36-Hour Management Course* (New York: McGraw-Hill), 1989, pp. 179, 184, 185.

Bittel, Lester R., and Jackson E. Ramsey, editors. *Handbook for Professional Managers* (New York: McGraw-Hill), 1985, pp. 194, 196.

Business Week (July 13, 1992). "Equifax Vows to Get It Right," p. 38.

Business Week (November 18, 1991). "This Inspector Gets Under a Plane's Skin," p. 69.

Comins, Jr., Frederic M. "Renewal at K-mart," a letter to the editor of *Harvard Business Review* (September–October 1992), p. 176.

Garland, Susan B. "Keeping a Sharper Eye on Those Who Pass the Hat," *Business Week* (March 16, 1992), p. 39.

Henkoff, Ronald. "Inside America's Biggest Private Company," *Fortune* (July 13, 1992), p. 88.

Lubove, Seth. "'I Hope My Luck Holds Out,'" *Forbes* (July 20, 1992), p. 120.

Mangan, Doreen. "When It's Time to Ban Smoking," *Your Company* (Spring 1992), p. 6.

Nation's Business (August 1992). "Getting What They Owe You," p. 53.

Odiorne, George; Heinz Weihrichl; and Jack Mendleson. *Executive Skills: A Management by Objectives Approach* (Dubuque, IA: Brown), 1980, pp. 26–28.

Seidman, L. William, and Steven L. Skancke. *Productivity: The Proven Path to Excellence in U.S. Companies* (New York: Touchstone), 1990, pp. 44, 45–46.

Walton, Richard E. "From Control to Commitment in the Workplace," *Harvard Business Review* (March–April 1985), pp. 76–84.

Walton, Sam, with John Huey. *Sam Walton: Made in America* (New York: Doubleday), 1992, pp. 248–249.

GLOSSARY OF TERMS

concurrent control   A control that applies to processes as they are happening.

control process   A four-step process that consists of (1) establishing standards, (2) measuring performance, (3) comparing measured performance to established standards, and (4) taking corrective action.

control system   A system in which feedforward, concurrent, and feedback controls operate in harmony to ensure that standards are enforced, that goals are reached, and that resources are used effectively and efficiently.

controlling   The process through which standards for the performance of people and processes are set, communicated, and applied.

critical control point   An area of operations that directly affects the survival of a firm and the success of its most essential activities.

feedback control   A control that focuses on the outputs or results of operations.

feedforward control   A control that prevents defects and deviations from standards.

standard   Any established rule or basis of comparison used to measure capacity, quantity, content, value, cost, quality, or performance.

C A S E   P R O B L E M
Warnaco's Linda Wachner

As of the summer of 1992, Linda Wachner was the only female CEO of a Fortune 500 industrial company. She is considered to be America's most successful female executive. People who work with her know her to be a dynamic, sometimes abrasive personality. She has made her company, Warnaco, extremely successful in a highly competitive, recessionary environment. "Wachner has learned to run her company with a near-fanatical devotion to three guiding principles: Stay close to the customer, keep on top of the business, and watch the till." She and everyone who works for her carry a notebook with the words "Do It Now" printed on the cover.

Since taking the top spot in 1986 (when she and financier Andrew Galef teamed up to buy Warnaco), Linda has dropped the company's weakest lines of apparel and focused on the two that are most profitable: intimate apparel and menswear. In 1991 "intimate apparel produced 60% of Warnaco's $562 million in sales and about 69% of the $195.4 million in gross profits." Along with its own brands, Warnaco has licensing agreements with popular designers like Bob Mackie and Valentino to produce apparel under their names. Five of its regular customers are the Limited, May Department Stores, J.C. Penny, Dillards, and Victoria's Secret. The company began sales to Wal-Mart and K Mart in 1992. The menswear division brings in about 32% of sales under labels like Christian Dior, Ralph Lauren, and Jack Nicklaus.

In line with her principles, Wachner

pores over the selling reports that come in from many of her retail accounts. And she shops—roaming store aisles around the country, shooting the breeze with the salespeople, picking up firsthand intelligence on which products folks are buying and why. She works hard at building relationships with the merchants who stock her wares, spending countless hours with them to find out how she can expand her business within their stores. Says Leslie Wexner, chairperson of the Limited, "Linda is always willing to go the extra mile. I can't get some of my vendors to fly from Pittsburgh to Columbus."

Once every week, Linda meets with her seven key executives by way of a one-page fax from each. Each gives her an overview of the key problems and successes in his or her area. These reports—along with the monthly sales projections and daily cash receipts—are vital to tracking Warnaco's processes.

Q U E S T I O N S

1. Which of Wachner's three principles are related to controlling? In what ways are they related to each other?

2. Do you think it is important for a CEO to visit with customers regularly? Why?

3. What kind of feedforward, feedback, and concurrent controls does Wachner use?

For more on Linda Wachner, see Susan Caminiti, "America's Most Successful Businesswoman," *Fortune,* June 15, 1992, pp. 102–106, 108.

Control Techniques

LEARNING OBJECTIVES

After reading and discussing this chapter, you should be able to:

- Define this chapter's essential terms
- Describe the contents of balance sheets and income statements and how managers use these tools
- Explain why financial ratios are useful to managers
- Describe the importance of financial responsibility centers
- Discuss the purpose of a budget, the types of budgets, and the approaches to budgeting
- Describe five marketing control techniques
- Describe five human resource controls

audit

balance sheet

budget

financial budget

financial ratio

financial responsibility center

flexible budgeting

human asset accounting

income statement

operating budget

ratio

zero-based budgeting

MANAGEMENT IN ACTION
Hacking Long-Distance Fraud

stimates of telephone-fraud losses in the United States range from $500 million to $4 billion each year. Most fraud is committed on a grand scale by hackers who break into a company's private telephone network and then make long-distance calls.

One method the hackers use is to penetrate a voice-mail system and then gain access to the phone system connected to it. For example, a hacker cracked the private network of the Christian Broadcasting Network and made $40,000 worth of calls to Pakistan. Such fraud is sometimes committed by hackers who sell cut-rate phone calls to immigrants. Many such calls were placed from pay phones in Times Square, where hackers sell stolen long-distance–calling codes. The sight of long lines of callers waiting at each phone to use the stolen codes was not unusual. New York Telephone no longer accepts long-distance calls placed from public telephones in Times Square. Another way thieves gain access to calling codes is simply by

Controlling the phone lines *is a monumental task. Service providers must continuously be on the lookout for hackers.*

watching legitimate users as they punch in their calling-card numbers.

Corporations are fighting back. Communications managers program their telephone networks not to accept certain types of incoming calls and outgoing calls to certain destinations. To prevent access to voice-mail systems, they install complex passwords. Corporations are cooperating with police and phone companies to lay traps to catch repeat offenders.

Phone companies are helping to prevent fraud by implementing software that spots unusual calling patterns. One report sums up the effectiveness of these approaches: Sprint Corporation's average loss fell more than 90% in 1991–1992, to less than $2,000 per case. Tele-Choice, Incorporated, estimated that losses from phone fraud could fall 60% in 1992–1993. In another recent move to prevent misuse, AT&T cut off access to 800-numbers from more than 1,000 phone lines that were suspected of being involved in fraud.

Another deterrent to phone crime is the imposition of stiff penalties. Prosecution in regard to phone fraud is becoming more vigorous. The courts have handed out substantial fines and jail terms to offenders.

Companies without insurance against the losses from phone fraud can be out thousands of dollars. Sprint, for a fee, insures losses over $25,000 and up to $1,000,000. AT&T covers losses over $12,500 if customers discover the fraud before AT&T does. MCI covers 30% of a customer's first loss. ▲

▶ A hacker cracked the private network of the Christian Broadcasting Network and made $40,000 worth of calls to Pakistan. Sometimes hackers sell cut-rate phone calls to immigrants.

For more about phone fraud, see Mark Lewyn, "Phone Sleuths Are Cutting Off the Hackers," *Business Week,* July 13, 1992, p. 134.

The Importance of Control Techniques

Chapter 15 examined controlling as a management function. This chapter will explore several important control techniques that are used throughout the functional areas of a business. Among these techniques are feedforward, concurrent, and feedback controls. As you read about each technique, consider its purpose for managers and at which level of management the control would be most useful. Bear in mind that the control techniques are tools that measure the progress of people and processes toward achievement of individual and organizational goals. Control techniques provide the quantitative and qualitative information needed for sound decisions. Such information must be processed and interpreted by people who understand the activities they undertake to control.

As you recall from Chapter 5, strategic planning helps managers answer four questions: (1) Where is the organization now? (2) Where do top managers want it to be? (3) What trends and changes are occurring in the competitive marketplace? and (4) How can managers best achieve objectives and respond to perceived opportunities and threats? Answers emerge through development of a strategic plan—the same plan that provides guidance for designing controls. The plan identifies the company's key resources and their effective allocation. Control techniques must then be put into place to monitor resources, processes, trends, and changes. Controls must be chosen or designed to meet specific needs and then integrated into a system that avoids both overcontrol and nonessential duplication of control.

Control techniques are designed to provide the proper kinds and quantities of information at each management level. Budgets, for instance, are a means of control that also provide information. A budget created for an entire organization gives the CEO the summary information he or she needs to plot trends and identify deviations from standards. The information provided by a departmental budget differs markedly from that in the organizational budget. The budget for the marketing department, for example, tells the marketing chief what he or she needs to know about sales, advertising, distribution, and other key marketing functions. The team leader or supervisor uses the budget to determine what funding has been approved for his or her operations and personnel.

The number, types, and design of control techniques vary with each level of management and with each manager and operation. Those who use the controls must determine how much data they need and then design controls of sufficient integration and flexibility to provide accurate data in a timely way.

Management Control Systems

As plans are hierarchical, so are controls. An organization needs an overall control system, and so do subsystems. A firm's strategic plan guides the creation of the overall control system; subsystem plans do the same at their own levels.

The subsystems that require integrated and flexible control techniques are finance, marketing, operations (production), human resources, management information systems (MISs), and other management support activities. Among management support activities are legal services, computer services, and central filing services. This chapter will focus on control techniques used by finance, marketing, and human resource managers. Chapter 18 will discuss methods for operations management, and Chapter 19 will addresses techniques appropriate for management information systems.

Finance and Budgets

Finance managers need information about all aspects of the organization to determine its ability to meet monetary obligations. To prepare short- and long-term forecasts, managers prepare budgets for one month and six months and for one, two, and five years. Finance managers work with marketing personnel and others to project income and expenditures and then prepare projected and actual financial statements. Various formulas and ratios aid in the analysis of financial information.

Marketing

Marketing functions such as advertising, selling, distribution, and research can be expensive and must be adequately controlled. Managers use various techniques to ensure that marketing plans and resources are used effectively. The techniques include market research, test marketing, and various ratios, sales quotas, and stockage levels.

Operations

Operations, in the context of control techniques, refers to production activities. Typical production functions in need of control include product design; procurement of raw materials and other resources; production layout and flow; the handling of supplies, work in process, and finished goods; and efforts to improve quality and productivity. (Although controls such as budgets do affect manufacturing operations, discussion of specific control techniques for manufacturing is saved until Chapter 18.)

F O C U S   O N   Q U A L I T Y
Quality a Key Issue in the Burger Battle

All organizations must control their operations and stay ahead of their competition. For a mass merchandiser of name-brand merchandise, product and service quality must be maintained at all costs. A comparison of two fast-food franchisers makes the point. In 1955, McDonald's opened its first franchise in Des Plaines, Illinois. In 1967, General Foods Corporation bought the 700 franchises in the Burger Chef chain for $16 million. From 1967 to 1971, McDonald's net income increased by 285% to over $27 million. In the same period, Burger Chef created a $83 million loss for General Foods. Why the difference?

Within two years after its acquisition by General Foods, Burger Chef's key managers were replaced by General Foods managers who did not know the fast-food business. General Foods reduced Burger Chef outlets from 1,200 to 1,000 and introduced a new building design, logo, and wrappers to keep burgers warmer longer. From 1971 through 1974, however, sales increased but market share shrank. Why?

First, Burger Chef's operations were spread thinly over 39 states, making supervision and promotional support difficult. Second, Burger Chef failed to diversify its products when McDonald's and other rivals began producing fish sandwiches and double and triple hamburgers. Third, unlike McDonald's, Burger Chef did not adequately screen or properly train its franchisees. Finally, Burger Chef declined because it failed to emphasize product quality, cleanliness of outlets, and cheerful quick service. ▲

For more about marketing controls, see Robert F. Hartley, *Marketing Mistakes,* 5th edition (New York: Wiley), 1992, pp. 258–276.

Human Resources

Staffing involves all activities needed to manage human resources effectively and efficiently. This chapter will review the key control techniques and statistical measurements that track human resources and human resource activities.

Financial Controls

Financial resources are central to management: Without control over adequate funds, an organization cannot survive. Each financial activity requires specific, relevant control techniques. Some types of organizations (banks, for instance, or the Internal Revenue Service) require unique and elaborate fiscal controls. The controls such organizations use are unlike those of manufacturers and retailers. This chapter will examine control techniques common to all types of businesses.

Financial Statements

Nearly all organizations use two primary financial statements, the balance sheet and the income statement. The **balance sheet** identifies the assets of an organization—what it owns and the nature of the ownership—at a fixed *point* in time. The **income statement** presents the difference between an organization's income and its expenses to determine whether the enterprise operated at a profit or a loss over a specified *period* of time. Each provides a measure of feedback and concurrent control over financial and related activities. Both are used to prepare budgets and other kinds of plans and controls and to monitor the organization's financial health.

The Balance Sheet   Exhibit 16.1 presents the balance sheet of the Excel Corporation, a hypothetical medical-supply company, for one full year of operations, its *fiscal year*. (Like a calendar year, a fiscal year contains 365 days. A fiscal year, however, can begin at any time. The fiscal year for the U.S. government, for example, is from October 1 to September 31.) The balance sheet presents three categories of financial data—assets, liabilities, and stockholders' equity—as they exist on a specific date. The word *balance* in the term *balance sheet* derives from

Exhibit 16.1

Balance sheet of the Excel Corporation.

Excel Corporation
Balance Sheet
December 31, 199_

Assets

Current Assets		
Cash	$ 17,280	
Accounts Receivable	84,280	
Inventory	41,540	
Prepaid Expenses	12,368	
Total Current Assets		$155,468
Fixed Assets		
Building (Net)	$ 33,430	
Furniture and Fixtures (Net)	13,950	
Land	14,000	
Total Fixed Assets		$ 61,380
Total Assets		$216,848

Liabilities

Current Liabilities		
Notes Payable	$ 10,000	
Trade Accounts Payable	41,288	
Salaries Payable	400	
Taxes Payable	14,000	
Total Current Liabilities		$65,688
Long-Term Liabilities		
Mortgage Payable	$ 8,000	
Bonds Payable	3,280	
Total Long-Term Liabilities		$ 11,280
Total Liabilities		($ 76,968)

Stockholders' Equity

Common Stock (1,000 shares at $100 par value)	$100,000	
Retained Earnings	39,880	
Total Stockholders' Equity		$139,880
Total Liabilities and Stockholders' Equity		$216,848

the fact that the total assets must equal (balance) the sum of stockholders' equity and liabilities. Thus, the equation that describes a balance sheet is Assets equals Liabilities plus Stockholders' Equity.

Assets are the resources owned by a business. They usually fall into one of two categories, current or fixed. *Current assets* are cash or items that are normally converted into cash within one year from the date of the balance sheet. *Fixed assets* are assets not intended for sale or conversion to cash. Fixed assets include land, buildings, and the equipment used to conduct the activities of the business.

Liabilities are what a company owes—its current and long-term debts. *Current liabilities* are debts due and payable within one year of the date of the balance sheet. *Long-term liabilities* are those due after one year from that date. Included as liabilities are the claims by outsiders (creditors) on the assets of a business.

The difference between the value of the organization's assets and its liabilities equals the owners' interests in the assets of the business—their *equity.* Since a corporation is owned by stockholders, its equity is called *stockholders' equity.* In a sole proprietorship or partnership, the equity portion of the balance sheet is usually called *owner's equity.* To illustrate, assume that a sole proprietor buys a delivery truck that costs $10,000. The proprietor pays $3,000 in cash for the truck and arranges to borrow $7,000. The business owner now possesses an asset worth $10,000 but has also incurred a liability, or debt, of $7,000. The difference between the truck's value and the debt created to purchase it is $3,000—the amount of the proprietor's money that was used to purchase the truck. The proprietor's equity is $3,000.

Even as the balance sheet is being prepared, of course, changes occur that alter the mix of assets, liabilities, and equity. The utility of the balance sheet lies in the fact that it allows analysts to make comparisons from year to year and identify trends. In addition, the balance sheet yields information used to calculate various measures of the company's financial health and of management effectiveness. You will learn about some of these measures later in this chapter.

The Income Statement   Exhibit 16.2 presents the Excel Corporation's income statement, which summarizes the firm's accumulated income and expenses for a one-year period. The content of an income statement, like the content of a balance sheet, can be expressed as an equation. The equation that describes an income statement is Income minus Expenses equals Profit or Loss.

Managers use income statements as tools for reviewing the expenses and revenue of a business on an ongoing basis. These tools can be prepared to reflect any necessary time frame—a day, a week, a month, and so on. An income statement includes seven important categories:

1. Net sales, or the revenue from sales minus returns and allowances

2. Cost of goods sold, or the costs connected with making or acquiring goods that the organization has sold

3. Gross profit, or the measure of operating profits (obtained by subtracting the cost of goods sold from net sales)

4. Operating expenses, or overhead expenses (such as rent, advertising, utilities, insurance, and compensation paid to personnel not engaged in producing goods) that reduce gross profit

Excel Corporation
Income Statement
Year Ended December 31, 199_

Revenue

Sales	$778,918	
(Less Returns and Allowances)	(14,872)	
Net Sales		$764,046

Cost of Goods Sold

Beginning Inventory, January 1	$ 37,258	
Plus Net Purchases	593,674	
Goods Available for Sale	630,932	
(Less Ending Inventory, December 31)	(41,540)	
Cost of Goods Sold	$589,392	
Gross Profit on Sales		$174,654

Operating Expenses

Selling Expenses	$ 69,916	
General and Administrative	45,100	
Research and Development	9,970	
Total Operating Expenses		($124,986)
Net Income Before Taxes		($ 49,668)
(Less Federal and State Income Taxes		(18,315)
Net Income		$ 31,353

5. Net income (or loss) before taxes, the profit or loss of the business (obtained by subtracting operating expenses from the gross profit)

6. Taxes, the percentage of net income paid to governments

7. Net income, the profit left after paying taxes (the literal "bottom line")

Like a balance sheet, an income statement yields information needed to track the health of the organization it describes. The major purpose of the income statement is to measure trends in costs and income, noting growth or decline in each category.

Financial Ratio Analysis

A **ratio** expresses the relationship between numbers. The fraction ½ is a ratio. Ratios can be used to express the relationship between numbers in several ways: in words (as in "one to two" or "one part of two parts"), as a percentage (50%), or as a decimal (0.5).

A **financial ratio** involves selecting two critical figures from a financial statement and expressing their relationship as a ratio or percentage. Financial ratios help accountants and others measure a company's progress toward goals and assess its financial health. On the surface a firm may appear to be sound, its balance sheet reflecting impressive assets. But if the ratio of current assets to current liabilities is poor (less than 2 to 1), the company may have difficulty raising enough cash to meet short-term debts. Ratios can be involved in one of two types of comparisons. First, this year's ratio can be compared with the same kind of ratio for a past year. Or, a ratio describing one company can be compared with the same kind of ratio that describes a competitor.

Exhibit 16.3 lists frequently used ratios, describing how they are calculated and for what purposes they are used. This chapter will focus on four of the most common types: liquidity, profitability, debt, and activity ratios.

Liquidity Ratios   To measure the ability of a firm to raise enough cash to meet short-term debts, managers use liquidity ratios. To derive the most common liquidity ratio—the *current ratio*—the manager simply divides the figure for current assets by the figure for current liabilities (both figures are available on the company's balance sheet). To calculate the current ratio for the Excel Corporation

Exhibit 16.3

Commonly used financial ratios.

Ratio	Obtained by	Purpose
Current assets to current liabilities	Dividing current assets by current liabilities	To determine a firm's ability to pay its short-term liabilities
Net profits to net sales	Dividing net profits after taxes by net sales	To measure the short-run profitability of the business
Net profits to tangible net worth	Dividing net profits after taxes by tangible net worth (the difference between tangible assets and total liabilities)	To measure profitability over a relatively long period
Net profits to net working capital	Dividing net profits after taxes by net working capital (operating capital on hand)	To measure the ability of a business to carry inventory and accounts receivable and to finance day-to-day operations
Net sales to tangible net worth	Dividing net sales by the firm's tangible net worth	To measure the relative turnover of investment capital
Net sales to net working capital	Dividing net sales by net working capital	To measure how well a company uses its working capital to produce sales
Collection period (receivables to credit sales)	First, dividing annual net sales by 365 to determine daily credit sales; then, dividing notes and accounts receivable by average daily credit sales	To analyze the collectability of receivables

Exhibit 16.3 *(continued)*

Ratio	Obtained by	Purpose
Net sales to inventory	Dividing annual net sales by the value of the firm's merchandise inventory as carried on the balance sheet	To provide a yardstick for comparing the firm's stock-to-sales position with that of other companies or with industry averages
Fixed assets to tangible net worth	Dividing fixed assets (the depreciated book value of such items as buildings, machinery, furniture, physical equipment, and land) by the firm's tangible net worth	To show what proportion of a firm's tangible net worth consists of fixed assets (Generally, this ratio should not exceed 100% for a manufacturer and 75% for a wholesaler or retailer.)
Current liabilities to tangible net worth	Dividing current liabilities by the firm's tangible net worth	To measure the degree of indebtedness of the firm (Generally, a business is in financial trouble when this ratio exceeds 80%.)
Total liabilities to tangible net worth	Dividing current plus long-term liabilities by tangible net worth	To determine the financial soundness of the business (When this ratio exceeds 100%, the equity of the firm's creditors in the business exceeds that of the owners.)
Inventory to net working capital	Dividing merchandise inventory by net working capital	To determine whether a business has too much or too little working capital tied up in inventory (Generally, this ratio should not exceed 80%.)
Current liabilities to inventory	Dividing current liabilities by inventory	To determine whether a business has too little or too much current debt in relationship to its inventory (If current debt is excessive, the firm may have to dispose of inventory quickly, at unfavorable prices, to meet its obligations.)
Funded liabilities to working capital	Dividing funded liabilities (long-term obligations such as mortgages, bonds, serial notes, and other liabilities that will not mature for at least one year) by net working capital	To determine whether the firm's long-term indebtedness is in proper proportion to its net working capital (Generally, this ratio should not exceed 100%.)

Source: Adapted from *1970 Key Business Ratios* (New York: Dun & Bradstreet, 1971). Reprinted by permission of Dun & Bradstreet Credit Services, a company of The Dun & Bradstreet Corporation.

by using the balance sheet shown in Exhibit 16.1, divide total current assets ($155,468) by total current liabilities ($65,688). The result is 2.37 to 1. This ratio means that Excel possesses $2.37 in cash (liquid assets) for each dollar incurred in current debt. Because most experts consider any ratio higher than 2 to 1 to be adequate, Excel may be considered fiscally healthy. Ratios lower than 2 to 1 indicate that a company is overburdened with short-term debt.

Profitability Ratios   Managers use profitability ratios to study a company's profits from several perspectives. To determine profits generated from sales, divide net profits after taxes by net sales. To calculate the profit generated from the owner's investment, divide net profits after taxes by tangible net worth. Using Excel's income statement, the company's profit ratio on sales ($31,353 in profit divided by $764,046 in net sales) is 0.041, which translates to 4.1% profit. In other words, the owners of Excel kept $4.10 for every $100 in sales their firm generated. To determine the adequacy of this ratio, Excel managers may compare it with the profitability ratios of competitors. During a recessionary period in which competitors are losing money, a 4.1% return on sales is probably more than adequate.

Debt Ratios   A debt ratio expresses an organization's capacity to meet its debts. To calculate a debt ratio, divide total liabilities by net worth (total stockholders' equity). In terms of the Excel Corporation, this means dividing $76,968 by $139,880 to yield a ratio of 0.55, or 55%. This result means that Excel is financed by 55% debt. If the industry average is 65%, Excel should be able to borrow additional funds on the commercial market. But, if the industry average is considerably below this level, borrowing may be difficult. Any banker that Excel approaches for a loan might think that Excel was overdependent on other peoples' money. Of course, when deciding to approve a loan, creditors consider other factors besides ratios—including the company's management and competitiveness.

Activity Ratios   Activity ratios shed light on a firm's key internal areas to reveal performance. If managers wish to assess inventory levels, for example, several different activity ratios are helpful: inventory to net working capital, current liabilities to inventory, and average inventory levels to total sales. These relationships indicate whether inventory levels are too high in relation to sales and whether too much money is tied up in inventories. When inventories are high, managers are often tempted to make hasty sales that yield a less-than-normal profit.

Activity ratios can monitor many important activities. The manager wishing to know how quickly orders are being processed, for example, can select a week and divide the number of orders filled by the number of orders received. By recording ratios for particular activities over extended time periods, the manager can spot trends and plan needed changes.

Financial Responsibility Centers

All management control relies upon *responsibility accounting,* a simple idea: Each manager is responsible for a part of the company's total activity. A manager's unit and its related activities should contribute to the enterprise. A unit's contributions could be vital services, revenues, or the manufacturing of a product. A **financial**

responsibility center is any organizational unit that contributes costs, revenues, investments, or profits. The unit manager who accepts the obligation to achieve certain goals is responsible for reporting progress toward them. The author of a respected planning handbook (Dudick, 1983) summarized the notion of fiscal control and responsibility in this way:

> Internal financial reports should follow management's lines of responsibility. Careful evaluation is necessary to determine whether present financial reports track the results that are controllable by the individual held responsible for them. Reasonable assurance should exist that reported information is reliable, that transactions are recorded appropriately, and that corporate assets are safeguarded.

Exhibit 16.4 defines the principal financial responsibility centers in large businesses.

Each manager's organizational unit within a firm's fiscal structure functions as a financial responsibility center. For each center, top managers must specify the specific financial objective and then decide how to measure progress toward it. Because each manager contributes to unit and company-wide cost control and profitability, selection of each objective is important. Profit, for instance, should be used as a measure of financial responsibility only when profit increases as the direct result of actions for which the manager is responsible (Vancil, 1975).

Exhibit 16.4 reported that the sales manager who manages a revenue center is responsible for profit generated by sales, not by cost reductions. Similarly, the production manager who leads a cost center is responsible for costs, not revenue.

- **Standard cost centers.** A production department in a factory is an example of a standard cost center. In a standard cost center, the standard quantities of direct labor and materials required for each unit of output are specified. The supervisor's objective is to minimize the variance between actual costs and standard costs. In addition, he or she is usually responsible for a flexible overhead expense budget that the manager uses, once again, to minimize the variance between budgeted and actual costs.

- **Revenue centers.** A sales department in which the manager does not have authority to lower prices to increase volume is an example of a revenue center. The resources at the manager's disposal are reflected in the expense budget. The sales manager's objective is to spend no more than the budgeted amount and produce the maximum amount of sales revenue.

- **Discretionary expense centers.** Most administrative departments are discretionary expense centers. There is no practical way to establish the relationship between inputs and outputs in a legal department or information processing department, for example. Managers can only use their best judgment to set budgets. The department manager's objective is to spend the budgeted amount to produce the best (though still unmeasurable) quality of service possible.

- **Profit centers.** A profit center is a unit such as a product division in which the manager is responsible for achieving the best combination of costs and revenues. The objective is to maximize the bottom line, the profit that results from the manager's decisions. A great many variations on this theme can be achieved by defining "profit" as only those elements of cost and revenue for which the manager is responsible. Thus, a sales manager who is allowed to set prices may be responsible for gross profit (actual revenue less standard direct manufacturing costs). Profit for the marketing manager of a product line, on the other hand, might reflect deductions for budgeted factory overhead and actual sales-promotion expenses.

- **Investment centers.** An investment center is a unit in which the manager is responsible for the magnitude of assets employed. The manager makes trade-offs between current profits and investments to increase future profits. To help themselves appraise the desirability of new investments, many managers of investment centers think of their objective as maximizing return on investment or residual income (profit after a charge for the use of capital).

ISSUES AND ETHICS
What Are the Obligations of a Whistle-Blower?

n July 1992 the General Electric Company pleaded guilty in U.S. District Court to criminal charges involving conspiracy, money laundering, submitting false claims, and failure to make and keep accurate books and records. The crimes arose from sales of jet engines to the Israeli military. As punishment, GE agreed to pay $69 million in fines. A senior division vice president said, "Our systems should have caught [the wrongdoing] but they did not." From his perspective, the crime occurred primarily because the company lacked adequate controls to prevent or detect it.

The crimes were brought to light by a whistle-blower, the former manager of GE's aircraft engine business in Israel. The informant chose to tell federal authorities about the misdeeds rather than use the company's internal system to report noncompliance. The whistle-blower waited several years before notifying the government of his suspicions, because he was gathering the evidence he needed to file suit. Under the False Claims Act, employees whose tips result in fines and assessments from U.S. contractors can receive up to 25% of the sums collected. In addition, the act prohibits reprisals against those who report misdeeds. When asked why he did not use the company's internal compliance system, the GE whistle-blower replied, "I did a lot of research to see what happened to people who went up the chain of command and reported wrongdoings. All I found was they lost their jobs, their security; they lost everything."

Do you agree with the executive who asserted that the problem occurred because of lack of controls? What do you think of the whistle-blower's actions? Should he have informed company management as soon as he found something amiss? What would you have done in his place? ▲

For more about whistle-blowing, see Amal Kumar Naj, "GE's Drive to Purge Fraud Is Hampered by Workers' Mistrust," *Wall Street Journal*, July 22, 1992, p. A1.

Only the manager of a product division, who is responsible for both revenues and costs, can be held accountable for the unit's generated profits. Identifying responsibility centers, then, focuses managers' energies on controlling those factors actually within their scope of influence.

In 1992, the president of General Motors charged J. Ignacio Lopez de Arriortua with a specific objective: to cut costs in GM's internal parts factories within one year. Lopez and his staff reviewed contracts and bids from all GM's suppliers. Under his direction, GM buyers demanded double-digit price cuts, and his cost center cost-cutting teams showed internal and external suppliers how they could become more efficient producers. By September 1992, about 25% of GM's suppliers, including internal parts operations, had been replaced with new, less costly sources (White, 1992).

Financial Audits

Financial information is only as good as the data and interpretation on which it is based. **Audits** are formal investigations conducted to determine if financial data, records, reports, and statements are correct and consistent with the organization's policies, rules, and procedures. Audits may be conducted by insiders or outsiders.

Internal Audits Most companies maintain controls to determine if people are handling corporate financial activities according to policy and procedural, legal, and ethical guidelines. A superior's regular appraisals of subordinates function as a kind of internal audit. Most accounting systems incorporate controls to guarantee adherence to procedures, as do regular reviews by teams of internal auditors.

The accompanying Issues and Ethics feature discusses a lack of financial controls that proved a major embarrassment to General Electric. To prevent further embarrassment, General Electric supplemented its internal audit mechanisms with a program to motivate employees to promptly report suspected misconduct to company officials (Naj, 1992).

Internal audits keep problems in-house, and they are likely to be conducted by people who know operations well. Those who conduct internal audits may lack objectivity, however, and they may also lack the power to penetrate cover-ups.

External Audits The annual external audit is an American business tradition. An external audit is conducted by an independent public accounting firm. Such firms are staffed with certified public accountants (CPAs) who provide expert accounting and management services. Federal regulations require publicly traded companies to conduct certified external audits each year. The managers of many nonpublic companies choose to have their companies undergo external audits. The presumed objectivity of the audit enhances the organization's credibility with stockholders, creditors, investors, and key insiders, and such audits often uncover important information.

A certified external audit includes thorough inspection and analysis of policies, procedures, and records, and such tests as the auditors believe may be applicable to the situation. When they are satisfied, the audit team manager certifies that the financial data presented in the firm's financial reports is in keeping with generally accepted accounting practices and procedures and government regulations.

Budget Controls

The primary financial control used to manage operating organizations is a budget. As both a plan and a feedforward control, a **budget** provides estimates (projections) of revenues and expenses for a given period of time. A budget serves as the standard for measuring the firm's performance, because it allows managers to compare actual revenues and expenses to projections.

When forecast revenue is insufficient to support projected spending (expenditures), revenue must be increased or supplemented by borrowing or the use of savings (reserves). The alternative is to reduce expenditures. Conversely, if expenditures rise more quickly than the revenue needed to support them, spending must be reduced to avoid the need to borrow or to deplete reserves. Throughout 1992 and well into 1993, many large U.S. companies reduced spending to avoid borrowing and the depletion of reserves. Airlines (American, Delta, and United), manufacturers (Ford, IBM, and United Technologies), and retailers (Sears & Roebuck) laid off thousands of employees, closed facilities, and canceled or delayed capital spending.

Budgets serve managers in four important ways:

- They expedite allocation and coordination of resources for programs and projects.

- They operate as a powerful monitoring system when supplemented with periodic budget updates.

- They provide rigorous control guidelines for managers by setting limits on expenditures.

- They facilitate evaluation of individual and department performance.

Budget status reports allow managers to make timely activity adjustments. Exhibit 16.5 presents a sample budget status report. It includes the approved budget for certain items and actual expenditures for the first two quarters. Note that spending for long-distance telephone calls (line 5) is 25% over budget at the end of the second quarter. The manager of this department must take timely corrective action to avoid a shortfall during the last quarter.

Exhibit 16.5

A sample budget status report.

Line No.	Category	Approved Budget January 1	Budget Report April 1		Budget Report July 1	
	Salary Expense	*Actual*	*Actual*	*% Used*	*Actual*	*% Used*
1	Professional	$160,000	$40,000	25%	$ 80,000	50%
2	Administrative	60,000	15,000	25%	30,000	50%
3	Clerical Support	32,000	8,000	25%	16,000	
	Total Salary Expenses	$252,000	$63,000	25%	$126,000	50%
	Operating Expense					
4	Basic Telephone Service	$ 2,000	$ 500	25%	$ 1,000	50%
5	Long-Distance Telephone Service	2,000	1,000	50%	1,500	75%
6	Insurance	8,000	2,000	25%	4,000	50%
7	Utilities	12,000	4,000	33%	9,000	75%
8	Printing	9,000	1,500	17%	3,000	33%
9	Copying	15,000	3,000	20%	6,000	40%
10	Software	15,000	10,000	67%	10,000	67%
11	Office Supplies	5,000	1,000	20%	2,000	40%
	Total Operating Expense	$ 68,000	$23,000	34%	$ 36,500	54%
	Total Salary and Operating Expenses	$320,000	$86,000	27%	$162,500	51%

The Budget Development Process

Budgeting requires (1) setting goals, (2) planning and scheduling to reach the goals, (3) identifying and pricing resources, (4) locating needed funds, and (5) adjusting goals, plans, and resources to match actual fund availability. Some organizations involve all their people in these tasks. Others involve managers only. Either way, budgets must be prepared and adhered to at each level and in each unit of an organization.

Budget preparers can follow one or more of the four standardized approaches: top-down, bottom-up, zero-based, or flexible budgeting. Following a standardized approach helps ensure consistency in the process.

Top-Down Budgeting   In top-down budgeting, senior managers prepare budgets and distribute them to lower levels, with or without input from below. Managers who use this method may plan and control without the cooperation and knowledge of their subordinates. These managers may miss or neglect significant information about opportunities and risks—information that others could provide and that should be assessed during budget building.

Bottom-Up Budgeting   Sometimes called grassroots budgeting, the bottom-up system taps the knowledge and experiences of all organization members. The men and women closest to the planned activities contribute to building the budget that affects them. In harmonious dialogue, participants come to understand one another's priorities, limits, perspectives, and goals. They negotiate the inevitable compromises (few departments get all the resources their managers would like). And, as input moves up the hierarchy, various views are consolidated to create an inclusive framework. A compelling advantage of this process is that it earns support for the budget from the people who will be governed by it.

Many companies today are decentralizing, forming autonomous units and divisions. Corporate headquarters provides overall guidance and goals, but the divisions set their own priorities and run their own operations. They also construct their own budgets, partly because downsized organizations no longer maintain the large staffs required for top-down budgeting.

Zero-Based Budgeting   In some companies budget preparers begin their job by looking at last year's budget and building on the numbers it contained. The preparers factor in relevant recent experience, and a new budget emerges. Some managers simply increase last year's numbers by some percentage, on the assumption that what went before should continue. Such budgeting does not force managers to examine their operations and explore more efficient ways of operating. **Zero-based budgeting** eliminates such complacency by requiring preparers to launch each new budget from a clean sheet of paper (or, more likely, a blank computer spreadsheet). The head of each financial responsibility center must justify every dollar requested in light of the coming year's strategic plans and goals, not simply explain changes from previous years.

Zero-based budgeting requires managers to list their goals for the fiscal period and then identify the people and other resources they need to achieve the goals. They must also list the costs of all resources. The managers choose priorities and create alternatives for accomplishing the unit's part in the overall strategic plan. In discussions with higher-level managers, requests and plans from each unit are studied in light of the overall availability of resources and the organization's strategic objectives. Once agreement about resource allocation is reached, the budget is created. The key to zero-based budgeting is that the process is repeated for each fiscal period.

Flexible Budgeting   All approaches to budget building can utilize **flexible budgeting**, in which set levels of expense are correlated with specified output levels. The expense levels permit managers to judge whether expenses are acceptable at a given level of output. Managers can then adjust expenses accordingly (Heyel, 1982).

Flexible budgeting sets "meet or beat" standards with which expenditures can be compared. Incentives should be provided to managers at every level to meet and beat budget targets. Unit expenses within budgeted amounts are usually permitted. Managers who exceed guidelines must present compelling reasons or face curbs on their spending.

Sam Walton (1992) used flexible budgeting to build his Wal-Mart empire:

> I tried to operate on a two percent general office expense structure. In other words, two percent of sales should have been enough to carry our buying office, our general office expense, my salary, Bud's salary—and after we started adding district managers or any other officers—their salaries too. Believe it or not, we haven't changed that basic formula from five stores to two thousand stores. In fact, we are actually operating at a far lower percentage today in office overhead than we did thirty years ago.

When asked how he arrived at his 2% rule, Walton admitted that he just "pulled it out of the air." Wal-Mart's success is due in no small measure to its founder's obsession with controlling costs.

Operating Budgets

Operating budgets are financial plans and controls for each financial responsibility center's revenues, expenses, and profits.

Revenue Budgets   The organization as a whole as well as each revenue center uses revenue budgets, which forecast total revenues from all anticipated sources over a given time. Sears may forecast its revenues by store, line of merchandise, and region. States and cities forecast revenues from various taxes and fees—license and permit fees, sales tax, and property tax, for example.

Expense Budgets   Like revenue budgets, expense budgets are developed for each cost center and the whole organization. Expense budgets refer to several standard categories of costs. *Fixed costs* are facility-related expenses that an organization incurs regardless of the amount of activity in any function. Fixed costs include rent, real estate taxes, insurance premiums, wages and salaries of administrative and support personnel, interest payments, and payments on long- and short-term debts. *Variable costs* relate directly to operations and vary with revenue and production levels. The cost of utilities (typically, telephone, electricity, gas or heating oil, waste disposal, and water) is a variable cost. Other variable costs include the costs of raw materials and supplies, wages and salaries paid to people engaged in production and marketing, and advertising expenses. *Mixed costs* are costs that contain fixed and variable elements. For example, suppose a janitor maintains office and factory buildings. Part of the janitor's salary will be allocated to administration as a fixed cost and part will be allocated to production as a variable cost. Travel expenses are sometimes mixed costs. The travel expenses of administrators may be fixed expenses whereas those of sales and production people may be variable expenses.

Profit Budgets   Profit budgets simply merge revenue and expense budgets to calculate derived profit for the organization and each profit center. IBM operates product and service profit centers, as do most large retailers. Commercial bank profit centers are established according to the types of loans they grant—real estate, consumer, or commercial, for example. Profit budgets are useful in gauging manager performance. In whatever the business, where profits fail to reach projected levels, the responsible manager must increase them or risk losing his or her line, department, or division.

Financial Budgets

Financial budgets detail how each financial responsibility center will manage its cash and capital expenditures. Financial budgets include cash budgets and capital expenditures budgets.

Cash Budgets   Often called cash flow budgets, cash budgets project the amount of cash that will flow into and out of an organization and its subsystems during a fixed period. Line items include cash left over from the previous period, cash revenue from sales, and monies secured through borrowing. A cash budget also accounts for outlays—cash payments for all resources, including borrowed funds. Cash flow budgets project time frames during which managers expect expenses to outstrip revenues. Such periods call for a dip into investments or for loans. Any excess cash on hand during any period can be invested, thus yielding additional revenue.

Capital Expenditures Budgets   Managers use capital expenditures budgets to project the short- and long-term funding needed to acquire capital goods. Capital goods include machinery, office equipment, buildings, vehicles, computers, and other expensive assets that will take more than one year to pay for.

Only sound coordination of capital goods expenditures with ongoing expenses sustains operations. When sufficient funding cannot be found from the cash budget or from borrowing, managers may lease needed capital items. Raising capital can be an exercise in creativity. Aircraft maker McDonnell Douglas helps small airlines and countries raise the capital they need to purchase airliners by giving marketing assistance to its would-be customers. McDonnell Douglas representatives actively solicit U.S. buyers for the products or services its customers offer, and the representatives bring the sellers and buyers together.

Marketing Controls

Under the marketing umbrella are product design, packaging, pricing, sales, distribution, and customer service. Among the control techniques marketing managers use to prevent problems and monitor operations, this chapter will examine market research, test marketing, marketing ratios, sales quotas, and stockage.

Market Research

Market research is a feedforward control technique. It consists of gathering and analyzing geographic, demographic, and psychographic data. The analysis helps planners decide what potential and current customers want and need so that the planners can design products and services to meet those needs (Bittel and Ramsey, 1985). Market researchers gather information from varied public and private sources. These sources include published materials, personal and telephone interviews, direct-mail questionnaires, and focus groups.

Great Plains Software of Fargo, North Dakota, runs some fifty focus groups nationwide. Marketing and development staff from the company visit the groups as often as monthly to discuss current and projected needs with customers who use the company's software every day (Finegan, 1992). Combined with in-depth phone interviews with users, customer satisfaction surveys, and vendor feedback, focus-group input has allowed Great Plains Software to add hundreds of new features to its accounting package. (The case problem at the end of this chapter will discuss this company in detail.)

Market research draws upon data developed by professionals in academic, government, and commercial settings. *Demographic data* refer to peoples' income, age, gender, occupation, marital status, or education. *Geographic data* describe where people live by region, neighborhood, or type of housing. *Psychographic data* relate to cultural origin, religion, political philosophy, and personal interests. Researchers study needs and wants and the buying habits and motives of different population segments. Possessing such knowledge about current and potential customers allows managers to tailor products, advertising, sales, and distribution systems to individuals and groups.

Market research has generated many product innovations and identified discrete target markets. Imaginative research led pet food companies to formulate dog and cat food to appeal to owners with pets of different ages. Where Henry Ford once offered only a single standard model in "any color so long as it's black," market research has spawned a dizzying array of vehicles—from Rolls-Royce limousines and zippy Miata convertibles to minivans of every description, all with an array of options. David Daniel, CEO of Evian, decided to make his company's bottled water the most expensive brand on the market, because Evian market research indicated that buyers of bottled water equate price with quality. The research also indicated that people prefer plastic bottles with resealable caps. Evian has more than doubled its sales since introducing these changes in 1989 (Lubove, 1990).

Test Marketing

Suppose a new product or service has been conceived and a prototype developed. Planners may decided to test-market the new item—that is, introduce it to a limited market on a small scale to assess its acceptance. McDonald's launches new menu items on a limited basis through careful test marketing. First, candidate states, cities, and towns are chosen. Next, advertising and in-store displays promote the new offerings. Then, customers who try the new product are asked for their opinions. 3M Corporation began test marketing for Post-It notes in-house. The program began with the distribution of custom-made packets of the product to managers throughout the home office. The CEO also sent samples of Post-It notes to other CEOs of Fortune 500 companies. Soon demand outstripped 3M's capacity to supply the product; then marketing took over. This product now contributes over $400 million to 3M sales each year.

One disadvantage of extensive test marketing is that it can tip a company's hand to competitors. A smaller version of the practice has become popular for companies in highly competitive industries. These firms involve small groups of users or potential users and restrict their sampling of options. Working closely with users in a controlled environment, marketing and production people assess the marketability of a new product and make decisions on the basis of the users' feedback, however limited. Managers at Panasonic, Motorola, and Sony favor this method. Honda managers consider the company's dealers and customers the most reliable source of marketing information.

No matter which test-marketing methods are employed, planners analyze the results of testing to determine if the company should proceed with manufacturing and distribution and if modifications to the new product or service are needed. Test marketing limits the risks a company faces when introducing something new, and it increases the new item's prospects for success.

Marketing Ratios

As heads of financial responsibility centers who are responsible for profitability, marketing managers must track and control their costs. Along with supervising the sales force and reviewing income statements, marketing managers regularly calculate various ratios to monitor ongoing operations and determine needs for improvement. Frequently used measures include the ratio of profit to sales, costs of selling to gross profit, sales calls to orders generated and profitability of each order, and changes in sales volume to price changes. Marketing managers also calculate the ratio of bad debts to total credit granted, and sales volume to production capacity for the entire organization and its individual product lines. In addition, market share and order turnaround time are two common measures.

In many industries, total market share ranks as the critical standard of success. Market share performance often drives a marketing manager's decision making. Thomson Electronics of France is driven by market share and has made several important decisions to expand its market share in the U.S. market. Under the brand names General Electric and RCA, Thomson sells television sets in the United States. These two brands currently hold about 20% of the color television market. Joseph Clayton, chief of marketing for Thomson, plans to concentrate on wide-screen television—sets with screens of at least 30 inches. His strategies for taking a bigger market share for these sets included re-designing RCA sets in 1992 and GE sets in 1993, doubling his company's promotion budget, and being the first to introduce a wide-screen TV as soon as broadcast technology will permit (Therrien, 1992).

Japanese companies aim to dominate a market, sometimes at the cost of little or no profit. This strategy has led to charges of "dumping"—selling goods in a foreign market at less than the cost of manufacture or less than fair market value at home. America's Big Three car makers frequently charge their Japanese rivals with dumping, and global trade negotiators wrestle with the topic in tariff negotiations.

The focus on total market share has paid off in consumer electronics, where large Japanese firms have all but eliminated U.S. manufacturing. Nintendo follows this strategy in the computer games market. Its trade practices effectively keep large retailers from stocking competitors' games. A retailer who does stock competitors' products may find that he or she has trouble getting Nintendo games. Retailers who cut the price of Nintendo products find themselves stripped of their status as authorized outlets.

Sales Quotas

In many organizations each salesperson operates with a sales quota—a minimum dollar amount of sales within a specific time period to justify his or her salary. Many salespeople work on a commission-only basis, earning money in direct proportion to and as a fixed percentage of the value of the goods or services they sell. If commissioned salespeople make no sales, they get no pay. Commissions and quotas stimulate salespeople to meet or exceed specific quantity goals, but they can also lead to abuses. Overly aggressive salespeople may harass customers or sell them things they cannot afford or do not want. But managers usually favor quotas. Quotas ensure that professionals try their best and feed the ambition of those who want to succeed and advance.

Stockage

The level of inventory for any item is called *stockage.* Stockage is important to business success. You cannot sell what you do not have and you cannot produce when components are not on hand. In addition, maintaining inventories is expensive, as Exhibit 16.6 shows. Money tied up in inventories is unavailable for other uses. Retailers and manufacturers must track their inventories to ensure that they do not run out of needed items. They must reduce the number of slow-moving items or eliminate the items altogether. Retailers quickly learn to devote most of their best display areas to the items that yield the largest profits, either individually or by volume. By tracking stockage levels, managers can determine normal usage rates, maintain minimum levels, and set efficient reorder points.

Today large retailers and manufacturers endeavor to keep as little stock as possible. Many now rely upon just-in-time (JIT) inventory control—that is, they require their suppliers to deliver inventory just in time to meet production or sales

Exhibit 16.6

The costs of maintaining inventories.

1. Costs of producing or acquiring inventory items
2. Costs of loss to obsolescence, damage, or theft
3. Freight charges
4. Security costs (guards, alarm systems, insurance)
5. Storage costs (buildings and maintenance)
6. Administrative expenses (wages and salaries of those who run storage facilities, keep track of inventory, and inspect and move inventory)
7. Costs of computerized inventory control system
8. Costs of maintenance and operation of storage equipment
9. Costs connected with procurement and inspection of and payment for inventory items

demands. Wal-Mart, K Mart, and Sears maintain computer links that allow their suppliers to track sales of the items they produce, and ship items as needed to prevent stores from running out. On the manufacturing floor, JIT systems send items to each production stage as necessary. The notification to move materials along comes from operator signals or computerized inventory control processes. (Chapter 18 will say more about controlling inventories.)

Human Resource Controls

Human resource managers employ diverse control techniques. Among the most frequently used are human resource statistics, human asset valuation, performance appraisals, attitude surveys, and management audits. Each is intended to provide information about the productivity of the work force and the quality and quantity of individual and group performance.

Human Resource Statistics

Companies need to gather and store data about the composition of their work force, compliance with equal opportunity guidelines, employee turnover and absenteeism, and effectiveness of recruiting and compensation efforts. Companies need data about managerial and individual effectiveness, levels of job satisfaction and motivation, and employee safety and health. Many companies create databases containing facts about employees' skills, training levels, evaluations, formal education, and job experiences. Such information facilitates recruiting, promotion, and other employment decisions. Though data in all these categories is important, this section will focus on two standard measures: turnover and absenteeism. (Work force composition and safety will be discussed in relation to management audits.)

Turnover   The number of employees who leave an organization during a specific period of time is known as employee turnover. Some turnover occurs through attrition—retirement, resignation, illness, and death. Some turnover is seasonal and planned—farm laborers are hired to harvest a crop, and many salesclerks are hired only for the holiday shopping rush. Some turnover results from economic conditions and competitors' actions that decrease a firm's sales and its ability to support its work force. Resulting layoffs may be permanent or temporary. Substantial turnover results from bad management. In many cases, people lost to turnover must be replaced, and replacing people is costly. It is normally in a company's best interest to retain its most valuable employees for as long as possible.

The rate of turnover often serves as a measure of an organization's internal environment—its morale, stress, and managerial skill levels. Each organization, and each subsystem, needs to determine its acceptable turnover, or an acceptable number of people who must be replaced compared to the total work force. To determine an acceptable ratio, most companies study their own past and the experiences of other companies in their industries. Some businesses, such as the fast-food and hospitality industries, experience unusually high turnover rates, sometimes exceeding 100%. Managers must analyze the causes of turnover carefully and determine which among them are signs of trouble. Then managers must act to eliminate those causes.

Absenteeism   Absenteeism is the percentage of an organization's work force not at work on any given day. All organizations must maintain a realistic standard for absenteeism, say 5%. As with turnover, managers must assess the causes for absences and judge their validity. Many companies find that 90% of their absenteeism is caused by less than 10% of their work force members. At any given time, absenteeism that exceeds the standard may or may not be a sign of trouble. Circumstances such as a widespread flu outbreak or a natural disaster that prevents people from getting to work may temporarily and legitimately raise absenteeism. Many managers try to prevent absenteeism by encouraging 100% attendance; they offer financial rewards and set realistic and equitable attendance policies.

Human Asset Valuation

Various monitoring devices help managers assess the value of each employee to a company. One approach focuses on accounting. Another projects the long-range potential (promotability) of each person. **Human asset accounting** tracks the money spent to recruit, hire, train, and develop employees. This type of accounting treats each person as an asset, not an expense. Expenditures for the development of human assets are considered investments, not unlike the investments made to build an office or factory building. Managers who use human asset accounting realize that each person represents a sizable investment of company resources, and these managers tend to be committed to retaining good people. Many managers with this view keep balance sheets that list employees as assets. (These balance sheets are not for tax purposes.) When someone leaves, the corresponding investment is deducted from the total, showing a net loss of assets.

In an approach less common than human asset accounting, managers attempt to assign a dollar value to each employee's contribution to company profits. Such calculations are not easy to make. They consist of creating general categories of employees and assigning dollar amounts to each category on a percentage basis. Arbitrary as such an approach may be, it does attempt to focus attention on people as resources, not simply expenses.

Performance Appraisals

Perhaps the most important control device employed by human resource managers is the use of a regularly scheduled legal, objective, and equitable appraisal system. The focus of such a system must be on comparing people's performances to standards established for them and then sharing the results. Appraisal standards are feedforward control devices; the appraisals themselves are concurrent and feedback devices.

Domino's Pizza uses a computer test to gauge employees' effectiveness and alertness before they are allowed to take on their duties. When drivers are hired they are given a hand-eye coordination test. The results are recorded as that person's standard for acceptable performance. On reporting to work each day, the driver takes the same machine-based test. The results (answers and reaction times) are compared to those for their first test. The driver who fails to meet those standards may be assigned to alternative duties for that day or given the day off. The point is to keep people away from potentially dangerous and difficult-to-operate equipment when they are not in top form.

Attitude Surveys

An attitude survey shows how employees feel about their employer. It can highlight what is going right in the workplace and where problems exist. Top managers usually hire an outside consulting firm to conduct such a survey. The fact that the polls are objective and can be answered anonymously encourages employees to respond to them.

Attitude surveys ask questions about key processes, units, and personnel in an organization, and they can be tailored to the specific unit being evaluated. Questions should help companies pinpoint areas of dissatisfaction and gather suggestions about how to improve people, procedures, and policies. Sample questions are "How well does your boss respond to your requests for assistance?" and "What are the sources of stress for you on your job?"

After the answers are collected and analyzed, the results are given to management. For best results, the results should be shared (with nothing held back) with all employees. Data gathered from the surveys—facts about employees' gender, marital status, age, and job categories—become useful for determining which programs or changes are best for which group.

Management Audits

The Occupational Safety and Health Administration (OSHA) and the Equal Employment Opportunity Commission (EEOC) require regular recording, reporting, and disclosure of statistics about employment. Both agencies set standards and procedures for the workplace. In many cases, managers must also comply with state regulations about employment.

To ensure that regulations are being followed, managers should conduct regularly scheduled management audits, or compliance audits. In addition they must continually track and record statistics about safety, health, and compliance with equal employment opportunity guidelines. Violations of government employment regulations are punishable by significant sanctions.

EEOC guidelines require employers with 15 or more employees to maintain a work force representative of the mix of women and protected groups found in their community. The guidelines mean that women and protected groups must represent a certain portion of the work force at all levels. A company guilty of discrimination in the past must commit to affirmative action to quickly bring underrepresented groups into the organization. Managers in each subsystem must monitor compliance. They may have to set specific targets and construct specific programs to make up for the underrepresentation of protected groups.

Computers and Control

One of the major revolutions in the control function has been the application of computers to nearly every business process. More than two-thirds of employees now work to some degree with a computer as part of their daily routines, and all employees are affected by computer use. The most important contribution that computers have made to the control process is data. Computers can provide data more quickly, cheaply, and accurately than traditional means.

Computers facilitate communications throughout and among organizations and their members, placing data in the hands of anyone who needs it. Moreover, they can do so in "real time"—the time in which an event is actually happening. Although computers can be of tremendous benefit to the controlling function, they do pose potential problems. Gregory and Van Horn (1984) listed several issues that managers must consider when they evaluate the use of computers as control elements:

- Benefits versus cost of the system. The quality and quantity of the information received from the computer system must be greater than the cost of developing, installing, and maintaining it. (To be effective, all controls must produce more than they cost.)

- Technological environment. Computer technology changes rapidly. How can the company keep abreast of the latest developments? How can the company adapt its operations to these developments and keep employees up-to-date? What will be the cost of doing so?

- Impact of the computer on personnel. Introducing computers means change. How will the switch to computers affect people? What jobs, if any, will be replaced or created? What retraining will be necessary? What will managers need to know to interact with the computer? What specialists will

GLOBAL APPLICATIONS

The Courtship of British Airways and USAir

British Airways announced in July 1992 that it was prepared to offer $750 million to create an alliance with Virginia-based USAir. The deal would have given British Airways a 44% ownership of USAir's convertible preferred stock and a 21% ownership of the company's common stock. Under American law, a foreign airline cannot own more than 25% of a U.S. carrier's voting stock, but it can own up to 49% of its preferred stock. USAir needed cash badly; the organization had lost about $150 million from 1991 to 1992.

Joint operations with USAir would benefit British Airways, which could fly passengers from Europe into New York and then route them around the States on USAir flights. In exchange for survival and financial stability, USAir would have given to British Airways its current routes to England. (USAir would have retained its routes from the United States to Paris and Frankfurt, however.) The proposed agreement also called for a "supermajority" of the USAir board to approve significant decisions. Airline industry insiders asserted that this agreement would have given British Airways veto power over all major decisions, including those involving investments, financing, and the appointment of key officers.

The matter of American access to British markets has long been an issue of contention between the two countries. Nevertheless, the U.S. Department of Transportation approved the merger, allowing the two airlines to continue to explore ways in which they could benefit from more closely coordinated finances and operations. ▲

For more information about British Airways and USAir, see John Newhouse, "The Battle of the Bailout," *New Yorker,* January 18, 1993, pp. 42–51.

be needed? How will they interact with existing personnel? Who will design the systems? Managers must answer these and other questions so that they can plan an effective approach to those affected.

- Centralized versus decentralized computer system. Managers must eventually decide on one system or the other. This is not an easy decision. Centralized systems provide many advantages: All activities are carried out in one location, equipment and staff are not duplicated, costs are minimized, and proximity facilitates coordination and decision making by system users. In comparison to centralized systems, decentralized systems often offer users greater access to equipment and information, which results in greater control and timeliness of information. Regardless of which approach an organization takes, computers must be available when they are needed by those who need them. Users and technical specialists should work together to design a coordinated approach to operating the system.

Future Trends

In the increasingly competitive world marketplace, controlling is taking on much more significance. Managers see the following trends:

- Information systems are now networks linked with and without wires. As departments and divisions are linked across functional barriers, all personnel should have access to needed information. This access must be supplied to insiders as well as outsiders.

- Control systems will be put into place to reduce unnecessary delays caused by paperwork and noncomputerized processes.

- Quality control is assuming an increasingly important position and becoming the responsibility of all personnel.

- Most jobs will require computer literacy and demand regular interaction between employees and machines, either computer-controlled devices or computers themselves.

C H A P T E R   **S** U M M A R Y

- Control techniques are management tools used to prevent, identify, and deal with deviations from standards. Each has a specific application.

- Primary financial control techniques include the income statement and the balance sheet, which yield data needed to calculate financial ratios.

- Financial ratios measure liquidity, profitability, debt, and related activities. The ratios allow managers to assess the organization's financial health.

- Financial responsibility centers focus on costs, revenues, expenses, profits, or investments. A manager can be held accountable for profits only if they increase as the direct result of actions for which the manager is responsible.

- Both internal and external financial audits are needed to ensure that procedures and policies are followed.

- Budgets compare revenues to expenses for a fixed period of time and are prepared by one or more of these methods: top-down, bottom-up, zero-based, or flexible budgeting.

- Operating budgets are financial plans and controls for financial responsibility centers' revenues, expenses, and profits. Financial budgets include cash budgets and capital expenditures budgets.

- Marketing control techniques include market research, test marketing of products and services, marketing ratios, sales quotas, and stockage. The just-in-time inventory approach involves maintaining low levels of inventory and reordering stock just before it is needed.

- Human resource controls focus on various statistics. They treat humans as assets, evaluate performances, and survey attitudes; they include audits to ensure compliance with government mandates and company policy. Computers are becoming increasingly important as controls. Managers who are considering the installation of computer systems must take care to evaluate the costs and the impact on personnel.

S K I L L - B U I L D I N G

Apply the questions that follow to a job you hold now or one you held in the past. Answer each as candidly and completely as you can.

1. What specific financial control techniques have you encountered on the job? How did they affect you and your area of influence?

2. What specific kind of budget did you have to work with? How was it prepared?

3. What marketing control devices do you have firsthand knowledge of? How did you come by that knowledge?

4. What kind of human resource control device have you applied to other people where you work? Which one(s) were applied to you?

5. What part did computers play in the situations you described in the preceding four questions?

R E V I E W   Q U E S T I O N S

1. Review this chapter's essential terms and look up the meanings of those you cannot define.

2. Describe the contents and utility of income statements and balance sheets.

3. Describe the uses of the four kinds of ratios the chapter discussed.

4. Briefly describe how each kind of financial responsibility center is important to a business.

5. Describe the two primary budget types and their uses.

6. Describe the four ways of developing a budget.

7. What do managers accomplish with each of the five marketing control techniques?

8. What do managers accomplish by using each of the five human resource management control techniques?

R E C O M M E N D E D   R E A D I N G

Billings, John. *Controlling with Computers: Control Theory* (New York: McGraw-Hill), 1989.

Day, Charles R. "20% Is a Lousy Return: The Economic Implications of Workers Are Pretty Scary," *Industry Week* (December 3, 1990), pp. 28–33.

Fabozzi, Frank J. *Managing Institutional Assets* (New York: Harper Business), 1989.

Giffin, John. *Inventory Control* (New York: Wiley), 1989.

Hansen, Donald B. *Management Accounting* (Boston: PWS-Kent), 1990.

Hartley, Robert F. *Marketing Mistakes,* 5th edition (New York: Wiley), 1992.

Ishikawa, Kaoru. *What Is Total Quality Control?* David J. Lu, translator (Englewood Cliffs, NJ: Prentice-Hall), 1985.

Kaplan, Robert S., and David P. Norton. "The Balanced Scorecard—Measures That Drive Performance," *Harvard Business Review* (January–February 1992), pp. 71–79.

Rappaport, Alfred. "CFOs and Strategists: Forging a Common Framework," *Harvard Business Review* (May–June 1992), pp. 84–91.

Zinn, Walter. "Should You Assemble Products Before an Order Is In?" *Business Horizons* (March–April 1990), p. 88.

R E F E R E N C E S

Bittel, Lester R., and Jackson E. Ramsey, editors. *Handbook for Professional Managers* (New York: McGraw-Hill), 1985, p. 550.

Dudick, Thomas S., editor. *Handbook of Business Planning and Budgeting* (New York: Van Nostrand Reinhold), 1983, pp. 22, 74.

Finegan, Jay. "Taking Names," *Inc.* (September 1992), p. 129.

Gregory, Robert H., and Richard L. Van Horn. "Value and Cost of Information," *Systems Analysis Techniques,* J. Daniel Auger and Robert W. Knapp, editors (New York: Wiley), 1984, pp. 473–489.

Heyel, Carl, editor. *The Encyclopedia of Management,* 3rd edition (New York: Van Nostrand Reinhold), 1982, p. 328.

Lubove, Seth. "Perched Between Perrier and Tap," *Forbes* (May 14, 1990), p. 120.

Naj, Amal Kumar. "GE's Drive to Purge Fraud Is Hampered by Workers' Mistrust," *Wall Street Journal,* July 22, 1992, p. A1.

Therrien, Lois. "Thomson Needs a Hit, and It's Up to Nipper to Go Fetch," *Business Week* (July 6, 1992), p. 80.

Vancil, Richard F. "What Kind of Management Control Do You Need?" *Harvard Business Review on Management* (New York: Harper & Row), 1975, p. 481.

Walton, Sam, with John Huey. *Sam Walton: Made in America* (New York: Doubleday), 1992, p. 231.

White, Joseph B. "GM's Lopez Says He Will Accelerate, Expand Cost-Cutting Despite Criticism," *Wall Street Journal,* September 30, 1992, p. A8.

G L O S S A R Y O F **T** E R M S

audit A formal investigation conducted to determine if records and the data on which they are based are correct and conform to policies, rules, procedures, and laws.

balance sheet A listing of the assets of a business and the owners' and outsiders' interests in them. The equation that describes the content of a balance sheet is Assets equals Liabilities plus Stockholders' Equity.

budget A plan and control for the receipt and spending of income over a fixed period.

financial budget   The details of how a financial responsibility center will manage its cash and capital expenditures.

financial ratio   The relationship of two critical figures from financial statements. A financial ratio may be expressed in terms of a ratio, decimal, or percentage. Financial ratios help managers measure a company's financial health and its progress toward goals.

financial responsibility center   An organizational unit that contributes to an organization's costs, revenues, profits, or investments.

flexible budgeting   Budgeting in accordance with established standards against which expenditures will be compared. Flexible budgeting also refers to controlling expenses to conform to an established budget.

human asset accounting   Treating employees as assets, not expenses, by recording money spent on people as increases in the value of those assets.

income statement   A report that presents the difference between an organization's income and expenses to determine whether the firm operated at a profit or a loss over a specified period.

operating budget   A financial plan and control for each financial responsibility center's revenues, expenses, and profits.

ratio   The expression of the relationship between numbers. Ratios are often expressed in terms of percentages or decimals.

zero-based budgeting   A budgeting system that starts from scratch for each fiscal period in all spending categories. Planners must justify all amounts requested for the coming period.

C A S E   P R O B L E M
Doug Burgum's Great Plains Software

Fargo, North Dakota, may seem an unlikely place for a computer software manufacturer. But it is from Fargo that a fast-growing company, Great Plains Software, has spread its accounting software throughout America and Canada. Doug Burgum, a native North Dakotan, became interested in the company in 1984, when Great Plains hired him as a consultant. Burgum had a Stanford MBA and several years of experience as a management consultant. He saw the 20-person company as an excellent vehicle for putting his management philosophy to use. Burgum and his family bought the company.

Burgum brought his talents home to create a company centered on customer service. His strategy is "to gather momentum and market share slowly but steadily [by focusing on customer service]; by cementing that attitude into the Great Plains culture, he reasoned, he could begin to diffentiate his company from its competitors."

One of the most important tools Great Plains uses to implement Burgum's philosophy is a state-of-the-art customer list that gives the company a major marketing advantage. His customers are "the legions of small and midsize businesses, more that 400 companies, running their accounting systems on Great Plains products." The company began to build customer profiles from practically the beginning of the firm, in 1983.

The company has an ingenious way of getting information about customers. Inside its software modules is code that blocks use of the product after the first 50 transactions. The user has to contact Great Plains to get a 10-digit code to unlock the software. "When customers call in for their keys, Great Plains [asks] some 20 market-research questions. Among other things, it [gathers] names and information on locations, business sectors, and company sizes." This system has not caused any customers to complain, and it gives the company much-needed information about who its customers are and their needs. It forms the beginning of the company's primary effort to build long-term relationships with its customers and "partners."

Burgum's partners are "the 1,500 resellers (accounting firms and computer consultants), the 1,000 installers, and the 345 software developers who represent and work with Great Plains across the country."

To stay close to customers, Great Plains conducts in-depth telephone interviews with new customers. The company sponsors focus groups around the country, and it actively solicits feedback from partners. Through these means the company has received thousands of recommendations for new products and suggestions about improvements to existing ones. All customers are assigned to one of the company's authorized resellers and installers, who are paid commissions on sales and for supplying upgrades, training, and installation expertise.

All information about customers is stored in databases that are accessible to anyone in the company. "Depending on the need, the data can be manipulated to serve everything from software development, to lead tracking, to sales. Always, though, the information is used to mutually benefit company and customer alike." Imaginative use of information has turned customer support centers into profit centers that contribute about 20% of revenues with the sale of support contracts to users.

Support quality justifies support plans with high prices. Maintenance contracts begin at $125 per year and range up to $1,525, depending on options chosen. Some 70% of customers purchase a support plan and about 85% of those renew their plans each year. Support customers are pleased with their access to help; they are guaranteed a response to their inquiries within three hours. More than half the 1,100 calls per day are handled immediately. A Great Plains computer has been programmed to identify the caller, determine the kind of software he or she has, and route the call to the proper support specialist. The cost for this sophisticated system exceeded $1 million but soon paid for itself in phone-bill savings.

Great Plains Software has grown for 11 consecutive years. For five years running, accountants who rate PC-based accounting systems have awarded the company top honors.

Q U E S T I O N S

1. What marketing controls is Great Plains using? How have they helped the company?

2. What kind of profit center is mentioned in the case? What accounts for its success?

3. How is the company using computers to help it control operations?

For more about Great Plains Software, see Jay Finegan, "Taking Names," *Inc.,* September 1992, pp. 121–122, 125–126, 129–130.

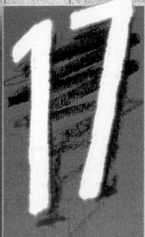

Total Quality Management and Productivity

LEARNING OBJECTIVES

After reading and discussing this chapter, you should be able to:

- Define this chapter's essential terms

- Explain how quality, productivity, and profitability relate

- Name the seven philosophers of management that this chapter discusses and identify the contribution that each made to total quality management (TQM)

- Explain why all members of an organization, at every level, must commit to TQM

- Discuss the three kinds of partnerships needed to make TQM successful

- Explain three ways in which the federal government influences levels of business productivity

- Describe three ways in which individual employees affect an organization's productivity

- Describe three ways in which management affects an organization's productivity

- Explain the link between productivity and research and development

benchmark

continuous-improvement process (CIP)

flexible manufacturing

kaizen

process improvement team

productivity

project improvement team

quality

quality audit

quality circle

quality control (QC)

quality control audit

quality function deployment (QFD)

quality improvement team

research and development (R&D)

statistical process control (SPC)

statistical quality control (SQC)

throughput time

total quality management (TQM)

MANAGEMENT IN ACTION

Quality Gains at Whirlpool

Whirlpool, an international manufacturer of major household appliances, runs a plant in Benton Harbor, Michigan, that is showing others how to improve productivity and quality. Productivity gains in 1991 meant an extra $2,700 in pay to each of the plant's 265 employees. With this productivity bonus, workers averaged $26,400 in pay and took home new attitudes about their work and their employer.

The Benton Harbor plant makes parts for Whirlpool washers and dryers. Since 1988, productivity there has increased more than 19%. Quality has improved even more, dropping from 837 defects per million to a mere 10 per million. Even though the plant and the equipment in it were aging, Whirlpool achieved this success by overhauling its manufacturing process and teaching its workers how to improve quality.

Before the reforms of 1988, workers looked forward to downtime, when machines failed or parts were delayed. They hid inferior parts from inspectors. Management and the labor union were enemies. Bitter strikes and lockouts marred labor relations. Things got so bad that the company reduced jobs by 1,000

Quality is in the details: *Whirlpool manufacturing used a gainsharing program to pass the rewards of quality on to workers.*

and tore down most of the factory. Top managers told remaining workers that their job security depended on improving output.

The main ingredient in the subsequent success at the plant was a gainsharing arrangement, which was hammered out in 1988 through compromises and the help of a private consultant. As productivity rose, a pool of money was created in which all workers shared equally. The workers' share of the pool is determined by the quality of their output, as measured by the number of rejected parts. From 1988 through 1991, the gainsharing program increased the average worker's wage by 12% (this increase was in addition to regular annual and cost-of-living hikes). The program helped workers realize that a company can raise their pay only by increasing productivity or raising prices.

Changes in the attitudes of managers and workers were also key to the turnaround at Benton Harbor. The company made a new commitment to training, teaching workers how to improve quality. In a learning center above the factory, workers can learn everything from general math skills to the handling of precision tools. Management emphasized quality over quantity and set up teams to take on shared tasks.

> Raising quality is important. With less time wasted on making bad parts, productivity increases. The cost of scrapping bad parts drops. And if more parts are made correctly, less inventory has to be kept on hand. Then, with output increasing, the company can gradually pare the payroll through attrition.

Productivity gains at Benton Harbor have resulted in lower costs. Similar gains at other Whirlpool facilities have made the company a leader among appliance manufacturers, substantially increasing the company's profits. Whirlpool has plowed its gains

▶ The workers' share of the pool is determined by the quality of their output, as measured by the number of rejected parts.

into programs for increasing research and improving distribution. Its prices have remained stable for several years, and stable prices have helped keep the company competitive. ▲

For more about Whirlpool and quality, see Rick Wartzman, "A Whirlpool Factory Raises Productivity—and Pay of Workers," *Wall Street Journal*, May 4, 1992, pp. A1, A4.

Quality, Productivity, and Profitability

Profitability results when money remains from sales after bills are paid. The Whirlpool case, discussed in this chapter's Management in Action feature, shows that profitability depends on the quality of products and services and a firm's ability to produce them efficiently. The two management revolutions of the 1990s are the drives to improve quality and productivity while holding down prices. The pressure is on every producer to be more efficient and quality-oriented. Whirlpool's experience demonstrates that good quality and high productivity can help a company sell at competitive prices and succeed in world markets. "No matter how high the quality, if the product is overpriced it cannot gain customer satisfaction" (Ishikawa, 1985).

Productivity and Quality Defined

Productivity, in its most common form, is the relationship between the amount of input needed to produce a given amount of output and the output itself. Productivity is usually expressed as a ratio between these two items. Dividing output by input yields a productivity index (PI), which can be used to make comparisons and to identify trends.

Quality has many definitions. According to Joseph M. Juran, "quality is 'fitness for use.'" He quickly added that such a brief definition is inadequate "because there are many uses and users. There are many short phrases to choose from, but the short phrase is a trap. There is no known short definition that results in a real agreement on what is meant by quality. The word quality has multiple meanings" (Juran, 1988).

Juran linked two major concepts to quality: "product performance [which generates] product satisfaction" and "freedom from deficiencies; [deficiencies produce] product dissatisfaction." *Performance* can mean, for example, the ability to fill an order quickly, without errors. It can also refer to the handling and acceleration of an automobile. Customers often use performance characteristics as a factor in making buying decisions: Customers compare competing products and services. "Because of the competition in the marketplace, a primary goal for product performance is to be equal or superior to the quality of competing products" (Juran, 1988). Customer dissatisfaction with a product or service is based on defects or deficiencies. These cause the customer to reject the product or service or to complain about it. The result for the vendor is the need to rework products or accept returns. "For quality in the sense of freedom from deficiencies, the long-range goal is perfection. A product [may] have no deficiencies and yet be unsalable because some competing product has better product performance" (Juran, 1988).

W. Edwards Deming saw quality differently. He wrote that quality can be defined only in terms of the supplier, producer, user, or customer. Both management decisions and customer judgments affect quality (Deming, 1986). New users or producers often need time to decide if a product, project, process, or service delivers the desired features and quality. Deming (1986) paraphrased his teacher, Walter A. Shewhart:

> The difficulty in defining quality is to translate future needs of the user into measurable characteristics, so that a product can be designed and turned out to give satisfaction at a price that the user will pay. This is not easy, and as soon as one feels fairly successful in the endeavour, he finds that the needs of the consumer have changed, competitors have moved in, there are new materials to work with, some better than the old ones, some worse; some cheaper than the old ones, some dearer.

Philip B. Crosby defined quality as "conformance to requirements." Conformance, wrote Crosby, "demands that products and services be measured against known and reliable customer requirements to ensure that they will, in fact, meet the customer's needs." Further, conformance "must be based on continuously updated data that reflect current, objective measures of customer needs" (Hunt, 1992). Crosby (1979) wrote:

> Requirements must be clearly stated so that they cannot be misunderstood. Measurements are then taken continually to determine conformance to those requirements. The nonconformance detected is the absence of quality. Quality problems become nonconformance problems and quality becomes definable [and controllable].

The American Society for Quality Control published a definition of quality that reflects the work of Deming, Shewhart, and Crosby. To this definition, we make two small additions, which are shown in the bracketed phrases that follow. **Quality** is "the totality of features and characteristics of a product or service [or process or project] that bear on its ability to satisfy stated or implied goals [or requirements of the producers or users of the outcomes]" (Johnson and Winchell, 1989).

Quality goals come from an organization's designers and producers and the internal and external producers, users, or customers. Features and characteristics are those aspects of the product, service, process, or project that lead to satisfaction

1. **Performance,** or a product's primary operating characteristic. Examples are the acceleration of an automobile and the picture clarity of a television set.

2. **Features,** or supplements to a product's basic functioning characteristics. Power windows are features of a car.

3. **Reliability,** or the probability of not malfunctioning during a specified period.

4. **Conformance,** or the degree to which a product's design and operating characteristics meet established standards.

5. **Durability,** or the measure of a product's life.

6. **Serviceability,** or the speed and ease of repair.

7. **Aesthetics,** or how a product looks, feels, tastes, and smells.

8. **Perceived quality,** or quality as seen by a customer.

Source: Reprinted by permission of *Harvard Business Review*. Adapted from "Competing on the Eight Dimensions of Quality," by David A. Garvin, *Harvard Business Review*, November–December 1987. Copyright 1987 by the President and Fellows of Harvard College. All rights reserved.

or dissatisfaction. Satisfaction is the degree of conformity between the user's expectations and their fulfillment.

Exhibit 17.1 shows eight dimensions of quality. Keep these dimensions in mind as you explore the concept of quality throughout the first half of this chapter.

The Quality-Productivity-Profitability Link

W. Edwards Deming stated that companies that improve quality can accrue fundamental benefits. Such companies decrease costs by reducing mistakes and waste, reducing the need to rework parts, and improving productivity. Improving quality, said Deming, can also help companies capture markets, ensure their future, and provide more jobs. To Deming, improving quality caused a chain reaction of benefits: "Continual reduction in mistakes, continual improvement of quality, mean lower and lower costs. Less rework in manufacturing. Less waste—less waste of materials, machine time, tools, human effort" (Walton, 1986). Exhibit 17.2 presents a visual representation of Deming's chain reaction.

Philip B. Crosby (1984) wrote: "Quality improvement is built on getting everyone to do it right the first time (DIRFT). But the key to DIRFT is getting requirements clearly understood and then not putting things in people's way." Another management expert (Barry, 1991) expressed a similar view: "When you focus on total quality management to achieve management excellence, you create the condition not only of high productivity but also high quality, which gives you a greater return [higher profitability]."

Exhibit 17.2

Deming's chain reaction: the quality-productivity-profitability link.

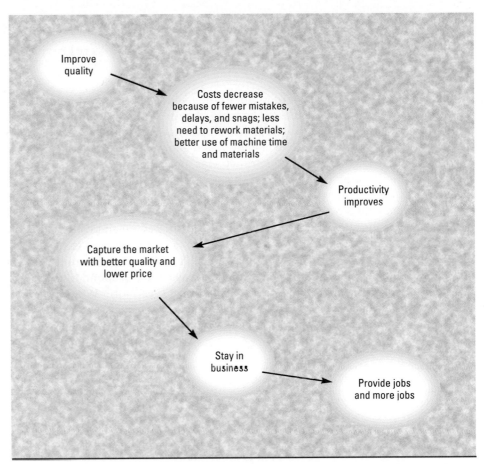

Source: W. Edwards Deming, *Out of the Crisis* (Cambridge, MA: Massachusetts Institute of Technology, Center for Advanced Engineering Study), 1986, p. 3.

Focusing on quality incurs costs. You must spend money to make money. On the other hand, money spent on quality can be a sound investment if it saves an organization from having to spend a relatively greater amount on repairing defects. "The cost of quality is the cost of avoiding nonconformance and failure. Maintaining quality helps you avoid compounding costs you would incur from the deviation of not doing the right thing the first time" (Barry, 1991). Crosby (1979) identified the cost of quality as "the expense of doing things wrong. It is the scrap, rework, service after service, warranty, inspection, tests, and similar activities made necessary by nonconformance problems."

At the Xerox Corporation managers take three measurements to determine the cost of quality. They determine the cost of conformance, the cost of nonconformance, and the cost of lost opportunities (Hunt, 1992). Conformance requires continual measurement of work outputs against known customer requirements. Nonconformance costs are those connected with not meeting customer needs and time lost by having to go back and do things over. Lost opportunities are customers and profits lost because of lack of quality.

Chipping Paint Reveals Faulty Research

rom 1985 to 1992, the Ford Motor Company's popular series of trucks received an extra heavy-duty coat of paint, applied without the company's conventional primer coat. The change was made because testing showed that the primer was not needed. Within months of the change, paint started flaking off.

Ford studied the problem for about two years and determined that the sun's ultraviolet rays broke down the adhesion of gray, silver, and metallic blue paints. In 1992 Ford returned to using a primer coat. The company acknowledged that its decision to bypass the primer caused a defect that could in time affect tens of thousands of trucks. Some have been repainted at company expense; some need repainting but are out of warranty.

Ford refused to recall the trucks for fear of overwhelming Ford dealers. The general manager of the Parts and Service Division stated Ford's approach to the problem: "Our position is that where people have a paint problem, they raise their hand. We'll take a look at their truck and tell them whether it's their problem or our problem." In June 1992 the citizens' group Center for Auto Safety threatened to file a complaint with the Federal Trade Commission unless Ford agreed to recall and repaint the flawed trucks.

If you were running Ford's TQM effort, how would you respond to this problem? Has the company done enough? Why? Refer to Ford's mission statement, which is presented in Exhibit 17.7. Do you see any conflict between what the company says it will do and what it has done in this instance? ▲

Source: *Chicago Tribune,* August 2, 1992, "Ford Owner Fumes Over Paint Defect," sec. 1, p. 19.

The Philosophy of Total Quality Management

The Creation of TQM

Robert Costello, an engineer and former GM executive, was Undersecretary of Defense for Acquisitions when he built on the work of Deming, Juran, Crosby, and others to create **total quality management** (**TQM**) for the Department of Defense. The department's TQM Master Plan, issued in August 1988, defined TQM as:

> a strategy for continuously improving performance at every level, and in all areas of responsibility. It combines fundamental management techniques, existing improvement efforts, and specialized technical tools under a disciplined structure focused on continuously improving all processes. Improved performance is directed at satisfying such broad goals as cost, quality, schedule, and mission need and suitability. Increasing user satisfaction is the overriding objective.

Exhibit 17.3 presents the seven-step model the Department of Defense developed to illustrate TQM. In step 1 the organization establishes the TQM environment. In step 2 the mission for each component or subsystem of the organization is defined. Step 3 requires the setting of performance improvement opportunities; the strategic planning process is established. In step 4 managers or managers and their subordinates define improvement projects and plans for action. In step 5 the projects are implemented through use of the appropriate tools and

Exhibit 17.3

The seven-step TQM model.

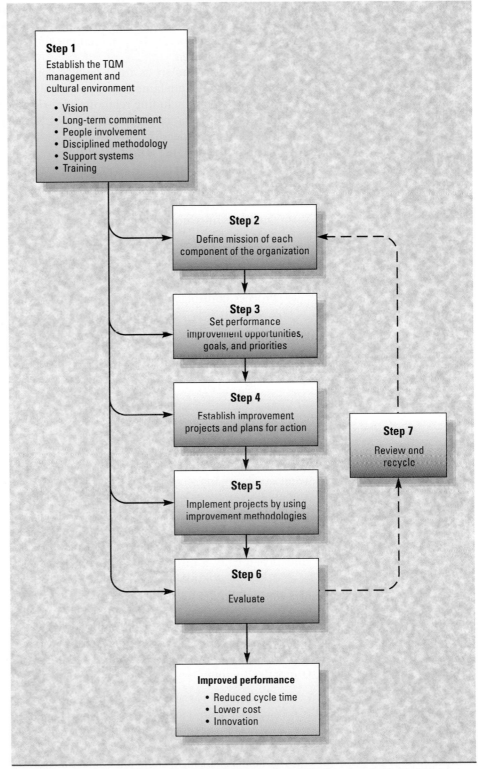

Source: Department of Defense, Quality and Productivity Self-Assessment Guide for Defense
Organizations (Washington, DC: Department of Defense), 1990.

techniques. (You will read more about implementation later in this chapter.) Step 6 is the evaluation phase, in which results—cycle times, costs, efficiency, and innovation—are evaluated. Step 7 mandates feedback so that processes can be continuously improved.

TQM is also known as total quality control (TQC), especially in Japan. (Japanese companies are famous for applying the concepts and tools of TQM to all company processes, including relations with suppliers and internal and external customers.) At 3M, the concept is known as Managing Total Quality. At Xerox, TQM is known as Leadership Through Quality. No matter the name, the concepts and methods are the same (Hunt, 1992):

- Quality improvements create productivity gains.

- Quality is defined as conformance to requirements that satisfy user needs.

- Quality is measured by continual process and product improvement and user satisfaction.

- Quality is determined by product design and achieved by effective process controls.

- Process-control techniques are used to prevent defects.

- Quality is part of every function in all phases of the product life cycle.

- Management is responsible for quality.

- Relationships with suppliers are formed for the long term and are quality-oriented.

As Thomas J. Barry (1991) wrote: "TQM/TQC is a journey, not a destination. It is a systematic, strategic process for organizational excellence."

The Components of TQM

Total quality management, or TQM, has two basic components: quality control and quality function deployment. As Ishikawa (1985) reported, Japanese Industrial Standards define **quality control** (**QC**) as a "system of production methods which economically produces quality goods or services meeting the requirements of consumers. Modern quality control utilizes statistical methods and is often called statistical quality control."

A key part of quality control as it is currently practiced is the commitment and participation of all members of an organization, from top to bottom. All members are involved in the design, development, production, and servicing of a product that is satisfying to the customer (Ishikawa, 1985). The concept of designing quality into a product is key to **quality function deployment** (**QFD**), a disciplined approach to solving quality problems before the design phase of a product. As Hunt (1992) wrote:

> the foundation of QFD is the belief that products should be designed to reflect customer desires; therefore, marketers, design engineers, and manufacturing personnel must work closely together from the beginning to ensure a successful product. The approach involves finding out what features are important to customers, ranking them in importance, identifying conflicts, and translating them into engineering specifications.

QFD was developed by Professor Yoji Akao of Japan. His purpose was to create a method of planning and executing product development across functional lines. QFD "links customer expectations to the technical considerations of the designer and manufacturer,... transforming customer wants and needs into quantitative terms" (Hunt, 1992). QFD uses a matrix that relates customer requirements and features of competitors' products to functional design characteristics and customer satisfaction. The process begins with surveys to identify what features and performance characteristics customers value. If a competing product already exists, a sample is purchased and disassembled to determine its particular characteristics. The best of the competing products becomes a **benchmark**—the product to meet or beat in terms of design, manufacture, performance, and service. Interdepartmental teams identify the weaknesses of the benchmark and develop improvements that the new product will incorporate (*Business Week,* Special Quality Issue 1991, pp. 22–23).

Toyota used QFD to design and build the Lexus LS 400. In the initial stages of product design, Toyota purchased competing cars from Mercedes, Jaguar, and BMW. Toyota engineers tested the cars rigorously, disassembled them, and studied the parts. The engineers were convinced that Toyota could match or exceed 11 performance goals, including goals relating to weight, fuel economy, aerodynamics, and noise. Toyota continued to refine the design and the manufacturing process that would produce the LS 400. The company spent $500 million in development costs, which included expenditures for new, more precise machine tools and innovative use of materials. The result was a quality product; according to J. D. Power & Associates, the car is a top-rated performer (*Business Week,* October 22, 1990).

Major Contributors to TQM

From almost the beginning of mass production in America, quality was a concern for managers. In early factories, a large number of unskilled laborers performed the work, producing interchangeable parts under the supervision of engineers. As the number of defective parts increased, most manufacturers realized that they were losing money to the costs connected with poor quality. "In its early days, quality control was a dimension of cost control, with emphasis on eliminating waste" (Hart and Bogan, 1992). By the end of World War I, inspection and inspectors were standard fixtures in most industrial plants. The inspectors were charged with the duty of weeding out defective parts before they were shipped to customers (Shewhart, 1939).

The paragraphs that follow briefly discuss the contributions of those who, along with Costello and Akao, offered ways to counter the problems of quality associated with mass production.

G. S. Radford   In 1922, Radford published *The Control of Quality in Manufacturing,* in which he advocated inspection as the cornerstone of industrial quality control. In his view, "it was the inspector's job to examine, weigh, and measure every item prior to its being loaded on a truck for shipment" (Hart and Bogan, 1992). Radford believed that maintaining quality was a management responsibility and that quality should be considered during the design stages of a product (Garvin, 1988).

Walter A. Shewhart   In 1931, Shewhart published *Economic Control of Quality of Manufactured Product.* Shewhart recommended that scientific methods and quantitative measures be applied to quality control. He and his colleagues at Bell Laboratories created what is now called statistical quality control and statistical process control. **Statistical quality control** (**SQC**) is the use of statistical tools and methods to determine the quality of a product or service. **Statistical process control** (**SPC**) is the use of SQC to establish boundaries that determine if a process is in control (predictable) or out of control (unpredictable) (Gabor, 1990). Shewhart was a teacher and mentor of W. Edwards Deming and Joseph M. Juran, both of whom worked at Bell Laboratories.

W. Edwards Deming   Perhaps the best-known advocate of total quality management is W. Edwards Deming. Exhibit 17.4 presents Deming's 14 points, a checklist of ways to improve quality. (Later in this chapter, in Exhibit 17.10, you will see Deming's list of seven "deadly diseases," or common barriers to quality control.) The model you studied in Exhibit 17.2, Deming's chain reaction, may be the most commonly used quality-related model in Japan.

Deming went to Japan in 1947 at the invitation of the Supreme Command for the Allied Powers. His assignment was to help in the preparations for the 1950 census of occupied Japan. The Union of Japanese Scientists and Engineers, organized to help rebuild Japan, contacted Deming and asked for his assistance. The rest is history; Deming became a driving force for quality in Japan. Along with Juran, he helped to make Japanese products the quality leaders around the world. Japan's most esteemed awards for quality bear his name.

Joseph M. Juran   Juran's book, *The Quality Control Handbook,* published in 1951, argued that quality should not be considered merely an expense. Quality, said Juran, should be viewed as an investment in a firm's profitability. Juran's argument is that managers must design quality into products, services, and processes by planning for quality. He divides quality management into three parts, or what he called the trilogy:

- Quality planning. This aspect of management involves budgeting and business planning.

- Quality control. In this part, managers control costs, expenses, and inventory.

- Quality improvements. This aspect of management involves cost reduction and profit improvement.

Juran outlined the processes necessary to achieve quality planning, quality control, and quality improvements in his book *Juran on Planning for Quality* (1988). Exhibit 17.5 presents Juran's "Quality Planning Road Map," which he suggested that managers use in conjunction with the trilogy. Juran believed that managers play a crucial role in quality. He estimated that "approximately 80 percent of the problems identified with breakthrough analysis, including defect rates, are correctable only by improving the management control system. The remaining 20 percent are attributable to the actions of the operating work force" (Walton, 1986).

Exhibit 17.4

Deming's 14 points for improving quality.

1. **Create a constancy of purpose for improvement of product and service.** Rather than to make money, the purpose of a company is to stay in business and provide jobs through innovation, research, constant improvement, and maintenance.

2. **Adopt the new philosophy.** Americans are too tolerant of poor workmanship and sullen service. We need a new "religion" in which mistakes and negativism are unacceptable.

3. **Cease dependence on mass inspection.** American firms typically inspect a product as it comes off the assembly line or at major stages along the way; defective products are either thrown out or reworked. Both practices are unnecessarily expensive. In effect, a company is paying workers to make defects and then correct them. Quality comes not from inspection but from improvement of the process. With instruction, workers can be enlisted in this improvement.

4. **End the practice of awarding business on the price tag alone.** Purchasing departments customarily operate on orders to seek the lowest-priced vendor. Frequently, this leads to supplies of low quality. Instead, buyers should seek the best quality in a long-term relationship with a single supplier for any one item.

5. **Improve constantly and forever the system of production and service.** Improvement is not a one-time effort. Management is obligated to continually look for ways to reduce waste and improve quality.

6. **Institute training.** Too often, workers have learned their jobs from other workers who were never trained properly. They are forced to follow unintelligible instructions. They cannot do their jobs well because no one tells them how to do so.

7. **Institute leadership.** The job of a supervisor is not to tell people what to do nor to punish them, but to lead. Leading consists of helping people do a better job and of learning by objective methods who is in need of individual help.

8. **Drive out fear.** Many employees are afraid to ask questions or to take a position, even when they do not understand what their job is or what is right or wrong. They will continue to do things the wrong way or not do them at all. The economic losses from fear are appalling. To promote better quality and productivity, people must feel secure.

9. **Break down barriers between staff areas.** Often a company's departments or units are competing with each other or have goals that conflict. They do not work as a team so they can solve or foresee problems. Worse, one department's goals may cause trouble for another.

10. **Eliminate slogans, exhortations, and targets for the work force.** These never helped anybody do a good job. Let workers formulate their own slogans.

11. **Eliminate numerical quotas.** Quotas take into account only numbers, not quality or methods. They are usually a guarantee of inefficiency and high cost. A person, to hold a job, meets a quota at any cost, without regard to damage to the company.

12. **Remove barriers to pride of workmanship.** People are eager to do a good job and distressed when they cannot. Too often, misguided supervisors, faulty equipment, and defective materials stand in the way of good performance. These barriers must be removed.

13. **Institute a vigorous program of education and retraining.** Both management and the work force will have to be educated in the new methods these points promote, including teamwork and statistical techniques.

14. **Take action to accomplish the transformation.** It will require a special top-management team with a plan of action to carry out the quality mission. Workers cannot do it on their own, nor can managers.

Source: Mary Walton, *The Deming Management Method at Work* (New York: Perigee), 1990, pp. 17–19. Reprinted by permission of the Putnam Publishing Group. Copyright 1990 Mary Walton.

Exhibit 17.5

*Juran's quality planning
road map.*

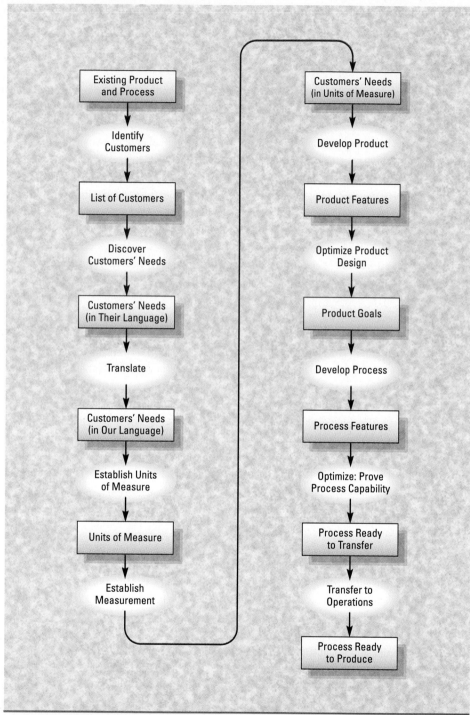

Source: Joseph M. Juran, *Juran on Planning for Quality* (New York: Free Press), 1988, p. 15. Copyright 1988 Juran Institute, Inc. Reprinted by permission of The Free Press, a division of Macmillan, Inc.

Juran is relentless in his desire for quality. "Whenever a basic cause leading to a quality failure is identified, Juran insists that the planning-control processes be altered to permanently prevent the cause from occurring again" (Hunt, 1992). Out of this view and Deming's teachings, the Japanese developed the idea of a **continuous-improvement process** (CIP), the never-ending search for ways to improve everyone and everything. The Japanese word for this process is **kaizen**.

Armand V. Feigenbaum   Following up on Juran's contributions was Armand Feigenbaum, manager of quality control for General Electric headquarters in the 1950s. As Hunt (1992) reported, Feigenbaum advocated total quality control, which he defined as

> an effective system for integrating the quality development, quality maintenance, and quality improvement efforts of the various groups in an organization so as to enable production and service at the most economical levels which allow for full customer satisfaction.

Feigenbaum believed that "quality was too central to a company's identity to be entrusted to an isolated corps of inspectors. For a total response, every single employee and vendor had to be brought into the process" (Hart and Bogan, 1992; Feigenbaum, 1956). Although quality involved everyone, Feigenbaum believed that managers who were specialists in quality control should take charge of the quality effort. Today the approach differs. Top managers want every employee to be a quality control expert and committed to quality in all their undertakings.

Philip B. Crosby   Philip Crosby was a 40-year employee of AT&T, a company that has contributed much to management know-how and technological breakthroughs, and a vice president of ITT for 14 years. In his books Crosby asserted that everyone needs to be trained by quality experts in quality control, quality assurance, and total quality management.

The first part of creating an environment that integrates quality principles and tools is to determine the organization's current level of management maturity. For this purpose, Crosby devised the grid shown in Exhibit 17.6, the quality management maturity grid. The left column lists six measurement categories. Across the top are the five stages through which a company passes on its way to ensuring quality as a regular part of its operations, products, and services. After the organization has identified its present stage, Crosby offers a 14-step program to move it to the final stage—Certainty.

Crosby has popularized quality through his down-to-earth language and approaches. He and Thomas J. Peters have accelerated national awareness of the importance of quality to our lives, our economy, and the perpetuation of our standard of living.

Thomas J. Peters   Author, lecturer, consultant, and professor, Tom Peters has given us a look at companies that are doing the right things. Peters has sounded alarms and taught average Americans about the need to get better at everything we do, to become more like our competitors by imitating them, learning from them, and trying to stay ahead of the trends.

Exhibit 17.6

Crosby's quality management maturity grid.

	Stage I **Uncertainty**	Stage II **Awakening**	Stage III **Enlightenment**	Stage IV **Wisdom**	Stage V **Certainty**
Management Understanding and Attitude	No comprehension of quality as a management tool. Tend to blame quality department for "quality problems."	Recognizing that quality management may be of value but not willing to provide money or time to make it all happen.	While going through quality improvement program learn more about quality management; becoming supportive and helpful.	Participating. Understand absolutes of quality management. Recognize their personal role in continuing emphasis.	Consider quality management an essential part of company system.
Quality Organization Status	Quality is hidden in manufacturing or engineering departments. Inspection probably not part of organization. Emphasis on appraisal and sorting.	A stronger quality leader is appointed but main emphasis is still on appraisal and moving the product. Still part of manufacturing or other.	Quality department reports to top management, all appraisal is incorporated, and manager has role in management of company.	Quality manager is an officer of company; effective status reporting and preventive action. Involved with consumer affairs and special assignments.	Quality manager on board of directors. Prevention is main concern. Quality is a thought leader.
Problem Handling	Problems are fought as they occur, no resolution; inadequate definition; lots of yelling and accusations.	Teams are set up to attack major problems. Long-range solutions are not solicited.	Corrective-action communication established. Problems are faced openly and resolved in an orderly way.	Problems are identified early in their development. All functions are open to suggestion and improvement.	Except in the most unusual cases, problems are prevented.
Cost of Quality as % of Sales	Reported: unknown Actual: 20%	Reported: 3% Actual: 18%	Reported: 8% Actual: 12%	Reported: 6.5% Actual: 8%	Reported: 2.5% Actual: 2.5%
Quality Improvement Actions	No organized activities. No understanding of such activities.	Trying obvious "motivational" short-range efforts	Implementation of the 14-step program with thorough understanding and establishment of each step	Continuing the 14-step program and starting Make Certain.	Quality improvement is a normal and continued activity.
Summation of Company Quality Posture	"We don't know why we have problems with quality."	"Is it absolutely necessary to always have problems with quality?"	"Through management commitment and quality improvement we are identifying and resolving our problems."	"Defect prevention is a routine part of our operation."	"We know why we do not have problems with quality."

Source: Philip B. Crosby, *Quality is Free: The Art of Making Quality Certain* (New York: Mentor), 1979, pp. 32–33. Reprinted by permission of McGraw-Hill, Inc.

The Irony of America's Approach to Quality

Most of the advocates of quality that this chapter has discussed are Americans. It is ironic, then, that American businesses are the most recent converts to their gospels. What did it take to make the top managers of U.S. industries realize the importance of quality? It took the dramatic inroads of foreign competitors. These competitors practically wiped out some U.S. industries; in others they captured huge portions of traditionally domestic markets. It took the quality of Japanese and German products to change U.S. standards of quality. It took the oil embargo of the early 1970s to change Americans' thinking about customer needs and their connection to product design and manufacture. It took the Japanese expertise at adapting new technologies to show Americans the importance of bringing innovations to market quickly.

In short, it took crises and competitors' success to show us what we had known once but had forgotten because of U.S. domination of world markets following World War II. From 1945 until the early 1970s, American companies were nearly the only sources for needed products. Obviously, that is no longer the case. From the 1970s through the 1980s, major U.S. industries have been abandoned. U.S. jobs have been lost to foreign competitors or moved offshore to foreign producers. Have American managers finally understood the messages sent by so many for so long? Will the quality produced by U.S. businesses improve through the 1990s and beyond? The signs are everywhere that they have and it will.

The Implementation of Total Quality Management

As Townsend and Gebhardt (1992), writers who address quality issues, observed:

> Partial understanding of and involvement in quality can produce only partial success or total failure. The only chance for a quality process to truly succeed is for a company to simultaneously attack all the issues: leadership, participation, and measurement.

Commitment Throughout an Organization

To be successful, TQM requires a 100% commitment from everyone. Many past attempts by companies to improve quality did not work because the efforts were neither company-wide nor committed and were too dependent on too few people.

Commitment at the Top   International Telephone and Telegraph implemented a major TQM program that proved very successful. Philip Crosby (1979) claimed that a vital element of the company's success with TQM was the commitment of top managers. The first step in his 14-step program requires top managers to discuss the need for quality improvement with management staff. Leaders should emphasize the need for defect prevention and, to highlight top managers' commitment to quality, issue a written policy about the subject. Managers must recognize that everyone has to be personally committed to participating in a TQM program. They will remain committed as long as management can show progress toward improvement.

In 1981 Deming was invited by Ford president, Donald E. Petersen, to speak to Ford executives. Refusing to talk about quality as it related to automobiles, Deming insisted on talking about Ford's management philosophy and corporate culture. Deming cross-examined executives to learn their thinking about quality. When asked to define quality, none could. When asked about their roles in quality assurance, managers talked about administration, not what Deming had in mind: commitment from the top to facilitate quality improvement. When asked by managers why America was having trouble competing with the Japanese, Deming answered with rage, "The answer is—MANAGEMENT!" (Gabor, 1990).

Ford was one of the first American companies to embrace Deming's teachings about quality. As Donald E. Petersen wrote, "I agreed with Dr. Deming's philosophy of management, and I especially liked the emphasis he placed on the importance of people. In fact, we hired him as a consultant, and I made a point of meeting with him myself roughly once a month" (Petersen and Hillkirk, 1991). Early efforts at implementing TQM at Ford included teaching all employees, not just quality control inspectors, how to use statistical process control. As Petersen observed, "When something's going wrong, 80 percent of the time there's something wrong with the way your production system or process is functioning" (Petersen and Hillkirk, 1991).

Later, Ford's TQM program dealt with removing fear from the workplace, developing trust in people, and building a supportive structure for the concept of continuous improvement. Ford executives began to ask questions: "What's our culture?" "What do we stand for?" As Petersen put it, "Dr. Deming's philosophy, expressed in his 'Fourteen Points on Management,' helped many of us zero in on some of the key concepts we wanted to express" (Petersen and Hillkirk, 1991). As a result, Ford executives rewrote their mission, value statements, and guiding principles. Exhibit 17.7 shows the new version.

Commitment at the Middle   Commitment to quality cannot begin and end with top management. Midlevel managers need to be active participants in planning for quality and quality control. Further, they must have the authority and responsibility to execute plans and deal with problems. Empowered managers, in turn, must empower those over whom they have authority.

Once middle managers are involved, they must work well together. "Besides pulling midlevel managers and supervisors into the quality process, companies need to develop systems that encourage and ensure cooperation. Cooperation among managers is essential for effective problem solving" (Hart and Bogan, 1992). As Ishikawa and others have pointed out, horizontal communication is vital to cooperation, because most processes flow horizontally. Managers can use various methods to encourage cross-functional cooperation and communication. These include creating cross-functional teams, rearranging work flow and reassigning tasks, developing incentives and rewards to encourage cooperation, and creating accountability for internal customers.

Commitment at the Bottom   Because TQM is everyone's responsibility, supervisors, team leaders, and workers must have a say in planning and executing plans. A common means of soliciting feedback from workers at all levels is the quality circle. A **quality circle** is a team of employees (usually workers and their supervisors or team leaders) who meet to define and solve a problem that they are close to. The members of a quality circle are volunteers, and they agree to use their

Exhibit 17.7

Ford's mission, values, and guiding principles.

MISSION

"…to improve continually our products and services to meet our customers' needs, allowing us to prosper as a business and to provide a reasonable return for our stockholders, the owners of our business."

VALUES

"How we accomplish our mission is as important as the mission itself. Fundamental to success for the company are three basic values":

- People—"Our people are the source of our strength. They provide our corporate intelligence and determine our reputation and vitality. Involvement and teamwork are our core human values."

- Products—"Our products are the end result of our efforts, and they should be the best in serving customers worldwide. As our products are viewed, so are we viewed."

- Profits—"Profits are the ultimate measure of how efficiently we provide customers with the best products for their needs. Profits are required to survive and grow."

GUIDING PRINCIPLES

- "Quality comes first. To achieve customer satisfaction, the quality of our products and service must be our number-one priority.

- "Customers are the focus of everything we do. We must strive for excellence in everything we do: in our products, in their safety and value—and in our services, our human relations, our competitiveness, and our profitability.

- "Employee involvement is our way of life. We are a team. We must treat each other with trust and respect.

- "Dealers and suppliers are our partners. The company must maintain mutually beneficial relationships with dealers, suppliers, and our other business associates.

- "Integrity is never compromised. The conduct of our company worldwide must be pursued in a manner that is socially responsible and commands respect for its integrity and for its positive contributions to society. Our doors are open to men and women alike, without discrimination and without regard to ethnic origin or personal beliefs."

Source: Donald E. Petersen and John Hillkirk, *A Better Idea: Redefining the Way Americans Work* (Boston: Houghton Mifflin), 1991, p. 13.

knowledge and experience to solve the problem. Members of the circle may also address issues other than quality.

Process teams and product teams are cross-functional groups that combine talents and energies to identify and solve problems and improve the execution of tasks. Some are self-managing; others are guided by managers. All facilitate quality control and communication. They speed the planning and execution phases of programs.

F O C U S   O N   Q U A L I T Y

Top Managers' Roles in Building Quality

r. Kaoru Ishikawa, one of Japan's leading authorities on quality control, believes that without leadership from the top, total quality management cannot succeed. He outlined the following list of duties for top managers:

1. Become an expert on quality and quality control.

2. Establish policies that define the positions the company will take in regard to total quality control. Establish "quality first" as the basic policy.

3. Take the leadership in quality control.

4. Integrate quality control through strategic planning and training.

5. Monitor to be certain that quality and quality control are according to plan.

6. Define top managers' responsibilities in regard to quality assurance, and give the company a solid system for ensuring quality.

7. Establish a system of cross-functional management to enhance horizontal communication.

8. Drive home the concept that "the next function is the customer." Since each process exists to serve the one that follows it, each process must assure work and product quality. Maintain a customer focus.

9. Top management must lead in introducing change and innovation. ▲

For more about Ishikawa's views, see Kaoru Ishikawa, *What Is Total Quality Control?* David J. Lu, translator (Englewood Cliffs, NJ: Prentice-Hall), 1985.

Most employees desire a participative style of leadership and, once trained and experienced, operate best under it. By removing fear of failure and blame for mistakes from a workplace and giving workers the authority, training, and incentives to promote quality, managers can release workers' creativity and ingenuity. Workers feel free to look for and try new approaches and to become risk takers. As discussed earlier, this was clearly the case at Whirlpool.

Motorola is a recognized leader in America's quality revolution. It was the winner of the first Malcolm Baldrige National Quality Award in 1988 and is committed to aggressive programs for quality and product innovations. Motorola has developed a "philosophy that allows each employee to contribute insights to the achievement of quality standards. The Participative Management Program (PMP) assumes that under the right conditions, employees will suggest better ways to do their jobs" (Hart and Bogan, 1992). All employees below top managers are members of PMP teams. Each is continuously at work to reduce defects and cycle times, either the time from order receipt to shipment for existing products, or the time from conception to delivery for new products. Targets to reduce defects and cycle times are the basis for rewards (Hart and Bogan, 1992).

Changes to the Corporate Culture

Commitment to TQM means changes in managers' thinking, methods, and approaches to the identification and solution of problems. These modifications mean changes to the corporate culture. Attitudes, beliefs, values, philosophies, and habits must undergo analysis and change if TQM is to succeed. A publication of Motorola, *The New Truths of Quality,* lists "old truths" and "new truths" about quality. For example, the old truth says "To err is human." The new truth says "Perfection—total customer satisfaction—is the standard."

According to Philip Crosby (1984), establishing a TQM culture means describing "the future as we would like it to be and then [marching] on down the yellow brick road. Only when the management team becomes educated and sets out on its mission of changing the culture of the company can it hope to reap the rewards such a change produces."

Joseph Juran (1988) cautioned that moving to a TQM environment means change and that change can breed resistance and fear. The existing culture in an organization provides support and social networks. "Any proposed changes are a potential threat to the stability of the pattern and thereby are a potential threat to the well-being of the members of the culture." Juran provided a list of rules to minimize resistance to change within an organization:

1. Provide participation.

2. Provide enough time.

3. Keep proposals free of excess baggage.

4. Work with the recognized leadership.

5. Treat people with dignity

6. Take the other person's point of view.

7. Look at the alternatives.

Thomas J. Barry (1991) believed that the existing culture needs to be clearly defined and communicated before management tries to produce a TQM environment. "First we must determine the existing organizational culture," Barry wrote, "and then we may determine how a TQM approach will fit it. TQM will nurture the organizational culture to produce a working environment in which people willingly take ownership for their work." Barry believed that those who work in TQM cultures:

1. Listen to customers to learn their requirements

2. Identify the cost of quality

3. Do the right thing the first time

4. Commit to continual improvement

5. Take ownership of quality at all organizational levels

6. Provide or are guided by executive leadership

The Forging of Partnerships

Partners share authority and responsibility. A TQM environment and culture thrives on committed teams of partners who work toward the vision of quality. Teams will be successful only if managers empower them by sharing authority, listening to team members, and acting on their recommendations.

The criteria for the Malcolm Baldridge National Quality Award encourage companies to use teams. Teams are ideal tools for "involving managers and workers in the quality process, for instilling quality values, and for problem solving" (Hart and Bogan, 1992).

A TQM environment requires partnerships of insiders and outsiders. All participants must be working for the same ends and focused on quality and requirements.

Internal Partnerships   In addition to various standing and ad hoc committees, most companies that commit to TQM maintain three kinds of teams: a quality improvement team, a process improvement team, and a project improvement team. All need a clear purpose, trained leadership, a structured environment, and guidelines or rules about the scope of their authority.

A **quality improvement team** is usually a group of people from all the functional areas of a company. The group meets regularly to assess progress toward goals, identify and solve common problems, and cooperate in planning for the future. The purpose of such a team is to facilitate operations by providing the support needed and enhancing coordination efforts. Team leaders should enjoy quick and easy access to top managers so that management strategies can be adjusted to meet changing conditions. Members "should represent the company to the outside world, schedule the education program [to bring quality improvement to internal operations], and create company-wide events [to highlight the importance and successes of efforts at quality improvement]" (Crosby, 1984). Large corporations may have several quality improvement teams, one for each operation or operational area. Small companies may have just one.

A **process improvement team** is made up of members who are involved with a process—getting the payroll out, making a part, or sorting the mail, for example. Team members meet to analyze how they can improve the process. They focus on measuring the effectiveness and efficiency of each step, reducing cycle times, and identifying and correcting causes for variations in the quality of inputs and outputs.

A **project improvement team** is usually composed of a group of people involved in the same project—installing a new computer system or creating a new product, for example. Members of the team determine how to make the project better. Project improvement teams usually include those who are or will be customers or consumers of the project's output. These users may be insiders or outsiders.

Investigations by all three types of teams may lead to contact with outsiders if outsiders are the sources of problems or if they can provide answers to problems. All three types of teams need feedforward, concurrent, and feedback controls to help them with their missions. All need reliable feedback and input from their customers, current or potential. To supply feedback, many companies use customer response surveys. Exhibit 17.8 shows a typical feedback tool that a company could use to gather customer responses about the quality of its products and dealer services.

External Partnerships   A focus on customer needs and requirements should be established at the beginning of product design and continue as the focus throughout manufacturing and delivery. Companies need to communicate regularly with outside stakeholders to keep the stakeholders informed and to

---

Exhibit 17.8

Excerpts from a typical customer response survey.

We value your opinions! Please the take time to complete this short questionnaire so we can better serve you:

Product name and model number _____

Dealer name and city _____

How would you rate your satisfaction with:	Very Satisfied	Somewhat Satisfied	Neither Satisfied nor Dissatisfied	Somewhat Dissatisfied	Very Dissatisfied
1. Your overall experience owning our product?	☐	☐	☐	☐	☐
2. The product design and characteristics (appearance, ease of use, etc.)?	☐	☐	☐	☐	☐
3. The overall quality of your purchase (reliability, workmanship, freedom from repair, etc.)?	☐	☐	☐	☐	☐
4. The clarity of the instruction booklet?	☐	☐	☐	☐	☐
5. The overall level of service received from your dealer?	☐	☐	☐	☐	☐
6. Courtesy of the dealer personnel?	☐	☐	☐	☐	☐
7. Convenience of the store hours?	☐	☐	☐	☐	☐
8. Convenience of the store location?	☐	☐	☐	☐	☐
9. Knowledge and expertise of the dealer personnel?	☐	☐	☐	☐	☐
10. Availability of dealer personnel?	☐	☐	☐	☐	☐
11. Explanation of the warranty and the extended service agreement?	☐	☐	☐	☐	☐

	Very Good	Good	Fair	Poor	Very Poor
12. Considering your experience, what are the chances that you will return to this dealer for another purchase?	☐	☐	☐	☐	☐

What could we do to improve your purchase, ownership, and service experience?

_____

_____

_____

solicit their input. Suppliers are often involved as members of quality, process, and project improvement teams. This book has already stressed the need for partnership with suppliers. Such partnership is crucial in some industries. Most automobile companies depend on suppliers for more than 70% of the parts they put into their cars. Most retailers depend on suppliers for 100% of their inventories. Many manufacturers and retailers are linked by teams and computers to their key suppliers. The manufacturers involve the suppliers in some decisions. When evaluating input from suppliers (and suppliers' suppliers), evaluators should look for the same commitment to quality that they themselves maintain, or the final product will not meet customers' requirements. To achieve maximum results, companies must be willing to share information, such as customer feedback, with their suppliers.

The Swiss chemical company, Ciba-Geigy, learned a tough lesson in quality when it received negative feedback from one of its largest customers, Milliken & Company, a top clothing maker. Milliken warned that it would no longer purchase Ciba-Geigy textile dyes if Ciba-Geigy did not improve quality. Bernardo De Sousa, CEO at Ciba-Geigy, was shocked. An investigation revealed that the company's processes for achieving quality were woefully inefficient. In addition, mistakes in product shipments, inventory shortages, and other errors were costing the company 20% of sales. "We needed new tools to increase productivity, improve our processes, and change our attitudes," said De Sousa (Levine, 1991).

Quality Audits

An audit is an important control device. Whether done by insiders or outsiders, audits monitor progress—or lack of it—toward measurable goals. A **quality audit** determines if customer requirements are being met. If they are not, the auditors discover why not. A quality audit can focus on a particular product, process, or project. It can be performed by a team of insiders or by outsiders—by a consultant or quality improvement team, for example.

A **quality control audit** asks two basic questions: How are we doing? and What are the problems? It focuses on "the way . . . the factory builds quality into a given product, control of subcontracting, the manner in which customer complaints are handled, and the methods of implementing quality assurance at each step of production, starting from . . . new product development" (Ishikawa, 1985).

Both quality audits and quality control audits use visual quality assurance tools. Exhibit 17.9 shows one of these tools, a control chart that monitors a process that yields frequent outputs. Both types of audits also use quality assurance techniques. Some of these techniques include brainstorming, statistical process control, concurrent engineering, quality-cost analysis, benchmarking, robust design, and quality function deployment.

The Removal of Barriers

This chapter has already mentioned some of the obstacles that can impede implementation of TQM. Resistance to change is one. In addition, Exhibit 17.10 lists seven "deadly diseases" that Deming said can infect management and impose barriers to TQM.

Deming also cited seven obstacles to the successful implementation of TQM (Walton, 1986). The first of Deming's obstacles is the hope for instant results once

Exhibit 17.9

Control chart used to monitor performance of a process.

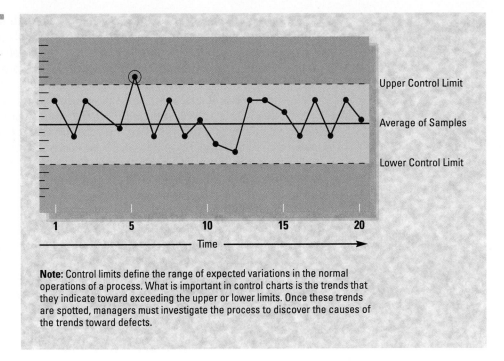

Upper Control Limit

Average of Samples

Lower Control Limit

1   5   10   15   20

Time

Note: Control limits define the range of expected variations in the normal operations of a process. What is important in control charts is the trends that they indicate toward exceeding the upper or lower limits. Once these trends are spotted, managers must investigate the process to discover the causes of the trends toward defects.

Exhibit 17.10

Deming's seven deadly diseases: common barriers to quality control.

The following "diseases" can form barriers to total quality management:

1. Lack of constancy of purpose to plan products and services that will have a market, keep the company in business, and provide jobs.

2. Emphasis on short-term profits. Short-term thinking can be fed by fear of an unfriendly takeover or by bankers and owners who focus on dividends.

3. Evaluation of performance, merit rating, or annual review.

4. Mobility of management (job hopping).

5. Management that uses visible figures only, with little or no consideration for figures that are unknown or unknowable.

6. Excessive medical costs.

7. Excessive liability costs that are swelled by lawyers who work on contingency fees.

Source: W. Edwards Deming, *Out of the Crisis* (Cambridge, MA: Massachusetts Institute of Technology, Center for Advanced Engineering Study), 1986, pp. 97–98.

efforts at promoting quality begin. Attempts to improve things take time and preparation. Obstacle 2 is the assumption that technology alone can solve quality control problems. Remember that Whirlpool made quality gains not by applying high technology, but by working with people. GM found out in the 1980s that spending billions for the latest in robotics and sophisticated machinery was not the answer to improving quality. A company-wide effort that involves everyone simultaneously is the only answer.

The third obstacle is reliance on an off-the-shelf solution, a cookie-cutter approach to quality control and improvement. Each company is unique. Each situation calls for a tailored approach in line with established principles.

Obstacle 4 is the excuse that the uniqueness of a company's problems renders a TQM program impossible. There is no real choice. Companies must become quality-oriented and customer-focused or lose out to those that do.

Obstacle 5 is the assumption that the quality control department should handle problems of quality. In tandem with the sixth obstacle—the view that "we installed quality control"—obstacle 5 is an excuse for laziness or unwillingness to do what must be done. Quality is everyone's job.

The last of Deming's obstacles to implementing TQM is the misconception that, once products or processes meet specifications, the purpose of quality control has been achieved. Deming pointed out that "not only may products meet specifications yet vary widely in quality, but in addition, 'the supposition that everything is all right inside the specifications and all wrong outside does not correspond to this world'" (Walton, 1986).

The American Quality Foundation Study   In partnership with the accounting and consulting firm of Ernst & Young, the American Quality Foundation conducted a $2-million study of 584 firms in the United States, Canada, Japan, and Germany. The purpose of the study was to specify why quality programs fail. As Fuchsberg (1992) reported, the study revealed that

> many businesses may waste millions of dollars a year on quality-improvement strategies that don't improve their performance and may even hamper it. Some highly popular management tools may be hurting rather than helping companies. The success of certain practices depends on a company's current performance.

According to the study, efforts at quality control yield the best results when they begin with a few select practices and integrate others as appropriate.

The study proposed three models for improving quality at companies at three performance levels: lower, medium, and higher. (The rankings were based on profitability, productivity, and quality measures.) The list that follows (Fuchsberg, 1992) presents recommendations for companies at each level.

- Lower performers. Emphasize teams across and within departments, and increase training of all sorts. Do not use benchmarking or encourage wide participation in quality-related meetings.

- Medium performers. Simplify such corporate processes as design, and focus training on problem solving. Do not select suppliers based on their reputation; choose them through competitive bidding and by certifying their quality efforts.

- Higher performers. Use benchmarking to identify new products and services. Encourage company-wide quality meetings. Do not increase departmental teams—they could inhibit cooperation across functions.

The study found that empowering employees works best for higher performers and for giving customer representatives the ability to resolve customer issues more quickly. Every organization can use what the study called "universal

Quality assessment is one of the judging criteria of the Malcolm Baldridge National Quality Award. Here a Cadillac worker conducts a quality check against parts. Cadillac, IBM, and Federal Express have all been recipients of the award.

truths: explaining the corporate strategic plan to employees, customers, and suppliers; improving and simplifying production and development processes; and scrutinizing and shortening cycle time" (Fuchsberg, 1992).

The Nature of Productivity

Most of what has been said about quality applies to productivity as well. Commitment to productivity must begin at the top. Then everyone at every level must coordinate their searches for a better way to do everything. They must continuously strive to improve. Goals must be stated and people and cultures shaped to take on the new challenges. Gains and losses need to be measured, strategies created, tools and techniques defined and used, and people rewarded for their efforts. When quality is viewed as conformance to standards, then lack of quality means a conformance failure has occurred. Any failure may mean customer dissatisfaction and the need to rework, make good on a warranty, or face a lawsuit.

Efforts to improve product and process quality improve productivity and vice versa. In addition, improving productivity paves the way for improvements in employees' and citizens' standards of living and quality of life. The money saved through increased productivity can be made available for use in incentive programs and as pay increases. (Think back to the Management in Action feature in this chapter: At the Whirlpool plant, workers' bonuses were entirely from funds created by their efficiencies.) Government figures indicate that since 1980, the earnings and standard of living of the top third of Americans have increased while those of the middle third have stayed about even and those of the bottom third have decreased. Improvements in productivity could mean bigger paychecks where bigger paychecks are needed most.

Measures of Productivity

Productivity is a simple concept: It is the relationship of a given amount of output to the inputs it requires. One management writer (Belcher, 1987) explained how this relationship can change:

> We increase productivity by improving that output/input ratio; that is by producing more output, or better output, with a given level of input resources. Production represents the top half of the equation; we cannot reach a conclusion about productivity without considering the changes in inputs that were required to improve that output.

Measuring the productivity of a manufacturer is fairly easy and can be done numerically. Measuring the productivity of a service organization, however, is not so simple. How do you measure the productivity of a bank, a staff department, a government agency, or an individual manager? Also, if gains in productivity yield declines in product or process quality, has a gain really occurred?

Productivity can be measured by two kinds of indexes: a single-factor index and a combined-factors index. The single-factor index uses any of the following factors as a unit of input: hours of labor (the most common), hours of machine time, tons of materials, or dollars of invested capital. A combined-factors index, sometimes called a multifactor index, integrates such inputs as labor, materials, and capital in a formula and uses it as an overall measure of an organization's total productivity gain or loss. Whichever index is used, it must be as simple as possible and thoroughly understandable to those who must read and react to it (Chew, 1988). Each firm must develop its own productivity measures as well as use the traditional measures of its industry.

Productivity indexes such as hours of labor and dollars of invested capital can be used to compare countries, industries, or companies within an industry. They can also be used to compare plants within a company, departments within a plant, and people or units within a department. Productivity indexes are even applied to people not directly involved with producing what the company sells. As one management writer stated, "Engineers, supervisors, and other white-collar employees make significant contributions to manufacturing productivity" (Chew, 1988). Peter F. Drucker wrote that "The single greatest challenge facing managers in the developed countries of the world is to raise the productivity of knowledge and service workers" (Drucker, 1991).

The primary purpose of all productivity indexes is to focus managers' attention on critical aspects of all production efforts and processes. Productivity indexes help managers plot trends and spot those parts of the organization that are displaying unusually strong or poor performance. Indexes are just one kind of tool companies use to help themselves improve. No index is a perfect measure in and of itself, but an imperfect measure is often better than no measure (Chew, 1988).

American Productivity

According to U.S. Department of Commerce figures from 1945 to 1965, America's productivity rose at an average annual rate of 3.2%. From 1965 through 1973, productivity grew at an annual average rate of 2.4%. From 1978 to 1982, the rate averaged –0.2%. From 1982 to 1988, it grew again at an average of 1.3%. For the period from 1989 to 1991, productivity grew by less than 1%. Exhibit 17.11 shows

Exhibit 17.11

Productivity in the United States as measured in output per hour of labor with annual changes in percent, 1981–1991.

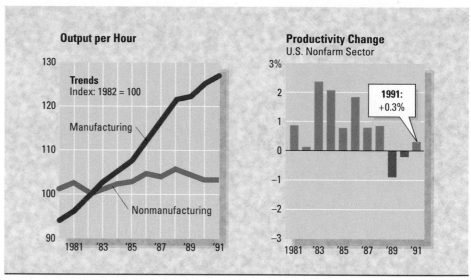

Source: U.S. Department of Commerce.

America's manufacturing and nonmanufacturing (service) productivity from 1981 to 1991, based on output per hour of labor invested. Note that productivity for 1982 is used as the base year—it equals 100 on the scale.

   The downward slide in America's productivity growth is reflected in its gross national product (GNP) and gross domestic product (GDP). The GNP measures goods and services produced by American-owned businesses anywhere in the world. The GDP measures goods and services produced in the United States regardless of who owns the business. Thus, Ford's European operations are part of the GNP but not the GDP; Honda's U.S. production is part of America's GDP but not the GNP. The GDP has become the standard of measurement for U.S. economic output since 1991. Exhibit 17.12 shows the trends in both measures from 1989

Exhibit 17.12

Gross national product and gross domestic product of the United States, and changes in GDP, 1989–1991.

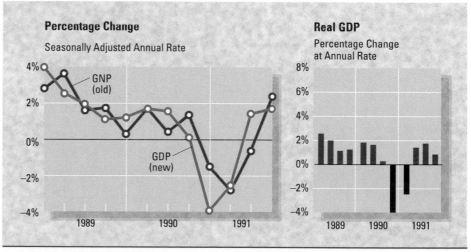

Source: U.S. Department of Commerce.

through 1991. In 1991 the GNP was about $5.5 trillion. The GDP was about 1% less. It should be noted that from 1990 into 1992, the U.S. economy was in a recession.

America has been playing catch-up with leading competitors since the 1970s. As Kupfer (1992) explained:

> In the 1970s, while Americans concentrated on volume, the Japanese focused on cost. When the U.S. turned its eyes to cost, Japan moved on to quality. Now that the quality revolution has taken hold here, Japan is embracing what Harvard Business School professor David Garvin calls 'post just-in-time manufacturing.' This involves speeding product development as well as production, with the goal of halving the time it takes to roll out a new manufactured good.

The name of the latest game in manufacturing is to be first to the market with the most recent innovations and adaptations of the newest technologies.

Although America is still the most productive country in the world, Germany and Japan are gaining—and improving their productivity at a faster rate. These countries have been able to improve their productivity so quickly for three reasons: (1) They have been able to adapt rapidly to products and manufacturing processes; (2) compared to Americans, their citizens have a higher rate of savings, which gives them a significant edge in capital formation; and (3) they spend more per capita on capital equipment and other aids to productivity (Kupfer, 1992). Exhibit 17.13 compares growth in capital investment, GDP, and personal savings rates in America and in its chief competitors, Germany and Japan.

Exhibit 17.13

Trends in personal savings rates, GDP, and capital investment for the United States, Germany, and Japan.

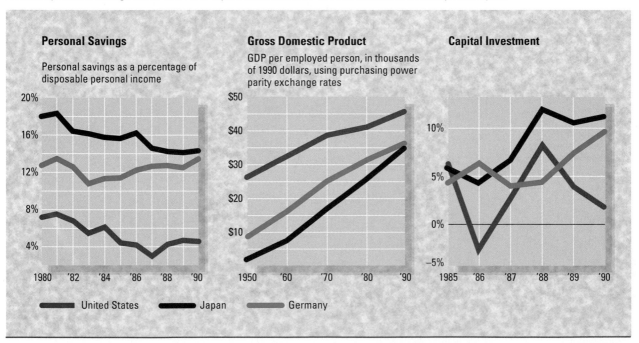

Source: U.S. Department of Commerce.

One reason for the recession that struck the United States in 1990 was the enormous amount of debt that corporations and individuals accumulated throughout the 1980s. From 1984 to 1990, American corporations added $1.1 trillion in debt to their organizations. The debt burden—interest that had to be paid—ate up nearly $150 billion, or 70%, of what could have been corporate profits in 1991. On average, Americans owed 95% of their income in 1990, up from 69% in 1982 (*Wall Street Journal,* April 13, 1992). This personal-debt burden slowed the recovery from the recession—most Americans had no choice but to restrict their spending and use their disposable incomes to reduce their indebtedness. They did so—at record rates in both 1991 and 1992—but the result was a slowdown in consumer purchases.

Factors That Affect Productivity

Productivity is affected most directly by capital equipment improvements, research and development, technological advances, investment in human resources, and general management expertise (Altany, 1990). As the Property and Casualty Division of United Services Automobile Association (Belcher, 1987) put it:

> Productivity improvement isn't just working harder, it's working smarter. It means devising a method to get the best return on our investment in people, facilities, equipment and other resources. Improving productivity means finding better ways to do more with the resources we have. We must strive to improve all levels of company operations and maintain our performance in profits and growth. In short, we need to provide quality products through distribution systems which are customer-convenient and operator-efficient.

Notice that this statement of purpose regarding productivity includes a strong reference to quality.

To plan for productivity, managers must understand what affects productivity. Employee output is not just a matter of how efficiently and effectively employees work. The government, employees, unions, and management all have an impact on productivity. The remainder of this chapter examines the impacts of these groups and how a company can manage its efforts to improve productivity.

Government

Governments affect productivity through decisions about levels of taxation, spending, regulations, and capital investment.

Government Spending   The federal government spent about $1.4 trillion during its 1992 fiscal year, or about 25% of the nation's GDP. It had to borrow about $400 billion to spend that much, boosting the national debt (federal deficit) to about $4 trillion. The budget included about $200 billion for interest on that total debt—about 15% of total federal spending. The Congressional Budget Office projects annual deficits of $300 billion or more during the remainder of the twentieth century. See Exhibit 17.14 for a brief summary of federal spending and deficits from 1973 to 1993.

Except during recessions, when demand for products and services falls, ever-increasing levels of government spending and debt contribute to inflation—

Exhibit 17.14

U.S. goverment spending, revenues, and deficits, 1973–1993.

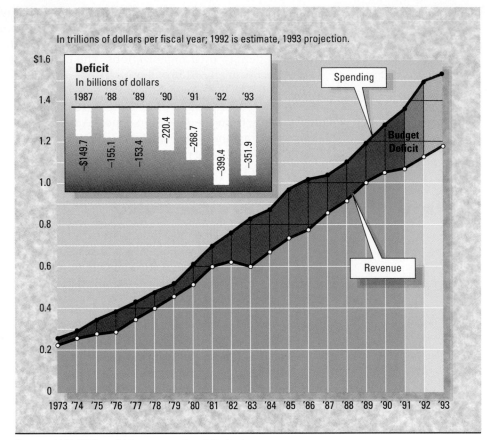

Source: U.S. Office of Management and Budget.

the erosion of buying power—and to the level of interest rates charged to borrowers. Although inflation has been fairly low (an average of 4% per year) since 1990, interest rates in America have hovered about 3 percentage points higher than German and Japanese interest rates. The relatively high U.S. interest rates make it relatively expensive for American businesses to borrow funds. Boston University economist Laurence Kotlikoff (Spiers, 1992) wrote: "Every time the public sector buys paper to publish regulations or hires an administrator, that reduces resources available for saving and investment by the more efficient private sector."

Government Regulation   In 1992, 122,406 employees in 52 federal regulatory agencies administered tens of thousands of federal rules at a cost of $13 billion (Warner, 1992). The 1993 federal budget proposed an additional $1 billion for regulators. One analyst (Warner, 1992) observed:

> Complying with federal regulations costs small businesses billions of dollars and millions of worker hours each year. It is estimated that the [Americans with Disabilities Act of 1991] will cost taxpayers as much as $20 billion annually, while the [1990 Clean Air Act amendments] will add at least $25.6 billion to the cost of doing business.

Professor Weidenbaum of Washington University in St. Louis reported: "About 150,000 small companies may have to spend more than $10,000 each for pollution permits under the 1990 Clean Air Act" (Saddler, 1992).

Few will argue that regulations are needed to benefit citizens and protect the environment. But it must be noted that the financial and time burdens placed on businesses by federal, state, and local regulations affect productivity. Furthermore, U.S. regulations do not burden our international competitors. Indeed, it is clear that to avoid these burdens, many companies have exported jobs.

Government and Capital Investment   The state of the economy affects what business and government can spend on capital improvements (road repair, bridge and dam construction, and the like). In 1989 (the latest year for which figures are available), spending on capital improvements by all levels of government in the United States totaled 1.6% of GDP. This level was below that of countries whose businesses compete with American businesses. The recession of the early 1990s has kept spending to very low levels. This chapter will discuss capital improvement spending by businesses in a later section.

Employees

In early 1992 two Japanese officials created a storm of protest in America by speaking their minds about America's lagging competitiveness. Yoshio Sakurauchi, the speaker of the lower house of the Japanese parliament, said that American workers were lazy and illiterate. The Japanese prime minister, Kiichi Miyazawa, said: "I have felt that the ethic of working by the sweat of one's brow has seemed to be lacking" among Americans in recent years (Chipello and Lehner, 1992). Today, American workers have never been better educated. The average American works 44 hours per week for pay; the average Japanese worker works 52. Davis and Milbank (1992) provided their own perspective of working America:

> Americans work just as many hours as they have for decades, absenteeism is down, and families as a whole work more because more women have jobs outside the home. Among families headed by married couples, 65 percent have two or more people at work, . . . 6.2 percent are holding down two jobs; many of them say they need the work to meet routine living expenses and pay off debt.

A person's work ethic is psychological and spiritual. Davis and Milbank (1992) reported:

> Just because Americans show up for work doesn't mean that their heart is in it—that they are finding fulfillment in labor or doing their best. Interviews with workers around the country turn up a lot of disenchantment among people who feel abused by their employers and by society at large.

Layoffs and cutbacks, downsizing and outsourcing have left their mark on those who remain in companies. Fear can replace commitment; alienation can replace enthusiasm. "Disaffection is especially strong among women and minorities because of pregnancy, race and sex discrimination, and sexual harassment," contends Barbara Otto, national program director for 9 to 5, the national association of working women (Davis and Milbank, 1992).

Before an employer can expect to make his or her work force more productive, all employees must be efficient and effective in reading, writing, arithmetic, and responsibility, "the four R's." Unfortunately, America's labor force increases by more than two million illiterate adults per year. One study (*Chicago Tribune*, June 5, 1992) highlighted the impact of illiteracy on small businesses:

> More than 10 million workers in small businesses have serious problems with reading, writing, mathematics, and other basic skills, impairing job performance. Those workers represent up to 40 percent of the small business workforce. Half of America's five million small businesses report skill problems that merit programs, but only up to five percent have programs.

Basic literacy—a fourth-grade education—is pathetically inadequate for today's best-paying and information-intensive jobs. The Educational Testing Service, which develops and administers the Scholastic Aptitude Test (SAT), rated American 13-year-olds at the bottom in math and science when compared with Asian, Canadian, and European children of the same age group (Labich, 1992).

Growth in quality and productivity requires that businesses empower their employees. But empowering an individual demands that he or she be able to take on new authority and responsibilities. As Sherman (1991) reported:

> Giving workers more power and responsibility is another way of saying that they will be thinking, judging, and deciding more. Workers who don't read well, and therefore don't think well, may not be able to handle the added responsibility. Reading turns out to be strongly connected to many of the most important skills in business—among them speech and writing, the primary forms of human communication. Management experts say that communicating often and clearly with workers will be among every manager's key skills in the coming years, while in an interconnected world, skillful communication outside one's company becomes steadily more important.

Managers at many companies know that the key to quality and productivity lies with empowered workers. Since 1982 Ford has given skills training to over 32,000 employees. One of the nation's leading publishers of educational materials, Simon & Schuster, anticipates selling $500 million per year in remedial reading and basic skill-building programs to industry. Quality and productivity leader Motorola spends millions annually to improve its workers' and managers' skills (Sherman, 1991). Company efforts to raise quality and productivity depend on committed workers who do not waste time, steal from their employers, withhold effort, use drugs and alcohol on the job, or resist needed change. The best efforts and millions of dollars in capital equipment cannot overcome such barriers. People are both the causes of and cures for most of a company's productivity and quality problems.

A poll published by the Gallup Organization and National Opinion Research Center asked workers this question: "Would you agree, strongly agree, disagree, or strongly disagree with the following: I am willing to work harder than I have to in order to help this organization succeed." The majority said yes: 52% agreed, 38% strongly agreed, 9% disagreed, and 1% strongly disagreed (Lublin, 1992).

Unions

Historically, labor unions have had little appreciation for plans and programs to make union members partners with managers. Many union leaders and members suspected that plans for process, product, and service improvements were simply schemes to get more work from members or reduce the number employed. Union leaders feared that agreeing to such plans would lead members to accuse them of selling out to management.

Unions thrived for decades by giving their members protection from arbitrary management actions, by winning ever-increasing raises (made possible by the fact that American firms had little real competition abroad), and by securing numerous job-security provisions. But the commercial environment of today demands that a business have the freedom to experiment and re-design, enlarge, or enrich workers' jobs. When markets call for short runs of specialized products, when demand is unpredictable, or when a company must change its organization and direction rapidly, old-style job definitions and work rules no longer apply. The shift to information-based and service-based jobs has cut into labor's ability to find new members. The loss of traditional manufacturing jobs and managers' willingness to hire permanent, nonunion workers during strikes have cut into membership rolls as well.

The MIT Commission on Industrial Productivity studied eight American industries for two years, beginning in 1986, to learn about their productivity and competitiveness. The commission made these recommendations regarding labor relations (Dertouzos, Lester, and Solow, 1990):

1. Break the traditional adversarial pattern of industrial relations, which produces low levels of productivity and quality.

2. Involve employees in shop-floor problem solving and in flexible teams that do away with traditional narrow job descriptions.

3. Enhance long-term trust and cooperation by including labor in strategic managerial decisions; to take part, labor must commit to building a more cooperative and flexible labor/management relationship.

4. Standardize the push for continuous improvement, investment in human resources, lifelong learning by employees, workers' involvement in problem solving, and cooperation with managers in designing and implementing long-term strategies.

Labor relations are improving in many companies, of course. Remember that at Whirlpool labor initially opposed changes to work rules. Now, however, workers wholeheartedly endorse the new ways.

Management

One of the most basic ways in which management can boost productivity is by providing the technology and equipment that employees need to do their jobs well. In 1991, U.S. businesses spent $529.2 billion on capital improvements—that is, improvements to plants, machinery, and equipment. According to the U.S. Department of Commerce, American businesses plan to spend $553.9 billion in 1992. As Spiers (1991) reported:

> The most compelling argument for decent equipment growth is the continued drive for productivity improvement. Business has clearly used the recession to target unit labor costs, which means not only laying people off but also lifting the output per hour of those remaining with efficient new machine tools and the like.

In 1989, for the first time, Japanese businesses outspent American businesses in capital improvements. Although the Japanese econony is half the size of the U.S. economy, Japanese businesses in effect paid for twice as many capital improvements as American enterprises. Japan's record-level spending for capital improvements has allowed it to reduce its spending slightly during the recession while America plays catch-up once again.

Ford Motor Company is spending $5 billion on a program to upgrade all the engines and transmissions it makes in North America. "Ford hopes the capital improvements will keep it a step ahead of Toyota. Specifically, Ford wants to make its new compacts to at least meet or beat the Toyota Camry" (Casey, 1992). The investments Ford has made in its plant in Batavia, Ohio, will make the facility more efficient, increasing production capacity to 550,000 four-speed transmissions per year. Ford invested in more than 400 machines, some with advanced computerized monitoring, to produce the transmissions. Part of the money being spent in Batavia will pay to teach hourly employees how to operate the new equipment. The education will help Ford start production faster and with fewer errors (Casey, 1992).

In areas other than capital investment, what contributions are American managers making to productivity? The MIT Commission on Industrial Productivity uncovered problems in this regard (Dertouzos, Lester, and Solow, 1990). Management, the study asserted, is using outdated strategies that focus on too short a time horizon. Furthermore, the study concluded, managers are not contributing sufficiently to technological or human resource development and they are guilty of failures of cooperation. The commission made the following recommendations to managers:

1. Put products and manufacturing processes ahead of finance.

2. Establish new measures of productive performance.

3. Focus on the effective use of technology in manufacturing.

4. Embrace product customization and production flexibility.

5. Innovate production processes.

In addition, the commission urged managers to focus on quality. Managers must measure current and future processes and progress, commit to delivering a quality product in a timely way at a competitive price, flatten the hierarchy, integrate functions, cooperate with suppliers, adopt the best practices, and understand foreign cultures (Dertouzos, Lester, and Solow, 1990). Implementing these suggestions is a worthy challenge.

Management That Promotes Productivity

This section will examine five key issues that contribute to improvements in productivity: top-level commitment, sound management practices, research and development, modern manufacturing, and time management.

Top-Level Commitment

As with quality improvements, commitment from those at the top of an organization is vital to starting to improve productivity and continuing the process. Strategic plans must build productivity improvement into the organization's culture and programs. Managers must assess their corporate culture and devise ways to change it to promote productivity. They must establish goals and mount strong, funded programs to reach them. CEOs must make a genuine personal commitment and be willing to oversee, now and in the future, the organization's push for productivity gains. The commitment begins with an appraisal of where the company is now. Managers must establish rigorous measurements along with coordinated controls. They must devise imaginative training programs to thoroughly prepare everyone for their roles. And efforts to improve productivity must be integrated with efforts to improve quality.

Sound Management Practices

Along with the tools and techniques already discussed throughout this text, management must focus on the long term. Managers must abandon two destructive practices: rewarding people for short-term performance and planning for one year rather than five. At the same time, managers need to drastically shorten time cycles for new-product development and new processes. In 1992 GM announced that it will change a production process to boost productivity. The company will reduce the number of basic vehicle frames it uses from 20 to 7. The large number of frames has hindered the company's efforts to reduce costs and the time it takes to bring new models online (Patterson, 1992). For similar reasons, Chrysler may drop its Plymouth nameplate after 1995.

Many managers have been able to boost productivity by reducing the number of suppliers to a trusted few—suppliers who share the company's vision of productivity and quality. In return for the suppliers' loyalty, the managers should prepare to stick by them in every suitable way. A surprising way to boost productivity is to forge links with competitors (horizontal partnerships that the Japanese call *keiretsu*). Such partnerships can shorten the time it takes to meet regulatory challenges and develop and adapt new technologies. "Horizontal groups provide security and stability to promote the risk-taking and long-term investment often shunned by U.S. companies. And by collaborating on research and production, *keiretsu* members regularly deliver new products ahead of lone-wolf rivals" (*Business Week,* January 27, 1992). Ford, GM, Chrysler, IBM, Microsoft, Apple, and Motorola are but a few companies that have forged alliances with competitors to create American versions of *keiretsu.*

Another way to improve productivity is to empower workers, create and fully utilize self-managing teams, and train and retrain employees to keep them growing and participating. CEO Gordon Forward of Chaparral Steel emphasized this approach to productivity. Forward dedicated himself and his company to three principles: Create a classless corporation, empower through universal education, and give employees freedom to act (Dumaine, 1992). Workers at Chaparral receive a salary and bonus based on individual performance, company profits, and skills learned. Workers are expected to take the initiative and do what has to be done. The company makes sure that at least 85% of its 950 employees are taking courses. The employees cross-train in such subjects as electronics and credit history. Sales, credit, shipping, and billing are in one place; everyone knows each others' jobs. This makes staying close to the customer a lot easier. Employees continue to generate money-saving ideas and display the motivation to succeed (Dumaine, 1992). Chaparral Steel is now the world's lowest-cost steel producer.

Learning can take place outside organizations as well as within. Managers must stay up-to-date about educational offerings outside their companies and, when needed, be instrumental in creating learning opportunities to explore new fields. In May 1992 a seminar for 1,500 managers and engineers focused on computer-integrated manufacturing. The sessions covered all aspects of how computer-run factories should work and what strategies managers need to run them. The seminar brought various specialists together and showed them how to integrate what they know with what others know and how to facilitate cooperation (Van, 1992). Such integration provides an important key to productivity and quality improvement.

Like many forward-looking companies, Motorola sponsors competitions among its teams. They compete in projects designed to raise quality, reduce production time, and improve efficiency. Each year the company showcases the teams' ideas and presents awards to those that created the best innovations (Van, 1991). Such competitions can be an excellent way to foster productivity and continuous improvement.

Research and Development

From research projects come new materials, machines, methods, technologies, and products. **Research and development** (**R&D**) consists of investing money and time to guarantee an organization's future. In 1990, American industry spent a total of $70 billion on R&D, up by about 7.5% from 1989. In 1991, American corporations spent $74 billion on R&D, up by about 7% from 1990 (*Business Week,* June 29, 1992).

As the Special Quality Issue of *Business Week* (1991, p. 170) reported, in times of tight money, R&D may suffer.

> As everything from drugs to cars gets more complex, the cost of R&D is soaring just as profits in many industries are falling. Companies are compensating by trying to make R&D more efficient, often by focusing their research on fewer areas, setting up joint ventures with erstwhile competitors—or both. At the same time, global competition is forcing companies to launch R&D centers abroad—both to snare foreign talent and to open new markets—and this is creating new management headaches.

Federal as well as state governments help America's R&D efforts by funding basic and applied research projects. The federal government funded research through American colleges and universities to the tune of nearly $15 billion in

Research and development
*is a company's investment in
its own future. Increasing
costs and reduced revenues,
however, have squeezed R&D
budgets and put pressure on
management to fund only
"sure bets" that will yield a
quick return on investment.*

1992, up from about $13 billion in 1991. From such research over the years have come the polio vaccine, nuclear fission, genetic engineering, the discovery of the relationship between chlorofluorocarbons (CFCs) and the destruction of the earth's ozone layer, and countless other technological innovations both good and problematic (*Chicago Tribune*, June 23, 1992). According to the federal Accounting Office, many foreign and domestic companies maintain financial links with universities. These links give the companies rights or licenses to use various R&D discoveries (*Chicago Tribune*, May 24, 1992).

Companies must build cultures that foster innovation and nourish creative people. Bell Atlantic has started a program to encourage creative employees to pursue innovative ideas (Dumaine, 1991).

> To spur new ideas, Bell Atlantic started what it calls its Champion Program. Any employee with a good idea may leave [his or] her regular job for a while, at full pay and benefits, and receive training in such skills as writing a business plan and organizing a development schedule while also receiving money to invest in the idea. The employee becomes the idea's champion, with a strong incentive to develop it, and can invest 10% of the revenues (subject to certain caps) if the product gets to market. Champion has generated two patents, with 11 more pending since Bell began the program in 1989. Ideas from program participants have led to a successful new device for trouble-shooting telephone switching problems and a phone small enough to fit in your ear.

Technology transfer is the key to converting laboratory discoveries into marketable products. Technology can be transferred quickly when researchers work side by side with product designers and manufacturing experts. At Hewlett-Packard, CEO Frank Carrubba spends most of his time in meetings that "bring his researchers into contact with one another and with the world outside" (Bylinsky, 1990). His researchers do R&D with a capital *R* and small *d;* his divisions do R&D with a small *r* and a capital *D.* Du Pont divides its research lab into "centers of excellence," each specializing in one technology. "Within each unit, scientists doing basic research work alongside product experts from the divisions" (Bylinsky, 1990). This collaboration has resulted in new products, such as a catalyst for producing a chlorofluorocarbon-like substance that does not destroy ozone.

Modern Manufacturing

The hallmarks of manufacturing as it is emerging around the world include:

- Direct links to customers and suppliers
- Flexible production lines capable not only of handling large or small runs of specialized products, but also, within minutes, of being reconfigured to produce another product
- Short cycle times
- Horizontal product, project, and process teams
- Just-in-time delivery of vital materials
- Cleanliness
- Decentralized pockets of highly skilled employees working with computer-guided machines
- An intense focus on efforts to improve quality and productivity in every process and operation

In addition, manufacturing facilities are becoming showrooms for outsiders and laboratories for insiders.

American producers and others are moving toward the latest in efficient and cost-effective manufacturing facilities. Chrysler Corporation has invested about $1 billion to build the Chrysler Technology Center (CTC), a twenty-first–century research and factory complex in Auburn Hills, Michigan. When the facility is completed in 1994, 7,000 designers, engineers, and others will perform research, build and test prototypes, try out new production techniques, and evaluate technologies of all sorts. The CTC includes an assembly plant to build and modify prototypes; a facility that can simulate the noise, vibration, and harshness of different road conditions; a facility that can simulate weather conditions; and a wind tunnel to test the aerodynamics of new models. The facility will also contain classrooms, lecture halls, and an auditorium. "By bringing all of its car people together, Chrysler hopes to improve creativity and communication while reducing the time it takes to move a vehicle from the drawing board to the showroom" (Nauman, 1992). No person will be more than a ten-minute walk from any other. Such proximity should allow engineers and production experts to solve problems quickly and easily. "Besides the increased productivity and more competitive products it hopes the CTC will facilitate, Chrysler thinks it has created a better place to work" (Nauman, 1992).

Banking on its all-new trio of LH models for 1993, Chrysler has invested $600 million to make certain that they are built well. The primary production facility for the line is in Brampton, Ontario. The Brampton plant employs 3,000

GLOBAL APPLICATIONS
Prizes for Quality

In **1951,** the Union of Japanese Scientists and Engineers created two prizes: the Deming Application Prize for companies, and the Deming Prize for individuals. Both prizes recognize achievements in quality control in Japan. Both bring great honor to those who win them, and many people compete for them rigorously. The competition enriches the competitors and the companies they work for, because the pursuit of quality brings about improvements.

A company that applies for the Deming Application Prize must conduct a total quality control audit. An audit is also performed by the experts on the Deming Application Prize Subcommittee, which rates the company as a whole and various units within the company. The subcommittee also rates the company's policies and objectives, education and training, quality control programs, and future plans.

In America, companies compete annually for the Malcolm Baldridge National Quality Award, which was created by an act of Congress in 1987. It is named in honor of the late U.S. Secretary of Commerce, and it is similar to Japan's prizes. The Baldridge examines the "seven pillars" of product and service quality: leadership, information and analysis, strategic quality planning, human resource development and management, quality and operational results, and customer focus and satisfaction.

In 1992, AT&T became the first company to win two Baldridge awards in one year. Its Universal Card Services division won in the service-sector category and its Transmission Systems unit won in the manufacturing sector. In describing the 1992 competition, a *Wall Street Journal* article reported:

> Seventeen of the 90 companies seeking Baldridge awards reached the competition's final stage, in which quality experts visit corporate facilities to follow up on lengthy written applications. Culminating the six-month review, a nine-member panel of independent judges recommends winners. But to gain Commerce Department approval, finalists must pass a background check to determine their suitability as corporate role models. ▲

For more about the Malcolm Baldridge National Quality Award, see Christopher W. L. Hart and Christopher E. Bogan, *The Baldridge: What It Is, How It's Won, How to Use It to Improve Quality in Your Company* (New York: McGraw-Hill), 1992; and Gilbert Fuchsberg, "AT&T Becomes First Company to Win Two Malcolm Baldridge Quality Awards," *Wall Street Journal,* October 15, 1992, p. C12.

---

workers. It relies on machine tools that can produce parts with closer tolerances than those found on the Nissan Maxima, Toyota Camry, or Ford Taurus. Among the facility's several innovative techniques is a new underbody assembly operation that uses 28 people and eliminates the need for them to work in awkward positions. "All underbody components, including the engine, transmission, rear suspension, fuel tank and exhaust system are installed on a metal pallet raised to the car's unibody structure. A machine automatically inserts 21 bolts to secure the components to the car and simultaneously fastens them. The pallet then is lowered to begin the process again" (*Chicago Tribune,* June 21, 1992). The plant has a new electrical testing setup to check on the functions of the electrical systems as they are being built. The staff at the plant includes a team that implements employees' ideas to boost efficiency. If a worker needs a modification of some kind, the change can be implemented quickly. The first 1,000 cars will go to Chrysler's Dollar and Thrifty car-rental fleets for testing. Chrysler managers plan to produce initial runs slowly, making certain that all the bugs are out (*Chicago Tribune,* June 21, 1992).

A truly modern factory can produce several products on the same assembly line at high speeds and for short runs, an approach called **flexible manufacturing**. In a flexible manufacturing system, the many parts of the factory are linked by computer so that they can respond quickly to changing needs. "The ultimate flexible factory could be programmed to roll out many different types of products, made on the same day to customer order, eliminating expensive inventories" (Neikirk, 1987). In addition to responding to individual customers, flexible computer-integrated manufacturing (CIM) equipment allows a manufacturer to respond rapidly to changes in the marketplace. A company that decides to move into CIM must "coordinate design and manufacturing functions to minimize the number of parts and labor needed to make a product." When IBM decided to make its own computer printers, engineers reduced the number of parts from 150 to 62. They lowered the number of parts for its typewriters from 3,000 to 1,000 and increased the reliability of both products by doing so. IBM's manufacturing facilities demonstrate another hallmark of flexible manufacturing—just-in-time delivery of parts (*New York Times,* January 11, 1987).

Time Management

In the world of business, time really *is* money. By reducing the time it takes to do anything, a firm becomes more productive. Companies that are close to their customers know that timely deliveries are crucial to maintaining good customer relations and to retaining customers. Warehousing and storage problems can be all but eliminated with carefully planned delivery schedules. The Walgreen Company maintains a computer-based inventory system called SIMS (strategic inventory management system) that tracks sales in each of its stores. Periodically the warehouse prepares an order to replace sold items. In six minutes (four times more quickly than before SIMS) the order is packed and ready for shipment. The items are stacked in the order that they will fill the shelves at the receiving outlet. Compared to the system SIMS replaced, the new system has saved Walgreen Company about $200 million (Ryan, 1991).

As information can be the key to timely delivery, it can also be the key to timely changes in production. Benetton, the Italian fashion company, links its retail outlets, warehouses, factories, and suppliers. "Information on hot-selling items and colors is available immediately and can be used to adjust production schedules to catch rapidly changing trends in the market." This kind of close-to-the-customer philosophy keeps Benetton competitive in both price and style (Clark, 1989).

Timeliness in decision making is as important as timely delivery and production. IBM has created software to streamline the decision-making process. The software allows people to respond simultaneously to any topic on an agenda. After trying the software, Ray Fletcher, general manager of information systems for Southern New England Telecommunications, said: "This system is four times as productive as [a conventional meeting] and takes much less time. That's almost as good as having no meetings at all" (Deutsch, 1990). The success of the electronic meetings lies in the fact that they encourage honesty from participants, who are anonymous. Electronic meetings provide an environment that supports a free flow of uninterrupted thought, and they produce a printed record of results.

Levi Strauss & Co. stays in touch with its retailers by using LeviLink, a computerized inventory control system. Such up-to-date information allows them to respond quickly to trends in the marketplace.

Throughput time is a term often used in discussions of timeliness. **Throughput time** is the "weighted average time through the process of all the units of a representative batch or order" (Schmenner, 1990). Doing things correctly from the beginning reduces throughput time. Managers can also shorten throughput times by ensuring an efficient flow of parts from suppliers and to workstations, applying corrections quickly, eliminating bottlenecks, and providing continual training to keep employees focused on operations (Schmenner, 1990).

Future Trends

The following trends in quality and productivity are quickly becoming apparent in American business and industry:

- Production by teams of workers and islands of automated equipment will continue to grow. These approaches are now being incorporated into clerical jobs.

- The drive to improve productivity and quality in the service sector will soon receive as much interest as improving quality and productivity in the manufacturing sector.

- Look for increases in worker-training budgets in nearly every industry. As more businesses commit to TQM and productivity improvement, managers quickly realize the need to train workers and continue training them—in every level of the company.

- Trends toward downsizing and outsourcing will continue, but the exportation of jobs to lower labor costs will decrease. Wage gaps are narrowing very quickly around the world. Distribution times and quality will determine where outsourcing will take place.

- More American companies will apply for the Malcolm Baldridge Award, which is taking on the importance it deserves in terms of how it can enhance a company's image.

CHAPTER SUMMARY

- Quality must be measured in terms of standards. Standards should be developed according to criteria established by internal and external users and customers.

- Quality affects productivity. Both affect profitability. The drive for any one of the three must not interfere with the drive for the others. Efforts at improvement need to be coordinated and integrated. The real cost of quality is the cost of avoiding non-conformance and failure. Another cost is that associated with poor quality—of losing customers and wasting resources.

- The improvement of quality and productivity involves processes that never end.

- To implement a strategy of continuous improvement, companies need a commitment from everyone, at every level. Without the total commitment and supervision of top management, efforts to improve quality and productivity will fail.

- Committing to total quality management and productivity improvement means committing to change in an organization's culture.

- Without strong partnerships between insiders and outsiders, efforts at improvement will not work.

- Government, individuals, unions, and management affect efforts at improving productivity and quality. All need to be committed to the efforts.

- Companies can improve productivity by securing the commitment of top-level managers, implementing sound management practices, using R&D effectively, adopting modern manufacturing techniques, and improving time management.

SKILL-BUILDING

The following statements are designed to explore your understanding of total quality management.

	Agree	Disagree
1. When something goes wrong, it is best for managers to determine who was at fault.	☐	☐
2. Quality may be defined as excellent, good, fair, or poor for a product or service.	☐	☐

	Agree	Disagree
3. A manager concerned about quality in his or her department should develop a departmental program for improvement.	☐	☐
4. TQM relies heavily on trained, skilled inspectors operating from a central location.	☐	☐
5. When things go wrong, workers' attitudes are usually at fault.	☐	☐
6. One measure of the quality of a process is its ability to satisfy customer requirements.	☐	☐
7. With TQM, achieving quality standards is the most important goal.	☐	☐
8. TQM requires a never-ending search for a better way.	☐	☐
9. When an organization commits itself to TQM, it will improve its productivity.	☐	☐
10. TQM requires a one-step-at-a-time approach.	☐	☐

Answers: 1. D; 2. D; 3. D; 4. D; 5. D; 6. A; 7. D; 8. A; 9. A; 10. D

R E V I E W   Q U E S T I O N S

1. Review this chapter's essential terms and look up the meanings of those you cannot define.

2. In what ways are quality, productivity, and profitability linked?

3. This chapter discussed the work of Radford, Shewhart, Deming, Juran, Feigenbaum, Crosby, and Peters. What did each contribute to the philosophy of total quality management?

4. Why does successful implementation of a TQM program depend on commitment from everyone in an organization?

5. What three kinds of partnerships are needed to make TQM successful?

6. In what three ways can the federal government affect productivity in America?

7. What are three ways in which individuals can affect an organization's drive to improve productivity?

8. What are three ways in which top managers can affect the productivity of their organization?

9. How are efforts at research and development linked to productivity improvement?

R E C O M M E N D E D   **R** E A D I N G

Albrecht, Karl, and Ron Zemke. *Service America!* (New York: Warner), 1985.

Belcher, Jr., John G. *Productivity Plus* (Houston: Gulf Publishing), 1987.

Berry, Leonard L. "Five Imperatives for Improving Service Quality," *Sloan Management Review* (Summer 1990), pp. 29–38.

Burt, David N. "Managing Suppliers Up to Speed," *Harvard Business Review* (July–August 1989), pp. 127–135.

Crosby, Philip B. *Quality Is Free: The Art of Making Quality Certain* (New York: Mentor), 1979.

Hart, Christopher W. L., and Christopher E. Bogan. *The Baldridge: What It Is, How It's Won, How to Use It to Improve Quality in Your Company* (New York: McGraw-Hill), 1992.

Hunt, Daniel V. *Quality in America* (Homewood, IL: Business One Irwin), 1992.

Juran, Joseph M. *Juran on Planning for Quality* (New York: Free Press), 1988.

Pirsig, Robert. *Zen and the Art of Motorcycle Maintenance* (New York: Morrow), 1974.

Walton, Mary. *Deming Management at Work* (New York: Putnam), 1990.

Wilham, Sandy. *Forging the Productivity Partnership* (New York: McGraw-Hill), 1990.

R E F E R E N C E S

Altany, David. "The Race with No Finish Line," *Industry Week* (January 8, 1990), pp. 105–106.

Barry, Thomas J. *Management Excellence Through Quality* (Milwaukee: ASQC Press), 1991, pp. ix, 3, 7, 19.

Belcher, Jr., John G. *Productivity Plus* (Houston: Gulf Publishing), 1987, pp. 3, 27.

Business Week (January 27, 1992). "Learning from Japan," p. 54.

Business Week (October 22, 1990). "A New Era for Auto Quality," pp. 88–89.

Business Week (June 29, 1992). "On a Clear Day You Can See Progress," p. 104.

Business Week (Special Quality Issue 1991). "A QFD Snapshot," pp. 22–23.

Business Week (Special Quality Issue 1991). "A Tighter Focus for R&D," p. 170.

Bylinsky, Gene. "Turning R&D into Real Products," *Fortune* (July 2, 1990), pp. 73, 74.

Casey, Mike. "Ford Emphasizing 4 on (Plant) Floor," *Chicago Tribune,* May 10, 1992, sec. 17, p. 9.

Chew, W. Bruce. "No-Nonsense Guide to Measuring Productivity," *Harvard Business Review* (January–February 1988), pp. 114, 115, 118.

Chicago Tribune (June 21, 1992). "Chrysler Gives Its New Trio of LH Cars Everything It's Got," sec. 17, p. 16.

Chicago Tribune (May 24, 1992). "GAO: Tax-Paid Research Going to Businesses," sec. 1, p. 6.

Chicago Tribune (June 23, 1992). "Universities Put Teaching in Back Seat," sec. 1, p. 1.

Chicago Tribune (June 5, 1992). "Workers Lack Three R's, Hurting Small Firms, Study Says," sec. 3, p. 3.

Chipello, Christopher J., and Urban C. Lehner. "Miyazawa Calls U.S. Work Ethic Lacking," *Wall Street Journal,* February 4, 1992, p. A10.

Clark, Kim B. "What Strategy Can Do for Technology," *Harvard Business Review* (November–December 1989), p. 98.

Crosby, Philip B. *Quality Is Free: The Art of Making Quality Certain* (New York: Mentor), 1979, pp. 11, 15, 17, 39, 80, 112–113.

Crosby, Philip B. *Quality Without Tears* (New York: Plume), 1984, pp. 59, 99–100, 106–107.

Davis, Bob, and Dana Milbank. "If the U.S. Work Ethic Is Fading, 'Laziness' May Not Be the Reason," *Wall Street Journal,* February 7, 1992, pp. A1, A5.

Deming, W. Edwards. *Out of the Crisis* (Cambridge, MA: Massachusetts Institute of Technology, Center for Advanced Engineering Study), 1986, pp. 167–168, 169.

Dertouzos, Michael L.; Richard K. Lester; and Robert M. Solow. *Made in America: Regaining the Productive Edge* (New York: Harper Perennial), 1990, pp. 44, 99, 132–134, 148–150, 151.

Deutsch, Claudia H. "Business Meetings by Keyboard," *New York Times,* October 21, 1990, sec. F, p. 25.

Drucker, Peter F. "The New Productivity Challenge," *Harvard Business Review* (November–December 1991), p. 69.

Dumaine, Briane. "Closing the Innovation Gap," *Fortune* (December 2, 1991), pp. 61–62.

Dumaine, Briane. "Unleash Workers and Cut Costs," *Fortune* (May 18, 1992), p. 88.

Feigenbaum, Armand V. "Total Quality Control," *Harvard Business Review* (November–December 1956), pp. 95–98.

Fuchsberg, Gilbert. "'Total Quality' Is Termed Only Partial Success," *Wall Street Journal,* October 1, 1992, pp. B1, B7.

Gabor, Andrea. *The Man Who Discovered Quality* (New York: Penguin), 1990, pp. 47–48, 126–127.

Garvin, David A. *Managing Quality: The Strategic and Competitive Edge* (New York: Free Press), 1988, p. 5.

Hart, Christopher W. L., and Christopher E. Bogan. *The Baldridge: What It Is, How It's Won, How to Use It to Improve Quality in Your Company* (New York: McGraw-Hill), 1992, pp. 5, 8, 77, 96, 128–130.

Hunt, Daniel V. *Quality in America* (Homewood, IL: Business One Irwin), 1992, pp. 23, 43, 64–70, 74, 76, 268–269, 286.

Ishikawa, Kaoru. *What Is Total Quality Control?* David J. Lu, translator (Englewood Cliffs, NJ: Prentice-Hall), 1985, pp. 44, 45, 98, 125–128, 186.

Johnson, Ross, and William O. Winchell. *Management and Quality* (Milwaukee: ASQC Press), 1989.

Juran, Joseph M. *Juran on Planning for Quality* (New York: Free Press), 1988, pp. 4–5, 268, 269–270.

Kupfer, Andrew. "How American Industry Stacks Up," *Fortune* (March 9, 1992), pp. 32, 71.

Labich, Kenneth. "What Our Kids Must Learn," *Fortune* (January 27, 1992), p. 64.

Levine, Jonathan B. "It's an Old World in More Ways Than One," *Business Week* (Special Quality Issue 1991), p. 26.

Lublin, Joann S. "Trying to Increase Worker Productivity, More Employers Alter Management Style," *Wall Street Journal,* February 13, 1992, p. B1.

Nauman, Matt. "Next Generation of Automaking Under One Roof," *Chicago Tribune,* May 10, 1992, sec. 17, p. 5.

Neikirk, William. "U.S. Manufacturers Wary of Automation," *Chicago Tribune,* July 5, 1987, sec. 1, pp. 1, 14.

New York Times (January 11, 1987). "Revving Up the American Factory," sec. 3, p. 1.

Patterson, Gregory A. "GM to Cut Number of Vehicle Frames to Seven from 20," *Wall Street Journal,* May 15, 1992, p. A2.

Petersen, Donald E., and John Hillkirk. *A Better Idea: Redefining the Way Americans Work* (Boston: Houghton Mifflin), 1991, pp. 6–7, 8, 9–11.

Ryan, Nancy. "Simplicity Is Walgreen's Cure for the 1990s," *Chicago Tribune,* January 21, 1991, sec. 17, p. 3.

Saddler, Jeanne. "Small Businesses Complain That Jungle of Regulations Threatens Their Futures," *Wall Street Journal,* June 11, 1992, p. B1.

Schmenner, Roger W. "The Merit of Making Things Fast," *The Best of MIT's Sloan Management Review* (1990), p. 30.

Sherman, Stratford P. "America Won't Win Till It Reads More," *Fortune* (November 18, 1991), p. 202.

Shewhart, Walter A. *Statistical Method from the Viewpoint of Quality Control* (Washington, DC: Graduate School of the Department of Agriculture), 1939, pp. 2–4.

Spiers, Joseph. "Do Americans Pay Enough Taxes?" *Fortune* (June 1, 1992), p. 67.

Spiers, Joseph. "Equipment Spending Is Up," *Fortune* (December 6, 1991), pp. 21, 24.

Townsend, Patrick L., and Joan E. Gebhardt. *Quality in Action* (New York: Wiley), 1992, p. 17.

Van, Jon. "Competition in Syllabus at Engineers, Short Course," *Chicago Tribune,* May 19, 1992, sec. 3, pp. 1, 6.

Van, Jon. "Firms Tool Up with Information," *Chicago Tribune,* November 5, 1991, sec. 1, p. 12.

Wall Street Journal (April 13, 1992). "The Outlook: Huge Private Debts Will Slow Recovery," p. A1.

Walton, Mary. *The Deming Management Method at Work* (New York: Perigee), 1986, pp. 19–20, 25–26, 72.

Warner, David. "How Do Federal Rules Affect You?" *Nation's Business* (May 1992), p. 56.

G L O S S A R Y   O F   T E R M S

benchmark A standard by which something can be measured or judged; the level to match or exceed in design, manufacture, performance, and service.

continuous-improvement process (CIP) The ongoing search for incremental betterment. The Japanese term for continuous-improvement process is *kaizen.*

flexible manufacturing An approach to manufacturing that includes high-speed assembly lines that can produce several different products.

kaizen *See* continuous-improvement process.

process improvement team A group assigned to cooperatively assess a process and make it better.

productivity   The relationship between the amount of input needed to produce a given amount of output and the output itself. Productivity is usually expressed as a ratio.

project improvement team   A group engaged in executing a project; the purpose of the team is to make the project better.

quality   The totality of features and characteristics of a product, service, process, or project that bear on its ability to satisfy stated or implied goals or requirements of producers and users of the outcomes.

quality audit   A determination of how well customer or consumer requirements are being met by an organization, product, service, or process. A quality audit includes implementation of corrections.

quality circle   A small group of employees who meet as volunteers to improve their unit's processes, products, and services.

quality control (QC)   An economical system of production that produces quality goods or services meeting the requirements of customers. Quality control employs statistical measures and methods and is often called statistical quality control (SQC).

quality control audit   A check of quality control efforts that asks two questions: How are we doing? and What are the problems?

quality function deployment (QFD)   A disciplined approach to solving problems of quality before the design phase of a product; research discovers and ranks customer needs to be translated into design specifications.

quality improvement team   A team composed of people from all functional areas of a company who meet regularly to assess progress toward goals, identify and work to solve common problems, and cooperate to plan for the future.

research and development (R&D)   The investment of resources to guarantee an organization's future through the discovery or acquisition of processes, materials, or products to be used in the short and long term.

statistical process control (SPC)   The use of statistical tools and methods to measure and predict variations. Statistical process control establishes boundaries to determine if a process is in control (predictable) or out of control (unpredictable).

statistical quality control (SQC)   The use of statistical tools and methods to determine the quality of a product or service.

throughput time   The weighted average time of all the parts of a process that produces a representative batch or order.

total quality management (TQM)   A strategy for continuously improving performance at every level and in all areas of responsibility throughout an organization.

CASE PROBLEM
Roger Staubach, Quality in Action

Roger Staubach is a Heisman Trophy winner. When he was quarterback for the Dallas Cowboys, he led the team to four National Football Conference championships and two Super Bowl victories. The former football star has brought the dedication that he learned in sports to his real estate business—and he is winning there, too.

Staubach started learning the real estate business before he retired from sports. During his off-seasons, Staubach worked for a large real estate firm in Dallas, moving from one department to another to learn the business. In 1982 he formed his own real estate consulting and service business. His company helps clients plan, acquire, lease, and finance real estate ventures.

Staubach's firm specializes in representing tenants only. He had a rough start but soon established a reputation for integrity and hard work. One client was so impressed that he went to work for Staubach. He is now president and chief operating officer of The Staubach Company, and he oversees total quality management at the 11 offices of the firm.

Staubach knew that the desire for commissions could interfere with a TQM effort. He implemented a new system in which the client, not the pay, would be the first concern and responsibility of employees. His system was unique in the real estate business. "Under the plan, employees are paid an annual salary plus a bonus geared largely to client satisfaction as measured through the use of a formal survey procedure." Employees work in teams of specialists designed to handle any client problem. Staubach began to survey his 200 customers' needs, recognizing that by doing so he would be exercising a fundamental principle of TQM: Stay close to the customer. Like other managers committed to TQM, Staubach watches the money and sets the example for his employees. "I fly first class, but I buy my own upgrades, and I stay in the most reasonable hotels."

A cornerstone of The Staubach Company's TQM effort is what he calls the "Double EE Standard of Excellence." This means exceeding customer expectations through high levels of excellence and ethical behavior. He issues his customers a "guarantee of quality" that gives the customer the right to reduce agreed-upon fees if the customer is not satisfied. Since offering his guarantee in 1983, only one client has requested a reduction. The chief of quality at The Staubach Company says, "You can never get enough quality. It's something you have to keep working on each and every day."

QUESTIONS

1. As an employee on a Staubach team, how would you like the compensation system?

2. What partnerships has Staubach formed in his TQM effort?

3. Do you think that The Staubach Company will achieve TQM? Why?

For more about Staubach's operation, see Albert G. Holzinger, "How to Succeed by Really Trying," *Nation's Business,* August 1992, pp. 50–51.

18

Operations Management

LEARNING OBJECTIVES

After reading and discussing this chapter, you should be able to:

- Define this chapter's essential terms
- Discuss the nature and importance of operations strategy and operations management
- Discuss the nature and importance of product and service design planning
- Describe the four main strategies for facility layout
- Discuss the nature of process and technology planning
- Explain the factors in facility location planning and capacity planning
- Describe the role of operations control in achieving quality and productivity
- Discuss the purpose of design controls
- Discuss the importance of managing and controlling materials purchasing
- Explain how EOQ, MRP, MRPII, and JIT differ
- Discuss the importance and methods of schedule controls
- Describe the importance and methods of product control

acceptance sampling
aggregate planning
capacity planning
cellular layout
computer-aided design (CAD)
computer-aided
    manufacturing (CAM)
computer-integrated
    manufacturing (CIM)

control sampling
critical path
design control
design for manufacturability
    and assembly (DFMA)
detailed inspection and tests
economic order quantity
    (EOQ)
facilities layout
finished-goods inventory
fixed-position layout

flexible manufacturing system
    (FMS)
Gantt chart
inventory
just-in-time (JIT) inventory
    system
manufacturing resource
    planning (MRPII)
master schedule
materials requirement
    planning (MRP)
network scheduling

operations management
operations strategy
program evaluation and
    review technique (PERT)
process layout
product control
production layout
purchasing
qualification testing
raw materials inventory
reorder point (ROP)
robotics
work-in-process inventory

M A N A G E M E N T ▪ I N ▪ A C T I O N
Allen-Bradley's Factory of the Future

Allen-Bradley's new manufacturing center in Milwaukee says as much about the company's devotion to customer satisfaction as it does about the company's mastery of computer-integrated manufacturing (CIM). "This is not another CIM facility," states Glenn Eggert, vice president of operations for Allen-Bradley's Industrial Control Group. "This is a capability—a capability to get customized benefits within a mass-production structure. It allows us to provide quality products in a cost-effective way."

The 27,500-square-foot factory is a technological masterpiece that transforms ideas into reality. The facility, which cost $9.5 million, embodies Allen-Bradley's Electronic Manufacturing Strategy, or EMS1. The strategy was designed to

High-tech manufacturing of a high-tech product allows Allen-Bradley to respond to customer needs with cost-effective quality.

help the company get more solid-state products to market more quickly while not compromising the company's philosophy of putting the customer first.

EMS1 has resulted in construction of what many experts believe is the best manufacturing process to date. Using a continuous-flow assembly line, the facility can automatically assemble six or more different types of circuit boards on a single integrated line. This capability is unequaled in the industry. Boards can be produced in lots as small as one, and as many as 10 different types of circuit boards can be in production at one time. Currently, the facility turns out more than one thousand panels in a 40-hour workweek. Those panels may contain more than five hundred thousand integrated circuits, resistors, capacitors, memory chips, and other electronic components.

That's not all. The plant can move the panels with incredible efficiency. A conveyor system can carry each panel through all the process options, including surface mounting, robotics assembly, and soldering. Or, a panel can bypass a process that is inappropriate. In addition, Allen-Bradley has incorporated in-line testing to keep defective products out of customers' hands.

Allen-Bradley has staffed the operation with four self-directed EMS1 work teams. The teams are composed of enthusiastic veteran employees who trained under the direction of EMS1 managers and instructors from the Milwaukee School of Engineering.

Already the advantages of EMS1 have made the system a standout in manufacturing. Production reports note that EMS1 has reduced total product-introduction time "from as long as three years to as little as five months." Also, a circuit board can move through the operation in as little as one day. It took a board weeks to move through the previous operation, a manual batch-assembly process. ▲

For more about the factory of the future, see Joseph F. McKenna, "Not a Facility, But a Capability," *Industry Week,* June 15, 1992, pp. 60–61.

The Nature of Operations Management

The Management in Action feature that begins this chapter shows how Allen-Bradley is refining and restructuring its technology to gain the upper hand in the marketplace. The many companies that are making these changes have discovered that strategic success relates directly to the efficiency and responsiveness of their production operations (Morley, 1992). In turn, these companies are going on the offensive by using their operations management strategies (strategies such as Allen-Bradley's EMS1) as competitive weapons to change the way they develop products and services.

Innovative managers do not just manage people; they also manage the technical resources and processes associated with the production of goods and services. This chapter is devoted to a discussion of the processes, decisions, and systems involved in manufacturing and service operations. After defining operations management, the chapter will examine how companies plan operations. The second part of the chapter will examine operations control.

Operations Strategy and Management Defined

Operations strategy is the part of the strategic plan that defines the role, capabilities, and expectations for operations. **Operations management** consists of the managerial activities and techniques used to convert resources (such as raw materials and labor) into products and services (Adam and Ebert, 1989). The terms *production* and *operations* are commonly applied to manufacturing processes. It is important to remember, however, that operations management applies to all organizations, not just manufacturers.

Every organization produces something. Companies such as Allen-Bradley, Caterpillar, and Nike produce physical goods. On the other hand, Sheraton Hotels,

Exhibit 18.1

The flow of operations.

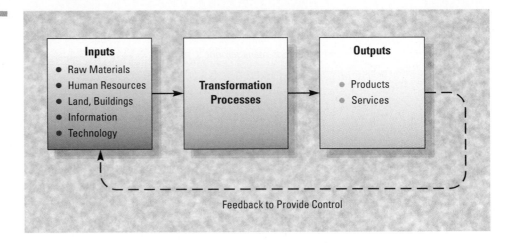

Trans World Airlines, and the University of Michigan produce services. Organizations that produce goods and those that produce services encounter similar operational problems:

- Each is concerned with converting resources into something saleable.

- Each must acquire materials or supplies to achieve that conversion.

- Each must schedule the process of conversion.

- Each must control processes and ensure quality.

With these similarities in mind, examine Exhibit 18.1, which illustrates the flow of operations. Notice that every organization takes inputs and transforms them into outputs, either products or services.

The Importance of Operations Management

The heart of an organization is its production of saleable goods or services. Some managers, such as those at Allen-Bradley, have discovered that the success of their companies is directly related to the effectiveness of their operations system. In addition, managers now realize that when developing strategic plans, they must include a component that consists of operations strategy. Without effective operations strategy and management, few organizations would survive (Adam and Swamidass, 1989).

No matter the company, the goal is to squeeze the bottom line for more profits. Managers cannot increase profits if operations management is left out of strategic planning or if the goal of operations is simply to keep pace with the industry. Operations management must be viewed as a competitive weapon to be used with marketing and finance. In this capacity the process of operations management often leads to new strategic concepts (Hayes and Wheelwright, 1984). The results can be lower prices or better quality, performance, or responsiveness to consumer demand. When operations management receives proper emphasis, marketing and financial strategies are not the only tools of competition (Hill, 1985).

Exhibit 18.2

The role of operations strategy and operations management.

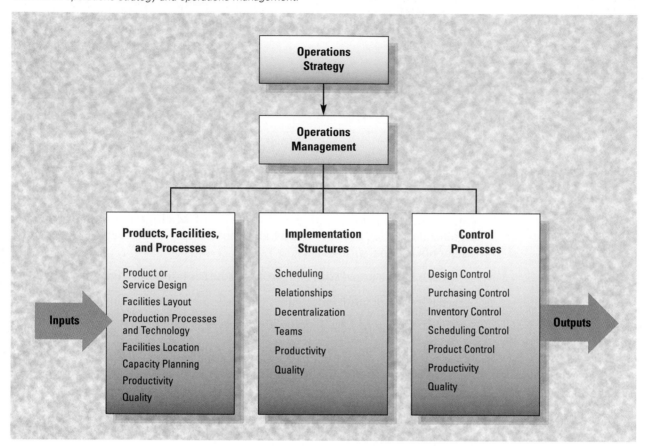

Exhibit 18.2 illustrates the pervasive role that operations management plays in an organization. Note that operations management embraces product, facility, and process design; implementation structures; and control processes. In all areas of operations management, the focus is on improving productivity and quality.

Operations Planning

The starting point of any undertaking is planning. In the case of an organization's operations, the planning stage involves decisions about product or service design, facilities layout, production processes and technology, facilities location, and capacity planning.

Product or Service Design

Historically, product and service design planning has not been acknowledged as part of operations management. Managers have discovered, however, that the

Organizational planning, the best way to start a successful venture, involves decisions about product or service design, facilities layout, production processes and technology, facilities location, and capacity planning.

goals of operations management (competitiveness, response time, and production efficiency) are well served by a design concept called **design for manufacturability and assembly (DFMA)**. This concept involves designing products for effective performance while considering how they will be manufactured and assembled.

In the past, many product engineers designed with a lack of thought—some would even say with disdain—for product manufacture and assembly. Product engineers handed finished designs to manufacturing engineers. More often than not, the products the designs specified could not be assembled easily and, during production, they had to be inspected for quality. The design-centered approach also led to products that contained a greater number of parts than necessary.

DFMA calls for design by teams consisting of designers, manufacturers, and assemblers. Because these specialists have a say in product design, actual production of the product becomes more efficient. At Westinghouse's Thermo King, product-design teams include engineering, marketing, and manufacturing personnel (Morley, 1992). General Motors used the DFMA approach to produce the Buick Le Sabre. The design teams included process and product engineers, financial experts, marketing people, inside and outside suppliers, and operators from the assembly center at Buick City in Flint, Michigan. The result of the teams' work: The new Le Sabre contains 40% fewer parts and takes 20% less time to assemble than the old model. As a GM manager observed (Moskal, 1992):

> We now have a much more effective functional execution of car building. It makes engineering more effective. It makes materials management more effective and the assembly center more effective. That is because we are using the total technical voice of the division plus the knowledge of outside suppliers.

Quality	Excellence of the car, including serviceability
Reliability	The degree to which the car fulfills its intended purpose
Durability	The degree to which the car withstands performance demands
Mass	The total weight of the car
Safety	The degree to which the car increases the protection of occupants
Manufacturability	The degree to which the car can be manufactured and assembled within existing operational capacity
Time to market	The time from product design until the car is ready for sale to the consumer
Total cost	The total amount of materials, labor, transportation, design, and overhaul expenses associated with the design

DFMA product design involves four criteria: producibility, cost, quality, and reliability. Producibility is the degree to which the product or service can be manufactured for the customer within the organization's operational capacity. The criteria of cost includes the costs of labor, materials, design, overhead, and transportation. Quality, in the eyes of the producer, is the excellence of the product or service. In the eyes of the consumer, quality is the serviceability and value gained by purchasing the product. Reliability is the degree to which customers can count on the product or service to fulfill its intended purpose. Exhibit 18.3 summarizes the eight major benefits of the DFMA approach, against which designs are evaluated at General Motors. (Notice that the last three relate to operations.) At General Motors, these benefits serve as the basis for evaluating all new designs.

Auto makers are not the only companies using DFMA. At Federal Express and UPS, service-design decisions are now made by teams that include members from materials handling, transportation, computer services, and customer service. The results of DFMA include fewer questions when the service begins and fewer modifications after the service has been implemented for a while (Brown, 1992).

The criteria of producibility, cost, quality, and reliability should apply to the design of services as well as to the design of products. In addition, service design calls for another criterion: timing. This criterion relates to the customer's requirements for timeliness. At Federal Express, the customer wants the package the next day, not two days later.

Facilities Layout

After design, the next step in operations management is to plan the actual production. This involves, among other things, determining the **facilities layout**—the physical arrangement of equipment at the manufacturing site and how the work will flow. There are four main types of layouts to choose from: process, production, cellular, and fixed position. Exhibit 18.4 illustrates these four options.

Exhibit 18.4

The four options of facilites layout.

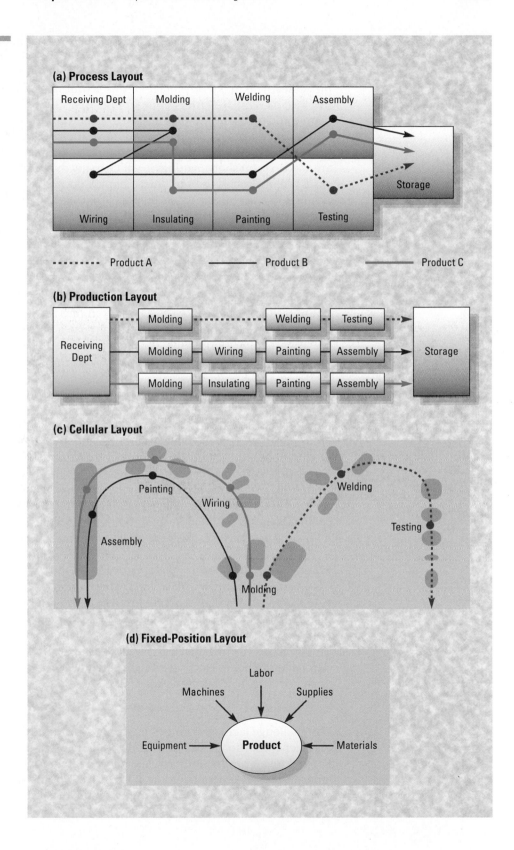

(a) Process Layout

Receiving Dept	Molding	Welding	Assembly

Wiring　　Insulating　　Painting　　Testing

Storage

- - - - - - - - Product A ———— Product B ———— Product C

(b) Production Layout

Receiving Dept → Molding → Welding → Testing → Storage

Molding → Wiring → Painting → Assembly

Molding → Insulating → Painting → Assembly

(c) Cellular Layout

Painting　Wiring　Welding　Testing　Assembly　Molding

(d) Fixed-Position Layout

Machines　Labor　Supplies

Equipment → **Product** ← Materials

Process Layout   In a **process layout**, all the equipment or machines that perform a similar task or function are placed together (see Exhibit 18.4a). A product is moved from process to process as needed—all products may not require all processes. The major advantage of this layout is its potential for reducing costs. Because all similar work is done in one area, the process layout requires fewer people and pieces of equipment than a decentralized arrangement. One limitation of the process layout is the need to move the product through several different processes. Each move costs time and money. In manufacturing, process layouts are used in print shops, settings in which many different products (such as business cards, color brochures, and bound books) do not require the same processes. A hospital is a service-oriented business that uses a process layout. The layout is appropriate because patients receive many different types of services.

Production Layout   In a **production layout**, machines and tasks are arranged according to the progressive steps by which the product is made (see Exhibit 18.4b). This layout is efficient when the business produces large volumes of identical products. Car manufacturing on an assembly line is perhaps the best-known example of a production layout. Other examples include computer manufacturing and appliance assembly. A hospital might use a production layout when doctors are undertaking a large-scale vaccination effort, for example. In this case, many patients moved through a line, each receiving the same treatment.

Cellular Layout   The **cellular layout** combines some of the characteristics of process and production layouts. In a cellular arrangement, all the equipment required for a sequence of operations on the same product is placed together in a group called a cell (see Exhibit 18.4c). The cellular groupings allow efficient handling of materials, tools, and inventory. In addition, the cellular layout facilitates teamwork; workers are physically close enough to work together to solve problems (Daft, 1991). A recent survey of manufacturers indicated that in the next five years, the use of the cellular layout will double (Miller, 1992). In service settings, the cellular layout is used where many workers, as teams, see to the needs of a group. A hospital ward is an example of a cellular layout.

Fixed-Position Layout   Exhibit 18.4d also shows a **fixed-position layout**. It is used when, because of size or bulk, the product remains in one location. Tools, equipment, and human skills are brought to the product. Organizations that build planes and ships use this form of layout. The fixed-position approach is sound for bulky products and custom-ordered goods, but not for high-volume manufacturing. This type of layout is used in a hospital operating room, where a number of specialists gather to work on a single patient.

Production Processes and Technology

The challenge facing operations managers is to identify the proper blend of people and technology to use in transforming inputs into finished products and services. For any given production task, several conversion methods are available—some labor intensive, others equipment intensive. The nature of the product, and the objectives and resources of the organization, are critical factors in choosing one method over another.

A fixed-position layout, *where resources are brought to bear at the product location, is appropriate for large projects like those assembled at Boeing, the world's largest manufacturer of commercial jetliners.*

The growing trend today is toward the use of sophisticated technology in manufacturing. This type of manufacturing—associated with the "factory of the future"—relies increasingly on equipment that works almost unaided by employees. The technologies most responsible for revolutionizing manufacturing processes include robotics, CAD/CAM, flexible manufacturing systems, and computer-integrated manufacturing.

Robotics The use of programmed machines to handle production constitutes **robotics.** The machines, or robots, are constructed to do the work of employees. They weld, deliver materials and parts, load and unload, and more. Robots provide greater precision than humans; therefore, they enhance quality. The disadvantages of robots include capital expenditures, maintenance costs, and malfunctions. Apple Computer has been one of the leading organizations in robotics experimentation and implementation. At the Apple plant in Cupertino, California, robots place parts into inventory as well as retrieve parts for use in manufacturing.

CAD/CAM Among the most widely adopted technologies in manufacturing today are **computer-aided design** (**CAD**) and **computer-aided manufacturing** (**CAM**). A survey of manufacturers revealed that 50% employ CAD and 26% use CAM (Miller, 1992). CAD allows engineers to develop new products by using a computer monitor to display and manipulate three-dimensional drawings. The assistance of the computer has helped some engineers cut design time in half. In addition, the CAD system allows the engineers to visualize the effects of a design change. Some of the companies that use CAD are Rockwell International, GE, and New Balance (a manufacturer of athletic shoes). The design engineers at New Balance use CAD to simulate stress on a jogging shoe. By seeing the effects of

Robotics *have taken over many of the most tedious or hazardous tasks in auto manufacturing. As well as welding and painting, the robotic arm can perform more delicate operations like assembling brake shoes.*

stress, the engineers can design a shoe that withstands it. Prior to using CAD, each new shoe design had to be built before it could be tested.

CAM involves the use of computers to guide and control manufacturing processes. The computer is programmed to direct a piece of equipment to perform a certain action, such as drilling holes or pouring steel. Compared with human control, computer control results in less waste, lower costs, higher quality, and improved safety. Chaparral Steel uses CAM throughout manufacturing. Computers monitor the temperature of liquid steel, make adjustments to each batch, control the pouring of the molten metal, and direct the cutting of rods and bars (Dincen, 1992).

Flexible Manufacturing Systems   A flexible manufacturing system (FMS) is an automated production line. The machinery is coordinated by computers. The automated line controls assembly, welding, tightening, and adjusting. In addition, an FMS allows rapid adjustment of the assembly process, so the production line can produce more than one model. General Motors is installing an FMS at its plant in Lordstown, Ohio. At the plant, GM will be able to mass-produce four different car models (Treece, 1992).

An FMS automates the entire production line by controlling and providing instructions to all the machines. The greatest advantage of an FMS is that through computer instructions, the system can be adapted to produce a different product. (The adaptability of an FMS is the characteristic that distinguishes it from CAM.) The computer instructs the machines to change parts, machine specifications, and tools.

Computer-Integrated Manufacturing   Originally, computer-integrated manufacturing meant controlling production machinery through a system of interconnected computers. Such a system was supposed to make human labor unnecessary. Today, however, **computer-integrated manufacturing** (**CIM**) is a computerized system that orchestrates people, information, and processes to produce quality outputs efficiently. Allen-Bradley's EMS1 program, discussed in this chapter's Management in Action feature, is a CIM operation that involves automation and team concepts.

A recent survey asked manufacturing executives to rank the benefits of CIM. More than 50% cited lower manufacturing costs as the primary benefit. The next most frequent answers included flexibility (48%), responsiveness to the market (43%), production control (42%), and higher quality (41%) (Sheridan, 1992).

Computers and the Delivery of Services Computers have revolutionized delivery as well as manufacturing. The widespread access to information that computers provide has allowed businesses to improve the quality of customer service. For example, computerized point-of-sale terminals constantly update inventory records; the up-to-date records facilitate rapid response to customers' needs. At Schneider National, a major trucking firm, data sent from computers in the cabs of trucks allow dispatchers to monitor the load status and location of each rig. Dispatchers know which trucks are in the vicinity of a customer and when each will be empty. Computers also enhance the ability to track orders. At UPS and Federal Express, computerized monitoring of shipments has allowed both companies to improve delivery time and quality of service.

Facilities Location

In considering the placement of facilities, managers must ask two important questions: Should the firm have one or two large plants, or several smaller ones? Where should the facilities be located?

The decision about the number of plants depends on the company's long-range objectives and distribution strategies, financial resources, and equipment costs. The choice about location depends on a number of factors: the location of the market where the product will be sold, availability of labor skills, labor costs, proximity to suppliers, tax rates, construction expenses, utility rates, and quality of life for employees (Straub and Attner, 1991). To make the decision, the company must undertake a cost-benefit analysis. When TRW chooses among two or more potential locations, it analyzes the costs of land, transportation, relocation, construction, zoning, and taxation. Then planners examine perceived benefits—proximity to customers, quality of work life for employees, and labor supply (Robbins, 1992). Finally, they divide total benefits by total costs for each potential location.

Capacity Planning

A critical element in operations management is **capacity planning**—determining an organization's capability to produce the products or services necessary to meet demand. Capacity planning is essentially a matter of trying to convert sales forecasts into production capabilities. Decisions about capacity should be made carefully. Too little capacity means that the organization cannot match demand and that it will lose customers. The reverse—excess capacity—results in facilities and equipment that sit idle while incurring costs.

To increase production capacity, companies have a number of options. They can build new facilities, create additional shifts and hire new staff, pay present staff overtime, subcontract work to outside firms, and refit existing plants. New GM president Jack Smith, following a model he initiated in Europe, wants to put his company's U.S. plants on round-the-clock schedules. Chrysler recently adopted this approach at its St. Louis plant. With no additional capital investment, the new schedule boosted plant capacity by 50,000 minivans (Treece, 1992). Recall from Chapter 6 that Cooper Tire & Rubber Company refurbishes old plants when its operations call for more capacity (Taylor, 1992). If a company must decrease capacity, its options include laying off workers, reducing the hours of operation, and closing facilities.

Capacity is a dynamic variable in operations management. It changes from month to month as well as year to year. Producers attempt to plan capacity to avoid boom-and-bust cycles of plant expansion followed by layoffs and the reduction of operations. The key determinant in capacity planning is the demand for goods and services. (As discussed in Chapter 6, managers can determine demand by using forecasting techniques.) If a company is operating with stable demand, managers should provide plant capacity equal to monthly demand. Suppose, however, that seasonal fluctuations, uncertain economic conditions, or other factors result in unstable demand. In this situation, managers should build a small plant to meet normal demand, and add extra shifts or subcontract work during peak periods (Williams, 1990).

The Management of Operations

Once managers have made the strategic planning decisions about design, layout, process and technology, location, and capacity, the operations management team needs to develop specific plans for the overall production activities. This involves aggregate planning, master scheduling, and structuring for operations.

ISSUES AND ETHICS
What Happens to the Workers?

With global competitors on every side and more pressure being placed on the bottom line, every manager wants to produce more at less cost and faster than anyone else. The answer seems to be automation, computers, and robotics.

But if that is the answer, there's another question: In this stampede to automate, what happens to the workers? There do not seem to be many choices for the workers at auto plants and other mass-production operations. These sites seem natural candidates for transformation into the factories of the future.

Are there ethical questions involved in automation? What consideration, if any, should be given to the workers who are replaced by machines? Are there any ethical concerns relating to the economic welfare of affected communities? ▲

The Aggregate Plan

Aggregate planning involves planning production activities and the resources needed to achieve them. It draws the "road map" for operating activities for a period of time up to one year.

Aggregate planning begins with consideration of the demand forecast for products or services and study of the capacity of the operations. By examining demand and capacity, the operations management team sets production rates, inventory levels, materials requirements, and labor needs. The result of this process is a general operating (aggregate) plan. For a restaurant, such a plan would show the total number of customers to be served, but not the specific meals each would consume. For a facility that makes cooking ranges, the plan would show the total number of ranges to be produced, but not the color of each one. Details come later. When completed, the aggregate plan serves as the basis for the master schedule (Williams, 1990).

The Master Schedule

The **master schedule**, derived from the aggregate plan, specifies the quantity and type of each item to be produced and how, when, and where it should be produced (Robbins, 1991). Exhibit 18.5 illustrates the development of a master schedule from an aggregate plan. Materials requirements are derived from the master

Exhibit 18.5

The development of a master schedule from an aggregate plan.

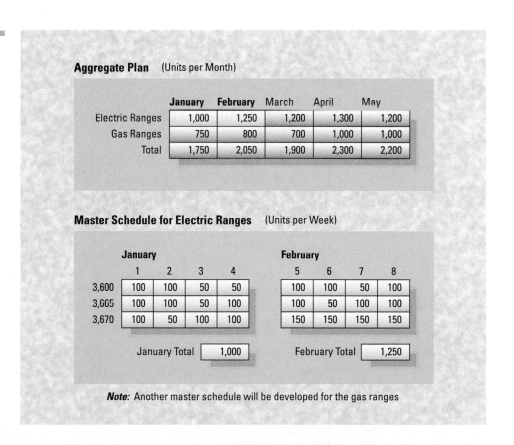

Aggregate Plan (Units per Month)

	January	February	March	April	May
Electric Ranges	1,000	1,250	1,200	1,300	1,200
Gas Ranges	750	800	700	1,000	1,000
Total	1,750	2,050	1,900	2,300	2,200

Master Schedule for Electric Ranges (Units per Week)

	January				February			
	1	2	3	4	5	6	7	8
3,600	100	100	50	50	100	100	50	100
3,665	100	100	50	100	100	50	100	100
3,670	100	50	100	100	150	150	150	150

January Total	1,000

February Total	1,250

Note: Another master schedule will be developed for the gas ranges schedule, and the schedule affects inventory levels. These two points will be discussed later in this chapter.

The Structure for Implementing Production

One more element of operations remains to be planned: the structure for implementing production. In this regard, the operations management team must decide how to organize the department, whether and how to incorporate teams, the nature of authority relationships, and the extent of decentralization. These concepts have been discussed in earlier chapters; the point here is that the operations management team must address each one in the context of operations. The desired result is an integrated, flexible organizational structure that can respond to changes in the aggregate plan.

Controls for Quality and Productivity

The driving forces in the organizations of today are productivity and quality. Or, quality and productivity. The order is irrelevant; the two cannot be separated.

Traditionally, managers viewed productivity in terms of greater output. They did not give much thought to whether the units of output were usable or not. Enlightened managers now realize that productivity is related to saleable, high-quality units of output, whether the outputs are products or services.

The costs associated with poor productivity relate to quality. These include the costs of scrap, repair, and downtime. Such costs are directly observable during production. Quality is also related to the costs incurred before manufacturing begins. These expenses include the cost of incoming materials, purchasing, and inventory (Holt, 1990).

All these factors fall within the purview of operations management. To achieve high quality and productivity, managers use a number of operational controls. These include controls of design, materials, inventory, scheduling, and products.

Design Control

The team approach to product design, discussed earlier in the chapter, provides an opportunity for designers to insert quality and performance controls before a product is produced. **Design control** focuses on creating new products engineered for reliability, functionality, and serviceability.

For example, the characteristics of materials to be used in manufacturing can be examined to be sure up front that they meet production standards. This orchestrated process should ensure a well-functioning final product.

The team approach can be expanded to integrate marketing research specialists, who can provide the connection between consumer needs and production capabilities. The team can then incorporate quality, as defined by the consumer, at the design stage.

Materials Control: Purchasing

An integral component of an operations management control system, materials control is achieved through effective purchasing. **Purchasing** is the acquisition of needed goods and services. The goal of the purchasing agent is to acquire them at

Verifying Quality

epublic Engineered Steel came to life when the LTV Corporation sold its steel bar division to employees through an employee stock ownership plan. At that time the new owner-employees made a pledge to customers: Republic would continue the tradition of introducing advances that would help customers lead their industries.

In fulfillment of that pledge and in a bid to remain a long-term competitor, Republic has introduced a quality verification system that is the first of its kind. The new system, the Quality Verification Line (QVL), is the first fully integrated system in the American steel industry. The QVL can inspect and verify the precise internal and external quality of bar products. The system cost $12.5 million.

The QVL can automatically check the surface, straightness, diameter, length, weight, and chemical composition of each bar. And, as if this were not enough, the line bundles, tags, and labels each bar, readying it for shipment.

The system also provides detective skills. The data gained from operation of the QVL permits Republic to trace defects to their origin and eliminate the cause. ▲

For more about quality verification, see Joseph F. McKenna, "Ohio Steelmaker Claims a Quality First," *Industry Week,* February 17, 1992, p. 52.

---

optimal costs from competent and reliable sources. What an organization produces depends on the inputs—the materials and supplies. Therefore, purchasing is critical for the following reasons:

- If the materials are not on hand, nothing can be produced.

- If the right quantity of materials is not available, the organization cannot meet demand.

- If the materials are of inferior quality, it is difficult or costly to produce quality products.

The goal of purchasing control is to ensure the availability and acceptable quality of material while balancing costs. Maintaining relations with reliable sources is one strategy for achieving this goal.

The advent of total quality management (see Chapter 17) has shifted the emphasis of materials purchasing control. Traditionally, controls focused on— in order of emphasis—quantity, time, and quality specifications. Now quality has the same priority as quantity.

Managers are initiating two practices to reflect this change. First, they are building long-term relationships with suppliers. This creates a partner for the producer and a sure source of sales for the supplier. The practice of building long-term relationships contrasts starkly with the traditional practice of pitting vendors against one another. The traditional practice was a short-term approach that often led to financial savings and quality reductions.

The second new practice related to quality is the shifting of the responsibility for quality to suppliers. Contracts are developed on the understanding that the

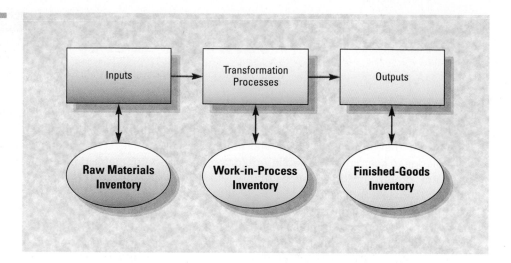

supplier inspects materials and equipment before shipping and that what the producer buys is guaranteed to have minimum defects.

Kingston Technology Corporation designs and manufactures memory, processor, and storage upgrades for computers, laser printers, and workstations. The company implements both new purchasing strategies. The firm builds long-term partnerships with vendors. Kingston has never canceled a purchase order. The firm works with suppliers to schedule the manufacture and delivery of memory chips, and Kingston purchasers do not grind down suppliers on price. Instead, the purchasing agents prefer a consistent supply and quality. In return for Kingston's steady business, suppliers guarantee to meet quality specifications (Welles, 1992).

Inventory Control

The goods an organization keeps on hand are called **inventory**. Inventory control is critical to operations management because inventory represents a major investment. Most organizations have three types of inventory: raw materials, work-in-process, and finished goods. Each type is associated with a different stage of the production process, as Exhibit 18.6 shows.

The **raw materials inventory** includes the materials, parts, and supplies an organization uses as inputs to production. The raw materials for a Hewlett-Packard laser printer include the printer engine, circuit boards, and the power supply. At a Wendy's fast-food restaurant, the inventory includes meat patties, buns, tomatoes, and lettuce. Raw materials inventory is the least expensive type of inventory because the organization has not yet invested any labor in it. Nevertheless, an excessive raw materials inventory ties up cash unnecessarily.

Work-in-process inventory consists of the materials and parts that have begun moving through the production process but are not yet a completed product. At Hewlett-Packard, the toner and drum assembly and the shell of a laser printer are work-in-process inventory. Because labor has been expended to produce work-

Work-in-process, these television components are a considerable inventory investment at Thomson Consumer Electronics, the largest TV plant in the world.

in-process inventory, this type of inventory represents a greater investment than raw materials inventory.

The **finished-goods inventory** consists of the products that have completed the entire production process but have not yet been sold. Assembled and boxed Hewlett-Packard printers, for example, stored in a warehouse before shipping are finished-goods inventory. This inventory, of course, represents the greatest investment of all three types.

The Importance of Inventory Control   At one time, managers prided themselves on maintaining large inventories. Inventories were regarded as measures of wealth. Today managers realize that a large inventory can indicate wasted resources. Money not tied up in inventory can be used elsewhere. The goal of inventory control is to sustain the proper flow of materials while maintaining adequate inventory levels and minimum costs.

With this goal in mind, organizations have four specific techniques for inventory management. They are: economic order quantity, materials requirement planning, manufacturing resource planning, and just-in-time inventory systems. The following paragraphs discuss each method in detail.

Economic Order Quantity   The **economic order quantity (EOQ)** is the order quantity that minimizes ordering and holding costs based on the rate of inventory use. Ordering costs are the costs of placing an order. Ordering costs include, for example, the costs of postage, receiving, and inspections. Holding costs are the costs of keeping the inventory on hand. These expenses include the costs of storage space, financing, and taxes (Daft, 1991).

The EOQ may be derived by calculation. The formula for EOQ is

$$\sqrt{\frac{2 \times D \times C}{H}}$$

where D represents demand, or annual usage rate; C represents ordering costs; and H represents holding costs.

Suppose the manager of a small shop that manufactures valves needs to order 1-inch valve gaskets. A review of records indicates that ordering costs for the gaskets amount to $20, the annual holding cost is $12, and the annual demand for the gasket is 1,815. The formula to calculate the EOQ in this case is

$$\sqrt{\frac{2 \times 1{,}815 \times 20}{\$12}} = 77.8$$

The best order quantity, then, is 78.

The next question facing the manager is when to order. This is determined by calculating the **reorder point** (**ROP**). The formula for ROP is

$$ROP = \frac{D}{Time} \times Lead\ Time$$

Assuming that gaskets can be delivered five days after the order is placed, the manager determines the ROP by using the following calculation:

$$ROP = \frac{1{,}815}{365} \times 5 = 24.86,\ or\ 25$$

This formula tells the manager that, because the time to receive new orders is five days, at least 25 gaskets should be in inventory at all times. Any time the number of gaskets drops to 25, a new order for 78 gaskets should be placed.

EOQ can result in substantial savings and improvement in inventory management. It forces managers to evaluate usage rates, ordering costs, and holding costs. The major disadvantage of EOQ is that it focuses on optimal order quantity while ignoring quality. Another disadvantage of EOQ is that it does not take into account supplier performance.

Materials Requirement Planning   EOQ is useful so long as each inventory item, as in the valve example, is independent of others. But when demand for one inventory item depends on other inventory items, EOQ is no longer applicable. Such is the case for Boeing, for example. To produce one hundred 747s, each of which includes some three million parts, Boeing must have a vast number of discrete components on hand. One technique for managing such an inventory is **materials requirement planning** (**MRP**). This production planning and inventory system uses forecasts of customer orders to schedule the exact amount of materials needed to support the manufacture of the desired number of products.

An MRP program begins with a master schedule of planned production. (Recall that a master schedule uses sales forecasts to determine the quantities of finished goods required in a specific time period.) The next step is to use a computer to analyze product design and determine all the parts and supplies needed to manufacture the finished product. This information is then merged with existing inventory records. The quantities of each item on hand are identified, and usage rates are calculated. Then the system can determine ordering times and quantities. In essence, MRP incorporates EOQ, perpetual inventory control, and statistics to provide a comprehensive system for purchasing materials and scheduling various production activities to meet projected customer orders (Daft, 1991).

MRP results in purchasing on time and according to actual needs. In most cases MRP means a reduction in inventory and fewer production stops due to lack of stock. These changes save money. The major limitation associated with MRP is the extensive organizational commitment it requires. To use MRP properly, an organization must develop adequate support systems and skilled personnel. The system cannot be implemented in a piecemeal fashion.

Manufacturing Resource Planning   An even more sophisticated system than MRP is **manufacturing resource planning** (**MRPII**). MRP is used to manage inventory; MRPII, on the other hand, is a comprehensive planning system. It emphasizes planning and controlling all of a firm's resources—its finances, capital, and marketing strategies—as well as production and materials management (Migliorelli and Swan, 1988). MRPII creates a model of the overall business, allowing top managers to control production scheduling, cash flow, human resources, capacity, inventory, purchasing, and distribution. Because of its comprehensiveness, MRPII can be used effectively for strategic planning. At the Stanley works in New Britain, Connecticut, the MRPII system not only ensures that the next product is being manufactured at the right time, but it also coordinates the warehouse management system (Holt, 1990).

The value of MRPII lies in its comprehensiveness. It is a strategic management system that links the entire organization. Because it is very expensive to implement, only large companies can afford to use it. In addition, it must be custom-designed for the user, which involves a major commitment of the organization's time and human resources.

Just-in-Time Inventory Systems   Another technique for inventory control is designed to reduce inventory by coordinating supply deliveries with production. This technique, called the **just-in-time** (**JIT**) **inventory system** originated in Japan. The JIT concept is sometimes referred to as the *kanban* system, the stockless system, or the zero-inventory system.

With the JIT approach, suppliers deliver exact quantities of materials directly to manufacturers as the manufacturers need them. There is no buffer of "safety" inventory. There is no warehousing or in-process handling. The benefits managers expect to receive from JIT include reduced inventory and setup time, better work flow, shorter manufacturing time, and less consumption of space. They often reap unexpected benefits, however. When a company changes to a JIT system, managers are often able to identify production problems that were masked by inventory reserves, slack schedules, and devices that workers developed to keep up the required flow (Marenghi, 1992).

A JIT system depends on reliable suppliers that must meet strict delivery schedules. When the system works, it works well. At Caterpillar, the JIT system—and the cooperation of suppliers—has resulted in the company's ability to supply components to Caterpillar customers within 72 hours of receiving the order, 99.9% of the time (Hall, 1983). But when the supplier has trouble, the result is production stoppages. In 1992, the Saturn plant in Lordstown, Ohio, was shut down as a result of labor strikes against suppliers.

Schedule Control

Another important element of operations control is schedule control—techniques for scheduling operations and tracking production. There are two basic scheduling techniques: Gantt charts and network scheduling.

Gantt Charts   An early pioneer in scientific management, Henry L. Gantt, was the first to devise a reliable method for reserving machine time for jobs in production. The method promotes the orderly flow of work from one process to the next, with a minimum of lost time or delays. His method involved a tool called a **Gantt chart**. As you can see by studying Exhibit 18.7, a Gantt chart tracks a project from beginning to end, comparing the time estimates for the steps involved with the actual time they require and adjusting the starting and ending times of steps if necessary.

Exhibit 18.7 presents a Gantt chart for a manufacturing department. The processes it tracks are machining, assembling, and shipping. To aid the production manager in monitoring the progress of each process and making any required adjustments, the chart presents two sets of information: (1) the planned time for each task, represented by the area enclosed in brackets, and (2) the actual

Exhibit 18.7

A Gantt chart for a manufacturing department.

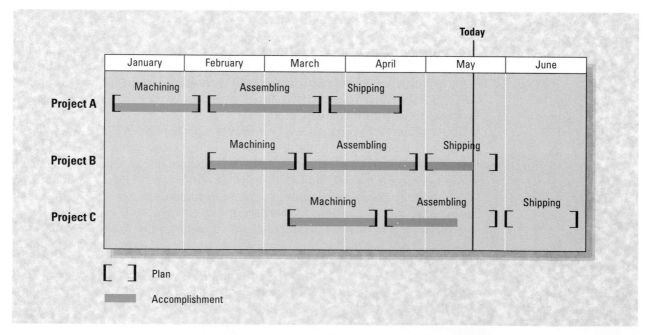

completion time, represented by a solid bar within each set of brackets. The length of the line indicates how much of the task is complete.

Gantt charts work best for scheduling and tracking sequential events, the completion times of which will determine the total time for an entire project. Gantt charts are not appropriate for highly complex projects that require many different kinds of sequential operations that begin or run simultaneously.

Network Scheduling   Managers use **network scheduling** to schedule and track projects in which events and activities are interrelated. This technique for scheduling and controlling uses events and activities that have time estimates assigned to them. Exhibit 18.8 presents a network diagram. Events, represented by circles, indicate the starting point of some production operation, such as delivery of materials. Activities, or processes, are represented by lines with arrows. The length of a line indicates the length of time required to complete the process.

Exhibit 18.8

A network diagram showing how to replace a pipeline.

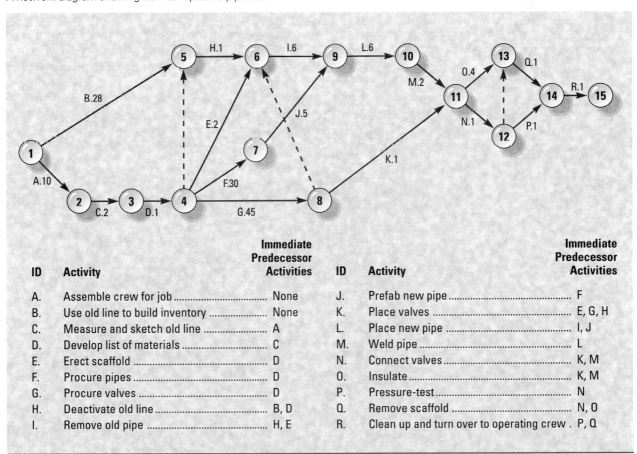

ID	Activity	Immediate Predecessor Activities
A.	Assemble crew for job	None
B.	Use old line to build inventory	None
C.	Measure and sketch old line	A
D.	Develop list of materials	C
E.	Erect scaffold	D
F.	Procure pipes	D
G.	Procure valves	D
H.	Deactivate old line	B, D
I.	Remove old pipe	H, E

ID	Activity	Immediate Predecessor Activities
J.	Prefab new pipe	F
K.	Place valves	E, G, H
L.	Place new pipe	I, J
M.	Weld pipe	L
N.	Connect valves	K, M
O.	Insulate	K, M
P.	Pressure-test	N
Q.	Remove scaffold	N, O
R.	Clean up and turn over to operating crew	P, Q

Source: *Production-Inventory Systems: Planning and Control,* 3rd edition, by Elwood S. Buffa and Jeffrey G. Miller, pp. 611, 622. Reprinted by permission of the publisher. Copyright Richard D. Irwin, Inc., Homewood, IL.

The network diagram in Exhibit 18.8 shows the schedule for a project that involves 15 events and 18 activities. Event number 1 marks the start of activities A and B. The notation "A.10" means that activity A is scheduled for 10 days. Event number 2 marks the end of activity A and the beginning of activity C, which is scheduled to take two days. To construct this network, the manager had to list each activity, estimate the time for each, and identify the immediate predecessors for each activity. Note that an activity cannot be started until its predecessor has been completed. Note, too, that some activities can take place simultaneously.

The **program evaluation and review technique** (**PERT**), an adaptation of network scheduling, assigns four time estimates to activities: optimistic, most likely, pessimistic, and expected. The expected time (the amount of time the manager thinks the activity will actually take) is based on a probability analysis of the other three time estimates.

The PERT method, originally devised at the Lockheed Corporation for planning complex aerospace development projects, provides managers with a graphic view of the details of a project from initiation to completion. It functions as a control device by helping the manager spot trouble areas and see when a project is falling behind schedule. The manager can take corrective action before the delay becomes critical.

One benefit of a PERT network is that it helps managers identify the **critical path**—the longest possible path or least direct route from the beginning to the end of a network diagram. Given current time estimates, the critical path shows the longest time a job could take. Exhibit 18.9 shows the calculations that define the critical path for the pipeline project introduced in Exhibit 18.8. The critical path represents the earliest possible completion time for the project—65 days—assuming that the worst combination of events occurs.

Awareness of the critical path equips a manager with the ability to really control a project. For example, a delay in the completion of activity B by one

Exhibit 18.9

Calculation of the critical path.

Activity	Time in Days
A	10
C	2
D	1
G	45
K	1
O	4
Q	1
R	1
Critical Path =	**65 Days**

day will not affect the total project's completion time. On the other hand, if activity G takes 47 days instead of 45, the entire project will be 2 days off schedule unless the manager takes some corrective action. By maneuvering to ensure that the length of the critical path does not increase, the manager can maintain effective control of the project.

Product Control

At one time, the entire concept of operations control focused on inspection of the physical product. With the advent of TQM, inspection was placed in a new perspective, as only one part of controlling. Now **product control** encompasses controls from purchasing to end use. It involves reducing the probability and cost of poor quality and unreliable products. Product controls focus on inspection and testing techniques.

Acceptance Sampling   Any inspection of a representative group of products that takes place prior to the beginning of a new phase of production constitutes **acceptance sampling**. The inspection may be done prior to the receipt of raw materials, when subassemblies are completed, after critical processes of manufacturing, and prior to shipping finished goods. The data from the sample is used to evaluate all items in the group. Acceptance sampling is used to make cost-effective evaluations of large numbers of items. The evaluations determine whether entire batches are accepted or rejected. The increase in acceptance sampling has lead to the rapid development of statistical software (Daniel, 1992).

Detailed Inspection and Tests   Rather than a sampling approach to product control, some operations conduct **detailed inspection and tests** on every finished item. Medicines, for example, are tested in this way. The goal of the technique is to identify all parts that do not meet standards and to pinpoint inadequate processes. As you read in the Focus on Quality feature in this chapter, Republic Engineered Steel introduced the Quality Verification Line that automatically checks the internal and external quality of bar steel and allows managers to trace defects to their origin.

Control Sampling   The purpose of **control sampling** is to detect variations in production processes and workmanship. The technique involves periodic tests to uncover problems with equipment, worn tools, bad parts, or personnel. When managers know about problems, they can correct them. Unlike acceptance sampling, which is used to decide whether a batch is acceptable or not, control sampling is used to correct problems as they occur.

Qualification Testing   In **qualification testing**, a sample product is checked for performance on the basis of reliability and safety. New car models are driven hundreds of thousands of miles so that engineers can test the overall car and its components. Thousands of golf balls are hit by automated golf clubs so that engineers can check on the quality of the balls and the reliability of their flight. The goal of qualification testing is to ensure that a product, as a class, performs as it should. The purpose of detailed testing is to ensure that each version of a product meets established standards.

The Three K's—*Kiken, Kitsui,* and *Kitanai*

At a time when thousands of auto workers in the United States are losing their jobs, Japan's world-beating auto makers cannot find enough people to fill their manufacturing facilities. With Japan's rising prosperity, young people seem to be shunning assembly-line work, which many view as monotonous, fast-paced, and tiring. When they think of manufacturing jobs, they think of the "three K's": *kiken* (dangerous), *kitsui* (difficult), and *kitanai* (dirty). Most Japanese young people prefer jobs in the service sector.

As a result, many Japanese manufacturing companies are trying to improve the image of factory work by creating "friendly factories" that will be pleasant for the workers. At Nissan's newest facility, which a company brochure calls Human Land, automation has done away with the conveyer belt. Each car sits on its own dolly, which can be raised or lowered at each workstation so that workers do not have to bend or stretch much. The factory is brightly lit by natural sunlight that filters in through skylights, and air conditioners keep the temperature at 77 degrees. Human Land incorporates a great deal of automation. Robots handle most of the painting and welding, the two dirtiest jobs. The automation not only makes the work easier, but it improves efficiency as well.

At another factory, Nissan is experimenting with a "silver line," a heavily automated assembly line that makes work easier for workers over 50 years old. Such a line will allow the manufacturer to recruit workers from Japan's rapidly aging population.

At Mitsubishi, many workers traditionally lived in shared dormitory rooms. Now, to attract workers, the

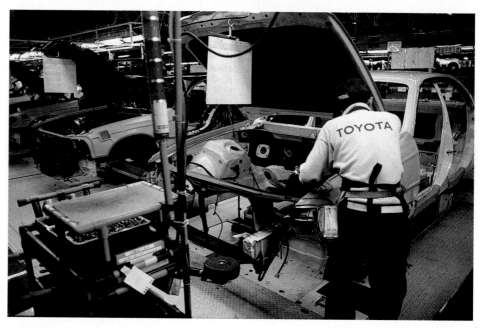

Safe, easy, and clean *are job qualities that Japanese auto manufacturers would like to promote in order to attract young people who are put off by work thought of as dangerous, difficult, and dirty.*

company is offering unmarried workers their own rooms. Toyota, Japan's largest auto company, is borrowing excess workers from two steel companies and plans to eliminate unpopular late-night work at a new plant.

Several companies are taking what is still a relatively radical step in Japan—they are letting women work in their factories. In general, the women's jobs are physically undemanding. Female employees inspect vehicles, for example.

By making these changes and others to attract the next generation of assembly workers, Japanese auto makers are doing their best to integrate the latest technology and the labor supply. ▲

For more about the three K's, see Andrew Pollack, "An Industrial Evolution," *Dallas Morning News,* July 20, 1992, p. 8D.

Future Trends

As the emphasis on automation and work teams continues, the following trends in operations management will be evident:

- Among the newer technologies, computer-aided manufacturing—CAM—will become the most widely adopted.

- The use of computer-integrated manufacturing—CIM—will increase. After a decade of trying to use computers alone to control manufacturing, managers are beginning to balance the use of computers, information, and human resources.

- In the area of facilities layout, more organizations will adopt a cellular configuration to coincide with newly created manufacturing teams.

- The continuous development of new processes and technologies will require workers to change their work processes frequently. To do this, they will have to be better trained and educated than they are today.

- The rapid movement toward automation in manufacturing will change workers' focus. Rather than wanting job security on the production line, workers will be concerned about keeping a job anywhere in their organization. This change in attitude will cause workers to be increasingly accepting of different assignments and training.

C H A P T E R S U M M A R Y

- Strategic success is directly related to the efficiency and responsiveness of production operations. Operations management helps make production efficient.

- Operations management applies to organizations that produce services as well as those that produce goods.

- Product design according to the precepts of an approach called design for manufacturability and assembly (DFMA) enhances competitiveness, response time, and efficiency.

- The four types of facility layouts are process, production, cellular, and fixed position.

- The new technologies that are revolutionizing manufacturing processes include robotics, computer-aided design (CAD), computer-aided manufacturing (CAM), flexible manufacturing systems (FMSs), and computer-integrated manufacturing (CIM). Computers are also responsible for revolutionizing the delivery of services.

- Managers use cost-benefit analysis to make decisions about facility location.

- Capacity planning involves determining the organization's capability to produce the number of products or services to match demand.

- The operations management team needs to develop specific plans for the overall production activities. This involves aggregate planning, master scheduling, and structuring for operations.

- Design control focuses on incorporating reliability, functionality, and serviceability into product design.

- The goal of purchasing control is to ensure availability and acceptable quality of materials while balancing costs.

- Inventory control is critical because inventory represents a major investment. The four methods for inventory control this chapter discusses—EOQ, MRP, MRPII, and JIT—have different purposes and strengths.

- Schedule controls are designed to structure and track production. Gantt charts are useful for scheduling consecutive tasks. Network scheduling using PERT helps managers schedule multifaceted projects by identifying the project's critical path.

- Product control encompasses controls from purchasing to the end user, focusing on testing and inspection techniques. The four types of product controls are acceptance sampling, detailed inspection and tests, control sampling, and qualification testing.

S K I L L - B U I L D I N G

To help you apply the concepts associated with operations management and control, visit a print shop, a bakery, or a manufacturing facility. During the visit, consider these questions:

1. What type of inputs (such as raw materials, human resources, land and buildings, information, technology) does the organization appear to use in its transformation processes?

2. What type of facilities layout does the company use for the production of goods or services? Sketch the layout.

3. Why did the company choose its location? What factors might managers have analyzed when they made the choice?

4. What parts of the operation are automated? How does automation affect the organization's ability to produce goods or services?

5. What is the organization's total monthly capacity? In other words, how many goods can the firm produce or how many customers can it serve in one month?

6. What items does the firm keep in inventory? Why?

7. What methods of product control does the firm use?

R E V I E W   Q U E S T I O N S

1. Review this chapter's essential terms and look up the meanings of those you cannot define.

2. What is operations management? Why is operations strategy important?

3. Why is design for manufacturability and assembly important in terms of overall operations management?

4. When should a process layout be used? Why?

5. What benefits can CAD or CAM technology provide for a manufacturer?

6. What factors should managers consider when selecting a facility location? What is the role of a cost-benefit analysis in the decision?

7. What is the role of operations control in achieving quality and productivity?

8. What is the purpose of design control?

9. Why is it important for an organization to control materials purchasing?

10. How do EOQ and JIT systems control inventory?

11. What is the purpose of a Gantt chart? What is the purpose of PERT scheduling?

12. What is the difference between acceptance sampling and control sampling?

R E C O M M E N D E D   R E A D I N G

Bass, Thomas. "Road to Ruin," *Discover* (May 1992), pp. 56–62.

Bassett, Glen. *Manufacturing Strategies for Today* (Westport, CT: Greenwood), 1991.

Cook, L. P. *No Down Time: Six Steps of Industrial Problem Solving* (Reading, MA: Addison Wesley), 1991.

Gardner, Dana. "Design's Watchword for the 1990s: Speed," *Discover* (May 1992), pp. 56–62.

Heizer, Jay, and Barry Render. *Production and Operations Management: Strategy & Tactics,* 2nd edition (Needham Heights, MA: Allyn and Bacon), 1991.

Lynch, Terrence. "How to Make Factory Design Pay Off," *Design News* (February 24, 1992), pp. 63–67.

Montgomery, Douglas C. *Introduction to Statistical Quality Control,* 2nd edition (New York: Wiley), 1991.

Ricciuti, Mike. "Connect Manufacturing to the Enterprise," *Datamation* (January 15, 1992), pp. 42–44.

Schlack, Mark. "IS Has a New Role in Manufacturing: The New Role of Information Systems Managers in Manufacturing Departments," *Datamation* (January 15, 1992), pp. 38–39.

R E F E R E N C E S

Adam, Jr., Everett E., and Ronald J. Ebert. *Production and Operations Management,* 4th edition (Englewood Cliffs, NJ: Prentice-Hall), 1989.

Adam, Jr., Everett E., and Paul M. Swamidass. "Assessing Operations Management from a Strategic Objective," *Journal of Management* (June 1989), pp. 181–204.

Brown, Tom. "Managing for Quality," *Industry Week* (July 20, 1992), p. 28.

Daft, Richard L. *Management,* 2nd edition (Homewood, IL: Dryden Press), 1991, pp. 575–577, 581.

Daniel, Mel. "Statistical Software Rings in Quality," *Computer World* (January 6, 1992), p. 64.

Dincen, Steve. "Can American Steel Find Quality?" *Industry Week* (January 26, 1992), p. 37–39.

Hall, R. W. *Zero Inventories* (Homewood, IL: Dow Jones-Irwin), 1983.

Hayes, R. H., and S. C. Wheelwright. *Restoring Our Competitive Edge: Competing Through Manufacturing* (New York: Wiley), 1984.

Hill, T. *Manufacturing Strategy: The Strategic Management of the Manufacturing Function* (London: Macmillan), 1985.

Holt, David H. *Management: Principles and Practices,* 2nd edition (Englewood Cliffs, NJ: Prentice-Hall), 1990, pp. 550, 564–565.

Marenghi, Catherine. "Stanley Hammers on Quality," *Computer World* (February 6, 1992), p. 62.

Migliorelli, Marcia, and Robert T. Swan. "MRP and Aggregate Planning—A Problem Solution," *Production and Inventory Management Journal* 29, no. 2 (1988), pp. 42–44.

Miller, William H. "CAD Comes Into Its Own," *Industry Week* (May 18, 1992), p. 62.

Morley, Brad. "Management's Competitive Weapon," *Industry Week* (May 18, 1992), p. 44.

Moskal, Brian S. "GM's New Found Religion," *Industry Week* (May 18, 1992), pp. 46–52.

Robbins, John. "TRW Relocation on the Horizon," *Dallas Morning News,* February 14, 1992, p. C1.

Robbins, Stephen P. *Management,* 3rd edition (Englewood Cliffs, NJ: Prentice-Hall), 1991, p. 638.

Sheridan, John H. "The CIM Revolution," *Industry Week* (April 20, 1992), pp. 32–36.

Straub, Joseph, and Raymond Attner. *Introduction to Business,* 4th edition (Boston: PWS-Kent), 1991, pp. 241–244.

Taylor, Alex. "Now Hear This, Jack Welch," *Fortune* (April 6, 1992), p. 94.

Treece, James B. "General Motors: Open All Night," *Business Week* (June 1, 1992), pp. 82–83.

Welles, Edward O. "Built on Speed," *Inc.* (October 1992), pp. 82, 84, 88.

Williams, Frederick P. *Production Operations Management* (Boston: Houghton Mifflin), 1990, p. 32.

G L O S S A R Y O F T E R M S

acceptance sampling A product control technique involving inspection of a representative group of products before a new stage of production.

aggregate planning The planning of production activities and the resources needed to achieve them. Aggregate planning is an element of operations management.

capacity planning Determining an organization's capability to produce the number of products or services to meet demand. Capacity planning is an element of operations management.

cellular layout A facilities layout option in which equipment required for a sequence of operations on the same product is grouped into cells.

computer-aided design (CAD) A design technique that uses a computer monitor to display and manipulate proposed designs for the purpose of evaluating them.

computer-aided manufacturing (CAM) Using computers to guide and control manufacturing processes.

computer-integrated manufacturing (CIM) A technology in which computers coordinate people, information, and processes to produce quality products efficiently.

control sampling A product control technique designed to detect variations in production processes and workmanship.

critical path The longest sequence of events and activities in a network production schedule; the longest time a job could take.

design control An area of operations control that involves incorporating reliability, functionality, and serviceability into product design.

design for manufacturability and assembly (DFMA) Considering, during product design, how products will be manufactured and assembled.

detailed inspection and tests A product control technique in which every finished item receives an examination or performance test.

economic order quantity (EOQ) An inventory technique that helps managers determine how much material to order by minimizing the total of ordering costs and holding costs based on the organization's usage rate.

facilities layout   The element of operations planning concerned with the physical arrangement of equipment and work flow.

finished-goods inventory   Inventory consisting of completed products that have not yet been sold.

fixed-position layout   A facilities layout option in which the product stays in one place and the equipment, tools, and human skills are brought to it.

flexible manufacturing system (FMS)   A technology in which an automated production line is coordinated by computers. A line controlled by an FMS can produce more than one product.

Gantt chart   A graphic scheduling and control tool that helps managers plan and control a sequence of events.

inventory   The goods an organization keeps on hand.

just-in-time (JIT) inventory system   A technique for inventory control designed to eliminate raw materials inventories by coordinating production and supply deliveries.

manufacturing resource planning (MRPII)   A comprehensive planning system that controls the total resources of a firm.

master schedule   An element of operations management that specifies the quantity and type of each item to be produced and how, when, and where it should be produced.

materials requirement planning (MRP)   A planning and inventory system that uses forecasts of customer orders to schedule the exact amount of materials needed for production.

network scheduling   A graphic technique for scheduling projects in which activities and events are interrelated.

operations management   The managerial activities directed toward the processes that convert resources into products and services.

operations strategy   The element of the strategic plan that defines the role, capabilities, and expectations of operations.

program evaluation and review technique (PERT)   A network scheduling technique for planning and charting the progress of a complex project in terms of the time it is expected to take—an estimate that is derived from probability analysis.

process layout   A facilities layout option in which all the equipment or machines that perform a similar task are placed together.

product control   A component of operations control that reduces the probability and costs of poor quality and unreliable products by implementing controls from purchasing to end use.

production layout   A facilities layout option in which machines and tasks are arranged according to the progressive steps through which the product is made.

purchasing   The acquisition of goods and services at optimal costs from competent and reliable sources.

qualification testing   A product control technique in which products are tested for performance on the basis of reliability and safety.

raw materials inventory   Inventory consisting of the raw materials, parts, and supplies used as inputs to production.

reorder point (ROP)   The most economical point at which an inventory item should be reordered.

robotics   The use of programmed machines instead of people to handle production tasks.

work-in-process inventory   Inventory consisting of parts and materials that have begun moving through the production process but are not yet assembled into a completed product.

C A S E   P R O B L E M
The Downside of JIT

ust-in-time (JIT) inventory systems, pioneered by the Japanese, have swept through dozens of manufacturing and service industries. The concept is simple... for the manufacturers. Rather than keeping plenty of parts and other supplies in stock in case they may be needed, companies obtain the supplies just as they are needed in the factory. This technique has reduced stockage and cut costs for thousands of manufacturing and service firms.

What is a solution for manufacturers creates problems for suppliers, however. Demanding JIT delivery schedules increase both risks and costs. Suppliers who fail to deliver products at the promised time simply lose their customers. The rigors of the JIT approach can decrease a supplier's profitability.

Surveys reveal that each rescheduling of a delivery costs a supplier an average of $150. Suppose a firm receives 100 orders a year and the orders are worth $1 million. The firm makes a pretax profit of 10% ($100,000). If the firm has to reschedule each delivery date twice, the supplier's profit declines by 30%, or $30,000.

Businesses caught in the downside of JIT tend to adopt "fire-fighting" strategies, usually in vain. The most popular strategy is to maintain a "hot list"—a stockpile of products that the supplier finds particularly hard to deliver on time. But if the hot-list items make up 10% to 20% of a supplier's production, its entire manufacturing schedule starts to go awry, making deliveries of all its products unreliable.

Q U E S T I O N S

1. Based on the supplier-manufacturer relationship presented in this case, has the goal of JIT been achieved? Why?

2. From the ultimate consumer's view, is there a downside to JIT? Why?

3. What options are available to the supplier?

For more about the downside of JIT, see "I Want It Now," *The Economist,* June 13, 1992, pp. 78–79.

P · A · R · T

Special Concerns

Information Management Systems

L E A R N I N G   O B J E C T I V E S

After reading and discussing this chapter, you should be able to:

- Define this chapter's essential terms
- List and describe the seven characteristics of useful information
- Describe the characteristics of an effective management information system (MIS)
- Discuss the guidelines for establishing an MIS
- Discuss the purposes of decision support systems
- Describe the kinds of resistance to implementing an MIS that an organization can experience
- Discuss emerging information technologies and their potential for improving organizational productivity

application program

artificial intelligence (AI)

batch processing

computerized information
   system (CIS)

data

database

data center

decision support system
   (DSS)

distributed data processing
   (DDP)

end-user computing

executive information system
   (EIS)

expert system

group decision support
   system (GDSS)

information

key indicator management
   (KIM)

management information
   system (MIS)

networking

operating system

transactional processing

MANAGEMENT IN ACTION

Computers in the Transport Industry

Computers accomplish an endless variety of tasks. When suitably linked and powered by sophisticated software, computer systems can collect, catalog, store, process, and distribute limitless information. Computers enable managers to do everything from budgeting to satellite tracking. Few industries make more productive use of the computer's prodigious capabilities than transportation. From designing, building, and navigating jetliners to scheduling a taxicab's oil changes, computers help transport managers ensure that people and goods move safely, swiftly, and profitably.

The Norfolk Southern Railroad created its "Computer Aided Reporting System" in 1987 at a cost of $5 million. The system quickly paid back its investment. The heart of CARS beats in more than 500 pocket-sized computers, radio-linked directly with the company's central computers. CARS keeps records up-to-date, tracks rolling stock, and keeps tabs on parts and maintenance operations.

Today's airline operations are inconceivable without computer systems. Its immensely powerful SABRE (Semi-Automated Business Research Environment) reservation and marketing system has

Tracking the movement and condition of freight cars is just one of the many uses for computers in the transportation industry.

played a significant part in American Airlines' dominance in U.S. air travel. The NAVSTAR satellite-based, computer-aided global positioning system (GPS) tells pilots of globe-girdling flights their exact position, while on-board computers allow them to plot the most efficient routes and control settings. Maintenance- and flight-crew scheduling, inventory tracking, weight and balance, and documentation requirements all rely upon computerized systems.

The Boeing Company, the world's largest builder of airliners, employs sophisticated computers for every phase of its vast operations, from CAD modeling of preliminary ideas to tracking each finished ship throughout its service life. Among the most interesting applications are optical imaging systems, which can transform drawings and specifications of components into digitized images. The images can be stored and recalled quickly and easily wherever they are needed.

For trucking firms and independent truckers, computer systems support every phase of operations, from choosing the best engine/transmission combinations for particular fleet assignments to scheduling drivers, loads, and maintenance. Whereas many railroads and airlines create their own application software, trucking firms can purchase off-the-shelf programs from a variety of vendors. One trucking company, Overnight Transportation, uses software created by Control Software, Inc. The program is powerful enough to help the company control some 23,000 pieces of equipment. Cecil Cowan, Overnight's manager of systems and planning, comments about the system: "It gives us the ability to track all of our equipment costs, parts, inventories, manage our fuel and fluids." According to Cowan, "You can get cost per miles on your equipment. You've got a complete history of the repairs on your equipment. You can use it to spot trends." UPS, Federal Express, and DHL have all used computers for years to keep track of parcels from the moment they are received to the time they are delivered. ▲

▶ Few industries make more productive use of the computer's capabilities than transportation.

For more about contemporary computer applications, see Shawn Tully, "Can Boeing Reinvent Itself?" *Fortune,* March 8, 1993, pp. 66–73; and Tony Seidman, "Computers track parts and maintenance," *Chicago Tribune,* September 1991, sec. 7, p. 9A.

Information and the Manager

Regardless of the size of their enterprise, managers must have data and up-to-date information on many subjects from varied sources to make effective and efficient decisions. **Data** are unprocessed facts and figures that—until they are sorted, summarized, processed, and distributed to those who need them—are of little value to managers. Data include such things as parts numbers, price lists, sales figures, costs of inventories and supplies, and customer complaints. **Information** is data that have been deliberately selected, processed, and organized to be useful to an individual manager (Mandell, 1988). Examples of information are reports about a focus group, a proposal for a new project, and financial statements. The systems mentioned in the opening case not only process data but select, sort, store, and disseminate information to managers. Managers then use that information to manage resources, monitor maintenance activities, and track costs and trends.

In this chapter we consider the need for management information systems, what such systems can accomplish, how they are implemented and run, and what types of systems are now in use. We'll also sample something of the cutting edge in information technologies. But so rapidly is this field developing, by the time the ink is dry on these pages significant improvements will be available to managers (see this morning's *Wall Street Journal*). Although not every manager is called upon to implement or operate an MIS, in today's environment every manager must be well informed enough about them to be able to assist colleagues who are formally responsible for the system. And every manager should be able to competently contribute input and effectively obtain and use the system's outputs. Managers, of course, should be the best judges of how well the system is meeting their needs.

Characteristics of Useful Information

To be useful, information must be understandable, reliable, relevant, complete, concise, timely, and cost-effective. Information that meets these criteria, as described in Exhibit 19.1, must then be placed in the hands of those who need it.

Exhibit 19.1

Characteristics of useful information.

- **Understandable information** is in suitable (correct) form and uses appropriate terms and symbols that the receiver will know and interpret properly. When jargon, abbreviations, shorthand notations, and acronyms are used, the person receiving the information must be able to decode them.

- **Reliable information** is accurate, consistent with fact, actual, and verifiable. The sources of the information, and people who gather and process it, must be trustworthy. Reliable information will be as free from filtering and rephrasing as possible. Sales figures that have not been adjusted for returns and refunds are not reliable. Stating the value of a company's assets without showing the claims against them by others inaccurately portrays the real financial situation.

- **Relevant information** pertains to a manager's area of responsibility and is essential for the manager to have. Information about maintenance costs of the company's truck fleet is needed by only a few managers. Irrelevant information can waste a manager's time.

- **Complete information** contains all the facts that a manager needs to make decisions and solve problems. Nothing vital is left out. Managers with incomplete information are handicapped. Although information cannot always be complete, every reasonable effort should be made to obtain it.

- **Concise information** omits material that is extraneous. Just enough—no more, no less—is received by those in need. Giving managers a 200-page computer printout to wade through wastes their time. Summaries of key information, leaving out the details and supporting documents, may be all that is needed. Whenever appropriate, information should be displayed using visual devices such as charts, graphs, and tables. A standard used in the law offers a sensible guideline: Include only that which is necessary and sufficient.

- **Timely information** comes to managers when they need it. Premature information can become obsolete or be forgotten by the time it is actually needed. Information arriving after the time of need is likewise useless. Timeliness is one reason why so many managers rely on computers; they help managers to monitor events as they happen and obtain the real-time information and instant feedback necessary for spotting trends and reacting promptly to circumstances and events.

- **Cost-effective information** is gathered, processed, and disseminated at reasonable cost. A weekly detailed survey of all of a company's customers might delight the sales manager, at least until the survey costs were matched against revenues. A scientifically conducted periodic survey of consumers is likely to yield comparable results at more acceptable cost.

Types of Information Needed by Managers

Managers require a wide variety of information, depending on their positions. Functional information—about marketing, production, finance, and personnel—is needed by both line and staff managers. Information gathered or generated by staff personnel—legal, public relations, computer services, or research and development—may be useful to some line managers as well. Production managers need timely information about inventories, schedules, materials and labor costs, and the maintenance and serviceability of machines and equipment. Supervisors in marketing need sales figures (by stores, departments, and products), order-processing times, inventory levels, delivery schedules, and market-research findings. Finance and accounting managers need financial statements, payroll figures, accounts-receivable and -payable numbers, asset valuations, budgets, and cost data. Regardless of the information needed, an organization's management information system must provide it effectively and efficiently to those in need. Says one authority succinctly, "Information provides the substance for coordinating every aspect of the management process" (Bittel, 1989).

Top-level managers need information on economic conditions, competitors, legal and political developments, technological innovations, customers' needs for and acceptance of the company's products and services, and progress of operational units toward the organization's goals. Middle managers need information on their particular divisions' operations, including sales, costs, production output, personnel employed, and budget status. The primary difference between what is needed at the top and what is required in the middle lies in the source of information. Much of what top management requires comes from external sources. Most of what middle managers require comes from internal sources—observations, meetings, and reports.

Lower-level managers and autonomous teams need information and feedback about daily, weekly, and monthly activities. The sales manager needs to know how the salespeople are spending their time and the results they generate. Production people need to know the figures on waste, quality, productivity gains, units produced, and schedules met. Personnel may require daily and weekly figures on safety, attendance, new hires, interviews conducted, and job openings. And with today's emphasis on empowering workers and staying close to the customer and suppliers, feedback from these sources is essential for quick responses to their and the organization's needs.

As the need for new information grows and the organization evolves, so too must the ways in which it gathers, processes, stores, and disseminates information. The information system must be continually updated to provide what is needed.

Management Information Systems

A **management information system** (**MIS**) is a formal collection of processes that provides managers with suitable quality information to allow them to make decisions, solve problems, and carry out their functions and operations effectively and efficiently. Says one management writer, "MIS procedures include collecting, analyzing, and reporting past, present, and projected information from within and outside the organization." Another writer compares the MIS to the system model that was examined in Chapter 3:

The MIS is a system that exists as a subsystem of the organization. It gathers and transmits data (input); it combines and files data (conversion); and it retrieves, formats, and displays information (output). In addition, MISs have managers who monitor progress and take corrective action to solve problems and keep the system going (Virga, 1987).

Information provided to managers through their MIS helps them to plan, organize, staff, direct, and control both resources and operations. Information provides input to follow ongoing operations and their results. Information helps to highlight problems and potential problems by putting managers in touch with present conditions and developing trends. And information gives managers the data they will need to do future research and to make future plans, both strategic and operational. Exhibit 19.2 diagrams the components of a management information system.

Guidelines for Developing an MIS

Developing an MIS usually begins with a survey of those who will be served by it. By starting with an assessment of user needs, the system can be suitably equipped and designed. In work settings with no prior MIS, system designers may encounter

Decision making *is a manager's most important activity. The information system needs to support managers by providing timely and accurate information in an organized format.*

Exhibit 19.2

A simplified MIS for an oil company.

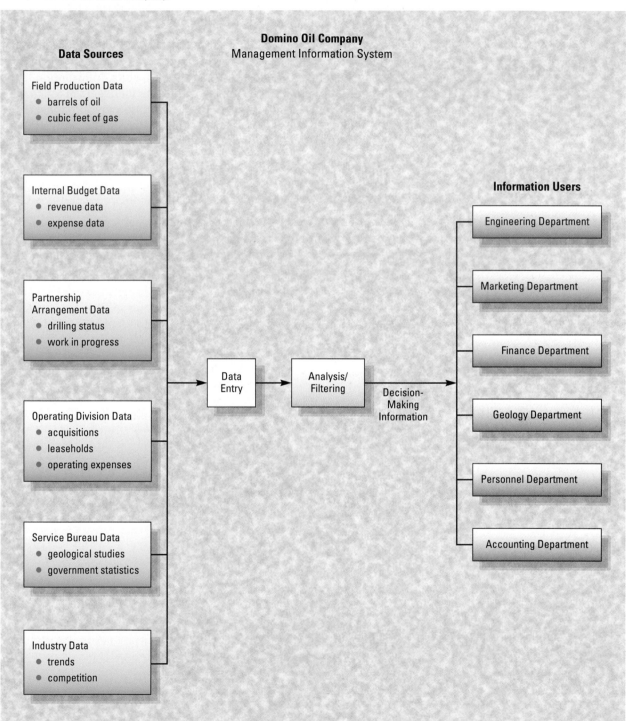

Domino Oil Company
Management Information System

Data Sources

Field Production Data
- barrels of oil
- cubic feet of gas

Internal Budget Data
- revenue data
- expense data

Partnership
Arrangement Data
- drilling status
- work in progress

Operating Division Data
- acquisitions
- leaseholds
- operating expenses

Service Bureau Data
- geological studies
- government statistics

Industry Data
- trends
- competition

Data Entry

Analysis/ Filtering

Decision-Making Information

Information Users

Engineering Department

Marketing Department

Finance Department

Geology Department

Personnel Department

Accounting Department

resistance among employees due to fear of the unknown or fear of change. Some workers may perceive a loss of their authority to "techno-experts." In order to ensure acceptance, wise managers will thoughtfully address such concerns before attempting to institute the system. Needs assessments can help to improve existing systems by revealing problems and specific needs not currently being met. From the outset, the MIS should be integrated harmoniously into the organization's portfolio of management resources.

When establishing or improving an MIS, the following guidelines should prove useful.

- Involve users in the system's design. Where computers will form the heart of the system, users should be consulted on choices of hardware and software. Make certain that components are user-friendly and fully compatible—able to communicate with one another. Because the information specialists (such as system-design people and MIS personnel) will not be using the information they help to prepare and disseminate, they need the guidance of those they are to serve.

- Establish clear lines of authority and direction for the MIS personnel. If the group is to operate a centralized MIS serving the entire organization's needs, place it under the control of a top-level manager—a chief information officer. If decentralization is chosen, establish unambiguous links and guidelines for those on lower levels to use while running their data centers; link them to the top for control, coordination, and guidance. Many firms use a standing committee for this purpose, composed of department heads, MIS supervisors, or a mixture of both.

- Establish clear procedures for gathering, sorting, interpreting, displaying, storing, and distributing data and for interacting with the system. Structure reduces fear and helps to guarantee security, uniformity, quality, and productivity.

- Where technical specialists are used, ensure that both they and the managers they support fully understand the specialists' functions and roles. Leave no doubt that the specialists serve in an advisory capacity.

- Build an MIS staff consistent with service requirements. Keep the staff members flexible and their skills current with suitable training and professional development. Avoid under- and overstaffing; both degrade service quality.

Characteristics of an Effective MIS

An MIS must be designed to meet specific user needs; it provides information and links an organization's parts. To provide useful information, an MIS, like controls, should possess three characteristics (Sihler, 1971):

- Meet organizational objectives. Does the system relate to and reinforce the goals of the organization? Are the system and objectives congruent, or do they conflict? Is the system cost-effective?

- Provide information flow. Does the system relate well to the organizational structure? Does information flow acceptably to those who generate and use it? Is coordination and consolidation of information effective and easy?

- Deliver the right quality and quantity of information. Do managers receive information necessary and sufficient to do their jobs? Do they receive too little? Too much? Does the information tell them what they need to know about activities they control and can influence?

Computerized Information Systems

Because the computer is an affordable, portable, and efficient tool, a growing proportion of U.S. businesses large and small use it throughout their operations, including management information systems. The result, as one observer sees it, is that

> almost all forms of organizations are dependent on digital computer technology to process information. With the tremendous advances in microcomputers, office automation, robotics, telecommunications, and computer-aided manufacture and design, computer technology is affecting almost all aspects of business…. Computers have become so important to some firms that the successful administration of the information system can mean life or death for the organization (Mensching and Adams, 1991).

A **computerized information system** (**CIS**) is an MIS built upon computer hardware and software to collect and process data and store and disseminate the resulting information. The functions of a CIS are shown in Exhibit 19.3. Computerized information systems may be centralized or decentralized. After a brief examination of both types, we will examine computer operations.

The centralized computer information system is under top management's direction and control.

> Its primary function is to assist other units of the organization to function in a more effective and efficient manner. Unless the information systems area also sells computing services to external users, it will not produce an end product or generate external revenue. Hence, it is of the utmost importance that the managers within the information systems area understand the operations of their client departments and the company as a whole (Mensching and Adams, 1991).

A CIS functioning both at the top and at other management levels is said to be decentralized. Each unit of a decentralized CIS is called a **data center**, and operates to serve its unit's members with their own sets of hardware, software, and specialists (machine operators and programmers). The basics for operating a decentralized CIS include:

> At a minimum there must be data exchange standards established so that files can be easily transferred. For the sake of economy and efficiency, many firms find it best to establish company-wide standards such as those for hardware and software compatibility. Not only does this allow for the exchange of data but, more importantly, it encourages the sharing of resources and the uniformity of reports (Mensching and Adams, 1991).

Function	Description
Computer Operations	Runs the system; involves starting jobs, mounting the proper input and output volumes, and responding to problem conditions
System Programming	Installs and maintains the operating system and associated system software
Data Entry	Entering data in machine-readable form
Application Program Development	Writing new application systems
Application Program Maintenance	Correcting and updating existing application systems
Data Management	Assuring data security, access, integrity, and useability
Communications Management	Configuring and maintaining the network
End-User Computing	Helping and educating users

Source: James R. Mensching and Dennis A. Adams, *Managing an Information System* (Englewood Cliffs, NJ: Prentice-Hall), 1991, p. 56. Reprinted by permission of the publisher. Copyright 1991 Prentice-Hall.

Decentralized CISs result in **end-user computing**: the use of information technology (IT) by people who are free from control by top management. Although end-user computing can stimulate innovative problem solving and decision making, it does present managers with collateral problems.

The first problem concerns control. Efforts must be made to coordinate multiple end-users' computing efforts in order to avoid duplication of work and consequent waste. Top management and other units must be encouraged to share useful approaches with one another and keep informed of projects and processes.

A second problem concerns possible duplication of expensive software and hardware. Planners must ensure that such components are fully compatible—able to efficiently share and exchange data through suitable interfaces and networks.

The third problem lies in orderly, authorized access to both the organization's systems and to its **database** (sometimes called data bank)—a collection of data arranged for ease and speed of retrieval. Databases rank among some organizations' most valuable assets; loss or impairment may shut down the enterprise cold. Imagine American Express or the New York Stock Exchange or Pacific Bell with their computers down. A lack of trained users, or inadequate controls over access and scheduling, renders systems and components vulnerable to damage or compromise.

Databases may be created internally, by outsiders, or both. Accessing outside databases can be useful but expensive. Because external users are commonly billed by the amount of time they are in contact with a commercial data source, one of a firm's database users may be able to acquire information and then share it with others within the organization, thus avoiding duplication in time and billing.

Among outside sources is PC Globe, whose software atlas includes digitized maps and data for some 200 countries, among them the newly liberated countries of Eastern Europe as well as the Baltic States and the nations that once composed the Soviet Union. This database contains a wealth of statistics and graphs of interest to managers dealing with the global economy (Reid and Hume, 1992).

The remainder of this chapter concentrates on management information systems that are at least partially computerized and thereby qualifying as full or partially computerized information systems.

Computer Operations

Computer hardware consists of input devices, a control unit, a central processing unit (CPU), storage devices, and output devices. A computer system also includes software—the programs that give the hardware the instructions for processing and storing data. Computer software encompasses two fundamental classes of programs: operating systems and application programs. An **operating system** comprises "an extensive and complex set of programs that manages the operation of a computer and the application [programs] that run on it" (Keen, 1991). Computer manufacturers design their computers to run on one or more operating systems. Some 100 million personal computers (PCs) were estimated to be in use in early 1993, many in business settings. The great majority of the IBM-compatible PCs use Microsoft's MS-DOS for their operating system; recent additions to the field include Microsoft Windows and IBM's OS/2. Apple Macintosh computers employ a different operating architecture altogether, and large IBM machines (mainframes and minicomputers) run on MVS and DOS/VSE operating systems.

Application programs are programs designed to execute specific sets of tasks such as word processing, graphics design, accounting and finance, production operations and marketing, personnel and inventory control, and many more. Some are specially designed (and programmed) in-house, whereas others may be purchased commercially from a vast array of options. Among well-known off-the-shelf programs are WordPerfect, Lotus 1-2-3 (spreadsheet), dBase, and Design CAD 3. Custom-developed programs include many of Boeing's design and engineering packages, Norfolk Southern's computer-aided reporting system, and American Airlines' SABRE. System designers first consider the software that will meet the company's needs, then select equipment that can run that software. Care must be taken to ensure that all equipment and software can be used interchangeably by user groups and units within the company. In the case of the American Airlines reservation system, outside users such as travel agents must be able to access it as well.

Data Processing Modes

Two data processing modes are commonly used in the business setting: batch processing and transactional processing. Under **batch processing**, data are collected over time and entered into data banks according to prescribed policies and procedures. For example, a clerk may collect orders from outside salespeople and enter them into the order database at the end of each week. In **transactional processing**, data are received about a company's ongoing operations and entered into data banks as each transaction occurs. In order to accomplish the intended utility of transactional processing, certain kinds of information must be entered into the system in real time or as close to real time as possible. Without such immediacy, these data will be unavailable to users and managers when needed. Bank automated-teller machines (ATMs) record transactions in the computer's memory as they occur; travel agents book reservations directly into the database. Most CISs are built around transactional processing to yield the best results.

Linking Computer Systems

The electronic linking of two or more computers is called **networking** (not to be confused with the informal system of personal contacts often used in career development, as discussed in Chapter 21). Such linkage allows computers to communicate directly through cables (in local area networks, or LANs), via microwave transmission, or by fiber optics. As organizations decentralize into data centers, the requirement to operate with networks grows. Typical network linkages include suppliers with customers, designers and engineers with production staffs, and among divisions and headquarters of global operations.

For greatest effectiveness, a CIS can communicate outside an organization as well as among insiders. External compatibility requirements influence the kind of software and hardware that planners choose. Wal-Mart and K Mart use **distributed data processing** (DDP) in their linkups with suppliers. In such systems the company and its suppliers can share information and tap into common databases to monitor and modify transactions. DDP, sometimes called electronic data interchange, allows quick contact and response times. The resulting cycle compression usually increases productivity.

CIS Tools for Managers

Effective managers use every available asset to accomplish their jobs. Few assets rival the computer for sheer utility in helping managers plan, organize, staff, direct, and control. Among the great strengths of computer technology is the ability to automate the data processing that underlies a sound MIS. The power and flexibility of most computer systems is limited only by the imagination of their users. The editors of a respected management handbook, however, caution their readers to remember that "computers do not have the feelings, perceptions, or flexibility of the human mind" (Virga, 1987).

Decision Support Systems   To harness the immense quantities of data now accessible to managers, imaginative thinkers have devised a specialized variant of a CIS, the **decision support system** (DSS). This analytic model joins the manager's experience, judgment, and intuition with the computer's data access, display, and calculation strengths (Virga, 1987). The DSS allows managers to interact with linked programs and databases through the keyboard. DSS programs are available off-the-shelf or may be tailored in-house. With such a system, a marketing manager may ask the computer, "What happens to sales if we lower prices by 10 percent?" The system will manipulate the model and stored data, then present likely outcomes: production volume, sales, inventories, revenues, and costs.

Specialized end-user decision support programs include the **expert system**, software that stores the knowledge of a group of authorities for access by nonexperts faced with the need to make topic-related decisions (Mensching and Adams, 1991). To build such a system, information specialists study an expert's way of analyzing an issue or solving a problem; then they write a program that simulates the expert's methods and techniques. Expert systems are a kind of artificial intelligence, which is discussed in Future Trends at the end of this chapter.

Yet another variant decision support system is the **group decision support system**, or **GDSS**. The GDSS allows a group focusing on a problem, like a product or process design team, to interact with one another and exchange information, data, and ideas. GDSSs are used in brainstorming and problem-solving sessions and to facilitate conferencing of all kinds. For example, a group of participants, assembled anonymously from terminals in their offices or in remote locations, may interact in real time under the direction of a moderator as ideas and questions are presented.

It should be emphasized that a DSS is an analytical *support* system, not a maker of decisions (Bittel and Ramsey, 1985). Observe two experts, a "DSS allows the manager to examine more thoroughly a problem and experiment with many different solutions. This tends to give the manager more confidence in the decision. But, due to the multitude of possibilities to explore, it usually does not make the decision process any quicker" (Mensching and Adams, 1991).

General Mills utilizes a DSS by making appropriate data available to autonomous factory teams so that they can make their own decisions:

> At some beverage plants, for example, four shifts of 20-person teams are informed of marketing plans and production costs. "They have at their fingertips all the data that would normally be held by management," says Daryl D. David, a human resources director. The self-managed teams do everything from scheduling production to rejecting products not up to quality standards, and they receive bonuses based on plant performance. Some 60% of General Mills' plants have been converted to such high-performance work systems. The approach has produced significant gains in productivity, and the company is now moving to spread it to all operations (*Business Week,* 1992).

Executive Information Systems   An **executive information system** (EIS) is a decision support system custom designed to facilitate executive decision making. Typical executive uses include forecasting; strategic planning; performing risk and cost-benefit analyses; running business game simulations; linear programming; monitoring quality, productivity, ethics, and social responsibility efforts; and monitoring critical success factors and stakeholder expectations (Crockett, 1992). EISs and DSSs "are particularly useful when they are able to access the databases used by other organizational information systems as well" (Bittel and Ramsey, 1985).

A sophisticated EIS can integrate many levels of information and abstraction. Users may draw upon data derived from a division, department, function, individual employee, or discrete transaction. Moreover, the exponentially expanding resources of external databases may be accessed electronically. From the vast library of legal citations of Mead Data's LEXIS or the *Wall Street Journal* to book and periodical holdings of immense university libraries, managers have the world of information at their keyboards to assist in researching problems and making decisions (Mensching and Adams, 1991).

Implementing a CIS: Overcoming Resistance

Proper establishment of a CIS requires guidance and support from top management. Coordinated with a comprehensive needs assessment, managers must create goals, standards, and schedules, and sufficient funding must be committed to staff and equip the system. These actions determine choices of hardware, software, and databases. An appropriate organization, the number of systems that will be created, the degree of autonomy that each will have, and reporting and control relationships must be determined. Perhaps programmers and information specialists should be hired; staff must be trained both to create and to operate the system, and the job descriptions of present staff should be modified and expanded. All these issues mean change, and change can generate resistance.

Apprehension is common among employees encountering a CIS for the first time; they perceive threats to their authority, job security, career, and social relationships. People fear they may lose status, that their interactions with others will change. Managers worry that their futures suddenly depend on the performance of a computer staff. To help overcome these concerns, line managers can be given control over decentralized data centers placed within their units. The system can be tailored to ensure that these managers are active players, less dependent on information specialists.

Other employees may worry that computers will render them expendable, or that they lack the technical expertise to adapt to the new technology. Information systems *do* require basic computer literacy and familiarity with the software for people who will use them; nevertheless, nearly everyone with a willingness to learn can acquire the skills needed to access and use the hardware and software of a new CIS. Furthermore, whereas some existing jobs may be eliminated, new ones will inevitably be created. Management should provide suitable retraining, wherever possible, and offer the new positions to valued employees. Well in advance, workers should be told just what changes are coming and precisely what the changes will mean to them personally. When managers provide ample information to their people, enthusiastic interest and support drive out fear and speculation.

Comfortable with old ways of doing things, many employees (including some at the top) resist any change to their work habits. The task of managers is to convince these people, and everyone affected by the new system, that the organization and all its members will benefit from the new system. Each person needs to know how the new system will serve his or her needs more effectively and efficiently. All those affected need to know why change is necessary and should be included the decisions that will effect the change. It takes time, patience, and money to get the system up and running and the people comfortable with new methods and technologies.

Managing Information Systems

To manage a CIS effectively, an organization must confront three challenges: to develop users, to integrate the components, and to evaluate the effectiveness and efficiency of the information system. These issues are examined in the following section.

Developing Users

When designing a DSS or EIS, information specialists must spend time with future users in order to design systems that mimic the users' thought processes and analytic techniques. As these developmental conferences are in progress, managers can learn from the information specialists what they can expect the system to do for them and what they will need to know in order to use the system properly. Then users can begin training, to acquire the necessary knowledge and skills.

Most managers rely on several techniques to aid them in their problem solving and decision making. One approach is management by exception—looking for and focusing on deviations from standards and norms. Decision support systems can be designed to identify the deviations and report them promptly to managers. Increasingly sophisticated advances in computer graphics permit translation of exceptions and other critical factors into remarkably useful visuals—not shopworn shaded bars and pies, but interactive displays in commanding color video.

The **key indicator management** (**KIM**) monitoring system provides core measures of the company or unit operations that are indispensable for managers' decision making. Reports are designed so that for each measure and target, progress toward the identified target is shown (Janson, 1980). Rather than reviewing an entire operation, the manager can concentrate on the indicator. If the indicator is off target, the manager investigates further.

Exhibit 19.4 shows one application of a KIM. Note that the key indicator has been identified as sales orders, which are measured by average order amount in dollars; the target or goal is $500. At a glance the manager can see that the results for the month, the year to date, or the past year have not reached the goal. The target was exceeded, however, at some time during the last 12 months.

Integrating Components

Integration—networking and sharing—is usually required to some extent among CISs throughout an organization. Integration allows people at the next workstation or halfway around the world to communicate with one another and to access stored and remote databases; it allows units to use one another's software and hardware. Integration requires that users know each other's systems and components and possess the proper access codes (passwords) that allow entry into a program or database.

Equipment and software packages must be compatible. Compatibility must also extend to the systems of appropriate outside users.

Design and redesign of a CIS must allow for interunit communication and shareability. Designers identify who must communicate with whom, what they must be able to share, where they are located, how best to connect them, what equipment each user has, and how much it will cost to install the system. Consistent guidelines and standards for system operation must be devised. And care must be

Exhibit 19.4

Key indicator management applied to sales performance.

Order Size	Indicator	Measure	Target	This Month	Year to Date	Past Year	Range: Past 12 Months	
							High	Low
The amount of the individual sales orders serves as an indicator of both the energy used in promoting the product and the meeting of market potential	Sales orders	Average order amount (dollars)	$ 500	$ 350	$ 400	$ 475	$ 600	$ 325

taken to avoid duplication of effort or appropriation of redundant components; such wastes must be eliminated when they are discovered.

For efficiency and effectiveness, functions and processes need to be linked both by networks and by physical proximity. Many companies today are organizing around processes, not functions, by grouping personnel and equipment in close proximity. This horizontal focus allows processes to be managed by a person or team, through the use of integrated components, from start to finish.

Evaluating Effects

The CIS that does not result in improved management is not functioning properly, and possible causes for disappointment abound. An information system may appear to fail because managers expect too much from it. Information systems are tools to facilitate, not substitute for, decision making. Their success depends upon imaginative conception and skilled application: machines can do only what they are programmed to do; systems can produce only what they are designed to produce. Limitations placed on system designers will limit system performance.

Companies that do not hire talented system professionals, that fail to properly train their users, or that invest in poor-quality equipment and software will be operating in an inefficient and problematic environment. An inadequately designed system will remain so, no matter how accurate the data entry. Poorly trained users will make mistakes and fail to utilize system capabilities. People who fear or resent the system or who feel that it or their employer has done them a disservice may decide to (or even inadvertently) sabotage the system. Unhappy workers who know they will be laid off or fired have been known to delete files or unleash a computer virus. Employees who feel that the system will erode their authority or monitor their activities may act to subvert the system by entering false data or altering stored information. Substandard equipment is prone to malfunctions and incompatibility with other components.

I S S U E S   A N D   E T H I C S
Putting Out the Fire with Gasoline

n a January 1992 article titled "Biggest Business Goofs of 1991," *Fortune* magazine included the following report:

Angry over leaks of what it considered proprietary information from employees to a reporter from the *Wall Street Journal,* [a major consumer products manufacturer] (armed with a subpoena and police cooperation) set out in June [1991] to find the leaker by combing phone records of citizens around its headquarters city. Eight hundred thousand of them. The member of the police force who ran the investigation just happened to be a part-time employee with the company. The search failed to uncover a leaker but it did manage to bring the public's wrath down on the company. After condemnation from a local newspaper and business press, the company's chairman said, "We created a problem that was larger than the one we were trying to solve."

What do you think about this company's actions? If you worked for the firm, how might your attitude at work change? If you were this company's chairman, how would you have handled the incident? ▲

For more on this topic, see Alan Farnham, "Biggest Business Goofs of 1991," *Fortune,* January 13, 1992, p. 83.

People who feel frustrated by the CIS and their own inabilities to use it properly may decide to bypass it, relying on the old, less automated ways of doing things. And when the system does not yield the results people believe or assume it should, they may work around it and come up with their own methods and solutions, leaving the system underutilized and lacking justification for its funding and personnel.

Finally, as managers and organizational needs change, the information system must be adapted as well. Nothing remains static. Systems must be flexible to provide for the new and to eliminate their inefficiencies. Users must be continually asked how the system is serving them, and their answers used to improve CIS operations.

Emerging Information Technologies

In this section we examine recent innovations that affect information systems. Some break new ground, others represent improvements to existing technologies. All offer ways to improve quality and productivity in organizations.

Computer Hardware

Deep into 1993 the cost of computers continued its dramatic decline begun a year earlier. Increasingly powerful computers are found in even the smallest mom-and-pop operations. Notebook-sized machines (laptops and palmtops) are proliferating like bubbles on a pancake. Able to accompany their busy users virtually anywhere as well as to communicate with desktops, mainframes, and mini-computers by any of several technologies, these are remarkably versatile little machines. Some even allow their users to input and manipulate data using wireless pens for pointing or writing. All these features expand the appeal of computers, even to people uncomfortable with keyboarding.

Application programs are designed to assist in the performance of specific tasks. This database integrates employee photos so that personnel departments can facilitate security, badging, and management reviews.

Innovations of size and breadth of task seem endless. Liquid crystal display (LCD) technology has made the flat TV and computer screens possible. Olivetti & Company has produced PCs using reduced-instruction-set computing (RISC)—a speedy technology usually found in more-powerful workstation computers; they also recently announced a 2.2-pound PC about half the size of a notebook computer (Hooper, 1992). In 1992 Apple Computer introduced a PC called Newton

> that takes its orders from hand-printed entries, which are deleted to the sounds of crumpling paper. By using an electronic pen and printing on its screen such [messages] as 'Fax Bob, meeting Wednesday,' Apple's hand-held computer, which is the size of a videocassette, is designed to automatically fax data and make an entry for a meeting in its computerized appointment calendar without any additional steps. In addition, the Newton can be used as a sophisticated calculator and includes an automatic telephone-dialing feature (Yamada, 1992).

In 1992 IBM became the first manufacturer to produce a fingernail-sized chip able to store 16 million bits of data—equivalent to some 1,600 pages of typewritten, double-spaced text—four times the capacity of common four-megabit chips (*Chicago Tribune*, 1992). IBM has used them in its AS-400 minicomputers, which sell for just under $1 million.

The supercomputer maker, Thinking Machines, introduced in 1992 a new system for storing huge amounts of data. It has a system that integrates disks more tightly than most computers do, vastly increasing the speed of data access and storage while breaking the bottlenecks imposed by conventional input/output (I/O) architecture (*Wall Street Journal*, 1992). This technology allows a disk system to reach a speed of 4,000 megabytes per second, or 40 times faster than the current 100 million characters per second.

Cordless cellular phones that transmit by microwave add still another dimension. Through modems (the device that permits computers to communicate via telephone lines) they become effective computer input/output devices. Today phone manufacturers as well as computer makers are building modems right into their hardware. Microcom Inc. of Massachusetts sells a 4.5-pound cellular phone in a bag with its modem: the user simply plugs the phone into the computer and dials (Weber, 1992).

Computer Software

A catalogue of innovative software is beyond the scope of hardcover publishing. Dozens of breathless computer periodicals and newsletters can barely summarize each month's bushel baskets of powerful new programs. Whether you'd like the complete *Oxford English Dictionary on Historical Principles,* voice-activated language translators, any of Adobe's more than 1,300 typefaces, or a package to calculate the complete weekly payroll and corporate taxes for a company with 15,000 employees, next-day delivery is only a toll-free phone call and a credit card away.

Allstate Insurance, Sears & Roebuck, McDonald's, AT&T, and IBM are equipping handicapped employees with software that allows them to become fully productive members of their organizations. Allstate lets Mike Baubkus, senior staff systems programmer and a quadraplegic, use speech-recognition software from Dragon Systems to control programs that create memos, reports, electronic mail, and spreadsheets. With DragonDictate, from 200 words entered by the user, the computer builds a base to recognize 30,000 words spoken by the user (Engdahl, 1992). Applications are endlessly expanding.

Software packages exist to detect viruses (programs, usually maliciously designed, that replicate themselves into other programs stored in a computer, causing various malfunctions) in computer databases. One way to keep out viruses is to carefully monitor and limit access to databases. In addition to passwords and

FOCUS ON QUALITY
Chips That Find Fault, but Forgive

Geneneral Electric is designing quality into a new generation of computer chips. Its goal is to solve the frustrating problem faced when a computer component fails. Every computer user fears that occasion when the monitor screen goes blank or displays some grim message, like FATAL ERROR.

"'Fault-tolerant' computers that can keep running even when a component fails" have been around awhile. But they require additional cost and space [because] they rely on extra components, like microprocessors, that back up primary systems. But General Electric has created "'self-healing' computer chips that police themselves for errors caused by faulty circuit elements and correct the problems without halting data processing." The GE chip does not require much of an increase in the size of the systems it is part of and has the "additional capability to detect and correct errors built right into the chips." The chips are less expensive than the redundant systems they replace.

GE has applied for patents and expects to use the new chips in its own lines of such products as aircraft engines and medical systems—equipment that must have high reliability. GE hopes to license its technology to others in the future. ▲

For more about self-correcting microchips, see Amal Kumar Naj, "GE Chip Finds, Corrects Errors, Company Says," *Wall Street Journal,* April 16, 1992, p. A20.

tokens, ID cards and numbers, computer-security software now allows a computer to recognize a user's voice, the map of blood vessels in one's eye, one's fingerprint, and one's lip print (*Fortune*, 1991).

Silicon Graphics Inc., a California-based software maker, has developed packages used by scientists and engineers to produce three-dimensional color images (Zachary, 1992). Xerox has found a method by which facsimile machines can be used as keyboards for input to remote computers.

> Dubbed PaperWorks, the software allows users to retrieve, store, distribute, and organize documents without having to be near their personal computers— all on a single sheet of fax paper. Users make check marks with a pen or a pencil in boxes on the sheet and then fax the form to their PC, which carries out the instructions (Pac, 1992).

Many new PCs now come equipped with a built-in fax board.

A variety of operating systems software—the programming that guides the inner operations of the computer—has given users new variants of the graphical user interface (GUI, or 'gooey' for short). Introduced in the 1980s by Apple Computer for its popular Macintosh machines, the GUI system uses a mouse (a button-activated hand-held input device supplementing the conventional computer keyboard) to move an on-screen arrow among icons that represent functions. Recent innovations have brought the GUI to the IBM-compatible world through IBM's OS/2 2.0 and Microsoft's Windows 3.1 (Rogers, 1992).

Networking

Local area networks (LANs) began as cable hookups among a company's PCs and workstations. When companies added new terminals or moved existing ones, new cable had to be installed. When rented facilities were abandoned, cable was left behind. Added to these costs the expense of renting cable access, companies often found networking a very expensive proposition. Today's LANs are no longer cable-dependent. Full-speed wireless LANs are now possible with NCR Corporation's WaveLAN, which uses radio frequencies and an antenna to transmit two million bits per second across 200 feet. Motorola introduced a cableless network called Altair that uses Ethernet—a leading networking environment. The system can transmit three million bits per second across as much as 250 feet indoors. InfraLAN, made by the British company BICC, uses infrared light, transmitting at four million bits per second over an 80-foot range (Wood, 1991).

Integrated Services Digital Network (ISDN) offers dedicated phone lines that can be used for voice, fax, data, and video transmissions. These lines use digital signals instead of electric impulses along wires. Most use fiber optics and convert electrical signals to light impulses. A Chicago TV station employs ISDN to record its voice-over announcements between programs—using an announcer who lives in Arizona (Blankenhorn, 1991).

Virtual Reality

This technology blends television, computers, software, and microprocessors to present the user with a three-dimensional model in which he or she can navigate. Users wear a headset with television screens for viewing. As the users move, the software adjusts the images they see to those movements.

G L O B A L   A P P L I C A T I O N S
International Piracy of Intellectual Property

tealing someone's ideas is still stealing. When someone appropriates a maker's software—loads it into a computer without buying it from an authorized source—it is called pirating. According to Nancy McSharry, an analyst at International Data Corporation in Massachusetts, "Our assumptions are that basically 20% of the software in the United States is pirated. In Western Europe, though, it's more like 50% to 60%. In Asia, 80% of software is pirated. There we're looking at a major problem." McSharry notes that a precondition for Italy's entry into the European Community was that its government move to reduce the pirating problem.

"In the U.S., piracy penalties can be a fine as high as $100,000 for each registered program." Since 1990, "Software Publishers Association, an industry watchdog group, has filed more than 100 lawsuits and collected more than $1 million in penalties from companies for software piracy." When people pirate software, they usually don't have the manuals and backup support that comes with it. If they have a problem, they are on their own. Also, when you load someone else's software into your computer, you run the risk of loading a virus that may have been picked up in the other person's usage. That could mean losing much more than the amount of a fine. ▲

For more on software pirating, see Michael Bane, "Pirating on Wane in U.S. but Prevalent Elsewhere," *Chicago Tribune*, November 17, 1991, sec. 19, p. l0.

Architects use virtual reality to take people on a tour: clients can experience what it will be like to walk up to, around, and through a building that has not yet been built. Scientists use virtual reality to view a molecule up close. The molecule takes on the size of any room they happen to inhabit. In America, Europe, and Japan, kitchen installers and remodelers use it to help the customer choose cabinets and appliances and visualize how they will look in the new kitchen.

Future Trends

The following innovations will affect management information systems in the near future:

- Sanyo has developed a superconducting transistor that is 10 times faster than existing semiconductors and uses far less power. It could appear in high-speed supercomputers soon.

- Motorola has teamed with United Parcel Service to create the first nationwide cellular mobile data network. In 1993, it gives UPS the ability to instantly locate any of its packages on the ground or in the air.

- French researchers have built on U.S. inventions and come up with a new type of flat display screen they call field emission display, or FED. It is cheaper, lighter, and easier to read than conventional LCD screens and should appear soon on all kinds of miniature electronic devices.

- Digital Equipment Corporation has developed a more powerful chip, called Alpha, which can process 64 bits of information at one time, twice the capacity of current microprocessor chips.

● In addition to these trends, technology is moving ever closer to **artificial intelligence** (**AI**)—developing the capability of machines to learn, sense, and think for themselves. Such a goal requires enormous computing capabilities coupled with great speed.

Thinking Machines Corporation has moved in this direction with a new line of supercomputers that uses hundreds of RISC-based microprocessors chained together to solve little parts of big problems simultaneously, a technique called parallel processing. The typical computer works sequentially—one step, then another. This new supercomputer is capable of nine billion calculations per second. The smallest version costs more than $1 million, but the firm claims to have orders for computers that can handle hundreds of billions of calculations per second (*Chicago Tribune*, 1991).

Fields related to artificial intelligence include voice-recognition systems, speech synthesis programs, expert systems, computer vision, and robotics. But most research in AI is focused on giving computers decision-making capability. "In fact, advances in one branch of AI, neural network technology, suggest that machines may not only have the capability to mimic human decision making, they may actually be able to learn and reason like humans." When computers are "programmed with a set of rules and a knowledge base, the system can then make logical inferences as well as routine calculations" (Wade, 1993).

C H A P T E R   **S** U M M A R Y

■ Managers depend on a constant flow of information from a variety of sources to carry out their duties.

■ Data can be used when processed into information—data that have been selected and prepared for users.

■ For information to be useful, it must be understandable, reliable, relevant, complete, concise, timely, and cost-effective.

■ The kinds of information needed by managers vary with their duties and positions in the company.

■ Management information systems (MISs) provide needed information in a timely, effective, and efficient manner. They usually require the services of talented information specialists to design and operate them.

■ Developing and evaluating the MIS depends upon user inputs and feedback.

■ Computerized information systems depend on computers in the hands of information specialists and end users. MISs that use computers experience gains in speed, accuracy, and reliability.

- Computers depend on operating systems that run the machines' internal operations, and application programs that allow the user to perform specific tasks. Computers can work and access data and information in real time—as things actually occur.

- Implementing the CIS depends on a commitment from top management and decisions about how to control its operations. They can be centralized or decentralized.

- Decision support systems assist managers in their efforts to make decisions and analyze problems.

- Major problems encountered when organizations establish a CIS include fear for one's job, career, social relationships, and authority. To work best, CISs need the input and support of those they are established to serve.

- Unless components are integrated and compatible, they will not interface, and communications throughout the organization will be compromised.

S K I L L - B U I L D I N G

The following questions are designed to test your knowledge of management information systems and how companies should work with them. Use any experience you may have with such systems from a current or past job when answering each question.

		Yes	No
1.	I know exactly what services my company's MIS offers and what it can do for me.	☐	☐
2.	Within the last year I have been asked for my opinion about and ratings of our MIS.	☐	☐
3.	I have sometimes sought necessary information on my own and from sources outside my company's MIS.	☐	☐
4.	I sometimes get information I do not need from my MIS.	☐	☐
5.	The information specialists in the MIS know my needs and generally meet them.	☐	☐
6.	I find it easy to discuss my needs with the information specialists because they listen.	☐	☐
7.	The commercial software my MIS uses has been purchased from authorized sources.	☐	☐
8.	My company has properly trained me to use the MIS and its services.	☐	☐
9.	Using the MIS has made my job easier and more productive.	☐	☐
10.	The MIS has helped to add quality to my outputs.	☐	☐

R E V I E W   Q U E S T I O N S

1. Review this chapter's essential terms and look up the meanings of those you cannot define.

2. What seven characteristics make information useful to managers?

3. What kinds of information do executives need? Middle managers? Marketing managers?

4. What characteristics make an MIS effective?

5. What major guidelines should a company follow when establishing an MIS?

6. What are the major kinds of decision support systems? What can they do for a manager?

7. What kinds of resistance can an organization expect from employees when it decides to establish and MIS?

8. What are the major emerging technologies discussed in this chapter, and how can they influence managers' productivity?

R E C O M M E N D E D   R E A D I N G

Benjamin, Robert I., and Jon Blunt. "Critical IT Issues: The Next Ten Years," *Sloan Management Review* (Summer 1992), pp. 21–32.

Billings, John. *Controlling with Computers: Control Theory* (New York: McGraw-Hill), 1989.

Crockett, Fess. "Revitalizing Executive Information Systems," *Sloan Management Review* (Summer 1992), pp. 39–47.

Keen, Peter G. W. *Every Manager's Guide to Information Technology: A Glossary of Key Terms and Concepts for Today's Business Leader* (Boston: Harvard Business School Press), 1991.

Lederer, Albert L., and Aubrey L. Mendelow. "Information Systems Planning: Top Management Takes Control," *Business Horizons* (May–June 1989), pp. 59–69.

Lockwood, Russ. "Systems That Dazzle," *PC Sources* (August 1992), pp. 179–180, 184–185, 190–191, 194–196.

Mensching, James R., and Dennis A. Adams. *Managing an Information System* (Englewood Cliffs, NJ: Prentice-Hall), 1991.

Nonaka, Ikujiro. "The Knowledge-creating Company," *Harvard Business Review* (November–December 1991), pp. 96–104.

Silk, David, and Tony Knight. *Managing Information* (New York: McGraw-Hill), 1989.

Stankovic, John A. "Real-Time Computing," *Byte* (August 1992), pp. 154–160.

R E F E R E N C E S

Bittel, Lester R. *The McGraw-Hill 36-Hour Management Course* (New York: McGraw-Hill), 1989, p. 229.

Bittel, Lester R., and Jackson E. Ramsey, editors. *Handbook for Professional Managers* (New York: McGraw-Hill), 1985, pp. 220, 222.

Blankenhorn, Dana. "Phones look like computer networks," *Chicago Tribune,* November 17, 1991, sec. 19, p. 4.

Business Week (August 31, 1992). "Management's New Gurus," p. 50.

Chicago Tribune (February 19, 1992). "IBM beats the Japanese with new memory chip," sec. 3, p. 3.

Chicago Tribune (November 10, 1991). "Computers close in on sacred goal," sec 7, p. 8.

Crockett, Fess. "Revitalizing Executive Information Systems" *Sloan Management Review* (Summer 1992), p. 41.

Engdahl, Lora. "New technologies lower the barriers," *Chicago Tribune,* March 15, 1992, sec 19, p. 3.

Farnham, Alan. "Biggest Business Goofs of 1991," *Fortune* (January 13, 1992), p. 83.

Fortune (December 16, 1991). "Computer Security: New Ways to Keep Hackers Out," p. 14.

Hooper, Laurence. "Olivetti Unveils Mini-PC at 2.2 Pounds; July Debut Set and U.S. Partner Sought," *Wall Street Journal,* May 19, 1992, p. A11.

Janson, Robert L. "Graphic Indicators of Operations," *Harvard Business Review* (November–December 1980), pp. 164–170.

Keen, Peter G. W. *Every Manager's Guide to Information Technology: A Glossary of Key Terms and Concepts for Today's Business Leader* (Boston: Harvard Business School Press), 1991, pp. 156–157.

Mandell, Steven L. *Information Processing and Data Processing,* 3rd edition (St. Paul, MN: West), 1988, p. 9.

Mensching, James R., and Dennis A. Adams. *Managing an Information System* (Englewood Cliffs, NJ: Prentice-Hall), 1991, pp. 1–2, 19, 54, 295, 296.

Pae, Peter. "Xerox Corp. Turns Facsimile Machines Into Computer Keys," *Wall Street Journal,* March 24, 1992, p. B14.

Reid, T. R., and Brit Hume. "PC Globe's software atlas will bring the world to your computer keyboard," *Chicago Tribune,* May 31, 1992, sec. 7, p. 6.

Rogers, Michael. "Windows of Opportunity," *Newsweek* (April 27, 1992), p. 63.

Sihler, William H. "Toward Better Management Control Systems," *California Management Review* 14, no. 2 (1971), p. 33.

Virga, Patricia H., editor. *The NMA Handbook for Managers* (Englewood Cliffs, NJ: Prentice-Hall), 1987, p. 312.

Wade, Winston J. "Knowledge in a Box," as printed in *The Best of Chief Executive,* J. P. Donlon, editor (Homewood, IL: Business One Irwin), 1993, p. 283.

Wall Street Journal (October 15, 1992). "Thinking Machines Introduces a Faster Storage Technology," p. B6.

Weber, Thomas E. "Cutting the Cord," *Wall Street Journal,* May 18, 1992, p. R8.

Wood, Lamont. "LANs needn't spawn wire tangles," *Chicago Tribune,* November 17, 1991, sec. 19, p. 7.

Yamada, Ken. "Apple Introduces 'Newton' Featuring Printing by Hand," *Wall Street Journal,* May 29, 1992, p. B3.

Zachary, G. Pascal. "Apple Is Seeking to Boost Power of Macintosh Using IBM Chip," *Wall Street Journal,* March 9, 1992, p. B6.

GLOSSARY OF TERMS

application program A computer program designed to execute specific sets of tasks such as word processing.

artificial intelligence (AI) The ability of a machine to perform those activities that are normally thought to require intelligence; giving machines the capability to learn, sense, and think for themselves.

batch processing A computer procedure in which data are collected over time and entered into databases according to prescribed policies and procedures.

computerized information system (CIS) An MIS built upon computer hardware and software to collect and process data and store and disseminate the resulting information.

data Unprocessed facts and figures.

database A collection of computerized data arranged for ease and speed of retrieval; sometimes called data bank.

data center A unit of a decentralized CIS that operates to serve its unit's members with their own sets of hardware, software, and specialists (machine operators and programmers).

decision support system (DSS)   A specialized variant of a CIS; an analytic model that joins a manager's experience, judgment, and intuition with the computer's data access, display, and calculation processes; allows managers to interact with linked programs and databases via the keyboard.

distributed data processing (DDP)   Computer systems in which two or more using organizations can share information and tap into common databases to monitor and modify transactions; sometimes called electronic data interchange.

end-user computing   The use of information technology (IT) by people who are not controlled and directed by top management.

executive information system (EIS)   A decision support system custom designed to facilitate executive decision making; may include forecasting, strategic planning, and other elements.

expert system   A specialized end-user decision support program that stores the knowledge of a group of authorities for access by nonexperts faced with the need to make topic-related decisions.

group decision support system (GDSS)   A variant decision support system that allows groups focusing on a problem to interact with one another and to exchange information, data, and ideas.

information   Data that have been deliberately selected, processed, and organized to be useful to an individual manager.

key indicator management (KIM)   A monitoring system that focuses on core measures of the company or unit operations that are indispensable for managers' decision making.

management information system (MIS)   A formal collection of processes that provides managers with suitable quality information to allow them to make decisions, solve problems, and carry out their functions and operations effectively and efficiently.

networking   The electronic linking of two or more computers.

operating system   An extensive and complex set of instructions that manages the operation of a computer and the application programs that run on it.

transactional processing   A computer procedure in which data are received about a company's ongoing operations and entered into data banks as each transaction occurs.

C A S E   P R O B L E M
Telephone Information Services

he nation's seven Baby Bells—the seven regional phone companies—already have some networks in place that carry voice mail and teleconferencing for businesses. Some offer news, sports, banking, and other information-related services. In some states their fiber-optic cables provide networking capabilities for high schools, colleges, and universities to talk with one another and share resources from libraries, research, and professors.

The Baby Bells are barred by federal law from owning the programs that are transmitted. This law has caused them to seek partners in the business community. One such arrangement is with Dow Jones & Company and Atlanta-based BellSouth. The partnership is testing voice mail for mobile-phone customers in Los Angeles that would give current news about finance, economic issues, and commodities trading. AT&T, U S West, and the cable company Telecommunications Incorporated are testing a pay-per-view and movie service in the Denver area. U S West will provide the transmitting signals that will link cable companies. Ameritech, based in Chicago, has initiated a set of facsimile services that, among other things, let users send simultaneous faxes from a single machine and collect fax messages sent to their subscribers when phone links are busy.

The Baby Bells' biggest asset is the databases on their subscribers and the services they have subscribed to. Several of these companies have begun innovative services based on their business directories.

Southwestern Bell, headquartered in St. Louis, is exploring operator-assisted directories that will help customers looking for a specific service find several options. Pacific Telesis, based in San Francisco, is testing a new form of directory assistance in which operators give callers more than just a business's phone number; they give its hours, address, ZIP code, and cross streets.

The Baby Bells' entrepreneurship has not gone unnoticed by their actual and potential rivals, including newspapers, cable companies, on-line computer services companies, and even American Telephone & Telegraph. These and other organizations are seeking legislation that will restrict the phone companies in their efforts to expand their information services.

Q U E S T I O N S

1. What additional services can you think of that might be offered by the Baby Bells?

2. What are some potential problems for phone companies that get into the media business?

3. Why do you think the federal government has prohibited phone companies from owning the programming that travels across their fiber-optic, electrical, and microwave lines?

International Management

LEARNING OBJECTIVES

After reading and discussing this chapter, you should be able to:

- Define this chapter's essential terms

- List three reasons why businesses establish foreign operations

- Discuss the importance of international trade to the U.S. economy

- Identify the characteristics of multinational corporations

- Describe components of the international manager's five environments

- Describe the complexities of planning for global operations

- Describe three phases of a company's move from domestic operations to a multinational structure

- Discuss three problems associated with staffing an international company

- Describe three problems associated with directing a cross-cultural work force

- Describe two control problems faced by multinational corporations

balance of trade

cross-cultural management
direct investment

embargo
global structure
globalization

international division
international management
multinational corporation
quota
tariff

M A N A G E M E N T   I N   A C T I O N
Blockbuster Entertainment

Blockbuster Entertainment Corporation, founded in 1987 and headquartered in Florida, operates 2,037 stores in the United States and 952 offshore, including Chile, Mexico, Venezuela, Spain, Japan, and Australia. Outlets in these countries are owned entirely by foreign nationals. Blockbuster's largest foreign presence is in Britain, where nearly all its 790 outlets are owned by the company. With a forecasted 1992 income from video rentals of $1.25 billion, Blockbuster Is the largest video-rental chain in the United States, even though it has only 15% of the market. By 1995 Blockbuster expects to earn about 25% of its revenue from foreign operations, an increase of about 20% from 1992. By that same year, it expects to operate 3,000 outlets in the United States.

President Joseph R. Baczko, past head of the international division of Toys R Us, is in charge of Blockbuster's overseas expansion. With "952 stores in nine foreign countries [he] plans to add at least 1,200 more stores by 1995." Blockbuster began its international expansion in London in 1990. In 1991 the firm entered into a joint venture with Den Fujita in Japan to run 15 stores. In 1992 it bought Britain's largest video-rental company, Citivision PLC, for cash and company stock. "Under the name Ritz, Citivision operates around 775 stores in Britain and 23 in Austria." Blockbuster is planning to use the British chain as its vehicle for expansion into other European countries. Joint-venture negotiations are already ongoing in Italy, Germany, and France. Expansion is under way in Japan, Chile, Spain, and Venezuela.

Its partner, Philips Electronics based in Holland, increased its ownership stake in Blockbuster to 7.9% in 1992 with a stock purchase worth $66 million. Philips owns a music and video chain called Superclubs with 500 outlets in the U.S. that Blockbuster would like to acquire. Blockbuster has used its U.S. stores in order to help Philips test-market its "new compact-disk interactive technology (CDI), a seductive multimedia system that stores video, sound, text, and graphics on a compact disc."

Along with plans to increase its overseas operations, the company is considering several types of diversification to include "music retailing and the creation of mini-amusement parks with virtual-reality

Expanding its horizons *around the globe, Blockbuster plans to increase its international operations and diversify its activities.*

'rides,' in which computer simulators produce the effects." According to Chairman H. Wayne Huizenga, the company's effort to diversify is due to a maturing video-rental market and the pay-per-view system now offered by cable services and soon to be available from telephone companies. ▲

▶ Along with plans to increase its overseas operations, the company is considering several types of diversification to include "music retailing and the creation of mini-amusement parks with virtual-reality 'rides.'"

For more about Blockbuster, see Gail DeGeorge and Jonathan B. Levine, "They Don't Call It Blockbuster for Nothing," *Business Week,* October 19, 1992, pp. 113–114.

The Nature and Scope of International Business

American businesses mirror a global economy, regardless of how large or small they may be. Many small businesses employ a cross-cultural work force. Immigrants now make up more than 9% of the total U.S. population and account for 39% of its population growth from 1980 to 1990 (*Business Week,* July 13, 1992). Most businesses find that some part of their inputs comes from across national boundaries. A significant portion of the outputs of large companies flows across national borders. Today companies need the flexibility to purchase inputs from sources offering the highest quality, greatest dependability, and lowest cost, whether they originate overseas or down the street.

Recent Changes in International Business

As probably never before in American history, managers must pay attention to what goes on in economies all around the globe. The world is changing more rapidly every day, and the changes are monumental. As communism lost its hold in the former Soviet Union, the various Soviet republics became independent nations once again. East Germany has been reunited with West Germany to form the single Federal Republic of Germany. The 12 nations of the European Community (EC) plan to become a united states of Europe with a common currency, banking system, and removal of most barriers to trade. China has opened its doors to new capitalist ventures. Mexico and other countries in Latin and South America are moving toward more-open economic systems with the privatization of many government-owned operations. Mexico, the United States, and Canada have recently negotiated the North American Free Trade Agreement (NAFTA). These and other changes mean vast economic opportunities for citizens around the world, and companies from Asia, Europe, and North America are moving swiftly to take advantage of them.

Organizations in every country need the freedom and flexibility to act quickly in anticipation of, or in reaction to, changes taking place around the world. Each day the values of countries' currencies fluctuate, offering advantages and disadvantages. As the value of the U.S. dollar falls against a foreign currency, American goods and services become cheaper and more appealing to the citizens in that country. As the value of the dollar rises against that of a foreign currency, that country's products and services become more appealing to U.S. consumers. These shifts in currency values affect manufacturers, retailers, banks, and many other businesses as well.

Most large corporations from around the world, like Blockbuster and Philips, have found it necessary to join forces with others to share research, develop new ventures, and promote the sales of their products and services. In April 1992, Matsushita Electric joined forces with Nestle S.A. of Switzerland to market a new espresso coffee system in Japan. Matsushita will provide the machines, which it will manufacture in Europe, while Nestle provides the coffee in capsules. Nestle owns the capsule technology and will establish a unit in Japan to distribute the coffee (*Wall Street Journal,* April 24, 1992). General Motors is investing $75 million in a joint venture with FSO of Poland to build up to 35,000 Opel Astras each year in an FSO factory near Warsaw. GM will gain a foothold in Poland's 200,000-car-per-year market, and FSO will gain needed technology, an upgraded factory, and jobs for local workers. GM has already invested more than $300 million in Hungary for assembly and engine building, and about $611 million in the former East German city of Eisenach (Aeppel, 1992).

The Extent of International Business

In 1992, 139 American corporations were among the Fortune 500 largest global service companies (Martin and Moran, 1992). The top 50 U.S. exporters (all manufacturing companies) for 1991 together exported $130.4 billion in goods and services, or about 13% of their total sales, according to *Fortune*'s annual survey (Eiben, 1992). American international merchandise trade—imports and exports of goods—accounts for better than 80% of U.S.-owned manufacturing output (*Business Week,* August 10, 1992). Exhibit 20.1 shows the 10 largest U.S. corporations ranked by sales.

Of the world's 500 largest foreign corporations in 1991, 195 were Japanese—including eight of the top 10, according to the Forbes International 500 Survey (Kichen, 1992). Among the top 10 foreign global corporations appear British Petroleum and Royal Dutch/Shell Group. Exhibit 20.2 shows the 10 largest foreign corporations ranked by sales. The world's seven largest economies—those of the United States, Japan, Germany, France, Italy, the United Kingdom, and Canada—produced 63% of the world's goods and services in 1991, down from 66% in 1990 (Kichen, 1992). But many corporations rival other *countries* in economic might. As one writer puts the fact, "of the top 100 economies in the world, 47 are corporations, not countries" (Yates, December 13, 1991). According to the Conference Board, a New York–based research group, "General Motors Corporation is not only the world's largest company, it also is the 20th-largest economic unit on the planet, beating out most of the world's 130-plus nations. Sixteen of the top 100 economies in the world are U.S. firms; Japan placed 11 corporations on the list" (Yates, December 13, 1991). Ranked by their 1991 gross national products (GNPs), the five

Exhibit 20.1

The 10 largest U.S.-based corporations ranked by 1992 sales.

Rank	Company	Business	Sales
			($ in billions)
1	General Motors	Motor vehicles	132.77
2	Exxon	Petroleum, chemicals	103.54
3	Ford Motor Co.	Motor vehicles	100.78
4	IBM	Computers	65.09
5	General Electric	Jet engines, plastics, medical systems	62.20
6	Mobil	Petroleum, chemicals	57.38
7	Philip Morris	Tobacco, foods, beverages	50.15
8	E. I. Du Pont de Nemours	Specialty chemicals	37.64
9	Chevron	Petroleum, chemicals	37.46
10	Texaco	Petroleum, chemicals	37.13

Source: "The Fortune 500," *Fortune,* April 19, 1993, p. 184.

largest economies in the world are the United States ($5.2 trillion), Japan ($2.9 trillion), Germany ($1.27 trillion), France ($1 trillion), and Italy ($872 billion) (Yates, December 13, 1991).

Globalization and Its Opportunities

The trend for the near future is clear. As one writer sums it up, "The buzzword for the 1990s clearly is globalization" (*Business Week,* June 15, 1990). **Globalization** embraces many activities: exporting products and services; locating operations outside one's national borders; using foreign partners to help in research and development and to sell products and services around the world; and tailoring strategies, management functions, and products and services to meet the needs of customers worldwide.

As discussed in the Management in Action section, Blockbuster and its foreign partner, Philips, have formed a joint venture with Den Fujita in Japan and are negotiating others in France, Germany, and Italy in the video-rental market. Globalization requires that managers think beyond national borders and see all world markets as part of one global economy. L. Patrick Lupo, group chief executive for DHL Worldwide Express, observes: "It is the most competitive companies who are the quickest to take advantage, and to use their resources globally. Those who are left behind may never catch up" (*Business Week,* June 15, 1990). Susan C. Schwab, then assistant secretary of commerce and director general of the United States and Foreign Commercial Service, added, "The only way an American company can really be certain of its competitive position in this [global] market is to be able and prepared to compete with its foreign competition on their own turf as well as in other world markets" (*Business Week,* June 15, 1990).

Exhibit 20.2

The 10 largest foreign corporations ranked by sales.

Rank	Company	Country	Business	Sales
				($ in billions)
1	C Itoh & Co.	Japan	Trading	154.56
2	Sumitomo	Japan	Trading	149.53
3	Marubeni	Japan	Trading	140.46
4	Mitsubishi	Japan	Trading	135.88
5	Mitsui & Co.	Japan	Trading	133.63
6	Royal Dutch/Shell Group	Netherlands	Energy	102.80
7	Nissho Iwai	Japan	Trading	84.87
8	Toyota Motor	Japan	Automobiles	71.91
9	Hitachi	Japan	Electronics	58.23
10	British Petroleum	UK	Energy	57.68

Source: "The *Forbes* Foreign Rankings," *Forbes,* July 20, 1992, p. 242.

Author Tom Peters believes that being a global company requires managers to make a long-term commitment to understanding the rest of the world, to knowing what is going on beyond their home borders. Globalization requires that engineers and designers visit and live in foreign markets (Peters, 1989). In their book, *Managing Across Borders,* authors Christopher Bartlett and Sumantra Ghoshal urge companies to structure their product development, manufacturing, and marketing organizations differently in different countries at different times, according to the needs of businesses, markets, and products.

This is what Bausch & Lomb did with much success throughout the mid-1980s and is still doing today. In 1991 more than half of all new designs for its Ray Ban line were developed locally for international markets. In Asia the glasses were redesigned to better suit Asian faces, and sales increased dramatically. In China, where average earnings are far below those of citizens in other markets, Bausch & Lomb changed its strategy by lowering prices and relying instead on high volume. It worked, and higher earnings were the result (Jacob, 1992).

The Reasons for Globalization

Companies may have little choice about going global. Their markets may simply be saturated at home and the only chance for growth may lie outside their borders. Blockbuster sees this happening, hence its expansion to overseas markets. Or the best sources for needed inputs—labor, raw materials, and state-of-the-art equipment—may lie outside their home bases, making foreign-based production and sales facilities a logical choice.

In general, companies go international and global because of two basic motivations: proactive or reactive. *Proactive motives* include the search for new

Domino's Pizza has 530 stores in 31 different international markets, including this store in France with its two-wheeled delivery fleet. The pizza stays the same, just the toppings differ: Japanese pizza can be ordered with seafood.

customers and expanded markets, necessary raw materials and other resources, tax advantages, lower costs, and economies of scale. This last motive seeks to maximize the efficiency gained from investments to build factories, conduct research, and incur other costs of expanding sales to many additional markets either alone or with foreign partners. The drive to reduce costs has led to setting up operations in such countries as Malaysia, Indonesia, China, Mexico, and the Philippines, which offer lower wages and fewer restrictions on business. In these countries, workers on average earn one-fourth to one-fifth what workers are paid in the United States, Germany, and Japan. This chapter's Global Applications feature highlights the proactive motives driving some of Taiwan's businesses to relocate to areas that offer cost advantages.

Reactive motives include the desire to escape from trade barriers and other government regulations (GM has moved production facilities from Mexico City to northern Mexico to escape that city's tough environmental laws); to better serve a customer or group of customers (many Japanese auto parts suppliers, for instance, have moved to the United States to be near the Japanese auto companies they supply); and to remain competitive. Fear of potential trade restrictions has prompted U.S. auto makers to expand their presence in Europe and has led Japanese auto makers to build plants in America. Boeing of Seattle is America's largest exporter, but it has no factories outside the United States. Boeing does rely heavily, however, on foreign manufacturers for many components for the planes it builds. To some extent, these suppliers give the aircraft builder protection from foreign trade restrictions.

The most important reason for expanding globally is that it provides a powerful additional source of growth. "While U.S. companies hunkered down to tough out an anemic recovery in the domestic market [in 1991], U.S. exports rose to a new record—pushing America past a flagging Germany as the world's champion exporter" (Eiben, 1992). America's largest exporter for 1991 was Boeing. It earned $17.9 billion (more than half its over $29 billion in total sales) in sales of aircraft and related goods and services to foreign markets (Eiben, 1992).

The Impact of Globalization on Business

Going global—doing business outside one's home country through integrated operations—means dealing with political, legal, sociocultural, economic, and technological environments that are unfamiliar and unique. As a result, the kind of managers needed to staff foreign and home-office operations will change. Their education and experience should prepare them to live and work in those countries or cultures in which they will do business. Marketing, production, finance, and all other business functions will change, taking on a flavor and style appropriate for the foreign environment. The movement of goods, money, and people across borders regularly calls for skills the company may not ordinarily possess. Stakeholders' interests must be protected from the threats posed by foreign governments and environments. Products and services must be tailored to the needs of foreign customers. One reason that American-made cars do not sell well in Japan, England, and Australia is because they are designed with the controls on the left side of the car even though drivers in these countries—who drive on the left side of the road—need a right-hand orientation for controls.

Globalization means change. It also means a drive among businesses to achieve world-class products and services with competitive quality and productivity. Intense competition from abroad has caused American employers to downsize, outsource, reorganize, cut costs, create partnerships with foreign firms, and spend billions on training. The price to America's economy has been enormous. Although the competitiveness of American companies has increased, their ability to provide well-paying jobs has not. The 500 largest industrial companies laid off 3.7 million workers from 1981 to 1992—about a 25% reduction. Now the service sector is undergoing its own revolution to increase productivity, which will mean additional job losses. "As established service companies face global competition, much of it in the form of direct investment by foreign service companies in the United States, they are starting to cut back white-collar jobs with a vengeance," says Morgan Stanley senior economist Stephen Roach (O'Reilly, 1992).

The movement to become more efficient and competitive has led to a decline in wages for the average employed American. In 1979 the median wage for full-time workers was $409.13 per week. In 1989 that figure stood at $398.88. Although 13.6 million jobs were added to our economy from 1979 to 1989, about 5 million of them paid less than $250 per week, or about $13,000 per year after adjusting for inflation. That wage is below the government's official poverty level for a family of four (O'Reilly, 1992).

Other international trends will affect jobs. The North American Free Trade Agreement comprising Canada, Mexico, and the United States was concluded and sent to Congress in August 1992. Many trade barriers have been negotiated out of existence.

> This will no doubt create U.S. jobs as exports to Mexico [and Canada] increase— but it will also send more lower-skilled ones south. Meanwhile, the seven major industrial countries are trying to expand the 108-nation General Agreement on

Tariffs & Trade (GATT), which will leave labor-intensive industries such as textiles more vulnerable to foreign rivals. And countries such as Malaysia and China are rapidly boosting exports. All this 'will have a dramatic impact on lower-skilled workers in the United States,' predicts Edward E. Leamer, a trade economist at the University of California at Los Angeles (UCLA) (*Business Week,* August 10, 1992).

Signs are beginning to appear that the trend toward shipping high-paying jobs overseas may be reversing. According to a study by the National Association of Manufacturers, 5% to 7% of American manufacturers are investing in their work forces to keep the high-paying jobs at home (*Business Week,* August 10, 1992).

More and more innovative U.S. companies are starting to realize that rather than continue to dumb-down tasks and save money by cutting wages, they'd be better off striving to hire, train, and reward a better-prepared work force. Flexible, responsive delivery of products and services rather than mass production is the new watchword in the global economy, and only highly skilled employees can quickly master these challenging new processes (*Business Week,* August 10, 1992).

Another factor reversing the trend of U.S. job loss is that wages are rising in many countries, making some of them much less competitive (Taiwan, for example). Other reasons why many manufacturers are bringing their exported jobs back to America and working to keep them here are outlined below.

- Recent gains in productivity have made higher domestic wage levels possible.

- The shift to competition through service—quick responses to customer needs and reduced time delays for deliveries—means that suppliers need to be near customers.

- The necessity to keep product development and manufacturing close for quick decision making and shortening of cycle times.

- Bad experiences with foreign governments, regulations, workers, and other problems.

- The movement to buy American and to sell American-made as a product feature (Faltermayer, 1991).

Globalization and the U.S. Economy

The U.S. Balance of Trade   The difference between the goods and services flowing into a country and those flowing out is a nation's **balance of trade**. Trade can be measured on goods—merchandise trade—and on goods and services—the current account method of measuring. Since 1976 America has experienced a negative balance by both measures, importing a greater dollar value of goods and services than it exports. Exhibit 20.3 shows the U.S. merchandise trade balance from 1970 through 1992. From 1975—the last year in which America had a positive balance of trade—through 1991, America accumulated a trade deficit of about $1.8 trillion.

Exhibit 20.3

U.S. balance of merchandise trade from 1970 to 1992.

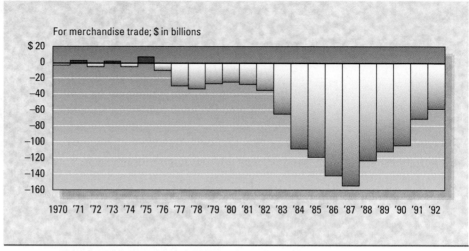

For merchandise trade; $ in billions

Sources: Federal Reserve Board; U.S. Department of Commerce.

It should be noted that both balance of trade measures do not record the sales of goods and services by U.S. producers to their overseas facilities or from them to the world.

> U.S. companies are manufacturing an ever broader array of products in overseas subsidiaries, producing sales that are an important part of their global business but [which] don't get counted as exports. Philip Morris [America's 12th largest exporter in 1991] took in over $13 billion of [overseas] sales, far more than its $3.1 billion of exports (Faltermayer, 1991).

The National Research Council, a part of the National Academy of Sciences, urges the federal government to enact a broader measure of exports that will more accurately reflect America's trade situation.

The U.S. government's bipartisan Competitiveness Policy Council states, "Our prosperity depends, to a considerable degree, on whether we can compete effectively in the world market—including, of course, within the United States itself—against competition from abroad" (Yates, June 15, 1992). While several thousand U.S. companies are seeking world markets aggressively, and tailoring their products to foreign customers, the report goes on to criticize the overall effort:

> Too many American corporations . . . have taken the route of setting up offshore manufacturing plants, rather than competing in foreign markets from the American bases, a strategy that would benefit the American economy much more. . . . Much of corporate America has yet to respond to the global nature of today's economy. Of 360,000 U.S. manufacturers, only 2% are exporting, and a relative handful of [those, some] 2,000 American firms[,] account for 80% of U.S. [manufactured] exports (Yates, June 15, 1992).

Exhibit 20.4 shows the movement of imports and exports of both goods and services—the current account measure—from 1989 through projections for 1992 and the first half of 1993. This is a much broader measure than the merchandise

Exhibit 20.4

U.S. trade in goods and services, 1989 through 1993.

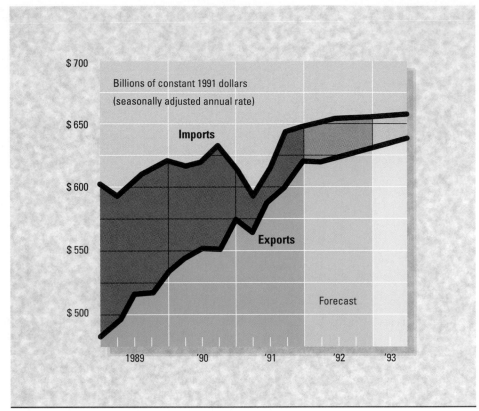

Sources: Federal Reserve Board; U.S. Department of Commerce.

trade measure. For example, the current account measure for 1991 includes the nearly $50 billion received from Arab nations, Japan, and Germany to reimburse America for the liberation of Kuwait in 1990. For 1991, America's current account showed a deficit of $29 billion (Brownstein, 1992).

According to data from the U.S. Department of Commerce, the top five U.S. export markets for 1991 were Canada ($85.1 billion), Japan ($48.1 billion), Mexico— a country growing in importance to the United States as both a source of inputs and a buyer of outputs—($33.3 billion), the United Kingdom ($22.1 billion), and Germany ($21.3 billion). The top five sources of imports for 1991 were Japan ($91.6 billion), Canada ($91.1 billion), Mexico ($31.2 billion), Germany ($26.2 billion), and Taiwan ($23 billion). The United States' largest trade imbalance is with Japan— $43.5 billion for 1991, or about two-thirds of the total U.S. trade deficit. This deficit made up the largest portion of Japan's nearly $78-billion trade surplus with the world for 1991 (*Time*, 1992). America maintained a favorable balance of trade with the 12 nations of the European Community in 1991 of about $17 billion. America's largest surplus with an individual country was with the Netherlands—$8.7 billion. America's leading imports are automobiles, petroleum, chemicals, agricultural commodities, and electrical and industrial equipment. Major exports are aircraft, agricultural commodities, chemicals, motor vehicles, and office, data-processing, and telecommunications equipment.

FOCUS ON QUALITY
World-Class Turnaround for Hurco

Hurco, an Indiana-based machine-tool manufacturer, learned that quality was the answer to entering foreign markets. According to Brian McLaughlin, president and CEO, "It became very clear to our company very early on that if you weren't aggressive in international markets you weren't going to survive. The global market for machine tools is $43 billion per year, and the U.S. market accounts for only 7% of that. You must be a global trader today, and your products must be world class." The company was close to bankruptcy in 1987, building shoddy goods with a "lack of focus on the customer." Now half of Hurco's total sales come from exporting its $40,000 to $150,000 computer–numerically controlled milling machines. How did the turnaround take place?

Hurco established a company-wide commitment to total quality control. It redesigned its products with the help of customer feedback. It empowered its workers to make the tough decisions about what changes were needed, how best to bring about those changes, and how to improve its products and services. The company invested in a state-of-the-art high-tech manufacturing center and completely changed its corporate culture.

Hurco listens to its customers and its employees. Workers take pride in doing things right the first time. Installers, who used to dread their work because so many defects in Hurco equipment could be expected, now look forward to getting their company's equipment up and running for a satisfied customer. ▲

For more about global business, see Ronald E. Yates, "American firms wake up to world market demands," *Chicago Tribune,* June 15, 1992, sec. 1, pp. 1, 16.

Foreign Investments in America   Each year investors from around the world purchase land, buildings, businesses, securities, and various rights from Americans. In 1992, for instance, a group of Japanese investors paid about $100 million for the Seattle Mariners baseball team. When foreign-born nationals and foreign businesses invest their money in U.S. assets, the federal government records the major purchases as foreign **direct investments.** In 1991, according to the U.S. Department of Commerce, the cumulative investments made by foreigners in the United States totaled $2.49 trillion, up 10.7% from 1990. "Britain remained the largest owner of direct assets in the United States in 1991 with holdings of $106.06 billion. Japan was second with holdings of $86.66 billion." (Direct assets are defined as at least 10% ownership of a business. The government uses as its measures the value of a company's stock owned by foreigners and the "current replacement costs of assets to value investments" [*Chicago Tribune,* July 3, 1992]). According to U.S. Department of Commerce data, total foreign direct investments in the United States for 1991 alone totaled $22.6 billion, down from $65.9 billion in 1990 (Yates, June 10, 1992). The drop in dollars invested is a reflection of the recession of the early 1990s and the rising popularity of the EC as a place to invest. The largest investors in the United States in 1991 were the Japanese with $5.07 billion, the French with $4.75 billion, and the Canadians with $2.65 billion (Yates, June 10, 1992). In addition to this direct investment, foreigners are helping to finance America's more than $4-trillion federal debt by owning over $460 billion in U.S. government obligations.

In 1992 Honda, Nissan, Mazda, Mitsubishi, Toyota, Subaru, and Isuzu all had plants operating in the United States, as did their major suppliers. Competition by states for foreign businesses is intense. Illinois gave $88 million in services, tax advantages, and direct cash expenditures for training and site improvements to Mitsubishi/Chrysler to build their Illinois plant. Kentucky has given $284 million in similar aid to Toyota (Franklin, 1990). Most recently, South Carolina has agreed to millions in assistance to help BMW of Germany to build its plant. The reason for this competition is jobs. Japanese businesses employ 200,000 Americans in the Midwest and another 160,000 elsewhere in the United States. The largest Japanese employer is Matsushita Electric, with more than 21,250 employees. Sony is second with 18,000, and Toyota is third with 16,400 (Franklin, 1990).

Some industries are significantly affected by foreign investments. The U.S. airline industry is one example: British Airways owns 15% of United and 49% of Northwest; Ansett Airlines has a 20% stake in America West; SAS holds 10% of Texas Air; and Japan Airlines holds a 20% share in Hawaiian (Storch, 1989). The tire business in America is almost totally owned by foreign firms. Michelin of France owns B. F. Goodrich and Goodrich/Uniroyal and operates five plants of its own in the United States. Bridgestone of Japan bought Firestone's tire operations and also has plants in the United States. Pirelli of Italy owns Armstrong Tire, Continental of Germany owns General Tire, and Sumitomo of Japan owns Dunlop. Two major tire makers remain in American hands: Goodyear/Kelley-Springfield and Cooper Tire & Rubber (Pantages, 1989).

American Investments Abroad   In 1992 the Department of Commerce reported that cumulative American investments overseas totaled $2.11 trillion, up 6.6% from 1990 (*Chicago Tribune*, July 3, 1992). At the beginning of 1992, U.S. firms had invested more than $900 million in Eastern Europe. Another area favored by U.S. businesses is Japan. In addition to having Japanese partners,

International business is the watchword today; it is fitting, then, that IBM—International Business Machines—is one of the largest U.S. investors in overseas operations.

U.S. manufacturers and service-based companies have production and marketing operations of their own in Japan. Among the largest are IBM, Texas Instruments, 3M, Hewlett-Packard, Motorola, Disney, McDonald's, and Coca-Cola (*Chicago Tribune*, July 3, 1992). Ford owns 24% of Mazda, and that company puts Ford nameplates on 12% of the cars it sells in Japan (Rapoport, 1990). The output of U.S.-based companies in Japan exceeds the output of Japanese-based companies in the United States (Peters, 1990).

The Overseas Private Investment Corporation (OPIC) is a federal agency (within the U.S. International Development Cooperation Agency—IDCA) that sells risk insurance to U.S. companies moving to foreign environments. It protects U.S. private investments in 116 countries for up to 20 years. Its insurance covers losses due to political upheaval, government seizures, and the inability to convert local currencies into dollars. Its first policy for the newly independent countries of Eastern Europe was sold to General Electric to insure $100 million of its investment in the Tungsram Company, Hungary's government-owned light-bulb maker (Hearn, 1990).

In recent years, Mexico has been a center for foreign investment, much of it along the Texas–New Mexico border with Mexico. In this northern area of Mexico are located nearly 2,000 *maquiladora* plants employing nearly 500,000 Mexicans (Baker, 1990). *Maquiladora* assembly operations, the result of special legislation by the Mexican government, may be 100% owned by foreigners. The facilities assemble and export finished products and parts using cheap ($10 to $20 per day) Mexican labor. Along with such American investors as GM, RCA, Zenith, Ford, Chrysler, and others are the Japanese, Germans, and Koreans (Sanderson and Hayes, 1990). Northern Mexico is rapidly becoming a major automobile-manufacturing center, with GM, Ford, Chrysler, Volkswagen, and Nissan already producing cars there, and Toyota, Honda, Mercedes-Benz, and auto suppliers making plans to locate there in the future (*Business Week*, March 16, 1992).

The Multinational Corporation

Companies can do business in foreign countries in many ways. Some simply maintain sales offices in other lands; others only buy materials from companies in other countries. Those companies with operating facilities, not just sales offices, in one or more foreign countries are called **multinational corporations** (Heyel, 1982). Curiously, America's largest exporter in 1991, Boeing, is not a true multinational. Although it sells its airplanes around the world and purchases supplies abroad, it does not have any of its own manufacturing and assembly operations outside the United States. Some multinationals are government-owned or -supported enterprises. Airbus of Europe—a consortium formed by France, Germany, Great Britain, and Spain—is one example; it has won about 30% of all orders for new airplanes from 1989 to 1992 (Labich, 1992).

In general, there are two kinds of multinationals: those that market products and services in relatively unaltered states throughout the world (*standardization*), and those that modify their products and services and adjust their marketing to appeal to specific groups of consumers in specific geographical areas (*customization*). Products that illustrate the first category include sporting goods, soft drinks, cigarettes, chemicals, oil products, liquors, certain types of clothing (Lee jeans, for example), and transportation services. Both Pepsi and Wrigley's chewing gum are sold around the world, with only their packaging, promotion, and labeling altered to suit foreign tastes. Examples of customization include computer software programmed to work in foreign languages; cars manufactured to meet different countries' safety and pollution regulations and driver preferences; fast-food menus altered to cater to cultural tastes; and cosmetics formulated to complement the skin tones and coloring of different populations. McDonald's adjusts its menus and food service to suit the tastes of foreign customers; Mary Kay cosmetics are altered to suit foreign preferences as well.

Companies that attempt to sell the same product to different nationalities soon discover problems. In the realm of laundry products, "Germans, for example, demand a product that's gentle on lakes and rivers and will pay a premium for it. Spaniards want cheaper products that get shirts white and soft. And Greeks want smaller packages that allow them to hold down the cost of each store visit" (Browning, 1992). Whirlpool has discovered in its European experience that "Not only are kitchen appliances different from one country to another, but consumers also react differently to advertising messages from one country to the next" (Nelson, 1992).

Characteristics of Multinationals

Even though multinationals around the world differ in sales volumes, profits, markets serviced, and number of subsidiaries, they do share some common characteristics. One common trait is the creation of foreign affiliates, which may be wholly owned by the multinational or jointly held with partners from foreign countries. Blockbuster owns almost all of its outlets in Britain and Austria and half of those in Canada; most of the others are franchises or joint ventures that grant foreign nationals the right to do business under the company's name. One writer describes the relationship of multinationals to their affiliates in this way:

> The foreign affiliates are linked with the parent company and with each other by ties of common ownership and by a common global strategy to which each affiliate is responsive and committed. The parent company controls the foreign affiliates via resources which it allocates to each affiliate—capital, technology, trademarks, patents, and [people]—and through the right to approve each affiliate's long- and short-range plans and budgets (Phatak, 1992).

Most of the large corporations discussed throughout this text in cases and features exemplify multinationals with affiliates in foreign countries—IBM, Motorola, Hewlett-Packard, Ford, and Johnson & Johnson among them.

Another common characteristic of multinationals is that their management operates with a global vision and strategy, seeing the world as their market. Top managers coordinate long-range plans and usually allow the foreign affiliates to work with great autonomy, leaving the day-to-day management up to those on the spot and closest to the problems in foreign markets. Bausch & Lomb is but one example. Affiliate operations are integrated and controls are exercised through management reports, frequent meetings and communications between headquarters and affiliates, and the setting of objectives both independently and in conjunction with headquarters. Foreign affiliates become the training grounds for group and company top management as well as the sources for them.

A third characteristic is the tendency of multinationals to choose certain types of business activities. Most multinationals are engaged in manufacturing. The rest tend to cluster around the petroleum industry, banking, agriculture, and public utilities (Phatak, 1992).

A fourth characteristic is the tendency to locate affiliates in the developed countries of the world—Western Europe, Canada, South Korea, Taiwan, Japan, and the United States. "It is estimated that about two-thirds of the world's direct investments are in the developed countries (Phatak, 1992). Less-developed countries (LDCs) tend to be seen as sources for raw materials and cheap labor, and as markets for fairly inexpensive consumer products that can be mass produced to standardized designs.

A fifth characteristic is the adoption of one of three basic strategies regarding staffing. The first is a high-skills strategy in which the company exports products, not jobs. "Rather than push pay to the lowest common denominator, companies such as Deere, Ford, and Motorola are training workers to improve their skills, boost productivity [and quality]—and keep jobs at home" (*Business Week,* August 10, 1992). The second is to "dumb-down jobs" and shift the work to cheap-labor countries. This has been the choice for the majority of companies around the world. The third strategy is to mix the first two: "for every Motorola or Ford, a trendsetter such as AT&T is turning high-paying jobs into low-wage ones. Even those that upgrade worker skills, such as Ford Motor Co. and General Electric, still shift work to cheap-labor countries—thus pursuing both approaches" (*Business Week,* August 10, 1992).

The International Manager

The managers of those businesses that are part of international trade have become engaged in **international management**—managing resources (people, funds, inventories, and technologies) across national boundaries and adapting management principles and functions to the demands of foreign competition and environments. The demands on such managers have never been greater than they are today. They must love a challenge—the challenge of working in the ever-changing contexts of international trade. Managers must thrive on the unexpected, the new, the different, and the unique. If they are to work abroad, people need a love of or sincere interest in the host country's people, culture, traditions, and history. They must have an adequate knowledge of the host country's language, business customs, economy, and commercial laws. Above all, they need to be open, flexible, and patient human beings.

The international manager can be a native of the country in which he or she is working, a native of the parent company's country, or a native of a third country. Most multinational corporations employ a mixture of the three in their domestic and foreign operations. (Some countries require by law that a certain number of their citizens be employed in the management ranks of the operations they host.) Before sending a manager to a foreign country, the parent company will usually give the manager a certain amount of training. Courses and seminars in the host country's language, customs, laws, history, and culture will help prepare managers and their families for what awaits them. In larger multinationals, newly arrived managers and their families participate in orientation activities in the host country.

Most new managers have a chance to understudy for a time with experienced managers before they take on full responsibility.

The Environments of the International Manager

The environment in which managers in an international company function is far more complex than domestic management settings. The key task for top management in a multinational company is to develop and maintain an in-depth understanding of the environments of every country in which it has operations, affiliates, suppliers, and customers. Five basic environments must be monitored: political, legal, economic, sociocultural, and technological. Each environment is constantly undergoing change. Exhibit 20.5 summarizes the components of each environment. The discussion that follows focuses on the key issues of each.

The Political Environment

Political environments can foster or hinder economic development and direct investment by native and foreign investors and businesses. The political and economic philosophies of a nation's leaders can give rise to laws that promote domestic commerce and raise barriers to trade with the outside world. In July 1992 House Majority Leader Richard A. Gephardt, for instance, urged legislation that would tax U.S. firms that move to Mexico; revenues would fund training for workers left behind in the United States (*Business Week*, August 10, 1992).

The stability of a nation's government and the extent of its support by the people will affect decisions by outsiders to seek commercial opportunities or to avoid investments. Various citizen groups with vested interests—farmers, manufacturers, and distributors—can organize civil protests and promote protectionist legislation to safeguard their particular interests. Japanese farmers have pressured their government successfully for years to keep foreign agricultural commodities such as rice out of the country. The farmers don't want competition; they have been selling their domestic rice for six times the price of California rice for years (Ono, 1992). When the Tokyo discount liquor-store chain, Kawachiya Shuhan Company, imported sake (traditional Japanese rice wine) made in California with California rice, the chain was able to sell the wine more cheaply than the Japanese product. The company soon encountered resistance from Japanese brewers. The president of the chain, Yukio Higuchi, says that "all five U.S. brewers, which are affiliates of Japanese sake makers and wholesalers, have refused to supply his stores—or any Japanese liquor store—with the U.S.-made sake. Higuchi suspects liquor makers, fearing that the cheaper sake would threaten the high prices of Japanese sake, have joined forces against him" (Ono, 1992).

The Legal Environment

Each country has its own unique set of laws that affect commerce. Contract law and methods for enforcing contracts differ from one country to another. Laws designed to protect the rights of individuals and labor unions differ as well. Just as managers working in America need to be certain that their actions will not violate any of the many laws that bear on conducting business, so, too, must international managers in each host country.

Exhibit 20.5

Components of the international environment.

POLITICAL ENVIRONMENT	
Form of government	Social unrest
Political ideology	Political strife and insurgency
Stability of government	Governmental attitude toward foreign firms
Strength of opposition parties and groups	Foreign policy

LEGAL ENVIRONMENT	
Legal tradition	Patent and trademark laws
Effectiveness of legal system	Laws affecting business firms
Treaties with foreign nations	

ECONOMIC ENVIRONMENT	
Level of economic development	Membership in regional economic blocks (EC, LAFTA, CIS)
Population	Monetary and fiscal policies
Gross national product	Nature of competition
Per-capita income	Currency convertibility
Literacy level	Inflation
Social infrastructure	Taxation system
Natural resources	Interest rates
Climate	Wage and salary levels

SOCIOCULTURAL ENVIRONMENT	
Customs, norms, values, and beliefs	Social institutions
Languages	Status symbols
Attitudes	Religions
Motivations	Demographics and Psychographics

TECHNOLOGICAL ENVIRONMENT	
State-of-the-art in various industries	CAD, CAM, and CIM
Research and development	Host countries' levels of acceptance and utilization
Recent innovations	Presence of educated work force in host countries
Robotics	Potential partners around the globe

Source: Adapted from Arvind V. Phatak, *International Dimensions of Management,* 3rd edition (Boston: PWS-Kent, 1992), p. 9. Reprinted by permission of the publisher. Copyright 1992 Wadsworth, Inc.

Dorothy Manning is a cultural consultant specializing in preparing CEOs for cross-cultural assignments. Operating out of Boston, she charges hundreds of dollars per day per executive. Her specialty is knowing what legal customs exist and how the executive should respect them. The following are just a few of Manning's no-nos (*Chicago Tribune,* August 5, 1990).

- Never discuss business over dinner in France.

- Don't pass documents with the left hand in Saudi Arabia (where the left hand is used for bathroom functions).

- Don't expect written contracts in most Moslem countries; a handshake is considered binding on the parties.

- Don't expect the contract with South Korean businesspeople to spell out all the details. Written contracts are typically documents that change as conditions do.

Some companies erect trade barriers such as quotas, tariffs, and embargoes. **Quotas** limit the import of a product to a specified amount per year. Japanese auto makers have agreed to restrict their imports into America to a specific number of cars each year for several years to help redress the trade imbalance between the United States and Japan.

Tariffs are taxes placed on imported goods in order to make them more expensive and thus less competitive. The goal is to protect domestic producers. Under the 1992 NAFTA, comprising Mexico, Canada, and the United States, Mexican tariffs on imported agricultural commodities will be phased out over a period of years. Under the terms of the treaty, which Congress has not yet ratified, the United States would have 15 years before markets would be totally open to Mexican sugar, peanuts, frozen orange-juice concentrate, and some other fruits and vegetables (Gunset, 1992).

Embargoes keep a product out of a country either for a specified period of time, or entirely. Following NAFTA's five-year phase-in, Mexico would still bar U.S. imports of soybeans for three months annually, when Mexican farmers are harvesting their crops (Arndt, 1992). Embargoes are sometimes used as sanctions to enforce political policy. The United States permanently embargoes sensitive nuclear materials as part of its support of nonproliferation treaties. Embargoes were also enacted by the United States and other countries to pressure South Africa to change its racial policies, and to pressure the governments of Iran and Iraq (Arndt, 1992).

The Economic Environment

When companies analyze their options for establishing operations in a foreign country, they must consider such factors as the stability of the country's currency; its infrastructure; the availability of necessary raw materials and supplies; levels of inflation, wages, interest rates, and taxes; proximity to customers; and climate. When Disney was looking for a place in Europe to build its Euro Disney theme park, it chose 5,000 acres outside of Paris because that city is a premier tourist attraction. The choice was a wise one; many European tour operators are selling packages that combine visits to both Paris and Euro Disney (*Wall Street Journal,* April 10, 1992). In the 1980s, Whirlpool, the appliance maker, wanted to expand its operations overseas.

It used "many factors, including ease of access, growth potential and government regulation. Europe got the green light in 1987, when the Netherlands-based conglomerate Philips N.V. made overtures about spinning off its appliance business" (Adler, 1992). In 1988 Whirlpool formed a joint venture with Philips, then bought out its partner's interests in 1991, by which time 37.5% of Whirlpool's revenue came from sales in Europe, up 5.5% since 1988 (Adler, 1992).

The Sociocultural Environment

This environment of the international manager includes such concerns as a people's traditions, languages, customs, values, religions, and levels of education—in marketing terms, demographics and psychographics. To accomplish their companies' objectives, international managers work daily in the cultures of different nations and regions, which differ from their own culture. Understanding the host country's people and their values and how to appeal to them has helped Amway expand its operations overseas.

Capitalizing on the Hungarian population's "longtime habit of moonlighting, the government's benign view of Amway's training in free enterprise, and the [appeal] of being a typically American import," Amway recruited 44,000 Hungarians to be distributors. According to Klaus Tremmel, the head of Amway Hungaria Marketing Ltd., the company 'is using the same appeals that have brought 150,000 former East Germans into the company's family: in a time of growing unemployment and falling living standards, this business gives people the opportunity to influence their income. Success through individual initiative is our byword'" (Ingram, 1991). Amway tapped into these peoples' growing desire to embrace capitalism.

Before American managers go abroad, it is imperative that they understand the cultures of countries in which they must operate and how those cultures compare to America's. To gain this understanding, the manager must first be aware of what makes American culture what it is. Exhibit 20.6 shows five dimensions of American society.

After analyzing American culture, the international manager must evaluate the culture in the country or region where he or she will be doing business. One suggested approach is to use the following five factors (Phatak, 1992).

- Material culture. The international manager needs to evaluate the technology and the technological know-how in a host country, the manner in which the country makes use of these abilities, and the resulting economic benefits to society.

- Social institutions. The influence on individuals of social institutions—family, schools, social class, religions, political parties—needs to be analyzed. These strongly affect individuals' work ethic and their ability and willingness to work in groups.

- Humans and the universe. The values and beliefs of people in other cultures may be influenced greatly by religion, customs, and traditional superstitions. The international manager needs to understand that these elements are an integral part of the culture.

Exhibit 20.6

Five basic dimensions of American culture pertaining to business.

- **Individualism.** The attitude of independence of people who feel that a large degree of freedom in the conduct of their personal life constitutes their individualism. The effects of individualism can be seen in self-expression and individual accomplishment. This value may not be shared in other cultures.

- **Informality.** Informality has two components. First, American culture does not place a great deal of importance on tradition, ceremony, or social rules. Second, the "style" in American culture is to be direct and not waste time in the conduct of meetings and conversation. Neither of these values may be significant when conducting business in Latin America or the Middle East.

- **Materialism.** There are two elements in Americam materialism. First, there is a tendency to attach status to physical objects—certain types of cars or designer clothing, for example. Second, because of vast natural resources, Americans are inclined to buy objects and then discard them while they still have a functional value. Both of these behaviors, if exhibited in other societies, may create problems for the international manager.

- **Change.** Although viewed as part of American culture, change is also perceived as something an individual can influence. That one person can bring about significant change is a fundamental tenet of American culture. In other societies, this same cultural value may not exist. Change is seen as inevitable but as a phenomenon that occurs naturally—a part of the overall evolution of people and their world. Change is accepted; it is predetermined. There is no deliberate attempt to influence it or bring it about.

- **Time orientation.** Time in American culture is seen as a scarce and precious resource. As a result, there is an emphasis on the efficient use of time. This belief dictates the practices of setting deadlines and of making and keeping appointments. But in other societies, time is often viewed as an unlimited and never-ending resource. This attitude explains why people in some cultures tend to be quite casual about keeping appointments or meeting deadlines.

Source: Adapted from Arvind V. Phatak, *International Dimensions of Management,* 3rd edition (Boston: PWS-Kent), 1992, pp. 44–48. Reprinted by permission of the publisher. Copyright 1992 Wadsworth, Inc.

- Aesthetics. The manager needs to understand the art, folklore, myths, music, drama, and native traditions of the culture. These factors can be important in interpreting the symbolic meanings of various communications such as gestures and visual representations. Failure to interpret such signals as the people of the culture do is bound to alienate the manager, causing problems of communication and professional socialization.

- Languages. A difficult factor for the international manager is language and dialects of main languages. He or she must understand the nuances of the languages, as words have connotations not spelled out in dictionary definitions. This logically extends to understanding which groups within a society are at odds with one another and which traditionally get along.

The Technological Environment

This environment contains the innovations that are rapidly occurring in all types of technology, from robotics to cellular phones. Before a company can expect to sell its goods in another country, the technologies of the two countries must be compatible. If, for example, GE makes a device that depends on fiber optics, that device cannot be sold in a country that lacks fiber-optic technology. Nor can companies that depend upon this technology locate in countries that lack it. This is one reason why AT&T has decided to invest, along with 46 other carriers from 34 countries, in a joint venture to lay an undersea fiber-optic cable across the Pacific Ocean to link the mainland United States with Hawaii, Guam, and Japan. The cable will permit 320 simultaneous phone calls, four times the capacity of any transoceanic system presently in place (*Wall Street Journal,* October 30, 1992). The cable will transmit voice, video, text, and data signals so essential to today's commercial communications, and should be operating by 1996.

American electronics companies are linking with Japanese and European rivals at an unprecedented rate in order to remain competitive in the global marketplace. Forty percent of U.S. electronics manufacturers maintain alliances with domestic competitors and more than 60% are affiliated in one way or another with overseas firms, according to the Ernst & Young Electronic Business '92 Survey of CEOs (Yates, April 26, 1992). The objective in electronics and most other industries is, says Stephen Almassy, national director of Ernst & Young's electronics industry service division, "to achieve world-class product development and delivery. The goal is to deliver—not necessarily build—the highest-quality products and bring them to market in the shortest possible time"(Yates, April 26, 1992).

Unless companies want to go it alone—with all the expenses in money, time, and bricks and mortar that decision carries with it—they must join forces with others to quicken the pace of research and development and to cut the costs connected with utilizing the latest technology. IBM and Toshiba created a partnership to develop and manufacture flat panel television screens, as reported in the *Chicago Tribune:*

> The joint venture, dubbed Display Technologies Inc. (DTI), already churns out 10,000 screens per month for the two computer giants. By sharing its technology, Toshiba gained access to IBM's superior skills in computer-integrated manufacturing. Just as important for both companies, however, was the ability to share the enormous cost and risks of developing what is proving to be an extremely difficult technology to perfect (Goozner, April 26, 1992).

The flat panel screen can be used in nearly every product requiring a visual display. When its price comes down and its size increases, it will rival television cathode-ray tubes. It is lighter in weight, uses less energy, takes up less space, and "can process digital signals, the likely future for all forms of communication" (Goozner, April 26, 1992).

Regardless of the kind of business a company is in, it must choose partners and locations possessing an available work force to deal with the applicable technology. The best equipment and state-of-the-art technology count for nothing unless the people chosen to use it in manufacturing possess the background and the willingness to learn how to use it properly. Many companies have chosen Mexico and Mexican partners because they find a willing and capable work force. GM's plant in Arizpe, Mexico, rivals its North American ones

ISSUES AND ETHICS
Pocketbook Patriotism?

onsumers across the country have recently shown rising support for the call to "buy American." But this is not as easy to do as it is to say. Is a Boeing 777 an "American" plane when it relies on 20 foreign suppliers (including seven in Japan who make most of the plane's fuselage) to make thousands of its components? Is Chrysler's best-selling minivan an American car when it is made in Canada? Are Honda Accords Japanese cars when they are made in Ohio?

What about the growing cry from Europeans to "buy European"? Will Europeans continue to buy GM and Ford products made in Europe? Hundreds of thousands of Americans and Europeans work for foreign-owned firms. Honda makes its Accord wagon entirely in America and began exporting it to Japan and seven other countries only in 1992. Will the Japanese see the Accord as a foreign product when they practice the art of buying locally?

What do you think about the call to buy American? What would be the result if consumers in every country supported and acted by this philosophy? How can you tell whether a product is American, Japanese, or Canadian? Is the distinction important? ▲

in quality. Says William J. Warwick, AT&T's president of microelectronics manufacturing, "The average education level in Mexico is about the ninth grade, but it doesn't take more than that to use [AT&T's] new manufacturing techniques" (*Business Week*, August 10, 1992).

Planning and the International Manager

Regardless of whether a manager is planning for domestic or international operations, forecasts of the future depend on assumptions. Planning on an international level involves the same planning elements discussed earlier in this text: assessing the environment, developing assumptions, and then forecasting based on those assumptions. Although the process is the same, planning in an international company will be more difficult because many more variables and environments must be considered.

Deciding How to Go International

There are four fundamental ways to sell products and services abroad. When deciding to "go global," any combination of the following strategies may be chosen.

- Export your product or service

- License others to act on your behalf (as sales agents, franchisees, or users of your processes and patents)

- Enter into joint ventures

- Build or purchase facilities outside your home country to conduct your business on your own

Maquiladora operations south of the U.S.–Mexico border, owned by such industrial giants as Zenith, Volkswagen, and Nissan, employ nearly 500,000 Mexicans. By the year 2000, as many as three million workers may be employed in this sector.

Most companies begin by exporting their goods through foreign distributorships that can successfully place the products on dealers' shelves or in consumers' hands. Before deciding on one or another course, however, a company must choose a target market.

Recreation Equipment Incorporated, the Seattle-based consumer co-op, used the first strategy in 1987. REI began to find unsolicited cash flowing from Japanese consumers looking for its lines of sporting goods. It got the message and began offering its catalog (printed in English and with prices in dollars) in advertising placed in Japanese outdoor-oriented publications. By 1991 REI had quadrupled its sales to the Japanese market and had 10,000 Japanese members (*Chicago Tribune,* June 21, 1992).

Coca-Cola is using the second strategy to expand into central and Eastern Europe. It will invest $1 billion with its licensed bottling affiliates through 1995 to achieve this expansion (*Chicago Tribune,* June 1, 1992). Harley-Davidson employed strategy number three. By joining with a Japanese sportswear company, Harley-Davidson now sells its logo apparel in an upscale area of Tokyo. In 1991, Harley sold $41 million in motorcycles to Japanese enthusiasts "many of whom are organized into touring clubs around their bike size and brand"(Goozner, February 11, 1992). The *maquiladoras* rising in northern Mexico are examples of the fourth strategy, as are the tire plants built in the United States by the French and Germans.

Assessing the External Variables

Managers in an international company must monitor the five environments we have already defined in each of the countries in which it operates to determine the presence of threats and opportunities. They must determine how these external environments will influence one another and how they will affect the company.

Managers must then choose goals and strategies and create programs to bring goals to reality. In developing plans the international manager monitors and assesses several key factors, including the following (Phatak, 1992):

- Political instability and risk. Changes in governments and their policies affect commerce, company plans and strategies, and the ability to conduct trade within and outside of the host country.

- Currency instability. Fluctuations in currency exchange rates mean changes in how companies conduct their operations. Large sums are at stake because a company's earnings are in local currencies and must be spent around the globe as well as within the borders of a host country.

- Competition from national governments. State-owned or state-controlled companies and industries often operate with sizable government subsidies and may not be expected or required to earn profits. This places any international competitor at a great disadvantage.

- Pressures from national governments. Companies have been accused of sending unsafe or environmentally unsound technologies and products to a host country, exporting technology and jobs, and interfering with domestic industries. It's important for corporations, like individuals, to be good citizens.

- Nationalism. National pride creates political ideologies that can inhibit commerce, especially from foreign-owned operations. From such ideologies can come trade restrictions, local ownership restrictions, and limits on how much money can be exported.

- Patent and trademark protection. Some countries will offer no protection; anyone's property is fair game. Others offer limited protection to foreign-owned enterprises. Some countries and industries are notorious for their piracy of ideas and technology.

- Intense competition. Lucrative markets will always be the focus of fierce competition from both domestic and foreign companies.

These variables illustrate that managers planning in the international marketplace are confronted with many complex issues and uncertainties; and inadequate assessment courts failure. Managers charged with assessing a company's possible entry into the global market must do their work thoroughly and competently to ensure the best prospects for success. Of special concern in assessing possible international operations are capital budgeting and long-term planning. Assessment may be assigned in-house to line or staff managers, or contracted out to private consultants (Shreeve, 1984).

Assessments lead to forecasts which managers then use to construct their plans. The aim of all these efforts is to create unity among managers of the multinational, and a commitment on behalf of the company to behave as a decent corporate citizen in its host countries. Corporate strategy determines how the organization will deploy its resources in order to achieve objectives. Top-level strategy also becomes the framework for the formulation of correlated strategies in the company's affiliates around the world. Exhibit 20.7 highlights the major areas in which global corporate objectives are needed and the areas toward which strategies are directed.

PROFITABILITY

- Level of profits
- Return on asset, investment equity, sales
- Annual profit growth
- Annual earnings per share growth

MARKETING

- Total sales volume
- Market share—worldwide, region, country
- Growth in sales volume and growth in market share
- Integration of host-country markets for marketing efficiency and effectiveness

PRODUCTION

- Ratio of foreign to domestic production volume
- Economics of scale via international production integration
- Quality and cost control
- Introduction of cost-efficient production methods

FINANCE

- Financing of foreign affiliates—retained earnings or local borrowing
- Taxation—minimizing tax burden globally
- Optimum capital structure
- Foreign exchange management—minimizing losses from foreign fluctuations

TECHNOLOGY

- Type of technology to be transferred abroad—new or old generation
- Adaptation of technology to local needs and circumstances

HOST-GOVERNMENT RELATIONS

- Adapting affiliate plans to host-government developmental plans
- Adherence to local laws, customs, and ethical standards

PERSONNEL

- Development of managers with global orientation
- Management development of host-country nationals

RESEARCH AND DEVELOPMENT

- Innovation of patentable products
- Innovation of patentable production technology
- Geographical dispersion of research and development laboratories

ENVIRONMENT

- Harmony with the physical and biological environment
- Adherence to local environmental legislation

Source: Arvind V. Phatak, *International Dimensions of Management,* 3rd edition (Boston: PWS-Kent), 1992, pp. 98–99. Reprinted by permission of the publisher. Copyright 1992 Wadsworth, Inc.

Organizing and the International Manager

Companies develop organizational structures to achieve objectives. As it extends its operations internationally and modifies its objectives, an organization must also adapt its structure. The structure chosen at any time in a firm's evolution depends on the extent of its operations abroad; the structure developed to simply market a product overseas must be changed when the company moves to actually produce the product abroad. Other influences on structure include the locations of foreign operations, their contributions to the parent company, and the degree of experience and competence possessed by both headquarters and host-country managers. The structure chosen must accommodate political, legal, economic, sociocultural, and technological differences between the host-country and parent-country operations. Choices about the degree of decentralization must continually be re-examined as operations unfold. Threshold issues to address when attempting to establish an international organization include the following:

- Achieving operational efficiency

- Creating the flexibility to respond to national and global changes

- Allowing units to share information and technology quickly

- Coordinating activities from various cultures

- Responding swiftly to changes in consumer needs and demands

- Differentiating operations by function, product, customers, or geography

- Developing management teams with common goals and shared visions

The structure of a company changing from a domestic to an international outlook generally evolves through three phases: the pre–international division phase, the international division phase, and finally the global structure phase (Phatak, 1992).

Pre–International Division Phase

Companies with a product or service that incorporates the latest technology, is genuinely unique, or is superior in features, performance, or price may consider themselves ready for entry into the international arena. For many companies the first strategy used to introduce the product to a foreign market is to find a way to export the product. The result is typically the addition of an export manager to the present marketing department. Companies with a broad line of products—such as a chemical manufacturer—may establish an export manager who reports directly to the CEO and works in a staff capacity with the individual product divisions to coordinate production and marketing. The export manager will determine the appropriate methods for foreign distribution and marketing—whether to place company employees in a host country or to work through agents (importers, distributors, or retailers) already established there. Exhibit 20.8 shows the addition of an export manager to an established domestic management structure.

International Division Phase

In time, pressures may mount through the enforcement of host-country laws, trade restrictions, and competition, to place the company at a cost disadvantage. In such an event, the company often decides to defend and expand its foreign

Exhibit 20.8

Organizational structure with export manager engaged in exporting to foreign markets.

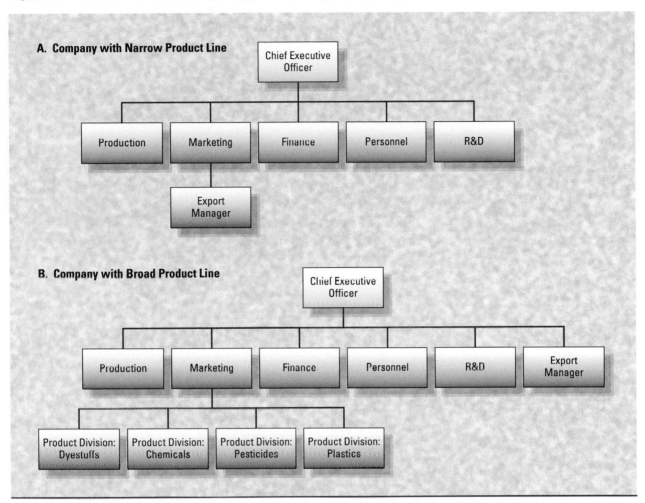

Source: Adapted from Arvind V. Phatak, *International Dimensions of Management,* 3rd edition (Boston: PWS-Kent), 1992, p. 139. Reprinted by permission of the publisher. Copyright 1992 Wadsworth, Inc.

market position by establishing marketing or production operations in one or more host countries. Exhibit 20.9 shows the result—the establishment of an **international division** with its head reporting directly to the CEO. The international division structure works well for companies in the early stages of global involvement. These firms typically display certain characteristics: "limited product diversity; comparatively small sales (compared to domestic and export sales) generated by foreign subsidiaries; limited geographic diversity; and few executives with international expertise" (Phatak, 1992).

In the early stages, centralization may be practiced to retain tight control over the international facilities. In time, decentralization begins, giving those closest to the problems and opportunities the authority needed to respond quickly to customer, political, and economic demands and challenges. As the on-site

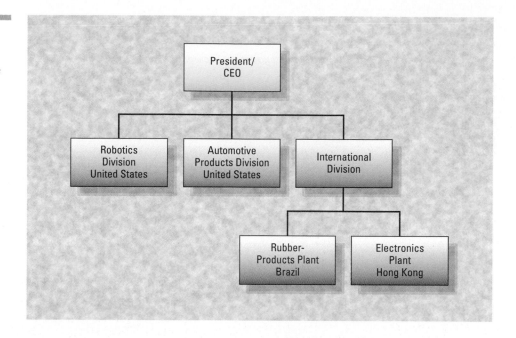

managers gain experience and expertise, they pass it on for future planning purposes and become trainers for those who will follow them in present or future overseas ventures. Many managers will pass through the international divisions on their way to regional and corporate headquarters jobs.

Global Structure Phase

As international operations achieve success, top management makes a greater commitment to them and begins to see the company in a global perspective. Most companies find that as their international operations expand, a greater percentage of revenues and profits begins to flow from them. Such is the case with Philip Morris, GM, Ford, Bausch & Lomb, and Motorola. International divisions enable companies to better serve more markets than would be possible without them. Such companies become nearly immune to most trade restrictions and function in closer proximity to their customers. These firms usually find themselves with an ever-increasing number of foreign nationals on their payrolls and running their operations, both in foreign markets and in the firms' various headquarters. Organizational culture begins to evolve as these forces for change are absorbed and take power.

According to research done by *Business International*, a company is ready to move away from an international division phase and toward a global structure when it meets the following criteria:

● The international market is as important to it as the domestic market

● Senior officials in the company possess both foreign and domestic experience

● International sales represent 25% to 35% of total sales

Exhibit 20.10a

A simplified corporate structure integrating worldwide product groups.

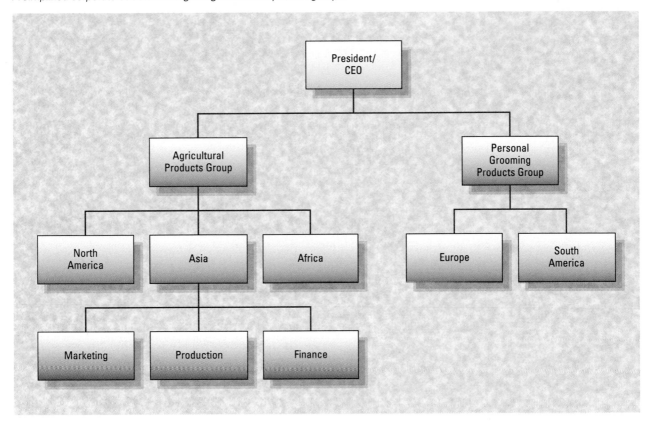

- The technology used in the domestic division has far outstripped that of the international division (*Business International,* 1970)

The shift to a **global structure** means a change in how decisions are made. Typically, decisions that were previously made by separate and autonomous divisions will now be made at a corporate headquarters for the entire enterprise. Corporate decisions now need a total-company perspective. The final structure will contain functional, product, and geographic features and may be based on worldwide product groups, worldwide area groups, or a mixture of the two. Each group becomes a profit center controlled by a vice president. The product-group structure works best for diverse and widely dispersed product lines and for companies with relatively high levels of technology or R&D operations. Product-group structure is illustrated in Exhibit 20.10a.

The regional or area approach works best with a narrow group of similar products and products that are closely tied to local consumer markets. Oil companies, specialty-food manufacturers, and rubber-products companies tend to adopt this structure. The functions of the international division are carried out by the regional managers who report directly to the parent headquarters (see Exhibit 20.10b). Ford of Europe, Inc., headquartered in a London suburb, is an

Exhibit 20.10b

A simplified corporate structure integrating regional divisions.

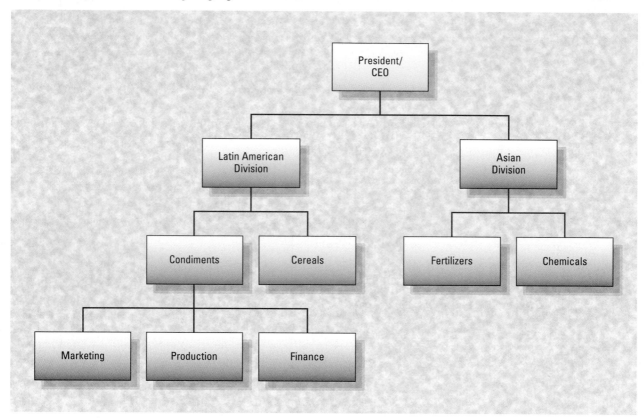

example of the regional approach. It oversees the conduct of the company's manufacturing operations in Northern Ireland, England, France, Belgium, Germany, Spain, and Portugal. Components and finished vehicles are routinely shipped from one nation to another, all coordinated from the London headquarters. The structure parallels Ford's North American operations (Arndt, 1989).

Staffing and the International Manager

The function of staffing is to identify and acquire qualified human resources to ensure the success of the organization. In an international company, staffing becomes far more complex because the search for talent knows no national boundaries.

Staffing Problems and Solutions

Finding qualified persons to fill jobs in host countries can be difficult, especially in developing or less-developed countries. During initial stages of expansion abroad, positions in host-country operations may have to be filled by transferring current employees from domestic operations. But, as a recent survey of multinational companies indicates, this is not always an adequate approach:

> Only 25% of U.S. managers are eager for foreign duty. Executives cite family responsibilities such as children's education, spouses' careers, or fears about living conditions abroad. Many also think foreign assignments will remove them from the corporate mainstream, hurting their careers. "It's difficult to be selective when [managers are] turning you down for many reasons," says David Weeks of the Conference Board (*Wall Street Journal,* June 16, 1992).

Eventually, through training and development programs conducted by the company or by outsiders, host-country citizens and others can be groomed for various jobs. Local conditions are also a factor. Finding executives for a multinational's operations in Mexico is particularly tough. With so many foreign companies already operating and many more coming, "The pool of qualified Mexican executives is so thin, and the demand so great, that competent Mexican managers often command greater salaries than their counterparts in the United States" (Moffett, 1992).

Different companies take different approaches to staffing foreign operations. Minnesota Mining & Manufacturing (3M) "brings dozens of foreigners every year from overseas units for stints at its St. Paul, Minnesota, headquarters. These 'inpatriates' receive as many financial benefits here as 3M's U.S. workers do when they go abroad" (*Wall Street Journal,* February 24, 1992). Honda believes that its "managers dispatched from the head office should be encouraged to become part of the community by understanding local culture and ways of thinking; to delegate authority to local personnel; and to create a sense of unity between management and labor so that everyone is working toward a common goal" (Sugiura, 1990).

The Japanese generally prefer to send a core of Japanese executives to head their foreign operations, but many are now moving toward giving host-country citizens, especially Americans, more important roles. Ronald G. Shaw is one of the new breed of Americans who serve as presidents and CEOs of Japanese subsidiaries in the United States. He is the CEO of Pilot Pen of America, a U.S. subsidiary of Pilot Corporation of Japan. In 1992 he became somewhat unique when he was appointed to the parent company's board of directors (Rosenberger, 1992).

General Electric may have the ideal international manager in place to run its recently acquired light-bulb manufacturing plant in Hungary. George F. Varga, who left his native Hungary as a teenager, is a veteran of overseas assignments, having worked in the United States, Spain, Holland, Switzerland, and Mexico. He speaks six languages and has western know-how in marketing and financial management. He replaced half the Hungarian managers with seasoned GE executives (his managers average over 18 years' service). "We didn't want the young tigers. We need people with sensitivity to perform a cultural marriage. We have the ideal team to sell our ideas to the Hungarians" (Tully, 1990).

"The ticket to an overseas job is a master's degree in international management," says Kathryn A. Vegso, director of the career services center of the American Graduate School of International Management in Glendale, Arizona. "You need to learn the culture, speak the language, have the connections, and know how to do the job" (Kleiman, 1990). Scott A. Scanlon, an editor of the monthly newsletter *Executive Search Review,* believes that three qualities are needed to be a manager in Eastern Europe, an area of likely business focus in the coming years: being able to speak the language, knowing the country's culture and business environment, and being trained in western management techniques (Schubert, 1990). Russell Reynolds, head of the American executive search firm that bears his name, calls Eastern European countries "hardship zones" because of the deprivations managers experience after taking up residency there. He is looking for talent to manage in these countries, in the Middle East, Southeast Asia, and less-developed countries (Schubert, 1990).

Inevitably, foreign nationals are rising through the ranks to head up headquarters staffs of American multinationals. "At General Motors Corporation, a Spaniard was named to head GM's worldwide purchasing, responsible for spending $30 billion a year. And Xerox Corporation named an executive vice president from Italy" (Lublin, 1992). A Swiss national, Fritz Ammann, recently won the top job at Esprit de Corps, a U.S. sportswear manufacturer based in San Francisco. Ammann previously ran a Paris shoe company and beat out seven other candidates, including four Americans. Joseph Canion, founder of Compaq, observed, "In this decade and beyond, as more and more [U.S.] companies are forced to be global companies, you are going to see more mixing of nationalities at the top." He ought to know. He lost his job to his assistant, German-born Eckhard Pfeiffer (Lublin, 1992).

Compensation

Compensating host-country personnel in line with parent-company practices seldom works. Traditions, legally mandated pay scales and benefits, differing tax rates and levels of inflation, different standards of living, the relative value of currencies, and host-country competitors all combine to make compensation a difficult issue with regard to foreign affiliates. The American customs of rewarding individuals and groups on the basis of short-term performance, and rewarding managers for their departments' or divisions' success, must be tempered with the contributions that international divisions make to the enterprise as a whole and the kinds of barriers that they had to overcome. Some cultures shun group compensation plans whereas others live by them. Some countries (Germany, for example) have strong unions while others have none. In addition, such factors as the value of seniority, the cost of living in a host country (Japan has the highest), and a manager's level of status must be considered, and compensation plans adjusted accordingly.

A brief look at some compensation issues and numbers will convey a general feel for the pay and benefit differences existing around the world. The average annual salaries in 1991 for an electrical engineer in five foreign countries were as follows: In Hungary, $10,000; in South Korea, $19,000; in Britain, $25,000; in Japan, $30,000; and in Belgium, $35,000 (Cronin, 1992). Perks for managers and salespeople in these countries—in addition to voluntary and legally mandated benefits—include the following: in Belgium, as elsewhere in Western Europe, a car, a cellular phone, and a discretionary expense account; in Japan, a company car for executives; in Great Britain, a company car equipped with telephone; in South Korea, pickup by a car pool, graduating to a company car and driver, and a generous expense account; in Hungary, a company car for managers and salespeople and payment in western currency (Cronin, 1992). Exhibit 20.11 compares the average hourly wages, including benefits, and average number of vacation days for selected countries.

Exhibit 20.11

Average hourly wages, including benefits, and average vacation days for selected countries, 1991.

Country	Average Wages*	Average Vacation†
Germany[1]	$25.14	18 days
Switzerland	24.12	22
Denmark	19.39	30
Canada	18.42	10
Japan	18.40	10
France	16.60	26
United States	15.88	10
United Kingdom	14.14	22
Spain	13.98	22

1. Figures apply to former West Germany. Wages in former East Germany are generally considered to be two-thirds as much.

Sources: *Institut der Deutschen Wirtschaft for figures as reported in "Unity's Cost: Germany's Big Bill for Helping East Rilos Workers," *Wall Street Journal,* May 15, 1992, p. A8; and †Hewitt Associates data as reported in Carol Kleiman, "U.S. employees come up short on vacation benefits," *Chicago Tribune,* March 29, 1992, sec. 8, p.1.

Directing and the International Manager

People around the world are similar but not the same. Different languages, cultures, traditions, and attitudes affect how they approach their work and communicate with others. These differences make directing foreign nationals a challenge for the international manager. Managers who are not natives of the countries in which they work need to pay particular attention to how they communicate and interact with foreign nationals. What should be kept in mind throughout this section is that most nations today comprise multiple nationalities, and their work forces reflect cross-cultural influences just as the American work force does. Most European nations are hosts to immigrants from around the world—Turks, Arabs, and Asians—as well as other Europeans. Many Asians, particularly Koreans, work in Japan. Blending of populations can be expected to continue as countries in Europe, Asia, and Latin America attract foreign labor and as multinational businesses expand their operations to more and more nations.

Employee Attitudes

John E. Rehfeld has worked in an executive capacity for two major Japanese companies in the United States. He points out two differences between traditional

U.S. and Japanese management attitudes. First, when something goes wrong in a Japanese company, the emphasis is on solving problems, not placing blame. Japanese managers want to know what went wrong and how to fix it. Second, when Japanese managers set a goal and achieve it, they keep going and don't wait for praise. "The Japanese simply are not interested only in absolute results; they are equally interested in the process and in how you can do it better next time. They not only plan something and do it but also stop to see the result to determine how it could be done better" (Rehfeld, 1990).

When GE took over the management of the Tungsram works in Hungary, it found 18,000 workers, about as many as it had in the rest of its own lighting division, which generated seven times the sales volume. "In the West the solution would be huge layoffs. But the Hungarians' deep fear of joblessness [prompted] GE to take a more modest approach." It chose to reduce worker ranks by early retirements and normal attrition. Hungarians are also used to being paid in cash and few have checking accounts. GE chose to continue stuffing pay envelopes with cash (Tully, 1990).

For years, foreign companies have sent their managers to the United States and Western Europe for schooling in western business techniques and western culture. In the 1990–1991 school year, 407,529 foreign students were enrolled in American universities. The top field of interest for these students is business and management. At Northwestern University's J. L. Kellogg School of Management, in Evanston, Illinois, 198 out of the 1,100 students seeking an MBA degree were foreigners (*Fortune,* November 18, 1991). Some companies couple formal schooling with their own education programs:

> Many [South] Korean executives have degrees from U.S. universities, but Chey Jong-Hyon, 62, chairman of Sunkyong, has found another way to tap into American management methods. Chey, who earned a master's degree in economics at the University of Chicago in 1961, set up what he calls the Office of the Chairman for Management and Planning in New York and hired 15 Americans headed by IBM veteran Ronald D. Olsen to staff it. Says Chey: "Koreans think they understand America, but they don't know what they don't know." His Americans not only teach Korean managers to operate better in the United States but help Sunkyong get into new businesses in Korea (Kraar, 1992).

Communication Problems

An international manager may be presented with a number of communication dilemmas. Not only words, but body language as well differs from one culture to another. For example, Arabs consider it an insult to cross your feet or legs or to show the bottoms of your shoes. In Spain, the "okay" sign using the thumb and forefinger is considered vulgar. Seating one's self at a formal meeting before those of a higher rank are seated may be acceptable in American businesses but is viewed as disrespectful in many other cultures.

The parent company may wish to transact business in English, but it will have to adjust to Japanese, Korean, German, Spanish, and other languages. A manager at headquarters who is Swiss and speaks German may meet with host-country managers who are Italian, French, American, and Mexican, or mixtures of several nationalities. One solution chosen by some companies is to have all

Stepping outside a familiar business environment to one that can seem alien is not a move all small or mid-sized companies can make. LL Bean has been testing the waters in Japan.

communications among managers take place in one language—usually English or French in American and Western European companies, and Japanese in Japanese companies. Relying on translators can be tricky. Host-country nationals may pretend to lack understanding when it is in their interest to do so. And many words in one language have no direct translation into others.

Even though English is becoming more and more the language of international business, and most educated people around the world learn it, affiliate managers must have a firm grounding in their host-country's language. There is simply no substitute for language fluency when it comes to directing the affiliate's work force, dealing with host-country unions and government officials, keeping abreast of local commercial and political affairs, and negotiating with suppliers and customers. Motorola, for example, gives language instruction to its managers before posting them in foreign countries.

As a final word on communications, consider the messages sent by the choice of a gift for a foreign colleague or business associate. This is an area with many potential problems. The choice of a gift can cause embarrassment or trouble for the giver if a country's customs and traditions are not understood. Exhibit 20.12 outlines a few rules for giving gifts to foreign associates.

Cross-Cultural Management

A relatively new field called **cross-cultural management** "studies the behavior of people in organizations around the world and trains people to work in organizations with employee and client populations from several cultures." It describes and compares organizational behavior within and across countries and cultures and

- Don't rely on your own taste.

- Don't bring a gift to an Arab man's wife; in fact, don't ask about her at all. Bringing gifts for the children is, however, acceptable.

- In Arab countries, don't admire an object openly. The owner may feel obligated to give it to you.

- Do not bring liquor to an Arab home. For many Arabs, alcohol is forbidden by religious law.

- Don't try to out-give the Japanese. It causes great embarrassment and obligates them to reciprocate even if they cannot afford it.

- Do not insist that your Japanese counterpart open the gift in your presence. This is not their custom and can easily cause embarrassment on the part of the recipient.

- As a courtesy, hold your gift with two hands when presenting it to a Japanese businessperson, but do not make a big thing of the presentation.

- Be careful when selecting colors or deciding on the number of items. The color purple is inappropriate in Latin America because it is associated with Lent.

- Avoid giving knives and handkerchiefs in Latin America. Knives suggest the cutting off of the relationship, and handkerchiefs imply that you wish the recipient hardship. To offset the bad luck, the recipient must offer you money.

- Logos should be unobtrusive.

- In Germany, red roses imply that you are in love with the recipient. Perfume is too personal a gift for business relationships.

- In the People's Republic of China, expensive presents are not acceptable and cause great embarrassment. Give a collective gift from your company to theirs.

- In China, a banquet is acceptable, but you will insult your hosts if you give a more lavish banquet than the one given you.

- A clock is a symbol of bad luck in China.

- The most important rule is to investigate first. After all, no one laughs at gift games. True, it is the thought that counts: the thought you give to understanding the culture and the taste of the people with whom you plan to negotiate.

"seeks to understand and improve the interaction of co-workers, clients, suppliers, and alliance partners from different countries and cultures" (Adler, 1991).

Managers of global enterprises interact regularly with people of differing backgrounds, educational systems, business training, and personal perspectives and biases. "Diversity exists both within and among cultures; but within a single culture, certain behaviors are favored and others repressed. The norm for a society is the most common and generally most acceptable pattern of values, attitudes, and behavior" (Adler, 1991). This section briefly examines some norms that managers must recognize and cope with.

Individualism Versus Collectivism   In general, Americans and citizens of many western countries like to think and act as individuals, preferring to gain their personal identities through achievements and individual efforts. But many societies, such as in Japan and several Latin American countries, are more group oriented. From an early age children are taught to work collectively and to derive a large portion of their personal identity from the group. Working with teams, especially those that need to be empowered and autonomous, may not be so easy in cultures that foster individualism.

Doing Versus Being   A *doing* orientation is an action orientation. Western culture fosters this outlook; citizens like to be rewarded for individual actions and behaviors. "Managers in doing oriented cultures motivate employees with promotions, raises, bonuses, and other forms of public recognition." By contrast, a *being* orientation "finds people, events, and ideas flowing spontaneously; the people stress release, indulgence of existing desires, and working for the moment.... they will not work strictly for future rewards" (Adler, 1991).

Some Asian cultures foster the being orientation. Rewards for individual performance are not popular. Employees focus on the value in a process rather than on the reward that results, and delight in doing it better each time. Employers are often viewed as surrogate parents and usually offer job security and collective benefits to encourage a family atmosphere and long-term commitment from employees. Progression in such companies is methodical, slow, and systematic, with few if any shortcuts or fast-track careers.

The Value of and Focus on Time   Some cultures value time more than others. To many people in the Middle East, time is not considered precious. Many people see work as a means to support life, not as a reason for living. Some cultures emphasize planning for the long term; others focus on the present or the past by following tradition.

Masculinity Versus Femininity   Geert Hofstede defines masculinity as the extent to which the dominant values in a society emphasize assertiveness and the acquisition of money and things and de-emphasize concern for people. He defines femininity as the extent to which the dominant values in society emphasize relationships among people, concern for others, and the overall quality of life (Hofstede, 1980). He sees the Scandinavian countries as feminine; he sees Mexico,

Japan, and much of Western Europe as masculine. Societies with feminine cultures "tend to create high-tax environments; extra money often fails to strongly motivate employees. Conversely, masculine societies tend to develop into lower-tax environments in which extra money or other visible signs of success effectively reward achievement" (Mexico for example) (Adler, 1991).

Controlling and the International Manager

The management function of control involves setting standards, measuring performances, applying standards to performances, and taking corrective actions as needed. These fundamentals do not change with multinational operations, but some specifics of controlling do. The next section focuses on the control characteristics and problems of international managers.

Characteristics of Controls

Multinationals use a variety of controls to monitor and adjust the performance of their foreign affiliates. These controls fall into two groups: direct and indirect. Direct controls include the use of such devices as periodic meetings, visits to foreign operations by headquarters staff, and staffing foreign affiliates with home-country nationals. Meetings are often held via satellite linkups and by teleconferencing between affiliate managers and top management. Periodically, host-country managers are called to headquarters to give firsthand reports on strategic progress.

Direct controls such as face-to-face meetings are sometimes difficult to arrange for managers of multinational corporations. Telecommunication links by phone, fax, and computer help companies to keep in touch.

Indirect controls include various kinds of reports sent daily, weekly, monthly, and yearly via fax and computer linkups. The main criteria used to measure performances by international affiliates are costs, return on invested capital, market share, and profits earned by product line and area of operations. In the same family of reports fall an entire array of budgetary and financial controls imposed by both local and corporate headquarters managers.

Control Problems

International controlling is complicated by everything from language to legal restrictions. Most companies rely on (1) regular reporting procedures and communications between affiliates and their headquarters, (2) progress toward

---

GLOBAL APPLICATIONS
Taiwan Comes Full Circle

Taiwan, a country about 1½ times the size of New Hampshire and containing about 20 million people, has been a source of cheap labor for manufacturers from around the world. It began its entrance into manufacturing with low-wage, low-technology assembly of relatively inexpensive items such as shoes, radios, and toys. For more than 20 years Taiwan has built a booming economy based primarily on small and medium-sized businesses. It has experienced rapid growth in personal income, land values, and gross domestic product. In 1982 the government opened a high-technology industrial park to help it capture better, higher-paying manufacturing jobs. Today the park has 138 companies—many from the West—employing 23,000 people, and is expected to double in size by 1996. "Taiwan now produces about 10% of the world's personal computers, with 40% of that coming from the park's 1,000 acres."

Taiwan's Acer Corporation, one of the 10 largest computer makers in the world, reflects Taiwan's current problems. Established in 1976, it has grown from 11 employees to more than 5,000 and to sales of over $1 billion. Dependent on U.S. and Japanese chips for its products, it is moving into the more sophisticated areas of computer manufacturing. But with the price wars in personal computers and rising labor costs, the company has lost money for two consecutive years. Rising land prices have made expansion expensive. And a growing middle class is demanding better environmental and labor laws. As a result, Acer and a host of high-tech companies are looking abroad to find lower-cost production centers. "More and more of Taiwan's businesses are running abroad in search of cheap labor. Taiwanese manufacturers have invested more than $5 billion in the People's Republic of China, and another $10 billion in Malaysia, Indonesia and Thailand."

The Taiwanese government is trying to attract more high-tech jobs and keep those it has. It wants to move from supplying parts to the world to building entire assemblies. This means keeping its talent and entrepreneurs at home and fostering high-tech research and development. Chen Li-ching, deputy director of the Hsinchu science-based industrial park, says, "The way we compete is with good engineers and well-trained technicians at a cost much lower than in the United States or Japan. An electrical engineer out of college earns the equivalent of $13,000 here." ▲

For more on Taiwan's contemporary economics, see Merrill Goozner, "Taiwan trying to harness power of high-tech base," *Chicago Tribune*, November 1, 1992, sec. 7, pp. 1–2.

goals that have been established with the affiliates' inputs, (3) regular screening of reported data by area and functional experts, and (4) regular on-site inspections by various corporate personnel, both staff and line.

At Thomson, S.A., the French electronics giant, controlling international operations means touching bases on a regular schedule with key managers (in much the same way that Wal-Mart keeps track of its far-flung operations). Thomson maintains four major product groups and operations in the United States, Canada, Central America, Europe, Australia, and the Pacific Rim nations. Regular meetings and seminars are held in France each year involving employees from all the company's divisions.

> The CEO of the consumer electronics division spends at least one week in the United States every month, plus a week in Asia every second month, plus, of course, commuting inside Europe. Two of the executive vice presidents in charge of the four world product groups are based in Indianapolis, while the other two are in Paris. They have to meet regularly as well as travel to their sales organizations (McCormick and Stone, 1990).

A final note on controlling human resources abroad: In many countries bonuses, pensions, holidays, and vacation days are legally mandated and considered by many employees to be their right. Particularly powerful unions exist in many parts of the world, and their demands restrict management's freedom to operate. Many countries have laws requiring that money be paid regularly into funds to provide for employee layoffs and terminations. Also, it can be quite expensive to fire or lay off a manager in many countries, as a study by William M. Mercer, a New York–based management consulting firm, has discovered. The cost of firing

> a 45-year-old middle manager with 20 years of service and a $50,000 annual salary, for example, varies in cost from $13,000 in Ireland to $130,000 in Italy. The amount is often much more than in the United States where a comparable worker doesn't have the same statutory protection. In Germany, managers receive six months' notice-period pay after working 12 years [*Fortune*, April 6, 1992]. And these expenses do not take into account the cost of finding a replacement.

Future Trends

Future globalization of business is likely to bring about these trends:

- Look for growing complaints about discrimination from employees of foreign-owned firms in the United States. These charges will focus on companies discriminating on the basis of sex and country of origin (favoring home-country personnel at the expense of Americans). Sexual harassment charges are likely to increase as well. In many cultures women are not given the protections that U.S. laws give them.

- The number of foreign students at American colleges and universities will continue to grow as more countries seek to develop and as more foreign companies seek international know-how and opportunities.

- The trend of exporting jobs will continue to diminish as wages and costs of doing business around the world rise and as calls for protection increase in many countries. Although firms will continue to seek the best sources for their inputs, they are realizing (as Taiwan has) that they must be active players in both R&D and product manufacturing to stay in the multinational game.

- The trend toward forming joint ventures among rivals both domestic and foreign will continue to increase in numbers and importance to all firms' survival.

- Certain Pacific Rim nations—the Philippines, Malaysia, South Korea, Indonesia, the People's Republic of China, and Vietnam—will continue to experience growth and attract new businesses. Their relatively low costs for land and labor will continue to attract Asian entrepreneurs.

C H A P T E R   S U M M A R Y

- Since the 1950s, American companies have invested billions annually in foreign businesses and nations, as have foreigners in U.S. ventures.

- The U.S. trade deficit is caused because the nation imports more than it exports.

- Multinationals are companies that own or jointly operate businesses and their affiliates in several countries. Multinationals can sell standardized products and services or customize them for each country's markets.

- The international manager must know the language, culture, laws, and customs of the host countries in which he or she operates.

- The international manager must position his or her company strategically in relation to the political, legal, economic, sociocultural, and technological environments of each country in which the company operates.

- Companies can sell products or services abroad in four ways: directly, by licensing them, by participating in joint ventures, or by creating or buying new facilities in other countries.

- In planning for the multinational company, managers must monitor and adapt to changes from many parts of the world. They must consider all the environments in which their organization does business.

- As companies expand operations abroad, the organizational structure typically evolves from the addition of a position responsible for marketing, to the creation of an international division, to the development of a global structure.

- Staffing for international operations can be handled at first by transferring home-country workers abroad, but eventually the company must develop skilled workers in the host country. Compensation laws and customs vary from country to country.

- Directing workers from many cultures is a challenge for international managers, who must deal with communication problems and differing attitudes and cultures.

- Controlling poses special challenges for companies engaged in international business because of the far-flung scope of operations and the differing influences of diverse environments. Controlling operations is nonetheless a crucial function for managers of multinational organizations.

S K I L L - B U I L D I N G

The following questions test your knowledge of this chapter's contents and your awareness of the U.S. economy's reliance on and interdependence with those of other countries. Answers appear at the end of the quiz.

1. Which of the following cars are currently produced in the United States?
   a. Chevrolet Lumina
   b. Mercury Sable
   c. Dodge Stealth
   d. Honda Accord Coupe
   e. Plymouth Voyager
   f. Chrysler LH sedans

2. In which country, America or Japan, are you most likely to find these practices?
   a. A commitment to lifetime employment by employers
   b. Promotions linked to seniority and training received
   c. Bonuses linked to individual efforts
   d. Confrontations between managers and workers
   e. A true, company-wide commitment to long-range planning, spanning 10 to 15 years
   f. A true spirit of competition between individuals on a variety of issues

3. Match the countries listed to the areas of the world.

(1)	Japan	a.	Middle East
(2)	Taiwan	b.	Central America
(3)	India	c.	Asia
(4)	England	d.	Africa
(5)	Bolivia	e.	Europe
(6)	Austria	f.	South America
(7)	Saudi Arabia	g.	Antarctica
(8)	Algeria	h.	North America

(Key: 1. Honda and Mercury 2. a. Japan; b. Japan; c. United States; d. United States; e. Japan; f. United States 3. Asia: Japan, Taiwan, India; Middle East: Saudi Arabia; Africa: Algeria; South America: Bolivia; Europe: England, Austria)

R E V I E W   **Q** U E S T I O N S

1. Review this chapter's essential terms and look up the meanings of those you cannot define.

2. What are two reasons why a company goes multinational?

3. What is the size of the U.S. balance of trade deficit? Why is international trade important for the U.S. economy?

4. What are the major characteristics of the multinational company?

5. What are the major components of each of the following international environments: political, legal, economic, sociocultural, and technological?

6. What makes planning so complex for multinationals? (consider the external issues discussed in this chapter)

7. What are the three organizational stages that a company passes through in going multinational?

8. What are three problems faced when attempting to staff international affiliates?

9. What are three problems connected with directing a cross-cultural work force?

10. What are the major control problems for a multinational corporation?

R E C O M M E N D E D   R E A D I N G

Adler, Nancy J. *International Dimensions of Organizational Behavior,* 3rd edition (Boston: PWS-Kent), 1991.

Axtell, Roger E. *Do's and Taboos of Hosting International Visitors* (New York: Wiley), 1990.

Business Week (July 13, 1992), "The Immigrants: How They're Helping to Revitalize the U.S. Economy," pp. 114–120, 122.

Choate, Pat. "Political Advantage: Japan's Campaign for America," *Harvard Business Review* (September–October 1990), pp. 87–103.

Lamont, Douglas. *Winning Worldwide: Strategies for Dominating Global Markets* (Boston: Business One Irwin), 1991.

Lane, Henry W., and Joseph J. DiStefano. *International Management Behavior,* 2nd edition (Boston: PWS-Kent), 1992.

Morita, Akio. "Partnering for Competitiveness: The Role of Japanese Business," *Harvard Business Review* (May–June 1992), pp. 76–83.

Phatak, Arvind V. *International Dimensions of Management,* 3rd edition (Boston: PWS-Kent), 1992.

Reich, Robert B. *The Work of Nations* (New York: Vintage), 1992.

Traverton, Gregory F., editor. *The Shape of the New Europe* (New York: Council on Foreign Relations Press), 1992.

Yip, George S. *Total Global Strategy: Managing for Worldwide Competitive Advantage* (Englewood Cliffs, NJ: Prentice-Hall), 1992.

R E F E R E N C E S

Adler, Alan L. "Whirlpool puts its brand on Europe," *Chicago Tribune,* March 30, 1992, sec. 4, p. 5.

Adler, Nancy J. *International Dimensions of Organizational Behavior,* 3rd edition (Boston: PWS-Kent), 1991, pp. 10–11, 17, 28, 57.

Aeppel, Timothy. "IIGM Sets Venture with Poland's FSO to Build Opels," *Wall Street Journal,* March 2, 1992, p. A4.

Arndt, Michael. "Ford is providing model for conquering new Europe," *Chicago Tribune,* December 11, 1989, sec. 4, pp. 1, 4.

Arndt, Michael. "Key issues remain in North American trade talks," *Chicago Tribune,* August 11, 1992, sec. 3, p. 3.

Baker, Stephen. "Along the Border, Free Trade Is Becoming a Fact of Life," *Business Week* (June 18, 1990), p. 41.

Browning, E. S. "In Pursuit of the Elusive Euroconsumer," *Wall Street Journal,* April 23, 1992, p. B1.

Brownstein, Vivian. "Exporters Will Keep Slugging," *Fortune* (April 20, 1992), p. 26.

Business International (1970). "Organizing the Worldwide Corporation," Research Report No. 69-4, p. 9.

Business Week (August 10, 1992). "The Global Economy: Who Gets Hurt," pp. 48, 50, 52, 66.

Business Week (July 13, 1992). "The Immigrants: How They're Helping to Revitalize the U.S. Economy," pp. 114–116.

Business Week (June 15, 1990). "Managing Global Expansion," pp. 9, 12.

Business Week (March 16, 1992). "Detroit South—Mexico's Auto Boom: Who Wins, Who Loses," pp. 98, 100–103.

Chicago Tribune (August 5, 1990). "In manners, no room for innocents abroad," sec. 7, p. 9C.

Chicago Tribune (July 3, 1992). "U.S. boosts debt to foreigners in 1991," sec. 3, p. 1.

Chicago Tribune (June 1, 1992). "Coke plans $1 billion for Europe," sec. 1, p. 11.

Chicago Tribune (June 21, 1992). "Co-op hits the jackpot in Japan," sec. 7, p. 8C.

Cronin, Michael P. "A Globetrotting Guide to Managing People," *Inc.* (April 1992), p. 122.

Eiben, Therese. "U.S. Exporters on a Global Roll," *Fortune* (June 29, 1992), pp. 94, 95.

Faltermayer, Edmund. "U.S. Companies Come Back Home," *Fortune* (December 30, 1991), p. 107.

Fortune (April 6, 1992). "Goodbyes Can Cost Plenty In Europe," p. 16.

Fortune (November 18, 1991). "More Foreigners at U.S. Colleges," p. 16.

Franklin, Stephen. "Despite costs, states still racing to lure Toyota," *Chicago Tribune,* October 29, 1990, sec. 4, pp. 1–2.

Goozner, Merrill. "Harley wears well in Japan," *Chicago Tribune,* February 11, 1992, sec. 3, p. 1.

Goozner, Merrill. "Venture tilts flat-screen technology Japan's way," *Chicago Tribune,* April 26, 1992, sec. 7, pp. 1, 4.

Gunset, George. "Trade accord productive for Midwest farms," *Chicago Tribune,* August 13, 1992, sec. 1, p. 1.

Hearn, Edward T. "U.S. insurer points to Eastern Europe," *Chicago Tribune,* March 11, 1990, sec. 7, p. 5.

Heyel, Carl, editor. *The Encyclopedia of Management,* 3rd edition (New York: Van Nostrand Reinhold), 1982, p. 495.

Hofstede, Geert. "Motivation, Leadership, and Organizations: Do American Theories Apply Abroad?" *Organizational Dynamics* (Summer 1980), pp. 42–63.

Ingram, Judith. "Amway sells a piece of the American Dream in Hungary," *Chicago Tribune,* November 21, 1991, sec. 3, pp. 1, 2.

Jacob, Rahul. "Bausch & Lomb: Trust the Locals, Win Worldwide," *Fortune* (May 4, 1992), pp. 76–77.

Kichen, Steve, editor. "The Forbes Foreign Rankings," *Forbes* (July 20, 1992), pp. 242–243, 246.

Kleiman, Carol. "Planning, not dreaming, will land that foreign job," *Chicago Tribune,* November 4, 1990, sec. 8, p. 1.

Kraar, Louis. "Korea's Tigers Keep Roaring," *Fortune* (May 4, 1992), p. 110.

Labich, Kenneth. "Airbus Takes Off," *Fortune* (June 1, 1992), p. 102.

Lublin, Joann S. "Foreign Accents Proliferate in Top Ranks As U.S. Companies Find Talent Abroad," *Wall Street Journal,* May 21, 1992, p. B1.

Martin, Thomas J., and Kevin S. Moran. "The Global Service 500," *Fortune* (August 24, 1992), p. 210.

McCormick, Janice, and Nan Stone. "From National Champion to Global Competitor: An Interview with Thomson's Alain Gomez," *Harvard Business Review* (May–June 1990), p. 135.

Moffett, Matt. "White-Collar Migrants Head Into Mexico," *Wall Street Journal,* March 27, 1992, pp. B1, B6.

Nelson, Mark M. "Whirlpool Gives Pan-European Approach a Spin," *Wall Street Journal,* April 23, 1992, p. B1.

O'Reilly, Brian. "The Job Drought," *Fortune* (August 24, 1992), pp. 62, 65.

Ono, Yumiko. "Japanese Liquor Dealer Imports Sake Made in U.S. Igniting a Controversy," *Wall Street Journal,* February 28, 1992, p. B3.

Pantages, Larry. "U.S. treads on Michelin's bid for Uniroyal," *Chicago Tribune,* October 22, 1989, sec 7, p. 16A.

Peters, Tom. "Global a state of mind, not a list of particulars," *Chicago Tribune,* October 23, 1989, sec. 4, p. 8.

Peters, Tom. "There are certain facts to consider before deciding that Japan is unfair," *Chicago Tribune,* April 23, 1990, sec 4, p. 7.

Phatak, Arvind V. *International Dimensions of Management,* 3rd edition (Boston: PWS-Kent), 1992, pp. 5, 55–62, 71–73, 136–146.

Rapoport, Carla. "Mazda's Bold New Global Strategy," *Fortune* (December 17, 1990), p. 109.

Rehfeld, John E. "What Working for a Japanese Company Taught Me," *Harvard Business Review* (November–December 1990), p. 169.

Rosenberger, Jane Ellen. "Japanese Firm Opens Door to Executive at U.S. Unit with Board Appointment," *Wall Street Journal*, March 27, 1992, p. B5.

Sanderson, Susan Walsh, and Robert H. Hayes. "Mexico—Opening Ahead of Eastern Europe," *Harvard Business Review* (September–October 1990), p. 32.

Schubert, Christian. "Executive recruiters facing tough time in Eastern Europe," *Chicago Tribune,* October 29, 1990, sec. 4, p. 3.

Shreeve, Thomas W. "Be Prepared for Political Changes Abroad," *Harvard Business Review* (July–August 1984), p. 112.

Storch, Charles. "Critics return fire in war on airline control," *Chicago Tribune,* October 1, 1989, sec. 7, p. 2.

Sugiura, Hideo. "How Honda Localizes Its Global Strategy," *Sloan Management Review* (Fall 1990), p. 78.

Time (June 22, 1992). "There's Plenty of Blame to Go Around," p. 27.

Tully, Shawn. "GE in Hungary: Let There Be Light," *Fortune* (October 22, 1990), p. 138.

Wall Street Journal (April 10, 1992). "Major Attraction: As Euro Disney Sets Opening, the French Go Goofy," p. A8.

Wall Street Journal (April 24, 1992). "Matsushita Electric Joins Nestle in Coffee Venture," p. A7.

Wall Street Journal (February 24, 1992). "3M Tries to Scotch 'Inpatriate!' Problems," p. B1.

Wall Street Journal (June 16, 1992). "Managers Balk at Overseas Assignments," p. A1.

Wall Street Journal (October 30, 1992). "AT&T Slates $402 Million for Pacific Cable Venture," p. B6.

Yates, Ronald E. "American firms wake up to world market demands," *Chicago Tribune,* June 15, 1992, sec. 1, pp. 1, 16.

Yates, Ronald E. "Economy size for companies," *Chicago Tribune,* December 13, 1991, sec. 3, p. 1.

Yates, Ronald E. "Foreigners' investment in U.S. plunges," *Chicago Tribune,* June 10, 1992, sec. 3, p. 1.

Yates, Ronald E. "Going abroad for allies," *Chicago Tribune,* April 26, 1992, sec. 7, pp. 1, 4.

G L O S S A R Y   O F   **T** E R M S

balance of trade   The difference between the goods and services flowing into a country and those flowing out.

cross-cultural management   An emerging discipline focused on improving work in organizations with employee and client populations from several cultures.

direct investment   The purchase of real property or other major assets by foreign nationals and foreign businesses in a country.

embargo   A government regulation enacted to keep a product out of a country for a time or entirely; often used as a political sanction to enforce a nation's foreign policy.

global structure   The arrangement of an organization's management decision making to efficiently and effectively operate in a multinational context; form may contain functional, product, and geographic features based on worldwide product or area units.

globalization   The aggregate processes of exporting products and services; locating operations outside one's national borders; using foreign partners to help in R&D and to sell products and services around the world; and tailoring strategies, management functions, and products and services to meet the needs of international customers; requires that managers think beyond national borders and see all world markets as part of a single global economy.

international division   A parent company's corporate unit, commonly a marketing or production operation, located in a host country offshore from the parent headquarters, and whose head reports directly to the CEO; common practice for companies in the early stages of international involvement.

international management   The process of managing resources (people, funds, inventories, and technologies) across national boundaries and adapting management principles and functions to the demands of foreign competition and environments.

multinational corporation   A company with operating facilities, not just sales offices, in one or more foreign countries; management favors a global vision and strategy, seeing the world as their market.

quota   A government regulation that limits the import of a product to a specified amount per year.

tariff   A tax placed on imported goods to make them more expensive and thus less competitive in order to protect domestic producers.

C A S E   P R O B L E M
Caterpillar's Don Fites

Donald V. Fites, chairman since 1990 of Caterpillar, the heavy-equipment manufacturer, may be an ideal international manager of an international company. He has a bachelor's degree in liberal arts, an MBA from the Massachusetts Institute of Technology, and overseas service of several years in South Africa, Brazil, Japan, Germany, and Switzerland. At age 58, his career with Caterpillar spans 36 years and started with his college graduation in 1956.

He began his career in marketing; his first overseas experiences were in selling Cat's products in South Africa. It was there that he learned the value of giving people in host countries the kind of autonomy they need to make sales and get close to their customers. He learned how out-of-touch his company's domestic marketing methods were for making sales overseas. Fites then worked 4½ years as marketing director of Caterpillar's construction-equipment joint venture with Mitsubishi in Tokyo. There he discovered the Japanese methods for product design and engineering. He saw firsthand how Japanese unions cooperated with management and how committed they were to their company's success. All three lessons served him well when he returned to Cat's headquarters in Peoria, Illinois.

In the 1970s Fites redesigned Cat's product development process by instituting "engineering with Japanese-style cross-functional teams. The teams included marketing, design, and manufacturing people, integrating the development process so plans wouldn't have to be passed back and forth among departments. Development time was cut in half." Since the mid-1980s the company, using teams, has boosted its productivity by 30%. Fites then redesigned worldwide marketing efforts. Remembering the troubles he had experienced in dealing with home-office control, when he became executive vice president of marketing in 1985 he "put more marketing staffers into the field and turned over authority for such market-sensitive matters as pricing to district offices."

In 1990, when Fites became chairman, he downsized the company by trimming the bureaucracy and creating more, smaller units. He also decentralized, pushing decision making lower in the management structure. Fites created 14 profit centers and demanded that each one earn a 15% return on assets. His most recent struggle has been with the United Auto Workers, the union that represents many of his company's employees. After five months of a bitter strike, Fites decided to hire nonunion employees to replace striking workers. That brought the union rank and file back to work without a contract and, in effect, has weakened the union's influence with the company's work force. An industry analyst sums up Fites's achievements: "He has completely changed the culture."

Q U E S T I O N S

1. What in Don Fites's background tells you he is equipped to run a multinational company?

2. What lessons did he learn from his overseas experiences?

3. What stages in Cat's international evolution can you identify?

For more about Caterpillar, see "Caterpillar's Don Fites: Why He Didn't Blink," *Business Week,* August 10, 1992, pp. 56–57.

21 Succeeding in Your Organization

L E A R N I N G   O B J E C T I V E S

After reading and discussing this chapter, you should be able to:

- Define this chapter's essential terms
- Discuss the nature of careers
- Describe what is meant by having a career perspective
- Identify and describe the four stages of career development
- Identify and discuss the five steps for career planning
- Discuss how a manager can understand his or her organization and why it is important to do so
- Identify and describe the abilities and actions that organizations value in managers
- Discuss the strategies associated with career management
- Discuss the organizational dilemmas experienced when personal and organizational interests are in conflict

burnout

career
career management

career perspective
career planning
job
mentor

organizational politics
organizational socialization
organizational visibility
psychological contract
sponsor
stress

M A N A G E M E N T   I N   A C T I O N
Armstrong, Davis, Eaton: A Trio of Successes

What two things do Michael Armstrong, Marilyn Davis, and Robert Eaton have in common? Besides being regarded as eminently successful in their management careers, each has recently made a major career move. These executives left the security and success of one organization to broaden their horizons in another.

Michael Armstrong had been an IBM lifer. After a brilliant rise at IBM, including building its European operations into a $26-billion powerhouse, he stunned "Big Blue" by announcing his departure to become CEO of Hughes Aircraft. The two important factors in his decision were IBM CEO John Akers's clear indications that Armstrong was not going to eventually get IBM's top spot, and assurances from GM Chairman Robert Stempel that Armstrong could run GM-owned Hughes Aircraft without much interference from the parent company.

Marilyn Davis left her spot as vice president of risk financing at American Express to become a senior director in the American Express Bank Ltd.—a private bank for wealthy individuals, their companies, and select financial institutions. With a goal of broadening her experience, Davis now reports directly to the bank's CEO and works on strategic, operational, and financial projects.

Robert Eaton went across town to begin his new career at Chrysler. After 29 years at General Motors, the last four as the head of European operations, Eaton was tabbed to be CEO of Chrysler to succeed the retiring Lee Iacocca. With his career advancement at GM blocked by a logjam of other qualified candidates, Eaton moved into an interesting situation—Iacocca will remain as chairman of the board and Robert Lutz, the chief internal candidate for the CEO position, remains as Chrysler's president.

The career moves made by Armstrong, Davis, and Eaton illustrate three major points of career management. First, each person is taking risks. Risk is associated with leaving a familiar environment for

Taking charge of your career *means finding the best arena for developing your talents and fulfilling your potential as a manager.*

► Managers need to constantly evaluate their positions and make a move if it is best for them.

one that is unknown. And there is always the risk of failure when taking on a different job with new challenges and expectations. Second, the decision by

Armstrong and Eaton to leave their firms to seek advancement in another organization illustrates that lifetime employment in one company is unlikely. To advance in a career, a person should not feel limited to any one employer. Third, the decision by each executive illustrates how managers need to constantly evaluate their positions and make a move if it is best for them. The decision may lead to increased responsibility, the opportunity to learn, and a step up the career ladder. ▲

For more on this trio of career moves, see Greg Bowens, "Mike Armstrong's Leap of Faith," *Business Week,* March 9, 1992, pp. 66–67; Alex Taylor, "Chrysler's Next Boss Speaks," *Fortune,* July 27, 1992, pp. 82–83; Alex Taylor, "Iacocca's Last Stand at Chrysler," *Fortune,* April 20, 1992, pp. 63–73; and Frank Moloy, "Power Surge," *Black Enterprise,* February 1992, pp. 99–104.

Managing to Success

Michael Armstrong, Marilyn Davis, and Robert Eaton have managed to achieve success in two areas: their jobs and their careers. In their positions at IBM, American Express, and GM, they were knowledgeable and got results. Each has also succeeded in managing his or her career—after all, one doesn't reach the heights they have reached by chance. Each developed his or her own career plan by focusing on the key elements: planning, preparation, and understanding the workings of organizations.

This chapter is about being successful in career management. First we will examine the nature of careers and then discuss the elements of career planning. The remainder of the chapter will examine personal career management and some associated dilemmas.

The Nature of Careers

One observer of the workplace puts the matter succinctly: "Some people have jobs, others have careers—it all depends on what you want, and how you approach it" (Vreeland, 1992). For some people, work is a **job**—a specific position they hold in an organization for which they are compensated. They take pride in it and do it well; but a job does not take on a long-term perspective, nor does it imply that the person doing it extends himself or herself beyond its requirements.

A **career**, on the other hand, is the sequence of jobs a person holds over a lifetime and the person's attitude toward his or her involvement in those jobs (Feldman, 1989). A career is a person's entire life in a work setting or settings. Because it encompasses a lifetime, a career reflects a long-term perspective and includes a series of jobs (Hall, 1986). A career also denotes involvement. People who have careers are so psychologically involved in their work that they extend themselves beyond its requirements.

A Career Perspective

An individual's probability of success in his or her career can be increased by adopting a career perspective. A **career perspective**, as illustrated in Exhibit 21.1, is a proactive strategy that involves an overall view of career progress or growth over time. It requires a person to adopt a broad vision that includes all the elements involved in a successful career—objectives, timetables, career stages, skills improvement, organizational politics, power, stress, and values. This can be accomplished through career planning, which places an emphasis on the activities involved in making career decisions, and career management, which emphasizes the activities and behaviors involved in career advancement.

Career Planning

One of the most important principles governing careers is that you alone are responsible for your career. Although you may be fortunate to work for organizations and managers who help you develop your career and advance, the hard fact is that you cannot sit back and wait for that to happen. All three of the executives in the Management in Action case moved to new companies when they saw the need. In addition, it is simply not enough to work hard and do well in your job. Those people who plan their careers greatly improve the chance of long-term success.

Career planning is the process of developing a realistic view about how one wants one's career to proceed, and then making plans to ensure that it follows that course. The process includes a series of activities to help make informed decisions: performing a self-assessment, identifying opportunities, matching skills to career-related activities, developing objectives and timetables, and evaluating progress. The process is important because it links personal needs and skills with career goals and opportunities.

Exhibit 21.1

Taking a career perspective.

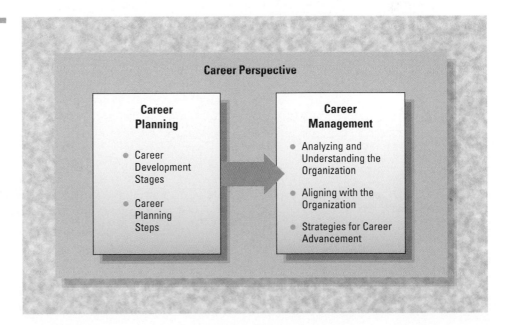

Planning one's careeer is a successful process because it is systematic. Such planning involves linking long- and short-term objectives, developing personal capabilities en route, and performing a focused analysis of progress. But it is not a one-time process. Career planning is ongoing; as the environment and organizations change, it is necessary to review, update, and adjust career plans periodically (Kunde, 1992). Michael Armstrong may not have imagined that he'd ever leave IBM—but when the time was right, he did just that.

Stages of Career Development

To understand how to plan a career, it is helpful to view how careers unfold. Most careers go through four distinct stages, each dealing with different issues and tasks (Hall, 1986). These four stages are illustrated in Exhibit 21.2. The tasks for each stage are listed in Exhibit 21.3.

Stage 1: Exploration and Trial   This first stage usually occurs between the ages of 15 and 25. For most people it begins with the decision to become serious about employment after having concentrated on education. This stage is a learning process, as it includes many firsts—the first job interview, first part-time job, first full-time job—and introduces the individual to the challenges associated with working. People in this stage face the issue of staying with an organization or moving to a job with another company.

Exhibit 21.2

The four stages of career development.

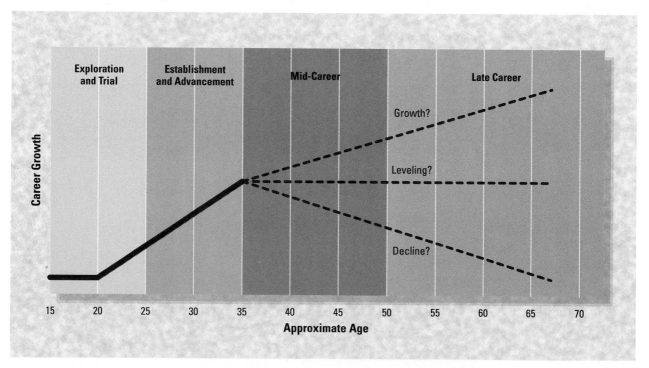

Stage 2: Establishment and Advancement   In this stage, normally between ages 25 and 35, people are involved in their first "real job." They experience success as well as frustration, and receive promotions and transfers. This is the period when most people take stock and start developing a career strategy—they begin to identify a field of specialization and weigh long-term success. For many, this stage includes offers for new jobs outside the organization.

Stage 3: Mid-Career   The mid-career stage most often occurs between the ages of 35 and 50. Most people don't face their first career dilemma until they reach this stage. A career may take any of three directions at this point: growth, leveling, or decline. If the direction is growth, the person is valued by the organization and is receiving promotions and increased responsibility. If the career levels off, the individual may receive transfers but not promotions; the person is secure, but with no growth in sight he or she often considers the option of a second career. If the career is in decline, the person is seen as surplus in the eyes of

Exhibit 21.3

Characteristics of the four stages of career development.

Stage	Task Needs
Exploration and Trial	• Varied job activities • Self-assessment
Establishment and Advancement	• Job challenge • Develop competence in a specialty area • Develop creativity and innovation • Rotate into new area after three to five years
Mid-Career	• Technical updating • Develop skills in training and coaching others (younger employees) • Rotation into new job requiring new skills • Develop broader view of work and role in organization
Late Career	• Shift from power role to one of consultation and guidance • Identify and develop successors • Begin activities outside the organization • Plan for retirement

Source: D. T. Hall and M. A. Morgan, "Career Development and Planning," *Contemporary Problems in Personnel,* revised edition. W. C. Hammer and Frank L. Schmidt, editors (Chicago: St. Clair Press), 1977.

the organization; he or she feels insecure and has a growing sense of failure. Such a person is likely to consider at least a move to a different company.

Stage 4: Late Career   The late-career stage—between the ages of 50 and retirement—is marked by a peak in prestige for those who experienced growth in the prior stage. Their value to the organization lies in their judgment and experience and their ability to share this knowledge with others. Such managers become reliable trainers of the next generation of managers. Plans need to be made to slow down, develop outside interests, and prepare for retirement.

For those whose careers level off or deteriorate in the mid-career stage comes the final realization that they have not made the impact on the organization that they intended, nor will they. One outcome is to stay on until retirement. A second option—which has become viable in companies that are downsizing— is early retirement (Serant, 1992).

Steps in Career Planning

The career-planning model can be used continually in one's employment life. Regardless of whether a person is on the outside looking in—just beginning a career—or trying to advance within an organization, the same steps apply (Plunkett, 1992). Exhibit 21.4 illustrates the steps in career planning.

Exhibit 21.4

The steps in career planning.

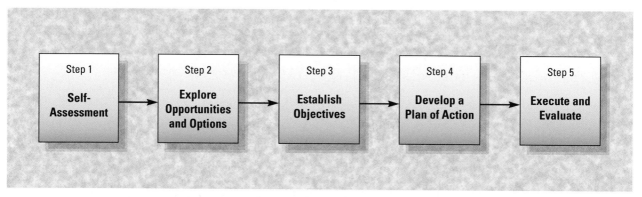

Step 1: Self-Assessment   Performing a realistic self-assessment is the first step in career planning. A thorough data-gathering process includes evaluating one's values, interests, skills, abilities, experience, and likes and dislikes. This step requires a clear and objective view of what one believes is important (values), what makes one happy at work, and what rewards are expected. Exhibit 21.5 provides an assessment checklist that can be used to identify skills and values.

At the beginning of a career, this step involves identifying initial skills and interests. As a career progresses and new opportunities surface, this step should be undertaken a number of times to ensure that one has retained his or her focus and to see if any additional training is needed. Exhibit 21.6 outlines 10 attributes that organizations look for in candidates when filling management positions.

Exhibit 21.5

An assessment checklist for identifying skills and values.

WHAT I DO WELL?

Check the items that apply to you:

☐ Organizing   ☐ Innovating
☐ Handling details   ☐ Making decisions
☐ Making things   ☐ Teaching others
☐ Researching   ☐ Supervising
☐ Creating   ☐ Dressing well
☐ Reasoning/logic   ☐ Persuading
☐ Writing   ☐ Communicating
☐ Drawing/painting   ☐ Dealing with criticism
☐ Computing/mathematics   ☐ Coordinating activities
☐ Dealing with others   ☐ Developing new skills
☐ Other (specify) _____

My five most important abilities are: _____

_____   _____

_____   _____

WHAT IS IMPORTANT TO ME

Check the items that apply to you:

☐ Helping others   ☐ Fast pace
☐ Working alone   ☐ Gaining knowledge
☐ Working with others   ☐ Creativity
☐ Making decisions   ☐ Change and variety
☐ Chance for advancement   ☐ Security
☐ Monetary reward   ☐ Recognition
☐ Physical challenge   ☐ Excitement
☐ Power and authority   ☐ Independence
☐ Improving society   ☐ Responsibility
☐ Competition   ☐ Intellectual challenge
☐ Other (specify) _____

My five most important abilities are: _____

_____   _____

_____   _____

Source: W. Richard Plunkett, *Supervision,* 6th edition (Needham Heights, MA: Allyn and Bacon), 1992, p. 39. Reprinted with permission of the publisher. Copyright 1992.

Exhibit 21.6

Ten attributes that organizations look for in applicants for management positions.

1. **Oral communication skills:** Effective expression in individual or group situations (includes gestures and nonverbal communication).

2. **Oral presentation skills:** Effective expression when presenting ideas or tasks to an individual or group when given time for presentation (includes gestures and nonverbal communication).

3. **Written communication skills:** Clear expression of ideas in writing and in correct grammatical form.

4. **Job motivation:** The extent to which activities and responsibilities available in the job correspond with activities and responsibilities that result in personal satisfaction.

5. **Initiative:** Active attempts to influence events to achieve goals; self-starting rather than passive acceptance; taking action to achieve goals beyond those called for; instigating change.

6. **Leadership:** Utilizing appropriate interpersonal styles and methods in guiding individuals (subordinates, peers, superiors) or groups toward task accomplishment.

7. **Planning and organization:** Establishing a course of action for self and/or others to accomplish a specific goal; planning proper assignments of personnel and appropriate allocation of resources.

8. **Analysis:** Relating and comparing data from different sources, identifying issues, securing relevant information, and identifying relationships.

9. **Judgment:** Developing alternative courses of action and making decisions that are based on logical assumptions and reflect factual information.

10. **Management control:** Establishing procedures to monitor and/or regulate processes, tasks, or the responsibilities of subordinates; taking action to monitor the results of delegated assignments or projects.

Source: Reprinted with permission from *HR* magazine, published by The Society for Human Resource Management, Alexandria, VA.

Step 2: Explore Opportunities and Options   The second step in career planning requires examining the opportunities that exist in the industry and within a company. At the beginning of a career, this involves determining the following points.

- What are the future prospects for the industry?

- What career opportunities exist in the industry?

- What jobs are available?

- What jobs relate to a career path?

Career development doesn't just happen, it must be managed. Setting long-term goals helps to shape the short-term decisions.

For a person in mid-career, the emphasis shifts to evaluating both inside and outside the organization:

- What are the future prospects for the company?

- What positions will open up in the company?

- What training and development is available?

- Who is being promoted?

- When are they being promoted?

- What is the job market?

In the new business environment of the 1990s, which emphasizes flatter organizational structures and team orientation, this step becomes even more critical. The answers to many of the questions—what career opportunities exist, what jobs relate to a career path, what positions will open up, who is being promoted—evolve on a day-to-day basis. For the career planner, the implications are clear: research thoroughly, build in flexibility, and constantly evaluate and update.

Step 3: Establish Objectives   Once the opportunities are identified, the career planner has to make short- and long-term decisions. The key is to make the long-term decisions first and then derive the short-term decisions from them. According to Professor Sal Davita, "The two issues of paramount importance are: what position do you want to hold the day you retire, and in what industry do you want to make a career?" The decision on the industry is critical for a few reasons.

F O C U S   O N   Q U A L I T Y

Advancement for Quality Workers

With a recognition that quality—quality work, quality effort, and quality results—are the product of a quality work force, many companies are restructuring their policies to maintain and advance proven employees. As an example, many companies are developing "family-friendly" policies such as flexible scheduling and family leave. The purpose is to remove work/family conflict that can limit the advancement of proven employees who are torn between two major commitments. The flexible scheduling and family leave facilitate a career focus and a family focus simultaneously.

Still other organizations, which maintain family-friendly policies, are changing the focus of implementation and interpretation. At Corning, a 17-member task force, ranging from vice presidents to engineers, has been looking at ways to remove barriers to advancement. The task force has developed a number of ideas, including:

- Make part-time work and family policies explicitly available for reasons that have nothing to do with motherhood, such as the need to spend time with an ailing parent. This broadens the policy to apply to all employees, rather than only to women.

- "Flexibility training" to help managers administer flexible scheduling fairly and stress flexibility in career planning as well. Instead of routinely promoting people who follow a traditional career path, the focus is on matching an employee's skills, interests, and ability to learn with the demands of the job.

At Xerox, company managers are being directed to emphasize results as a basis of promotion rather than time spent in the office, the number of transfers, or other corporate rituals. The company is not interested in whether a person puts in a 60-hour workweek just because a predecessor took 60 hours to do the job. Results are what count. ▲

For more on advancement for quality workers, see Sue Shellenberger, "Averting Career Damage from Family Policies," *Wall Street Journal,* June 24, 1992, p. B1.

First, an individual's abilities and interests are more or less suited to work in different industries. Second, industries vary in their future prospects. It is possible to change industries later in one's career, but doing so often sends a person back to lower levels in the hierarchy. The decision on the final position is important because by defining a career path, it provides direction (Davita, July 6, 1992).

Once these long-term objectives are established, other decisions follow:

- Which functional area of the organization needs to be learned about?

- What jobs and departments will lead to the ultimate objective?

- What skills are needed to attain the objective?

- What people and other resources are necessary to achieve the objectives?

- What work assignments will be valuable?

Step 4: Develop a Plan of Action   This step provides the detailed map for accomplishing the objectives. It requires determining how to specifically acquire the skills—whether formal education is necessary or if they can be learned by seeking a special project. The plan should include establishing specific timetables for completing training, reaching a new job level, and gaining new exposure in a company. This stage also identifies potential barriers and the resources for working around them.

Step 5: Execute and Evaluate　Once the plan is in place, it must be put into action. This is a matter of taking charge of one's career rather than waiting for things to happen. The second phase of this step is to follow up and evaluate progress on the plan. As the environment changes, adjusting the plan may become necessary. The evaluation should also consider individual growth, career progress, new assignments—those items that were targeted by objectives and developed in the plan of action. This execution phase—career management—is the next topic of discussion.

Career Management

The key to success is to take charge and actively manage one's career. **Career management** involves three elements: understanding the organization, aligning oneself with the organization, and implementing career-enhancing strategies.

Analyzing and Understanding the Organization

As noted in Chapter 9, all organizations are unique. Each develops its own methods, values, and rewards; each makes clear what it accepts and does not tolerate. Before a person can develop strategies for advancement, he or she must know the company—what abilities it values, what actions it rewards, and how it compensates its achievers; he or she must both accept the organization and be accepted by it. This critical phase has been identified by organizational psychologist Edgar H. Schein as the organizational socialization process.

Organizational Socialization　Regardless of whether it is a new employee's first company or fifth, he or she undergoes **organizational socialization**. In this process new members of an organization gain exposure to its values, norms, policies, and procedures. At the same time, they discover who wields power, what restrictions there are on behavior, and how to succeed and survive.

Exhibit 21.7 presents Schein's model for the process through which an employee becomes an accepted and conforming member of the organization. In Phase I, a job seeker forms impressions and expectations of the company. Phase II is the period of adjustment in which the new employee matches individual needs to those of the organization. Phase III marks the mutual acceptance of employee and organization. Not all employees survive these last two phases; faced with conflicts and compromises too great to overcome, employees who cannot adjust and conform may quit voluntarily or be asked to leave (Schein, 1978).

At the end of Phase III, the employee and the organization enter into a **psychological contract**, an unspoken agreement defining what people are expected to give the organization and what they can expect in return. Formed in the mind of the employee, it is based on experiences, promises, and personal observations of how the organization operates. The terms of the contract are the result of interactions between the employee and boss, the employee and co-workers, and

---

PHASE I

Entry

- Occupational choice
- Occupational image
- Anticipatory socialization to occupation
- Entry into labor market

PHASE II

Socialization

- Accepting the reality of the human organization
- Dealing with resistance to change
- Learning how to work: coping with too much or too little organization and too much or too little job definition
- Dealing with the boss and deciphering the reward system—learning how to get ahead
- Locating one's place in the organization and developing an identity

PHASE III

Mutual Acceptance: The Psychological Contract

Organizational acceptance	**Individual acceptance**
Positive performance appraisal	Continued participation in organization
Pay increase	Acceptable job performance
New job	High job satisfaction
Sharing organizational secrets	
Initiation rites	
Promotion	

Source: Edgar H. Schein, *Career Dynamics*. Reprinted with permission of the publisher. Copyright 1978 by Addison-Wesley Publishing Company, Inc.

---

the employee's firsthand experience with the organization's enforcements of the rules and behaviors it considers essential. A sense of fairness or equity must exist between employee and employer; each must believe that the other is doing his or her part and giving in proportion to what he or she expects to receive.

Determining What Is Valued and Rewarded   Organizational socialization provides the employee with the opportunity to identify and focus on what the organization values and rewards—what abilities are associated with advancement

*Being a **team player*** *and possessing communication skills is as important as being a hard worker.*

and what actions are perceived as valuable. Although it is critical to identify traits that a specific organization values, a survey of major organizations and leading CEOs (including Michael Eisner of Disney, Nancy Widman of CBS Radio, and John Reed of Citicorp) identified a number of abilities associated with advancement in a broad spectrum of companies (Hetzer, 1992):

- Communication skills. The ability to communicate one on one, in groups, and in writing.

- Interpersonal skills. The ability to work with others, relating well to people at all levels of the organization, understanding how others feel, and establishing networks.

- Competence. The ability to produce quality work, get results, be accountable, know the field, and perform consistently.

- Conceptual skills. The ability to focus on the big picture and understand all the interlocking pieces.

- Decision skills. The ability to handle more and increasingly complex problems.

- Flexibility. The ability to adjust to rapid change, new variables, and new environments.

Interviews conducted at Fortune 500 companies revealed that the actions most likely to be valued and rewarded in today's organization include the following:

- Hard work. Working hard means being willing to accept more responsibility, being committed, and being dedicated. It also involves working more hours than the standard workweek and producing high-quality results.

- Risk taking. This includes a willingness to move into unfamiliar areas of the business, taking on new assignments, and accepting increases in responsibility.

- Make contributions. This involves focusing on the critical parts of a job—quality and innovation. It also involves looking at the company's objectives, and seeing how the present position fits in and how it affects the bottom line.

- Team player. Being a team player presupposes a dedication to making the organization run more effectively, rather than focusing on just a job or a department. It involves being able to step back and align one's objectives with those of others rather than trying to dominate or isolate.

Assessment and Alignment

Having identified the abilities and actions that are valued and rewarded by the organization, it is necessary to assess both and possibly make a mid-course correction. One's actions and abilities must align with those the organization values. To assist this process, the employee must ask the following questions:

- How do my skills match those the organization values?

- Am I capable of the actions necessary?

- What other preparation, education, or training do I need?

It is equally important for the employee to be committed to continuous evaluation and skill building.

Strategies for Career Advancement

Knowing and understanding the organization provides the basis upon which to develop and implement strategies for career advancement. As shown in Exhibit 21.8, these strategies focus on creating visibility, developing mentor relationships, understanding power and politics, working with the boss, and managing stress.

Creating Visibility

Of course, one way to create visibility on the job is to perform effectively: People who do a good job get noticed. Unfortunately, performance evaluations and recommendations for promotion may involve a substantial degree of subjectivity. To make oneself stand out, a major strategy for career advancement is creating organizational visibility (Robbins, 1991).

Exhibit 21.8

Strategies for career advancement.

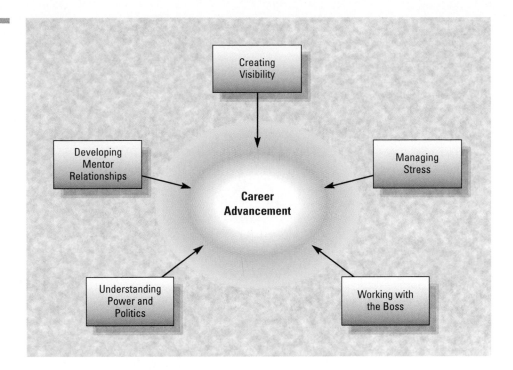

Organizational visibility is spotlighting and highlighting a person's abilities, talents, and contributions for those people in the organization who influence promotion and advancement. In addition to the subjective nature of evaluation, many individuals perform jobs that have low visibility—they work in remote locations or have limited contact outside a department. In order for talent to be recognized and rewarded, it is important that it be observed.

Volunteering Visibility   One approach to obtaining visibility is to volunteer for projects, task forces, and other high-profile assignments (Schlee, 1992). These assignments not only highlight talents and abilities, but provide young executives with developmental opportunities. To reach general-management responsibilities, it is preferable that individuals spend time in two of the major functions of an organization. Getting that range of experience can be accelerated by volunteering (Fiant, 1992). According to Mary Herbert, vice president and director of quality for the international operations at Motorola, "You have to go to management and say here's what I can do; here's why; let me try it" (Fischer, 1992).

Not every task force, project, or committee, however, should be targeted for volunteering. Rather, for career spotlighting the decision to volunteer should come after considering the following points:

- What new experience or knowledge can be gained?

- What will be the impact on one's immediate boss and the boss's success?

- What will be the impact on the organization?

- What will be the exposure to multi-level management?

The mentor relationship provides support and encourages development. Unfortunately, women often lack upper-management same-sex mentors.

Sponsorship   Another approach for gaining visibility is to find a **sponsor**—a person who will actively promote a subordinate's talents and look out for his or her organizational welfare. A sponsor is someone in the organization who is at least one position higher than the immediate boss, is successful, and who has a promising future.

Developing Mentor Relationships

Another key strategy for career advancement is to find a mentor. Whereas a sponsor actively promotes the abilities of and seeks opportunities for a protégé, a **mentor** is a senior employee who acts as a guide, teacher, counselor, and coach. A mentor takes a less experienced person under his or her wing and helps that person navigate the organization. A mentor should be someone who is successful and esteemed in the organization (Kram, 1985).

Mentor Programs   Mentoring is seen as so critical for success that many large organizations, such as Pacific Bell, have implemented formal mentoring programs. In this situation, a senior executive is formally appointed as a mentor to a few junior managers (Dubrin, 1990).

Mentors for Women and Men   The conventional model of mentoring that was created by and for men has not been as successful for women. First, there are few women in senior executive positions, making female mentors difficult to find. Second, when acting as mentors for women, men normally provide advice and information, but not the necessary emotional support. One solution has been to move to a dual-mentor relationship in which women managers identify both a male and a female mentor. Rather than receiving only one type of support, the dual-mentor relationship provides a balance—advice, information, and emotional encouragement (Siegel, 1992).

Understanding Power and Politics

In an ideal world, everybody would receive raises, promotions, and a fair share of desirable and not-so-desirable assignments—based entirely on merit. But in real life, many of these decisions are grounded in **organizational politics**—the unwritten rules of work life and informal methods of gaining power or advantage (Siegel, 1992). The politics of any organization result from the interaction between those in positions of influence and those seeking influence. These interactions are evidenced by power being acquired, transferred, and exercised on others.

The term *politics* offends many people—organizational veterans and novices alike—because it connotes cronyism and deception. But it is simply a matter of seeking an advantage. As noted management consultant and author Tom Peters says, "If you want to escape organizational politics—forget it. Politics is life. Politics involves investing in a relationship—investing time, energy, and emotions" (Peters, 1992).

Identify the Power Structure   Knowing that politics are a way of life, the first strategy is to identify the power structure in the organization. This means examining both the formal organizational structure and the workings of the informal organization. In this process one determines the following:

- Who are the people upon whom the leaders of the organization rely?

- What skills and knowledge do these people provide?

- Are you able to supply the same skills and knowledge?

- Could these people help you as sponsors or mentors?

Once key people are identified, the next step is to acquire power.

Acquiring Power   From a career management viewpoint, people obtain power—the ability to influence—in four ways:

- Developing expertise in areas critical to the company. Knowledge and reputation in a specific area can provide the opportunity to participate in projects and lend advice. In today's marketplace, expertise is valued in quality control, understanding consumer preferences, making teams successful, and working with ailing organizations to cure problems (Dowd, 1992).

- Developing a network of contacts. By developing a network of personal acquaintances, information can be acquired, support for new ideas can be gathered, and expertise for solving problems can be made available. Being a lone wolf will not get anyone ahead in organizational politics.

- Acquiring line responsibility. The position a person holds in an organization automatically carries certain power. But line managers—those whose work is tied directly to the primary purpose of the organization—have more power than staff groups. Nicole Williams, executive vice president of worldwide operations of SPSS, a $34-million software manufacturer in Chicago, claims that moving from a staff to a line position solidified her career. "It provided exposure and responsibility" (Hellwig, 1992).

- Solving others' problems. Career advancement is associated with positive support from as many areas as possible. A positive way to acquire power and support is to help someone else solve his or her problems. Whether the person is a colleague, someone in another department, or a superior, the result is the same—positive reviews and endorsements (Schlee, 1992).

Working with the Boss

A major strategy in career management involves learning to work with the boss. A career can be extinguished by not developing a positive alliance with a superior (Jensen, 1992).

Understand the Boss   In order to work with the boss, time must be spent determining and understanding the boss's priorities, objectives, and negative "hot buttons." The valued subordinate is one who understands that part of his or her job is relieving the boss's pressure, not adding to it.

Make the Boss Successful   The second element of working with the boss is to add to his or her success. After identifying the boss's goals and priorities, one should develop a set of sub-objectives that support the accomplishment of these major goals. This will keep objectives aligned, which is not only a good strategy for career advancement, but sound management.

Support Versus Buck the Boss   No boss/subordinate relationship is ideal. An expectation in any working relationship is that there will not always be agreement, operations won't necessarily run smoothly, and problems will inevitably surface. In such situations, there are several approaches:

- Provide solutions rather than register complaints. Identifying a problem is only the first step. The people who advance are those who develop an array of alternative solutions to problems.

- Practice constructive disagreement rather than rebellion. This is disagreement focused on a problem—not on a person—with the aim of identifying weaknesses and solutions. Once the discussion is over—win or lose—the job gets done. On the other hand, rebellion says "my way only." It also means that the disagreement doesn't end with the discussion—it will continue in other places with other people.

- Support the decision. Once the boss makes a decision, it is important for the subordinate to carry it out with the intention of making it work. Ignoring the decision or sabotaging it by not implementing it effectively will not endear the subordinate to the manager. In situations in which the decision may counter the organization's goals or be ethically questionable, it may be necessary to take the issue to someone other than the boss. In such a situation, a mentor can be valuable.

Managing Stress

Another cornerstone of career management is stress management. A manager's job is characterized by a rapid pace, conflicting deadlines, and multiple events. In addition all managers have responsibility for planning, organizing, and controlling the actions of their departments, and the amount of this responsibility increases as the manager moves up in an organization. Given these realities, it is obvious that stress is a part of the job.

The Nature of Stress   Stress is the physiological and psychological reaction of the body as a result of demands made upon it (Beehr and Bhagat, 1985). The demands may be emotional (role conflict, fear of unemployment, sexual harassment) or environmental (noise, or a lack of privacy or ventilation). People experiencing stress perceive, through their body's reactions, that the stressful situation is demanding beyond their ability to cope. People experience stress when they aren't finished with a project and the deadline looms, or when they are trying to solve a customer's problem but cannot reach a key decision maker.

***Under pressure** to perform, managers must develop stress management skills or risk burning out.*

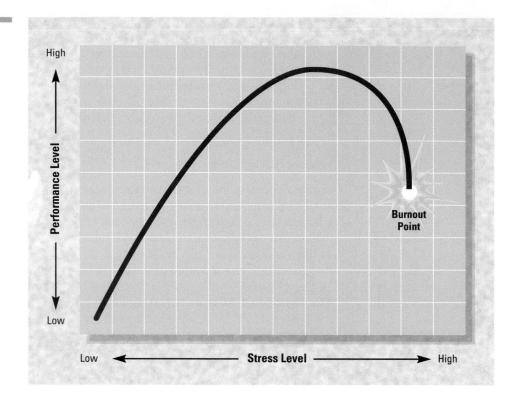

Positive and Negative Stress   Although stress is always discussed in a negative context, not all stress is negative. Moderate stress is a normal part of a manager's work. A deadline—determined three months earlier—to submit the year's budget forecast for approval inevitably causes stress as the date approaches. As shown in Exhibit 21.9, a moderate amount of stress has a positive effect on performance, as it provides motivation.

Extreme levels of stress, on the other hand, are negative and contribute to performance decline. As shown in Exhibit 21.9, if the periods of high stress are extended over a long period of time the result can be **burnout**—a state of emotional exhaustion as a result of overexposure to stress (Freudenberger, 1980). This chapter's Global Applications feature discusses extreme consequences of job stress.

The many possible causes of negative stress for managers are summarized in Exhibit 21.10. For career managers the most critical include the following (Maturi, 1992):

- Incongruence of values between the manager and the company

- Downsizing or layoffs that threaten security or long-range plans

- Limited opportunities for advancement

- Role ambiguity

- Leadership style incompatible with the immediate supervisor

Exhibit 21.10

Causes of negative stress for managers.

- Downsizing or other threats to security
- Limited opportunities for advancement
- Role ambiguity
- Interpersonal conflict
- Limited decision-making responsibility
- Leadership style incompatible with immediate supervisor
- Incongruence of values between the manager and the company
- Boredom or under-utilization
- Take-home work and erratic work schedule
- Constant change
- Task or work overload
- Unrealistic deadlines
- Sexual harassment
- Physical environment: noise, lighting, privacy, climate

Although the manager may be stressed by these situations, it is important to remember that he or she may in turn be the source of stress for others by causing these situations. When employees develop the following perceptions, managers are the source of the stress:

- Uncertainty about the specific responsibilities of the job

- Inability to make decisions or have decisions made when needed

- Work overload

- Unrealistic deadlines

- Lack of control over the things that affect the person in the work environment

Symptoms of Stress What are the signs that might indicate an excessive stress level? Common symptoms include anxiety, increased blood pressure, headache, backache, fatigue, insomnia, depression, irritability, muscular tightness, and inattention. What these signs don't indicate is the degree of wear and tear on the individual—emotionally and physically. The hidden effects can cost the organization through loss of productivity, absenteeism, and health care expenses. Excessive stress can also cost the individual his or her health and future.

Three types of strategies available for managing stress relate to the manager's own stress, that of employees, or organization-wide stress management programs. A manager's own strategy entails developing a balanced approach to life that includes plenty of rest, good eating habits, regular exercise, and the ability to anticipate stressors. Research findings emphasize the importance of relaxation, nutrition, and exercise as keys to stress management.

The other key is to identify personal stressors. Not all people react the same way to a situation. Knowing what causes stress allows a person preventive maintenance. A manager must also learn to delegate, to constructively disagree with the boss, and to consciously try to limit the hours spent working (Maturi, 1992). Managers helps themselves by learning to say no to work loads that are unacceptable and unrealistic.

Managers have an obligation to monitor employees and their environment for signs of stress. A manager can minimize stress by providing clear and current job descriptions and expectations, initiating timely and relevant feedback, facilitating employees' control over their own jobs, recognizing employee contributions, and encouraging work and personal support groups (Maturi, 1992).

Many companies have chosen to institute formalized stress management programs. Control Data's "Stay Well" program uses a combination of exercise, smoking cessation, hypertension screening and control, and nutrition counseling. Johnson & Johnson's "Live for Life" program emphasizes exercise, relaxation, and nutrition. Other organizations have provided:

- Facilities for physical exercise, ranging from jogging tracks to full gyms with instructors and organized classes

- Quiet rooms for meditating and reading

- On-site and off-site clinical psychologists or counselors

- Courses focusing on stress reduction and coping techniques (Maturi, 1992).

Stressbusters *like exercise, relaxation, and good nutrition help keep managers in the game. Many companies, such as Ford and General Foods, have built corporate fitness centers and encourage employees to take advantage of fitness courses.*

Organizational Dilemmas

Within career planning and management, an individual is often confronted with organizational dilemmas. The four dilemmas involve value conflicts, loyalty demands, decisions on advancement, and concerns for independence.

Conflicts Between Personal and Organizational Values

To have a successful career, a person's value system needs to fit that of the organization. Despite socialization, there are times when a person's values do come in conflict with those of the organization, resulting in dissatisfaction (Davita, April 13, 1992).

To minimize this possibility, managers need to do periodic self-analyses to determine their personal values and to select an organization that ensures compatibility. In addition, they should constantly analyze the demands of the organization against their personal values to monitor any conflict. But even with vigilant attention, organizations evolve and values may change. Or a person may not have analyzed the value system completely, and a conflict can occur (Davita, March 16, 1992). For example, a job that initially required minimal travel now requires the manager to be out of town for two weeks each month. This creates a conflict with the manager's values of home and family. Of course, each individual will resolve such a situation differently. Some will accept the development, thriving on the travel or hoping that the situation will change again shortly; others may switch jobs, feeling that the new demands are unacceptable. The point here is that circumstances do change and managers must be prepared to consult their own values and goals in responding to those changes.

I S S U E S A N D E T H I C S
Buy In or Get Out

Values are a basis for ethical behavior. This is true for both individuals and organizations. Noted management consultants and writers Tom Peters and Robert Waterman assert: "Every company takes the process of value shaping seriously... you either buy into the company's values or you get out."

Perhaps because of greater awareness of this truth, recent surveys have shown that more managers today than 10 years ago feel that they sometimes have to compromise their personal principles in order to conform to organizational expectations. The percentage of middle managers and executives who agreed with this statement jumped more than 58%. The percentage of managers who felt that their personal values were generally compatible with those of their organization declined by 10% over the same 10 years.

Why do you think the managers feel this way? Do you feel that this compromise in values could result in less-ethical behavior on the part of the individual managers and organizations? ▲

Personal values must be weighed carefully against the demands made by the organization. Each manager must decide where to draw the line.

Loyalty Demands

A dilemma intimately related to a person's value system is the question of loyalty. Often, early in a career, loyalty demands are made on a person by the immediate supervisor, whose conveys messages like "Don't make me look bad; protect me," or "Trust me; tell me about…"

Both of these messages are requests for loyalty. Both place a subordinate in a dilemma. The first loyalty demand—don't make me look bad, protect me—may not seem so unusual. Employees should naturally try to make the boss look good by doing excellent work. Likewise, protecting the boss by keeping him or her informed—no surprises—is a sound practice. But these demands go beyond that; they may involve covering up for weak performance or holding back information that would place a superior in a bad light. In such situations a manager needs to acknowledge what is happening and not be drawn into that behavior. A demand for loyalty—trust me, tell me about…—potentially places the subordinate in the position of being an informant on someone or of violating a confidence. The superior has gained information but at the same time has caused the subordinate to compromise his or her values. Such a demand for loyalty should be recognized for what it is and avoided.

Promotions are decided by a number of factors, not all of which are in the control of the employee. If progress up the corporate ladder stalls, due either to political or economic conditions, the choice to stay or leave becomes crucial.

Advancement Decisions

Another set of dilemmas is met in regard to advancement. They fall into two categories: (1) whether to take a position when it is offered, and (2) what to do when advancement does not occur.

Taking a new job offer may be problematic if it requires a person to move, uprooting a family or relocating to an undesirable location. The situation may be complicated by a spouse's career. Or the offer may come at a time when the manager believes he or she is not really ready. In this case the manager should talk to his or her mentor to get an objective appraisal of current skills and competence in regard to the new job. Having planned a career path from the start, the offer probably comes as no surprise to the manager; he or she should be prepared for the possibility. Still, it is necessary to make the decision. And that decision can come only after thorough discussion with one's spouse and a complete analysis of the costs and benefits—both professionally and personally—of the alternatives.

A situation where advancement does not happen may simply reflect the manager's own timetable for advancement—three years between promotions— not being met. Or the organization may believe the person is not promotable. In either case, the manager is faced with a dilemma—stay and possibly lose time if a promotion is not forthcoming, or leave and lose security and familiarity. Again, the best approach is a complete analysis of costs and benefits. Consideration should be given to one's stage in career development. How much has the manager invested in the organization? What are the chances of moving to another organization with immediate opportunity?

G L O B A L   A P P L I C A T I O N S
Work Stress in Japan

The **Japanese work ethic** is legendary. Workers—both salaried and blue-collar—throughout Japanese business and heavy industry are expected to work until the job is done, and then some. Ten- to 14-hour days and seven-day workweeks are commonplace. One outcomes of this pace is *karoshi.*

Karoshi—sudden death by heart attack or stroke triggered by overwork and stress—claims 10,000 Japanese each year. Until recently, because of the legal system in Japan, the issues of responsibility and compensation have been largely ignored. Decisions to award compensation for deaths attributed to *karoshi* occurred in only about one in every 700 claims. But now the regulations are being interpreted more broadly, and the number of monetary awards is increasing.

This has had a rippling effect through corporate boardrooms. Companies are trying to ease the pressure. At Matsushita Electric Industrial, mandatory vacations are being extended from 16 to 23 days a year. Other employers are starting to track employees' emotional health. A branch of corporate giant Nippon Telephone and Telegraph found that stress was making some workers ill and irritable. So to improve the emotional health of its employees, the company instituted periods of silent meditation. At Mitsui, general managers will be assessed on how well they set overtime hours, keep subordinates healthy, and encourage workers to take vacations. ▲

For more about work stress in Japan, see Karen Lowrey Miller, "Now Japan Is Admitting It: Work Kills Executives," *Business Week,* August 3, 1992, p. 35; and Gary Katzensten, "Why No Layoffs Is Nonsense," *Working Woman,* February 1992, pp. 100–101.

Independence and Sponsorship

A final dilemma faced by individuals is striking the balance between the need for independence and the advantages of sponsorship. The support of a sponsor sometimes carries a negative price tag; the person sponsored gives up a degree of independence to be on the team. Worse, if a sponsor is fired, the person sponsored may suffer similar consequences (Dubrin, 1990). A possible solution to the dilemma is to build relationships with many individuals and groups in the organization.

Future Trends

The following trends relating to careers and career management are likely in the next few years:

- Technology and economic competition will fundamentally change the structure of organizations and work. Competition will force most companies to employ fewer people in permanent and full-time jobs, and adopt more flexible ways of utilizing their labor pool.

- More work will be done on a contract, fee, part-time, or temporary basis. Companies will become a vehicle for organizing the work of others. The corporation core will comprise a well-paid, permanent corporate staff. Other work will be acquired via contractors and part-time workers.

- The number of women in senior positions will triple. The two barriers to access—preconceptions about performance capabilities and role stereotypes—will become less ubiquitous.

- The new business environment with its emphasis on flatter organizational structures and elimination of middle-management positions will reduce the number of opportunities for promotion and advancement.

- New career paths will emerge as companies eliminate levels of management, decentralize decision making, and capitalize on team efforts.

- Managers with cross-functional experience will be in demand. Both the team environment and flatter organizational structures will place a premium on broad backgrounds rather than specialization in a functional area.

- The ability to adapt to change will be a prized characteristic of managers. Flexibility in learning new methods of working and responding to the changing environment will increase the possibility of success and advancement.

C H A P T E R   S U M M A R Y

- A career comprises the series of jobs a person holds over a lifetime and the person's attitude toward these job experiences. It includes a long-term perspective, a sequence of positions, and a psychological involvement.

- A career perspective is a proactive strategy that takes a global view of career progress or growth over time as it develops.

- Career planning is the process of developing a realistic vision of how one wants one's career to proceed and then taking steps to ensure that it follows that course.

- A person's career normally evolves through four stages: exploration and trial, establishment and advancement, mid-career, and late career.

- Career planning involves five steps: self-assessment, explore opportunities and options, establish objectives, develop a plan of action, and execute and evaluate.

- Career management involves understanding one's organization, aligning oneself with what the organization values, and implementing career-enhancing strategies.

- Part of understanding an new company occurs during organizational socialization, the process in which new members gain exposure to an organization's values, norms, policies, and procedures.

- An individual must determine what abilities are associated with advancement and what values are rewarded, and then align his or her abilities and actions with what the organization values and rewards.

- To advance in an organization an individual must develop and implement strategies that focus on creating visibility, developing mentor relationships, understanding power and politics, working with the boss, and managing stress.

- Within the scope of career planning and management, an individual is often confronted with organizational dilemmas. These include conflict between personal and organizational values, loyalty demands, advancement decisions, and concerns for independence.

S K I L L - B U I L D I N G

An awareness of organizational politics can provide assistance in career management. How politically aware are you? For each question, determine your response. Directions for scoring and a rating follow the exercise.

1. During a departmental meeting, your boss criticizes a proposal you make—one he had privately praised a few days ago. You:

   a. Wait until the meeting is over and ask why he changed his mind

   b. Say nothing to him but let others know that he can be erratic

   c. Defend your idea during the meeting, then let it rest

   d. Be philosophical about his attitude

2. You're working late on a project and know the boss is also putting in some extra hours. You'll probably:

   a. Figure an excuse to walk by her office; you want to be sure she knows you're there.

   b. Try to avoid her; she may ask you about a deadline or perceive your staying late as a sign of poor time management.

   c. Wait until she leaves, then look through her desk and files in the hope of uncovering useful information.

   d. Pack up your work and finish it at home; why try to predict what she'll think?

3. An inexperienced newcomer joins the company in a position comparable to yours. Because he's so well connected, he's already being favored. Your first impulse is to:

   a. Invite him to lunch, offer help, and make friends.

    b. Invite him to lunch; tell him some things you have done for the company so that he will be properly impressed.

    c. Do nothing; after a while, his edge (influence, preferred treatment) will wear off.

    d. Note his weaknesses, then casually point them out to your peers; the talk will eventually filter up to management.

4. A colleague has left the company, and you've been offered her vacated office. It has a small window and is closer to the boss, whereas your present space is a bit bigger and nearer the elevator. Your first instinct is to:

    a. Make the switch; you'll be able to become friendlier with the boss.

    b. Graciously refuse the offer—the closer the flame, the hotter the fire.

    c. Take the office—whether you want it or not; why look ungrateful?

    d. Tell the boss that although you wouldn't mind switching, Employee X has been with the company longer; perhaps it should be given to him.

5. Check those topics you consider appropriate subject matter for conversation with officemates:

    a. Recent political scandals

    b. Personal investments

    c. Civil rights

    d. Religion

    e. Books, movies

    f. Whom you're voting for in the next election

    g. Medical and family problems

    h. Office gossip

6. You're a bit bored with your present job and decide to investigate other possibilities. Your first step is to:

    a. Ask a trusted co-worker to help you fine-tune your resume

    b. Work on your resume alone or hire a professional to help

    c. Tell personnel you'd like to be considered for other positions within your company

    d. Discreetly put the word out to a few friends that you're job hunting

7. Your superior is in danger of getting fired. How do you handle yourself?

    a. Openly support your boss to show the company how loyal you are

    b. Start looking for another job—the new boss may want to bring in her own staff

    c. Try to form new alliances—people who will stick up for you

    d. Meet with a senior executive and ask how secure your job is

8. You've just started work at a company with a very conservative corporate culture. Though it hasn't been stated, you get the feeling that your wardrobe is deemed inappropriate. Your solution?

   a. Invest in a new wardrobe—even if it means getting a small loan from your parents.

   b. Make do with the acceptable items in your closet; when you start earning bigger paychecks, you can splurge on clothes.

   c. Settle on an affordable compromise—buy one or two appropriate outfits and wear them occasionally.

   d. Approach management and let them know that you intend to maintain a professional look—then politely ask whether they occasionally relax the dress code.

9. At lunch your manager—who's also a friend—begins talking about problems he's having with his wife. Your response?

   a. Make him feel better by sharing some of your own spouse's behavior

   b. Offer advice—you may be able to give new perspective

   c. Listen, but try (subtly) to steer him away from the topic

   d. Tell him nicely that you'll both be happier if the two you don't get too personal

10. When it comes to getting credit at work, you're more likely to:

    a. Wait for acknowledgment

    b. Pursue recognition

    c. Assume you have the boss's approval unless you hear otherwise

    d. Subtly mention your achievements—it's important for people to know how hard you work

11. Which of the following qualities would you use to get ahead? (Choose as many as you wish.)

    a. Humor

    b. Charm

    c. Charisma

    d. Self-promotion

    e. Sex appeal

12. A woman in the office, known for wearing low-cut blouses and flirting with the boss, just received a promotion that you think you deserved. Your reaction?

    a. Quietly file a complaint with your company's upper management

    b. Flirt a little yourself—it can't hurt

    c. Quit—this is not a company you want a future with

    d. Schedule a meeting with the boss to evaluate your performance

13. In keeping with the 1990s' approach to salaries, your company has given you a new title but no raise. Your next move?

    a. Demand higher pay—there's always money for good people

    b. Grab the title, but let them know they owe you one

    c. Turn down the new title on principle

    d. Gladly accept the promotion

Scoring

1.	a-3	b-1	c-2	d-0	7.	a-0	b-1	c-2	d-3
2.	a-2	b-0	c-3	d-1	8.	a-2	b-0	c-1	d-3
3.	a-2	b-1	c-0	d-3	9.	a-1	b-0	c-2	d-3
4.	a-3	b-1	c-2	d-0	10.	a-0	b-2	c-1	d-3

5. Give yourself one point each if you checked items a or e; the rest are worth 0 points.

11. Give yourself one-half point for each answer marked.

12.	a-3	b-0	c-1	d-2

6. a-0   b-2   c-3   d-1

13. a-3   b-1   c-0   d-2

Rating on Organizational Politics

27 or more points	You are overly and overtly political. More emphasis on work and less on politics is needed.
16–27 points	You have a balanced approach: doing the job well and staying tuned in to the organization, corporate culture, and politics.
15 or fewer points	You are avoiding organizational politics. But politics exist; think about getting a mentor and increasing visibility.

REVIEW QUESTIONS

1. Review this chapter's essential terms and look up the meanings of those you cannot define.

2. What is the difference between a job and a career?

3. What are the four stages of career development?

4. What are the five steps involved in career planning?

5. Why is it important for a manager to understand his or her organization?

6. What abilities do organizations typically value in managers seeking advancement?

7. What is the importance of organizational visibility? How can it be achieved?

8. How does a decision on advancement present an organizational dilemma?

R E C O M M E N D E D   R E A D I N G

Block, Peter. *The Empowered Manager: Positive Political Skills at Work* (San Francisco: Jossey-Bass), 1991.

Daly, James. "Taming the Difficult Executive," *Computerworld* (March 16, 1992), p. 85.

Graham, Pauline. *Integrative Management: Creating Unity from Diversity* (Cambridge, MA: Blackwell, Basil), 1991.

Hosmer, La Rue. *The Ethics of Management* (Homewood, IL: Richard D. Irwin), 1991.

March, James G., and John P. Olsen. "Rediscovering Institutions: The Organizational Basis of Politics," *Society* (January–February 1992), pp. 88–91.

Russell, Anne. "Fine-Tuning Your Corporate Image," *Black Enterprise* (May 1992), pp. 72–80.

Simon, James. *Fifty Activities for Developing Management Skills* (Brookfield, VT: Gower), 1991.

Simms, Margaret. "Are Apprenticeships the Answer?" *Black Enterprise* (February 1992), p. 57.

Webber, Ross. *Becoming a Courageous Manager: Overcoming Career Problems of New Managers* (Englewood Cliffs, NJ: Prentice-Hall), 1991.

Weiner, Benjamin. "What Executives Should Know About Political Risk," *Management Review* (January 1992), pp. 19–22.

R E F E R E N C E S

Beehr, T. A., and R. S. Bhagat. *Human Stress and Cognition in Organizations: An Integrated Perspective* (New York: Wiley), 1985.

Davita, Sal. "Personal Values Affect Your Career Satisfaction," *Marketing News* (April 13, 1992), p. 16.

Davita, Sal. "The Two Most Important Decisions in Career Designing," *Marketing News* (July 6, 1992), p. 16.

Davita, Sal. "Value System Can Make or Break Your Career," *Marketing News* (March 16, 1992), p. 16.

Dowd, Maureen. "Power: Are Women Afraid of It—Or Beyond It?" *Working Woman* (May 1992), pp. 98–99.

Dubrin, Andrew. *Winning Office Politics: Dubrin's Guide for the 90's* (Englewood Cliffs, NJ: Prentice-Hall), 1990, p. 166, 167.

Feldman, Daniel C. "Careers in Organizations: Recent Trends and Future Directions," *Journal of Management* 15 (1989), pp. 135–156.

Fiant, Ray J. "Leadership Training for Long-Term Results," *Management Review* (July 1992), pp. 50–53.

Fischer, Anne B. "When Will Women Get to the Top," *Fortune* (September 21, 1992), p. 56.

Freudenberger, Herbert J. *Burnout: The High Cost of High Achievement* (Garden City, NY: Anchor), 1980, p. 13.

Hall, Douglas T. *Career Development in Organizations* (San Francisco: Jossey-Bass), 1986.

Hellwig, Basia. "Who Succeeds, Who Doesn't," *Working Woman* (May 1992), pp. 108–112.

Hetzer, Barbara. "Making Yourself Indispensable," *Working Woman* (August 1992), pp. 53–55.

Jensen, Blair. "How to Figure Out What Others Expect of You," *Computer World* (January 20, 1992), p. 1.

Kram, Kathy E. *Mentoring at Work: Developmental Relationships in Organizational Life* (Glenview, IL: Scott, Foresman), 1985.

Kunde, Diana. "Game Plan Assists in Scoring Career Goals," *Dallas Morning News,* April 3, 1992, pp. 1D, 14D.

Maturi, Richard. "Stress Can Be Beaten," *Industry Week* (July 20, 1992), pp. 23–26.

Peters, Tom. "If You Want to Escape Office Politics—Forget It," *Chicago Tribune,* July 27, 1992, sec. 4, p. 7.

Plunkett, W. Richard. *Supervision,* 6th edition (Needham Heights, MA: Allyn and Bacon), 1992, pp. 31–53.

Robbins, Stephen P. *Management,* 3rd edition (Englewood Cliffs, NJ: Prentice-Hall), 1991, p. 377.

Schein, Edgar H. *Career Dynamics* (Reading, MA: Addison-Wesley), 1978.

Schlee, Adele. "Feeling Invisible? Here's How to Get Clout," *Working Woman* (February 1992), pp. 36–37.

Serant, Clare. "Making the Switch," *Black Enterprise* (January 1992), p. 23.

Siegel, Alexander. "Making the Most of Mentors: Yours Differs from His," *Working Woman* (May 1992), pp. 1, 26.

Vreeland, Leslie. "Managing the Risks," *Working Woman* (April 1992), pp. 61–63.

Wentling, Rose Mary. "Women in Middle Management: Their Career Development and Aspirations," *Business Horizons* (January–February 1992), pp. 47–54.

G L O S S A R Y   O F   T E R M S

burnout   A state of emotional exhaustion as a result of overexposure to stress.

career   The series of jobs a person holds over a lifetime and the person's attitude toward his or her involvement in those job experiences; includes a long-term perspective, a sequence of positions, and a psychological involvement.

career management   The planning, strategy, activities, and behaviors involved in executing a career.

career perspective   A proactive strategy that involves a global view of career progress or growth over time.

career planning   The process of developing a realistic view about how one wants one's career to proceed and then taking steps to ensure that it follows that course.

job   A specific position a person holds in an organization.

mentor   A senior employee who acts as guide, teacher, counselor, and coach for a less experienced person in the organization.

organizational politics   The unwritten rules of work life and informal methods of gaining power and advantage.

organizational socialization   A process through which new members of an organization gain exposure to its values, norms, policies, and procedures.

organizational visibility   A strategy for career advancement that involves highlighting a person's abilities, talents, and contributions for those people in the organization who influence promotions and advancement.

psychological contract   The unspoken contract that marks the end product of the organizational socialization process and defines what people are expected to give to the organization and what they can expect to receive.

sponsor   An individual in the organization who will promote a person's talents and look out for his or her organizational welfare.

stress   The physiological and psychological reaction of the body to demands made on it.

C A S E   P R O B L E M
Career Obsolescence or Mismanagement?

Managers, like packaged goods, have shelf lives. They begin their careers with all the promise and potential in the world and with bright, shiny credentials—the latest technical knowledge, awareness of the management concepts in vogue, and cutting-edge ideas. With this competitive advantage they burst onto the scene in a new organization. Because of their freshly minted skills, they successfully complete "test" projects—assignments that have minor impact on the organization but that test the knowledge, skills, and resourcefulness of the managers.

The degree of difficulty and the importance of the projects continue to rise for those who are successful. Soon the new manager settles into a permanent position with the appropriate organizational amenities—a comfortable office, a desk and credenza, and a secretary. The job becomes the most important focus of the day, week, and month. Meeting deadlines, hitting projections, and adjusting to the organizational demands consume the manager's attention. There is little or no time to attend seminars, conferences, or professional-association briefings on new management concepts or technological advances. Associates may go to these, or possibly a subordinate is sent, but the manager cannot spare the time.

The immediate demands of the job are the number one priority. Old practices—eating lunch with people in other departments, playing daily racquetball games with the boss or golfing on the weekends—are scaled back. Information on the grapevine about power shifts in the organization doesn't seem as important as it once did, nor does it receive as much attention from the manager.

One day there is a rude awakening—and a summons. The manager, among others, is now excess. The skills, once valued by the organization, are no longer appreciated. The manager's shelf life is up. Caught in the downsizing move, the manager's career at this organization is over.

Q U E S T I O N S

1. What are the possible causes of this manager's downfall?

2. Does organizational politics play a role in this situation? How?

3. Is there a possibility that this manager did not continue to update skills? Why?

4. What strategies could this manager have employed to prevent this scenario?

For more on career obsolescence or mismanagement, see Stanley Bing, "Executive Shelf Life," *Esquire*, June 1992, pp. 69–70; and Adele Schlee, "Should You Change Your Job or Your Career," *Working Woman*, July 1992, p. 16.

Management Ethics and Social Responsibility

L E A R N I N G   O B J E C T I V E S

After reading and discussing this chapter, you should be able to:

- Define this chapter's essential terms
- Discuss four motives behind unethical conduct
- Discuss the three C's of ethics
- Discuss the relationship between the law and ethics
- Describe responsibilities businesses have to their stakeholders
- Describe the methods used to encourage both ethics and social responsibility in an organization
- Discuss the relationship between ethics and social responsibility

M A N A G E M E N T   I N   A C T I O N

Southern California Edison's John Bryson

Southern California Edison (SCE), a subsidiary of SCEcorp, a holding company, is one of the largest utilities in the United States. SCE supplies power to 10 million residents of Southern California, except for those living in San Diego and the city of Los Angeles. Pollution is a problem; the region's air is the dirtiest in the nation, exceeding federal air-quality limits two days of every three. The Chairman of SCEcorp, 49-year-old John Bryson, has worked as both an environmental lawyer and a government regulator. He has served as California's chairman of the Water Resources Board and as president of its public utilities commission. In this latter post, "Bryson once fined his [current] employer $6 million for stalling in negotiations with non-utility power companies." Now the leader of SCE, Bryson is committed to making his environment and his company greener—more environmentally friendly—through a variety of means.

The power to improve *the environment and keep customers and stockholders happy is in the hands of creative management.*

"The cornerstone of cleanup is a big campaign to promote conservation with what utilities call 'demand-side management,' or DSM, which often involves replacing inefficient electric [devices] with efficient ones." A utility that practices DSM can build its expenses into its rate base and pass the costs along to consumers through regulatory approval. The utility encourages consumers of electricity to become more energy efficient by issuing rebates for a portion of the costs of energy-saving devices. Another approach is aimed at commercial users, which SCE reimburses for the purchase of more efficient generators. As a result of these actions:

In all, SCE has invested over $105 million in conservation, a sum that may grow to $2 billion by the year 2000. Result: Growth in demand for new power will drop from 2.5% a year, the average in the 1980s, to near 1% in the 1990s. And all of that investment will earn the utility's authorized [return on investment] of 13%.

SCE is also committing to long-term efforts to reduce pollutants that are breaking down the ozone layer. To meet its ambitious goal of an 86% reduction by 1999, the company is spending $800 million to use natural-gas–fueled turbines instead of oil-burning generators. Another goal is to reduce carbon dioxide emissions to 90% of current levels by the year 2000 and to 80% by 2010. These goals meet or exceed both

❝ Many times there are great business opportunities in meeting environmental needs. ❞

— **John Bryson**, Chairman, SCEcorp

industry standards and the demands of the 1990 Clean Air Act. "Bryson also told his engineers to alter the design of some new facilities—like power lines and substations—to minimize the strength of electromagnetic fields they generate."

Another plan involves a partnership with Texas Instruments to create tiny photovoltaic cells that will be less expensive than current solar cells and that, when installed on the roofs of buildings, may supply solar power for as little as 15 cents per kilowatt-hour. This rate is expensive compared with the cost of most electricity, but is very competitive with the 30 cents per kwh that consumers must pay for peak-load periods. In addition, SCE is exploring the possibility of expanding the light-rail system in Southern California by "building, owning, and earning a return on the catenary cables and wires that would power [the system]."

John Bryson embraces his company's "no regrets policy." He pursues environmental goals "only if they can be justified for other reasons as well, or cost so little that shareholders will have 'no regrets' if a perceived threat turns out to be groundless. Says Bryson: 'many times there are great business opportunities in meeting environmental needs.' " ▲

For more about SCE and the environment, see Peter Nulty, "Finding a Payoff in Environmentalism," *Fortune,* October 21, 1991, pp. 79–80, 84.

Managing Ethically

Today's headlines are filled with reports of individual and corporate wrongdoing—companies that pollute the air, land, and water, or the savings and loan bailouts that will cost Americans an estimated $500-plus billion. The insider-trading scandals on Wall Street in the 1980s netted the major perpetrators millions in profits (and only limited jail terms). The United States Congress ran a so-called bank which gave members thousands of dollars in interest-free loans. And Dow Corning sold breast implants even though its "executives had for years ignored memos showing that it had known silicone could and did leak from its breast implants. The company now faces untold future liability, essentially for its failure to act ethically" (Widder, 1992).

Today's business climate does not make ethical conduct any easier than it has been in the past. As one writer notes,

> The U.S. press, broadcast and print, has become increasingly adept at uncovering corporate misdeeds. In the past few years most media have given much more coverage to business. Newspapers and magazines all over the United States now employ investigative reporters with MBAs and business experience to dig into the affairs of companies. The old advice is still the best: Don't do anything on the job you wouldn't want your mother to read about with her morning coffee (Labich, 1992).

Although few individuals would openly endorse cheating, stealing, telling lies, breaking rules, and overcharging customers, the reality is that people and companies do these things every day, often with the complicity or outright support of management. In this era of ferocious competition and economic turbulence, companies are downsizing, retrenching, outsourcing, and laying off workers in droves. Many people who remain in the workplace feel threatened and insecure. Nearly everywhere the pressure to perform grows more intense. "The message out there is: reaching objectives is what matters and how you get there isn't that important," says Gary Edwards, president of the Ethics Resource Center, a Washington, D.C., consulting firm (Labich, 1992). According to polls taken by ethicist Michael Josephson, who consults with some of America's largest public companies, 20% to 30% of middle managers have [at some time] written reports that are deceptive (Labich, 1992). Managers and employees who act unethically "are more often motivated by the most basic of instincts—fear of losing their jobs or the necessity to eke out some benefit for their companies. If that means fudging a few sales figures, abusing a competitor, or shortchanging the occasional customer, so be it" (Labich, 1992). Writes David Kidwell, dean of the Carlson School of Management at the University of Minnesota,

> In business, the bottom line and self-interest are driving this trend. There is nothing inherently unethical in making a profit in a capitalistic system. The 'moral dilemma' comes at crunch time, when there is a seeming choice between ethical actions and profits (Widder, 1992).

The news is not all bad, however. Many individuals and companies consistently conduct themselves with honesty and integrity (steadfast adherence to a strict moral or ethical code), and see to it that others for whom they are responsible act that way too. Many companies prosper while cultivating right conduct, equity, and an enlightened respect for the community and environment. Southern California Edison provides an example, as do corporate giants Johnson & Johnson, Hewlett-Packard, Motorola, Coca-Cola, 3M, Disney, McDonald's, and Merck (the nation's largest pharmaceutical manufacturer). Says Elliot Hoffman, a co-founder of Just Desserts, a small (240 employees) San Francisco upscale bakery,

> If business is to be the dominant social institution of the future, we have to mix social goals with business goals. The bottom line should include whether you hired more people and that you improved your products, your workplace, and your community—not just your profit (Schlender, 1992).

This chapter probes the responsibilities and obligations that businesses and their employees bear to themselves and others. We concentrate on a touchstone question: What is the best decision or course of action available to a person or an organization in each circumstance? Our assumption is that the best decision maximizes achievement of legitimate goals, conforms to high standards of legal and ethical behavior, and unambiguously affirms good corporate citizenship. We review principles and methods through which managers and their organizations may strengthen their personal and institutional capacity to act in an ethical and socially responsible manner.

Ethics in Context

The threshold management issue does not change: Managers must balance diverse and sometimes contradictory demands of multiple constituencies—employees, owners, customers, suppliers, and the community (local and regional)—while allocating and managing limited resources. Near the turn of the twenty-first century, two powerful factors imperil the balance.

First, never have so many conflicting demands been made so insistently on those who manage institutions and hold power; the construction industry, cigarette companies, the military, environmentalists, nuclear-power advocates, teachers, school boards, the Baby Boomers. The list of powerful special interests is matched only by the list of less powerful general interests: children, the poor and homeless, disadvantaged minorities, the undereducated, the elderly.

Second, the consequences of management decisions affect far more people and environments—and more profoundly—than ever before. Whether directing a medical research laboratory at work on cancer or AIDS, maintaining a fleet of 747s, commanding transoceanic supertankers, supervising a nuclear reactor at Chernobyl or an insecticide plant in Bhopal, leading the police department in Los Angeles, or plotting the future of General Motors, today's managers wield unprecedented influence over the world of today and tomorrow.

With the accelerating rate of change in our society and the explosion of information and technology, the pace of real events approaches that of a video game—with relentless hazards surfacing almost too fast to manage. Pressures to improve quality of products and operations, to increase productivity, to stay close to suppliers and customers, to value diversity, and to react swiftly to global changes all combine to compress the time managers and their organizations can take to make decisions and choose courses of action. Managers need guidelines to help them to cope with these pressures.

Ethics Defined

Ethics, you will recall from Chapter 2, is the branch of philosophy concerned with human values and conduct, moral duty and obligation. Ethics is concerned with what constitutes right and wrong human conduct, including actions and values, in light of a specific set of circumstances. **Business ethics** address these issues in the context of commerce and organizational conduct (Barry, 1986), and is the primary focus of this chapter. A person's or group's ethics are influenced by the morality of individuals. "Religious beliefs and training, educational background, political and economic philosophy, socialization through family and peer group influences and work experience all come together to produce a personal moral code of ethical values with associated attitudes" (Dunfee, 1984).

Ethical theory provides two principles that may guide our thinking about ethical conduct:

> There are two broad categories of ethical theories. Ethical theories may be based on consequential principles or nonconsequential principles. *Consequential* principles judge the ethics of a particular situation by the consequences of that action. Consequential ethics determines the "rightness" or "wrongness" of any action by determining the ratio of good to evil that the action will produce. The "right" action is that action that produces the greatest ratio of good to evil of any of the available alternatives....
>
> *Nonconsequential* principles tend to focus on the concept of duty. Under the nonconsequential approach, a person acts ethically if that person is faithful regardless of the consequences that follow from being faithful to that duty. If a person carries out his or her duties, the greatest good occurs *because* the duty of the individual is carried out. If each individual carries out his or her duty, society knows what to expect from each individual in any given situation (Davidson et al., 1990).

In his recent study of leadership, business writer Danny Cox compiled a list of 10 characteristics common to great leaders. The first is "cultivating a high standard of personal ethics." Cox feels that "at the core of any high standard of personal ethics is the declaration of personal responsibility. A person who refuses to accept responsibility lacks the ethical armor to stand against temptation" (Cox and Hoover, 1992).

Management and ethics professor George Dupuy of Georgia's LaGrange College suggests that a concern for ethics is not merely theoretical: "Ethics has always been an issue in business, but has become a more critical issue in recent years with serious abuses like Wall Street insider trading and the savings and loan fiasco. Continued ethical abuse is likely to lead to increased government regulations and decreased freedom in business" (Bell, 1992).

Robert C. Solomon and Kristine R. Hanson, business consultants on ethical issues, have discovered in their research that:

> Good business begins with ethics. The most successful people and companies are those that take ethics seriously. This is not surprising, since ethical attitudes largely determine how one treats employees, suppliers, stockholders, and consumers as well as how one treats competitors and other members of the community. Inevitably, this affects how one is treated in return. Ethical managers and ethical businesses tend to be more trusted and better treated and to suffer less resentment, inefficiency, litigation, and government interference. Ethics is just good business (Solomon and Hanson, 1985).

Ethical Dilemmas

Ethics is not prescriptive. No simple set of rules tells us how to behave morally or ethically in all situations. Codes of conduct—when they are documented—are written in the manner of company policies—as brief, general guidelines, and interpretation varies from one individual to the next. Like policies, codes are meant to give freedom of action within certain boundaries and require interpretation. Saul W. Gellerman, dean of the University of Dallas Graduate School of Management, queries and replies:

> How can you tell if a rule 'really' applies to what you are doing? How can you avoid crossing a line that is almost never defined precisely? The only safe answer is not even to move in the direction of the line. Here is where the *real* ethical dilemma begins to emerge, however. Because if you constantly played it safe, and never tested the limits of what you could and couldn't get away with, you'd risk being considered inefficient, or even gutless, by your superiors (Gellerman, 1992).

Managers constantly face **dilemmas**—situations that require a choice between options that are or seem equally unfavorable or mutually exclusive. Dilemmas involve uncertainty and risk over the rightness or wrongness of actions. Besides uncertainty about which course of action is ethical, an **ethical dilemma** also arises when all courses of action open to a manager are judged to be unethical. For example, a company's plant is simply unable to bring work in at a profit. Managers are considering three possible alternatives: (1) shut the plant down and outsource the work to subcontractors who will give the firm the costs it needs, (2) invest in computerization that will eliminate half the jobs but make the plant productive enough to continue to operate, or (3) seek wage and benefit concessions from all employees to bring costs into line. Any of these choices will impose immediate hardship on the employees of the plant and those who depend upon them—families, local merchants, and others.

When managers face such "gray areas," Professor Gellerman (1986) offers the following suggestions:

- When in doubt, don't.
- Don't try to find out "how far is too far."
- Superiors who push you to do things better, faster, cheaper will turn on you when you cross the line between right and wrong.

Gellerman offers this practical, concrete stratagem:

> When what you might or might not do is questionable, let the burden of the decision rest on someone who is paid to make the tough decisions. Make your boss earn his [or her] pay. You can't openly condone what policy prohibits. Neither can your boss. That's why bringing the question into the open keeps both of you honest (Gellerman, 1992).

Motivations for Unethical Conduct

Human behavior derives from discernible causes or motives that can be identified, acknowledged, and modified. For this reason the wise manager cultivates a continuous awareness of personal priorities, goals, values, needs, feelings, and assumptions. Such awareness allows a person to realistically assess the motivation that underlies choices and actions. Decisions frequently result from a combination of the readily apparent influences and the underlying factors not so readily apparent. Managers must consciously recognize the influence of underlying motivation in themselves and others.

Warns writer Verne E. Henderson, "Managers and executives who are... unaware of what motivates them are ethical accidents searching for a place to happen. [Motives] need to be examined from an ethical perspective." Henderson suggests that when colleagues—including a boss—recommend a course of action, we must consider their motives as well as our own. As reasons unfold, watch for rationalizations (self-satisfying but incorrect reasonings for one's behavior) that excuse and bury subtle warnings from our conscience. "An enduring and ethical business is dependent upon leaders whose motives [are known to others and] can be shared by everyone on the team" (Henderson, 1992). Gellerman believes that four basic rationalizations underlie unethical behavior by managers; these are outlined in Exhibit 22.1.

Some basic motives for stepping over the line between ethical and unethical conduct include fear of losing one's job, pressures from time and superiors to produce results, ambition to excel and advance one's career, revenge for a perceived wrong, and a tendency to ignore the consequences of one's actions—their impacts on others as well as on oneself. Gellerman points out that organizations can encourage (overtly or covertly) unethical behavior in employees in several ways (Gellerman, 1992):

- Offering unusually high rewards. "Huge bonuses and commissions can distort one's values, in much the same way that too much power can corrupt one's standards of decency. You can motivate people without corrupting them simply by keeping their rewards within the bounds of reason."

Exhibit 22.1

Four common rationalizations that can lead to misconduct by managers.

- A belief that the activity is within reasonable ethical and legal limits—that is, that it is not "really" illegal or immoral

- A belief that the activity is in the individual's or the corporation's best interests—that the individual would somehow be expected to undertake the activity

- A belief that the activity is "safe" because it will never be found out or publicized; the classic crime-and-punishment issue of discovery

- A belief that because the activity helps the company, the company will condone it and even protect the person who engages in it

Source: Reprinted by permission of the *Harvard Business Review.* Excerpt from "Why 'Good' Managers Make Bad Ethical Choices," by Saul W. Gellerman, July–August 1986. Copyright 1986 by the President and Fellows of Harvard College. All rights reserved.

GrandMet companies in the United States give more than $10 million in charitable contributions, with a further $6 million being donated in the form of product donations. Employees are encouraged to contribute time to community programs such as this recreational center for children.

- Threatening unusually severe punishments. "If people are desperate to avoid what they regard as a calamity, they will go to whatever lengths they must to avoid it. One's conscience will be anesthetized by terror, so the dirty business can be done."

- Emphasizing results and avoiding concern for the means employed by subordinates to achieve results.

In their capacity of setting an example for subordinates, managers teach more about ethics through their actions than they do through their words or what is written in a company's ethics code. An employee who is expected to turn a blind eye to a superior's unethical behavior receives the message loud and clear that ends are more important than means.

The Three C's of Business Ethics

Most people want to do the right thing for both themselves and others. Most people are honest and, if able to resist serious temptations or helped by others to cope with them, will remain so. Everyone has a conscience—a warning voice inside that tells one that an intended action might be wrong. Guilt, shame, fear, remorse, and dread are but a few of the emotions one experiences when faced with the temptation or ramifications of improper conduct.

According to authors Solomon and Hanson, "business ethics is nothing less than the full awareness of what one is doing, its consequences and complications." Their three C's of business ethics are *compliance, contributions,* and *consequences* (Solomon and Hanson, 1985).

I S S U E S   A N D   E T H I C S
Business and Education

A **1991 poll** by *Fortune* magazine of the Fortune Industrial 500 and the Service 500 asked about business support for education in America. Of the 1,000 companies surveyed, 301 responded. Their answers indicated that various kinds of programs were in operation to assist all levels of education—preschool through graduate school. Programs targeted school reform, teacher training, math and science education, dropout prevention, business/school partnerships, job preparation, and community partnerships.

Since American companies first responded to the crisis in public education nearly a decade ago, they have learned a few hard lessons. But more and more believe they are getting something for their money. In 1989 [the first year of *Fortune*'s survey] only 22% of companies felt their involvement had made a difference. [In 1991] 56% [did].

Nearly 25% of the companies responding donated $1 million or more to public education in 1991, up from 1990's 18%. In addition to money, "CEOs and their employees are also offering more of their time. Top management in 83% of the companies surveyed say they participated actively in educational reform, versus 70% [in 1990]."

What is the impact of corporate gifts on the rights of stakeholders? Why do corporations donate funds to aid education? Besides the donation of money and goods, what else can a business do to improve education in its community? ▲

For more about U.S. corporations and education, see Joel Keehn, "How Business Helps the Schools," *Fortune,* October 21, 1991, pp. 161–162.

Compliance involves living and behaving according to the law, corporate codes of ethics, company rules, principles of morality, community expectations, and such general concepts as equity and fair play. Managers must go further than simple obedience to what the law demands, however. Shortcuts in quality that lead to customer dissatisfaction with a product or service may be legal, but they are hardly encouragement for repeat business. Treating employees with respect and fairness is essential to building trust and a productive, stable work force. And remember that managers are not only accountable for their own actions; they are accountable for the actions of their subordinates as well.

To promote ethics, management has to forge credibility (the power to elicit belief), as Martin Marietta learned in its Orlando, Florida, electronics plant. The plant's production was of such poor quality that it was in danger of losing federal contracts. According to the company's president, A. Thomas Young,

> We had all the correct slogans, posters, and buttons emphasizing the importance of quality to our work force. We couldn't understand the lack of employee response until we realized we simply were not believed. It wasn't until we demonstrated to employees that we were serious about this ethical approach that improvements occurred. The company then spent a lot of money getting the right tools for workers and we went out on the shop floor and gave gifts to employees who stopped work rather than producing inferior products (Widder, 1992).

Contributions are what business gives back to society. They include giving customers value for their patronage, providing employment, helping individuals and society meet their needs, and making improvements to the quality of life for employees and the community as a whole, which includes making charitable contributions. In 1990 American corporations gave $7.8 billion to charities such as the United Way, the arts, and education (Gunset, 1991).

Gifts included cash, goods, and the services of corporate personnel. Gifts of time can help communities, local charities, and nonprofit groups with talent, expertise, and willing hands. Gifts of inventory and depreciated property can cut costs for nonprofit groups and enrich life for various groups' members. Each year American citizens give over $100 billion to nonprofit causes, which does not count the numerous hours donated to help worthy individuals and groups. Foreign-based multinationals join in the giving as well. In 1990, Japanese companies gave $300 million to nonprofit groups in the United States. British, German, and French companies gave a combined $60 million (Yates, 1991).

The consequences of individual and corporate actions can be either positive or negative. These ramifications may be intended or unintended, anticipated or unexpected. Two examples from 1992 will illustrate how consequences can be negative for companies, employees, and others.

- Inventor Robert W. Kearns was awarded $11.3 million from Chrysler Corporation for infringements on his patents "on an electronic control system for intermittent windshield wipers, or 90 cents for each of the 12.6 million vehicles with intermittent wipers that Chrysler built between May 1977 and August 1988 [the year his patents expired]. In 1990, Ford agreed to settle with Kearns for $10.2 million or 30 cents a vehicle plus interest for 20.6 million vehicles" (*Wall Street Journal,* June 12, 1992).

- "Rockwell International Corp. has agreed to pay an $18.5 million criminal fine to settle [10 criminal] charges that it violated federal waste-disposal and clean-water laws when it ran a U.S. nuclear-weapons plant [Rocky Flats] in Colorado" (Gutfeld, 1992).

The Importance of Organizational Controls

Corporate cultures (as explained in Chapter 9) sustain values and beliefs that influence how people relate to one another. Of course, several cultures exist in any one organization: corporate culture, promoted and exemplified by management action; and the subcultures, reflecting different work groups or discrete ethnic groups that arise from the work force. These subcultures may display differing, and ideally complimentary, sets of values and perceptions, but unity of viewpoint can be achieved: "In a pluralistic society, business is the one place where different cultures and personal values are forced to cooperate and compromise. It is the one place where a single and unifying ethic is essential" (Henderson, 1992). The corporate culture and the subcultures can support ethics and social responsibility or oppose them. And these cultures are influenced to a great extent by America's culture and subcultures. Exhibit 22.2 is a checklist for examining a corporation's culture. Every "no" response indicates that some changes are necessary to bring the company into an appropriate position to foster ethical behavior and social responsibility.

Exhibit 22.2

A checklist for determining if a corporate culture supports ethical behavior and social responsibility.

Is the company:	Yes	No
1. Concerned about quality in its services, products, and operations?	☐	☐
2. Concerned about its employees' quality of life?	☐	☐
3. Proud of its reputation in the industry?	☐	☐
4. Proud of its reputation in the community?	☐	☐
5. Focused on the needs of its customers?	☐	☐
6. Honest in its dealings with you?	☐	☐
7. Honest in its dealings with customers?	☐	☐
8. Honest in its dealings with others?	☐	☐
9. Fair and equitable in the ways in which it decides on promotions?	☐	☐
10. Fair and equitable in the ways in which it compensates employees?	☐	☐
11. Open in its communications?	☐	☐
12. Trusting in its relationships with employees?	☐	☐
13. Concerned with developing and keeping its employees?	☐	☐
14. Actively promoting ethical conduct in all its operations and employees?	☐	☐
15. Actively searching for ways to better serve its stakeholders?	☐	☐
16. Carefully monitoring how decisions are made and checking them for their concern for ethical behavior?	☐	☐

Management must control these cultures and see to it that they promote ethical and socially responsible conduct. The next section examines three types of controls that can be used: commitment of top management, codes of ethics, and compliance programs.

Commitment of Top Management   The importance of managers as role models and the fact that they teach through example has already been discussed. As with so many issues, ethical and socially responsible standards will not be met in an organization until they are part of top management's philosophy and backed by commitments of money and time. Ethical businesses don't just happen; they must be carefully planned and continuously monitored by committed executives and managers with the expertise to instill in all members of the organization the importance of ethical behavior.

> Measuring something makes it important even if it wasn't before. In the U.S. Army, the phrase is 'don't expect what you don't inspect.' The corporate equivalent is, 'what the boss watches well gets done well.' The same principle applies to the ethical side of enterprise. It only becomes important if and when it's measured (Henderson, 1992).

Gellerman (1992) asserts that the "first line of defense against unethical conduct is each individual's conscience." Managers "have to do everything [they] can to keep it awake. The second line of defense is to eliminate or minimize the circumstances that can overwhelm a conscience, or deceive it, or put it to sleep." He recommends three steps that top managers can take to discourage unethical behavior in their areas of responsibility:

- "Draw a clean line between the behavior you'll tolerate and the behavior you'll have to punish." This means establishing a code of ethics or conduct that management is willing to commit to and enforce.

- "Invest the time and money in making sure that those distinctions are understood and remembered." This requires training, constant oversight, and the establishment of rewards for ethical behavior.

- "Put the fear of God into would-be violators by conspicuously raising the risk of exposure." This means punishing wrongdoers fairly and swiftly. People will learn from each example of misbehavior and how it is handled by management.

Codes of Ethics   Although there is no generic code of ethics for business, individual organizations often find such codes useful. In 1992 the Conference Board, a business-funded research group, reported that "company codes of conduct are becoming increasingly sophisticated [and] nearly one-third of the 264 chief executives surveyed had issued a personal statement or [engaged in a] formal discussion of ethics issues in [1991]" (Widder, 1992). To be effective and influential in an organization's culture and command structure, codes of ethics must be specific enough to give concrete guidance and must be re-enforced by the examples set by key corporate figures. They must be written in such a way as to develop a clear understanding of a company's values and commitment to ethical behavior, both inside the organization and in relation to key outside stakeholders. Codes should deal directly with situations known by a company to have been problematic in the past.

Authors Solomon and Hanson (1985) outline the following characteristics for codes of ethics.

- They are visible guidelines for behavior at all levels

- They are an unchallengeable basis for firing an unethical employee, even when his or her action is not, strictly speaking, against either the law or the specific terms of the job

- They protect all personnel from the pressures of the market, which tend to incite desperation and unethical behavior

- They remind employees to look beyond the bottom line and they provide a touchstone for appeals through the hierarchy

Compliance Programs   Without some means to communicate and enforce codes of ethics and conduct, they will be just words on paper. Peter Madsen, executive director at Carnegie Mellon University's Center for the Advancement of Applied Ethics, separates ethics training into two areas:

- Compliance training that alerts people to policies, regulations, and laws that establish acceptable behavior within a company; and

- Cognitive thinking exercises that develop skills to allow people to think through various 'moral mazes' they may be confronted with in the workplace (*Human Resources Management,* 1992).

According to Andrew D. Sigler of Champion International, "You need a culture and peer pressure that spells out what is acceptable and isn't and why [and a program] involving training, education, and followup" (Byrne, 1988). To make such a program effective, the Business Roundtable, an advisory and research group comprising the chief executives of 200 major corporations, recommends that top management devote a greater commitment to ethics programs, boldly assert management's expectations through clearly written and communicated codes, and conduct surveys to monitor compliance (Byrne, 1988).

There are signs that American companies are getting serious about ethics:

> According to a survey of Fortune 1,000 companies conducted by Bentley College in Boston, over 40% of the respondents are holding ethics workshops and seminars, and about one-third have set up an ethics committee. Some 200 major U.S. corporations have recently appointed ethics officers, usually senior managers of long experience, to serve as ombudsmen (a person who investigates complaints, reports findings, and mediates fair settlements) and encourage whistle-blowing (Labich, 1992).

According to a 1991 Conference Board survey of 264 North American and European companies, "one out of 10 corporate boards now has a separate ethics committee" (*Wall Street Journal,* February 24, 1992). Some have full-time ethics officers reporting to them. At Raytheon Corporation a "hotline" provides employees access to an ethical specialist to consult with. Employees can "register complaints or ask about questionable behavior. Around 80% [of calls] involve minor issues that [the expert] can resolve on the spot or refer to the human resources department. About 10 times a month, a caller reports some serious ethical lapse that [the ethics officer] must address with senior management" (Labich, 1992).

Ethics programs can be very creative. Citicorp uses "an ethics board game, which teams of employees use to solve hypothetical quandaries. General Electric employees can tap into specially designed interactive software on their personal computers to get answers to ethical questions. At Texas Instruments, employees are treated to a weekly column on ethics over an international electronic news service" (Labich, 1992).

Professor Dupuy at LaGrange College has developed a condensed version of Friedrich Dürrenmatt's renowned 1956 play, *The Visit,* in which a wealthy woman returns to her hometown to take revenge on a person who hurt her when she was young. After buying the town's factories and shutting them down to cause a local depression, she offers $1 million to any person who agrees to kill the man who wronged her. After some soul-searching among the characters, a mob kills the man. After the performance, audience members participate with the cast to explore their values and ethics in relation to one another's. "Such self-discovery should be invaluable to participants when they confront ethical issues on the job," says Dupuy (Bell, 1992).

Legal Constraints

Competent managers cultivate an informed awareness of the role of the law in organizational and individual conduct. Because ours is a nation of laws, certain presumptions influence decision making at several levels. From the broadest context of constitutional rights to the minutest municipal regulation, companies and their managers are witting and unwitting creatures of the law. One group of business-law experts view the relationship of the law to ethics in this way:

> There is a basic problem facing any business in its efforts to be "ethical": there are no fixed guidelines to follow, no formal codes of ethics to set the standards. The legal profession has a Code of Professional Responsibility; the medical profession has its Hippocratic Oath; the accounting profession has a code of ethics; the real-estate industry has a code of conduct; other professions have codes to guide them. But business has no "roads map" of ethical conduct. The closest thing business has is the law. If a business obeys the law, it is acting legally, and it is seemingly meeting its minimum social requirements (Davidson et al., 1990).

Those minimum requirements offer only a structure, however, void of content and context. Says Peter Madsen:

> Laws and policies form an ethical foundation. But the law is a moral minimum. And no law or policy is going to cover every situation. Sooner or later organizations will have to rely on people to make choices when there is no on-point law or policy to follow. The best ethics training goes beyond legal compliance (*Human Resources Management*, 1992).

Author Vincent Barry adds,

> Although useful in alerting us to moral issues and informing us of our rights and responsibilities, law cannot be taken as an adequate standard of moral conduct. Conformity with law is neither requisite nor sufficient for determining moral behavior, any more than conformity to rule[s] of etiquette is. By the same token, nonconformity with law is not necessarily immoral, for the law disobeyed may be unjust (Barry, 1986).

Corporations and their employees take actions every day that affect the lives of countless people—from their constituents to their stakeholders. Laws can form boundaries and a basis for human and corporate conduct; law and ethics together define acceptable behavior. But ethics comprises more than legalities. Ethics "should protect and promote the interests of society in general and the corporation's constituents in particular. Good ethics strengthens the bonds of personal and social relationships" (Henderson, 1992). Southern California Edison, for example, has stayed ahead of legal demands in the area of pollution control by focusing simultaneously on the best interests of its customers and of society as a whole.

In Exhibit 22.3, a simple grid model relates law and ethics in four combinations, using for example the issue of smoking in the workplace. Such a model can be used to sort out alternative resolutions of any issue posing an ethical

Exhibit 22.3

Legal/ethical behavior model applied to the issue of smoking in the workplace.

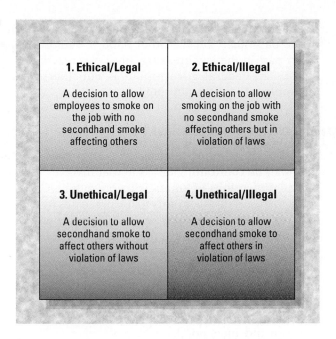

1. Ethical/Legal	**2. Ethical/Illegal**
A decision to allow employees to smoke on the job with no secondhand smoke affecting others	A decision to allow smoking on the job with no secondhand smoke affecting others but in violation of laws
3. Unethical/Legal	**4. Unethical/Illegal**
A decision to allow secondhand smoke to affect others without violation of laws	A decision to allow secondhand smoke to affect others in violation of laws

dilemma. For any example, unambiguously positive resolution occurs only with alternatives qualifying for quadrant 1 (ethical/legal), which poses no potentially negative consequences for decision maker, organization, or constituents. All other quadrants present a legal and/or ethical dilemma.

Based on the investigations following the collapse of many of the nation's largest savings and loan associations, then–FBI Director William Sessions said, "Experience demonstrates that insider abuse is a major factor in almost all of our investigations involving failed financial institutions" (*Chicago Tribune*, 1990). William Black, former director of the now defunct Federal Savings and Loan Insurance Corporation, said, "Evil triumphed because too many good men and women did nothing to stop the looting of thrifts" (*Chicago Tribune*, 1990).

Legal sanctions against individual and corporate criminal behavior can be significant. Since 1909 when the U.S. Supreme Court held that corporations can be "held liable, as individuals can be, for crimes involving intent," corporate liability has translated into fines and jail terms for corporate officials. More than half of the 50 states now have some form of corporate criminal liability law under which business owners can be prosecuted for criminal negligence. According to New York attorney Steven Alan Reiss, during the past 10 years the trend has been toward escalating criminal penalties that "can be drastically reduced if the company can show it has in place [a legal] compliance program" (Widder, 1992).

In November 1991 the trend toward harsh penalties for white-collar crime continued, as new federal guidelines went into effect. They "cover many offenses that can be committed by employees without a business owner's knowledge. Some of the new penalties [base fines range from $5,000 to $72.5 million] may be enough to destroy a small company" (Jacobs, 1992). Heavy penalties for a variety of offenses "including serious misrepresentation of a product by a salesperson and bribery of a public official by a subcontractor" are included. "If high-level managers were not involved in the crime and [they] have taken steps to ensure employees' compliance with the law, a firm could pay as little as 5% of the base fine." On the other hand, if senior managers "have encouraged or taken part in the law breaking, fines can reach 400% of the base rate" (Jacobs, 1992). The federal government is considering adding crimes against the environment to these new guidelines.

Guidelines for Acting Ethically

Someone struggling with a decision, torn between one or another course of action, may well be confronting an issue that involves ethics. The time to consider the ethical dimensions of an act is before acting. Companies and individuals must strive to make ethics a priority in the processes by which they make their decisions. Different people and groups invoke different criteria for determining if an intended action (or inaction) is the ethical course to follow. The Golden Rule states that we should treat others as we ourselves want to be treated. A variation is to do to others what they want you to do to them. Both work well if the people involved are moral and aware of prevailing social conventions. The utilitarian standard of the greatest good for the greatest number of people provides another ethical test, which works well if the consequences and circumstances surrounding the intended act are fully foreseen and understood.

Authors Solomon and Hanson (1985) offer the following rules for contemplating the ethical implications of intended actions:

- Consider other people's well-being, including the well-being of nonparticipants

- Think as a member of the business community and not as an isolated individual

- Obey, but do not depend solely on, the law

- Think of yourself—and your company—as part of society

- Obey moral rules

- Think objectively

- Ask the question, "What sort of person would do such a thing?"

- Respect the customs of others, but not at the expense of your own ethics

These rules remind us that we are all part of a larger community and that our actions affect others, whose interests must be considered. Keeping these rules in mind can help managers analyze the consequences of their actions before steps are taken. When one makes decisions without a moral and ethical base, he or she is adrift and may rely solely on self-interest and economics. People lacking a moral foundation put themselves, their organizations, and others at great risk. And although risk taking shows up in most managers' job descriptions, "they are paid to know which risks are worth taking. One risk that is definitely not worth taking is the risk of ruining the rest of your career" (Gellerman, 1992).

Management professor Kenneth Blanchard and noted cleric Norman Vincent Peale (author of *The Power of Positive Thinking*) have written a cogent book, *The Power of Ethical Management*. In it they offer a simple sequence of three tests for determining the ethical implications of intended actions (Blanchard and Peale, 1988):

- Is it legal? Will I be violating either civil law or company policy?

- Is it balanced? Is it fair to all concerned in the short term as well as the long term? Does it promote win-win relationships?

- How will it make me feel about myself? Will it make me proud? Would I feel good if my decision were published in a newspaper? Would I feel good if my family knew about it?

With these inquiries a manager can examine his or her intentions in private and with complete objectivity. When judging the ethical facets of a decision, a person must take ample quiet time, away from pressures and the biases of others, for unhurried reflection on the facts and implications of the decision.

The Nature of Social Responsibility

The notion that individuals and organizations have certain obligations, in addition to their business interests, to protect and benefit others and to avoid actions that could harm them is what constitutes **social responsibility** (Davis, 1975). One reason for the prevalence of this belief in the developed countries of the world is that societies have given businesses tremendous power and rely on them to meet various individual and societal needs.

Businesses are open systems, and most of what they do generates direct benefits and costs for their societies. At one time businesses did only what they

Social responsibilities are taken seriously at Smith & Hawken Co. Employees spent Earth Day creating urban gardens for the community.

had to do. Today society demands that businesses join in the urgent task of solving societies' problems. Corporations must nourish cultures that promote ethical conduct, and their owners and employees must act with an ethical perspective in order to be socially responsible. Being socially responsible does not mean making everyone happy. Businesses face conflicting demands, and at times a socially responsible action puts the needs of one group of stakeholders ahead of the needs of others—such as donating money to charity rather than paying stockholders higher dividends or giving employees higher raises. Such issues require managers to consider their duty (the course of action required of them by their position or by law) and the priorities of their specific obligations.

Author Rogene A. Buchholz expresses the need for businesses to act in a socially responsible way: "Corporations are more than economic institutions and have a responsibility to devote some of their resources to helping to solve some of the pressing social problems, many of which corporations helped to create" (Bucholz, 1989). Benjamin Franklin may have been the first American businessman to advocate such responsible conduct for businesses. Franklin believed that "public service and philanthropy were legitimate concerns… because it is good business to improve the health of the communities from which wealth is derived and because public problems can benefit from private solutions" (Watson, 1991).

Robert D. Haas, president and CEO of Levi Strauss, persuasively argues the case for businesses to cultivate social responsibility:

> Corporations can be short-sighted and worry only about our mission, products, and competitive standing. But we do it at our peril. The day will come when corporations will discover the price we pay for our indifference. We must realize that by ignoring the needs of others, we are actually ignoring our own needs in the long run. We may need the goodwill of a neighborhood to enlarge a corner store. We may need well-funded institutions of higher learning to turn out the skilled technical employees we require. We may need adequate community health care to curb absenteeism in our plants. Or we may need fair tax treatment for an industry to be able to compete in the world economy. However small or large our enterprise, we cannot isolate our business from the society around us. Nor can we function without its goodwill (Haas, 1984).

Approaches to Social Responsibility

American businesses adopt different approaches to the demands made upon them. Some businesses eagerly seek ways to accommodate societal needs, whereas others vehemently resist external obligations. Businesses can adopt any of three primary strategies to manage the issue of social responsibility: to resist, to react, and to anticipate.

The Resistance Approach   Companies adopt the **resistance approach** when they actively fight to eliminate, delay, or fend off the demands being made on them. In the earliest days of the Industrial Revolution, businesses were relatively unaffected by government regulation. Labor was cheap and plentiful. Businesses behaved pretty much as they wanted, exerting tremendous influence over their towns, industries, and governments. This early phase of business history was marked by resistance to government interference and active opposition to demands

Working Toward Cleaner Air

The **1990 Clean Air Act** requires private and governmental employers with 100 or more employees in heavily polluted areas to develop alternative employee transport programs that will reduce the use of one-passenger vehicles by at least 25% by 1994, and to translate those plans into action by 1996. Many states and companies have been at work on this problem for several years. Some maintain toll-free numbers and referral services that put motorists in touch with others who commute to common destinations, allowing them to form car pools. Public transit companies offer reduced fares for regular riders and offer a variety of additional incentives for people to use their service. Many transit operations are planning to extend their services to growing populations in suburban areas.

Baxter Healthcare maintains a campuslike headquarters in a Midwest suburb. The facility was built with commuters in mind and offers ample parking for all employees' automobiles, should they decide to drive to work. The community's public transport system does not directly serve the headquarters complex. In 1992 Baxter volunteered to be part of an areawide, combined government and business effort to promote clean air and to meet legal mandates. The company surveyed its several hundred employees to determine how dependent they were on automobiles, and solicited suggestions for alternate ways for commuting that had popular support. Major suggestions were car pools, telecommuting for those who could use it, chartered vans from regular public transit stations, four-day workweeks, and extension of public transit routes to provide direct access to corporate headquarters.

Whatever methods are adopted, they will depend on a commitment from Baxter's employees to use them, and probably some incentives from the company to encourage their use. Baxter believes that with its people behind the effort, it will be able to meet or exceed mandated goals ahead of schedule. The finalized program will receive a trial run and be evaluated through an additional survey. ▲

For more about companies' clean air efforts, see David Ibata, "Clean Air Act spurs businesses to give public transit a push," *Chicago Tribune,* November 3, 1992, sec. 2, p. 5.

---

from both insiders and outsiders. The emphasis was on maximizing profits and the self-interests of owners. The prevailing attitude was that managers owed their allegiance to owners, a view reinforced by the courts. In a 1919 decision, a Michigan court refused to let Henry Ford divert stockholder dividend payments to "certain socially beneficial programs." The court held that directors had an obligation to stockholders and could not renege on that duty (Davidson et al., 1990). Regulatory agencies were virtually nonexistent. No laws protected consumers or the environment, and both suffered as a consequence.

Even in today's regulatory environment and with so many of society's needs vividly apparent, some businesses persist in doing as little as possible—only what the law demands—and even that is done reluctantly. Previous chapters have cited examples of corporate efforts to resist stakeholders' demands. Another recent example occurred in 1992, when Toyota Motor Corporation encountered problems with its 1987 to 1991 Camry models—some 890,000 vehicles. The automatic door locks "could jam, and lock owners out of the car or trap occupants inside the vehicle." Toyota is cooperating with the investigation by the National Highway

Traffic Safety Administration, but the company (while admitting that some locks are faulty) maintains that a recall isn't warranted. Both the Center for Auto Safety (a consumer group) and *Consumer Reports* magazine wrote about the problem, and the Center recommended a recall (Mitchell, 1992).

The Reactive Approach   Businesses taking the **reactive approach** wait for demands to be made and then respond to them by evaluating alternatives. In 1992, in Chicago's Lincoln Park area just north of the city's center, neighbors complained about too many restaurants and bars in their neighborhood being open too late, whose patrons repeatedly caused disturbances. When their complaints went unheeded, neighborhood groups began a petition drive to place a referendum on the November 1992 ballot to ban the sale of alcohol in the area. Hundreds of people signed the petitions, causing the affected business owners to mount their own campaign. They went door-to-door in an effort to get people to remove their signatures. Eventually a compromise was worked out: the businesses agreed to hire off-duty police to patrol during the late evening hours to curtail the problems. But it wasn't until a real threat to these businesses arose that the owners took actions to meet community demands.

The Proactive Approach   Companies taking the **proactive approach** continually look to the needs of constituents, constantly staying in touch, sensing their needs, and trying to find ways to assist them. We have already mentioned companies assisting education with donated cash, services, and goods. Southern California Edison's proactive policies illustrate that being socially responsible can benefit both the constituents and the company. Just Desserts' Elliot Hoffman "teamed up with the San Francisco County Jail to turn a vacant lot adjoining his bakery into an elaborate organic garden tended by parolees, the homeless, and other folk" (Schlender, 1992). Prudential Insurance Company is the only corporation to have received an award given each year by the Business Enterprise Trust, a nonprofit organization that promotes socially responsible behavior.

> [Prudential] received the award for creating the Living Needs Benefit, an option allowing certain seriously ill policyholders to redeem most of their life-insurance benefits while still alive. Some one million of the company's three million North American policyholders have signed up for the free option; to date... Prudential has paid some $21 million on about 275 claims (Fuchsberg, 1992).

Simultaneously, the trust gave awards to three individuals as well as a lifetime achievement award to J. Irwin Miller, former chairman of Cummins Engine Company of Columbus, Indiana, calling him a pioneer of "models of business responsibility" for his many contributions to worthy causes (Fuchsberg, 1992).

Responsibilities to Stakeholders

Stakeholders are those who have an interest in or who are affected by how a business conducts its operations. In general, the stakeholders in most businesses include their owners and stockholders, employees, customers, suppliers, and communities. Society as a whole can be considered a stakeholder as well if the business is large enough to affect people and environments beyond its physical location.

Owners and Stockholders   A business and its employees owe their best efforts to owners. Assets must be conserved and used effectively and efficiently. Employees must do their best to maximize the return on invested capital and to generate a reasonable profit. Owners and employers should have the right to hire, train, reward, promote, discipline, and remove employees in accordance with ethical, moral, and legal restraints. Owners and employers should have the right to expect ethical, moral, and legal conduct from their employees.

Employees   Employees should enjoy equal access to the rights, responsibilities, and privileges afforded by employers. Employees need to receive fair and equitable compensation, to be dismissed only for just cause, and to be treated without discrimination. Employees should experience a quality of work life that provides satisfying jobs. They should receive competent guidance and direction in their work and be accorded due process in disputes.

Employees hold certain rights to freedom of expression, safety, adequate information, and privacy and confidentiality in regard to personal concerns. A growing trend in several areas of the country is to fire employees for their consumption of alcohol or tobacco (both on and off the job), and for working a second job (moonlighting). Several states, including Illinois, have addressed these privacy issues. Since July 1992, no employer in Illinois can fire an employee for engaging in a lawful activity away from work (Vitale, 1992). Numerous laws have been enacted on the local, state, and federal level to protect the health, privacy, and welfare of employees.

Customers   Businesses and their employees owe fair and honest representation of their products and services to their customers. Such products and services should encompass quality of design, manufacture, distribution, and sales. Consumers have a right to be warned of any hazards they may encounter while using a product or receiving a service. In short, customers have a right to be treated fairly and with respect. Many laws have been passed to protect consumers; government inspection of food, drugs, and cosmetics is one result of such consumer-protection legislation. Credit laws are another example. A 1992 case suggests the scope of these laws:

> Three companies that sell consumer credit data nationwide settled federal charges that they released such information without determining whether their customers were using the sensitive information legally [a violation of the federal Fair Credit Reporting Act]. Under the settlement, the companies agreed to undertake periodic audits to ensure that their customers are requesting and using the information for legitimate purposes (Saddler, 1992).

Suppliers   Suppliers and businesses should build relationships based on mutual trust. Suppliers deserve to receive needed information in time to render quality service and supplies. They, like all parties to business contracts, have the legal right to be treated according to the terms of their agreements.

In July 1992 General Motors made a startling announcement:

> GM would provide suppliers [worldwide through September 1993] not only with paid workers but also with leased factories for them to build parts. GM would

benefit in that a portion of any savings its suppliers realized in plant and production costs could be returned to GM to help it reduce costs (Mateja, 1992).

The offer came because, according to its contract with the United Auto Workers, GM pays laid-off workers 95% of their pay for 36 weeks. In the 37th week they join a job bank from which they may be assigned any position by a plant's Jobs Committee while they earn 100% of their pay.

Communities Those environments and their governments that are affected by a company's operations constitute its community. The quality of life in a community; its air, land, and water quality; and its specific needs all come into play. All its constituents, many of whom may be customers, deserve ethical, legal, and moral treatment. A suburban restaurant owner got complaints from neighbors about food-packaging debris on lawns and streets. He now employs a person full-time to patrol the neighborhood and pick up all litter within a square mile of the restaurant.

Pollution is a growing concern around the world; with mounting pressure to produce **green products**—those that minimize energy consumption and pollutive by-products connected with their manufacture and disposal. Auto makers have developed more fuel-efficient and cleaner-burning engines,

According to EPA estimates, Americans generate 195 million tons of trash in a year. Businesses such as Sears & Roebuck Co. and Procter & Gamble are attempting to deal with the problem by changing product design and packaging.

encouraged in no small measure by California's tough environmental laws and the Clean Air Act of 1990. Several American and Japanese car models are already equipped with "superclean" engines, and more are in the pipeline (*Wall Street Journal,* November 3, 1992).

The music-recording industry has bowed to pressures from several sources and agreed to phase out its "long box" packaging for compact disks (CDs). Beginning in April 1993 most CDs will be sold in the simple plastic "jewel boxes"; the only waste will be plastic shrink-wrap to prevent tampering (Cox, 1992). McDonald's reduced its packaging for similar reasons in the late 1980s. The fast-food chain has also made attempts to help individuals with vision, hearing, and speech impairments by adding Braille menus in 1979 and picture menus in 1988. McDonald's is the only major fast-food chain to offer these services (Ryan, 1992).

Government Regulation: Pros and Cons

Corporations have committed acts that harm the environment, consumers, communities, and society as a whole. Laws now in existence were brought about largely by these abuses. When society can't depend on the perpetrators to act appropriately, it must compel such action. But the enforcement of many laws depends more on individuals' commitments to social responsibility than it does on government agencies. Governments simply do not have enough money or people to adequately enforce their regulations. Society's best protection rests in an informed citizenry and a formed conscience in each and every owner and employee.

The costs of regulation are high and getting higher. Businesses spend billions of dollars and millions of hours reporting to governments and complying with legal mandates. In 1992 the federal Environmental Protection Agency estimated that the chemical industry "will spend $347 million in capital costs and $182 million a year in operating expenses to meet [1992's] new technology requirements for cutting... cancer-causing emissions" (Rosewicz, 1992). Although regulations, many argue, have made the United States less competitive around the world, they have also brought about needed reforms. It must be remembered that society grants businesses the right to operate. In return, society retains the right to proper treatment and a clean environment. When these fundamental rights are abused, we all suffer.

Unfortunately, after their products are produced and sold too many businesses do not consider the costs placed on society. Such costs include cleanups of all kinds and the pressing need to recycle. Our nation has created a Superfund to clean up the worst cases of toxic waste; in fact, it spends hundreds of millions of dollars each year to right the wrongs of irresponsible businesses and individuals. Some environmental damage can never be repaired, or will take more than money to make right. Cleaning up such environmental hazards as nuclear waste, toxic dumps, and oil spills will take years of commitment by dedicated individuals willing to invest the energy and talent required to remedy what has been done. The costs are borne by all of us through taxes.

But times are changing. A growing number of individuals and corporations are moving from a reactive to a proactive approach and becoming more socially responsible. These people are redesigning processes and products, recycling and repackaging for reduced waste, anticipating needs, and facing problems up front.

Businesses are finding that being good citizens pays off, with dividends that contribute to corporate bottom lines. Many companies have found that pollution prevention is better than pollution control. These organizations have made profits through their efforts to both prevent and reduce pollution. And a growing number of consumers are showing their willingness to pay a premium for products that are environmentally friendly.

Managing for Social Responsibility

Managers today must anticipate society's concerns and actively forecast and plan to meet its needs. They must make social responsibility a priority and, as with ethics, build a concern for it as a priority in their cultures and employees as well.

Top-Management Commitment

Executives in top management must commit the time and money necessary to make their organization socially responsible. They need to act as well as talk. They set the tone for their entire operation and establish its priorities. Authors Christopher B. Hunt and Ellen R. Auster (1990) recommend the following key elements to top managers who want to make their organizations proactive:

- Top-level commitment and support
- Corporate policies that integrate environmental issues
- Effective interfaces between corporate and business-unit staff
- High degree of employee awareness and training
- Strong auditing programs
- Establishment of responsibility for identifying and dealing with real and potential environmental problems

A checklist for implementing the proactive environmental management program is shown in Exhibit 22.4.

Many organizations have built in a variety of safeguards to promote social responsibility. They usually start with the commitment in words and deeds of top management. Policies are written or revised to include concerns for social responsibility as well as ethics. They create programs for promoting an active role for their organizations in meeting societal needs. Training is given to employees, emphasizing how they can contribute. They encourage people to participate in their communities by granting time off and other incentives. Most United Way campaigns, for instance, are staffed by managers on leave, whose salaries are paid by their business employer. General Electric has had a public policy committee staffed by members of its board of directors since 1970. It seeks to create social programs and keep track of their progress and achievements (Steiner, 1975). The larger the enterprise, the more likely it is to have a separate department to plan for and oversee organizational efforts to be socially responsible and to see to it that environmental, fair-employment, and safety and health regulations are followed (Buehler and Shetty, 1976).

Managers are the key to making ethics and social responsibility realities in their organizations. They need fully formed consciences based on sound values. They need to understand the motives that support their decisions and those of

Exhibit 22.4

A checklist for implementing a proactive environmental management program.

- Secure top-level commitment and long-term funding.

- Develop a corporate environmental policy statement.

- Assign a senior executive to champion the program.

- Assess areas of environmental exposure (i.e., conduct environmental audits and legal reviews).

- Appoint a manager with superior managerial skills and influence within the organization.

- Prioritize program goals and objectives.

- Revise corporate organizational structure to maximize the program's visibility, accessibility, and effectiveness.

- Develop formal reporting relationships within the department and across divisions.

- Identify key individuals in other divisions to serve as liaisons with the environmental department.

- Develop streamlined yet comprehensive management information and record-keeping systems.

- Develop formalized inspection programs.

- Develop training and education programs for environmental staff and key individuals in other divisions.

- Establish a career track for environmental professionals.

- Continually re-evaluate program needs and design.

Source: Christopher B. Hunt and Ellen R. Auster, "Proactive Management: Avoiding the Toxic Trap," *The Best of MIT's Sloan Management Review* (Cambridge, MA: The Sloan Management Review Association, MIT Sloan School of Management), 1990, p. 24. Reprinted by permission.

others. They need principles, rewards, examples, and other forms of guidance and support to keep their commitments to ethical and socially responsible actions. When an organization is truly committed to meeting its social responsibilities, it reflects this commitment in routine management decision making and ongoing planning efforts. And it monitors those efforts to ensure compliance.

The Social Audit

To be truly effective, social responsibility needs the backing of all owners, managers, and employees. It must be a consideration in daily decisions, not secondary to them. Managers and owners need to know what is being done to meet social obligations, what will be expected in the future, and what past results and contributions have been.

The **social audit** is a report on the social performance of a business. No uniform format currently exists, but most proactive firms have devised some

I t seems that some of America's global competitors don't wish to spend the time and money to do their own research and development. In 1992, Honeywell of Minneapolis received a court-awarded settlement of $124.1 million from "seven camera makers [mostly Japanese companies] it says infringed on its patented technology for autofocus lenses.... Agreements were negotiated separately with Kodak, Konica, Kyocera, Canon, Matsushita, Nikon, and Premier. In March, Honeywell won a [separate] $127.5 million settlement from Minolta. Honeywell also will get future royalties for camera sales through March 28, 1995, when its applicable autofocus patents expire." ▲

For more on this case, see "Honeywell to get $124 million in autofocus patent settlement," *Chicago Tribune*, August 22, 1992, sec. 2, p. 2.

---

method for auditing their efforts and for disclosing the results to both insiders and outsiders. Such an audit usually summarizes corporate activities under the following headings: charitable contributions, support of local community groups and activities, employment of protected groups, political contributions, pollution control and cleanup, health and safety measures, and efforts to improve the quality of work life for employees.

Progress may be stated in terms of goals set and met, in monetary terms, or both. Those who benefit are clearly labeled, and the extent to which they benefit is quantified when possible. The results of the social audit should be shared with all constituents and stakeholders so that awareness of and commitment to the programs can be reinforced. Programs that have been successful should be continued and expanded if the need still persists, and programs that yield few positive results should be eliminated so that more productive ones may be instituted. People who contribute to successes should be cited and rewarded.

Future Trends

Look for the following developments and think about potential impacts each may have on your job, career, and future:

- Personal privacy will remain an issue for the 1990s and will focus on such infringement aspects as computer monitoring, genetic screening, and testing for honesty, drug use, and AIDS. More laws will be passed to curtail these practices.

- The concern over exporting jobs and downsizing American manufacturing operations while expanding those operations outside U.S. borders will become greater; more companies will act to reverse this trend.

- Companies will continue to expand their efforts to be more socially responsible, and more firms will join this trend by moving from the reactive to the proactive approach.

- Look for some forms of the electric car to emerge from major automobile manufacturers by 1995. All are experimenting with prototypes; some blend electricity with gasoline- and propane-powered engines. Railroads are experimenting with propane-powered locomotives.

- Look for increases in the number of companies prosecuted for crimes against property and against nature.

- Prompted by the Americans with Disabilities Act, more companies will become proactive in their efforts to accommodate the handicapped.

C H A P T E R　**S** U M M A R Y

- Because the consequences of management decisions are greaterthan ever before, the duty of managers to act ethically is increasingly significant.

- Increased pressure from more sources coupled with decreasing time to make decisions means that guidelines to facilitate ethical decision making and behavior are especially important for business organizations.

- Ethics—viewing actions in light of standards of honesty and honorable conduct—affect countless business decisions.

- Ethical dilemmas arise when individuals are unsure of what course of action to follow. It is best to confront these dilemmas before deciding on a course of action.

- Fears, pressures, and ambition are among the motives that lead to unethical conduct.

- Three keys to ethical conduct are compliance with norms of behavior, making contributions to society, and recognizing the consequences of one's actions.

- Businesses face legal constraints on their actions, but ethics constitute more than just legal concerns.

- Managers hold the best interests of their society in trust. They bear inherent obligations to employees, owners, and their community, and have fundamental duties to all their organization's stakeholders.

- Today's businesses must integrate into their cultures, planning, and decision making a concern for ethics and social responsibility. For such concern to receive serious attention, it must be backed by strong commitment from top management.

- Once initiated, programs for ethics and social responsibility should be monitored and audited; successes should be noted and meaningful effort made to eliminate and prevent unethical and antisocial behaviors and attitudes.

The following questions are designed to determine your personal ethics and commitment to acting in a socially responsible manner. Answer each honestly to get an accurate picture of where you stand.

	Always	**Sometimes**	**Never**
1. I like to approach problem solving with a consideration of how my solution will affect others.	☐	☐	☐
2. When an action is legal it is acceptable to engage in it.	☐	☐	☐
3. When making decisions I like to bounce my thinking off of others.	☐	☐	☐
4. When considering actions, I think about their impact on society.	☐	☐	☐
5. One test I use for determining if my decisions are acceptable is to ask myself how I would feel if my thinking were made known to friends and family.	☐	☐	☐
6. I think that when a decision hurts one party so that another can benefit, it is an unethical decision.	☐	☐	☐
7. When I see someone at work stealing from the company, I let those in authority know about it.	☐	☐	☐
8. I think that if the company does not care about ethics or socially responsible behavior, doing so personally is not important to my career.	☐	☐	☐
9. When I see litter in the office at work I clean it up.	☐	☐	☐
10. I feel good about my actions.	☐	☐	☐

R E V I E W   **Q** U E S T I O N S

1. Review this chapter's essential terms and look up the meanings of those you cannot define.

2. What are four motives for the actions of managers who act unethically?

3. Why is it essential that each person in an organization act ethically? How can a company ensure that they do?

4. What is the connection between acting legally and acting ethically?

5. What are a company's responsibilities to each of its stakeholders?

6. What actions can a company take to ensure ethical and socially responsible conduct?

7. How are ethics and social responsibility related?

R E C O M M E N D E D   R E A D I N G

Andrews, Kenneth R., editor. *Ethics in Practice* (Boston: Harvard Business School Press), 1989.

Barry, Vincent. *Moral Issues in Business,* 3rd edition (Belmont, CA: Wadsworth), 1986.

Blanchard, Kenneth, and Norman Vincent Peale. *The Power of Ethical Management* (New York: William Morrow), 1988.

Fitzgerald, William Edward. *Arenas of Greed: The Great Chicago Commodity Market Scam* (New York: De Vin), 1990.

Henderson, Verne E. *What's Ethical in Business?* (New York: McGraw-Hill), 1992.

Hunt, Christopher B., and Ellen R. Auster. "Proactive Environmental Management: Avoiding the Toxic Trap," *The Best of MIT's Sloan Management Review* (Winter 1990), pp. 7–18.

Jackall, Robert. *Moral Mazes: The World of Corporate Managers* (New York: Oxford University Press), 1988.

Madsen, Peter, and Jay M. Shafritz, editors. *Essentials of Business Ethics* (New York: Meridian), 1990.

Solomon, Robert C., and Kristine R. Hanson. *It's Good Business* (New York: Athenaeum), 1985.

R E F E R E N C E S

Barry, Vincent. *Moral Issues In Business,* 3rd edition (Belmont, CA: Wadsworth), 1986, pp. 5, 9–10, 156.

Bell, David. "Stage set for ethics in business," *Chicago Tribune,* June 21, 1992, sec. 7, p. 8B.

Blanchard, Kenneth, and Norman Vincent Peale. *The Power of Ethical Management* (New York: William Morrow), 1988, p. 27.

Buchholz, Rogene A. *Fundamental Concepts and Problems in Business Ethics* (Englewood Cliffs, NJ: Prentice-Hall), 1989, p. 5.

Buehler, Vernon M., and Y. K. Shetty. "Managerial Response to Social Responsibility Challenge," *Academy of Management Journal* (March 1976), p. 69.

Byrne, John A. "Businesses Are Signing Up for Ethics 101," *Business Week* (February 15, 1988), pp. 56–57.

Chicago Tribune (April 12, 1990). "Crime major cause of S&L woes, FBI says," sec. 3, p. 1.

Chicago Tribune (August 22, 1992). "Honeywell to get $124 million in autofocus patent settlement," sec. 2, p. 2.

Cox, Danny, with John Hoover. *Leadership When the Heat's On* (New York: McGraw-Hill), 1992, p. 23.

Cox, Meg. "CD Marketers Will Eliminate Paper Packaging," *Wall Street Journal,* February 28, 1992, p. B1.

Davidson, Daniel V.; Brenda E. Knowles; Lynn M. Forsythe; and Robert R. Jespersen. *Business Law: Principles and Cases,* 3rd edition (Boston: PWS-Kent), 1990, pp. 107, 111, 112.

Davis, Keith. "Five Propositions for Social Responsibility," *Business Horizons* XVIII, no. 3 (June 1975). Adapted from article reprinted in Barry, 1986, p. 156.

Dunfee, Thomas W. "Employee Ethical Attitudes and Business Firm Productivity," *The Wharton Annual* (University of Pennsylvania: Pergamon Press), 1984, p. 76.

Fuchsberg, Gilbert. "Business People Aiding Society Win Accolades," *Wall Street Journal,* March 6, 1992, p. A3.

Gellerman, Saul W. *Motivation in the Real World* (New York: Dutton), 1992, pp. 265, 266–267, 269–271, 273–274.

Gellerman, Saul W. "Why 'Good' Managers Make Bad Ethical Choices," *Harvard Business Review* (July–August 1986), pp. 88–89.

Gunset, George. "Recession weighs on nonprofits," *Chicago Tribune,* June 8, 1991, sec. 2, p. 1. (Figures cited from the American Association of Fund-Raising Council.)

Gutfeld, Rose. "Rockwell to Plead Guilty, Pay Fine on Waste Disposal," *Wall Street Journal,* March 26, 1992, p. C20.

Haas, Robert D. Acceptance speech, Lawrence A. Wein Prize in Corporate Social Responsibility, Columbia University, New York (November 19, 1984) as recorded in Watson, 1991, pp. 321–322.

Henderson, Verne E. *What's Ethical in Business?* (New York: McGraw-Hill), 1992, pp. 62, 74–75, 202, 205.

Human Resources Management: Ideas & Trends in Personnel 273 (April 15, 1992). "The best ethics training goes beyond legal compliance by giving people skills needed to make value-based decisions," an interview with Dr. Peter Madsen (Chicago: Commerce Clearing House), p. 60.

Hunt, Christopher B., and Ellen R. Auster. "Proactive Environmental Management: Avoiding the Toxic Trap," *The Best of MIT's Sloan Management Review* (Winter 1990), pp. 7–18.

Jacobs, Deborah L. "Stiff New Penalties: Companies Can Be Fined For Workers' Misdeeds," *Your Company* (Winter 1992), p. 12.

Labich, Kenneth. "The New Crisis in Business Ethics," *Fortune* (April 20, 1992), pp. 167, 168, 172, 176.

Mateja, Jim. "GM offers workers free to parts suppliers," *Chicago Tribune,* July 18, 1992, sec. 1, pp. 1, 6.

Mitchell, Jacqueline. "Toyota Finds Itself in Jam on Door Locks," *Wall Street Journal,* August 19, 1992, p. B1.

Rosewicz, Barbara. "EPA Acts to Cut Toxic Emissions, Draws Criticism," *Wall Street Journal,* October 30, 1992, p. A5.

Ryan, Nancy. "McDonald's update for special menus," *Chicago Tribune,* March 12, 1992, sec. 3, p. 3.

Saddler, Jeanne. "Three Credit Data Firms Agree to Try to Keep Clients From Misusing Reports," *Wall Street Journal,* August 19, 1992, p. C9.

Schlender, Brenton R. "The Values We Will Need," *Fortune* (January 27, 1992), p. 77.

Solomon, Robert C., and Kristine R. Hanson. *It's Good Business* (New York: Athenaeum), 1985, pp. xiii–xiv, 20–21, 46–49, 146–148.

Steiner, George. "Institutionalizing Corporate Social Decisions," *Business Horizons* (December 1975), p. 18.

Vitale, Robert. "If it's legal, law says workers may do it on their own time," *Chicago Tribune,* July 1, 1992, sec. 2, p. 2.

Wall Street Journal (February 24, 1992). "Odds and Ends," p. B1.

Wall Street Journal (June 12, 1992). "Chrysler Must Pay Royalty to Pioneer of Wiper System," p. B4.

Wall Street Journal (November 3, 1992). "'Green' Cars Struggle to Gain Acceptance," p. B1.

Watson, Charles E. *Managing with Integrity, Insights from America's CEOs* (New York: Praeger), 1991, p. 321.

Widder, Pat. "More corporations learning that ethics are bottomline issue," *Chicago Tribune,* June 7, 1992, sec. 7, pp. 1, 6.

Yates, Ronald E. "Japanese firms invest in charity," *Chicago Tribune,* September 29, 1991, sec. 7, p. 4.

G L O S S A R Y   O F   T E R M S

business ethics   The rules or standards governing the conduct of persons or members of organizations in the field of commerce.

dilemma   A situation that requires a choice between options that are or seem to be equally unfavorable or mutually exclusive.

ethical dilemma   A situation that arises when all courses of action open to a decision maker are judged to be unethical.

ethics   The study of the general nature of morals and of the specific moral choices made by individuals; concerned with what constitutes good and bad human conduct, including actions and values.

green products   Those manufactures with reduced energy and pollution connected with their production and disposal.

proactive approach   A social responsibility strategy in which businesses continually look to the needs of constituents and try to find ways to meet those needs.

reactive approach   A social responsibility strategy in which businesses wait for demands to be made and then react to them, choosing a response by evaluating alternatives.

resistance approach   A social responsibility strategy in which businesses actively fight to eliminate, delay, or fend off demands being made on them.

social audit   A report on the social performance of a business.

social responsibility   The notion that, in addition to their business interests, individuals and organizations have certain obligations to protect and benefit other individuals and society, and to avoid actions that could harm them.

C A S E   P R O B L E M
Far Less of Phar-Mor

In **1992** it came to light that one of the founders of Phar-Mor, a rapidly growing pharmacy and general-merchandise discounter, stole "at least $10 million, which was funneled to [support his World Basketball League], and altered financial statements to cover losses." The privately held company fired several culprits: Michael I. Monus (vice chairman), Patrick Finn (the chief financial officer), two other employees, and its auditing firm, Coopers & Lybrand. The FBI was called in by Vice Chairman David Shapira, the company filed a suit against its auditors, and the operations of the WBL were suspended. Upon further investigation it was discovered that the company had not earned any profits in its operations since its founding in 1989—although income statements had shown profits—and in fact had incurred losses totaling $340 million. More than two dozen stores in the chain that had been listed as profitable were losing money. The company's net worth had been overstated as well. The apparent motive for the thefts was Monus's liability for league expenses—he owned about 60% of the 10 teams in the league.

The financial disaster put some of Phar-Mor's corporate partners—suppliers, investors, and lenders—in jeopardy, and the value of its stock fell dramatically. In August 1992 the company filed for bankruptcy protection under Chapter 11 of the Bankruptcy Act.

Some people questioned whether the board exercised proper monitoring of the company's management. It did not. "Phar-Mor's lenders have hired [their own] accounting firm to conduct their own audit of the company's books." Meanwhile the fired auditors have filed a countersuit, alleging that "Mr. Shapira was negligent [and that the fired executives and three others] injured and impaired... our ability to do our job." According to one of the company's distributors, "David [Shapira] never really got involved in Phar-Mor at all. It was [Monus's] show and David had little idea of specifics. At the trade conventions he wasn't there. Now he's got a real problem because he was the CEO and is going to be blamed for this."

Q U E S T I O N S

1. How could the embezzlement and fraud have gone undetected for several years?

2. What and who do you think are responsible for this disaster? In what ways was each responsible?

3. What effects can you foresee for Phar-Mor's stakeholders?

For more about Phar-Mor, see *Wall Street Journal,* "A Founder Embezzled Millions for Basketball, Phar-Mor Chain Says," August 5, 1992, p. A1; "Phar-Mor Fiasco Puts Shapira in Hot Seat," August 7, 1992, p. B1; and "Coopers & Lybrand Brings Countersuit Against Phar-Mor Over Firms Problems," August 20, 1992, p. A3.

References

Adam, Jr., Everett E., and Paul M. Swamidass. "Assessing Operations Management from a Strategic Objective," *Journal of Management* (June 1989), pp. 181–204.

Adam, Jr., Everett E., and Ronald J. Ebert. *Production and Operations Management,* 4th edition (Englewood Cliffs, NJ: Prentice-Hall), 1989.

Adams, J. Stacy. "Toward an Understanding of Equity," *Journal of Abnormal and Social Psychology* (November 1963), pp. 422–436.

Adler, Alan L. "Whirlpool puts its brand on Europe," *Chicago Tribune,* March 30, 1992, sec. 4, p. 5.

Adler, Nancy J. *International Dimensions of Organizational Behavior,* 3rd edition (Boston: PWS-Kent), 1991, pp. 10–11, 17, 28, 57.

Ady, Robert M. "Why BMW Cruised into Spartanburg," *Wall Street Journal,* July 6, 1992, p. 8.

Aeppel, Timothy. "IIGM Sets Venture with Poland's FSO to Build Opels," *Wall Street Journal,* March 2, 1992, p. A4.

Albanese, Robert, and David D. Van Fleet. "Rational Behavior in Groups: The Free-Riding Tendency," *Academy of Management Review* 10 (1985), pp. 244–255.

Alderfer, Clayton. *Existence, Relatedness, and Growth: Human Needs in Organizational Settings* (New York: Free Press), 1972.

Altany, David. "The Race with No Finish Line," *Industry Week* (January 8, 1990), pp. 105–106.

Amend, Patricia. "Job References Hard to Come by These Days," *USA Today,* February 2, 1990, p. 4B.

Argyris, Chris, and Don Schon. *Organizational Learning: A Theory of Action Perspective* (Reading, MA: Addison-Wesley), 1978.

Argyris, Chris. *Personality and Organization* (New York: Harper & Brothers), 1957.

Arndt, Michael. "Ford is providing model for conquering new Europe," *Chicago Tribune,* December 11, 1989, sec. 4, pp. 1, 4.

Arndt, Michael. "Key issues remain in North American trade talks," *Chicago Tribune,* August 11, 1992, sec. 3, p. 3.

Astley, W. Graham. "Organization Size and Bureaucratic Structure," *Organization Studies* 6 (1985), pp. 201–228.

Ayers-Williams, Roz. "Mastering the Fine Art of Delegation," *Black Enterprise* (April 1992), pp. 91–93.

Bahls, Jane Easter. "Getting Full-Time Work from Part-Time Employees," *Management Review* (February 1992), pp. 50–52.

Baker, Stephen. "Along the Border, Free Trade Is Becoming a Fact of Life," *Business Week* (June 18, 1990), p. 41.

Barnes, Louis B. "Managing the Paradox of Organizational Trust," *Harvard Business Review* (March–April 1981), pp. 107–118.

Barrett, Thomas M., and Richard J. Kilonski. *Business Ethics,* 2nd edition (Englewood Cliffs, NJ: Prentice-Hall), 1986.

Barry, Thomas J. *Management Excellence Through Quality* (Milwaukee: ASQC Press), 1991, pp. ix, 3, 5, 6, 7, 19.

Barry, Vincent. *Moral Issues In Business,* 3rd edition (Belmont, CA: Wadsworth), 1986, pp. 5, 9–10, 156.

Beck, Joan. "Matching the Workplace to the Work Force," *Chicago Tribune,* March 9, 1992, sec. 1, p. 15.

Beehr, T. A., and R. S. Bhagat. *Human Stress and Cognition in Organizations: An Integrated Perspective* (New York: Wiley), 1985.

Belcher, Jr., John G. *Productivity Plus* (Houston: Gulf Publishing), 1987, pp. 3, 27.

Bell, David. "Stage set for ethics in business," *Chicago Tribune,* June 21, 1992, sec. 7, p. 8B.

Bender, Marilyn, and Selig Altschul. *The Chosen Instrument: Pan Am, Juan Trippe, the Rise and Fall of an American Entrepreneur* (New York: Simon & Schuster), 1982.

Bennett, Amanda. "Executive Pay: A Little Pain and a Lot to Gain," *Wall Street Journal,* April 22, 1992, p. R1.

Benson, Tracy. "The New Leadership," *Industry Week* (June 1, 1992), pp. 12–16.

Bittel, Lester R. *The McGraw-Hill 36-Hour Management Course* (New York: McGraw-Hill), 1989, pp. 31–33, 34, 179, 184, 185, 229.

Bittel, Lester R., and Jackson E. Ramsey, editors. *Handbook for Professional Managers* (New York: McGraw-Hill), 1985, pp. 194, 196, 220, 222, 550, 634, 869.

Blake, Robert R.; Jane S. Mouton; Louis B. Barnes; and Larry E. Greiner. "Breakthrough in Organization Development," *Harvard Business Review* (November–December 1964).

Blanchard, Kenneth, and Norman Vincent Peale. *The Power of Ethical Management* (New York: William Morrow), 1988, p. 27.

Blankenhorn, Dana. "Phones look like computer networks," *Chicago Tribune,* November 17, 1991, sec. 19, p. 4.

Boyett, Joseph H., and Henry P. Conn. *Workplace 2000* (New York: Plume), 1991, pp. 330, 331.

Brenner, Joel Glenn. "The World According to the Planet Mars," *Dallas Morning News,* April 19, 1992, pp. 1H, 2H, 7H.

Brown, Donna. "HR: Survival Tool for the 1990s," *Management Review* (March 1991), p. 10.

Brown, Tom. "Managing for Quality," *Industry Week* (July 20, 1992), p. 28.

Brown, Tom. "Want to Be a Real Team?" *Industry Week* (July 20, 1992), p. 17.

Browning, E. S. "In Pursuit of the Elusive Euroconsumer," *Wall Street Journal,* April 23, 1992, p. B1.

Brownstein, Vivian. "Exporters Will Keep Slugging," *Fortune* (April 20, 1992), p. 26.

Buchholz, Rogene A. *Fundamental Concepts and Problems in Business Ethics* (Englewood Cliffs, NJ: Prentice-Hall), 1989, p. 5.

Buehler, Vernon M., and Y. K. Shetty. "Managerial Response to Social Responsibility Challenge," *Academy of Management Journal* (March 1976), p. 69.

Bulkeley, William M. "Computer Use by Illiterates Grows at Work," *Wall Street Journal,* June 9, 1992, p. B1.

Burns, Lawton R. "Matrix Management in Hospitals: Testing Theories of Matrix Structure and Development," *Administrative Science Quarterly* 34 (1989), pp. 349–368.

Burns, Tom, and G. M. Stalker. *The Management of Innovation* (London: Taristock), 1961.

Burton, Gene E. "Organizational Development—A Systematic Process," *Management World* (March 1976).

Business International (1970). "Organizing the World-wide Corporation," Research Report No. 69-4, p. 9.

Business Week (August 10, 1992). "The Global Economy: Who Gets Hurt," pp. 48, 50, 52, 66.

Business Week (August 31, 1992). "Management's New Gurus," p. 50.

Business Week (February 8, 1993). "IBM After Akers," pp. 22–24.

Business Week (January 27, 1992). "Just How Excessive Are the Pay Scales of U.S. CEOs?" p. 22.

Business Week (January 27, 1992). "Learning from Japan," p. 54.

Business Week (July 13, 1992). "Equifax Vows to Get It Right," p. 38.

Business Week (July 13, 1992). "The Immigrants: How They're Helping to Revitalize the U.S. Economy," pp. 114–116.

Business Week (June 15, 1990). "Managing Global Expansion," pp. 9, 12.

Business Week (June 29, 1992). "On a Clear Day You Can See Progress," p. 104.

Business Week (March 16, 1992). "Detroit South—Mexico's Auto Boom: Who Wins, Who Loses," pp. 98, 100–103.

Business Week (May 7, 1990). "Japanese Employers Are 'Locking Out' Their U.S. Managers," p. 24.

Business Week (November 18, 1991). "This Inspector Gets Under a Plane's Skin," p. 69.

Business Week (October 22, 1990). "A New Era for Auto Quality," pp. 88–89.

Business Week (Special Quality Issue 1991). "A QFD Snapshot," pp. 22–23.

Business Week (Special Quality Issue 1991). "A Tighter Focus for R&D," p. 170.

Business Week (Special Quality Issue 1991). "Questing for the Best," p. 9.

Byham, William C. "Self-Directed Work Team Magic," *Board-Room Reports* (June 15, 1992), pp. 1–8.

Bylinsky, Gene. "Turning R&D into Real Products," *Fortune* (July 2, 1990), pp. 73, 74.

Byrne, John A. "Businesses Are Signing Up for Ethics 101," *Business Week* (February 15, 1988), pp. 56–57.

Caggiano, Christopher. "Results from March: The *Inc.* FaxPoll," *Inc.* (June 1992), p. 24.

Campbell, Jeremy. *Grammatical Man: Information, Entropy, Language, and Life* (New York: Simon & Schuster), 1982, pp. 15–31.

Cartright, Dorwin, and Alvin Zandler. *Group Dynamics: Research and Theory,* 3rd edition (New York: Harper & Row), 1968.

Case, John. "Collective Effort," *Inc.* (January 1992), pp. 32–35, 38, 42–43.

Casey, Mike. "Ford Emphasizing 4 on (Plant) Floor," *Chicago Tribune,* May 10, 1992, sec. 17, p. 9.

Chandler, Clay, and Joseph B. White. "It's Hello Dollies at Nissan's New 'Dream Factory,'" *Wall Street Journal,* July 6, 1992, p. B11.

Chandler, Clay. "Honda's Middle Managers Will Regain Authority in New Overhead of Company," *Wall Street Journal,* June 15, 1992, p. 173.

Chew, W. Bruce. "No-Nonsense Guide to Measuring Productivity," *Harvard Business Review* (January–February 1988), pp. 114, 115, 118.

Chicago Tribune (April 12, 1990). "Crime major cause of S&L woes, FBI says," sec. 3, p. 1.

Chicago Tribune (August 5, 1990). "In manners, no room for innocents abroad," sec. 7, p. 9C.

Chicago Tribune (August 22, 1992). "Honeywell to get $124 million in autofocus patent settlement," sec. 2, p. 2.

Chicago Tribune (February 19, 1992). "IBM beats the Japanese with new memory chip," sec. 3, p. 3.

Chicago Tribune (July 3, 1992). "U.S. boosts debt to foreigners in 1991," sec. 3, p. 1.

Chicago Tribune (June 1, 1992). "Coke plans $1 billion for Europe," sec. 1, p. 11.

Chicago Tribune (June 5, 1992). "Workers Lack Three R's, Hurting Small Firms, Study Says," sec. 3, p. 3.

Chicago Tribune (June 21, 1992). "Chrysler Gives Its New Trio of LH Cars Everything It's Got," sec. 17, p. 16.

Chicago Tribune (June 21, 1992). "Co-op hits the jackpot in Japan," sec. 7, p. 8C.

Chicago Tribune (June 23, 1992). "Universities Put Teaching in Back Seat," sec. 1, p. 1.

Chicago Tribune (May 24, 1992). "GAO: Tax-Paid Research Going to Businesses," sec. 1, p. 6.

Chicago Tribune (November 10, 1991). "Computers close in on sacred goal," sec 7, p. 8.

Chipello, Christopher J., and Urban C. Lehner. "Miyazawa Calls U.S. Work Ethic Lacking," *Wall Street Journal,* February 4, 1992, p. A10.

Clark, Kim B. "What Strategy Can Do for Technology," *Harvard Business Review* (November–December 1989), p. 98.

Comins, Jr., Frederic M. "Renewal at K-mart," a letter to the editor of *Harvard Business Review* (September–October 1992), p. 176.

Cooper, Helen. "Carpet Firm Sets Up an In-House School to Stay Competitive," *Wall Street Journal,* October 5, 1992, pp. A1, A5.

Cox, Allan. "The Homework Behind Teamwork," *Industry Week* (January 7, 1992), p. 21.

Cox, Danny, with John Hoover. *Leadership When the Heat's On* (New York: McGraw-Hill), 1992, p. 23.

Cox, Meg. "CD Marketers Will Eliminate Paper Packaging," *Wall Street Journal,* February 28, 1992, p. B1.

Crockett, Fess. "Revitalizing Executive Information Systems," *Sloan Management Review* (Summer 1992), p. 41.

Cronin, Michael P. "A Globetrotting Guide to Managing People," *Inc.* (April 1992), p. 122.

Crosby, Philip B. *Quality Is Free: The Art of Making Quality Certain* (New York: Mentor), 1979, pp. 11, 15, 17, 39, 80, 112–113.

Crosby, Philip B. *Quality Without Tears* (New York: Plume), 1984, pp. 59, 99–100, 106–107.

Daft, Richard L. *Management,* 2nd edition (Homewood, IL: Dryden Press), 1991, pp. 154, 180, 246, 292, 404–410, 464–465, 575–577, 581.

Daft, Richard L. *Organization Theory and Design* (St. Paul, MN: West), 1983, p. 227.

Daft, Richard L. *Organization Theory and Design,* 3rd edition (St. Paul, MN: West), 1989.

Dallas Morning News (February 16, 1991). "Four Day Week—The Jury Is Still Out," p. D1.

Daniel, Mel. "Statistical Software Rings in Quality," *Computer World* (January 6, 1992), p. 64.

Davidson, Daniel V.; Brenda E. Knowles; Lynn M. Forsythe; and Robert R. Jespersen. *Business Law: Principles and Cases,* 3rd edition (Boston: PWS-Kent), 1990, pp. 107, 111, 112.

Davis, Bob, and Dana Milbank. "If the U.S. Work Ethic Is Fading, 'Laziness' May Not Be the Reason," *Wall Street Journal,* February 7, 1992, pp. A1, A5.

Davis, Keith, and John W. Newstrom. *Human Behavior at Work: Organizational Behavior,* 8th edition (New York: McGraw-Hill), 1989, pp. 213, 215, 262, 362–363, 364, 366–367.

Davis, Keith, and John W. Newstrom. *Human Behavior at Work: Organizational Behavior,* 9th edition (New York: McGraw-Hill), 1992, p. 105.

Davis, Keith. "Five Propositions for Social Responsibility," *Business Horizons* XVIII, no. 3 (June 1975). Adapted from article reprinted in Barry, 1986, p. 156.

Davita, Sal. "Personal Values Affect Your Career Satisfaction," *Marketing News* (April 13, 1992), p. 16.

Davita, Sal. "The Two Most Important Decisions in Career Designing," *Marketing News* (July 6, 1992), p. 16.

Davita, Sal. "Value System Can Make or Break Your Career," *Marketing News* (March 16, 1992), p. 16.

Deal, Terrence E., and Allan A. Kennedy. *Corporate Cultures: The Rites and Rituals of Corporate Life* (Reading, MA: Addison-Wesley), 1982, p. 25.

DeGeorge, Gail, and Jonathan B. Levine. "They Don't Call It Blockbuster for Nothing," *Business Week* (October 19, 1992), pp. 113–114.

Deming, W. Edwards. *Out of the Crisis* (Cambridge, MA: Massachusetts Institute of Technology, Center for Advanced Engineering Study), 1986, pp. 167–168, 169.

Dertouzos, Michael L.; Richard K. Lester; and Robert M. Solow. *Made in America: Regaining the Productive Edge* (New York: Harper Perennial), 1990, pp. 44, 99, 118, 132–134, 148–150, 151.

Detz, Joan. "The Adaptive Leader," *Success* (June 1987), p. 46.

Deutsch, Claudia H. "Business Meetings by Keyboard," *New York Times,* October 21, 1990, sec. F, p. 25.

Deutschman, Alan. "The CEO's Secret of Managing Time," *Fortune* (June 1, 1992), pp. 136, 140, 144, 146.

Dincen, Steve. "Can American Steel Find Quality?" *Industry Week* (January 26, 1992), p. 37–39.

Dobrzynski, Judith H. "IBM's Board Should Clean Out the Corner Office," *Business Week* (February 1, 1993), p. 27.

Dowd, Maureen. "Power: Are Women Afraid of It—Or Beyond It?" *Working Woman* (May 1992), pp. 98–99.

Drucker, Peter F. "The New Productivity Challenge," *Harvard Business Review* (November–December 1991), p. 69.

Drucker, Peter F. *The Practice of Management* (New York: Harper & Row), 1954, pp. 49–61, 55–83, 351.

Drucker, Peter. *Managing for Results* (New York: Harper & Row), 1964, p. 5.

Dubrin, Andrew J. *Fundamentals of Organizational Behavior* (New York: Pergamon), 1974, pp. 331–361.

Dubrin, Andrew J. *Winning Office Politics: Dubrin's Guide for the 90's* (Englewood Cliffs, NJ: Prentice-Hall), 1990, pp. 166, 167.

Dudick, Thomas S., editor. *Handbook of Business Planning and Budgeting* (New York: Van Nostrand Reinhold), 1983, pp. 22, 74.

Dumaine, Briane. "Closing the Innovation Gap," *Fortune* (December 2, 1991), pp. 57, 61–62.

Dumaine, Briane. "Procter & Gamble Shoots for the Top," *Industry Week* (January 6, 1992), pp. 24–25.

Dumaine, Briane. "Unleash Workers and Cut Costs," *Fortune* (May 18, 1992), p. 88.

Dunfee, Thomas W. "Employee Ethical Attitudes and Business Firm Productivity," *The Wharton Annual* (University of Pennsylvania: Pergamon Press), 1984, p. 76.

Dupuy, John. "Learning to Manage World-Class Strategy," *Management Review* (March 1992), pp. 40–43.

Eiben, Therese. "U.S. Exporters on a Global Roll," *Fortune* (June 29, 1992), pp. 94, 95.

Ellig, Bruce R. "Do You Have the Right Stuff?" *HR Magazine* (October 1991), p. 40.

Engdahl, Lora. "New technologies lower the barriers," *Chicago Tribune,* March 15, 1992, sec 19, p. 3.

Erdman, Andrew. "Staying Ahead of 800 Competitors," *Fortune* (June 1, 1992), p. 111.

Ettorre, Barbara. "Breaking the Glass . . . Or Just Window Dressing," *Management Review* (March 1992), pp. 16, 17.

Fallows, James. "Computers: Crash-Worthy Speedster," *Atlantic* (February 1993), pp. 103–108.

Faltermayer, Edmund. "U.S. Companies Come Back Home," *Fortune* (December 30, 1991), p. 107.

Farnham, Alan. "Biggest Business Goofs of 1991," *Fortune* (January 13, 1992), p. 83.

Federal Register 43, #156 (August 1978). "Uniform Guidelines on Employee Selection Procedures," pp. 38,295–38,309.

Feigenbaum, Armand V. "Total Quality Control," *Harvard Business Review* (November–December 1956), pp. 95–98.

Feldman, Daniel C. "Careers in Organizations: Recent Trends and Future Directions," *Journal of Management* 15 (1989), pp. 135–156.

Fiant, Ray J. "Leadership Training for Long-Term Results," *Management Review* (July 1992), pp. 50–53.

Fiedler, Fred E. "The Contingency Model—New Directions for Leadership Utilization," *Journal of Contemporary Business* 3, no. 4 (Autumn 1974), pp. 65–80.

Finegan, Jay. "Taking Names," *Inc.* (September 1992), p. 129.

Fisher, Anne B. "CEOs Think That Morale Is Dandy," *Fortune* (November 18, 1991), pp. 83–84.

Fisher, Anne B. "Morale Crisis," *Fortune* (November 18, 1991), pp. 70, 76.

Fisher, Anne B. "When Will Women Get to the Top," *Fortune* (September 21, 1992), p. 56.

Fleming, Peter C. "Empowerment Strengthens the Rock," *Management Review* (March 1992), pp. 34–37.

Fortune (April 6, 1992). "Goodbyes Can Cost Plenty In Europe," p. 16.

Fortune (April 20, 1992). "Pay Gap Between the Sexes (Cont'd)," p. 20.

Fortune (December 16, 1991). "Computer Security: New Ways to Keep Hackers Out," p. 14.

Fortune (May 18, 1992). "Getting Hot Ideas from Customers," p. 86.

Fortune (November 18, 1991). "More Foreigners at U.S. Colleges," p. 16.

Fourre, James P. *Quantitative Business Planning Techniques* (New York: American Management Association), 1970, p. 55.

Fox, William M. "Anonymity and Other Keys to Successful Problem-Solving Meetings," *National Productivity Review* (Spring 1989), pp. 145–146.

Franklin, Stephen. "Despite costs, states still racing to lure Toyota," *Chicago Tribune,* October 29, 1990, sec. 4, pp. 1–2.

Freudenberger, Herbert J. *Burnout: The High Cost of High Achievement* (Garden City, NY: Anchor), 1980, p. 13.

Fuchsberg, Gilbert. "'Total Quality' Is Termed Only Partial Success," *Wall Street Journal,* October 1, 1992, pp. B1, B7.

Fuchsberg, Gilbert. "Business People Aiding Society Win Accolades," *Wall Street Journal,* March 6, 1992, p. A3.

Fuchsberg, Gilbert. "Study Says Women Face Glass Walls as Well as Ceilings," *Wall Street Journal,* March 3, 1992, pp. B1, B8.

Gabarro, John J. "Retrospective Commentary," *Harvard Business Review* (November–December 1991), p. 108.

Gabor, Andrea. *The Man Who Discovered Quality* (New York: Penguin), 1990, pp. 47–48, 126–127.

Galbraith, Jay R., and Robert Kazanjian. *Strategy Implementation: Structure Systems and Process,* 2nd edition (St. Paul, MN: West), 1986.

Garland, Susan B. "Keeping a Sharper Eye on Those Who Pass the Hat," *Business Week* (March 16, 1992), p. 39.

Garvin, David A. *Managing Quality: The Strategic and Competitive Edge* (New York: Free Press), 1988, p. 5.

Gellerman, Saul W. "Why 'Good' Managers Make Bad Ethical Choices," *Harvard Business Review* (July–August 1986), pp. 88–89.

Gellerman, Saul W. *Motivation in the Real World* (New York: Dutton), 1992, pp. 265, 266–267, 269–271, 273–274.

Gersick, Connie J. G. "Marking Time: Predictable Transitions in Task Groups," *Academy of Management Journal* (June 1989), pp. 274–309.

Gnoffo, Jr., Anthony. "Taking Flight Simulators for a Ride," *Philadelphia Inquirer,* August 30, 1992, pp. D1, D7.

Goodman, Paul S., and Abraham Fredman. "An Examination of Adam's Theory of Inequity," *Administrative Science Quarterly* (December 1971), pp. 271–288.

Goozner, Merrill. "Harley wears well in Japan," *Chicago Tribune,* February 11, 1992, sec. 3, p. 1.

Goozner, Merrill. "Venture tilts flat-screen technology Japan's way," *Chicago Tribune,* April 26, 1992, sec. 7, pp. 1, 4.

Greenwald, John. "Is Mr. Nice Guy Back?" *Time* (January 27, 1992), pp. 42–44.

Gregory, Robert H., and Richard L. Van Horn. "Value and Cost of Information," *Systems Analysis Techniques,* J. Daniel Auger and Robert W. Knapp, editors (New York: Wiley), 1984, pp. 473–489.

Greiner, Larry E. "Evolution and Revolution as Organizations Grow," *Harvard Business Review* (July–August 1972), pp. 55–64.

Greiner, Larry E. "Patterns of Organizational Change," *Harvard Business Review* (May–June 1967), pp. 119–130.

Gunset, George. "Recession weighs on nonprofits," *Chicago Tribune,* June 8, 1991, sec. 2, p. 1.

Gunset, George. "Trade accord productive for Midwest farms," *Chicago Tribune,* August 13, 1992, sec. 1, p. 1.

Gupta, Anil K., and V. Govindarajan. "Business Unit Strategy, Managerial Characteristics, and Business Unit Effectiveness at Strategy Implementation," *Academy of Management Journal* 29 (March 1984), pp. 25–41; and Bourgeois III, L. J., and David R. Brodwin. "Strategic Implementation: Five Approaches to an Elusive Phenomenon," *Strategic Management Journal* 5 (October–December 1984), pp. 241–264.

Gutfeld, Rose. "Rockwell to Plead Guilty, Pay Fine on Waste Disposal," *Wall Street Journal,* March 26, 1992, p. C20.

Haas, Robert D. Acceptance speech, Lawrence A. Wein Prize in Corporate Social Responsibility, Columbia University, New York (November 19, 1984) as recorded in Watson, 1991, pp. 321–322.

Haigh, Christopher, editor. *The Cambridge Historical Encyclopedia of Great Britain and Ireland* (Cambridge, England: Cambridge University Press), 1985, p. 269.

Hall, Cheryl. "Golden Quest," *Dallas Morning News,* May 31, 1992, pp. 1H, 8H.

Hall, Cheryl. "The Brinker Touch," *Dallas Morning News,* March 3, 1992, p. 23H.

Hall, Douglas T. *Career Development in Organizations* (San Francisco: Jossey-Bass), 1986.

Hall, R. W. *Zero Inventories* (Homewood, IL: Dow Jones–Irwin), 1983.

Hamner, W. C. "Reinforcement Theory and Contingency Management in Organizational Settings," *Organizational Behavior and Management: A Contingency Approach,* H. L. Tosi and W. C. Hamner, editors (New York: Wiley), 1974, pp. 86–112.

Harmon, Theo, and William B. Scott. *Management in the Modern Organization* (Boston: Houghton Mifflin), 1970, p. 452.

Hart, Christopher W. L., and Christopher E. Bogan. *The Baldridge: What It Is, How It's Won, How to Use It to Improve Quality in Your Company* (New York: McGraw-Hill), 1992, pp. 5, 8, 77, 96, 128–130.

Hawken, Paul. "Problems, Problems," *Inc.* (September 1987), pp. 24–25.

Hayes, R. H., and S. C. Wheelwright. *Restoring Our Competitive Edge: Competing Through Manufacturing* (New York: Wiley), 1984.

Healey, James R. "Hughes Aircraft to Lay Off 9,000," *USA Today,* July 1, 1992, p. 1B.

Healey, James R., and Michelle Osborn. "Bush Contingent Takes Heat over CEO Pay," *USA Today,* January 8, 1992, sec. B, p. 1.

Hearn, Edward T. "U.S. insurer points to Eastern Europe," *Chicago Tribune,* March 11, 1990, sec. 7, p. 5.

Hellman, Paul. "Delegating Is Easy, Deputizing a Posse Is Tough," *Management Review* (June 1992), p. 58.

Hellwig, Basia. "Who Succeeds, Who Doesn't," *Working Woman* (May 1992), pp. 108–112.

Henderson, Verne E. *What's Ethical in Business?* (New York: McGraw-Hill), 1992, pp. 62, 74–75, 202, 205.

Henkoff, Ronald. "Inside America's Biggest Private Company," *Fortune* (July 13, 1992), p. 88.

Hersey, Paul, and Kenneth H. Blanchard. *Management of Organizational Behavior,* 4th edition (Englewood Cliffs, NJ: Prentice-Hall), 1982.

Herzberg, Frederick. "One More Time: How Do You Motivate Employees?" *Business Classics: Fifteen Key Concepts for Management Success* (Cambridge, MA: Harvard Business Review), 1975, pp. 16–17.

Hetzer, Barbara. "Making Yourself Indispensable," *Working Woman* (August 1992), pp. 53–55.

Heyel, Carl, editor. *The Encyclopedia of Management,* 3rd edition (New York: Van Nostrand Reinhold), 1982, pp. 328, 495.

Hill, Charles W. L., and Gareth R. Jones. *Strategic Management: An Analytical Approach* (Boston: Houghton Mifflin), 1989 [a review].

Hill, T. *Manufacturing Strategy: The Strategic Management of the Manufacturing Function* (London: Macmillan), 1985.

Hoerr, John, et al. "Privacy," *Business Week* (March 28, 1988), pp. 61, 65.

Hofstede, Geert. "Motivation, Leadership, and Organizations: Do American Theories Apply Abroad?" *Organizational Dynamics* (Summer 1980), pp. 42–63.

Holt, David H. *Management: Principles and Practices,* 2nd edition (Englewood Cliffs, NJ: Prentice-Hall), 1990, pp. 100, 174, 550, 564–565.

Holusha, John. "A New Soft Edge for 'Neutron Jack,'" *New York Times,* March 4, 1992, pp. C1, C3.

Hooper, Laurence. "Olivetti Unveils Mini-PC at 2.2 Pounds; July Debut Set and U.S. Partner Sought," *Wall Street Journal,* May 19, 1992, p. A11.

House, Robert J. "A Path-Goal Theory of Leader Effectiveness," *Administrative Science Quarterly* 16 (1971), pp. 321–338.

House, Robert J., and Terrence R. Mitchell. "Path-Goal Theory of Leadership," *Journal of Contemporary Business* 3, no. 4 (Autumn 1974), pp. 81–97.

Howard, Robert. "Values Make the Company: An Interview with Robert Haas, *Harvard Business Review* (September–October 1990), p. 140.

Howe, Neil, and William Strauss. "The New Generation Gap," *The Atlantic* (December 1992), pp. 67–89.

Huber, Janean. "The Big Picture: Learning from Big Business," *Entrepreneur* (June 1992), pp. 186–187.

Human Resources Management: Ideas & Trends in Personnel 273 (April 15, 1992). "The best ethics training goes beyond legal compliance by giving people skills needed to make value-based decisions," an interview with Dr. Peter Madsen (Chicago: Commerce Clearing House), p. 60.

Hunt, Christopher B., and Ellen R. Auster. "Proactive Environmental Management: Avoiding the Toxic Trap," *The Best of MIT's Sloan Management Review* (Winter 1990), pp. 7–18.

Hunt, Daniel V. *Quality in America* (Homewood, IL: Business One Irwin), 1992, pp. 23, 43, 64–70, 74, 76, 268–269, 286.

Inc. (October 1992). "Managing People," p. 33.

Ingram, Judith. "Amway sells a piece of the American Dream in Hungary," *Chicago Tribune,* November 21, 1991, sec. 3, pp. 1, 2.

Ireland, R. Duane; Michael A. Hill; and J. Clifton Williams. "Self-Confidence and Decisiveness: Prerequisites for Effective Management in the 1990s," *Business Horizons* (January–February 1992), pp. 36–42.

Ishikawa, Kaoru. *What Is Total Quality Control?* David J. Lu, translator (Englewood Cliffs, NJ: Prentice-Hall), 1985, pp. 44, 45, 98, 125–128, 186.

Jacob, Rahul. "Bausch & Lomb: Trust the Locals, Win Worldwide," *Fortune* (May 4, 1992), pp. 76–77.

Jacob, Rahul. "What Selling Will Be Like in the 90s," *Fortune* (January 13, 1992), p. 63.

Jacobs, Deborah L. "Stiff New Penalties: Companies Can Be Fined For Workers' Misdeeds," *Your Company* (Winter 1992), p. 12.

Jamieson, David, and Julie O'Mara. *Managing Workforce 2000: Gaining the Diversity Advantage* (San Francisco: Jossey-Bass), 1991, p. 21.

Janson, Robert L. "Graphic Indicators of Operations," *Harvard Business Review* (November–December 1980), pp. 164–170.

Jefferson, David J. "MCA to Extend Health Insurance to Gay Couples," *Wall Street Journal,* May 18, 1992, p. B5.

Jensen, Blair. "How to Figure Out What Others Expect of You," *Computer World* (January 20, 1992), p. 1.

Johnson, Ross, and William O. Winchell. *Management and Quality* (Milwaukee: ASQC Press), 1989.

Juran, Joseph M. *Juran on Planning for Quality* (New York: Free Press), 1988, pp. 4–5, 268, 269–270.

Katz, Robert L. "Skills of an Effective Administrator," *Harvard Business Review* (September–October 1974), pp. 90–102.

Keen, Peter G. W. *Every Manager's Guide to Information Technology: A Glossary of Key Terms and Concepts for Today's Business Leader* (Boston: Harvard Business School Press), 1991, pp. 156–157.

Keller, Maryann. *Rude Awakening: The Rise, Fall, and Struggle for Recovery at General Motors* (New York: William Morrow), 1989.

Keller, Robert, and Andrew Szilagyi. "A Longitudinal Study of Leader Reward Behavior, Subordinate Expectations, and Satisfaction," *Personnel Psychology* (Spring 1978), pp. 119–129.

Kenney, Charles C. *Riding the Runaway Horse* (New York: Little, Brown), 1992.

Kichen, Steve, editor. "The Forbes Foreign Rankings," *Forbes* (July 20, 1992), pp. 242–243, 246.

Kiechell III, Walter. "The Leader As Servant," *Fortune* (May 4, 1992), pp. 121, 122.

Kirkpatrick, David. "Breaking Up IBM," *Fortune* (July 27, 1992), pp. 44–45.

Kirkpatrick, David. "Here Comes the Payoff from PCs," *Fortune* (March 23, 1992), pp. 93, 96, 100.

Kleiman, Carol. "1990s Will See Opportunity for New Breed of Manager," *Chicago Tribune,* March 22, 1992, sec. 8, p. 1.

Kleiman, Carol. "Dealing with Harassment," *Chicago Tribune,* October 15, 1991, sec. 3, p. 1.

Kleiman, Carol. "Employee Reviews Merit Close Attention," *Chicago Tribune,* February 2, 1992, sec. 8, p. 1.

Kleiman, Carol. "Employer-Based Training Is a Growing Job Source," *Chicago Tribune,* January 12, 1992, sec. 8, p. 1.

Kleiman, Carol. "From Genetics to Honesty, Firms Expand Employee Tests, Screening," *Chicago Tribune,* February 9, 1992, sec. 8, p. 1.

Kleiman, Carol. "Planning, not dreaming, will land that foreign job," *Chicago Tribune,* November 4, 1990, sec. 8, p. 1.

Kleiman, Carol. "Some Firms Breaking Glass Ceiling," *Chicago Tribune,* April 13, 1992, sec. 4, p. 7.

Kleiman, Carol. "Worker Skepticism Aside, Firms Like Exit Interviews," *Chicago Tribune,* October 13, 1991, sec. 8, p. 1.

Koloday, Harvey F. "Managing in a Matrix," *Business Horizons* (March–April 1981), pp. 17–24.

Konrad, Walecia, and Andrea Rothman. "Can Wayne Calloway Handle the Pepsi Challenge?" *Business Week* (January 27, 1992), pp. 90, 91, 92.

Kotter, John P. *Organizational Dynamics: Diagnosis and Intervention* (Reading, MA: Addison-Wesley), 1978.

Kotter, John P., and James L. Heskett. *Corporate Culture and Performance* (New York: Free Press), 1992, pp. 11, 12, 94–96.

Kountz, Harold, and Cyril O'Donnel. *Management* (New York: McGraw-Hill), 1976, p. 375.

Kraar, Louis. "Korea's Tigers Keep Roaring," *Fortune* (May 4, 1992), p. 110.

Kram, Kathy E. *Mentoring at Work: Developmental Relationships in Organizational Life* (Glenview, IL: Scott, Foresman), 1985.

Kunde, Diana. "Game Plan Assists in Scoring Career Goals," *Dallas Morning News,* April 3, 1992, pp. 1D, 14D.

Kupfer, Andrew. "Apple's Plan to Survive and Grow," *Fortune* (May 4, 1992), pp. 68–72.

Kupfer, Andrew. "How American Industry Stacks Up," *Fortune* (March 9, 1992), pp. 32, 71.

Kuratko, Donald F., and Richard M. Hodgetts. *Entrepreneurship: A Contemporary Approach* (Chicago: Dryden Press), 1989.

Kurwin, Kathleen, and James B. Treece. "GM Is Meaner But Hardly Leaner," *Business Week* (October 19, 1992), pp. 30–31.

Labich, Kenneth. "Airbus Takes Off," *Fortune* (June 1, 1992), p. 102.

Labich, Kenneth. "The New Crisis in Business Ethics," *Fortune* (April 20, 1992), pp. 167, 168, 172, 176.

Labich, Kenneth. "What Our Kids Must Learn," *Fortune* (January 27, 1992), p. 64.

Lammers, Terry. "The New Improved Organization Chart," *Inc.* (October 1992), pp. 147–149.

Larson, Carl E., and Frank M. J. LaFasto. *TeamWork* (Newbury Park, CA: Sage), 1989.

Lawrence, Paul R., and Jay W. Lorsch. *Organization and Environment* (Homewood, IL: Richard D. Irwin), 1969.

LeFauve, Richard G. "The Saturn Corporation: A Balance of People, Technology, and Business Systems," *Looking Ahead* (the journal of the National Planning Association), vol. XIII, no. 4 (April 1992), pp. 14–23a.

Levine, Jonathan B. "It's an Old World in More Ways Than One," *Business Week* (Special Quality Issue 1991), p. 26.

Lewin, Kurt. "Frontiers in Group Dynamics: Concept, Method, and Reality in Social Science," *Human Relations* 1 (1947), pp. 5–41.

Lii, Jane H. "In the Cut-Throat World of Ice Cream, Flavormania," *New York Times,* August 7, 1992, p. F7.

Likert, Rensis. "From Production- and Employee-Centeredness to Systems 1–4," *Journal of Management* 5 (1979), pp. 147–156.

Likert, Rensis. *The Human Organization* (New York: McGraw-Hill), 1976.

Lindstrom, Robert. "Toy Town Turnaround," *California Business* (December 1991), pp. 30–35.

Loden, Marilyn, and Judy B. Rosener. *Workforce America! Managing Employee Diversity as a Vital Resource* (Homewood, IL: Business One Irwin), 1991, p. xvi.

Loomis, Carol J. "What If They Had Broken Up IBM Like AT&T," *Fortune* (July 27, 1991), p. 52.

Los Angeles Times, February 5, 1993, p. D3.

Losee, Stephanie. "Revolution from Within," *Fortune* (June 1, 1992), p. 112.

Lublin, Joann S. "Foreign Accents Proliferate in Top Ranks As U.S. Companies Find Talent Abroad," *Wall Street Journal,* May 21, 1992, p. B1.

Lublin, Joann S. "Trying to Increase Worker Productivity, More Employers Alter Management Style," *Wall Street Journal,* February 13, 1992, p. B1.

Lubove, Seth. "'I Hope My Luck Holds Out,'" *Forbes* (July 20, 1992), p. 120.

Lubove, Seth. "Perched Between Perrier and Tap," *Forbes* (May 14, 1990), p. 120.

Magnet, Myron. "Meet the New Revolutionaries," *Fortune* (February 24, 1992), p. 97.

Magnet, Myron. "The Truth About the American Worker," *Fortune* (May 4, 1992), pp. 49–52, 54.

Maier, Norman R. F. *Problem Solving Discussions and Conferences: Leadership Methods and Skills* (New York: McGraw-Hill), 1963, pp. 95–110.

Main, Jeremy. "The Battle over Benefits," *Fortune* (December 16, 1991), p. 91.

Mandell, Steven L. *Information Processing and Data Processing,* 3rd edition (St. Paul, MN: West), 1988, p. 9.

Maney, Kevin. "Texas Instruments 10-Year Quality Quest," *USA Today,* October 15, 1992, p. 6B.

Mangan, Doreen. "When It's Time to Ban Smoking," *Your Company* (Spring 1992), p. 6.

Marenghi, Catherine. "Stanley Hammers on Quality," *Computer World* (February 6, 1992), p. 62.

Martin, Thomas J., and Kevin S. Moran. "The Global Service 500," *Fortune* (August 24, 1992), p. 210.

Maslow, Abraham H. "A Theory of Human Motivation," *Psychological Review* 50 (July 1943), pp. 370–396.

Matega, Jim. "Chrysler Future Bright in Concept," *Chicago Tribune,* January 6, 1992, sec. 17, pp. 1, 5.

Matega, Jim. "GM offers workers free to parts suppliers," *Chicago Tribune,* July 18, 1992, sec. 1, pp. 1, 6.

Matteson, Michael T., and John M. Ivancevich, editors. *Management Classics* 2nd edition (Santa Monica, CA: Goodyear), 1981, pp. 18, 156, 232, 280.

Maturi, Richard. "Stress Can Be Beaten," *Industry Week* (July 20, 1992), pp. 23–26.

Mayo, Elton. *The Human Problems of an Industrial Civilization* (New York: Macmillan), 1933.

McClelland, David C. *The Achieving Society* (New York: Van Nostrand Reinhold), 1971.

McClelland, David C., and David Burnham. "Power Is the Great Motivator," *Harvard Business Review* (March–April 1976), pp. 100–110.

McCormick, Janice, and Nan Stone. "From National Champion to Global Competitor: An Interview with Thomson's Alain Gomez," *Harvard Business Review* (May–June 1990), p. 135.

McDermott, Peter. "Tough Decisions," *USA Today,* April 1992, p. 8B.

McGregor, Douglas. *The Human Side of Enterprise* (New York: McGraw-Hill), 1960, pp. 23–27, 33–48.

McKee, Bradford. "A Team Is As Strong As Its Weakest Link," *Nation's Business* (May 1992), p. 12.

McKee, Bradford. "Turn Your Workers into a Team," *Nation's Business* (July 1992), pp. 36–38.

Mensching, James R., and Dennis A. Adams. *Managing an Information System* (Englewood Cliffs, NJ: Prentice-Hall), 1991, pp. 1–2, 19, 54, 295, 296.

Merrill, Harwood F., editor. *Classics in Management,* revised edition (New York: American Management Association), 1970, pp. 10, 56, 188.

Migliorelli, Marcia, and Robert T. Swan. "MRP and Aggregate Planning—A Problem Solution," *Production and Inventory Management Journal* 29, no. 2 (1988), pp. 42–44.

Milbank, Dana. "On the Ropes: Unions' Woes Suggest How the Labor Force in the U.S. Is Shifting," *Wall Street Journal,* May 5, 1992, p. A1.

Miles, Raymond E. "Adapting to Technology and Competition: A New Industrial Relation System for the 21st Century," *California Management Review* (Winter 1989), pp. 9–28.

Miles, Raymond E., and Charles C. Snow. *Organizational Strategy, Structure, and Process* (New York: McGraw-Hill), 1978.

Miller, William H. "CAD Comes Into Its Own," *Industry Week* (May 18, 1992), p. 62.

Mills, Quinn D., and Mark D. Cannon. "Managing the New Work Force," *Management Review* (June 1992), p. 38.

Mintzberg, Henry. "The Manager's Job: Folklore and Fact," *Harvard Business Review* (July–August 1975), pp. 49–61.

Mintzberg, Henry. *The Nature of Managerial Work* (New York: Harper & Row), 1973.

Mitchell, Jacqueline. "Toyota Finds Itself in Jam on Door Locks," *Wall Street Journal,* August 19, 1992, p. B1.

Mitchell, Jim, and Jennifer Tiles. "Challenging the Imagination," *Dallas Morning News,* May 17, 1992, p. K3.

Moffett, Matt. "White-Collar Migrants Head Into Mexico," *Wall Street Journal,* March 27, 1992, pp. B1, B6.

Mohrman, Jr., Allan; Susan Resnick-West; and E. E. Lawler III. *Designing Performance Appraisal Systems: Aligning Appraisals and Organizational Realities* (San Francisco: Jossey-Bass), 1989.

Mondy, R. Wayne; Arthur Sharplin; and Shane R. Premeaux. *Management: Concepts, Practices, and Skills,* 5th edition (Boston: Allyn and Bacon), 1991, p. 116.

Morley, Brad. "Management's Competitive Weapon," *Industry Week* (May 18, 1992), p. 44.

Moskal, Brian S. "GM's New Found Religion," *Industry Week* (May 18, 1992), pp. 46–52.

Moskal, Brian S. "Sexual Harassment '80s Style," *Industry Week* (July 2, 1989), p. 24.

Moskal, Brian S. "The Buck Doesn't Stop Here," *Industry Week* (July 15, 1992), pp. 29–30.

Murray, Kathleen. "Unocal's New Man: Stegemeier Pares Debt, Refines Look of Company," *Orange County Register,* January 28, 1990, pp. K1, K2.

Murray, Kathleen. "Unocal's New Man: Stegemeier Pares Debt, Refines Look of Company," *Orange County Register,* January 28, 1991, p. Kl.

Nadler, David A. "The Fine Art of Managing Change," *New York Times,* November 29, 1987, p. F3.

Naisbitt, John. *Re-Inventing the Corporation* (New York: Warner), 1985, pp. 32–33.

Naj, Amal Kumar. "GE's Drive to Purge Fraud Is Hampered by Workers' Mistrust," *Wall Street Journal,* July 22, 1992, p. A1.

Nation's Business (August 1992). "Getting What They Owe You," p. 53.

Nauman, Matt. "Next Generation of Automaking Under One Roof," *Chicago Tribune,* May 10, 1992, sec. 17, p. 5.

Neikirk, William. "U.S. Manufacturers Wary of Automation," *Chicago Tribune,* July 5, 1987, sec. 1, pp. 1, 14.

Nelson, Mark M. "Whirlpool Gives Pan-European Approach a Spin," *Wall Street Journal,* April 23, 1992, p. B1.

Nelton, Sharon. "Winning with Diversity," *Nation's Business* (September 1992), pp. 18–21.

Nemetz, Patricia L., and Louis W. Fry. "Flexible Manufacturing Organizations: Implications for Strategy Formulation and Organization Design," *Academy of Management Review* (October 1988), pp. 627–638.

Neuborne, Ellen. "Retailer Takes Team Approach," *USA Today,* April 29, 1992, p. 5B.

New York Times (January 11, 1987). "Revving Up the American Factory," sec. 3, p. 1.

Newsweek (February 8, 1993). "Available: One Impossible Job," pp. 44–51.

Newsweek (November 9, 1992), pp. 54–57.

Nulty, Peter. "How to Live by Your Wits," *Fortune* (April 20, 1992), p. 119.

O'Reilly, Brian. "The Job Drought," *Fortune* (August 24, 1992), pp. 62, 65.

Odiorne, George; Heinz Weihrichl; and Jack Mendleson. *Executive Skills: A Management by Objectives Approach* (Dubuque, IA: Brown), 1980, pp. 26–28.

Oliver, Joyce Ann. "Mattel Chief Followed Her Vision," *Marketing News* (March 16, 1992), p. 15.

Ono, Yumiko. "Japanese Firms Don't Let Masters Rule," *Wall Street Journal,* May 4, 1992, B1.

Ono, Yumiko. "Japanese Liquor Dealer Imports Sake Made in U.S. Igniting a Controversy," *Wall Street Journal,* February 28, 1992, p. B3.

Ouchi, William G. *Theory Z: How American Business Can Meet the Japanese Challenge* (Reading, MA: Addison-Wesley), 1981.

Owens, Thomas. "Business Teams," *Small Business Report* (January 1989), pp. 50–58.

Pae, Peter. "Xerox Corp. Turns Facsimile Machines Into Computer Keys," *Wall Street Journal,* March 24, 1992, p. B14.

Pantages, Larry. "U.S. treads on Michelin's bid for Uniroyal," *Chicago Tribune,* October 22, 1989, sec 7, p. 16A.

Parker, Glenn. *Team Players and Teamwork* (San Francisco: Jossey-Bass), 1990.

Patterson, Gregory A. "GM to Cut Number of Vehicle Frames to Seven from 20," *Wall Street Journal,* May 15, 1992, p. A2.

Peace, William H. "The Hard Work of Being a Soft Manager," *Harvard Business Review* (November–December 1991), pp. 40–47.

Perry, John A., and Erna K. Perry. *Contemporary Society: An Introduction to Social Science* (New York: HarperCollins), 1991, p. 94.

Peters, Thomas J., and Robert H. Waterman. *In Search of Excellence: Lessons from America's Best-Run Companies* (New York: Harper & Row), 1982, p. 173.

Peters, Tom. "Global a state of mind, not a list of particulars," *Chicago Tribune,* October 23, 1989, sec. 4, p. 8.

Peters, Tom. "If You Want to Escape Office Politics— Forget It," *Chicago Tribune,* July 27, 1992, sec. 4, p. 7.

Peters, Tom. "Steps to Turn Workers into Business People," *Chicago Tribune,* November 25, 1991, sec. 4, p. 4.

Peters, Tom. "There are certain facts to consider before deciding that Japan is unfair," *Chicago Tribune,* April 23, 1990, sec 4, p. 7.

Peters, Tom. "Time-Obsessed Competition," *Management Review* (September 1990), pp. 16–20.

Petersen, Donald E., and John Hillkirk. *A Better Idea: Redefining the Way Americans Work* (Boston: Houghton Mifflin), 1991, pp. 6–7, 8, 9–11.

Phatak, Arvind V. *International Dimensions of Management,* 3rd edition (Boston: PWS-Kent), 1992, pp. 5, 55–62, 71–73, 136–146.

Pinchot, Gifford. *Entrepreneuring* (New York: Harper & Row), 1985.

Plunkett, Lorne C., and Robert Fournier. *Participative Management: Implementing Empowerment* (New York: Wiley), 1991, pp. 123–124, 126–127.

Plunkett, W. Richard. *Supervision,* 6th edition (Needham Heights, MA: Allyn and Bacon), 1992, pp. 5, 31–53, 70.

Porter, L. W., and E. E. Lawler. *Managerial Attitudes and Performance* (Homewood, IL: Richard D. Irwin), 1968.

Porter, Michael E. *Competitive Strategy: Techniques for Analyzing Industries and Competitors* (New York: Free Press), 1980, pp. 36–46.

Prescott, John E. "Environment: As the Moderator of the Relationship Between Strategy and Performance," *Academy of Management Journal* 29 (1986), pp. 329–346.

Prince, George. "Recognizing Genuine Teamwork," *Supervisory Management* (April 1989), pp. 25–36.

Quinlan, Tom. "Apple Shakes Up Marketing Division," *Info World* (March 16, 1992), pp. 1, 8.

Quinn, Robert E., and Kim Cameron. "Organizational Life Cycles and Some Shifting Criteria of Effectiveness: Some Preliminary Evidence," *Management Science* 29 (1983), pp. 31–51.

Rammrath, Herbert G. "Globalization Isn't for Whiners," *Wall Street Journal,* April 6, 1992, p. C27.

Rapoport, Carla. "Mazda's Bold New Global Strategy," *Fortune* (December 17, 1990), p. 109.

Reese, Jennifer. "The Big and the Bloated," *Fortune* (July 27, 1992), p. 49.

Rehfeld, John E. "What Working for a Japanese Company Taught Me," *Harvard Business Review* (November–December 1990), p. 169.

Reid, T. R., and Brit Hume. "PC Globe's software atlas will bring the world to your computer keyboard," *Chicago Tribune,* May 31, 1992, sec. 7, p. 6.

Reynolds, Larry. "Quality Circles," *Management Review* (January 1992), pp. 53–54.

Richman, Tom. "The Master Entrepreneur," *Inc.* (January 1990), p. 50.

Rigdon, Joan E. "Using Lateral Moves to Spur Employees," *Wall Street Journal,* May 26, 1992, pp. B1, B5.

Robbins, John. "TRW Relocation on the Horizon," *Dallas Morning News,* February 14, 1992, p. C1.

Robbins, Stephen P. *Management,* 3rd edition (Englewood Cliffs, NJ: Prentice-Hall), 1991, pp. 72, 286, 301, 377, 638.

Robbins, Stephen P. *Organization Theory: Structure, Design, and Applications,* 3rd edition (Englewood Cliffs, NJ: Prentice-Hall), 1990, pp. 210–232.

Robbins, Stephen P. *Organizational Behavior: Concepts, Controversies, and Applications,* 5th edition (Englewood Cliffs, NJ: Prentice-Hall), 1991, p. 209.

Robbins, Stephen. *Managing Organizational Conflict,* 3rd edition (Englewood Cliffs, NJ: Prentice-Hall), 1986, p. 321.

Rogers, Michael. "Windows of Opportunity," *Newsweek* (April 27, 1992), p. 63.

Rose, Frederick. "Chevron Develops Diesel-Fuel Formula That Meets California's New Standard," *Wall Street Journal,* June 3, 1992, p. A4.

Rosenberger, Jane Ellen. "Japanese Firm Opens Door to Executive at U.S. Unit with Board Appointment," *Wall Street Journal,* March 27, 1992, p. B5.

Rosewicz, Barbara. "EPA Acts to Cut Toxic Emissions, Draws Criticism," *Wall Street Journal,* October 30, 1992, p. A5.

Ryan, Nancy. "If What You Want Isn't What You Get— It's Free," *Chicago Tribune,* July 10, 1992, sec. 3, p. 1.

Ryan, Nancy. "Interaction on the Way for Offices," *Chicago Tribune,* June 9, 1992, sec. 3, p. 1.

Ryan, Nancy. "McDonald's update for special menus," *Chicago Tribune,* March 12, 1992, sec. 3, p. 3.

Ryan, Nancy. "Simplicity Is Walgreen's Cure for the 1990s," *Chicago Tribune,* January 21, 1991, sec. 17, p. 3.

Saddler, Jeanne. "Small Businesses Complain That Jungle of Regulations Threatens Their Futures," *Wall Street Journal,* June 11, 1992, p. B1.

Saddler, Jeanne. "Three Credit Data Firms Agree to Try to Keep Clients From Misusing Reports," *Wall Street Journal,* August 19, 1992, p. C9.

Sanderson, Susan Walsh, and Robert H. Hayes. "Mexico— Opening Ahead of Eastern Europe," *Harvard Business Review* (September–October 1990), p. 32.

Sayles, Leonard R., and George Strauss. *Human Behavior in Organizations* (Englewood Cliffs, NJ: Prentice-Hall), 1966, pp. 93–94, 238–246.

Schares, Gayle. "The New Generation at Siemens," *Business Week* (March 9, 1992), p. 47.

Schein, Edgar H. *Career Dynamics* (Reading, MA: Addison-Wesley), 1978.

Schein, Edgar H. *Organizational Psychology,* 2nd edition (Englewood Cliffs, NJ: Prentice-Hall), 1970, pp. 32–34.

Schein, Edgar H. *Process Consultation* (Reading, MA: Addison-Wesley), 1969, pp. 42–43.

Schlee, Adele. "Feeling Invisible? Here's How to Get Clout," *Working Woman* (February 1992), pp. 36–37.

Schlender, Brenton R. "How Sony Keeps the Magic Going," *Fortune* (February 24, 1992), pp. 77, 78.

Schlender, Brenton R. "The Values We Will Need," *Fortune* (January 27, 1992), p. 77.

Schlossberg, Howard. "Internal Marketing Helps Companies Understand Culturally Diverse Markets," *Marketing News* (January 21, 1991), pp. 7, 9.

Schmenner, Roger W. "The Merit of Making Things Fast," *The Best of MIT's Sloan Management Review* (1990), p. 30.

Schneidawind, John. "Firm Connects on VideoPhone," *USA Today,* January 8, 1992, p. 3B.

Schneidawind, John. "Four-Pronged Plan Saves PC Maker," *USA Today,* September 24, 1992, pp. 131–132.

Schriesheim, C. A., and B. J. Bird. "Contributions of the Ohio State Studies to the Field of Leadership," *Journal of Management* 5 (1979), pp. 135–145.

Schubert, Christian. "Executive recruiters facing tough time in Eastern Europe," *Chicago Tribune,* October 29, 1990, sec. 4, p. 3.

Schuler, Randall S. *Personnel and Human Resource Management,* 3rd edition (St. Paul, MN: West), 1987, pp. 41–43.

Schwartz, John. "Can the Ailing Giant Remake Itself?" *Newsweek* (December 28, 1992), pp. 46–47.

Seidman, L. William, and Steven L. Skancke. *Productivity: The Proven Path to Excellence in U.S. Companies* (New York: Touchstone), 1990, pp. 44, 45–46.

Serant, Clare. "Making the Switch," *Black Enterprise* (January 1992), p. 23.

Shartle, C. L. "Early Years of the Ohio State University Leadership Studies," *Journal of Management* 5 (1979), pp. 126–134.

Shaw, M. E. *Group Dynamics—The Psychology of Small Group Behavior,* 4th edition (New York: McGraw-Hill), 1985.

Sheils, Merry. "The Next Paradigm," *Chief Executive* (June 1992), p. 63.

Sheridan, John H. "The CIM Revolution," *Industry Week* (April 20, 1992), pp. 32–36.

Sherman, Stratford P. "America Won't Win Till It Reads More," *Fortune* (November 18, 1991), p. 202.

Shewhart, Walter A. *Statistical Method from the Viewpoint of Quality Control* (Washington, DC: Graduate School of the Department of Agriculture), 1939, pp. 2–4.

Shreeve, Thomas W. "Be Prepared for Political Changes Abroad," *Harvard Business Review* (July–August 1984), p. 112.

Siegel, Alexander. "Making the Most of Mentors: Yours Differs from His," *Working Woman* (May 1992), pp. 1, 26.

Sihler, William H. "Toward Better Management Control Systems," *California Management Review* 14, no. 2 (1971), p. 33.

Simnacher, Joe. "Boardroom Rumblings," *Dallas Morning News,* April 8, 1992, pp. 18–20.

Single, John L. "The Power of Expectations: Productivity and the Self-Fulfilling Prophecy," *Management World* (November 1980), pp. 19, 37–38.

Skinner, B. F. *Contingencies of Reinforcement* (New York: Appleton-Century-Crofts), 1969.

Small Business Reports (July 1988). "Group Decision Making: Approaches to Problem Solving," pp. 30–33.

Smith, Adam. *The Wealth of Nations* (New York: Modern Library), 1937.

Solomon, Caleb. "Amoco to Cut 8,500 Workers, or 16% of Force," *Wall Street Journal,* July 9, 1992, p. A3.

Solomon, Robert C., and Kristine R. Hanson. *It's Good Business* (New York: Athenaeum), 1985, pp. xiii–xiv, 20–21, 46–49, 146–148.

Sonnenburg, Paul, and William Schoneberger. *Allison: Power of Excellence, 1915–1990* (Malibu, CA: Coastline), 1990.

Spertus, Philip. "It's Easy to Fool the Boss," *Management Review* (May 1992), p. 28.

Spiers, Joseph. "Do Americans Pay Enough Taxes?" *Fortune* (June 1, 1992), p. 67.

Spiers, Joseph. "Equipment Spending Is Up," *Fortune* (December 6, 1991), pp. 21, 24.

Spragins, Ellen E. "An Employee Newsletter with Zing," *Inc.* (April 1992), p. 121.

Steers, Richard M., and Lyman W. Porter, editors. *Motivation and Work Behavior,* 4th edition (New York: McGraw-Hill), 1987, pp. 3–4.

Steiner, George. "Institutionalizing Corporate Social Decisions," *Business Horizons* (December 1975), p. 18.

Steinert-Threlkeld, Ton. "Computer Revenge a Growing Threat," *Chicago Tribune,* March 9, 1992, sec. 4, p. 3.

Stertz, Bradley A. "For LH Models, Chrysler Maps New Way to Sell," *Wall Street Journal,* June 30, 1992, p. B1.

Stewart, Thomas A. "The Search for the Organization of Tomorrow," *Fortune* (May 18, 1992), pp. 93–94.

Stodghill, Ron. "Managing AIDS," *Business Week* (February 1, 1993), pp. 48–52.

Stodghill, Ron. "Who Says Accountants Can't Jump?" *Business Week* (October 26, 1992), pp. 98–100.

Stoner, James A. F. *Management,* 3rd edition (Englewood Cliffs, NJ: Prentice-Hall), 1986, pp. 85, 354–357.

Storch, Charles. "Critics return fire in war on airline control," *Chicago Tribune,* October 1, 1989, sec. 7, p. 2.

Straub, Joseph, and Raymond Attner. *Introduction to Business,* 4th edition (Boston: PWS-Kent), 1991, pp. 124–125, 182, 241–244.

Sugiura, Hideo. "How Honda Localizes Its Global Strategy," *Sloan Management Review* (Fall 1990), p. 78.

Swanson, Stevenson. "Your Clunker May Actually Pay Dividends," *Chicago Tribune,* September 29, 1992, sec. 2, p. 1.

Tarpy, R. M. *Basic Principles of Learning* (Glenview, IL: Scott, Foresman), 1974, pp. 71–79.

Taylor, Alex. "Can GM Remodel," *Fortune* (January 13, 1992), pp. 26–28.

Taylor, Alex. "Chrysler's Next Boss Speaks," *Fortune* (July 27, 1992), pp. 82–83.

Taylor, Alex. "Now Hear This, Jack Welch," *Fortune* (April 6, 1992), pp. 94–95.

Teitelbaum, Richard S. "Timeliness Is Everything," *Fortune* (April 20, 1992), p. 120.

Therrien, Lois. "Thomson Needs a Hit, and It's Up to Nipper to Go Fetch," *Business Week* (July 6, 1992), p. 80.

Thomas, Kenneth W. "Conflict and Conflict Management," *Handbook of Industrial and Organizational Psychology,* Marvin Donnette, editor (Chicago: Rand McNally), 1976, pp. 889–935.

Thompson, Roger. "Costs for Firms Set a Record," *Nation's Business* (February 1992), p. 43.

Thompson, Roger. "Employers' Costs for Employees Soar," *Nation's Business* (May 1992), p. 62.

Time (June 22, 1992). "There's Plenty of Blame to Go Around," p. 27.

Time (November 23, 1992), p. 38.

Townsend, Patrick L., and Joan E. Gebhardt. *Quality in Action* (New York: Wiley), 1992, p. 17.

TPF&C Company. *TPF&C Letter* 225 (August 1990). (The cited text is abstracted from Towers Perrin and Hudson Institute. *Workforce 2000—Competing in a Seller's Market: Is Corporate America Prepared?* [Valhalla, NY: Towers Perrin], 1990.)

Treece, James B. "General Motors: Open All Night," *Business Week* (June 1, 1992), pp. 82–83.

Trimble, Vance H. *Sam Walton: The Inside Story of America's Richest Man* (New York: Signet), 1992, p. 109.

Tuckman, B. W. "Developmental Sequence in Small Groups," *Psychological Bulletin* 63 (1965), pp. 384–389.

Tully, Shawn. "GE in Hungary: Let There Be Light," *Fortune* (October 22, 1990), p. 138.

Tully, Shawn. "What CEOs Really Make," *Fortune* (June 15, 1992), p. 94.

United States Senate, Subcommittee on Labor of the Committee on Labor and Public Welfare. Equal Employment Opportunity Act of 1972 (March 1972), p. 3.

Uris, Auren. *Techniques of Leadership* (New York: McGraw-Hill), 1964, p. 58.

Van Fleet, David D. *Contemporary Management,* 2nd edition (Boston: Houghton Mifflin), 1991, pp. 250, 371.

Van, Jon. "Competition in Syllabus at Engineers, Short Course," *Chicago Tribune,* May 19, 1992, sec. 3, pp. 1, 6.

Van, Jon. "Firms Tool Up with Information," *Chicago Tribune,* November 5, 1991, sec. 1, p. 12.

Vancil, Richard F. "What Kind of Management Control Do You Need?" *Harvard Business Review on Management* (New York: Harper & Row), 1975, p. 481.

Velocci, Anthony L. "United Technologies Restructures in Bid to Boost Profitability, Competitiveness," *Aviation Week and Space Technology* (January 27, 1992), p. 35.

Verespej, Michael A. "John Akers' Mission: A New IBM," *Industry Week* (February 17, 1992), pp. 23–24.

Verespej, Michael A. "Pay-for-Skills: Its Time Has Come," *Industry Week* (June 15, 1992), pp. 22–30.

Verespej, Michael A. "Stern Hand," *Industry Week* (February 17, 1992), p. 25.

Verespej, Michael A. "Tough Times, Tough Decisions," *Industry Week* (February 17, 1992), pp. 21, 27–28.

Verespej, Michael A. "When Workers Get New Roles," *Industry Week* (February 3, 1992), p. 11.

Verity, John W. "Out of One Big Blue, Many Little Blues," *Business Week* (January 12, 1992), p. 33.

Verity, John W. "Room at the Top," *Business Week* (March 9, 1992), p. 32.

Virga, Patricia H., editor. *The NMA Handbook for Managers* (Englewood Cliffs, NJ: Prentice-Hall), 1987, p. 312.

Vitale, Robert. "If it's legal, law says workers may do it on their own time," *Chicago Tribune,* July 1, 1992, sec. 2, p. 2.

Vreeland, Leslie. "Managing the Risks," *Working Woman* (April 1992), pp. 61–63.

Vroom, Victor H. "A New Look at Managerial Decision Making," *Organizational Dynamics* (Spring 1973), p. 67.

Vroom, Victor H. *Work and Motivation* (New York: Wiley), 1964.

Wade, Winston J. "Knowledge in a Box," as printed in *The Best of Chief Executive,* J. P. Donlon, editor (Homewood, IL: Business One Irwin), 1993, p. 283.

Wall Street Journal (April 10, 1992). "Major Attraction: As Euro Disney Sets Opening, the French Go Goofy," p. A8.

Wall Street Journal (April 13, 1992). "The Outlook: Huge Private Debts Will Slow Recovery," p. A1.

Wall Street Journal (April 24, 1992). "Matsushita Electric Joins Nestle in Coffee Venture," p. A7.

Wall Street Journal (February 24, 1992). "3M Tries to Scotch 'Inpatriatel' Problems," p. B1.

Wall Street Journal (February 24, 1992). "Odds and Ends," p. B1.

Wall Street Journal (June 12, 1992). "Chrysler Must Pay Royalty to Pioneer of Wiper System," p. B4.

Wall Street Journal (June 16, 1992). "Managers Balk at Overseas Assignments," p. A1.

Wall Street Journal (November 3, 1992). "'Green' Cars Struggle to Gain Acceptance," p. B1.

Wall Street Journal (October 15, 1992). "Thinking Machines Introduces a Faster Storage Technology," p. B6.

Wall Street Journal (October 30, 1992). "AT&T Slates $402 Million for Pacific Cable Venture," p. B6.

Walton, Mary. *The Deming Management Method at Work* (New York: Perigee), 1986, pp. 19–20, 25–26, 72.

Walton, Richard E. "From Control to Commitment in the Workplace," *Harvard Business Review* (March–April 1985), pp. 76–84.

Walton, Sam, with John Huey. *Sam Walton: Made in America* (New York: Doubleday), 1992, pp. 169, 231, 247–249.

Want, Jerome H. "Corporate Mission: The Intangible Contributor to Performance," *Management Review* (August 1986), p. 47.

Want, Jerome H. "Managing Change in a Turbulent Business Climate," *Management Review* (November 1990), pp. 38–41.

Warner, David. "How Do Federal Rules Affect You?" *Nation's Business* (May 1992), p. 56.

Warner, David. "Regulations' Staggering Costs," *Nation's Business* (June 1992), p. 50.

Watson, Charles E. *Managing with Integrity, Insights from America's CEOs* (New York: Praeger), 1991, p. 321.

Weber, Thomas E. "Cutting the Cord," *Wall Street Journal,* May 18, 1992, p. R8.

Weintraub, Pamela. "Challenge and Response: Business Management in the 21st Century," *Omni* (January 1992), p. 36.

Welles, Edward O. "Built on Speed," *Inc.* (October 1992), pp. 82, 84, 88.

Welles, Edward O. "Captain Marvel," *Inc.* (January 1992), pp. 44–46.

Wentling, Rose Mary. "Women in Middle Management: Their Career Development and Aspirations," *Business Horizons* (January–February 1992), pp. 47–54.

West, Phil. "Here's a Suggestion for Managers: Listen to the Employees," *Chicago Sun-Times,* September 12, 1991, p. 61.

White, Joseph B. "GM's Lopez Says He Will Accelerate, Expand Cost-Cutting Despite Criticism," *Wall Street Journal,* September 30, 1992, p. A8.

Widder, Pat. "More corporations learning that ethics are bottomline issue," *Chicago Tribune,* June 7, 1992, sec. 7, pp. 1, 6.

Wilke, John R. "Digital's Offer to Employees Proves Popular," *Wall Street Journal,* June 1, 1992, p. B6.

Williams, Frederick P. *Production Operations Management* (Boston: Houghton Mifflin), 1990, p. 32.

Wilson, Larry. "Creating the Best Work Culture: How Managers Can Avoid the Trap of Ignoring the 'People' Skills in Dealing with Their Employees," *Nation's Business* (April 1992), p. 38.

Winters, Terry E., and Donald L. Murfin. "Venture Capital Investing for Corporate Development Objectives," *Journal of Business Venturing* (Summer 1988), p. 207.

Womack, James P.; Daniel T. Jones; and Daniel Roos. *The Machine That Changed the World: The Story of Lean Production* (New York: Harper Perennial), 1991, pp. 43–45.

Wood, Lamont. "LANs needn't spawn wire tangles," *Chicago Tribune,* November 17, 1991, sec. 19, p. 7.

Woodward, Joan. *Industrial Organization: Theory and Practice* (London: Oxford University Press), 1965.

Wrapp, Edward. "Good Managers Don't Make Policy Decisions," *Harvard Business Review* (September–October 1967).

Wrolstad, Mark. "For TI Defense Unit, It's Quality Time," *Dallas Morning News,* October 15, 1992, pp. 1D–2D.

Yamada, Ken. "Apple Introduces 'Newton' Featuring Printing by Hand," *Wall Street Journal,* May 29, 1992, p. B3.

Yates, Ronald E. "American firms wake up to world market demands," *Chicago Tribune,* June 15, 1992, sec. 1, pp. 1, 16.

Yates, Ronald E. "Economy size for companies," *Chicago Tribune,* December 13, 1991, sec. 3, p. 1.

Yates, Ronald E. "Foreign Firms Flock to Suburbs," *Chicago Tribune,* July 13, 1992, sec. 4, pp. 1, 2.

Yates, Ronald E. "Foreigners' investment in U.S. plunges," *Chicago Tribune,* June 10, 1992, sec. 3, p. 1.

Yates, Ronald E. "Going abroad for allies," *Chicago Tribune,* April 26, 1992, sec. 7, pp. 1, 4.

Yates, Ronald E. "Japanese firms invest in charity," *Chicago Tribune,* September 29, 1991, sec. 7, p. 4.

Yukl, Gary A. *Leadership in Organizations* (Englewood Cliffs, NJ: Prentice-Hall), 1981, p. 70, 121–125.

Zachary, G. Pascal. "Apple Is Seeking to Boost Power of Macintosh Using IBM Chip," *Wall Street Journal,* March 9, 1992, p. B6.

Glossary

acceptance sampling A product control technique involving inspection of a representative group of products before a new stage of production.

accountability The need to answer for the results of one's actions.

affirmative action A plan to give members of specific groups priority in hiring or promotion. An affirmative action plan cites specific goals and the time period in which they will be achieved. For organizations that have discriminated against particular groups in the past, affirmative action is mandatory. Other organizations institute affirmative action plans by choice.

aggregate planning The planning of production activities and the resources needed to achieve them. Aggregate planning is an element of operations management.

alternative A potential course of action that is likely to eliminate, correct, or neutralize the cause of a problem or maximize an opportunity.

analyzer strategy A business-level strategy based on maintaining the current market share while innovating in some markets.

application program A computer program designed to execute specific sets of tasks such as word processing.

artificial intelligence (AI) The ability of a machine to perform those activities that are normally thought to require intelligence; giving machines the capability to learn, sense, and think for themselves.

assessment center A place where candidates are screened for managerial positions. Screening in an assessment center usually involves extensive testing and hands-on exercises.

audit A formal investigation conducted to determine if records and the data on which they are based are correct and conform to policies, rules, procedures, and laws.

authority The formal legitimate right of a manager to make decisions, give orders, and allocate resources.

autocratic style A leadership approach in which a manager does not share decision-making authority with subordinates.

avoidance A conflict strategy in which a manager ignores a conflict situation.

balance of trade The difference between the goods and services flowing into a country and those flowing out.

balance sheet A listing of the assets of a business and the owners' and outsiders' interests in them. The equation that describes the content of a balance sheet is Assets equals Liabilities plus Stockholders' Equity.

batch processing A computer procedure in which data are collected over time and entered into databases according to prescribed policies and procedures.

behavioral school The management theory that focuses on people as individuals with needs and as members of work groups and a larger society. Managers who are adherents of the behavioral school view subordinates as assets to be developed.

benchmark A standard by which something can be measured or judged; the level to match or exceed in design, manufacture, performance, and service.

benefit Legally required or voluntary compensation provided to employees in addition to their salaries or wages.

Boston Consulting Group (BCG) matrix A planning tool that groups strategic business units into categories based on market growth rate and market share.

boundary spanning A manager's surveillance of external environments to identify current or likely events and determine how those events will influence plans, forecasts, and the organization.

brainstorming A method of shared problem solving in which all members of a group spontaneously contribute ideas focused on the subject problem or opportunity.

budget A single-use plan and control for predicting sources and amounts of income over a fixed period and how it is to be used.

bureaucracy An administrative system marked by diffusion of authority through a hierarchy. The positions in the hierarchy are clearly defined and held by career people subject to rigid rules of operation.

burnout A state of emotional exhaustion as a result of overexposure to stress.

business ethics The rules or standards governing the conduct of persons or members of organizations in the field of commerce.

business-level strategy The kind of plan that focuses on how each product line or business unit within an organization competes.

capacity planning Determining an organization's capability to produce the number of products or services to meet demand. Capacity planning is an element of operations management.

career management The planning, strategy, activities, and behaviors involved in executing a career.

career perspective A proactive strategy that involves a global view of career progress or growth over time.

career planning The process of developing a realistic view about how one wants one's career to proceed and then taking steps to ensure that it follows that course.

career The series of jobs a person holds over a lifetime and the person's attitude toward his or her involvement in those job experiences; includes a long-term perspective, a sequence of positions, and a psychological involvement.

cellular layout A facilities layout option in which equipment required for a sequence of operations on the same product is grouped into cells.

centralization A philosophy of organizing that concentrates authority within a selected portion of an organizational structure.

chain of command The unbroken line of reporting relationships, from the bottom to the top of an organization, that defines the formal decision-making structure.

change agent A person who implements change.

change Any alteration in the present work environment. The shift may be in the way things are perceived or in how things are organized, processed, created, or maintained.

classical administrative school The branch of classical management theory that emphasized the flow of information in factories and businesses.

classical management theory The theory of management that originated during the Industrial Revolution. Adherents of this theory pursue the "one best way" to perform tasks. Classical management theory developed into two separate branches: the classical scientific school and the classical administrative school.

classical scientific school The branch of classical management theory that focused on the manufacturing environment and work on the factory floor; emphasized the division of labor among specialists and the application of scientific methods to management.

closed system A system in which a person or organization can act without outside interference or concerns.

cohesion The measure of a group's solidarity—the degree to which the members cooperate and share the group's ideas.

cohesiveness The extent to which members are attracted to the team and motivated to remain together.

collaboration A conflict strategy in which a manager focuses on mutual problem solving by both parties. Parties seek to satisfy their interests by openly discussing issues, understanding differences, and developing a full range of alternatives.

collective bargaining   Negotiation between a union and an employer in regard to wages, benefits, hours, rules, and working conditions.

committee   A horizontal team designed to focus on one objective. Committee members represent functional areas. An ad hoc committee does one job and is then disbanded; a standing committee is permanent.

communication   The transmission of information and understanding from one person or group to another.

compensation   All forms of financial payment to employees. Compensation includes salaries, wages, and benefits.

competitors   Firms or individuals that offer similar products or services.

compressed workweek   A schedule that allows employees to fulfill weekly time obligations in less than the traditional five-day workweek.

compromise   A conflict-resolution strategy in which each party gives up something.

computer-aided design (CAD)   A design technique that uses a computer monitor to display and manipulate proposed designs for the purpose of evaluating them.

computer-aided manufacturing (CAM)   Using computers to guide and control manufacturing processes.

computer-integrated manufacturing (CIM)   A technology in which computers coordinate people, information, and processes to produce quality products efficiently.

computerized information system (CIS)   An MIS built upon computer hardware and software to collect and process data and store and disseminate the resulting information.

conceptual skills   The abilities to (1) view an organization as a whole and see how its parts relate and depend on one another and (2) deal with ideas and abstractions.

concurrent control   A control that applies to processes as they are happening.

conflict   A disagreement between two or more organization members or teams.

confrontation   A conflict strategy that forces parties to verbalize their positions and area of disagreement.

contingency model   A leadership theory that states that a manager should focus on either tasks or employees, depending upon the interaction of three variables—leader-member relations, task structure, and leader position power.

contingency planning   Developing plans that are activated if changes in circumstance cause the preferred plan to become infeasible.

contingency school   The branch of management theory based on the premise that managers should make decisions based on the facts and variables of each unique situation. This school suggests that managers draw freely on other schools to seek the most effective solution.

continuous-improvement process (CIP)   The ongoing search for incremental betterment. The Japanese term for continuous-improvement process is *kaizen.*

continuous-process production   A technology in which the entire conversion process is completed through a series of mechanical or chemical processes. Employees are not a part of the actual production.

control process   A four-step process that consists of (1) establishing standards, (2) measuring performance, (3) comparing measured performance to established standards, and (4) taking corrective action.

control sampling   A product control technique designed to detect variations in production processes and workmanship.

control system   A system in which feedforward, concurrent, and feedback controls operate in harmony to ensure that standards are enforced, that goals are reached, and that resources are used effectively and efficiently.

controlling   The process through which standards for the performance of people and processes are set, communicated, and applied.

corporate culture   The distinctive character of an organization, comprising its shared values, beliefs, philosophies, experiences, habits, expectations, norms, and behaviors.

corporate-level strategy   The kind of plan that charts the course of business for the entire organization.

cost-leadership strategy A business-level strategy that focuses on keeping costs as low as possible through efficient operations and tight controls.

critical control point An area of operations that directly affects the survival of a firm and the success of its most essential activities.

critical path The longest sequence of events and activities in a network production schedule; the longest time a job could take.

cross-cultural management An emerging discipline focused on improving work in organizations with employee and client populations from several cultures.

cross-functional team A team designed to bring together the knowledge of various functional areas to work on solutions to operational problems. A cross-functional team has an undefined life span that is not tied to accomplishment of a specific objective.

customer departmentalization Creating departments in response to the needs of specific customer groups.

customers Individuals and groups that use or purchase the various outputs of an organization, whether inside or outside the organization.

data center A unit of a decentralized CIS that operates to serve its unit's members with their own sets of hardware, software, and specialists (machine operators and programmers).

data Unprocessed facts and figures.

database A collection of computerized data arranged for ease and speed of retrieval; sometimes called data bank.

decentralization A philosophy of organizing and management that disperses authority within an organizational structure.

decision A judgment reached after consideration; a choice made from among available alternatives.

decision making The process of identifying problems and opportunities, developing alternative solutions, choosing an alternative, and implementing it.

decision support system (DSS) A specialized variant of a CIS; an analytic model that joins a manager's experience, judgment, and intuition with the computer's data access, display, and calculation processes; allows managers to interact with linked programs and databases via the keyboard.

decision tree A graphical representation of the actions a manager can take and how these actions relate to other events.

defender strategy A business-level strategy based on holding the current market share or even retrenching.

delegation The downward transfer of formal authority from one person to another.

Delphi technique A group decision-making technique in which equal participation is structured by the use of written questionnaires.

demotion A reduction in an employee's status, pay, and responsibility.

departmentalization Creating groups, subdivisions, or departments that execute and oversee the various tasks that management considers essential.

design control An area of operations control that involves incorporating reliability, functionality, and serviceability into product design.

design for manufacturability and assembly (DFMA) Considering, during product design, how products will be manufactured and assembled.

detailed inspection and tests A product control technique in which every finished item receives an examination or performance test.

development Efforts to acquire the knowledge, skills, and attitudes needed to move to a job with greater authority and responsibility.

diction The choice and use of words in speech and writing.

differentiation strategy A business-level strategy that attempts to set the organization's products or services apart from those of other companies.

dilemma A situation that requires a choice between options that are or seem to be equally unfavorable or mutually exclusive.

direct investment The purchase of real property or other major assets by foreign nationals and foreign businesses in a country.

discrimination Using illegal criteria while making employment decisions. Discrimination results in an adverse impact on members of protected groups.

disparate impact The result of using employment criteria that have a significantly greater negative effect on some groups than on others.

distinctive competitive advantage   An element of strategy that identifies the unique position the organization has in relationship to its competition.

distributed data processing (DDP)   Computer systems in which two or more using organizations can share information and tap into common databases to monitor and modify transactions; sometimes called electronic data interchange.

diversification strategy   A corporate-level strategy that allows the company to move into new products or markets.

division of labor   *See* specialization of labor.

divisional structure   An organizational design in which people are grouped according to products, geography, or customers.

dysfunctional conflict   Conflict that limits the organization's ability to achieve its objectives.

economic forces   Conditions in an economy that indirectly influence management decisions and the costs and availability of resources.

economic order quantity (EOQ)   An inventory technique that helps managers determine how much material to order by minimizing the total of ordering costs and holding costs based on the organization's usage rate.

effectiveness   Doing the right thing, an indispensable characteristic of a successful manager.

efficiency   The measure of a manager's performance in regard to the cost of attaining a goal.

embargo   A government regulation enacted to keep a product out of a country for a time or entirely; often used as a political sanction to enforce a nation's foreign policy.

empowerment   A method to increase motivation. Empowerment occurs when an individual receives autonomy, authority, and trust and is encouraged to break rules in order to get the job done.

end-user computing   The use of information technology (IT) by people who are not controlled and directed by top management.

equal employment opportunity   Legislation designed to protect individuals and groups from discrimination.

equity theory   A motivation theory that states that comparisons of relative input-outcome ratios influence behavior choices. A worker mentally calculates the ratio of input (efforts) to outcome (rewards) and then compares it to others' ratios to see if equity exists.

ERG theory   A motivation theory that establishes three categories of human needs: existence needs, relatedness needs, and growth needs.

ethical dilemma   A situation that arises when all courses of action open to a decision maker are judged to be unethical.

ethics   The study of the general nature of morals and of the specific moral choices made by individuals; concerned with what constitutes good and bad human conduct, including actions and values.

executive information system (EIS)   A decision support system custom designed to facilitate executive decision making; may include forecasting, strategic planning, and other elements.

executive team   A team consisting of two or more people who do the job traditionally held by one upper-level manager.

expectancy theory   A motivation theory that states that three factors influence behavior: the value of rewards, the relationship of rewards to necessary performance, and the effort required for performance.

expert power   Influence due to abilities, skills, knowledge, or experience.

expert system   A specialized end-user decision support program that stores the knowledge of a group of authorities for access by nonexperts faced with the need to make topic-related decisions.

external environment   All the forces outside an organization's boundaries that interact directly or indirectly with it.

facilities layout   The element of operations planning concerned with the physical arrangement of equipment and work flow.

feedback control   A control that focuses on the outputs or results of operations.

feedback   Evaluative or corrective information given to the person who performed an action or process. In interpersonal communication, information about the receiver's perception of the sender's message.

feedforward control   A control that prevents defects and deviations from standards.

financial budget   The details of how a financial responsibility center will manage its cash and capital expenditures.

financial ratio   The relationship of two critical figures from financial statements. A financial ratio may be expressed in terms of a ratio, decimal, or percentage. Financial ratios help managers measure a company's financial health and its progress toward goals.

financial responsibility center   An organizational unit that contributes to an organization's costs, revenues, profits, or investments.

finished-goods inventory   Inventory consisting of completed products that have not yet been sold.

first-line management   The lowest level of management. A first-line manager's subordinates are nonmanagement workers.

fixed-position layout   A facilities layout option in which the product stays in one place and the equipment, tools, and human skills are brought to it.

flexible budgeting   Budgeting in accordance with established standards against which expenditures will be compared. Flexible budgeting also refers to controlling expenses to conform to an established budget.

flexible manufacturing   An approach to manufacturing that includes high-speed assembly lines that can produce several different products.

flexible manufacturing system (FMS)   A technology in which an automated production line is coordinated by computers. A line controlled by an FMS can produce more than one product.

flextime   An employment alternative that allows employees to decide, within a certain range, when to begin and end each workday.

focus strategy   A business-level strategy in which an organization targets a specific market.

force-field analysis   A technique to implement change by determining which forces drive change and which forces resist it.

forecasting   A planning technique used to develop predictions about the future, which become the basis of plans.

formal communication channels   Management-designated pipelines used for official communication efforts. Formal communication channels run up, down, and across the organizational structure.

formal communication network   An electronic link between people and their equipment and between people and databases.

formal organization   The official organizational structure that top management conceives and builds.

formal team   A team created by upper-level managers to function as part of the organizational structure.

forming stage   The phase of team development in which team members are becoming acquainted.

free rider   A person who receives the benefits of team membership but does not do a proportionate share of work.

free-rein style   A leadership approach in which a manager shares decision-making authority with subordinates, empowering them to function without direct involvement from managers to whom they report.

functional authority   The authority to make decisions about specific activities that are undertaken by personnel in other departments.

functional definition   A principle that maintains that the nature, purpose, tasks, and performance of a department must determine its authority.

functional departmentalization   Creating departments on the basis of the specialized activities of the business.

functional structure   An organizational design that groups positions into departments according to similar skills, expertise, and resources.

functional-level strategy   The kind of plan that details the activities of the organization's major functional departments.

game theory   A mathematical simulation model in which a competitive situation is analyzed to determine the optimal course of action to counter a competitor's behavior.

Gantt chart   A graphic scheduling and control tool that helps managers plan and control a sequence of events.

geographical departmentalization   Creating departments according to territory.

global structure   The arrangement of an organization's management decision making to efficiently and effectively operate in a multinational context; form may contain functional, product, and geographic features based on worldwide product or area units.

globalization The aggregate processes of exporting products and services; locating operations outside one's national borders; using foreign partners to help in R&D and to sell products and services around the world; and tailoring strategies, management functions, and products and services to meet the needs of international customers. Requires that managers think beyond national borders and see all world markets as part of a single global economy.

goal-setting theory A motivation theory that states that behavior is influenced by goals. Goals, whether set by a manager or by a worker and manager together, tell the employee what needs to be done and how much effort he or she must expend.

grand strategy The overall plan of action developed at the corporate level to achieve an organization's objectives.

grapevine *See* informal communicaton channels.

green products Those manufactures with reduced energy and pollution connected with their production and disposal.

group decision support system (GDSS) A variant decision support system that allows groups focusing on a problem to interact with one another and to exchange information, data, and ideas.

groupthink In group decision making, a phenomenon in which members are so committed to the group that they become reluctant to disagree with other members. Groupthink can seriously compromise decision making.

growth strategy A corporate-level strategy adopted when managers of an organization want to create high levels of growth.

horizontal integration A strategy to consolidate competition by acquiring similar products or services.

horizontal team A team composed of members drawn from different departments.

human asset accounting Treating employees as assets, not expenses, by recording money spent on people as increases in the value of those assets.

human resource manager A manager who fulfills one or more personnel, or human resource, functions.

human skills The abilities to (1) interact and communicate with other people successfully and (2) understand, work with, and relate to individuals and groups.

hygiene factors The causes most closely identified with unhappiness on the job. These extrinsic factors, provided by management, can result in no job dissatisfaction when they are of high quality. They are not necessarily motivators for growth or greater effort, however.

income statement A report that presents the difference between an organization's income and expenses to determine whether the firm operated at a profit or a loss over a specified period.

influence The ability to sway people to one's will.

informal communication channels The informal networks that exist outside the formal channels. People use informal channels to transmit casual, personal, and social messages at work.

informal organization A network of personal and social relationships that arises spontaneously as people associate with one another in the work environment.

information Processed data that have been deliberately selected, and organized to be useful to an individual manager.

innovating When managers bring new technologies, knowledge, and methods to bear on the design, production, or application of products and services.

integration strategy A corporate-level strategy adopted when managers see a need to stabilize supply lines, reduce costs, or consolidate competition.

interaction chart A diagram that shows the informal organization.

internal environment All the elements within an organization's boundaries that help make it unique and that are to some extent under the control of management.

international division A parent company's corporate unit, commonly a marketing or production operation, located in a host country offshore from the parent headquarters, and whose head reports directly to the CEO; common practice for companies in the early stages of international involvement.

international forces Economic, political, sociocultural, technological, and natural forces anywhere in the world that affect or influence the decision making of managers and the abilities of organizations to fulfill missions and reach goals.

international management   The process of managing resources (people, funds, inventories, and technologies) across national boundaries and adapting management principles and functions to the demands of foreign competition and environments.

interpersonal communication   Face-to-face or voice-to-voice (telephone) conversations that take place in real time and allow instant feedback.

intrapreneurship   Entrepreneurship within an organization. A company that values intrapreneurship allows employees flexibility and authority in pursuing and developing new ideas.

inventory   The goods an organization keeps on hand.

jargon   The specialized technical language of a trade, profession, subculture, or other group.

job   A specific position a person holds in an organization.

job analysis   A study that determines the duties associated with a job and the human qualities needed to perform it. A job analysis results in the preparation or updating of a job description and job specification.

job depth   An element of job re-design that refers to the degree of discretion an employee has to alter a job.

job enlargement   Increasing the variety or the number of tasks a job includes, not the quality or the challenge of those tasks.

job enrichment   Designing a job to provide more responsibility, control, feedback, and authority for decision making.

job evaluation   A study that determines the worth of a job in terms of its value to an organization. Job evaluations are used to determine compensation levels.

job re-design   The application of motivational theories to the structure of work, to increase output and satisfaction.

job rotation   Temporarily assigning people to different jobs, or tasks to different people, on a rotating basis.

job scope   An element of job re-design that refers to the variety of tasks incorporated into a job.

job sharing   A technique to provide flexibility in work by permitting two part-time workers to divide one full-time job.

just-in-time (JIT) inventory system   A technique for inventory control designed to eliminate raw materials inventories by coordinating production and supply deliveries.

kaizen   A Japanese term used in the business setting to mean incremental, continuous improvement.

key indicator management (KIM)   A monitoring system that focuses on core measures of the company or unit operations that are indispensable for managers' decision making.

labor force   The people from which an organization can recruit qualified candidates for jobs.

large-batch technology   *See* mass-production technology.

leadership style   The perceived approaches and behaviors a manager uses to influences others.

leadership   The process of influencing individuals and groups to set and achieve goals.

legal and political forces   Statutes and case law that apply to all segments of communities at large and businesses in particular; includes specific regulations imposed by all levels of government.

legitimate power   Authority possessed by managers and derived from the positions they occupy in the formal organization.

life-cycle theory   A view of management that asserts that a leader's behavior toward a subordinate should relate to the subordinate's maturity level. The focus on tasks and relationships should vary as the subordinate matures.

limiting factors   Constraints that rule out potential alternatives.

line authority   Direct supervisory authority from superior to subordinate.

line department   A core work unit established to meet the major objectives of an organization and directly influence its success.

linear programming   A planning technique that uses an equation to determine the optimum combination of resources and activities.

management by objectives (MBO)   A planning technique that emphasizes collaborative goal setting by managers and their subordinates.

management by reaction   A management method that does not anticipate change but merely reacts to it.

management hierarchy   The levels of management, which are usually represented by a pyramidal structure.

management information system (MIS)   The coordinated arrangement of gathering, collating, and distributing information that allows managers to make decisions, solve problems, and carry out their functions and operations effectively and efficiently. The term is often applied to computer systems designed for work units and organizations.

management science   The study of complex systems of people, money, equipment, and procedures, with the aims of understanding how they function and then improving their efficiency and effectiveness.

management   The process of setting and achieving goals through the execution of five basic management functions that use human, financial, material, and information resources.

manager   Someone who directs the activities of others.

managerial grid   Blake and Mouton's two-dimensional model for visualizing the extent to which a manager focuses on tasks or employees.

managerial style   The individual way in which a manager goes about managing. Managerial style includes personal attributes and decision-making approach.

manufacturing resource planning (MRPII)   A comprehensive planning system that controls the total resources of a firm.

mass-production technology   A type of technology that produces a large volume of standardized products.

master schedule   An element of operations management that specifies the quantity and type of each item to be produced and how, when, and where it should be produced.

materials requirement planning (MRP)   A planning and inventory system that uses forecasts of customer orders to schedule the exact amount of materials needed for production.

matrix structure   An organizational design that utilizes the functional and divisional chains of command simultaneously in the same part of an organization.

mechanistic structure   A tight organizational structure characterized by rigidly defined tasks, formalization, many rules and regulations, and centralized decision making.

medium   The means by which a sender transmits a message.

mentor   A senior employee who acts as guide, teacher, counselor, and coach for a less experienced person in the organization.

message   The information that the sender wants to transmit.

middle management   Managers below the rank of vice president but above the supervisory level.

mission statement   The formal written statement of an organization's purpose.

mission   The explicit expression of an organization's central and common purpose, its reason for existing. A mission is sometimes called a vision.

morale   The attitude, or feelings, workers have about the organization and their total work life.

motivation factors   The conditions that can lead to an individual's job satisfaction. They are intrinsic to the job and offer satisfactions for psychological needs.

motivation   The result of the interaction of a person's internal needs and external influences. Motivation involves perceptions of equity, expectancy, previous conditioning, and goal setting. Motivation determines behavior.

multinational corporation   A company with operating facilities, not just sales offices, in one or more foreign countries; management favors a global vision and strategy, seeing the world as its market.

mutual trust   The ability to rely on someone based on his or her character, ability, and truthfulness.

natural forces   The climate, weather, geography, and geology that affect an organization.

needs   Physical or psychological conditions that act as stimuli for human behavior.

network scheduling   A graphic technique for scheduling projects in which activities and events are interrelated.

network structure   An organizational design option in which a small central organization relies on other organizations to perform manufacturing, engineering, or other critical functions on a contract basis.

networking   The electronic linking of two or more computers.

noise Anything in the environment of a communication that interferes with the sending and receiving of messages.

nominal group technique A group decision-making technique that creates a structure to allow equal participation by all members.

nonprogrammed decision A decision made in response to a situation involving unique circumstances, unpredictable results, and important consequences.

nonverbal communication Images, actions, and behaviors that transmit messages.

norm Any standard of conduct, code, or pattern of behavior perceived by a group to be important for its members.

norming stage The phase of team development in which disagreement and conflict have been resolved and team members enjoy unity and focus.

objective The desired outcome or target that an individual or an organization intends to achieve through planning.

open system A system in which an individual or organization must interact with various and constantly changing components in both the external and internal environments.

operating budget A financial plan and control for each financial responsibility center's revenues, expenses, and profits.

operating system An extensive and complex set of instructions that manages the operation of a computer and the application programs that run on it.

operational objective The specific result expected from first-level managers, work groups, and individuals.

operational plan A plan developed by a first-level supervisor as the means to achieve operational objectives and in support of tactical plans.

operations management The practice of applying management science tools and techniques to the processes that convert resources into products and services in the manufacturing and service industries.

operations research (OR) The use of models, simulations, games, break-even analyses, queuing theory, and other analytical tools to optimize performance.

operations strategy The element of the strategic plan that defines the role, capabilities, and expectations of operations.

opportunity A good chance for progress or advancement whose realization requires that a decision be made.

organic structure A flexible, free-flowing organizational structure that has few rules and regulations. An organic structure is characterized by decentralization—many decisions are made by on-the-job employees.

organization A group of two or more people that exists and operates to achieve common objectives.

organization chart A visual representation of the structure of an organization and how its parts fit together.

organizational climate The quality of the work environment as experienced by employees.

organizational culture A system of shared beliefs, values, and norms that define what is important to the organization, how people should behave, how they should interact with each other, and what they should be striving for.

organizational design The creation of or change to an organization's structure.

organizational development (OD) A process of conducting a thorough analysis of an organization's problems and then implementing long-term solutions to solve them.

organizational learning The ability to integrate new ideas into established systems to produce better ways of doing things.

organizational life cycle The observable and predictable stages of an organization's evolution.

organizational politics The unwritten rules of work life and informal methods of gaining power and advantage.

organizational socialization A process through which new members of an organization gain exposure to its values, norms, policies, and procedures.

organizational visibility A strategy for career advancement that involves highlighting a person's abilities, talents, and contributions for those people in the organization who influence promotions and advancement.

organizing Establishing an orderly use of resources by assigning and coordinating tasks.

orientation Introducing new employees to the organization by explaining their duties, helping them meet their co-workers, and acclimating them to their work environment.

participative style A leadership approach in which a manager shares decision-making authority with subordinates.

path-goal theory A view of management that asserts that subordinates' behaviors and motivations are influenced by the behaviors managers exhibit toward them. This theory suggests that leadership style should depend on the leader's influence and subordinate's perceptions, goals, rewards, and goal paths.

payback analysis A procedure that ranks alternatives according to how long each takes to pay back its initial cost.

perceptions Ways in which people observe and bases for their judgments about the stimuli they experience.

performance appraisal A formal, structured comparison between employee performance and established quantity and quality standards.

performing stage The phase of team development in which team members progress toward team objectives, handle problems, coordinate work, and confront each other if necessary.

perk A payment or benefit received in addition to a regular wage or salary. Executives usually receive perks.

personnel manager *See* human resource manager.

philosophy of management A manager's attitude about work and the people who perform it. A manager's philosophy influences the motivation approaches he or she selects.

plan The means to achieving an objective.

planned change A philosophy that involves trying to anticipate what changes will occur in both the external and internal environments and then developing a response that will maximize success.

planning Determining the objectives of an organization or work group and developing the overall strategies to achieve them.

policy A broad guideline created by top management to help managers and workers deal with ongoing and recurring situations or functions.

portfolio strategy A strategy focused on determining the proper mix of business units and product lines that fit together to provide a maximum competitive advantage.

power A person's ability to exert influence.

proactive approach A social responsibility strategy in which businesses continually look to the needs of constituents and try to find ways to meet those needs.

problem Any question raised for the purpose of solution, answer, or decision. A current condition that is not a desired or preferred condition.

procedure The set of step-by-step directions that describes how to carry out an activity or task.

process improvement team A group assigned to cooperatively assess a process and make it better.

process layout A facilities layout option in which all the equipment or machines that perform a similar task are placed together.

product control A component of operations control that reduces the probability and costs of poor quality and unreliable products by implementing controls from purchasing to end use.

product departmentalization Creating departments according to product.

product-development team A team organized to create new products.

production layout A facilities layout option in which machines and tasks are arranged according to the progressive steps through which the product is made.

productivity The relationship between the amount of input needed to produce a given amount of output and the output itself. Productivity is usually expressed as a ratio.

program A single-use plan for solving a problem or accomplishing a group of related activities needed to reach a goal.

program evaluation and review technique (PERT) A network scheduling technique for planning and charting the progress of a complex project in terms of the time it is expected to take—an estimate that is derived from probability analysis.

programmed decision A decision about a problem or situation that has occurred so often that the situation, solution, and outcome are predictable.

project improvement team   A group engaged in executing a project; the purpose of the team is to make the project better.

project team   A team organized to complete a specific task in the organization.

promotion   A job change that results in increased status, compensation, and responsibility.

prospector strategy   A business-level strategy based on innovation, risk, the pursuit of opportunities, and expansion.

psychological contract   The unspoken contract that marks the end product of the organizational socialization process and defines what people are expected to give to the organization and what they can expect to receive.

purchasing   The acquisition of goods and services at optimal costs from competent and reliable sources.

qualification testing   A product control technique in which products are tested for performance on the basis of reliability and safety.

quality assurance team   A team created to guarantee the quality of services and products, visit customers, and work with vendors.

quality audit   A determination of how well customer or consumer requirements are being met by an organization, product, service, or process. A quality audit includes implementation of corrections.

quality circle (QC)   A team of workers who meet voluntarily and regularly to improve their unit's processes, products, and services, and to identify quality issues and offer solutions.

quality control (QC)   An economical system of production that produces quality goods or services meeting the requirements of customers. Quality control employs statistical measures and methods and is often called statistical quality control (SQC).

quality control audit   A check of quality control efforts that asks two questions: How are we doing? and What are the problems?

quality function deployment (QFD)   A disciplined approach to solving problems of quality before the design phase of a product; research discovers and ranks customer needs to be translated into design specifications.

quality improvement team   A team composed of people from all functional areas of a company who meet regularly to assess progress toward goals, identify and work to solve common problems, and cooperate to plan for the future.

quality of work life (QWL)   A term used to describe managers' efforts to enhance the dignity of workers by improving their physical and emotional well-being and enhancing the satisfactions that work can provide.

quality   The totality of features and characteristics of a product, service, process, or project that bear on its ability to satisfy stated or implied goals or requirements of producers and users of the outcomes.

quantitative school   The branch of management thought that emphasizes mathematical approaches and measurability.

queuing model   A simulation used to help managers decide what length of waiting line, or queue, is preferable.

quota   A government regulation that limits the import of a product to a specified amount per year.

ratio   The expression of the relationship between numbers. Ratios are often expressed in terms of percentages or decimals.

raw materials inventory   Inventory consisting of the raw materials, parts, and supplies used as inputs to production.

reactive approach   A social responsibility strategy in which businesses wait for demands to be made and then react to them, choosing a response by evaluating alternatives.

reactor strategy   A business-level approach in which a business does not adopt a strategy, but responds to environmental threats randomly.

receiver   The person or group for whom a communication effort is intended.

recruiting   Efforts to find qualified people and encourage them to apply for positions that need to be filled.

referent power   Influence that comes to people because of the kinds of persons they seem to be— their traits, personalities, and attractiveness to others.

reinforcement theory   A motivation theory that states that a supervisor's reactions and past rewards and penalties affect behavior.

reorder point (ROP)   The most economical point at which an inventory item should be reordered.

research and development (R&D) The investment of resources to guarantee an organization's future through the discovery or acquisition of processes, materials, or products to be used in the short and long term.

resistance approach A social responsibility strategy in which businesses actively fight to eliminate, delay, or fend off demands being made on them.

resource deployment An element of strategy that defines how managers of a company intend to allocate its resources to achieve objectives.

responsibility The obligation to carry out one's assigned duties to the best of one's ability.

retrenchment strategy A corporate-level strategy adopted when managers of an organization want to reduce the size or scope of activities.

robotics The use of programmed machines instead of people to handle production tasks.

role A set of expectations for a manager's behavior.

rule A plan that aims to control human behavior or conduct at work.

sanction A penalty—such as a fine, suspension, or termination—used by management to influence workers' behavior; a reward or penalty used by informal groups to persuade members to conform to norms.

satisfice To make the best possible decision with the time, resources, and information available. A satisficing decision contrasts with an ideal one.

scope An element of strategy that specifies the size or position managers want a firm to have in the environment.

selection Evaluating applicants and finding those best qualified to perform a job and most likely to fit into the culture of the organization.

self-directed work team A self-managing team that is fully responsible for its own work. It sets goals, creates its own schedules and budgets, and coordinates work with other departments.

semantics The study of the meanings of words.

sender The person or group that initiates the communication process.

separation The voluntary or involuntary departure of employees from a company.

sexual harassment Unwelcome verbal or physical conduct of a sexual nature that (1) implies, directly or indirectly, that sexual compliance is a condition of employment or advancement, or (2) interferes with an employee's work performance.

simulation A model of a real activity or process.

single-use plan A plan that applies to activities that do not recur.

situation analysis A search for an organization's strengths, weaknesses, opportunities, and threats (SWOT). The search forms part of the strategic planning process.

small-batch technology A type of technology that produces goods in small amounts designed to customer specification.

smoothing A conflict strategy in which the manager diplomatically acknowledges that conflict exists but downplays its importance.

social audit A report on the social performance of a business.

social responsibility The notion that, in addition to their business interests, individuals and organizations have certain obligations to protect and benefit other individuals and society, and to avoid actions that could harm them.

sociocultural forces Pressures that individuals, groups, and communities put on managers and organizations.

span of control The principle of organizing concerned with the number of subordinates each manager directs.

specialization of labor The degree to which organizational tasks are subdivided into separate jobs.

sponsor An individual in the organization who will promote a person's talents and look out for his or her organizational welfare.

stability strategy A corporate-level strategy adopted when managers of an organization want it to remain the same.

staff authority Authority to serve in an advisory capacity.

staff department A work unit that, by providing advice or technical assistance, helps all departments meet the objectives of the organization.

staffing   Efforts designed to (1) attract, develop, reward, and retain the people needed to accomplish an organization's goals and (2) promote job satisfaction.

stakeholders   Groups directly or indirectly affected by the ways in which business is conducted and managers conduct themselves. Stakeholders include owners, employees, customers, suppliers, and society.

standard   Any established rule or basis of comparison used to measure capacity, quantity, content, value, cost, quality, or performance.

standing plan   A plan that is usually made once and retained over the years. A standing plan may be revised.

statistical process control (SPC)   The use of statistical tools and methods to measure and predict variations. Statistical process control establishes boundaries to determine if a process is in control (predictable) or out of control (unpredictable).

statistical quality control (SQC)   The use of statistical tools and methods to determine the quality of a product or service.

stereotype   Predetermined belief about a group of people.

storming stage   The phase of team development characterized by disagreement and conflict as individual roles and personalities emerge.

strategic business unit (SBU)   An autonomous business division operating within a corporation. An SBU has its own competitors, market, and product line.

strategic management   Top-level management's responsibility for defining the firm's position, formulating strategies, and guiding long-term organizational activities.

strategic objective   A long-term goal that relates to the future role or position of an organization. Strategic objectives are set by top-level management.

strategic plan   The steps by which an organization intends to achieve its strategic objectives.

strategic planning   The decision-making and planning processes that chart an organization's long-term course of action.

strategy formulation   The processes associated with the planning and decision making that go into developing a company's strategic objectives and strategic plans.

strategy implementation   The processes associated with executing the strategic plan.

stress   The physiological and psychological reaction of the body to demands made on it.

subculture   Within an organization, a unit that forms because people share values, norms, and beliefs.

superordinate objective   An objective that overshadows individual interests. A manager can appeal to superordinate objectives as a strategy for resolving conflict.

supervisor   *See* first-line management.

suppliers   Individuals and groups that provide the resources an organization needs to produce goods or services inside or outside the organization.

symptom   A signal that indicates a problem is present.

synergy   The increased effectiveness produced through combined action. When two parties participate in a synergistic relationship, the result of their cooperation is greater than the sum of both individual efforts.

system   A group of interacting, interrelated, or interdependent elements that form a complex whole.

tactical objective   A goal that states what a subunit must do to achieve a strategic objective. Tactical objectives are set by midlevel managers.

tactical plan   The steps by which the major units in an organization will achieve tactical objectives.

tariff   A tax placed on imported goods to make them more expensive and thus less competitive in order to protect domestic producers.

task force   A horizontal team composed of employees from different departments. A task force is designed to accomplish a limited number of objectives, and it exists only until objectives are met.

team   A group of two or more people who interact regularly and coordinate their work to accomplish a common objective.

team norm   A standard of behavior accepted by all team members.

team structure   An organizational design that places separate functions into a group according to one overall objective.

technical skills   The abilities to use the processes, practices, techniques, and tools of the specialty area a manager supervises.

technological forces   The combined effects of scientific discoveries, engineering applications, and inventions that result in new materials, products, systems, opportunities, problems, and challenges for organizations and individuals.

technology   The knowledge, machinery, work procedures, and materials that transform inputs into outputs.

test   Any criterion used as a basis for an employment decision.

Theory Z   The management view that mutual responsibility, loyalty, and regard between companies and their employees yields higher productivity and well-being for all. The theory was introduced by William G. Ouchi in 1981.

theory   An explanation that helps organize information and knowledge.

three-step approach   A technique of behavior modification consisting of three phases—unfreezing, changing, and refreezing—that is used to implement change.

throughput time   The weighted average time of all the parts of a process that produces a representative batch or order.

top management   Managers responsible for the overall management of an organization. Their tasks include establishing company-wide objectives, goals, and operating policies and directing the company in relationships with the external environment.

total quality management (TQM)   A strategy for continuously improving performance at every level and in all areas of responsibility throughout an organization.

training   Giving employees the knowledge, skills, and attitudes needed to perform their jobs.

transactional processing   A computer procedure in which data are received about a company's ongoing operations and entered into data banks as each transaction occurs.

transfer   Moving an employee to a job with similar levels of status, compensation, and responsibility.

understanding   The situation that exists when all senders and receivers agree about the meaning and intent of a message.

unit-production technology   *See* small-batch technology.

unity of command   The organizing principle that states that each person in an organization should take orders from and report to only one person.

unity of direction   The organizing principle that states that each task be directed by a single command position and that the person in that position have the authority to perform the task.

vertical integration   A strategy focused on gaining ownership of resources, supplies, or distributive systems that relate to a company's business.

vertical team   A team composed of a manager and subordinates.

Vroom and Yetton decision tree   A series of questions, in the context of a decision tree, that guide managers to a decision-making style appropriate for a specific situation.

waiting-line model   *See* queuing model.

work team   A team composed of multi-skilled workers. A work team does all the tasks previously done by individual members in a functional department or departments.

work-in-process inventory   Inventory consisting of parts and materials that have begun moving through the production process but are not yet assembled into a completed product.

zero-based budgeting   A budgeting system that starts from scratch for each fiscal period in all spending categories. Planners must justify all amounts requested for the coming period.

Index

Photo Credits

DATE